EARTH SCIENCE
A STUDY OF A CHANGING PLANET

by

Robert B. Daley
Jamesville-DeWitt Central School
DeWitt, New York

W. John Higham
formerly of
Vestal Central High School
Vestal, New York

George F. Matthias
Croton-Harmon High School
Croton-on-Hudson, New York

CEBCO • A DIVISION OF
ALLYN AND BACON, INC.
Newton, Massachusetts

ROCKLEIGH, NJ • ATLANTA • WARRENSBURG, MO • DALLAS • RANCHO CORDOVA, CA
LONDON • SYDNEY • TORONTO

Staff Credits

Katherine M. Kotik, Editorial Services
Martha E. Ballentine, Preparation Services Manager
Roger Powers, Book Manufacturing

Cover Design

Richard Hannus and L. Christopher Valente

Outside Credits

Susan Van Etten, Photo Research
Shay J. Mayer, Design Services

Cover Photo: An eruption of Kilauea volcano, on the island of Hawaii. This shield volcano rises to a height of 4,090 feet (1,247 meters). It forms part of the eastern slope of a larger volcano, Mauna Loa.

ISBN: 0-205-09841-X

Printed in the United States of America
 2 3 4 5 6 7 8 9 90 89 88 87 86 85

To the Student

To study the earth is a formidable task. On a human scale the sheer magnitude of the earth is hard to grasp. Its complexity and variety seem beyond understanding. How should we attempt to teach a subject of such scope?

The approach of this text is *investigative*. It stresses the chain of reasoning from observation to generalization. We challenge you to seek out direct experiences of earth phenomena; the text can then aid you in interpreting them.

Certain features have been built into the text, such as *Review Questions,* and *Review Exercises*. These are designed to help you reinforce what you have learned.

We trust that this approach will generate in each of you the enthusiasm and success that we have observed in our own experience with it.

The Authors

Contents

Prologue

A student's life is filled with books. We hope this book will help you to change. The major change we hope to accomplish is to help you develop a new way of looking at, and studying, the earth. You can then use your observations to make intelligent conclusions, or inferences. How can the study of earth science help you do that?

Scientists use the method of observation and inference to solve problems. Let's look at a recent example of earth scientists working together to solve some important mysteries.

Geochemists, who study the chemicals in rock, have found unusually high amounts of the element iridium in sedimentary rocks of a certain age, in the United States, China, and Europe. This element is normally very rare in earth materials. It is reported to be common in meteorites, and is thought to be common in comets and the deep interior of the earth, as well.

Paleontologists, who study ancient life, have observed evidence that extinctions of life have occurred on earth in a pattern that repeats every 26 to 30 million years. For example, 65 million years ago the dinosaurs disappeared from the planet. About 248 million years ago, 90% of all life seems to have died away.

Astronomers have always been bothered by the fact that their observations of the motions of the planets did not fit perfectly with the calculated

Comets are "dirty snowballs" made up of frozen gases, dust, and rock particles. Kohoutek, pictured above, completes one orbit around the sun every 75,000 years.

positions. Also, the sun seems to be unusual, since more than half the stars (suns) in the sky are binary stars—two stars linked together in their movements through space.

Now, blending together all these separate observations, a new theory has been proposed. A group of scientists have inferred that some object in space may be responsible for these observed phenomena. A companion star to our sun, or an additional tenth planet in the solar system, could cause a huge increase in the number of comets passing through the solar system. Some of these could collide with the earth. The peak of these collisions, occurring every 26 to 30 million years, would cause a 'great darkening' of the earth because of the huge amount of dust thrown up from the surface. Life would be severely affected, with some forms even being extinguished. According to this theory, after the dust had settled, carrying with it the iridium from the comet, life would again develop on earth for another 30 million years.

Thus, a series of *observations,* seemingly completely isolated from each other, have been woven together into a major *inference,* or theory, by some scientists curious about life on earth—how it began, how it changes, and what might happen to it in the future.

The process of observation and inference is the method that science has always used to investigate our world. It is the same method that you will use in your study of earth science this year.

TOPIC I
OBSERVATION AND MEASUREMENT OF THE ENVIRONMENT

The surface of Mars from the Viking I Lander, 1976.

CHAPTER 1
Observation and Measurement

You will know something about observing and measuring if you can:
1. Describe how observations are made.
2. Classify your observations and make meaningful inferences.
3. Make some measurements and state how accurate they are.

1973-1998: Twenty-Five Years of Space History
(Reprinted from *The New York Times*, March 1, 1998)

We on Earth have now become used to the idea of having neighbors on other planets. But what did the Martians think of Earth before we contacted each other? In honor of the twenty-fifth anniversary of the discovery of life on Earth by our Martian friends, we are reproducing the following articles. They are from the largest newspaper on Mars, the *Global Observer,* and trace the history of space travel and interplanetary contact from the Martian viewpoint. (We are indebted to the Martian expert in comparative linguistics, Professor $24C^2x_1$, for his invaluable assistance in making this translation into English.)

March 10, 1973

The latest readings from Earth-1, the first unmanned Martian spacecraft to travel to another part of our solar system, indicate that the planet Earth definitely shows signs of life, but probably not life as we know it on Mars. According to a spokesman for the Space Agency, the seasonal color changes observed by astronomers seem to be associated with the growth of plant life, some of it very large. From collected data it seems that any forms of life on Earth must exist in an atmosphere containing more than 20% oxygen and at temperatures as high as 50°C. The Space Agency is presently working on protective suits for the astronauts who will land on this dangerous planet in a few years.

May 2, 1973

Yesterday's amazing news bulletin announcing the definite existence of life on Earth has left most Martians wondering what is next. Readings taken by sensitive instruments on board Earth-1 prove without any doubt that some form of life exists on Earth. No detailed descriptions of Earth life can be given at this time, since even the best photographs taken from Earth-1 still show the planet at a distance of about 1,200 kilometers—too far away to see small details.

The "blue planet," as every Martian schoolchild calls Earth, is mostly covered by water. Signs of life, such as carbon dioxide in the atmosphere and traces of carbon compounds, probably show the existence of at least water plants. As mentioned in earlier reports, seasonal color changes probably show the existence of land plants. Some scientists think that animal life may also have developed, but this is only an educated guess with the information now available.

One thing that puzzles the scientists at the Space Agency is the apparent high concentration of life in the equatorial and middle regions of Earth and the lack of evidence of life in the more Martian-like polar regions. Evidently, answers to these questions will not be forthcoming until the landing of the first astronauts, now expected in the early 1980's.

* * *

October 15, 1991

Yesterday was a day like no other in the history of any country or planet. At exactly 13:43 Mars Universal Time two Martian astronauts lowered the gangway of Friendship-1 and stepped onto the third planet from the sun, Earth. As had been arranged in the voice contacts that have been going on since the discovery of Earth civilization in 1989, a greeting party of Earth leaders met our astronauts as they touched a foreign planet for the first time. Most observers expressed amazement at the similarity in appearance between Martians and the Earth people, even though there are minor differences, such as skin color and the number of fingers. . . .

OBSERVING YOUR ENVIRONMENT

How many times have you heard someone say, "Try to look at it *my* way!" The "news" articles you have just read were intended to give you a look at the earth from a viewpoint of someone very different from yourself—someone from another planet.

How would such a person describe you to his friends? How would you two learn about each other?

Think of the early explorers here on the earth. The first thing they were asked when they returned home from a foreign land was what they had *seen*. What about the first landing on the moon? People on the earth waited impatiently to *see* for themselves, through the miracle of television, what the surface of the moon was like.

If an Earthling met a Martian, the first thing they would probably do would be to *look* at each other. In the story above it was stated that the Martians were amazed at the similarities between Earth people and themselves. This is a simple *observation*— that is, a use of one of the senses to learn something about the environment. Sight, hearing, touch, taste, and smell are senses that give you information about your environment, or surroundings.

Of course, you generally have to do more than just look when you really want to find out about something. Suppose, for example, you wanted to compare your skeleton with that of the Martians. Would your senses give you any information about that? Yes, some direct observations could be made. For example, you could feel the bones in your arm and compare them with those in the Martian's arm. But wouldn't it be better if you could compare X-ray photographs of the bodies of both of you? You can often gain more detailed information about something by using *instruments* than you can with just your unaided senses.

Instruments are used when people need to extend their limited senses. All instruments, from a ruler to the most complicated scientific equipment, answer that need. They were invented when someone wanted to observe something and found that it couldn't be done without using something more sensitive and accurate than the human senses.

SUMMARY

1. Observations involve the interaction of your senses with the environment.
2. Powers of observation can be increased by the use of instruments to extend the human senses.

CLASSIFYING YOUR OBSERVATIONS

You can make all possible measurements and observations about a situation and still not understand what the information you have collected really means. To make some sense out of your observations, you might try to arrange them in groups. This is *classification*. For example, if you were given a tray of buttons and asked to classify them, you might sort them out by color, or by size, or by both color and size. There are often many ways to classify the same material.

After you have organized, or classified, the observations you have made, you may be able to conclude something from the organized information that you could not have stated on the basis of any of the separate observations. This interpretation of your observations is called an *inference*. An inference is a conclusion that follows logically from the information that you have. Detective work provides a good example of the difference between an observation and an inference. In searching for clues a detective may make many observations. But eventually he or she will try to put together the collected information and make an inference about the crime, such as when it occurred, or who committed it.

In the study of earth science you will have many chances to make observations and to draw inferences. It will be important for you to know the difference between these two processes of science.

Let's see how well you understand the meanings of the terms *observation* and *inference*. Below are some statements from the Martian newspaper articles. Which statements would you call observations, and which would you call inferences?

STATEMENT	OBSERVATION OR INFERENCE
1. According to a spokesman for the Space Agency, the seasonal color changes observed by astronomers seem to be associated with the growth of plant life . . .	1. This one should be easy. The "seasonal color changes" are observations; the statement says so directly. But the growth of plant life is an inference from those observations. The words "seem to be . . ." make that rather clear.
2. Any forms of life on Earth must exist . . . at temperatures as high as 50°C.	2. The temperature readings should be called observations, even though no thermometers were actually sent to the earth. It is quite possible to read the temperature of something far away by means of sensitive instruments. (For example, using the Mount Palomar telescope, the temperature of a match could be measured at a distance of about 40 kilometers.)
3. The "blue planet," as every Martian schoolchild calls Earth, is mostly covered by water.	3. That the earth is blue is definitely an observation. What about the statement that the planet is "mostly covered by water"? If you observe a substance that has all the properties of water, are you "observing" water? Or are you *inferring* the presence of water from the observations you made? The line between observation and inference is not always easy to draw.

SUMMARY

1. Classification is an organization of information in a meaningful way.
2. An inference is a conclusion based on available information.

Figure 1-1. The largest ball of string on record is one of 12 ft 9 in in diameter, 40 ft in circumference and weighing 10 tons, amassed by Francis A. Johnson of Darwin, Minn. between 1950 and 1978.

MEASUREMENTS

Most people are fascinated by records—the largest, the fastest, the most, etc. This interest in records is so widespread that the *Guinness Book of World Records**, from which Figure 1-1 is taken, is one of the world's best-selling books. Most of the records in the *Guinness Book* are measurements. Most observations in science are measurements, also. Just what is a measurement?

Units of Measurement. Every measurement consists of a numerical *quantity* and a *unit*. The description of the ball of string in Figure 1-1 includes three measurements—11 feet, 5 tons, 14 years. Feet, tons, and years are all *units* of measurement. The figures 11, 5, and 14 are the quantities of units in the measurements.

Two of the units in this example (feet and tons) are part of the system of measurement called the *English system*. This is the system still in common use in this country, so some of the examples in the next page or two are given in those familiar units.

However, almost all the rest of the world uses the *metric system of measurement**, and the United States is now changing over to that system, too. So we will be using metric units for the most part in this text.

Table 1-1. Metric units.

QUANTITY	UNIT	SYMBOL
Length	meter	m
Volume	liter	l
Mass	kilogram	kg
Time	second	s

METRIC PREFIXES

micro	1/1,000,000	one millionth
milli	1/1,000	one thousandth
centi	1/100	one hundredth
deci	1/10	one tenth
kilo	1,000	one thousand

---

*The metric system is also called the International System of Measurement, and metric units are called SI units, from the French name *Systeme International.*

Both the quantity of units and the name of the unit are usually needed if the measurement is to make any sense. However, in daily affairs, we often express measurements without stating the units. We can do that because everybody concerned knows which units are meant. For example:

"The weatherman reports that the temperature at 11:00 A.M. was 70. . ."

"Guess what, Sue! My weight was down to 102 this morning!" "Oh, Fran, I wish I had your will power!"

We know the temperature reading was measured in degrees Fahrenheit; we know Fran measured her weight in pounds. The units were understood in each case, and so the measurements had meaning.

Fundamental Units. All measurements, as we have already said, consist of a number and a unit. Certain units of measurement are called *basic,* or *fundamental*. This means that the unit is not a combination of other units.

The fundamental units have been defined by general agreement. For example, the unit of length in the metric system is the *meter*. Until recently, the meter was defined as the distance between two marks on a certain metal bar kept at the International Bureau of Weights and Measures near Paris, France. Today, the meter is defined in a more complex way. But the important point is that there is nothing in nature that tells us how long a meter *must* be. This is something that scientists have to decide among themselves. A meter could have been any length. But once decided, it becomes the fundamental unit of length that all scientists use. All measurements of length (or distance—which is the same thing) are expressed in terms of that unit or its equivalents.

Scientists have discovered that

Figure 1-2. Basic and derived units. With a single measurement of length, the referee can find the distance the ball was moved. Length is a basic unit. Two measurements are needed to find the speed of the car—distance traveled and time of travel. Speed is a derived unit.

there are several different fundamental units that are needed for the measurements they make. In your study of earth science, you will be concerned almost entirely with four of these fundamental units—the units of length, mass, time, and temperature.

Derived Units. Let us refer back to the weather report mentioned earlier. The temperature was 70°F. As we have just stated, the unit of temperature is a fundamental unit. Suppose the weather report continues:

" . . . The wind is from the northwest at 22 miles per hour, gusting to 35. . . ."

What is the unit of wind speed in this case? You can see that it is a compound unit, made from a unit of length (miles) and a unit of time (hours). The unit of speed is actually a unit of length divided by a unit of time. Units of speed are therefore not fundamental units. Such units are called *derived units.*

Consider another example that is not so obvious.

"Honey, would you pick up a quart of milk at the store?"

What is being measured by the unit "quart"? This is a unit of *volume*. Volume, however, is not a fundamental quantity. If we think of volume in terms of cubic inches or cubic centimeters, we see that volume is actually a measurement derived by combining units of length. The volume of a rectangular box, for example, is found by multiplying its length by its width by its depth. Every unit of volume can be converted to an equivalent product of three length measurements. For example, the liter is simply a convenient shorthand for 1,000 cubic centimeters (cm^3).

The fundamental units play such an important part in all of science that it is a good idea to take a closer look at them.

Length. Length is the distance between two points. The length of a line on a piece of paper, the length of a football field, the distance to another planet—all are determined by finding out how many times a standard measuring unit fits between two points.

Mass. Mass is usually defined as "the amount of matter" in an object. How do we measure "amount of matter"?

You may be thinking that there is no problem—you can find the mass of an object by weighing it. But isn't there something wrong with that? The weight of an object changes, depending on where it is. For example, you probably know that astronauts weighed much less on the moon than on the earth. Inside an orbiting satellite or in a "space walk" outside a spaceship, astronauts appear to be altogether "weightless" (see Figure 1-3).

Although astronauts may become weightless in a space vehicle, they do not lose their mass. The "amount of matter" in an object remains the same wherever it is. If a weightless astronaut floats across his cabin and collides with the wall, he will be forcibly reminded that he still has his usual mass. A mass resists a change in its motion—a property called *inertia*. The more rapid the change in motion, the greater the force of resistance. That is why collisions cause so much damage. Bringing a moving object to a sudden stop results in very large forces that depend on the mass of the object alone, not its weight.

Figure 1-3. Astronauts in a weightless condition.

Mass and Weight. Weight is not mass, but weight is still a convenient way of measuring mass. The reason for this is that weight is the pull of gravity on a body. This pull near the earth depends on just two things: (1) the distance of the body from the earth's center; and (2) the mass of the body. As long as we stay on the earth's surface, our distance from the earth's center is not going to change very much. Therefore, the weight of the things we measure simply depends on their mass. Unless we need extreme accuracy, we get a perfectly satisfactory measurement of mass on the earth by weighing. In fact, this is such a common and acceptable method of measuring mass that for most purposes mass and weight are expressed in the same units. But it is well to keep in mind the fact that mass and weight are actually two different properties of matter, even though they are numerically related.

Units of Mass. You may be wondering what the unit of mass is. By international agreement, the standard unit of mass is a certain piece of metal kept at the International Bureau of Weights and Measures. Everybody agrees that this body of matter has a mass of 1 kilogram. All other masses are found by comparing them, directly or indirectly, with that standard mass.

Time. Time can be described as our sense of things happening one after another. It is measured by observing a change in something. A clock is nothing more than a machine that regularly registers the swinging of a pendulum, the turning of a small wheel, the vibration of a tuning fork, etc. It does this by indicating numbers that we call hours, minutes, or seconds. You will see in Chapter 6 that time, as we usually think of it, is related to the apparent motions of the sun and stars.

Temperature. Through our sense of touch, we learn quite early in life that some things are hotter than others. Temperature is a measurement that tells us precisely how "hot" something is.

In this country the unit of temperature in ordinary use is the Fahrenheit degree (symbol, °F). On the Fahrenheit scale, the temperature of melting ice is 32°F and the temperature of boiling water at standard atmospheric pressure is 212°F. One Fahrenheit degree is 1/180 of the difference between those two temperatures.

In the metric system and in most scientific work, the Celsius degree is the unit of temperature (symbol, °C). On this scale the melting point of ice is 0°C and the boiling point of water is

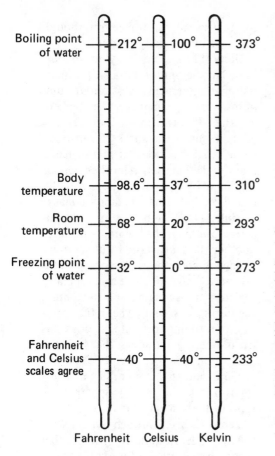

	Fahrenheit	Celsius	Kelvin
Boiling point of water	212°	100°	373°
Body temperature	98.6°	37°	310°
Room temperature	68°	20°	293°
Freezing point of water	32°	0°	273°
Fahrenheit and Celsius scales agree	–40°	–40°	233°

Figure 1-4. Fahrenheit and Celsius temperature scales.

100°C. One Celsius degree is 1/100 of the difference between those two temperatures.

If you live in one of the Northeastern or North Central states, you know from your own experience that temperatures can drop below zero. Temperature measurements below zero are shown as negative numbers (for example, –24°C).

There is no upper limit to temperatures. Temperatures in the interior of stars and in nuclear explosions range into the millions of degrees. There is,

however, a *coldest,* or *lowest,* possible temperature. The reason for this is that objects are made colder by taking heat energy out of them. When you have taken all the heat energy they have, you cannot lower their temperatures any further. This lowest possible temperature is the same for all matter, and it is called *absolute zero.* The temperature of absolute zero is —273.16°C (which we usually round off to —273°C).

The Kelvin scale of temperatures is a scale that uses Celsius degrees, but that has its zero point at absolute zero. On the Kelvin scale, 0°K is the lowest possible temperature, the melting point of ice is 273°K, and the boiling point of water is 373°K. Any temperature in °C can be converted to °K by adding 273.

The U.S. Weather Service is still using the Fahrenheit scale in its reports to the public, but most other scientific work is expressed either in Celsius or in Kelvin units of temperature.

Percentage Error. In making any measurement, the chances are that our results will not be absolutely accurate. We can often compare our results with some standard or accepted value to see how closely they agree. But how much error can be allowed before the results become meaningless?

As you may guess, the amount of error that is acceptable varies with the situation. Suppose you measure the distance on a map between your town and the next town and you get a result of 5 miles. If the actual distance is 5½ miles, the chances are this error will have no effect on a trip between the two towns. But if the same degree of

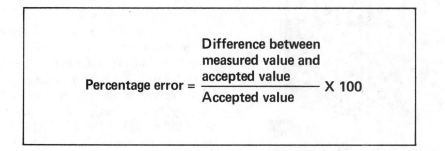

$$\text{Percentage error} = \frac{\text{Difference between measured value and accepted value}}{\text{Accepted value}} \times 100$$

error existed in the calculations used to send astronauts to the moon, those men would be in big trouble!

The amount of error in a measurement is the difference between the values you obtain and the true or accepted values. This is commonly given as *percentage error*. The formula for calculating percentage error is shown at the top of the page.

Suppose you measured the length of a table and obtained a result of 202 cm. A friend measured the same length and obtained a result of 198 cm. To calculate the percentage error in each of these measurements, you need to know the "correct" or "accepted" value of the length of the table. Let's suppose that you have the manufacturer's catalog and you find that the table is described as 200 cm in length. This is the accepted value. The calculations of percentage error of the two measurements are shown below. You and your friend have both made an error of 1%, but yours is an error on the high side, or a positive error, while your friend's error is on the low side, or a negative error.

Rounding Measurements and Calculations. The speed limit on most highways in the United States is 55 miles per hour. One mile is exactly equal to 1.609344 kilometers. If we multiply 55 by 1.609344 to change mi/hr to km/hr, we obtain 88.51392 km/hr as the equivalent of 55 mi/hr. Does this mean that when speed limit signs become

Your % of error =

$$\frac{202 - 200}{200} \times 100 = \frac{2}{200} \times 100 = 1\%$$

Your friend's % of error =

$$\frac{200 - 198}{200} \times 100 = \frac{2}{200} \times 100 = 1\%$$

Figure 1-5. U.S. highway sign of the future?

metric they may look like Figure 1-5?

You would probably agree that expressing the speed to so many decimal places is foolish. But how far should a calculation involving measurements be carried? Percentage error can help us decide.

The speedometer in a car is not a very accurate instrument. It probably has a percentage error of about 2%. This means that if you read your speed as 55 mi/hr, your measurement may be off by about 2% either way, or about 1 mi/hr. Your true speed may be anything between 54 and 56 mi/hr. You can't improve your percentage error by changing to km/hr. Your result must still be in doubt by 2%. If you multiply 55 mi/hr by 1.6 to change to km/hr, your result will be 88 km/hr—close enough for all practical purposes. So 88 km/hr is the speed limit we would expect to find on the sign.

In auto racing, a much higher degree of precision is used in determining speeds and records. Distances and times are measured with percentage errors as little as 0.001%. Speeds are calculated to within a thousandth of a mile per hour. For example, the speed of the winner in the 1972 Indianapolis 500-mile race was calculated to be 162.962 mi/hr. To convert this speed to km/hr, we would use the exact conversion factor and carry the result to the same number of decimal places as there are in the measurement. If you do the arithmetic, you should get a result of 262.262 km/hr. It makes sense to say that a speed record of 162.962 mi/hr is equal to 262.262 km/hr. It does not make sense to say that a speed limit of 55 mi/hr is equal to 88.51392 km/hr.

The number of figures or decimal places to keep in a calculation depends on how accurate your measurements are. It is wasted time and effort to carry out calculations to more places than your data has. In your laboratory investigations, keep this idea in mind. Your measurements will usually be made to two or three figures, or with a percentage error of about 1%. When using your measurements in a calculation, you should round off your results to the same two or three figures, or the same 1% margin of error.

For example, suppose you measure a block of wood to the nearest millimeter (0.1 cm), and obtain results like these:

length = 12.4 cm
width = 6.1 cm
height = 2.7 cm

If you use these measurements to calculate the volume of the block by the volume formula

V = length X width X height

you will get a result of 204.228 cm³. You have not really measured the volume with such high precision. Your result should be rounded to 204 cm³. You would use the rounded result in any further calculations you need to make.

SUMMARY

1. All measurements consist of a numerical value and a unit of measurement.
2. Some units of measurement are fundamental: they are not combinations of other units. Units of length, mass, time, and temperature are examples of fundamental units. Other units are derived: they are combinations of one or more fundamental units. Units of volume and speed are examples.
3. All measurements are comparisons of the quantity being measured with a standard unit. Scientists use the metric system of standard units.
4. Weight is a measure of the pull of gravity on an object and varies with location. Mass is the amount of matter in an object and does not vary with location. (For most measurements here on earth, we can substitute weight for mass.)
5. Any measurement is an approximation and must be considered to contain some error. The amount of error is usually given as the percentage error.

REVIEW QUESTIONS

Group A

1. What is involved in a direct observation of the environment?
2. How can you increase your powers of observation?
3. Describe three situations in which the use of instruments enables you to gather more information about the environment than would be possible with your unaided senses.
4. What is meant by the term *classification?*
5. If you were given a group of objects, explain, in general terms, how you would classify them.
6. What is an *inference?*
7. What is the difference between an observation and an inference?
8. What are the two parts of all measurements?
9. What is a *fundamental* unit of measurement? Give two examples.
10. What is a *derived* unit of measurement? Give two examples.
11. What system of standard units is used by scientists?
12. What is the difference between *weight* and *mass?*
13. What is *percentage error?*

Group B

1. a. What are some limitations to your direct observations of your environment?
   b. Give an example of an observation that could be made without using an instrument, but that would be improved by using one.
   c. Give an example of an observation that could not be made without the use of an instrument.
2. Give an example, preferably from your own experience, of how a group of observations led to an inference.
3. a. List two factors that can affect the accuracy of a measurement and explain how you would attempt to control each of them.
   b. Explain how a series of measurements could be *precise,* but not *accurate.*

Freezing water expands, causing crevices in pavement to widen. Traffic turns the crevices into pot-holes.

CHAPTER 2
Some Useful Measurements
of the Environment

You will know something about making measurements of the environment if you can:
1. Determine the density of a given sample of material.
2. Describe how the density of a material is affected by changes in temperature and/or pressure.
3. Explain how water differs from most materials when it changes state.
4. Use instruments to measure temperature, pressure, humidity, and wind speed and direction.

The full range of properties of the environment that can be observed and measured is enormous. That is why science is usually subdivided into specialties, with different investigators concentrating on different areas of study. That is also the reason for separating your science education into different subjects. This year you are studying earth science. In later years, you may take courses in biology, chemistry, physics, and so on. But since this is your year for earth science, you will be narrowing your scientific attention to matters of chief importance in that science. In this chapter we will take a look at some of the properties of the environment with which you will be particularly concerned.

DENSITY

You have already learned that some measurements are combinations of two or more of the basic quantities. One combined measurement that is important in earth science is *density*. Density is a measure of the *concentration* of matter (mass) in a given space.

You know from your experience that some things are heavier than others, and that the difference is more than just a difference in size or volume. If you had samples of many different materials, all the same volume, you could arrange them (classify them) by weight from heaviest to lightest. Since all the samples have the same volume, the heavier ones obviously have more mass packed into the same volume than the lighter ones have. This is what we mean by density. It is a characteristic of a material that does not depend on the size of the sample we have.

Now let's be a bit more precise about the meaning of the term den-

sity. Density is defined as the *mass per unit volume* of a sample of matter. That is, it is the mass of a single unit of volume. If we measure mass in grams and volume in cubic centimeters, density is the number of grams in 1 cubic centimeter.

Finding Density. It is easy to see that we don't have to obtain an exact cubic centimeter of a substance, and weigh that cubic centimeter, to find its density. If we know the volume of a sample, and we find its mass by weighing it, we can calculate the density by dividing the mass by the volume:

$$\text{Density} = \frac{\text{Mass}}{\text{Volume}}$$

In mathematical symbols:

$$D = \frac{M}{V}$$

Figure 2-1. The meaning of density. The density of a material is its mass per unit of volume. Density depends partly on the mass of the particles in a substance and partly on how closely they are packed. In *B* the density is greater than in *A* because there are more particles (with the same mass) in the same volume. In *C* the density is greater than in *A* because the particles in *C* have more mass.

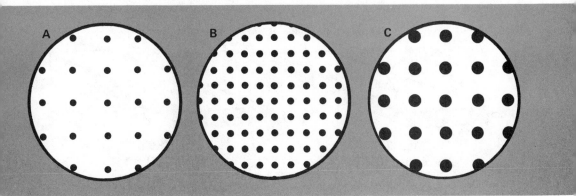

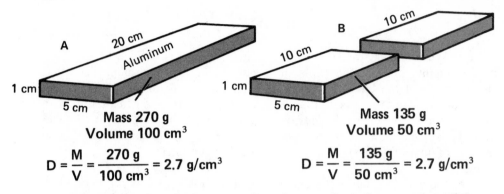

Figure 2-2. Density of pure samples. From these two illustrations you can see that the density of aluminum is the same regardless of the size, shape, or mass of the sample. This is true of any pure substance.

To understand the usefulness of the idea of density, look at Figure 2-2. In A, we see a bar of aluminum that has a mass of 270 grams and a volume of 100 cubic centimeters (100 cm³). Applying the density formula, we find that the density of the bar is 2.7 grams per cubic centimeter (D = 2.7 g/cm³).

In B, the bar has been cut into two pieces. Each piece now has only half the mass of the original piece—135 g. But the volume of each is also only half as large—50 cm³. When we calculate the density of each piece, it comes out to the same value—2.7 g/cm³.

This is, of course, not much of a surprise. We expect a pure material, such as aluminum, to be the same throughout. The ratio of its mass to its volume should naturally be the same no matter how large or small a piece we have. If we cut a piece precisely 1 cm³ in volume, it would have a mass of 2.7 g.

In short, the density of a piece of aluminum is always the same—2.7 g/cm³—regardless of its size, shape, or mass. On the other hand, the density of some other material would be different. In Figure 2-3, we see a bar of iron of exactly the same dimensions as the bar of aluminum in Figure 2-2. Its volume is therefore the same—100 cm³—but its mass is considerably greater—790 g. The density of iron is 7.9 g/cm³, almost three times as great as that of aluminum.

Each pure substance has its own particular density. Density is there-

Figure 2-3. Densities of two different substances.

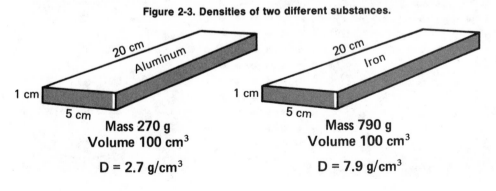

fore a characteristic that helps to identify a material. A piece of metal with a density of 2.7 g/cm³ is probably aluminum; a metal with a density of 7.9 g/cm³ is probably iron.

Can you apply the principle of density to the samples of matter in Figure 2-4? Arrange the materials in order of increasing density. Can you find two or more specimens that are probably the same material?

Figure 2-4. Arranging samples by density. Samples *C* and *D* are probably aluminum.

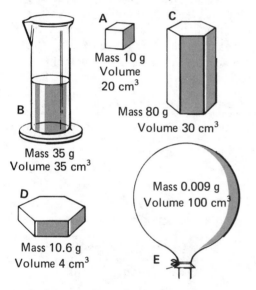

A
Mass 10 g
Volume
20 cm³

C
Mass 80 g
Volume 30 cm³

B
Mass 35 g
Volume 35 cm³

D
Mass 10.6 g
Volume 4 cm³

Mass 0.009 g
Volume 100 cm³

E

We have said that each substance has a definite density that is characteristic of the material. This is strictly true only when the temperature and pressure remain the same. This is an especially important requirement in the case of gases, as we shall see in a moment. It is also important to remember that only pure substances have a definite density. Materials such as rocks, which can be mixtures of several minerals in various proportions, will not have a very precise density. However, rock types will

have a certain average density that can help to identify them.

Changing the Density of a Substance. You have probably heard it said that cold air is heavier than warm air, and that is why cold air sinks and warm air rises. That statement can be made scientifically correct by changing the word "heavier" to "denser." Why is cold air usually denser than warm air? The following example may help you to understand the reason.

If a group of people try to crowd into an elevator, more of them can get in if they all stand still with their arms at their sides. But if they start a heated competition, moving their bodies and jumping up and down, not as many can get into the elevator. There

Figure 2-5. Density and temperature. More people will fit into the elevator if they are behaving calmly and "coolly" than if they are acting "heatedly." As temperature increases, density generally decreases.

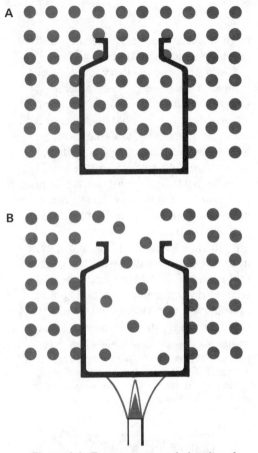

Figure 2-6. Temperature and density of a gas. In an open, unheated bottle *(A)* the density of the gas is the same as that of the surroundings. When the bottle is heated *(B)*, the molecules of the gas inside begin to move more rapidly, and some of them move out of the bottle. Thus the gas inside the bottle becomes less dense.

tends to make it more dense. These changes in density occur only if the gas is *able* to expand or contract. In a sealed container, heating a gas raises the pressure, rather than lowering the density, since the agitated molecules have no way to get out.

Solids and liquids also expand and contract with changes in temperature, but to a much lesser extent than gases. Therefore their densities are also affected to a much lesser extent.

Pressure is another factor that affects the density of gases. (Solids and liquids are also affected by pressure changes, but to a lesser extent.) Increasing the pressure packs the molecules of a gas closer together (see Figure 2-7). The gas contracts. This

Figure 2-7. Pressure and density of a gas. Increasing the pressure on a gas in a closed container causes an increase in the density of the gas because the molecules of the gas are packed closer together.

will be less mass (fewer people) in the same volume (the space in the elevator), and the "people density" will be less.

Something similar happens in a heated gas. Heating the gas adds energy to it. Its molecules begin to move more rapidly, they collide with more force, and they therefore tend to spread apart. Thus a heated gas tends to become less dense (see Figure 2-6). Removing energy by cooling the gas

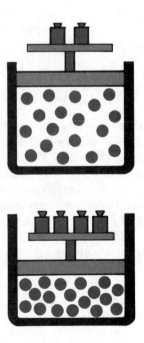

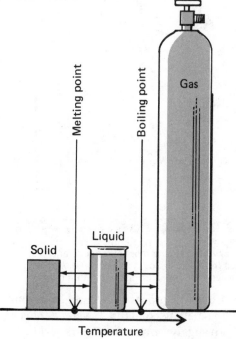

Solid | Liquid | Gas

Melting point

Boiling point

Temperature

Figure 2-8. Change in volume with change of state. Most common substances increase in volume (and decrease in density) as they change from a solid to a liquid and from a liquid to a gas. Water is an exception.

means that more molecules can fit in a given volume, and so the density is increased. If the pressure is reduced, the gas molecules move farther apart. The gas expands. So there are fewer molecules in a given volume, and the density is decreased.

Density and the States of Matter. As you know, heating or cooling a substance can cause other changes besides a change in volume or density. Heating may cause the material to melt, evaporate, or boil; cooling may cause it to condense or freeze. In other words, it may change its *physical state*, or *phase*.

The three states of matter are solid, liquid, and gas. Elements and many chemical compounds change state at definite temperatures, called their

melting and boiling points. As a substance changes state, its volume usually changes sharply also, especially between the liquid and gas states. Its density therefore changes in the opposite direction. These ideas are pictured in Figure 2-8.

What Figure 2-8 shows is true of most materials that exist in the three states. But the most common substance on the earth is an exception. That substance is water. Let us examine the behavior of water as its temperature and state change.

Water and Density. Water is the only substance that we find naturally in all three states on the earth. In fact, wherever the temperature is below the freezing point (0°C), we are likely to find all three of the states of water present at the same time.

In Figure 2-9, we see a photograph of water in the solid state (ice) floating in liquid water. This doesn't surprise us, because we are accustomed to the idea of ice floating in water. But if you think about it, you will realize that it is a very unusual phenomenon. An object floats in a liquid only if the object

Figure 2-9. The tip of an iceberg. Icebergs float because the ice (solid water) is less dense than the liquid water.

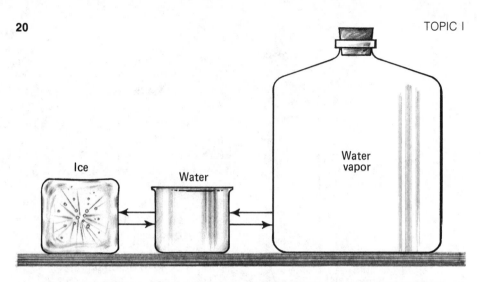

Figure 2-10. Change of state and volume of water. Unlike most other substances, water decreases in volume when it changes from a solid (ice) to a liquid. Like most other substances, it increases in volume when it changes from a liquid to a gas.

is less dense than the liquid. But as we have already stated, most substances are more dense in the solid state than they are in the liquid state. Therefore, a solid normally sinks in its own liquid. But here is a solid floating in its liquid. This means that ice must be less dense than water. The diagram in Figure 2-10 will help you see this important difference between water and other substances.

Figure 2-10 shows that the behavior of water as it changes from a liquid to a gas is normal. It does what other substances do, which is to become much less dense in the gaseous state.

But in the process of warming up from the melting point (0°C), water behaves strangely. Look at Figure 2-11. It shows a flask of water at various temperatures. The glass tube enables us to detect small changes in the total volume. Normally, a liquid expands as it is heated. But here we see that as the temperature of the water increases from 0°C, its volume *decreases* at first. Its volume does not begin to increase until its temperature passes 4°C.

What all this means is that the maximum density of water occurs in the liquid state, at a temperature of

Figure 2-11. Volume of water and temperature change. The volume of a given quantity of water is smallest at 4°C.

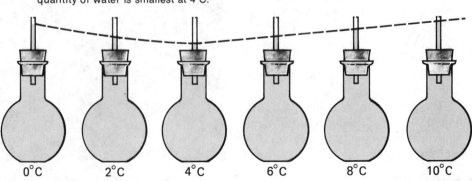

0°C   2°C   4°C   6°C   8°C   10°C

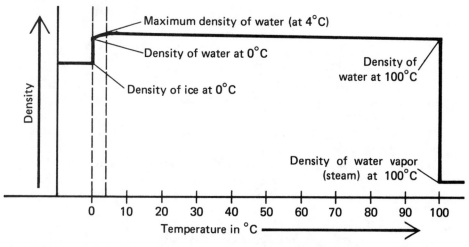

Figure 2-12. Density changes in water with change in state. Although the density of liquid water is greatest at 4℃, the amount of change between 0℃ and 100℃ is very little.

4°C. At 0°C, the density of water is slightly less than at 4°C, and the density of ice is even less than that. Changes in the density of water as its temperature and state change are shown graphically in Figure 2-12.

Importance of the Strange Behavior of Water. The following facts have some truly vital consequences: (1) Below 4°C water expands slightly and becomes less dense. (2) Ice is less dense than water at any temperature. If you were to measure the temperatures in a frozen pond, you would get readings something like those shown in Figure 2-13. The water at the bottom, which has to be the densest, must be at 4°C. The ice on top must

be at 0°C or lower. So the water in between must gradually increase in temperature from 0° to 4° as you go deeper.

Because water near 0°C is less dense than water at 4°C, and because ice, when it forms, floats on water, ponds and lakes freeze from the top down. Since the ice acts as an insulator for the water below it, most lakes do not freeze all the way through in winter. This means that water organisms can survive the winter quite nicely in the protected waters near the bottom. It means, also, that people are able to enjoy some ice skating much earlier in winter than they might otherwise expect.

Figure 2-13. Water temperatures in an ice-covered pond. Although the top of the pond is covered with ice, the water at the bottom of the pond is at a temperature of 4℃. This allows many aquatic organisms to survive over the winter.

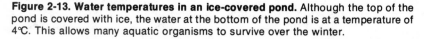

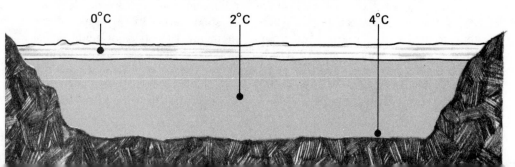

SUMMARY

1. Density is defined as the amount of mass in a unit volume and is expressed mathematically as Density = Mass/Volume.
2. The density of a pure substance is a characteristic that helps to identify it.
3. In most cases heating a substance decreases its density, while cooling it increases its density.
4. Increasing the pressure on a substance increases its density, while decreasing the pressure decreases its density.
5. The maximum density of most substances occurs in the solid state.
6. The maximum density of water occurs in the liquid state, at 4°C. The density of ice (water in the solid state) is less than the density of the liquid.

A WEATHER WATCH

Later in this course you will study about weather. As part of your study of that topic you may be asked to analyze and interpret weather data that you yourself have collected. In order to discover patterns or trends in the weather, you must have adequate data, so it is important that you begin your weather watch now, at the beginning of the course.

One of the points made in Chapter 1 was that there are many types of measurements that people cannot make with their unaided senses. These measurements require the use of instruments. Collecting data about the weather will require the use of instruments. Of course, you will be limited to those instruments that your school has available. The measurements that you will want to make include temperature, pressure, humidity, and wind velocity.

Temperature. As you probably know, the instrument used to measure temperature is the *thermometer*. In view of the enormous range of possible temperatures that scientists may want to measure, they need many different types of thermometers. Your window thermometer, for example, would not be much good for measuring the temperatures inside a furnace. However, for your needs in observing the weather, two basic types of thermometer will do.

1. *Liquid thermometers*. The common liquid-in-glass thermometer usually contains mercury or alcohol. The alcohol is often colored to make it easier to see. Heat energy is transferred to or from the thermometer, and the liquid in the tube expands or contracts.

One of the problems of the liquid thermometer is that it breaks easily. It is also obvious that a liquid thermometer cannot be used below the freezing point or above the boiling point of the liquid. So, a thermometer made entirely of solid parts is sometimes more practical.

2. *Bimetallic thermometers*. Bimetallic thermometers are made entirely of solid parts. In this type of thermometer, two strips of metal, usually brass and steel, are bonded together. When the strip is heated, the brass expands faster than the steel. This forces the strip to bend to one side.

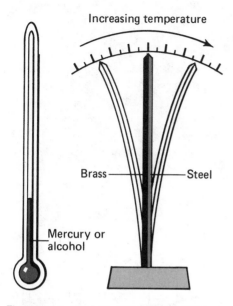

Increasing temperature

Brass ———— Steel

Mercury or
alcohol

Figure 2-14. A liquid and a bimetallic thermometer.

The bending of the strip moves a pointer or similar device and gives you a temperature reading (see Figure 2-14). One of the most important reasons for using this type of thermometer is that it can be easily attached to a recording instrument.

Pressure. The deeper you go into a body of water, the more pressure you feel. This occurs because there is more water packed above and around you, and its weight is pressing on you. Your eardrums are especially sensitive to pressure.

Pressure, however, is not simply a force. It is the amount of force exerted on a unit of area. Pressure can be expressed in such units as pounds per square inch or grams per square centimeter. The same total force can result in different intensities of pressure, depending on the area over which the force is spread. A clear demonstration of this fact can be obtained with a sharpened lead pencil. Press the eraser end against your

palm with moderate force. Then press the pointed end against your palm with the same force. There is much more pressure when the force is concentrated on the small area of the point—and you can feel the difference!

The atmosphere extends upward to a height of hundreds of kilometers above the surface of the earth. The weight of this air exerts pressure in the same way that water does. The amount of pressure exerted by the atmosphere varies with altitude. It is less at the top of a high mountain than it is at sea level, because the amount of air above you is less on the mountaintop. Atmospheric pressure also depends on weather conditions, so that at any location, the pressure changes constantly with the weather. There will be more about this in Chapters 10 and 11. Right now we are simply concerned with measuring air pressure.

Air pressure is measured with an instrument called a *barometer*. There are two types of barometers—mercurial and aneroid.

1. *Mercurial barometers.* The mercurial barometer is the one most commonly used by scientists. It consists basically of a narrow glass tube that is closed at one end, and a dish of mercury (see Figure 2-15).

The tube is filled with mercury and then put into the dish of mercury with the open end down. Not all the mercury runs out of the tube. Instead, a column of mercury about 76 cm high remains in the tube. The space above the mercury in the tube is a nearly complete vacuum.

The mercury is held in the tube by the force of the atmospheric pressure

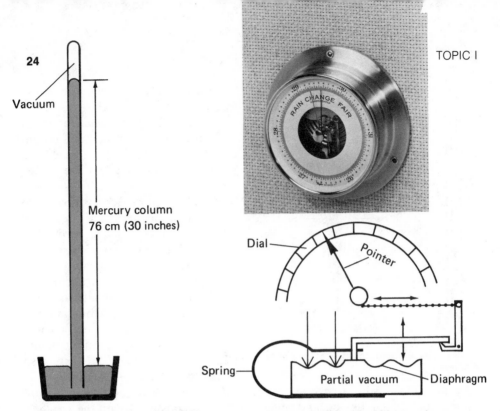

Vacuum

Mercury column
76 cm (30 inches)

Figure 2-15. A mercurial barometer.

Dial

Pointer

Spring

Partial vacuum

Diaphragm

Figure 2-16. An aneroid barometer.

pressing down on the surface of the mercury in the dish. When the air pressure drops, it can support only a smaller weight of mercury, and the level of mercury in the tube drops. (Now you know what is meant by a "falling barometer.") When the air pressure rises, the mercury level in the tube rises again.

2. *Aneroid barometers.* Mercurial barometers are very delicate. They are also difficult to carry from one place to another, and cannot be read very well unless firmly fixed in proper position. These characteristics limit their usage. As an answer to these problems, *aneroid* ("without liquid") *barometers* were developed. Aneroid barometers are not as accurate as mercurial barometers, but they are much more portable and resistant to breakage. Most home barometers are aneroid barometers.

An aneroid barometer consists of an airtight box from which some of the air has been removed (see Figure 2-16). Across the top of this box is a thin, flexible sheet of metal. An increase in air pressure pushes the sheet in. A decrease in pressure permits the sheet to move out. Thus this flexible metal sheet moves in and out in response to pressure changes. This movement is magnified by a mechanical system that also moves a pointer. The pressure is read by the position of the pointer against a marked dial. The scale on the dial is marked in the same units as the scale on a mercurial barometer.

Barometer Readings. Although the units of pressure are force per unit area, barometers are usually read in terms of the height of the mercury column that the air pressure can support. Thus standard atmospheric pressure at sea level is usually given as 76 cm. This is the height of the mercury column. (It is understood that the centimeter is not a unit of pressure, and that we are just using a convenient shorthand notation.) Since atmospheric pressure varies with altitude, barometric readings taken above or below sea level are corrected for this variation. Atmospheric pressure at sea level seldom falls below 71 cm, except possibly in the eye of a hurricane or tornado. High pressures rarely go above 79 cm.

In weather reports in the United States the barometric pressure is commonly given in *inches* of mercury, instead of in centimeters. Standard barometric pressure at sea level is 29.92 inches. Low readings rarely go below 28 inches, while high readings are rarely above 31 inches.

Another system for measuring air pressure uses a unit called a *millibar* (mb). This unit is derived from a unit of force called a dyne. Since this unit is no longer in favor with scientists, we won't go into a complete explanation of its meaning. Standard pressure at sea level is 1013.2 mb. Normal pressure varies from about 950 to 1050 mb. A comparison of barometric scales is shown in Figure 2-17.

Humidity. Humidity is the amount of water vapor, or water in the gaseous phase, in the air. Water vapor in the air comes from the evaporation of water from the earth's surface and from water vapor given off by living organisms.

The amount of water vapor that can be present in the air varies with temperature. The higher the temperature, the more water vapor the air can hold. Air containing the maximum amount

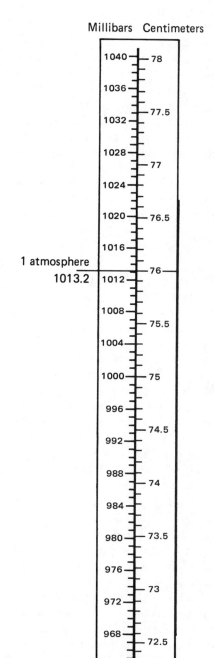

Figure 2-17. Barometric scales.

of water vapor it can hold at that temperature is said to be *saturated*.

The water vapor content of the air is often given in terms of *relative humidity* or *dew point*.

1. *Relative humidity*. Relative humidity is the ratio of the amount of water vapor in the air to the maximum amount that could be present at that temperature. It is expressed as a percent. Air containing one-half the amount of water vapor that it could hold at the temperature has a relative humidity of 50%. Absolutely dry air has a relative humidity of 0%, while saturated air has a relative humidity of 100%.

2. *Dew point*. As we have already mentioned, the amount of water vapor the air can hold decreases with falling temperature. If the amount of water vapor in the air remains the same, the relative humidity of the air increases as the temperature drops.

Think of what happens to a cold can of soda on a hot summer day. When you take it out of the refrigerator, the outside of the can is dry. But after it sits out in the air for a little while, the outside of the can becomes covered with drops of water. What has happened is that the air that is in contact with the can has become colder. This cold air cannot hold as much water vapor as the surrounding hot air, so some of the water vapor condenses on the can.

What this shows is that it is not necessary to add water vapor to increase the relative humidity of air. Decreasing its temperature will have the same effect. As the temperature of air drops, its relative humidity increases. Eventually the relative humidity becomes 100%, which

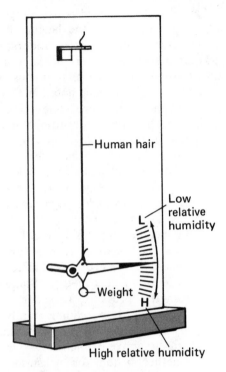

Figure 2-18. A hygrometer.

means that the air is saturated. The temperature at which air becomes saturated is called the *dew point*. It is the temperature at which water vapor begins to condense out of the air, forming drops of dew on surfaces in contact with it.

Measuring Relative Humidity. An instrument used to measure relative humidity of the air is called a *hygrometer* (see Figure 2-18). One type of hygrometer contains a thin bundle of human hair connected to a pointer. Hair is very sensitive to changes in relative humidity, lengthening with increased relative humidity, and shortening with decreased relative humidity. With this type of hygrometer, relative humidity is read directly from the position of the pointer on a scale (or similar arrangement).

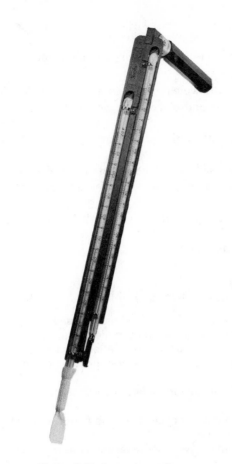

Figure 2-19. A psychrometer.

Another type of hygrometer is called a *sling psychrometer*. It is a simple instrument consisting basically of two ordinary liquid-in-glass thermometers fastened together. They are attached to a handle by which they can be whirled through the air (see Figure 2-19). One of the thermometers has a cloth sock or cover over its bulb, which is moistened before the instrument is used. This is the *wet-bulb thermometer*. The other thermometer has its bulb exposed to the air. It is called the *dry-bulb thermometer*.

As you whirl, or sling, the psychrometer, evaporation of water from

the cloth lowers the temperature of the wet-bulb thermometer. The temperatures of the wet-bulb and dry-bulb thermometers and the difference between them (the "wet-bulb depression") can be used to find both the relative humidity and the dew point of the air. Special tables and charts enable you to do this. (See page 539.)

Wind Velocity. Wind speed and wind direction are usually reported as one reading, which is called *wind velocity*. In terms of weather conditions and patterns it is important to know not only how hard the wind is blowing, but also from which direction it is blowing. It may make a great difference whether the wind is from the north or from the south.

The direction given is always the direction from which the wind is blowing. A north wind is coming from the north, and going toward the south.

An instrument used to measure wind speed is called an *anemometer* (see Figure 2-20). A *wind vane,* or *weather vane,* indicates wind direction.

Figure 2-20. An anemometer.

SUMMARY

1. The most common weather measurement is the measurement of air temperature.
2. Pressure is force per unit of area.
3. Atmospheric pressure is caused by the weight of the air above a given unit of area. The pressure at a given time and place decreases with increasing altitude.
4. Atmospheric pressure is most frequently expressed in terms of the height of the mercury column it will support.
5. Relative humidity is the ratio (expressed as a percent) between the amount of water vapor in the air and the maximum amount that could be present at the given temperature.
6. The dew point temperature is the temperature at which the air becomes saturated.
7. Wind velocity includes speed and direction.

REVIEW QUESTIONS

Group A
1. Define *density.* How is density expressed mathematically?
2. How can a measurement of density help to identify a substance?
3. How does heating or cooling a substance affect its density?
4. How does increasing or decreasing the pressure on a substance affect its density?
5. The maximum density of most materials occurs in which state—solid, liquid, or gas?
6. In which state does the maximum density of water occur? At what temperature does it occur?
7. What are the most common weather measurements?
8. Define the term *pressure.*
9. What causes atmospheric pressure?
10. How does atmospheric pressure vary with altitude?
11. What is *relative humidity?*
12. What is the *dew point?*
13. What two factors must be given in describing wind velocity?

Group B
1. You have just determined the density of a 50-gram sample of granite to be 2.5 g/cm³.
   a. What would be the density and the volume of a 100-gram sample of granite taken from the same location?
   b. What would be the density and the mass of a 40-cm³ sample of granite taken from the same location?
   c. What will be the effect on your determination of the density of a particular material if you use a larger sample of the material? If you use a smaller sample?

2. During an early spring morning the air temperature rises from 2°C (just above the freezing point) to 10°C. What effect does this rise in temperature have on the density of the air? Would the effect on the density of the soil be (greater than, the same as, less than) the effect on the density of the air? Why?

3. Water in the solid state (ice) floats in water in the liquid state. Would you expect a piece of solid lead to float in liquid lead? Explain your answer.

4. Suppose you wanted to keep a record of the following weather conditions: temperature, pressure, humidity, wind speed, and wind direction. Suppose also that you had to compile your record without the help of *any* equipment. Compare the accuracy and precision of your records with the records kept by a classmate who used ordinary weather instruments.

REVIEW EXERCISES

1. Choose a convenient location (at school, at home, outdoors). Examine the area carefully. Make a list of statements about the area. Now on another sheet of paper classify each statement as either an observation (0) or an inference (I). Have another student read your list of statements and classify them. Compare your classifications with his to see if they agree. Discuss any statements that you did not agree on.

2. Obtain an almanac or similar reference book from your library. Find ten facts (sports records, etc.) that involve measurements. Classify the measurements as fundamental (F) or derived (D). Try to identify the units involved in each measurement (time, length, etc.).

3. How accurate is your car's odometer (mileage meter)? Measure a certain distance on a road map. Now have someone drive over the same route. Using the map distance as the correct one, what was the percentage error in your odometer reading?

4. Find the density of a piece of modeling clay. (Hint: Think of the mathematical formula for density. How can you find mass? How can you find volume?) Now press or roll the clay into different shapes, and measure the density each time. Are all your density measurements equal? Should they be?

5. What is the density of water at room temperature? Is the density of ice really less than that of water? Can you think of a way to measure the density of ice accurately? (Hint: Ice floats in water, but will it float in liquids that are less dense than water? How can such liquids help you find the density of ice?)

TOPIC II
THE CHANGING ENVIRONMENT

The sudden release of energy, as in an earthquake, can be very destructive.

CHAPTER 3

You will know something about change in the environment if you can:
1. Explain how change can be described and measured.
2. Give some examples of cyclic changes.
3. Determine the direction of energy flow across an interface in a given example.
4. Apply what you have learned about change to the problems of environmental pollution.

The one thing we can count on in this universe is the occurrence of change. From moment to moment, from century to century, from one age to another, things change. They become different from what they were before. The earth scientist is interested in the changes that take place in the environment—the earth and the bodies of matter in the space around us.

CHARACTERISTICS OF CHANGE

The Events of Change. Every change or series of changes can be called an *event*. Events may occur almost instantaneously, as in the case of a lightning discharge or the breakdown of an atom. On the other hand, events may take place gradually over millions of years, as in the case of the wearing away of mountains and the drifting of continents. Regardless of the time span involved, an event is marked by some change in the properties of matter or in the properties of a system.

The earth scientist is interested, first of all, in *describing* the events of change that are occurring now and that have occurred in the past. Much detective work goes into figuring out just what these changes have been. But the earth scientist is even more interested in discovering the causes of change—the basic earth processes that explain the events that he describes. Your study of earth science will be concerned with both the events of change and the processes of change.

Frames of Reference for Change. Most changes that we observe and talk about are changes that occur in the course of time. That is, we observe that something is different from what it was like yesterday or last year. When looking back at past changes, such as the history of nations (or of mountains), we usually place the events of change on a time scale. In such cases, time becomes the *frame of reference* for describing the change.

There is, however, another kind of change that we observe, especially in earth science. It is the kind of change described by a sentence like the following:

> "As you travel westward from the Great Plains of Kansas into Colorado, the landscape undergoes a dramatic change."

Actually, the landscape of Colorado doesn't change during your trip. This is an observed change that results from a change of location. In other words, the frame of reference is space, rather than time.

Figure 3-1. The Grand Canyon. The erosion of the Grand Canyon is such a gradual process that it is almost impossible to measure the rate at which it is occurring.

In describing a changing weather pattern, the frame of reference likewise can be either time or space. "Rain ending tonight, followed by clear and colder weather." That might be a forecast for your community. The frame of reference is time. "Cloudy in the western part of the state, sunny toward the east." That is a changing weather pattern with space, or location, as the frame of reference.

Rate of Change. When describing a change with respect to time, it is often useful to know the *rate of change,* or how much of a change takes place within a given period of time.

Some of the processes we study in earth science, such as the phases of the moon, change at rates that can be easily and accurately measured. Others, such as the erosion of the Grand Canyon, occur so gradually and over such a long period of time that they are almost impossible to measure.

Graphing Change. A common way to represent change is in the form of a graph. A graph can give you a picture of what is happening. In this way it may be more useful for interpreting data than simple lists of numbers.

A graph shows you how one factor is changing with respect to another. Suppose you wanted to make a graph showing what happens to the temperature of a box of soil placed under a heat lamp for 10 minutes. You don't know what the temperature readings will be, but you do know that time will go from 0 to 10 minutes.

On this graph, time is the *independent variable.* You know in advance what the time measurement will be. The temperature readings, on the other hand, will vary with time. Thus temperature on this graph is the *dependent variable.* You know the values of the independent variable. The values of the dependent variable represent the data you are trying to find. You are drawing the graph because

Figure 3-2. Graphing change in temperature with time. The graph shows the general pattern of the relationship between temperature and time. This is a direct relationship.

TIME (in minutes)	TEMPERATURE (in °C)
0	11°
1	13°
2	16°
3	19°
4	22°
5	24°
6	25°
7	27°
8	30°
9	32°
10	33°

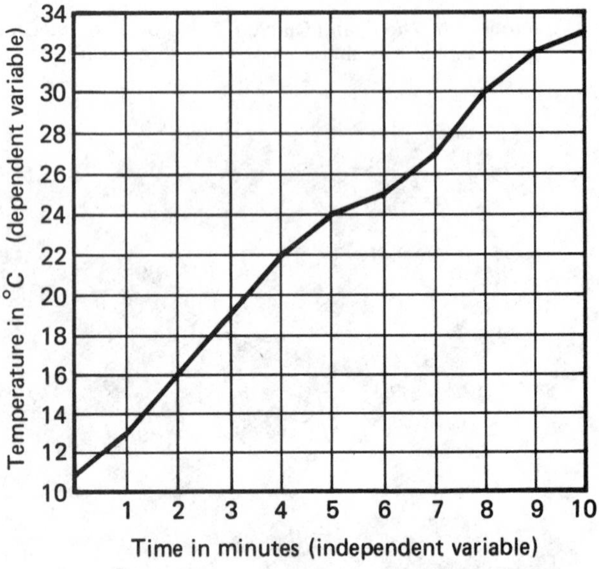

you want to see how the dependent variable changes.

In drawing a graph, the independent variable is generally shown along the horizontal axis and the dependent variable along the vertical axis (see Figure 3-2). The next thing you have to do is decide on the scales along the two axes. This will depend on the range of the variables, and upon the precision of the data. The scales must be chosen so that all your data will fit inside the borders of your graph paper. At the same time, you would like to make maximum use of all the space on your sheet. Since the time variable goes from 0 (the starting time) to 10 minutes, you can choose a scale that puts 10 min. near the right-hand end of the horizontal axis, with 0 near the left end. If, however, you are planning to *extrapolate* your graph (extend it beyond the range of your actual data), you would use a smaller scale, to leave room beyond the 10-minute mark.

Another consideration is the precision with which the data was measured. If (as in this case) the temperature readings were made to the nearest 2°, there is no point in having a vertical scale marked off in 0.1° intervals. Your data is not precise enough to give meaning to such a refinement. On the other hand, a scale marked off in 10° intervals would be too coarse. You would not be able to get as much information from your graph as the data actually contains.

Interpreting Graphs. An important feature of any graph is that it shows the general nature of the relationship between the two variables. In this case, the two variables—time and temperature—show a *direct relationship*. The temperature increases as time increases. The line of the graph slants upward from left to right. If the temperature decreased with passing time, the two variables would show an *inverse relationship*. The line of the graph would slant *down* from left to right.

Figure 3-3 is a graph of average ocean temperatures observed between the equator (0° latitude) and the

Figure 3-3. Variations in average ocean temperature with latitude. From this graph you can see that ocean temperature generally decreases with increasing latitude. This is an inverse relationship.

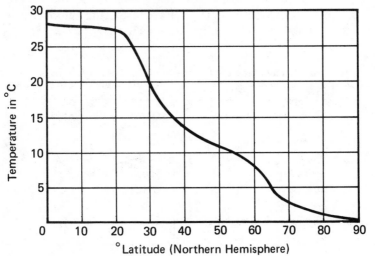

Figure 3-4. Some of the phases of the moon.

North Pole (90° north latitude). As you would expect, the temperature decreases as the latitude increases. This is therefore an inverse relationship, and the graph line slopes downward from left to right. Note, also, that this is an example of a change measured with reference to space, or location, rather than time.

Cyclic Changes. Figure 3-4 is a series of photos of the moon taken on different nights during a single month. Even if you have never given the subject much thought, you know that the appearance of the moon changes. These changes are called *phases,* and they follow a regular pattern, from crescent, through half-moon, through full moon, and back down to a crescent facing the other way. This cycle takes a quite definite period of time, and it repeats over and over in exactly the same way.

Table 3-1 gives the dates of the full moon for six consecutive months in a certain year. You can see that the full moons seem to occur at intervals of either 29 or 30 days. With an observed pattern like this you can try to foretell the future. What is your prediction of the date of the next full moon in this series? If you guessed Sunday, July 11, you hit it on the nose. But do you think you could predict full moon dates for the later months of that year? Probably not. The pattern of 29- and 30-day intervals is not regular enough to do this with only six months of data. Table 3-2 shows the actual observations.

Many changes in the environment go through an orderly series of events that repeat at regular intervals, like the phases of the moon. Such changes are called *cyclic changes*. The cycles of day and night, the seasons, and the

Table 3-1. Dates of the full moon during the first 6 months of a certain year.

Date	Day of Week	Interval
Jan 17	Saturday	
Feb 15	Sunday	29 days
Mar 16	Tuesday	30
Apr 14	Wednesday	29
May 13	Thursday	29
Jun 12	Saturday	30

Table 3-2. Dates of the full moon for the next 6 months of the year in Table 3-1.

Date	Day of Week	Interval
Jul 11	Sunday	29 days
Aug 9	Monday	29
Sep 8	Wednesday	30
Oct 8	Friday	30
Nov 6	Saturday	29
Dec 6	Monday	30

positions of stars and planets in the night sky are other examples of cyclic changes. Cyclic changes are observed with reference to space as well as to time. Ripple patterns produced in sand by waves or wind are often cyclic across a particular region (see Figure 3-5).

Some changes in the environment are not cyclic in nature. However, if you analyze them carefully, you may find that they follow a general pattern or trend. This information may enable you to make predictions about the future direction and nature of these changes.

Figure 3-5. Ripple patterns in the sand.

SUMMARY

1. Every change or series of changes can be called an event.
2. Either time or space can be the frame of reference for describing change.
3. Change is often described in terms of the rate at which it occurs.
4. Graphing is often used to examine how one factor changes with respect to another.
5. In cyclic changes events repeat with reference to time or space.
6. If a change is cyclic or follows a particular trend, it is often possible to predict the amount and direction of future change.

CHANGE, ENERGY, AND INTERFACES

One aspect of change that we haven't mentioned up to this point is the relationship between change and energy. Energy is defined as the capacity to do work. Most changes cannot occur unless a flow of energy also takes place.

Almost all changes involve a flow of energy from one part of the environment to another. The part from which the energy flows loses energy, while the part to which the energy flows gains energy.

Where do changes and energy flow occur in the environment? They often occur along boundaries where differ-ent materials or systems come to-gether. This type of boundary, where regions with different properties come together, is called an *interface*. Energy flow is generally across an interface.

Many interfaces are easy to recognize because they are sharp and distinct. An example is the interface between a stream and its bed (see Figure 3-6). At this interface, erosion occurs as kinetic energy from the water is transferred to soil and rock particles of the stream bed.

Sometimes, however, an interface is not so easily observed. Where is the

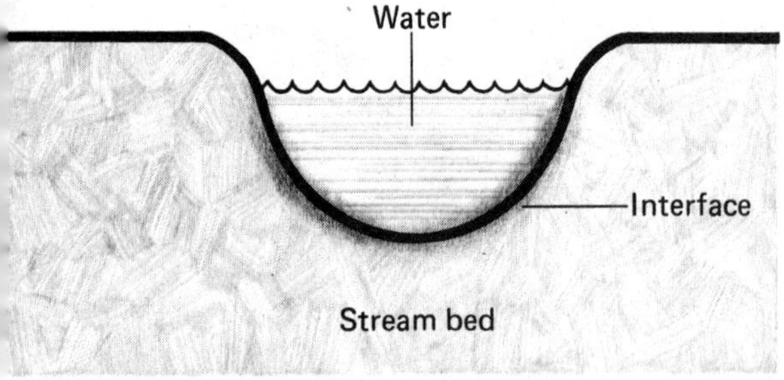

Water

Interface

Stream bed

Figure 3-6. Distinct interface between water and stream bed.

Figure 3-7. Diffuse interface between fog and clear air.

interface between the fog bank in Figure 3-7 and the clear air above it? Or where is the interface between the earth's atmosphere and the empty space beyond? The atmosphere gradually thins to almost nothing as you go higher in it, but it is hard to say just where the boundary is. Such "fuzzy" interfaces are said to be *diffuse*. You will encounter other diffuse interfaces in your study of earth science. But whether sharp or diffuse, it is at the interface that change usually occurs, and it is across the interface that energy associated with the change flows.

SUMMARY

1. Almost all changes involve a flow of energy from one part of the environment to another.
2. The boundary between regions with different properties is called an interface.
3. The exchange of energy and the processes of change occur at an interface.

ENVIRONMENTAL CHANGE

Figure 3-8 shows a tank with an inlet and an outlet for water and a control device for automatically regulating the flow of water into the tank. If the water level drops, the float opens the inlet valve to increase the flow of water. If the level rises, the float closes the valve to reduce the flow. In this way, the average level of the water in the tank is kept the same, even though changes are continuously occurring in the flow of water.

The conditions in the tank are called a state of *dynamic equilibrium*. In a dynamic equilibrium, changes are occurring, but there is a balance among the changes so that overall conditions remain the same. The natural environment is normally in a state of dynamic equilibrium. In a forest, for example, the numbers of various kinds of plants and animals tend to be about the same from year to year, even though the individual plants and

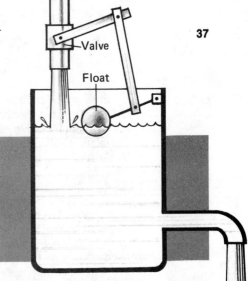

animals may change. This natural environmental equilibrium is often called the "balance of nature."

The environmental equilibrium may be upset frequently to a small extent or in a limited region, but in the course of time the natural balance is restored. Large-scale changes may be caused by natural disasters, such as volcanic eruptions or earthquakes, but even then a new equilibrium is eventually established.

Human activities, on the other hand, are tending more and more to cause permanent disruptions of the environmental equilibrium. What humans do to their environment may be compared to removing the float or turning off the water supply in the example of Figure 3-8. The forces that could restore the equilibrium are then no longer present.

Environmental Pollution. Pollution of the environment occurs when the concentration of a substance or form of energy becomes high enough to adversely affect people, their property, or plant or animal life. Things that pollute are called *pollutants*. Some pollutants are the results of natural processes—for example, ash from a volcano. Many others, however, are the result of human activities—for example, carbon monoxide from automobile exhausts.

Figure 3-8. Dynamic equilibrium. The tank shown here is in a state of dynamic equilibrium. The individual water molecules are constantly changing, but the average level of water in the tank remains the same.

Pollutants may be solids, liquids, gases, biologic organisms, or forms of energy, such as heat, sound, and nuclear radiation. Pollutants are found in the air, on land, and in water. The amount of pollution present varies with time and place. It is greatest in highly populated and highly industrialized areas, and least in lightly populated, unindustrialized areas.

As we continue to look into the processes of change on the earth, we will have more to say about this vital subject of pollution and the other effects of human actions on the environment.

SUMMARY

1. The environment is in a state of natural equilibrium. This equilibrium is frequently altered on a small scale, but is then restored by natural processes.
2. Human technology can cause large-scale disruption of large portions of the environment.
3. The environment is considered to be polluted when the concentration of a substance or form of energy reaches such a concentration that it adversely affects man, his property, or plant or animal life.
4. Pollutants are being added to the environment by natural processes and by the activities of individuals, communities, and industrial processes.

REVIEW QUESTIONS

Group A   1. In terms of change, what is an *event?*
      2. What are the *frames of reference* used for describing change?
      3. Give one example of space and one example of time as a frame of reference for describing change.
      4. Answer the following questions on the basic rules of drawing graphs.
         a. Which axis is used for the dependent variable? Which is used for the independent variable?
         b. How do you decide on the proper scale for a graph?
         c. Describe the general slope of a graph that shows a direct relationship between the variables plotted.
         d. Describe the general slope of a graph that shows an inverse relationship between the variables plotted.
      5. What is a *cyclic change?* Give some examples of cyclic changes.
      6. How is change related to energy flow?
      7. What is the boundary between regions with different properties called?
      8. Where do energy exchanges and processes of change occur?
      9. What is meant by *dynamic equilibrium?* How does this term apply to the environment?
     10. Are most natural changes in the environment small-scale changes or large-scale changes? What about changes caused by human technology?
     11. What is meant by *pollution?*
     12. What kinds of processes pollute the environment?

Group B   1. a.   Explain how you would go about proving or disproving that a change is taking place in some part of your environment.
         b.   Scientists attempt to give meaningful descriptions of change. In some situations, though, word descriptions are not enough for scientists. What else concerning change do they attempt to do?
         c.   What kind of relationship (direct or inverse) exists between the following: A — The masses and the volumes of a number of different water samples of various sizes; B — The masses and the mileages (average number of miles that can be driven on a gallon of gas) of a number of cars of various sizes.
      2. Which of the following are cyclic changes: (a) The change in water level caused by the ocean tides; (b) The change in the number of people living on earth at any given time since the year 1700.
      3. Energy from the sun warms the sand on a beach. What interface is involved in this energy transfer and what is the direction of the energy flow?
      4. "People are not the only polluters of the environment." Explain.

REVIEW EXERCISES

1. Make a list of ten changes that you have observed in your environment. Classify these changes according to their frame, or frames, of reference—either time, space, or both.
2. The data below show the time it takes for one type of earthquake wave to travel through the earth.

Distance of earthquake epicenter from observer	Travel time of earthquake waves
1,000 km	2 min
2,000 km	3 min 45 sec
3,000 km	5 min 30 sec
4,000 km	7 min
5,000 km	8 min 15 sec
6,000 km	9 min 30 sec
7,000 km	10 min 30 sec

Graph the data and answer the following questions:
a. Is this a cyclic or noncyclic change?
b. Is there a direct or an inverse relationship between the distance and the time?
c. What is the probable travel time for a distance of 10,000 km?

3. The data below show the position of a swinging pendulum as it was observed at 1-second intervals. Zero is the rest (vertical) position of the pendulum. Positive (+) distances are to the right; negative (−) distances are to the left.

Time in seconds	0	1	2	3	4	5	6	7	8	9	10	11	12
Distance from rest position (cm)	+10.0	0	-9.2	0	+8.4	0	-7.0	0	+6.6	0	-5.6	0	+5.2

Graph the data and answer the following questions:
a. Is the change of position of the pendulum cyclic or noncyclic?
b. What regular change in the pattern of the pendulum motion do you observe?
c. Predict the position of the pendulum at time 15 sec. At time 16 sec.

4. Make a list of ten pollutants that you have observed or that you know to exist in your environment. Classify them according to their source: natural (N), or man-made (M). Under those that are man-made, further identify the source of these pollutants by marking them: (I) for those caused by the activity of individuals; (C) for those caused by community activity; and (P) for those resulting from industrial processes.

Computer graphics are used to create sophisticated models of the earth.

CHAPTER 4
A Model of the Earth

You will know something about the earth as a planet if you can:
1. Describe various ways in which models are used.
2. Explain how the earth's shape and size are known.
3. Identify and describe the three parts of the earth's surface.

We are all accustomed to the "fact" that the earth is round. We take it so much for granted that we don't realize how hard it is to conceive of this idea without modern means of travel and observation. Yet 2,000 years ago, scientists (or "philosophers," as they were often called) had shown that the earth must be shaped like a ball. Eratosthenes (whom we will meet later in this chapter) had even calculated its size with remarkable accuracy. How could this be done without telescopes, radio, clocks precise to a billionth of a second, spacecraft, or even high-speed cars?

In this chapter and in the following chapters we are going to show you how the scientists of the past developed their model of the earth, using careful observation and simple instruments.

Since we are going to develop a model of the earth, the first thing we should do is make clear what we mean by the term model. *We should also find out what kinds of models we can use.*

MODELS

We can begin by saying that a model is anything that represents the properties of an object or a system. Some models are miniature copies of the things they represent, while other models represent things that cannot be seen.

Types of Models. There are a number of different kinds of models, and some of them we see every day.

1. *Physical and mechanical models. Physical models* are models that provide us with information through our sense of sight. Common examples include things like globes, dollhouses, and model planes and cars. An architect's drawing of a building is another example of a physical model.

Some physical models have working parts so that they can perform the same functions or movements as the original object. This type of model is called a *mechanical model.* A model electric train is a mechanical model.

In both physical and mechanical models, size is an important factor. In most models all parts of the model are made in the same proportions as the parts of the original. They are all made to the same *scale*. For example, if you were building a model car, you wouldn't make the model one-tenth as

Figure 4-1. An electric train—a mechanical model.

long as the actual car and only one-twentieth as wide. This would change the proportions of the car.

The blueprints for a skyscraper or an engineer's plans for a rocket engine must be exactly to scale and very accurate. But it is impossible to make a schoolroom model of our solar system to scale because of the differences in size between the sun and the planets and the great distances involved.

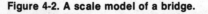

Figure 4-2. A scale model of a bridge.

42

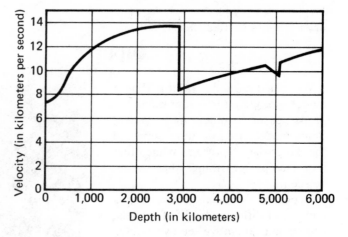

Figure 4-3. A graph showing how the velocity of one type of earthquake wave varies with depth below the earth's surface.

2. *Mental models.* Some models exist only in your mind. These are *mental models.* They are models of things that cannot be observed. There are many scientific concepts that cannot be illustrated with physical models. You cannot construct a physical model that shows you exactly what happens in an electric circuit when the current is turned on. But when you study physics and electricity you develop a mental model of this event. Another example of a mental model might be your idea of a friend's feelings.

3. *Mathematical models.* Scattered throughout this text are mathematical relationships, such as "density equals mass divided by volume," or "volume equals length times height times width." These relationships are usually expressed in mathematical symbols, such as D = M/V. These relationships, whether in words or symbols, are mathematical models that express certain properties of an object or system.

4. *Graphic models.* Graphs are commonly used to provide a picture of the relationship of one factor to another. For example, Figure 4-3 is a graph showing how the velocity of one type of earthquake wave varies with depth below the surface. Graphs are often used when no simple mathematical relationship between the factors can be found. But even when a mathematical relationship between two quantities is known, a graph may make it easier to see the nature of the relationship.

In this section we have talked about some of the kinds of models we use, both in science and in everyday life. What we call the models is not the important thing. What *is* important is to know *when* we are using a model and what we are using it for. We must always bear in mind that a model is not the real thing, but only a helpful device for trying to understand the real thing.

SUMMARY

1. A model is anything that represents the properties of an object or system.
2. Types of models include physical, mechanical, mental, mathematical, and graphic models.
3. The scale of a physical model is the ratio of the dimensions of the model to the dimensions of the real object.

THE SHAPE OF THE EARTH

Photographs of the earth taken from space have provided final proof that the earth is spherical in shape (see Figure 4-4). As we shall see later in this chapter, it is not a perfect sphere, but it is pretty close to one.

As we have already stated, scientists have known for over two thousand years that the earth is round. What observations led them to this conclusion? Let's begin with two everyday sights that, when you think about it, give us some evidence about the shape of the earth.

First, look around you as the sun is setting some evening. Notice how, as the sun slips below the horizon, the last sunlight lingers on the tops of the trees, then on hilltops, and finally, on clouds in the sky. (Jet plane condensation trails are startling when seen in a clear sky just after sunset.) The higher you are, the longer you can see the sun. People must have noticed this. What explanation could they have had?

Our second example involves a large object either disappearing or appearing over the horizon (see Figure 4-5). Suppose you are standing on shore watching a ship sail out to sea. As you watch, the ship begins to pass

Figure 4-4. The earth as seen from space.

over the horizon. It disappears from the bottom up. First the hull, or bottom, of the ship is lost from view. Then the rest of it gradually disappears. The last parts of the ship you can see are the smokestacks, then the smoke from the smokestacks, and then nothing. If a ship were sailing toward you from over the horizon, it would appear in the opposite order. You would first see the smoke, then the stacks, and finally the ship itself. (Of course, 2,000 years ago you would have seen sails and masts, not smokestacks.) How can you account for the way things disappear and appear over the horizon?

Figure 4-5. Evidence for the shape of the earth. As a ship moves away toward the horizon, its upper portions remain visible after the lower portions have disappeared. The drawing shows why this is to be expected if the earth's surface is curved. As the ship sails away, it gradually drops below the observer's line of sight.

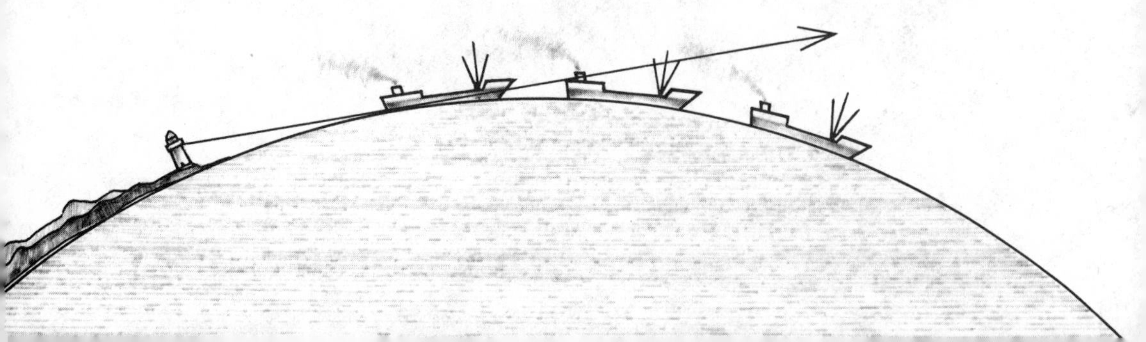

You may have jumped to the conclusion that these examples prove that the earth is round. They don't! The only inference you can really draw from these observations is that the earth is apparently curved, perhaps like an inverted saucer. They do not necessarily mean that the earth is a sphere.

Let's look at some other occurrences that give us evidence about the shape of the earth.

Eclipses. As you may know, there are two types of eclipses—eclipses of the sun and eclipses of the moon.

An eclipse of the sun (a solar eclipse) occurs when the moon passes between the earth and the sun. An eclipse of the moon (a lunar eclipse) occurs when the earth comes between the sun and the moon. In each case, one object cuts off the sun's light from the other.

The earth and the moon cast long, cone-shaped shadows in space (see Figure 4-6). These shadows can fall

Figure 4-7. The shape of the earth's shadow. The curved shape of the earth's shadow on the face of the moon during an eclipse suggests that the earth is round.

on another celestial object, just as your shadow might fall on another person's face. During a lunar eclipse the earth's shadow moves across the face of the moon, blacking it out. The shadow cast by the earth is larger than the moon. Therefore, you cannot see the whole of the earth's shadow on the moon. However, the part of the shadow that you can see is curved

Figure 4-6. The earth's shadow and eclipses of the moon. During a lunar eclipse the full moon enters and passes through the shadow that the earth casts in space.

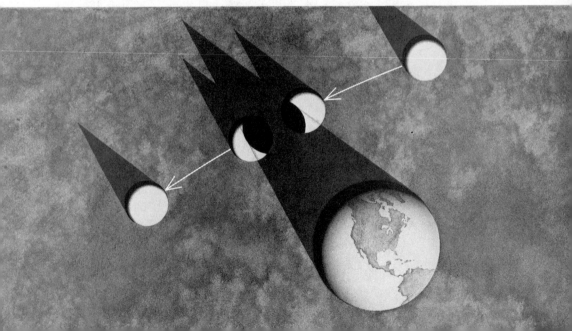

(Figure 4-7). This suggests rather strongly that the earth is circular in shape. However, this does not prove that the earth is a ball. It could be a flat disk, like a coin, and still cast a circular shadow.

Polaris. In the Northern Hemisphere there is one star that seems to remain stationary in the sky. All the other stars appear to move around this star in the course of 24 hours. Because it is almost directly over the North Pole, this stationary star is called the North Star, the pole star, or Polaris. At the equator, Polaris is always on the horizon. As you travel northward, it appears higher and higher in the sky—its angle with the horizon increases. At the North Pole, Polaris is directly overhead. Its angle with the horizon is 90°.

If you traveled directly north from the equator from a number of locations around the earth, you might notice an interesting fact. From each location, the altitude of Polaris increases the same amount for each kilometer of northward movement. The only reasonable explanation for these observations is that the earth is spherical in shape.

Precise Shape of the Earth. Observations of the kind we have described lead to the conclusion that the earth is a sphere. However, as the observations are made more precise, we find evidence that the earth is slightly flattened at the poles and slightly bulging at the equator. For example, on a truly spherical earth, the altitude of Polaris and the distance north of the equator should change exactly in step. They don't. Careful measurements show a small variation from perfect agreement.

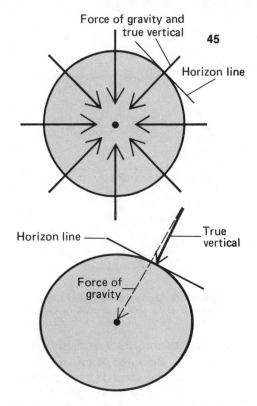

Figure 4-8. Force of gravity and the shape of the earth. The fact that the direction of the force of gravity is not a true vertical at every point on the earth's surface is evidence that the earth is not a perfect sphere.

Another measurement that we can make with high precision today gives similar results. This is the measurement of the force of gravity. According to Newton's theory of gravitation, the force of gravity on the surface of a perfect sphere is directed toward the center of the sphere. If the earth were a perfect sphere, the force of gravity would be straight down (at right angles to the horizontal) wherever you were on the earth's surface. Observations of gravity with very sensitive instruments show that this is not the case. The observations indicate that the earth is a slightly flattened sphere. Figure 4-8 shows why the force of gravity is not always vertical on a flattened sphere.

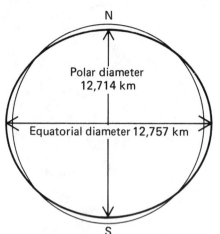

Figure 4-9. Exaggerated drawing of the shape of the earth. If drawn to scale, the drawing would look like a perfect circle.

Furthermore, on a perfectly spherical earth, the force of gravity should have the same strength at all places on the surface. Measurements of the force of gravity with an instrument called a *gravimeter* show that gravity is not the same everywhere on the earth. It is slightly less at the equator than at the poles. These observations agree with the conclusion that the earth is slightly flattened at the poles. Because of this flattening, an object near the poles is closer to the earth's center than one at the equator and therefore is acted upon by a slightly stronger gravitational force. (A more complete discussion on the force of gravity and how it depends on distance will come up later, in Chapter 7.)

The shape of a ball that is flattened at the top and bottom and bulging around the middle is called an *oblate spheroid*. This is the shape that the earth appears to have from the observations just described. However, you should keep in mind that the amount of flattening at the poles and bulging

at the equator is very slight, as shown by the small differences in diameters drawn through these two regions (see Figure 4-9).

SIZE OF THE EARTH

Among the ancient Greek philosopher-scientists, it was generally believed that the earth was a sphere. Aristotle used the fact that the visible stars shifted as you traveled north or south as evidence that the earth was spherical. He gave an estimate of its size (probably about 50% too large), but did not say how he had arrived at it. Eratosthenes is generally credited as the first man to make a scientific determination of the earth's circumference. He lived from about 275 to 195 B.C., and spent more than half his life in Alexandria, where he was head of the great library in that city. He was one of the greatest scholars of his time, an excellent mathematician, geographer, historian, and astronomer.

Figure 4-10. The angle of the sun at two different places on the earth's surface.

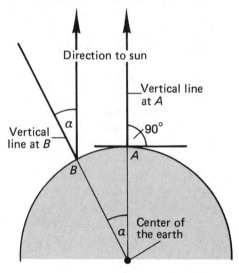

Eratosthenes knew that in the city of Syene in Egypt the noon sun was directly overhead at the summer solstice (the day the sun reaches its highest point in the sky). This fact was based on the observation that at noon that day the sun could be seen reflected from the water in a deep well.

Eratosthenes also knew that Alexandria, where he was located, was almost exactly due north of Syene, and that at noon at the summer solstice the sun was not directly overhead in Alexandria. Eratosthenes saw that he could use these observations to calculate the circumference of the earth.

To understand Eratosthenes' method for calculating the circumference of the earth, examine Figure 4-10. We assume there is an observer at *A* for whom the sun is directly overhead. For him the altitude of the sun is 90° from the horizon. An observer at *B* measures the angle of the sun at the same time. He finds the altitude to be less than 90°. The sun is assumed to be so far from the earth that its rays reaching any part of the earth are practically parallel. The apparent change in angle in going from *A* to *B* is entirely the result of the curvature of the earth's surface. This change in angular elevation of the sun is the same as the angle *a* at the center

of the earth. Angle *a* is some fraction of a full circle (360°), which we can calculate. The arc along the surface from *A* to *B* is the same fraction of the complete circle around the earth. If we know the distance from *A* to *B*, it is a simple matter to calculate the length of the full circle.

Now compare Figure 4-10 with Figure 4-11. You can see that Syene can serve as point *A* and Alexandria can serve as point *B*. So, all that Eratosthenes needed to do was to measure the angle of the sun at noon at the summer solstice in Alexandria. He found that the angle of the sun at that moment was a little more than 7° from the perpendicular, which corresponds to an arc of about 1/50 of a circle. He therefore could state that the circumference of the earth was 50 times the distance between Alexandria and Syene.

Eratosthenes expressed his estimate of the earth's size in units called *stadia* (singular, *stadium*). Taking the distance between Alexandria and Syene as 5,000 stadia, he obtained a value of 50 × 5,000, or 250,000, stadia as the circumference of the earth. Much has been made of the question of how close to our modern measurements he came. Nobody really knows, because nobody knows how long one stadium was. But this is quite

Figure 4-11. How Eratosthenes used the conditions at Alexandria and Syene to find the circumference of the earth.

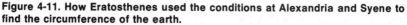

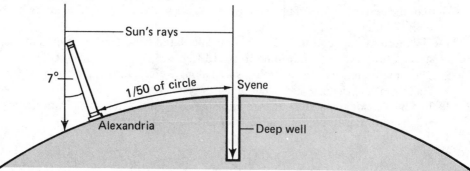

unimportant. Eratosthenes was not trying for great accuracy. He knew he couldn't get it. The fraction 1/50, and the distance 5,000 stadia, are plainly numbers that have been rounded off. What is important is the beauty and simplicity of the method and the good result it gave for that time. The circumference of the earth *is* very nearly 50 times the distance from Alexandria to Syene (Aswan).

Many hundreds of years passed before anyone made a more accurate determination of the size of the earth. Today we can measure the earth with great accuracy through the use of orbiting satellites. Its various dimensions are given in Table 4-1.

Table 4-1. Measurements of the earth.

	ACCEPTED	APPROXIMATE
Mass	5.975 X 10^{27} gm	6 X 10^{27} gm
Volume	1.08 X 10^{27} cm^3	1.1 X 10^{27} cm^3
Average density	5.52 gm/cm^3	5.5 gm/cm^3
Radius (N—S Pole)	6,378 km	6,400 km
Radius (equator)	6,346 km	6,400 km
Circumference (polar)	40,008 km	40,000 km
Circumference (equator)	40, 076 km	40,000 km

SUMMARY

1. Several simple observations can lead to the conclusion that the earth is curved.
2. Observations of Polaris at various distances north of the equator and from different locations around the earth lead to the conclusion that the earth is spherical.
3. Precise measurements of the force of gravity at varying locations indicate that the earth is an oblate spheroid—slightly flattened at the poles and slightly bulging at the equator.
4. The circumference of the earth can be calculated from measurements of the sun's altitude at the same time in two different locations.
5. The circumference of the earth measured along a circle through the poles is less than the circumference measured along the equator.
6. The best evidence about the size and shape of the earth comes from photographs and measurements taken from orbiting satellites.

PARTS OF THE EARTH

Now that we know something about the shape and size of the earth, we can continue to develop our model of this planet. Perhaps the next thing we should do is to describe the surface of the earth. We know that part of the earth's surface is land and part is water. We also know that the entire earth is surrounded by a layer of air. Thus the surface of the earth can be divided into a solid part, a liquid part, and a gaseous part.

The solid part of the earth's surface is called the *lithosphere*. The liquid part is the *hydrosphere*. And the gaseous layer surrounding the earth is the *atmosphere*. Although in the following paragraphs we will describe each of these "spheres" separately, you will learn in later chapters that the three are closely interrelated.

The Lithosphere. The term *lithosphere* refers to the solid rock that forms a continuous shell around the earth. The lithosphere extends under the oceans and all other bodies of water on the earth's surface. In most places the lithosphere is covered by a layer of soil or other loose material. But if you dig down deep enough, you hit solid rock. In some places the lithosphere is not covered by anything. One such place is shown in Figure 4-12.

The lithosphere has a thin, upper layer called the *crust,* in which the rocks are less dense than in the rest of the lithosphere. The thickness of the crust varies from about 10 km under the oceans to about 30 km under the continents. There is a sharp boundary, or interface, between the crust and the part of the lithosphere below it. The lower boundary of the lithosphere is less distinct, but it is believed to be a region about 100 km below the surface where the rocks are soft and plastic.

Figure 4-12. Stone Mountain, Georgia.

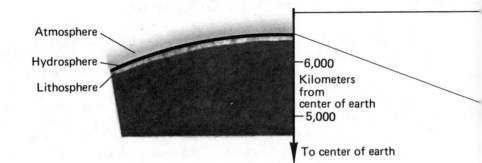

The Hydrosphere. The hydrosphere is the thin layer of water that rests on the lithosphere. It includes not only the water of the oceans, rivers, lakes, and streams, but also the water in the icecaps of the Arctic and Antarctic and all the water below the surface in spaces between soil and rock particles.

About 70% of the earth's surface is covered by water. But as you can see in Figure 4-13, the layer of water is so shallow compared with the diameter of the earth that it is really like a thin film. The average depth of the water layer is less than 4 kilometers, while the diameter of the earth is more than 12,700 kilometers.

The Atmosphere. The atmosphere is a thin layer of gases that surrounds the earth. Not counting the variable amounts of water vapor, the atmosphere is made up almost completely of nitrogen (about 78%) and oxygen (about 21%); the rest consists of very small amounts of carbon dioxide and chemically inert gases, such as argon and neon.

The atmosphere extends upward from the earth to a height of several hundred kilometers, gradually thinning out to nothing. This shell of gas is made up of various layers, each with its own characteristics. Most of the mass of the atmosphere is concentrated in the layers nearest the earth. That is, the air is most dense at sea level and becomes progressively thinner as you go higher.

Figure 4-13 shows the layers, or zones, of the atmosphere. There is no sharp line between one zone and the next, but the transition occurs over a fairly narrow change in altitude. The layers differ from one another in temperature, chemical composition, and other general characteristics.

SUMMARY

1. The lithosphere is a layer of solid rock that forms a shell around the earth.
2. The hydrosphere is a thin film of water that rests on the lithosphere and covers about 70% of the earth's surface.
3. The atmosphere is a shell of gases that surrounds the earth, extending upward for several hundred kilometers. It is layered, or stratified, into distinct zones, each with its own characteristics.

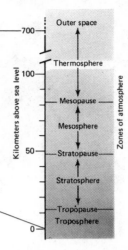

Figure 4-13. A cross section of the earth showing the three outer spheres. The drawing is not to scale.

REVIEW QUESTIONS

Group A

1. What is a *model?*
2. Identify and describe five different types of models.
3. What is meant by the *scale* of a physical model?
4. Describe two simple observations that lead to the conclusion that the earth is curved.
5. Explain how observations of Polaris indicate that the earth is spherical.
6. Explain how sensitive measurements of the force of gravity provide information about the shape of the earth.
7. Name and describe the actual shape of the earth.
8. Describe how measurements of the altitude of the sun at the same time at two different locations can be used to calculate the circumference of the earth.
9. From what do we obtain the best evidence for determining the exact size and shape of the earth?
10. What is the *lithosphere?*
11. What is the *hydrosphere?*
12. What is the *atmosphere?*

Group B

1. Describe two different types of models you could use to represent the earth. Explain how scale is involved in each of these models.
2. a. State one observation from which you might *infer* a round earth. Explain how this observation could also be interpreted as indicating a different shape for the earth.
   b. Is there any evidence that could be accepted as *proof* of the earth's shape?
3. Suppose you were to construct a model of the earth to scale, using 1 cm = 1000 km.
   a. How deep would the lithosphere appear on this model?
   b. How deep would the hydrosphere appear on this model?
   c. How deep would the atmosphere appear on this model?

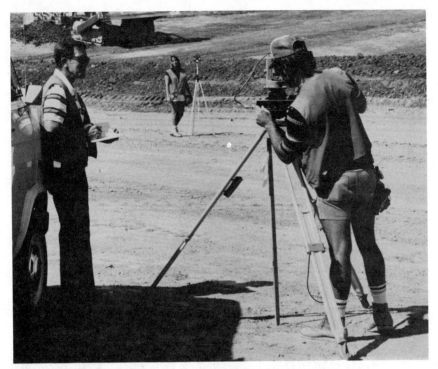

Land surveying teams use lasers to make precise measurements.

CHAPTER 5
Locating Positions on the Earth

You will know something about locating positions on the earth if you can:

1. Explain what is meant by a coordinate system and give examples of different types.
2. Name and describe the coordinate system used to find locations on the earth.
3. Describe the properties of regions of the earth in terms of fields.

Suppose you're on a ship in the middle of an ocean. How can you figure out where you are? How can you describe your location to someone else? In this age of travel, when the skies are filled with planes and the seas covered with ships, these questions are very important.

The system used to locate and describe positions on the earth must be a worldwide one used by all nations. And this is what we have. But before we learn about locating positions on the earth, we should learn something about the basic system used to describe locations on a flat surface.

COORDINATE SYSTEMS

Locating Points on a Flat Surface. Let's use a game to discover how the location of a point can be described so that anyone can find the point without question. On a piece of paper draw a square similar to the one in Figure 5-1. Place a point somewhere inside the square. How would you tell someone where the point is within the box?

If you measure the distance from the left-hand edge of the square to the point, you have one of the properties of the point. In Figure 5-1, the point is 2 cm from the left edge. Is this enough information to locate the point? Are there other points in the square that are 2 cm from the left edge? You're right if you see that many points could be at that distance—in fact, they would make another vertical line! So we need more information about the point to describe its location.

How far is the point from the bottom edge of the square? It is 3 cm up from the bottom. This distance is another property of the point. Now you have two measurements that you

can use to describe the location of the point. Is this enough information to describe its location? Try giving someone the two measurements you've made for your point, and see if they can locate the same point on a drawing of their own.

Coordinate Systems. What you have just discovered is a basic fact about locating points on a surface. It takes two numbers to do it. Any system for assigning two numbers to every point on a surface is called a *coordinate system.* The system you have just used is a *rectangular coordinate system.* It makes use of two reference lines at right angles to each other. You locate a point by telling how far the point is from each line. One line is called the *horizontal axis;* the other, the *vertical axis.* The two numbers for a particular point are called its *coordinates.*

A coordinate system is often shown as a grid (see Figure 5-2). In this case the units of measurement are marked on the grid, and you just count them off to obtain the measurements for a given point.

Figure 5-1. Fixing the location of a point inside a square. The distances from two adjacent sides of the square are enough to fix the location of a point inside the square.

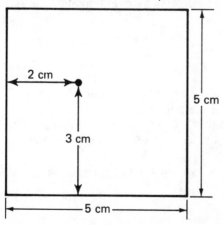

Figure 5-2. A grid for a rectangular coordinate system. The numbered grid lines help you find the coordinates of a point. A finer grid can be drawn to show fractions of units, such as fifths or tenths.

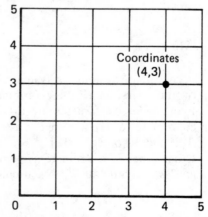

In Figure 5-2, the indicated point is 4 units from the vertical reference line and 3 units from the horizontal reference line. The *coordinates* for the point are (4, 3). (The numbers are always written in this order—the distance along the horizontal line first, the distance along the vertical line second.)

A rectangular coordinate system is a simple convenient one for flat surfaces. However, it is not the only possible coordinate system. For example, the two axes do not need to be at right angles. Figure 5-3 shows such a system. Another frequently used sys-

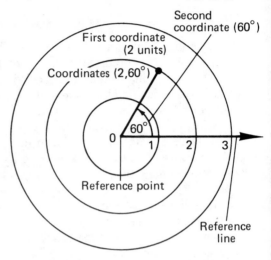

Figure 5-4. A polar coordinate system. In this system, one coordinate is a distance and the other is an angle.

tem has a central point as one reference and a line drawn from that point as the other reference. To find the coordinates of any point, you first draw a line to the reference point. The distance from the reference point to the given point is one coordinate. The angle between the connecting line and the reference line is the second coordinate. The distance and the angle together give a definite location for the point. This is called a *polar coordinate system*. Whatever the system, it always provides a different pair of coordinates for every point on the surface.

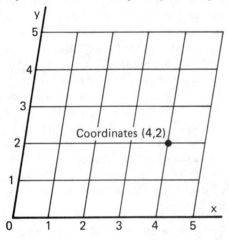

Figure 5-3. A coordinate system that is not rectangular. Distances to each axis are measured along lines that are parallel to the other axis.

SUMMARY

1. A coordinate system is a system of locating a point on a surface by means of two numbers, called the coordinates of the point.
2. Rectangular coordinates are a convenient system for a flat surface. The coordinates of a point are its distances from two reference lines that are at right angles to each other.
3. Other types of coordinate systems can be used for flat surfaces. They all give two coordinates for each point.

FINDING LATITUDE AND LONGITUDE

Locating Points on a Curved Surface. If we want to describe the location of a point on a curved surface, such as the surface of the earth, we have to invent a coordinate system to do it. Obviously, the system of rectangular coordinates that we used for a flat surface won't work on a sphere. We need a system of curved lines. The system that is generally used gives every point on the earth a pair of coordinates, called its *latitude* and *longitude*. Let's see how the system is set up.

The latitude-longitude system, by which we can locate any point on the earth's surface, consists of a grid of circular lines that covers the surface of the earth. There are east-west lines and north-south lines. So that you can see how this system was constructed, the first thing you should learn about are the reference lines for latitude and longitude.

The Equator and the Prime Meridian. The reference lines for the latitude-longitude system are the *equator* and the *prime meridian.*

The equator is a line around the earth connecting all points midway between the North and South Poles (see Figure 5-5). The plane of the equator is at right angles to the earth's axis (an imaginary line running through the earth from pole to pole).

The second reference line for the system is the prime meridian. A meridian is a semicircle (half a circle) on the earth's surface that connects the North and South Poles. There are many different lines that do this. But the prime meridian is a reference line, and it has to be the same for everyone if the system is to be useful. The meridian passing through Greenwich, England, where the Royal Observatory was located, was the one chosen as the prime meridian.

Latitude. Latitude is a measurement of angular distance north or south of the equator. This angle can be measured along the arc of a meridian. An arc from the equator to either the North or South Pole is 90°. Thus, at the equator, latitude is 0°. At the North Pole, latitude is 90°N, and at the South Pole, latitude is 90°S. You must remember to specify north or south when giving latitude.

The parallels of latitude are east-west lines above and below the equator made by passing planes through the earth parallel to the plane

Figure 5-5. The two reference lines for locating points on the earth by latitude and longitude.

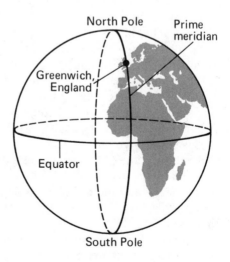

North Pole

Prime meridian

Greenwich, England

Equator

South Pole

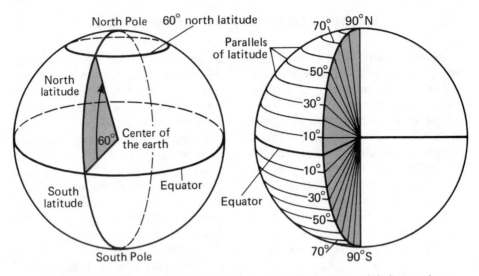

Figure 5-6. Parallels of latitude. The latitude of a point on the earth is its angular distance north or south of the equator, measured from the center of the earth. Points with the same latitude are on a circle parallel to the equator.

of the equator. The resulting circles are all parallel to the equator and parallel to one another, and they are all smaller than the equator (see Figure 5-6). The latitude is the same everywhere along a given parallel.

Measuring Latitude. In the Northern Hemisphere, latitude can be measured by measuring the altitude of Polaris. The latitude reading of a given location is equal to the altitude of Polaris at that location. For anyone at the equator, the altitude of Polaris is 0°. Thus latitude at the equator is 0°. At the North Pole the altitude of Polaris is 90°. Latitude at the North Pole is 90°N. If you are at a latitude of 45°N, the altitude of Polaris (the angle between the horizon and Polaris) will be 45°. If the altitude of Polaris is 37° at a certain location, the latitude of that location is 37°N.

Polaris cannot be seen in the Southern Hemisphere. So below the equator the altitudes of other stars are used to find latitude. In either hemi-sphere, if a very precise measurement of latitude is needed, then both the date and the time must be taken into account. There are astronomical tables that can be used to make such a calculation.

Longitude. Longitude is a measurement of angular distance east or west of the prime meridian. The *meridians of longitude,* like the prime meridian, are semicircles on the earth's surface connecting the North and South Poles. The longitude of the prime meridian is 0°. The meridian that is a continuation of the prime meridian has a longitude of 180°. Going east or west from the prime meridian, longitude increases up to 180°. Just as you must specify north or south with latitude, you must specify east or west with longitude.

The longitude of any given point on the earth's surface is the number of degrees (the angle) between the prime meridian and the meridian passing through that point. The angle is usu-

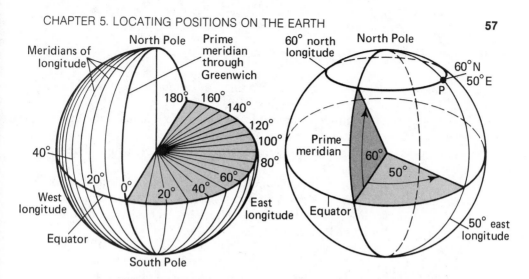

Figure 5-7. Longitude. The longitude of a point on the earth is the angular distance of its meridian east or west of the prime meridian, measured along the equator. Latitude and longitude are the two coordinates that fix the location of a point on the earth's surface. For example, only one point has a latitude of 60°N and a longitude of 50°E.

ally measured along the equator, but it can be measured along any of the parallels of latitude.

Measuring Longitude. High noon, the time at which the sun is at its highest point in the sky, occurs at the same time for all locations along a single meridian. The difference in time between high noon at any given point (local noon) and high noon at the prime meridian is the basis for measuring longitude.

The sun appears to move around the earth from east to west once every 24 hours. A complete circle has 360°. If you divide 360° by 24 hours, you find that the sun appears to move at the rate of 15° per hour. This means that if your longitude is 15° west of the prime meridian, your local noon will occur 1 hour later than noon at the prime meridian. It takes the sun 1 hour to move from the prime meridian to your meridian. In general, local noon occurs 1 hour later for each shift of 15° longitude to the west.

You can calculate longitude by finding the time difference between your local noon and noon at the prime meridian in Greenwich, England. If your local noon occurs before noon at the Greenwich meridian, then your longitude is east of the prime meridian. If your local noon occurs after noon at the Greenwich meridian, then your longitude is west of the prime meridian.

To find longitude, you must know what time it is in Greenwich, England, when it is noon where you are. This can be done either by having a clock that is set for Greenwich Time or by listening to radio signals that regularly give this information. If your local noon occurs at 5 P.M. Greenwich Time, then 5 hours have passed since noon at the prime meridian. During that 5 hours the earth will have rotated 5 x 15°, or 75°. Thus, your longitude is 75°W. If your local noon occurs at 11 A.M. Greenwich Time, your longitude is 15°E.

SUMMARY

1. The latitude-longitude system is a coordinate system using two sets of lines that make a grid covering the earth's surface.
2. The latitude and longitude of an observer can be determined by means of celestial observations.
3. The east-west lines are the parallels of latitude. The north-south lines are the meridians of longitude.
4. Latitude is a measurement of angular distance north or south of the equator.
5. Latitude in the Northern Hemisphere can be found by measuring the altitude of Polaris. For any location in the Northern Hemisphere, latitude is equal to the altitude of Polaris at that location.
6. Longitude is a measurement of angular distance east or west of the prime meridian.
7. To find longitude you must know the time difference between local noon and noon at the prime meridian.

DESCRIBING EARTH FIELDS

We already know something about the size and shape of the earth and how to locate our position on the earth. We are now ready to find some ways to describe other physical characteristics of our earth environment.

Fields. A field is a region of space in which there is a measurable quantity of a given property at every point. Magnetism is a good example of a field quantity. As you recall, objects made of iron or steel are attracted toward a magnet, and the force of attraction becomes stronger as the object approaches the magnet. We say there is a *magnetic field* in the space around the magnet. The strength of that field varies from point to point, depending on the distance from the magnet's poles. The earth has a gravity field around it. Objects are attracted toward the earth with varying force, depending on their distance from the earth's surface.

Figure 5-8. The magnetic field around a bar magnet. The field lines show the direction of the magnetic force. The closeness of the spacing of the lines indicates the strength of the magnetic force. This is a vector field, because the field quantity has both magnitude and direction.

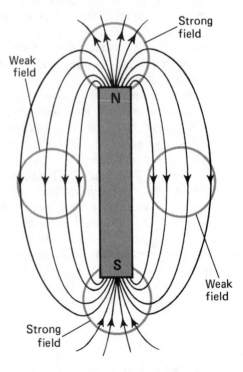

Strong field

Weak field

Weak field

Strong field

There are other kinds of measurable quantities that vary from place to place on or near the earth's surface. Each of these makes up a different kind of field. Among these measurable field quantities are atmospheric pressure, wind velocity, and temperature. The elevation of the earth's surface above or below sea level can also be thought of as a field, since there is a definite measurable elevation at each point of the surface.

Vector and Scalar Fields. Some types of fields can be completely described in terms of amount, or *magnitude*. Fields of this type are called *scalar fields*. Temperature, relative humidity, and atmospheric pressure are scalar fields. They can be completely described in terms of their size, or magnitude, alone.

Other types of fields cannot be described simply in terms of magnitude. Such fields need both magnitude and *direction*. Fields of this type are called *vector fields*. Wind velocity, gravity, and magnetism are examples of vector fields. A description of the wind must include not only the magnitude of its speed, but also the direction it's coming from. A problem that involves the force of gravity must also take into account the direction of this force.

Field Maps. When you are studying a particular field, it is often helpful to make a map of the region involved. On the map you can mark the various readings obtained for the property being studied.

Suppose you are walking down the street and suddenly notice the odor of barbecuing hamburgers. You have just entered a field. Farther down the street the smell becomes stronger, but by the time you reach the corner, the smell is weak again. If you take a shortcut through some backyards and go back toward the middle of the block, the smell becomes stronger and stronger. Eventually you may reach the source of the odor. If you're lucky, you'll be invited to help eliminate the cause of this field!

Figure 5-9 is a map showing part of the odor field from barbecuing ham-

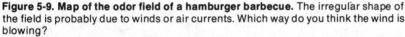

Figure 5-9. Map of the odor field of a hamburger barbecue. The irregular shape of the field is probably due to winds or air currents. Which way do you think the wind is blowing?

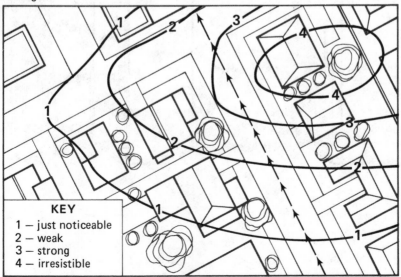

KEY
1 — just noticeable
2 — weak
3 — strong
4 — irresistible

burgers. The map key gives the meanings of the numbers used on the map. From the information on the map, can you tell where you would have the best chance of finding the hamburgers?

Isolines. On the map in Figure 5-9 you will notice that there are lines connecting all points having the same field value. These are *isolines*. Isolines connect points of equal value on field maps. Putting in isolines on a field map can give you a good idea of the shape of the field and the pattern of change within the field. For example, on weather maps all points showing the same temperature are connected by isolines. These isolines are called *isotherms*. They give you a clear picture of the temperature pattern within the map area.

Isosurfaces. Isolines show field conditions on a two-dimensional surface. For example, isotherms on a weather map generally show temperatures within the map area at ground level. But you can't tell from such a map what is happening at various levels above the ground. To get a three-dimensional picture of conditions within a field area, you must use isosurfaces. An *isosurface* is a surface (rather than a line) that passes through all points with the same field value.

Figure 5-10 is a model of the three-dimensional temperature field in a room with a refrigerator. In A, the isosurfaces show the temperature pattern around the refrigerator when its door is closed. Because warm air rises, the air is usually warmer near the ceiling of a room than near the

Figure 5-10. An example of isosurfaces in a model of a three-dimensional field. Each gray surface in the model shows points that have the temperature marked on the surface. When cold air flows out of the refrigerator, temperatures drop, causing each isosurface to bend upward.

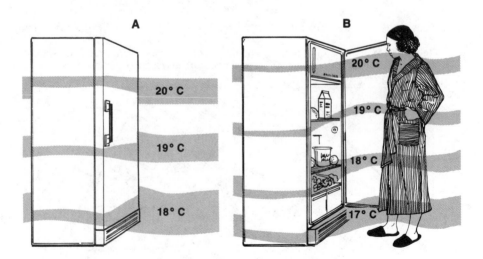

floor. Therefore, the higher isosurfaces represent points in the field at higher temperature. With the refrigerator door closed, the isosurfaces are fairly flat, but with a dip near the floor where heat is being given off. (A refrigerator keeps its interior cold by "pumping" heat to the outside.)

When the door is opened (B), cold air flows out of the refrigerator toward the floor. This causes the isosurfaces to bulge upward over the cold air.

Field Gradients. As we move from one point to another in a field, we usually find that the field quantity changes. The rate at which a field quantity changes as we go from one point in the field to another is called the *gradient,* or *slope,* of the field between those two points. The average gradient of a field over a given distance can be calculated from the formula below.

If the field quantity shows a large change in a short distance, the gradient is large, or steep. If the change is small over a fairly large distance, the gradient is small, or gradual.

An example of the calculation of a field gradient will be given in the discussion of contour maps on the following pages.

Time Changes in Fields. Field gradients usually apply to changes in fields when space is the frame of reference. It is assumed that the field as a whole is not changing with time. However, most properties of the environment do change in the course of time. Therefore, a field map may be accurate only for the time at which it was made. An example of an earth field that slowly changes with time is the earth's magnetic field. The elevation field is also changing on most of the earth's land surfaces.

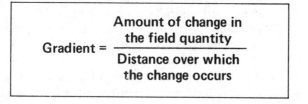

$$\text{Gradient} = \frac{\text{Amount of change in the field quantity}}{\text{Distance over which the change occurs}}$$

SUMMARY

1. A field is a region of space that has a measurable value of a given property at every point.
2. Scalar fields can be completely described in terms of magnitude.
3. Vector fields can be described in terms of magnitude and direction.
4. Isolines are lines on a field map connecting all points of equal value. They show field values on a two-dimensional surface.
5. An isosurface is a surface passing through all points of equal field value within a three-dimensional region of space. Isosurfaces show how the field varies both horizontally and vertically within the mapped region.
6. The gradient of a field is the rate at which field quantities change from place to place.
7. Field characteristics generally change with time.

CONTOUR MAPS

A *contour map,* or *topographic map,* is a map on which elevations of the surface are shown by means of isolines called *contour lines.* Each contour line passes through points that have the same elevation. The contour lines are drawn for a fixed difference of elevation, such as every 10, 20, or 50 feet. This difference between adjacent contour lines is called the *contour interval* of the map.

Figure 5-11 shows a drawing of a portion of the earth's surface that includes hills, valleys, streams, and a seashore. Below the drawing there is a contour map for the same region. To help you understand what a contour line means, the 200-foot contour is shown on the drawing. Imagine that all the land above the 200-foot level had been sliced off and that you were looking down on the top surface that was left. The 200-foot contour line on the map is the outline of the flat surface you would see. Similarly, each of the other contour lines is the outline of what you would see if the land were sliced off above that line.

Notice how the contour lines are bunched together along the steep sides of the cliffs, while they are widely spaced along the gentle slopes on the top of the cliffs. Another characteristic of contour lines is the way they bend when crossing streams or valleys. They always point upstream or toward higher elevations.

Topographic maps often contain symbols for or special ways of indicating various natural or manmade features of the surface, such as swamps, bodies of water, roads, and buildings.

The meaning of these symbols may be shown in a map *key.* Maps usually have a *scale* of distance. The scale tells you the relationship between a distance as measured on the map and the actual distance on the earth's surface. The scale is usually a line marked off in distance units, such as feet, kilometers, or miles. The map scale may also be shown as a ratio, such as 1 cm = 2 km. This means, for example, that two points that are 3.5 cm apart on the map are actually 7.0 km apart.

Maps almost always include an arrow indicating north. Maps are usually drawn with north at the top, but this is not always the case. If you are using a map to find the direction from one point to another, look first for the north arrow to be sure which way is north on the map.

Elevation Gradients. The earth scientist is a detective. He tries to reconstruct the past, that is, to figure out what happened to make the earth's surface what it is today. He also tries to predict future changes that are likely to occur. One of the chief forces that change the shape of the land is running water. The power of running water to change the land depends partly on its speed, and its speed depends on the steepness or gradient of its course. Thus the gradient of a particular region is often an important clue for the earth detective.

We have already seen how the contour lines on a topographic map indicate steepness in a general way. Where they are close together, the elevation changes rapidly over a short

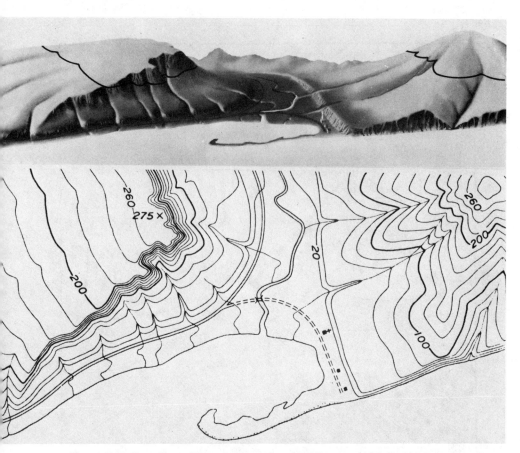

Figure 5-11. A portion of the earth's surface and its representation by a contour map. The contour lines for hundred-foot elevations are numbered and drawn heavier for greater ease in reading the map. Since there are five contour intervals for every 100 feet, we can see that the contour interval is 20 feet.

distance; that is, the surface has a steep gradient. Where they are widely spaced, the gradient is gradual. But a topographic map can give us more precise information about the rate of change of elevation. By using the map scale and the contour interval, we can calculate a numerical value for the gradient of the surface.

As an example, let us find the average gradient between points A and B on the map in Figure 5-12. The contour interval is 20 feet. We see that the elevation from A to B changes from 140 feet to 20 feet, a difference of 120 feet. Using the map scale, we find that

the distance from A to B is 2 miles. The gradient is then:

$$\frac{120 \text{ feet}}{2 \text{ miles}} = 60 \text{ feet/mile}$$

Profiles. Another important clue for the earth scientist is often the shape of the land between two points. By this we mean the shape we would see if the land were sliced vertically along the line between the two points. This shape is called a *profile*. A profile is actually a graph of elevation against distance along a line. A profile can be drawn quite accurately using the information on a topographic map.

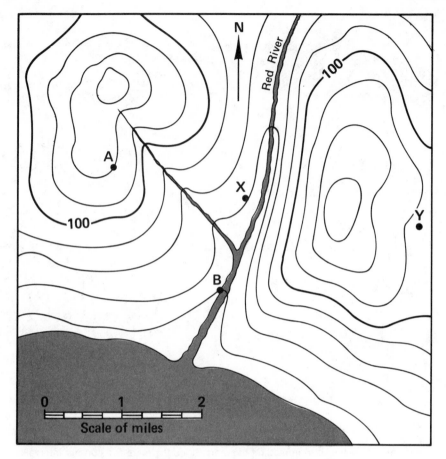

Figure 5-12. A contour map.

As an example, let us construct a profile between points X and Y on the map in Figure 5-12. The line from X to Y will be the horizontal axis of our profile graph. The vertical scale of the graph will have to include elevations up to the maximum that the line crosses, which is between 180 and 200 feet. In Figure 5-13A we see the axes of the graph ready for use.

Now we lay the edge of a card along the X-Y line on the map, and we mark the edge of the card wherever it crosses a contour line. We also label the marks with the elevation of the corresponding contour line. This is il-

lustrated in Figure 5-13B.

The next step is to copy the marks from the card on to the horizontal axis of the graph, as in Figure 5-13C. This process puts the marks on the graph axis the same distance apart as the points where the X-Y line crosses the contour lines on the map.

We now draw a line vertically upward from each point on the axis to the elevation corresponding to that contour line. Finally, we draw a smooth curve connecting the tops of the vertical lines (see Figure 5-13D). This is the profile of the surface between X and Y.

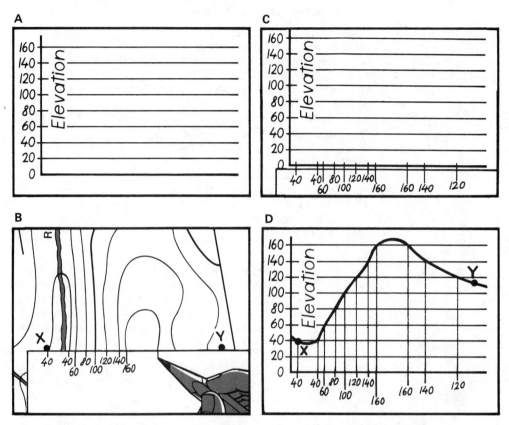

Figure 5-13. Constructing a profile between points *X* and *Y* on the map in Figure 5-12.

SUMMARY

1. A contour map is a map showing the elevation field of a portion of the earth's surface.
2. The contour lines on a contour map pass through points that have the same elevation.
3. Where contour lines are closely spaced, the gradient, or slope, of the surface is steep. Where contour lines are widely spaced, the gradient or slope is gradual.
4. A profile, or vertical section, of the surface along any chosen line can be constructed from the information in a contour map.

REVIEW QUESTIONS

Group A   1. What is a coordinate system?
2. What type of coordinate system is convenient for flat surfaces?
3. How many coordinates are necessary to locate a point on a surface?
4. What system of coordinates is used to locate positions on the earth's surface?
5. What are the reference lines of the latitude-longitude system?
6. What is latitude and how is it found?
7. What is longitude and how is it found?
8. What is a *field*?
9. How can you describe a *scalar* field?
10. How can you describe a *vector* field?
11. What is an *isoline*?
12. What is an *isosurface*?
13. What is a *field gradient*?

Group B   1. a. What basic parts are common to all coordinate systems?
   b. We use coordinate systems in many ways during our everyday experiences. Some of these experiences are locating streets and houses in cities, locating places on road maps, constructing mathematical graphs. Explain how each of these makes use of a coordinate system. Can you think of other examples?
2. Suppose you are planning to make a long trip. What changes could you expect to observe because your latitude changes? Because your longitude changes?
3. a. Three common fields that we are familiar with are gravitational, magnetic, and temperature. List three fields used in weather reporting and three fields used in pollution reporting.
   b. What kinds of information are available on a contour map that are not available on a standard road map?

REVIEW EXERCISES

1. In calculating the circumference of the earth, Eratosthenes made two assumptions—first, that the earth was round, and second, that the sun was very far away. But what if these assumptions had been wrong? Let's assume that the earth is flat. Can you figure out how near the earth the sun would have to be for the sun to be directly overhead at Syene but 7½° from the vertical at Alexandria?

   To begin with, you'll need a piece of graph paper, a protractor, and a ruler. With these instruments you can draw a scale model and measure off the distance to the sun. Start by choosing the scale you're going to use. We know that the distance from Syene to Alexandria was assumed to be 5,000 stadia. So pick a length on your graph paper to represent this distance. Next put in the sun's rays at both locations. At Syene the sun was directly overhead, so draw a vertical (90°) line from that point. At Alexandria the sun's rays were at an angle of 7½°. Mark off the angle with the protractor, and draw in the line representing the sun's rays at Alexandria. Where the two lines representing the sun's rays meet, would be the sun. How far would the sun have to be from the earth to satisfy members of the Flat Earth Society?

2. List three examples of physical models not mentioned in the text. List three examples of mechanical models not mentioned in the text.

3. Give an example of the use of scale in making models. Find a model of something and identify the type of model it is. Describe the accuracy of the scale of the model to the real object. Use actual measurements if possible.

4. Suppose you are on a ship somewhere in the Atlantic Ocean. You take sightings on Polaris and find that its altitude is 48°. You're told that a certain star is on the prime meridian at midnight Greenwich time. This star is on your meridian at 3 A.M. G.M.T. What is your latitude and longitude?

5. Base your answers to the following questions on the diagram below.

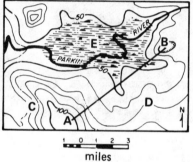

miles

a. What is the contour interval of the map?
b. From which direction does the river in the map flow?
c. Which of the four diagrams below best represents the profile view along line *AB*?

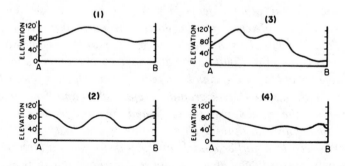

d. What is the straight-line distance in miles from *A* to *B*?
e. What is the greatest possible elevation of point *B*? What is the lowest possible elevation of point *B*?
f. What is the approximate gradient in feet/mile at points *C, D,* and *E*?

TOPIC IV
EARTH MOTIONS

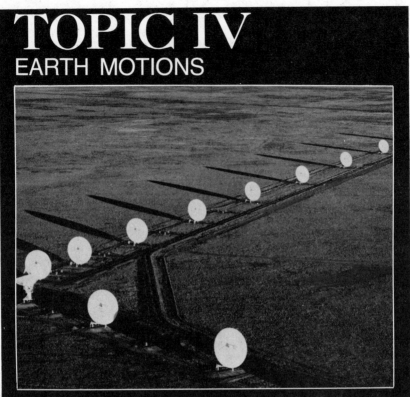

With radio telescopes, such as the Very Large Array in New Mexico, we can "see" much further into space than with optical telescopes.

CHAPTER 6
Motions in the Sky

In this chapter we will examine some of the observations with which we can form a model of the earth's environment—the space around us, the other objects in it, and the way those objects move. To an observer on the earth, the earth appears to be stationary, while the sun, moon, stars, and planets revolve about it. This is the model that nearly all scientists and other educated people accepted for thousands of years. Then, starting about 400 years ago, this model was gradually replaced by another. Today, it is that other model, with the earth and the other planets revolving about the sun, that we all accept as established "fact."

Why was that earlier model satisfactory for such a long time, and why was it finally given up and replaced by almost its opposite? Let us look at the evidence, think it through, and draw our own conclusions.

You will know something about motions in the sky if you can:

1. Make observations of the apparent motions of the stars and describe a star's "life-cycle" in terms of the H-R diagram.
2. Describe the apparent motions of the sun with respect to the stars observed during the course of 1 year, and the pattern of change in its daily motion across the sky.
3. Describe the apparent motion of the moon with respect to the stars and the cycle of the moon's phases.
4. State the relationship between units of time and celestial observations.

CELESTIAL OBSERVATIONS

Making Celestial Observations. One of the objectives of this chapter is to enable you to *collect* data from the sky. This objective cannot be accomplished unless you go outside and do some of your own stargazing. No matter how skillfully we may describe a certain observation, it can never be as vivid and meaningful as a firsthand experience. We feel very strongly that the study of earth science should be a series of firsthand experiences. So, we encourage you to be curious enough to gain the experiences for yourself.

When you do go stargazing, you may make some unexpected discoveries. Most people enjoy the sight of the stars on a clear night. But very few know that the stars change position during the night, or that the stars they can see in July are quite different from those they can see in January. Yet it can be very satisfying to know the names of the brighter stars, to know where and when to look for them, and to recognize them as old, dependable friends.

The Celestial Sphere. As you look at the nighttime sky, it appears like a large dome, or hemisphere, over your head. The highest point is directly overhead. This point is called the *zenith*. The edge, or rim, of the hemisphere is the *horizon*. These are labelled in Figure 6-1. Note that your position is at the center of the diagram. This model of the sky is called the *celestial sphere*. We see only the half of it that is above the horizon at any one time. The stars, moon, and planets seem to be located on the sphere, all at the same distance from the earth. The actual distances of

Figure 6-1. The celestial sphere. At any given time, an observer on the earth can see half of the celestial sphere.

Visible half of the celestial sphere

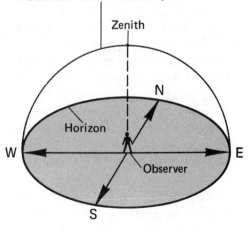

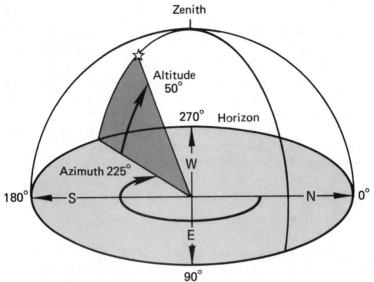

Figure 6-2. Altitude and azimuth. To describe the location of a celestial object you need two measurements, or coordinates. In the system shown, these are the altitude—the angular distance of the object above the horizon—and the azimuth—the angular distance around the horizon from some reference point (in this case, due north).

these objects from earth are so great that our depth perception cannot tell us which ones are farther and which ones are closer.

However, we can describe where a celestial object appears to be at a given moment. To do this, we measure two angular distances. One of the measurements is the distance above the horizon *(vertical angle),* called *altitude;* the other is the distance around the horizon from some reference point *(horizontal angle),* called *azimuth.* These measurements can be made using the techniques shown in Figure 6-2.

Using Star Maps. Figure 6-4 shows the night sky as it appears to an observer at a latitude of 42° north. To use the map, hold it over your head with the arrow marked "N" pointing north. Match this with the real stars.

The center of the map is the zenith—the point directly overhead.

Stars near the edge of the map are close to the horizon, in the direction indicated along the outside of the diagram. For example, the two brightest stars in the constellation Orion (Rigel and Betelgeuse) are just over the horizon and directly to the east. A line drawn from the zenith to the horizon passes near all the stars you see as you face that point on the horizon and let your gaze travel up to the zenith. Thus, if you face northwest, you will find the star Vega (the second brightest we see in our latitudes) about one-quarter of the distance up from the horizon to the zenith. With a little practice you can learn which part of the sky corresponds to each region of the map.

Notice that the east and west points on the horizon are shifted toward the north in this diagram, and the horizon is an ellipse rather than a circle. This has been done so that the paths of the stars on the map become circles around Polaris. As we will soon see, these are the paths the stars seem to follow during the night.

To find north you can use a magnetic compass. But it is more convenient to learn to find Polaris, the Pole Star, by means of the "pointer" stars in the bowl of the Big Dipper. Figure 6-3 shows how to do this. Face the Pole Star and you will be facing due north.

Star Paths During the Night. Figure 6-4 is a star map for the sky at about 8 P.M. (Standard Time) in the middle of November. The brightest stars and the best-known constellations for this season of the year are labeled on the map. On a clear night go to an unobstructed area away from bright lights, and you should be able to find them all.

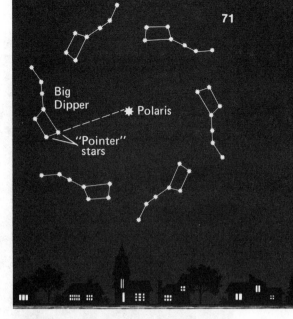

Figure 6-3. Using the "pointer stars" of the Big Dipper to find Polaris. The position of the Big Dipper depends on the time of night and the season of the year.

Figure 6-4. Star map for 8 P.M., November 15th, at about 42° north latitude.

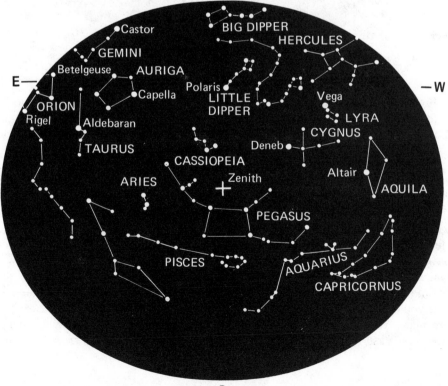

Figure 6-5. Star map for 10 P.M., November 15th.

Figure 6-5 is a map for the same date, but 2 hours later—about 10 P.M. Compare the two diagrams carefully to see what changes you can find.

Notice that some stars near the eastern horizon (for example, the constellation Orion) have risen above the horizon. Stars that had been in the western part of the sky have set (constellation Hercules). Most of the stars have simply moved to new locations. One star, however, the Pole Star, has not moved.

If you observed the stars for an entire night, you would see many stars rise in the east, while others were set-

ting in the west. All the stars would appear to move across the sky, although the Pole Star would move so little as to appear practically stationary. The actual paths of these motions could be recorded on photographic film by means of a time exposure with a camera. In a time exposure, the camera is in a fixed position and the shutter is open. Anything that moves during the period of the exposure will produce a blurred image across the film. This image will trace the apparent path of the object. In the case of a time exposure of stars, the star paths are thin lines, called *star trails*.

If the camera is facing the Pole Star, the star trails are quite interesting. They form parts of circles around the Pole Star as a center. We see such a time exposure photo in Figure 6-6. An exposure made in any other direction is less revealing. Figure 6-7 *A, B,* and *C* show time exposures of the stars taken toward the east, west, and south (but not in that order). Can you match each picture with its compass direction? You are a first-rate observer if you matched *A* with west, *B* with south, and *C* with east.

The star trails in the three photos of Figure 6-7, if examined carefully, will be seen to be curved. However, it is not easy to see whether they have any relation to each other or to the Pole Star. The situation will be clearer if we take a look at star trails at other latitudes.

Observing Stars at Other Latitudes. You may remember from Chapter 4 (page 56) that the altitude of the Pole Star depends upon your latitude. If you are at latitude 90°N (that is, at the North Pole), the Pole Star is directly overhead. At the North Pole, not only do the stars near the Pole Star make circular trails, but *all* the stars do so. All the star trails for an observer at the North Pole are full circles in the sky, and they are all parallel to the horizon (see Figure 6-8).

At the equator, or latitude 0°, the Pole Star is on the horizon, due north. For an observer on the equator, all the star trails are half-circles, and they all meet the horizon at right angles (see Figure 6-9).

We can now understand the star trails in intermediate latitudes, such as ours. These trails are also circular. However, the circles are inclined to

Figure 6-6. Star trails around Polaris.

Figure 6-7. Star trails at eastern, western, and southern horizons (not in that order).

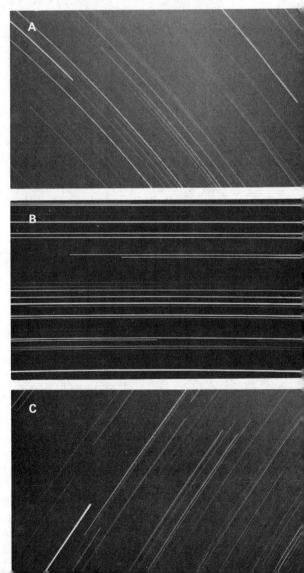

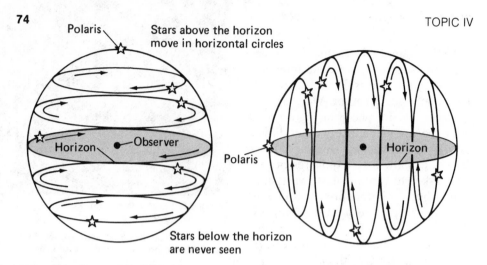

Polaris — Stars above the horizon move in horizontal circles

Horizon — Observer

Polaris — Horizon

Stars below the horizon are never seen

Figure 6-8. Apparent motion of the stars when observed at the North Pole.

Figure 6-9. Apparent motion of the stars when observed at the equator.

the horizon. Stars near the Pole Star make small circular trails that are completely visible. The trails of other stars meet the horizon at an oblique angle. In the case of stars in the southern sky, only a small part of the circle is visible above the horizon (see Figure 6-10).

Apparent Daily Motion of the Stars. We have now discovered that the stars appear to move in circles. Furthermore, if you examine Figures 6-4 and 6-5, which show the stars at two

Figure 6-10. Apparent motion of the stars when observed at about 45° north latitude.

These circular star trails are observed completely

Only a small portion of these star trails are ever observed

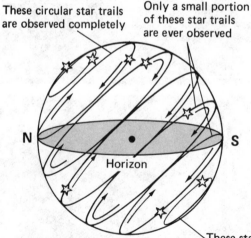

N

S

Horizon

These stars are never seen

different times, you will notice something else of importance. Although all the stars moved, they did not change their positions relative to each other. The stars of the Big Dipper are in the same position relative to each other, and the Big Dipper as a whole is in the same position relative to other stars and constellations. The apparent motion of the stars is not only circular, but also uniform.

You may have noticed our frequent use of the word "appears" or "apparent" in connection with the observed motion of the stars. We have done this to stress the fact that we *observe* a change of position. A change of position is usually caused by the motion of *something,* but it need not be the object we are observing. As you drive along a road, the trees, houses, telegraph poles, and hills appear to change their positions. However, you don't believe these objects have actually moved. You infer that the *apparent* motion is caused by the "real" motion of the car you are in. We see the stars appear to move relative to us as observers. Again we infer that

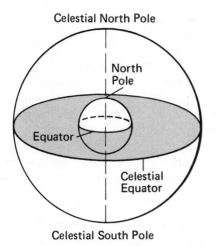

Figure 6-11. Celestial equator and poles. The celestial equator is a projection of the earth's equator, and the celestial poles are projections of the earth's North and South Poles.

something moved. Was it the stars? Was it ourselves? Or was it both? These questions are not easy to answer.

Apparent Motion of the Celestial Sphere. We can now describe the apparent daily motion of the stars in a simple way. We imagine that the celestial sphere is the expansion of the earth's surface outward to some great distance. This sphere has a *celestial equator* that is a projection of the earth's equator, and two *celestial poles* that are projections of the earth's poles, as shown in Figure 6-11. Each star has a fixed location on the celestial sphere. If we imagine the sphere rotating around an axis through the poles of the earth, each star will be carried along its star trail as observed from the earth. If we time the apparent motion of the celestial sphere, we find that its apparent rate of rotation is once a day; that is, 360° in 24 hours, or 15° per hour.

Locations on the Celestial Sphere. Figure 6-12 shows how the positions of the stars on the celestial sphere can be described. Each star trail is a circle parallel to the celestial equator. It is exactly equivalent to a parallel of latitude on the earth's surface. Its angular distance north or south of the celestial equator can be measured in degrees. This angular distance is called *declination;* instead of describing it as "north" or "south," we use a + sign for declinations to the north and a − sign for declinations to the south.

We can also imagine lines on the celestial sphere similar to meridians on the earth. These are circles passing through the celestial poles and crossing the celestial equator at right angles to it. To measure "longitude" on the celestial sphere, we need a "merid-

Figure 6-12. Locating stars on the celestial sphere. Stars are located on the celestial sphere by two coordinates—the angular distance above or below the celestial equator (called declination) and the angular distance from the reference meridian (called right ascension).

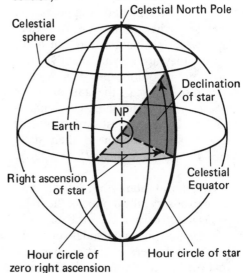

ian" to serve as zero. Note that a "meridian" through any star could have been chosen for this purpose. But astronomers have picked another reference point. It is determined by the sun's apparent motion among the stars, and will be explained later.

A different term is used for the measurement of this point. It is called *right ascension* (R.A.). Instead of expressing it in degrees, it is customary to express it in hours, minutes, and seconds of time. However, since 24 hours of rotation is equal to 360°, each hour of right ascension is equal to 15° of angular distance. The meridian through any star is called its *hour circle.*

Earlier, we suggested that you observe the sky for an entire night to become aware of the apparent westward motion of the stars. If you were to continue this observing during an entire year, you would notice another change.

While the stars seem to travel daily on circular paths from east to west, or counterclockwise as we look at the Pole Star, each night they appear to be slightly farther toward the *west* than they were the night before. In other words, they are moving slightly faster than one revolution per day. After a period of one year, the stars are back where they started, the cycle completed. This apparent westward shifting of the stars in addition to their daily motion is called *annual,* or yearly, motion.

Our Local Star—the Sun. If you tried to observe the motion of the stars, as suggested earlier, you probably wondered what you would find if you could see them better. It just so happens that you have one you can observe very

easily—the sun. All the stars you can see (and others visible only through telescopes) are similar to our sun.

First of all, stars produce their energy by *nuclear fusion.* Our sun converts 600 million metric tons of hydrogen into 596 million metric tons of helium every second. The 4 million metric ton difference is matter that is converted into energy. Other stars undergo different nuclear reactions, but all convert matter into energy by nuclear fusion.

In 1910, two astronomers independently developed a system for classifying stars by their temperature and brightness. The H-R Diagram was named in honor of the Danish astronomer Ejnar Hertzsprung and the American astronomer Henry Norris Russell. The key to this classification is the spectral type of the star, primarily determined by analyzing its light through a spectroscope. You will learn more about the electromagnetic spectrum in Chapter 8.

Figure 6-13 shows the H-R Diagram, with the sun marked where its temperature and brightness locates it on the graph. You can see that the sun is a rather ordinary star, not very hot and not very bright. It belongs in the band labeled Main Sequence stars. Other stars are brighter than the Main Sequence stars, and are classed as Giants or Supergiants. Still others are hotter, but dimmer. These are grouped as the Dwarf stars. Astronomers use the H-R Diagram to explain the life sequence of stars.

According to the diagram, what does the future hold for our own star, the sun? If it is converting its major element, hydrogen, into helium at such a tremendous rate, will it soon

Figure 6-13.

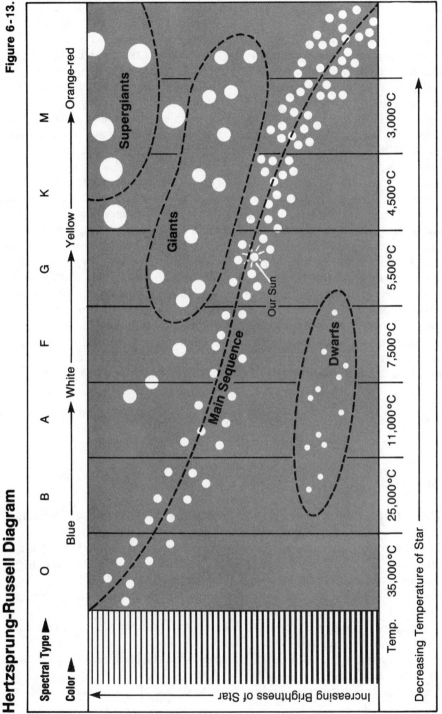

fade out of existence? Here is how astronomers see the life story of the sun, including its remaining years.

It began as a protostar, with gravity pulling gas and dust together. At some critical point, the early star began to warm and glow. After millions of years, the sun became a Main Sequence star, where it has been for about 4.5 billion years. In another 5 billion years, it will make another change.

When much of its hydrogen has been converted into helium, the sun will begin to grow bigger, redder, and brighter, becoming a Red Giant. The interior of the sun will then be almost completely composed of helium. Nuclear reactions will begin to occur in the outer layers of the sun. Because of the increased reactions, the amount of energy released will increase, perhaps by as much as 100 times. The intensity of the sunshine on Saturn will be as great as it is presently on Earth, and, of course, it will be tremendously greater on Earth.

After that, the sun will shrink, and become bluer and dimmer. It may then go through a variable stage, expanding and contracting many times; or it might become a *nova,* a star whose outer layers have blown off like a giant firecracker. If it does not destroy itself, however, it will continue to shrink, eventually turning into a fading white dwarf. From the Earth in this far distant time, a very cold person will see the sun only as a bright star in the sky. Its light will be only 1/10,000 as bright as it is now. As a result, the planets will be invisible to this future earthling, and the moon, with so little light to reflect, will be a pale and ghostly object in the dark sky. However, before you become too worried, remember that all of this will take place billions of years from now.

SUMMARY

1. The apparent daily motion of stars is from east to west in circular paths, centered on an extension of the earth's axis, and parallel to the equator.
2. The daily rate of apparent motion of stars is uniform at about 15° per hour.
3. Stars can be located by a system of coordinates similar to the system of latitude and longitude for locating places on the earth.
4. The stars also have an apparent annual motion from east to west in addition to their daily motion.
5. The energy of a star is a product of nuclear fusion reactions that convert one element into another and release energy.
6. An H-R Diagram shows the relationship between the brightness of a star and its temperature.
7. The sun is an average star, and is classified on the H-R Diagram as a Main Sequence star.

MOTIONS OF THE SUN

Motion of the Sun Among the Stars.
What is the apparent path of the sun among the stars? Since we cannot see the stars when the sun is in the sky, we cannot directly observe the position of the sun on the celestial sphere. However, we can figure out its position indirectly by making a series of observations over a period of time.

In the early morning of any day, shortly before sunrise, we can see the stars that are somewhat to the west of the sun. These are the stars that have just risen in the east. Then, as the sky brightens, the stars fade from view. Stars very close to the sun's position rise too late to be visible.

In the early evening, shortly after sunset, we see the stars that are somewhat to the east of the sun. These are the stars that are just about to set in the west. Again, we have missed a few stars very close to the

sun that set before the sky became dark enough for us to see them. We have missed seeing a few stars on either side of the sun, but we now know that the sun was among them.

As the days pass, the stars gradually shift westward with respect to the sun. Or looked at another way, the sun gradually shifts eastward with respect to the stars. After a few weeks, the sun is among a different group of stars. Now, in the early morning we can see the stars that we missed during the earlier observations. The entire group where the sun had been now rises before the sun. We can therefore figure out where the sun must have been among them at that time.

In this way, we can plot the sun's apparent path among the stars. When we do this, we obtain a circle called the *ecliptic* (see Figure 6-14). It takes

Figure 6-14. The ecliptic. It takes the sun one year to make a complete circuit of the ecliptic—its apparent path among the stars. This path crosses the celestial equator at two points, called the equinoxes.

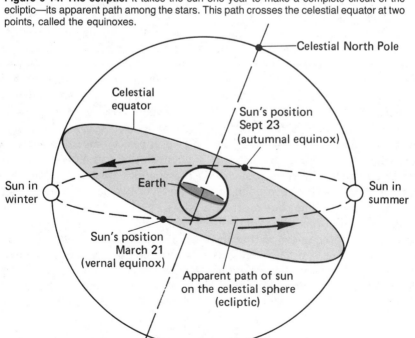

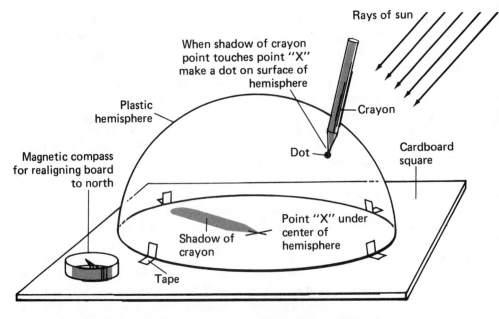

Rays of sun

When shadow of crayon
point touches point "X"
make a dot on surface of
hemisphere

Plastic
hemisphere

Crayon

Dot

Cardboard
square

Magnetic compass
for realigning board
to north

Point "X" under
center of
hemisphere

Shadow of
crayon

Tape

Figure 6-15. Observing the sun with a model of the celestial sphere.

the sun one year to make one complete circuit of the ecliptic. The center
of the ecliptic is the center of the
earth. The plane of the ecliptic is inclined at an angle of 23½° to the plane
of the celestial equator. Therefore,
the ecliptic (the path of the sun among
the stars) crosses the celestial equator
at two points. In other words, the sun
is on the celestial equator twice during
the year.

One of these dates is March 21, a
date called the *vernal equinox*. The
point where the ecliptic crosses the
celestial equator at the vernal equinox
has been chosen as the zero point for
right ascension. The hour circle
through this point has a right ascension of zero. You can see that at the
vernal equinox the sun has a declination of zero (it is on the celestial
equator), and a right ascension of zero
(it is on the zero hour circle).

Observing the Sun During the Day.
Up to this point we have been considering observations made mainly at
night. Now let's make some daytime
observations. Let's look at the
brightest object in the sky—the sun.
We don't really mean this last statement the way it sounds. *Never look
directly at the sun!* The intensity of
the sunlight is so great that you risk
permanent damage to your eyes even
glancing directly toward a bright sun.
Telescopes or binoculars increase the
chance of injury. You may have seen
the heating effect of sunlight brought
to a focus by a lens or reflector. These
devices can be used to *cook* food or
melt metals!

There are several ways you can observe the sun, however. Figure 6-15
shows one method of observing the
sun's position and recording it on a
model of the celestial sphere. If the

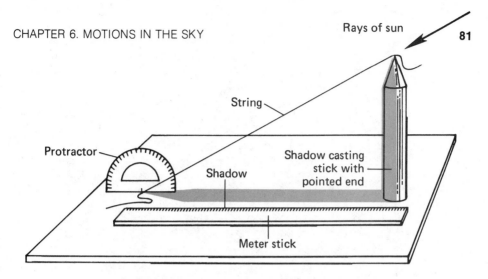

Figure 6-16. Observing the sun by measuring shadows.

materials are available, this method works very well.

Figure 6-16 shows another simple method. You can mark the end of the shadow at various times. Later you can measure angles, if you need this information. Frequently, the pattern produced by the positions of the shadow points is all the information you need.

Making observations of the sun can be just as fascinating as stargazing. The pastime can continue year-round. In fact, some of the observations that you might want to make *should* be done year-round.

Apparent Size of the Sun. One interesting observation of the sun that can be made with a very simple apparatus is the change in its apparent diameter. This can be done by using a pinhole in a card to project an image of the sun on a screen, as shown in Figure 6-17. If this is done at different times of the year, the diameter of the image is observed to vary in a cyclic manner. The change is not large—about 3% from maximum to minimum—but it is not difficult to measure. This observation could mean that the actual size of the

sun changes in the course of a year. Or it could mean that the sun remains the same size, but its distance from the earth changes. The second hypothesis seems the more likely explanation.

Figure 6-17. Observing the apparent change in the size of the sun.

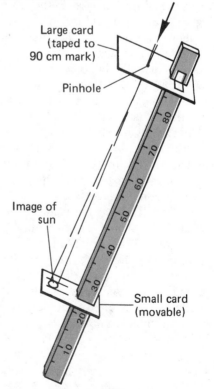

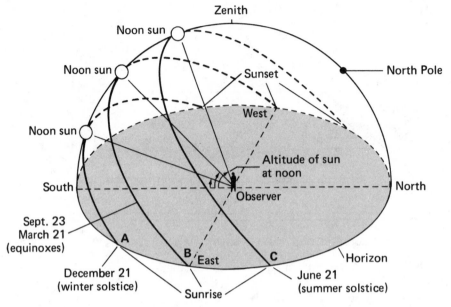

Figure 6-18. Sun's daily path at 42° north latitude for three different seasons of the year.

Motion of the Sun During the Day. Even the most casual observer realizes that the sun rises in the morning and sets at night. But if you ask someone where on the horizon does the sun rise and where does it set, the answers usually become much less definite. If you ask where the sun is in the sky at noon, many people will tell you that it is overhead. If you ask, "Directly overhead?," most people will think so, or again their answers are unsure. The first observations that we need are ones that will help answer our questions with certainty.

Figure 6-18 shows the results of observing the sun's position in the course of one day at latitude 42°N. If you observe the sun's path on September 23, the path labeled *B* is traced. The positions of sunrise, noon, and sunset are labeled. The sun's altitude at noon on September 23 is 48°.

If you observe the sun's path again about December 21, path *A* is traced. Sunrise on December 21 is in the southeast, and sunset is in the southwest. At noon the sun's altitude is only 24.5°.

If you observe the sun's path about March 21, it again follows path *B*. The noon altitude is 48° again. If you observe the sun's path about June 21, path *C* is traced. Sunrise on June 21 is in the northeast, and sunset is in the northwest. At noon, the altitude of the sun is 71.5°.

We now have some definite observations relating to the questions we raised earlier in this section. And we find that the answers are not simple. Where does the sun rise and set? It depends on the time of year, or season. Where is the sun at noon? Again, it depends on the season, but it is never overhead for an observer at 42° north latitude. The closest it gets to

DATE	EQUATOR 0°	TROPIC OF CANCER 23.5°N	NEW YORK STATE 42°N	ARCTIC CIRCLE 66.5°N	NORTH POLE 90°N	RELATIONSHIP OF EARTH TO SUN'S RAYS	SEASONAL EVENT
Sept. 23 Autumnal equinox	90°	66.5°	48°	23.5°	0°		**Fall begins** Equal day and night Sun on horizon at poles
Dec. 21 Winter solstice	66.5°	43°	24.5°	0°	Not visible		**Winter begins** Area north of Arctic Circle in constant darkness Direct rays at 23.5° S
Mar. 21 Vernal or spring equinox	90°	66.5°	48°	23.5°	0°		**Spring begins** Equal day and night Sun on horizon at poles
June 21 Summer solstice	113.5° or 66.5° above the north horizon	90°	71.5°	47°	23.5°		**Summer begins** Area north of Arctic Circle in constant light. Direct rays at 23.5° N Noon sun at equator appears in North

Table 6-1. Altitude of the sun at noon for several locations and at different times during the year.

being overhead is June 21, when it lacks 18.5° of being directly overhead.

Nevertheless, the sun's path through the sky each day does have certain regular features. The sun rises from the horizon in the morning somewhere between north of east and south of east. It moves along the arc of a circle at a rate of 15 degrees per hour. It reaches its highest altitude at noon. And it sets at the horizon as far north or south of west as it rose north or south of east. The daily path is symmetrical about a N-S line.

Table 6-1 on page 83 shows noontime altitudes for several locations on earth. Notice that the sun is directly overhead (90°) for people at the equator on September 23 and March 21. At 23.5° N (the Tropic of Cancer) the sun is overhead only on June 21. On December 21, the sun is not overhead at any of the locations in the table, but it *is* overhead at 23.5° S (the Tropic of Capricorn).

Table 6-1 includes diagrams of the sun's rays in relation to the earth's surface. They will help you visualize the effect of the changing altitude of the sun and its relation to the seasons.

The shifting of the sun's vertical rays (noontime altitude = 90°) from 23.5°N to 23.5°S means that only the area in between those two latitudes will have the noon sun directly overhead at some time during the year.

The locations of the Tropics of Cancer and Capricorn are determined by the maximum northward (Cancer) or southward (Capricorn) positions of the vertical noontime sun. The Arctic and Antarctic Circles are the maximum distances from the poles that can have 24 hours of daylight. (See Figure 6-19.)

Length of Daylight. In the summertime, we enjoy many hours of daylight, while in the winter, darkness may have fallen before we get home from school or work. These facts are

Figure 6-19. Altitude of the sun and number of hours of daylight.

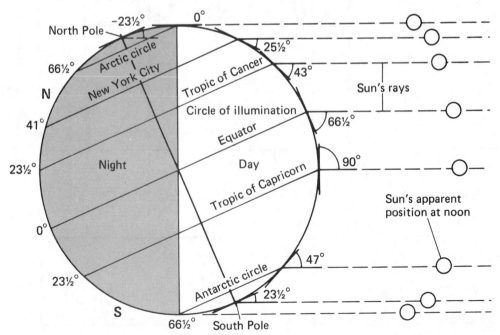

to be expected from the other observations we have made.

Refer again to Figure 6-18. How do the horizon-to-horizon lengths of the arcs *A, B,* and *C* compare? If the sun moves along each one at the rate of 15°/hour, how will this affect the length of daylight? Path *C* is long enough to cause daylight to last for nearly 16 hours at 42°N. Path *A* provides us with daylight for only about 8 hours. If we move nearer to the North Pole, the length of path *C* will increase, because more of it will be above the horizon. Therefore, the daylight will be even longer at latitudes nearer to the North Pole.

Above 66.5°N, daylight occurs for 24 hours when the sun is traveling along path *C*. This condition is also pictured in Table 6-1 for June 21.

SUMMARY

1. The sun has an apparent annual motion through the stars from west to east along a circle whose plane is inclined at an angle of 23½ degrees to the plane of the celestial equator.
2. The apparent diameter of the sun varies in a cyclic manner during the year.
3. The sun's apparent daily path through the sky is an arc.
4. The sun's apparent daily path varies with the seasons.
5. The noontime position of the sun is never directly overhead farther north than 23.5° north latitude.
6. The points of sunrise and sunset vary with the seasons.
7. The length of daylight varies with the seasons.

MOTIONS OF THE MOON

Observing the Moon. When you are stargazing, gaining the firsthand experience we mentioned earlier, you will often have an opportunity to study the moon. In fact, observing the stars is difficult when the moon is bright and high in the sky—so you may as well turn your attention to the moon at such times.

We are all so familiar with photographs of the moon from close range, and from the moon's surface itself, that studying it from the earth may seem rather a letdown. But viewing the moon through a telescope is still an enjoyable pastime, and observing the changing positions and phases of the moon is fascinating even without a telescope.

Path of the Moon Through the Stars. Most people are probably even vaguer about the apparent motions of the moon than about those of the sun. Have you given the subject much thought? Where and when does the moon rise and set? How are these events related, if at all, to its phases? When is the last time you saw a crescent moon at midnight? (If you can't recall, it is not because you have a poor memory!)

If you start recording observations of the moon on as many consecutive nights as you can, you will soon note

DAY	RIGHT ASCENSION hrs. min.		DIFFERENCE (in minutes)	PHASE	APPARENT DIAMETER
1	13	15		Full	33.0
2	14	10	55		33.0
3	15	09	59		33.0
4	16	11	62	Old Gibbous	33.0
5	17	15	64		32.5
6	18	21	66		32.5
7	19	24	63	3rd Quarter	32.0
8	20	23	59		31.5
9	21	18	55		31.0
10	22	09	51		30.5
11	22	56	47	Old Crescent	30.5
12	23	40	44		30.0
13	0	23	43		30.0
14	1	06	43		29.5
15	1	49	43	New	29.5
16	2	34	45		29.5
17	3	21	47		29.5
18	4	11	50		29.5
19	5	02	51	New Crescent	29.5
20	5	56	54		29.5
21	6	50	54		30.0
22	7	45	55	1st Quarter	30.0
23	8	38	53		30.5
24	9	30	52		31.0
25	10	20	50		31.5
26	11	10	50	New Gibbous	32.0
27	12	00	50		32.5
28	12	51	51		33.0
29	13	44	53		33.0
30	14	42	58	Full	33.5
31	15	43	61		33.5
32	16	48	65		33.5

(to nearest .5 minutes)

Table 6-2. Right ascension and phases of the moon for 32 successive days.

that the moon rises about an hour later each night. In other words, the moon moves noticeably eastward among the stars in the course of one day. This motion can be more precisely described by recording its right ascension at the same time each night.

Table 6-2 shows such data for 32 successive days. To help interpret this data, the *change* in right ascension each day is also listed. We see that the moon moves steadily eastward through the stars at a rate that varies from a minimum of 43 minutes of R.A. in one day to a maximum of 66 minutes, averaging about 50 minutes per day during this period of observation.

Time for One Complete Circuit. How many days are required for the moon to return to approximately its same position among the stars (that is, to the same R.A.)? On Day 1, the R.A. was 13 hr 15 min. On Day 28, the R.A. was 12 hr 51 min. On Day 29, it was 13 hr 44 min. So the moon was back at 13 hr 15 min at some time between Day 28 and Day 29. Since we started on Day 1, the time for one complete cycle was between 27 and 28 days in length. Closer analysis of the data leads to a value of about 27⅓ days.

Phases of the Moon. Table 6-2 also shows the changes in the appearance of the moon's face during the period of observation. As you know, these changes in appearance are called the *phases* of the moon. The period of observation started on a day when the phase of the moon was full. When the

moon returned to the same place among the stars (the same R.A.) on Day 28, it was not at the same phase as it was on Day 1. The phase did not become full again until some time on Day 30.

How many days elapse between successive full phases? Using the procedure above, we subtract 1 from 30 and obtain 29 days. More precise observations produce a value of about 29½ days. Thus, the period of time between successive full phases is *longer* than the period of time for the moon to arrive back at the same R.A. *by more than two days!* Our model of celestial motions must account for this observation.

Apparent Diameter of the Moon. Since it is quite safe to look directly at the moon, there are various simple methods for observing its apparent diameter. Table 6-2 includes data on the moon's apparent diameter. It can be seen that the apparent diameter goes through a cycle of variations.

SUMMARY

1. The moon's motion is eastward through the stars at a nearly uniform rate of 50 minutes of R.A. per day.
2. The moon takes about 27⅓ days to complete its cycle of motion through the stars and return to the same R.A.
3. The moon's appearance goes through a cycle of phases that is about 2 days longer than its cycle through the stars.
4. The moon's apparent diameter varies in a cyclic manner.

TIME

The Meaning of Time. We always seem to be interested in time. Time comes into our conversations in many ways. Here are some examples: "What a *time* we had!" "What *time* is

it?" "He got a hit every *time* he was at bat." "I need *time* to think."

It is hard to tell exactly what we mean by time, but it clearly has something to do with events. Time is a sys-

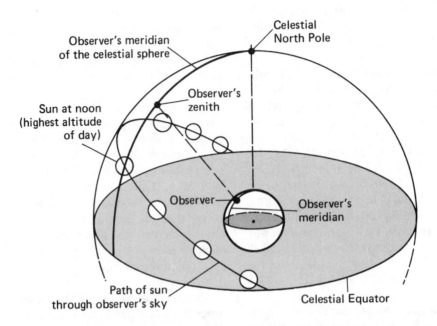

Figure 6-20. Solar noon. Solar noon at any given location occurs when the sun is centered on the meridian passing through that location. The sun reaches its highest altitude of the day at that time.

tem for arranging events in the order of their occurrence. We all talk about events that happened yesterday, or last month, and events that we expect to happen tomorrow, or next year. We are also able to state times with great precision. A class starts at 10:40 A.M. and ends at 11:20 A.M. An athlete runs 1500 meters in 3 minutes and 34.9 seconds. What do we mean by such times? How are they determined? You may say that we use clocks and calendars to measure time. But how do we set the clocks to the "right" time, and how do we know if they continue to tell the right time? In other words, what is the reference standard that we use to measure intervals of time?

Sun Time and Star Time. A circle on the celestial sphere that passes through the poles and through the point directly overhead is the observer's *meridian.* The moment the sun is centered on the meridian is called *noon.* It is also the moment the sun reaches its highest altitude of the day (see Figure 6-20). The time from one noon to the next is called a *solar day.* The clocks we use are adjusted to measure solar days. They divide the day into hours, minutes, and seconds.

We could also use the daily motion of the stars to mark off intervals of time. The time between the instant a star crosses the meridian during one night and the instant it crosses the meridian the next night is called a *sidereal day* ("sidereal" comes from a Latin word meaning "star").

As we have seen (page 76), at any given time by a solar clock, a star is a little farther along to the west on each

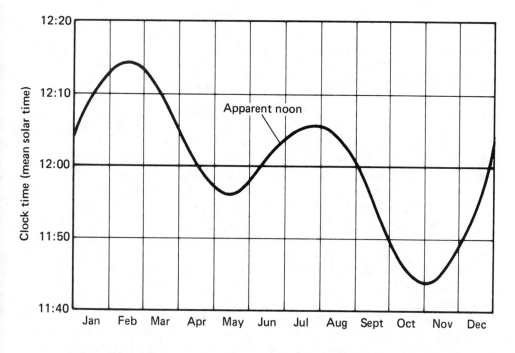

Figure 6-21. Difference between apparent solar noon and mean solar noon throughout the year.

successive night. If a star crosses the meridian at 8:00 P.M. one night, it will be past the meridian by 8:00 P.M. the next night. In other words, it crosses the meridian before 8:00 P.M. the second time. Thus we see that a sidereal day (from meridian to meridian for a star) is shorter than a solar day (from meridian to meridian for the sun). The actual difference is about 4 minutes of time.

Average (Mean) Solar Day. We have said that our clocks are adjusted to match the length of a solar day. However, we find that no clock can be made to keep exactly in step with the sun every day. Some days the clock seems to run a little fast; it reads 12:00 noon before the sun gets to the meridian. Other days it runs slow. The sun crosses the meridian before 12:00

noon. All clocks seem to have the same "error" on the same days. We therefore infer that it is not the clocks that are wrong, but the sun. That is, the apparent solar day varies in length. However, the variation follows a definite pattern through the year. It is possible to fix our clocks to measure an *average* solar day, so that the variations between clock time and solar time will cancel out over a year. The length of day that does this is called a *mean solar day.*

The variation between apparent solar time and mean solar time can be observed by noting the time at which the sun reaches its highest altitude (apparent noon) each day for a year. Figure 6-21 is a graph of the results of such a series of observations. We see that apparent noon (or "high noon") occurs at exactly 12:00 noon by the clock only four times during the year—about April 15, June 11, September 2, and December 24. At all other times, apparent noon is either earlier or later than noon by the clock. In February, apparent noon occurs almost 15 minutes late. At the end of October, apparent noon is more than 15 minutes early. However, the changes from one day to the next are small. Furthermore, the graph is a smooth curve that comes back to its starting point at the end of the year and repeats itself year after year. This means that our clocks are measuring the correct *mean* solar time.

The sidereal day does not fluctuate in this way during the year. Each sidereal day is exactly the same in length. However, it would be inconvenient to have our clocks keep sidereal time. Solar noon would occur at a different time by the clock each day. Any particular clock time, say 9:00 A.M., would occur in the morning at one season of the year, but it would be in the middle of the night at some other season. All things considered, mean solar time works best for everyday affairs.

The Year. Figure 6-21 can also help us understand what is meant by one year. The curve in this graph represents a repeating cycle. The time it takes for the sun to go through this cycle once is called one *solar year*. This period of time is also called a *tropical year*. We can mark off a period of one solar (or tropical) year by noting two successive times at which the sun reaches the same noontime altitude, and is moving in the same direction (that is, its altitude is either increasing or decreasing). Or we could use the time between two successive maximum altitudes (called *summer solstices),* or minimum altitudes *(winter solstices).*

In actual practice, scientists have selected the time from one vernal equinox to the next as the duration of one solar year. (You will recall that the vernal equinox is the moment the sun crosses the celestial equator. At this moment, the altitude of the noontime sun at the equator is 90°.)

A year can also be defined as the time it takes the sun to return to the same position among the stars during its annual eastward motion. This would be the time the sun takes for one complete circuit of the ecliptic. This period is called one *sidereal year.* Because of a complex phenomenon called the precession of the equinoxes, a solar year and a sidereal year are not exactly the same. The sidereal year is about 20 minutes longer than the solar year. Again, for human convenience, we prefer the solar year for regulating the calendar, since we like to have the seasons fall in the same months year after year.

Moon Time and the Month. The cycle of the moon's phases was a very common basis for the yearly calendar in ancient times. One month was the interval from one full moon to the next. There were 12 months in a year, each with its own name. The month was not an exact unit of time, because the cycle of phases is not an exact number of days. It is about 29½ days, so any month might have either 29 or 30, depending on when the full phase was reached. Furthermore, the year is longer than 12 months, although shorter than 13. In order to keep the names of the months in step with the seasons, one of the months was repeated every two or three years. You can see that this was a rather awkward arrangement.

Our modern calendar also has a 12-month year, but the months are not related to the phases of the moon in any way. The lengths of the months in days have been adjusted so that one year is almost exactly 12 months.

SUMMARY

1. The frames of reference for measuring time are based mainly on apparent celestial motions.
2. Mean solar time differs from apparent solar time by an amount that varies throughout the year.

REVIEW QUESTIONS

Group A

1. Describe the apparent daily motion of the stars.
2. What is the daily rate of apparent motion of the stars?
3. Describe the annual, or yearly, motion of the stars.
4. What is the source of a star's energy?
5. How is the sun classified on the H-R diagram?
6. Describe the apparent annual motion and apparent diameter of the sun during the course of a year.
7. What is the maximum latitude at which the noontime sun is ever directly overhead?
8. Are the points of sunrise and sunset, and the length of daylight constant throughout the year?
9. Describe the moon's apparent daily motion through the stars.
10. How long does it take the moon to complete its cycle of motion through the stars and return to the same R.A.?
11. How long does it take the moon to complete its cycle of phases?
12. Does the moon's apparent diameter remain constant?
13. By what amount of time does mean solar time differ from apparent solar time?

Group B

1. Describe how you can show that a star has moved by making two observations.
2. What simple observations can you make of the sun to show that it apparently moves during a day? During a year?
3. a. What simple observations can you make of the moon to show that it apparently moves?
   b. Our time-keeping system is based mainly on the sun. Why don't we keep time using the stars or moon?
   c. Atomic clocks are being used to measure time. What advantage do they have over the sun?

The equatorial rings and ringlets of Saturn are made up of ice particles.

CHAPTER 7
Models of Celestial Motions

You will know something about models of celestial motions if you can:
1. Explain the apparent motions of the planets.
2. Explain the observed motions of fluids at the earth's surface.
3. Describe a geocentric model of the motions of celestial objects.
4. Describe a heliocentric model of the motions of celestial objects.
5. Describe the cyclic changes in kinetic and potential energy of an object in orbit.

In Chapter 6 we gave our attention to the apparent motions of the stars when they are observed through the night and through the year. We also examined the apparent motions of the sun and the moon. To some extent we were repeating the observations of the earliest astronomers. We collected much data, and noticed several patterns of regularity in the observed motions.

Like those early scientists, we can begin to wonder what it all means. What is actually going on out there that can explain what we see? In other words, what "model" of the earth, the sun, the moon, and the stars can account for the observed motions? This chapter will be devoted to the construction of such a model. But first we will need to add certain information about celestial objects called planets—a word that comes from a Greek word meaning "wanderer."

MOTIONS OF THE PLANETS

There are several celestial objects that look like stars, but don't quite behave like stars. To the naked eye they seem to be points of light, just as stars do. But unlike stars, they do not keep a fixed position relative to the celestial sphere. As their Greek name tells us, they wander. We will take a detailed look at the wandering of typical planets very shortly.

Another trait of these wanderers is that they seem to have a measurable size. When viewed through a telescope, they become circular objects with a definite diameter. Except for the sun, all stars, even when viewed through the most powerful telescopes, appear only as bright points of light.

The apparent brightness of a planet is not always the same, as is the case with most stars. The brightness increases and decreases in a periodic fashion. Furthermore, when a planet appears brighter, it also appears larger. These observations strongly suggest that the planets approach the earth and then recede from it in a cyclic manner. Our model of the heavens will have to account for those observations.

Some of the planets have markings or features that can be seen with a telescope. These features move across the face of the planet in a constant direction and in a periodic manner. A likely explanation for these observations is that the planets are rotating spheres. This idea will have to be part of our model.

Eastward Motion of the Planets. Table 7-1 (page 94) shows some of the data presently available about our solar system. These data could be cor-

rected in the future. As in almost all areas of science, astronomers are constantly improving their equipment and looking for new ways to gather information. Observations from satellites, free of interference from the earth's atmosphere, are providing more detail and even some new data for astronomers. Some of the most startling data have been received from automated space vehicles designed to travel through the solar system, and in some cases, to continue on into space beyond the planets.

But what can some of the simplest observations tell us about the model we wish to develop? Are the motions of the planets in the sky identical with that of the stars? If not, the difference must become part of our model, and the explanation of those differences must be a part of it also.

All of the planets do, in fact, show the same eastward motion as that of the stars. However, all of the planets *also* show a strange pattern at various times in their motion across our sky. Mars, for example, takes about two years to make a complete eastward trip through the sky and return to the same point relative to the stars. For about three months, however, Mars appears to move *westward* relative to the stars. This apparent "backward" or *retrograde* motion is seen in the movement of all the planets at different times. Furthermore, two of the planets, Mercury and Venus, are peculiar in that they never get very far from where the sun is among the stars. When we finally construct our model of the solar system, these observations must be explained.

	DISTANCE From the Sun in A.U.*	MASS Earth=1	VOLUME Earth=1	PERIOD OF REVOLUTION	NUMBER OF SATELLITES	PERIOD OF ROTATION	DIAMETER Earth=1	AVERAGE DENSITY (g/cm³)	INCLINATION**
MERCURY	0.39	0.05	0.06	88 d	0	58 d	3000 mi 0.38	5.4	0°
VENUS	0.72	0.81	0.88	225 d	0	243 d	7700 mi 0.97	5.3	177°
EARTH	1.0	1.0	1.0	365 d 1.0 y	1	24 h 1.0 d	8000 mi 1.0	5.52	23.5°
MARS	1.52	0.1	0.15	1.9 y	2	1.0 d	4200 mi 0.53	4	25°
JUPITER	5.2	318	1318	11.9 y	15	9.8 h	89,000 mi 11.2	1.3	3°
SATURN	9.5	95	769	29.5 y	20	10.2 h	74,000 mi 9.47	0.7	27°
URANUS	19.2	15	67	84 y	5	10.8 h	30,000 mi 3.75	1.3	98°
NEPTUNE	30.0	17	58	165 y	2	15.7 h	28,000 mi 3.50	1.64	30°
PLUTO	39.4	0.1?	0.06?	248 y	0	6.4 d	3,600 mi 0.45?	4?	?

* 1 A.U. (Astronomical Unit) = 92,955,700 mi = 149,600,000 km, or 1 Earth-Sun distance.
** of the planet's axis to the plane of its orbit.

Table 7-1. Data about the solar system.

Distances of the Planets. One of the data columns in Table 7-1 lists the distance of the planets from the sun. It is also possible to measure the distance to each of the planets from the earth. These measurements yield some interesting results.

First of all, the distance from the earth to each planet varies in a cyclic manner: first near, then far, then near again. Additionally, the time of each planet's approach to the earth varies from the others. For example, the closest approach of Venus to the earth is not at the same time as Jupiter, or any of the other planets.

All the planets do have at least one observation in common. The time of each planet's closest approach to the earth is also at or near the time of its most rapid apparent retrograde motion.

This observation is very important to the development of our model. Telescopic observations allow astronomers to measure the diameters of the planets, as can be seen in Table 7-1. This measurement, however, depends on when it is taken. The diameter measurements for the planets vary in a cyclic manner, just like the distance measurements. As a matter of fact, the largest apparent diameter for each planet is observed at the time of its closest approach to the earth. Remember that this is also the time of the planet's most rapid apparent retrograde motion.

All of the motions and measurements just mentioned form a pattern. Of course, discovering what the pattern means for the purpose of our model may not be easy.

SUMMARY

1. The planets have a generally eastward motion relative to the stars, but periodically move westward for a time.
2. The apparent size of the planets and their distance from the earth vary in a cyclic manner.

TERRESTRIAL OBSERVATIONS

In the previous section all observations of motions were made in the sky; they were *celestial* observations. There is much evidence of motions to be collected on the earth itself; these are *terrestrial* observations.

These observations will have to be explained by our model of earth motions.

Foucault Pendulum. If a very long pendulum is suspended and allowed to swing back and forth, you will see it

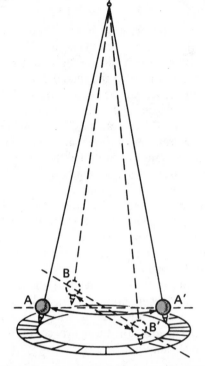

Figure 7-1. Apparent motion of a Foucault pendulum. An observer sees a pendulum swing in the direction A-A'. Several hours later the pendulum has changed its direction of swing to the line B-B'.

gradually change the direction of its swing (see Figure 7-1). After several hours the pendulum in the illustration will have changed its direction from A-A^1 to B-B^1. The amount of change can be measured and given as a rate. For example, if the pendulum shifted 10° in 1 hour, the rate of change would be 10°/hr.

The rate of change in the direction of a pendulum on the earth depends on its latitude. At the equator (latitude 0°) the rate of change is zero. The pendulum continues to swing in the same direction. At the poles (latitude 90°) the rate of change is 15°/hr. Notice that this is the same as the apparent rate of rotation of the celestial sphere. At intermediate latitudes, the rate of change is between 0° and 15° per hour. For example, at 42°, it is 10.5°/hr. In the Northern Hemisphere the Foucault pendulum shifts in a clockwise direction when viewed from above. In the Southern Hemisphere the pendulum shifts in a counterclockwise direction.

Coriolis Effect—*Projectile motion.* Projectiles, such as unsteered rockets, ballistic missiles, or shells from long-range cannons, have paths that seem peculiar. These projectiles appear to veer away from the point toward which they were aimed. In the Northern Hemisphere the shift is always to the *right* of the target. In the Southern Hemisphere it is always to the *left* of the target. This change in direction is called the *Coriolis effect.*

Ocean currents. Ocean currents appear to have a pattern of curving toward the right in the Northern Hemisphere and toward the left in the Southern Hemisphere.

Winds. Surface winds around high and low pressure areas have distinctive patterns in the Northern Hemisphere (see Figure 7-2). They have the opposite pattern in the Southern Hemisphere.

SUMMARY

1. A swinging pendulum changes its direction of motion in a manner that is predictable.
2. The path of a freely moving fluid at the surface of the earth or of a projectile appears to undergo a horizontal deflection.

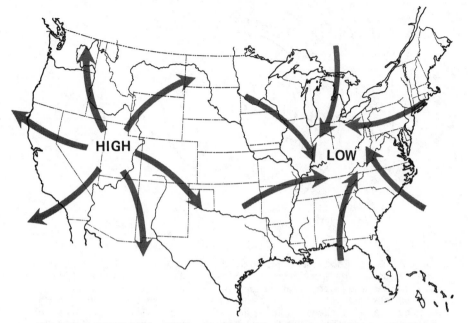

Figure 7-2. The Coriolis effect and winds. Winds blow out from high pressure regions in the atmosphere and in toward low pressure regions. The Coriolis effect deflects these winds to the right in the Northern Hemisphere, with the result that there is a counterclockwise pattern around centers of low pressure and a clockwise pattern around centers of high pressure. These directions are reversed in the Southern Hemisphere.

GEOCENTRIC MODEL OF THE UNIVERSE

"Seeing is believing." It is very human to believe what we see. If we see the sun, the moon, and the stars rise in the east each day, cross the sky, set in the west, and come up again the following day, it is only natural to assume that that is what is actually happening. Therefore, the earliest models of the heavens placed the earth at the center of the universe (or the "world," as it was called). In this model, all the celestial bodies moved around the earth in circles. We call this a geocentric model (*geo-* meaning "earth").

The Celestial Spheres. In the early Greek form of the geocentric model, the celestial bodies were believed to be fixed in transparent spheres. The

stars were all in the same sphere, which was the largest or most distant one. The sun, moon, and planets were in smaller spheres. All the spheres revolved around the earth, which was at their center. Differences in the speeds of the spheres accounted for the changing positions of the heavenly bodies among the stars.

The Geocentric Model of Ptolemy. About 2,000 years ago, the Greek astronomer Ptolemy developed a detailed model of the universe based on the idea of revolving spheres. In order to account for the irregular motion of the planets, Ptolemy's model included smaller spheres or circles called *epicycles*. Each planet was located on its own epicycle, and moved uni-

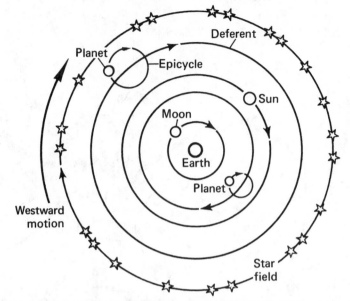

Figure 7-3. Geocentric model of the motions of celestial objects. In this model the earth is stationary. The moon, the sun, and the fixed stars revolve about the earth in circular orbits at different distances and speeds. Each planet revolves in a small circle called an epicycle, while the center of its epicycle moves around the earth along a circle called a deferent. In this diagram you are looking down on the earth from above the North Pole. From this position the celestial objects revolve about the earth in a clockwise (or westward) direction.

formly around the center of the epicycle. Meanwhile, the center of the epicycle was carried uniformly around the earth by one of the spheres.

The model (illustrated in Figure 7-3) can be summarized as follows:

1. The earth is located at the center of the system and does not move.

2. The stars are located on a transparent sphere that rotates once each day from east to west. The axis of rotation extends through the earth at its poles.

3. The sun, the moon, and each planet are carried by separate spheres of different radii. These spheres also rotate from east to west around an axis passing through the earth's poles. However, they rotate at slightly slower speeds than the sphere of the stars. As a result, these bodies have a general eastward drift relative to the stars.

4. Each planet is located on an epicycle that rotates at a fixed rate. The center of the epicycle is carried around the earth at a fixed rate by the planet's sphere, which is called the planet's *deferent*.

5. The deferents and epicycles of the different planets generally rotate at different rates, but the deferents of Mercury and Venus rotate at the same rate as the sun's sphere.

Observations Explained by the Geocentric Model. As we saw in Chapter 6, the stars appear to move as though fixed in a celestial sphere that rotates about the earth once a day. Ptolemy's model therefore explains the daily motion of the stars, because in this model there is an actual sphere of the stars doing just what the celestial sphere appears to do.

The daily motion of the sun, moon, and planets is likewise explained by the daily rotation of their spheres or deferents. Although this rotation is from east to west, it is somewhat slower than the rotation of the celestial sphere. Therefore these bodies drift slowly eastward relative to the stars—a retrograde motion—as shown in Figure 7-4.

However, it is the center of the planet's epicycle that is shifting uniformly to the east. The planet itself is revolving about that center. Therefore, there are times when its motion along its epicycle will carry it westward faster than its deferent is carrying it eastward. At such times, it will appear to drift westward among the stars—a retrograde motion.

Thus the model explains, in a general way, the features of the apparent motion of the celestial objects. It also explains the changing brightness and apparent size of the planets, since the distance of a planet from the earth varies as it travels along its epicycle.

Difficulties of the Geocentric Model. The test of any model is its success in predicting observations. The chief problem of the Ptolemaic model was that it could not be made to give exact predictions of future positions of the planets. Through the centuries, as more and more data accumulated, the astronomers kept tinkering with the model to make it work better. They added epicycles on top of epicycles to get better agreement with their observations. They moved the center of rotation of the planetary spheres to a point in space away from the earth, and had this point revolve about the earth. By the year 1500, the model had become very complicated, and it still did not work well.

When a scientific model or theory has to be made ever more complicated in order to fit new observations, there is likely to be something basically wrong with it. Scientists and

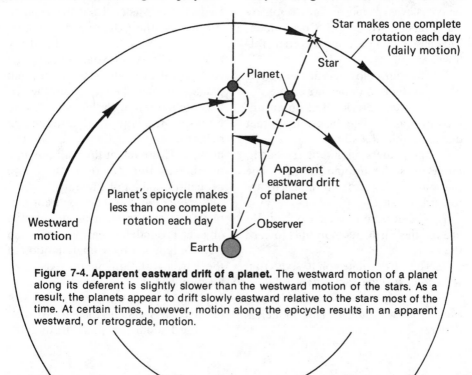

Figure 7-4. Apparent eastward drift of a planet. The westward motion of a planet along its deferent is slightly slower than the westward motion of the stars. As a result, the planets appear to drift slowly eastward relative to the stars most of the time. At certain times, however, motion along the epicycle results in an apparent westward, or retrograde, motion.

philosophers have always believed that the universe is fundamentally simple. A few basic rules, laws, or principles ought to be enough to explain everything—if we can only be clever enough to find them. The increasing complexity of a theory is usually a sign that it is time to look for a fresh idea.

Another difficulty with a model that has a stationary earth is that it does not account for the terrestrial motions described earlier in this chapter. These are modern observations, however, that did not affect the scientific thinking at the time we are referring to (16th century).

SUMMARY

1. A geocentric model of the universe can explain the general features of the apparent motion of the stars, sun, moon, and planets.
2. The geocentric model becomes very complicated when attempts are made to have it predict planetary positions accurately.
3. The geocentric model does not explain terrestrial motions, such as the rotation of a pendulum's direction and the curvature of the paths of projectiles, winds, and ocean currents.

THE HELIOCENTRIC MODEL

In 1543, a new model of the heavens was proposed in a book by the Polish astronomer Copernicus. This model can be summarized as follows:

1. The sun is located at the center of the system and does not move.

2. The stars are located on an unmoving sphere. The sphere is a great distance from the sun.

3. The planets, including the earth, move in circles around the sun. The motions as viewed from the earth are toward the east.

4. The moon moves in a circle around the earth. Its motion is toward the east.

5. The earth rotates on its axis from west to east once each day.

We call this a *heliocentric* model (*helio-* means "sun"). This model is illustrated in Figure 7-5.

Observations Explained by the Heliocentric Model. Like the geocentric model, the Copernican heliocentric model accounts for the daily motion of the celestial bodies, the eastward drift of the sun, moon, and planets through the stars, and the retrograde motion of the planets. It also explains the apparent changes in brightness and diameter of the planets. However, it does all this in a much simpler fashion than the geocentric model of Ptolemy.

1. *Daily motion.* The apparent motion from east to west of all celestial objects around the earth once each day is explained by a single motion of the earth—rotation on its axis from west to east.

2. *Eastward motion of the sun through the stars.* As the earth travels eastward along its path around the

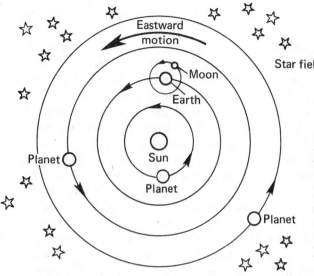

Figure 7-5. Heliocentric model of the motions of celestial objects. In the heliocentric model proposed by Copernicus, the sun and the stars are stationary. The earth and the planets revolve about the sun in circular orbits. The moon revolves about the earth. The earth rotates on its axis once a day. As we look down on the model from above the North Pole, all motions are counterclockwise, or eastward.

sun, the sun each day appears to be in front of a different set of stars, which are slightly to the east of those of the day before. As the earth makes one complete circuit around the sun in one year, the sun appears to make one complete circuit around the celestial sphere along the ecliptic.

3. *Motion of Mercury and Venus.* These two planets travel along orbits inside the earth's orbit around the sun. When they are traveling along the portions of their orbits that pass behind the sun, they appear to move from a point west of the sun, eastward past the sun to a point to the east of the sun. Then they reverse direction and move westward past the sun to a point again to the west of the sun. Since the earth is also moving eastward while this is happening, the two planets share the annual eastward motion of the sun along with their cyclic movement east, and west of the sun (see Figure 7-6).

4. *Motion of the other planets.* All the planets other than Mercury and Venus have orbits outside that of the

Figure 7-6. The apparent changes in position, size, and phase of Venus. In this drawing we are on the earth looking toward the sun. As Venus moves past the sun on the far side of its orbit, we see nearly all of its lighted face, but its apparent size is smallest. As it moves to the east of the sun, its apparent size increases, but we see less of its lighted face. Then as Venus continues along the near side of its orbit, it appears to move westward, to increase in size, and to have a crescent shape. The cycle of changes then reverses as the planet completes it circuit of the sun on the westward side of its orbit.

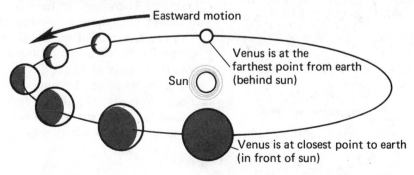

earth, most of them at great distances from the earth. The planets move eastward along their orbits, the more distant ones moving more slowly. The apparent eastward motion of the planets against the background of the stars is the result of this actual eastward motion. However, the earth is moving around the sun faster than any of these outer planets. Therefore, once each year the earth overtakes each planet and passes it in an eastward direction. During this time, the planet appears to move westward in relation to the stars—a retrograde motion (see Figure 7-7).

Figure 7-7. Apparent motion of Mars. This diagram shows how the position of Mars with respect to a distant star appears to change as viewed from the earth. Because of the star's great distance, the direction from the earth to the star remains practically the same, but the direction to Mars changes. Therefore, the position of Mars with respect to the star appears to change as shown.

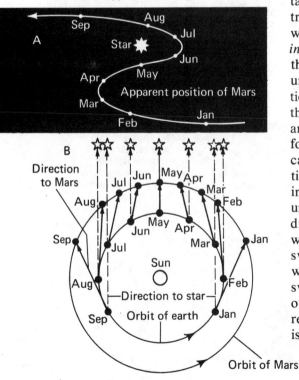

5. *Changing brightness and apparent diameter of the planets.* As the earth travels around its orbit, its distance from each planet varies. This accounts for the variations in apparent brightness and diameter in a simple and accurate manner.

6. *Terrestrial motions.* The geocentric model with a stationary earth cannot explain the changing direction of a pendulum or of projectiles and moving fluids on the earth. These motions would have to be treated as something unrelated to the apparent motions of the heavens. On the other hand, the heliocentric model with a rotating earth does account for these terrestrial motions. When one theory can explain two phenomena, while another theory explains only one of them, we tend to prefer the theory that does the more complete job.

In order to understand how the rotation of the earth explains the terrestrial motions that we are considering, we have to refer to the principle of *inertia*. Inertia is a property of matter that causes it to move in a straight line unless a force acts to change its direction. Imagine a pendulum swinging at the North Pole. (see Figure 7-8). At any moment it is swinging back and forth along a certain meridian. Because of its inertia, the pendulum continues to swing in the same direction in space. But the earth is rotating under it. Therefore, as time passes, different meridians come into line with the direction of the pendulum's swing. To an observer on the earth who is turning with it, the direction of swing seems to be changing continuously. Actually, the pendulum's direction in space remains the same. It is the observer who is turning.

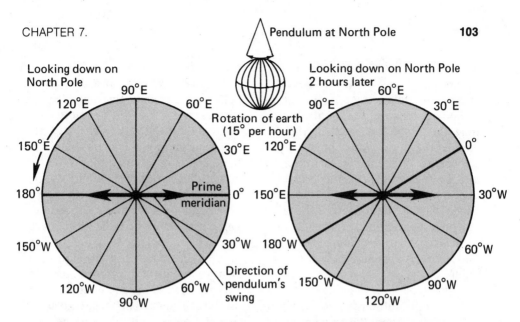

Figure 7-8. **Apparent rotation of a swinging pendulum at the North Pole.** To an observer at the North Pole, the direction of swing of a pendulum appears to change at the rate of 15°/hr. Actually, it is the earth that is rotating at 15°/hr. while the pendulum continues to swing in the same direction in space.

A pendulum at the pole is the simplest case. It is easy to see why the apparent rate of change of the pendulum's swing is the same as the rate of the earth's rotation, but in the opposite direction. As the pendulum is brought down to lower latitudes, its direction of swing continues to change, but at a slower rate. The rate finally becomes zero at the equator. It is not as easy to understand these more complicated cases. Mathematical analysis, however, shows how the change in direction is related to the earth's rotation.

The change in direction of a projectile is also easiest to understand by imagining the projectile starting at the North Pole and headed south along a particular meridian, as in Figure 7-9. As the projectile moves south in a constant direction, the earth is turning eastward under it. Suppose it travels south to the 60° parallel in 1 hour. In 1 hour, a point on the earth's surface at

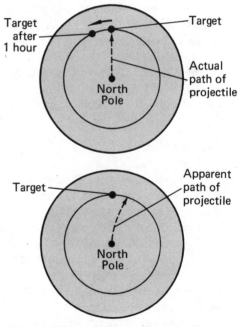

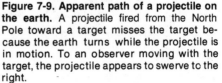

Figure 7-9. **Apparent path of a projectile on the earth.** A projectile fired from the North Pole toward a target misses the target because the earth turns while the projectile is in motion. To an observer moving with the target, the projectile appears to swerve to the right.

60° latitude moves eastward 839 km. If this point was on the projectile's original meridian (that is, the projectile was aimed at the point), by the time the projectile reached the 60° parallel the point would have moved 839 km to the east. To an observer moving with the earth, the projectile appears to veer to the west. It lands at a point 839 km to the west of the point at which it was aimed. Looking along the path of the projectile from its starting point, it appears to veer to the right.

A projectile appears to veer to the right at any latitude in the Northern Hemisphere, no matter in what direction it is fired. As in the case of the pendulum, the reason is not as obvious as in the simple case we just described. Mathematical analysis is needed to show how the rotation of the earth causes this apparent change in direction.

Difficulties of the Heliocentric Model. The Copernican heliocentric model that we have been examining is much simpler than the Ptolemaic geocentric one, and it works much better. It explains some observations (terrestrial motions) that the Ptolemaic does not. But still the Copernican model has problems. If the earth is revolving around the sun in a circular orbit, the distance to the sun should always be the same. Yet observations of the sun's apparent diameter indicate that the distance to the sun does change by a few percent in a cyclic manner in the course of each year. Furthermore, the sun's apparent speed along the ecliptic varies during the year. This seems to mean that the earth's speed along its orbit varies. It is hard to understand why an object in a circular orbit should speed up and slow down as it goes along.

Likewise, if the moon is revolving about the earth along a circle, its distance from the earth should remain the same at all times and its speed should be constant. Yet its apparent diameter and speed also vary in a cyclic manner.

SUMMARY

1. Apparent motions of celestial objects can be generally explained by a heliocentric model of the universe.
2. Apparent terrestrial motions of the objects are *not* explained by a geocentric model in which the earth is stationary.
3. Apparent motions of celestial objects are generally explained by a heliocentric model in which the earth moves around the sun and rotates around its axis.
4. Apparent terrestrial motions of objects *are* explained by a model in which the earth is rotating.
5. The heliocentric model is simpler than the geocentric model.
6. A heliocentric model with circular orbits does *not* explain the apparent cyclic variations in size and speed of the orbiting bodies.

IMPROVING THE HELIOCENTRIC MODEL

The Copernican model was superior to the Ptolemaic model. It was simpler, and it predicted future positions of the planets much more accurately. But as we have just seen, it did not explain the apparent changes in size and speed of the sun and the moon. And as more accurate observations of the motions of the planets were gathered, it was found that the model did not agree with the detailed data. Let us see how the model was improved.

Tycho Brahe. Tycho Brahe was a Danish astronomer who was born a few years after the publication of Copernicus' theory. Brahe devoted his life to making detailed and accurate records of the positions of the planets and other celestial objects. With the financial support of the king of Denmark, Brahe built the first observatory in history and equipped it with the best instruments that he could devise (the telescope was unknown at the time). With these instruments and painstaking techniques of observation, Brahe accumulated a vast collection of data on the positions of the planets.

Johannes Kepler. Johannes Kepler was Brahe's assistant. He was a brilliant mathematician as well as an astronomer. Kepler believed strongly in the correctness of the heliocentric model. Working with Brahe's tables of observations, he began a long attempt to make the data fit the circular orbits of the Copernican theory. Within a few years, however, he became certain that this could not be done. Kepler now began to try orbits of other shapes. One mathematical shape that

he tried was the ellipse, and he discovered that motion of the earth and the planets along elliptical orbits could be brought into good agreement with Brahe's observations.

The Ellipse. An ellipse looks like a flattened circle. The line drawn across the widest part of an ellipse is called its major axis. There are two points along this axis called the *foci* (singular: *focus*) of the ellipse. The sum of the distances between any point on the ellipse and the two foci is the same for all points on the ellipse. Figure 7-10 shows how an ellipse can be drawn. The two pins are at the foci of the ellipse. Since the string has a fixed total length, and the distance between the pins remains the same, the combined length of the two other sides of the triangle also remains the same. Thus we know that the curve satisfies the rule of the ellipse. By changing the distance between the foci, and the length of the string, ellipses of different sizes and different amounts of flattening can be drawn.

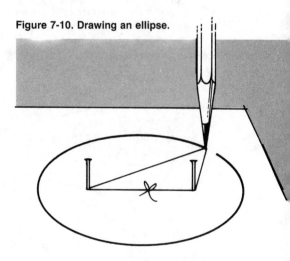

Figure 7-10. Drawing an ellipse.

The amount of flattening of an ellipse is measured by its *eccentricity*. The eccentricity of an ellipse is given by the following formula:

$$\text{Eccentricity} = \frac{\text{Distance between foci}}{\text{Length of major axis}}$$

For example, if the foci of an ellipse are 2 cm apart and the length of the major axis is 10 cm, the eccentricity of the ellipse is 2/10 = 0.2.

In Kepler's version of the heliocentric model, the orbit of each planet is an ellipse with the sun at one focus. Since the focus is off center, the distance between the planet and the sun varies as the planet moves. The same is true of the earth's orbit around the sun and the moon's orbit around the earth. With ellipses of the right dimensions, Kepler found that the motions of the planets could be brought into excellent agreement with Brahe's observations. The observed variations in apparent size (or distance) of the sun and the moon were also accounted for by the elliptical orbits.

Orbital Speed. Look back at the data in Table 6-2, on page 86. This table shows a cycle of changes in the moon's apparent size. Now let us see how *far* the moon appeared to move in one day when it was smallest (farthest away from the earth). It was smallest from the 14th to the 20th days. Between the 16th day and the 17th day the moon moved from an R.A. of 2 hrs. 34 min. to an R.A. of 3 hrs. 21 min. The difference is about 47 minutes.

What distance did the moon travel when it was largest (closest to the earth)? It was largest on the 32nd day. Between the 31st day and the 32nd day the moon moved from an R.A. of 15 hrs. 43 min. to an R.A. of 16 hrs. 48 min. The difference is about 1 hr. 03 min. So it appears that when the moon is closer to the earth it moves farther. This means it is moving faster, since both observations were made during the period of one day.

Kepler observed the same kind of difference in orbital speed for the planets. This discovery meant that the rate of motion of a planet (its velocity) was always changing. It would be greatest at *perihelion* (closest approach to the sun) and least at *aphelion* (greatest distance from the sun).

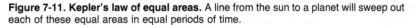

Figure 7-11. Kepler's law of equal areas. A line from the sun to a planet will sweep out each of these equal areas in equal periods of time.

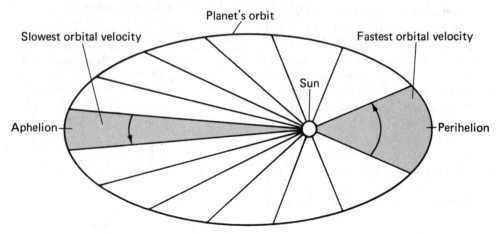

Law of Equal Areas. Kepler discovered another law that relates the changing velocity of the planet to the ellipse: Each planet revolves so that a line from the sun to the planet sweeps over equal areas in equal periods of time. Figure 7-11 illustrates the law. This law also applies to any satellite in orbit around any central object.

Law of Planetary Periods. Kepler studied the velocity and distance relationship more closely and was able to express the relationship between them with a mathematical model, or equation. In the equation, T represents the time it takes a planet to make one complete revolution around its orbit. R represents the average distance of the planet from the sun. T_1 and R_1 are values for one planet, T_2 and R_2 are values for another planet. The equation is:

$$\frac{T_1{}^2}{T_2{}^2} = \frac{R_1{}^3}{R_2{}^3}$$

The average distance of a planet from the sun is equal to half the length of the major axis of its orbit. For the earth, this distance is 149,600,000 km. It is called one astronomical unit (A U) and is often used for measuring distances in the solar system.

SUMMARY

1. In Kepler's modification of the heliocentric model, the earth and the planets move around the sun in elliptical orbits.
2. The sun is at one focus of each orbit.
3. The orbital speed of each planet, including the earth, is greater when the planet is nearer the sun.
4. The variation in orbital speed is such that a line from a planet to the sun sweeps across equal areas in equal times.
5. The greater the average distance of a planet from the sun, the slower its average speed and the longer its period of revolution.

OTHER OBSERVATIONS

In Chapter 6 we mentioned several observations of the sun and the moon that a celestial model must explain. Some of these have already been covered in the discussion of the heliocentric model. Now we will consider others that still need to be accounted for.

The Moon. In Chapter 6 (page 87) we compared the cycle of the moon's apparent position among the stars with the cycle of its phases. We found that one complete cycle through the stars takes about 27⅓ days. One complete cycle of phase changes takes about 29½ days. We noted at the time that our model of the heavens has to account for this difference. By referring to Figure 7-12 we can understand how the heliocentric model does this.

The half of the moon facing the sun is always illuminated by the sun's rays. The other half is dark. As the moon travels around the earth, we see a changing fraction of the lighted half.

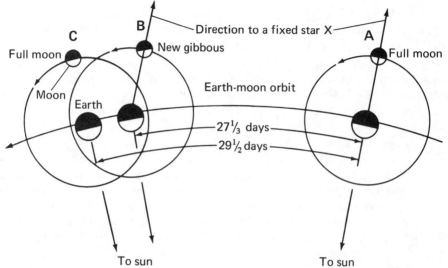

Figure 7-12. One phase cycle of the moon. At position A, the moon is full. At position B, the moon has made one complete revolution about the earth. However, the moon does not become full until it reaches position C, about two days later.

We see a full moon when the moon is on the side of the earth opposite the sun and in line with the earth and the sun. This situation is shown at A in Figure 7-12. (If the sun, earth, and moon were actually in a straight line, the moon would be in the earth's shadow and would be eclipsed. This does happen occasionally, but most of the time the moon is above or below the earth's shadow as it passes behind the earth.)

At B in the diagram, the moon has made a complete circuit of its orbit. It is seen in the same position relative to the stars. But it has not yet become full again. During the 27⅓ days that this circuit took, the earth moved along its orbit around the sun. The line from the earth to the sun is now in a different direction. It takes a little over 2 days more before the moon is again in line with the earth and the sun, and is therefore again full. By this time it has moved on to a new position relative to the stars. That is,

it is well into a second circuit of its orbit.

Changes in Apparent Solar Day. Because the earth moves along its orbit, the cycle of the moon's phases takes longer to complete than the cycle of its position relative to the stars. For similar reasons, the apparent solar day is longer than the sidereal day. The earth has to turn a little more than one complete rotation in order to bring the sun over the same meridian each day, as illustrated in Figure 7-13. When the earth is moving more rapidly along its orbit, it has to turn more to complete a solar day than when it is moving more slowly. Thus the changing speed of the earth is one of the causes for the changing length of the solar day during the year.

The Sun. In the course of a year, the path of the sun across the sky each day changes in a cyclic manner. The altitude of the sun at noon also changes in a cyclic manner. The noon sun can reach an altitude of 90° (be

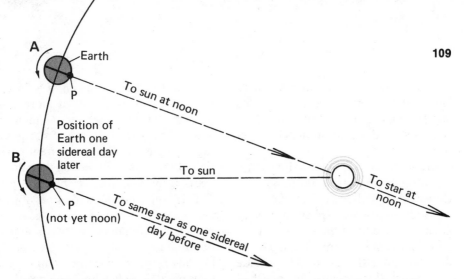

Figure 7-13. The length of a solar day. At position *A*, it is noon at point *P* on the earth. At position *B*, the earth has made one complete rotation relative to the stars. One sidereal day has passed, but it is not yet noon at point *P*. The earth must turn a little more to bring point *P* in line with the sun, when it will be noon again at point *P*. One solar day is therefore longer than one sidereal day.

directly overhead), but this happens only at latitudes between 23½° N and 23½° S.

Our model of earth motions explains these observations by having the axis of the earth tilted at an angle of 23½° to the vertical with respect to the earth's orbit (see Figure 7-14). As the earth travels along its orbit, the axis always points in the same direction in space. That is, the axis points

to the same spot among the stars. During one part of the earth's orbit, the North Pole is inclined *away* from the sun. It is winter in the Northern Hemisphere at that time. The angle of the noon sun is its lowest of the year, the arc of the sun's path is shortest, and the duration of daylight is least.

Six months later, the North Pole is still pointing in the same direction in space, but is now inclined toward the

Figure 7-14. Seasonal effect of the tilt of the earth's axis. In the Northern Hemisphere, the angle of the noon sun and the duration of daylight are least in winter, greatest in summer.

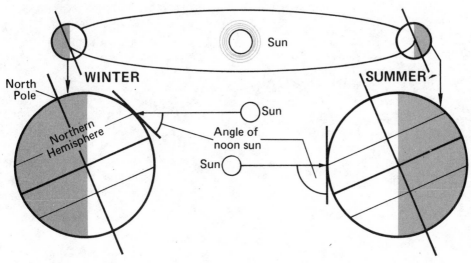

sun. It is now summer in the Northern Hemisphere. The noon sun reaches its highest angle, the arc of the sun's path is longest, and the duration of daylight is greatest.

Distances of the Stars. Most early scientists, including Ptolemy and Copernicus, believed that the stars were all on a single sphere at a very great distance from the earth. In their models, the stars were all at the same distance from the earth. They made this assumption because no one had ever seen stars move relative to one another. If the stars were at different distances, and therefore moving on different spheres, it would be expected that they would shift in apparent positions, just as the planets do.

In modern times, it has become possible to observe very small, cyclic shifts in the positions of some stars. According to our modern model of the heavens, these shifts in apparent position occur because of the earth's motion along its orbit around the sun. Figure 7-15 shows the relative posi-

tions of the earth, the sun, a "close" star, and a background of more distant stars at two times about 6 months apart. As the earth moves from position 1 to position 2, the apparent position of the close star among the others shifts from position A to position B.

This apparent shift of one object relative to others as the observer moves is called *parallax*. An example of parallax is easily observed by holding one finger up at arm's length and looking at it first with one eye, then with the other. As you change your view from one eye to the other, your finger appears to change its position against the more distant background.

The diameter of the earth's orbit is about 300,000,000 km. Yet the parallax of the *nearest* star caused by the shift of the earth by this distance is only about 1/5000 degree. This means that even the nearest star is an enormous distance from the earth—actually more than 40,000,000,000,000 km. Astronomers therefore use a special unit of distance—called a *light-*

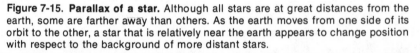

Figure 7-15. Parallax of a star. Although all stars are at great distances from the earth, some are farther away than others. As the earth moves from one side of its orbit to the other, a star that is relatively near the earth appears to change position with respect to the background of more distant stars.

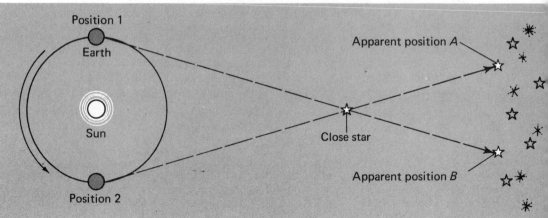

year—for expressing the distances of stars. A light-year is the distance light travels in one *year,* at its speed of 300,000 kilometers per *second.* The nearest star, Alpha Centauri, is more than 4 light-years from us.

Star distances are difficult to imagine. The sun is one star among the billions that make up our *galaxy*—a large group of stars concentrated in one region of space. Our galaxy is estimated to be 100,000 light-years across. Other galaxies are scattered about throughout the universe at even more incredible distances—some measured in hundreds of millions of light-years. Needless to say, such distances are *not* calculated from parallax measurements! They are estimated on the basis of a large number of interconnected astronomical observations, too complex to be summarized here.

SUMMARY

1. The difference between the time for the moon to complete a circuit of the stars and the time to complete a cycle of phases is due to the motion of the earth along its orbit around the sun.
2. The length of the apparent solar day varies because of the changes in the speed of the earth in its orbit.
3. The changes in the sun's daily path across the sky, its noon altitude, and the duration of daylight throughout the year are the result of the tilt of the earth's axis relative to the earth's orbit.
4. Distances to the stars vary over a wide range and are all very large.

FORCE AND ENERGY IN THE CELESTIAL MODEL

In the minds of the ancient Greek philosophers, circular motion was the most natural motion. To them, the circle was the simplest, most "perfect" shape. There was no need to explain *why* the celestial objects moved in circles. Conditions in outer space being perfect, there was no reason for these objects to move in any other way.

This view of the circle as a "natural" shape for celestial orbits continued right up to the time of Copernicus. Uniform motion along circular paths required no explanation. But then Kepler showed that the planets did not move in circular orbits, but in elliptical ones. Besides, they moved at varying speeds, depending on where along the orbit they were at the time. Here was something unexpected and "unnatural." Here was something that needed to be explained. What *causes* the planets to follow elliptical orbits at changing speeds?

Galileo. At about the same time that Kepler was discovering the laws of planetary motion, another brilliant scientist, Galileo, was studying the motions of objects on the earth. In particular, he was seeking the laws of motion for falling bodies. At that time, most scientists accepted Aristotle's belief that heavy objects fall faster than light ones. Galileo did not believe this to be the case. He believed, correctly, that light bodies such as sheets of paper and feathers fall more slowly than heavy objects only because the resistance of the air has a greater relative effect on the light objects.

There is a legend that Galileo dropped two cannon balls of different weights from the Leaning Tower in Pisa to show that they would reach the ground together. Whether or not he did this, it is known that he performed many experiments with balls rolling down inclined planes. From these experiments he learned that the weight of a ball did not affect the time it took to roll down an incline. All balls rolled down the same inclined plane at the same rate. He discovered also that the speed of the rolling balls increased uniformly with time, and that the distance they rolled increased as the square of the time.

From these observations Galileo concluded that objects changed the speed of their motion only when acted upon by a force. If no force acts on a body, it remains at rest if it is at rest, or it continues to move at constant speed in a straight line. This is the principle of inertia that was mentioned earlier in this chapter. It is the key idea for understanding the motion of anything.

Newton. Isaac Newton was born in the year that Galileo died (1642). Newton was one of the world's greatest geniuses, and he made important discoveries in many branches of science and mathematics. He is probably best known for his laws of motion and the theory of grativation that explains the motion of the planets.

Newton was familiar with Galileo's work on falling bodies. Galileo had stated that a moving body continues moving in a straight line at constant speed unless a force acts on it to change its motion. Newton was familiar also with Kepler's discoveries, and knew that the moon moved around the earth and the planets moved around the sun in elliptical orbits. He wondered what force could cause this constantly changing direction of motion.

According to Newton's own account, he was thinking about this problem while sitting under an apple tree. An apple fell from the tree and hit him on the head. The idea that the earth exerted a force of gravity that caused objects to fall was an old idea. The new idea that came to Newton's mind was the possibility that the force of gravity might extend outward into space—even as far as the moon. If that were so, then the moon was actually falling toward the earth all the time.

Of course, the moon doesn't fall *to* the earth—only *toward* it. Without the force of gravity, the moon would fly away from the earth along a straight-line path. The constant force of gravity keeps pulling the moon away from a straight-line path and into the curved path that it actually follows (see Figure 7-16).

The Law of Gravitation. Newton's idea of gravity means that there is a field of force around the earth. Any object in the field of force will be acted on by the force. This field is a vector field, which means that at every point in space the force has both a *magnitude* and a *direction*. The direction of the earth's gravity field is

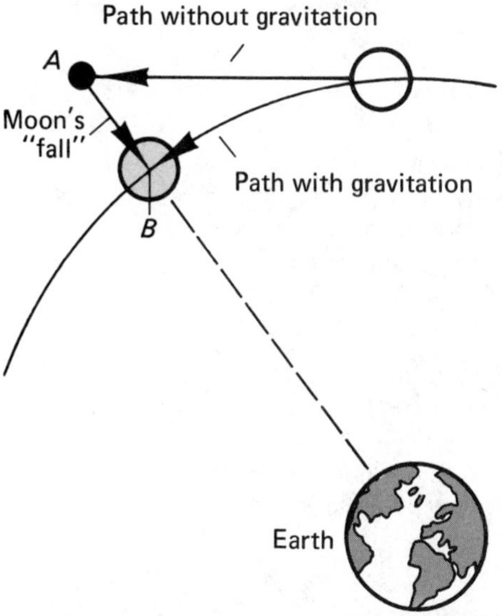

Path without gravitation

A

Moon's "fall"

Path with gravitation

B

Earth

Figure 7-16. How gravitation keeps a moving satellite in its orbit. If the moon stopped moving along its orbit, it would fall to the earth. If there were no gravitation, the moving moon would fly away in a straight line. Because of gravitation, the moving moon neither falls to the earth nor flies away. It continuously "falls" into its orbit.

always toward the center of the earth.

Newton's calculations led him to conclude that the magnitude of the force of attraction would depend on three factors:

1. The mass of the object (M_1).
2. The mass of the earth (M_2).
3. The distance between the centers of the two masses (R).

Newton suggested a mathematical model (equation) that relates all three factors to the force (F) that is produced. The equation is:

$$F = \frac{G\,M_1\,M_2}{R^2}$$

G is known as the gravitational constant. The mathematical model stated in words is:

The force of attraction between two masses is directly proportional to the product of the masses, and inversely proportional to the square of the distance between their centers.

Newton suggested that this force extended *throughout the universe*. Any two objects anywhere in the universe would be attracted to each other by the gravitational force between them. This principle is known as the *universal law of gravitation*.

Elliptical Orbits and the Law of Gravitation. Newton's theory of a force of gravitation extending outward through space from every body of matter was a startling one for his time. He dared not publish it without strong evidence for its correctness. The best evidence would be to show that the law of gravitation, combined with the laws of force and motion, explains the elliptical orbits of the moon and the planets. Mathematically, this is very difficult to do, because the distances and therefore the forces are constantly changing as the orbiting body moves. To solve the problem, Newton had to invent a new branch of mathematics, which is called calculus. Using the new method of calculation, Newton was able to show that when a small body revolves about a larger one under the influence of its gravitational field, the orbit of the small body is an ellipse with the large body at one focus. In other words, Newton's model of a gravitational field of force does account for the observed motions of the moon and all the planets.

Energy Transformation and Orbital Motion. If we summarize what we know about objects in motion in orbit, the following facts can be listed:

1. Objects in orbit move in elliptical paths.

2. The *distance* from the orbiting object to the "stationary" object is constantly changing.

3. The speed of the orbiting object

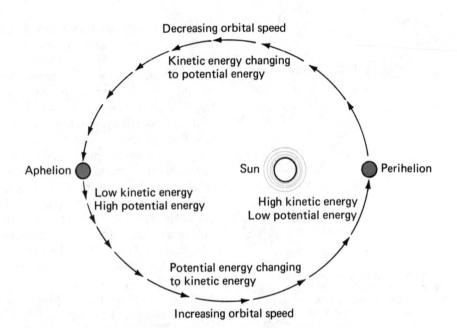

Figure 7-17. Cyclic changes in potential and kinetic energy of a planet in an elliptical orbit.

is constantly changing. It is greatest when the distance is least, and least when the distance is greatest.

The moon's energy of motion, or kinetic energy, is greatest when the moon is closest to the earth, because its speed is greatest at that time. As the moon moves farther away from the earth, it slows down. You might picture the moon as being "higher" above the earth in this position. Its kinetic energy is smaller, but because of its position it has more "stored" energy, or potential energy. As the moon then "falls" back toward the earth, its speed and kinetic energy increase while its potential energy decreases.

The same kind of energy transformation occurs while the earth or any planet travels in orbit around the sun (see Figure 7-17).

SUMMARY

1. A force of attraction exists between any two objects; this is called the force of gravitation.
2. The gravitational force is proportional to the product of the masses and inversely proportional to the square of the distance between their centers.
3. Cyclic energy transformations take place as an object moves along an elliptical orbit. Kinetic energy is changed to potential energy when the object's orbital speed is decreasing, and the reverse transformation occurs when the orbital speed is increasing.

REVIEW QUESTIONS

Group A   1. Is the motion of the planets through the star field uniform?
2. Is the distance to a planet constant, or does it vary? If it does vary, what sort of variation does it show?
3. How do we know that the planets rotate?
4. Why does a long, swinging pendulum appear to change its direction of motion with time?
5. What happens to the path of a freely moving fluid or a projectile at the surface of the earth?
6. Describe the geocentric model of the universe.
7. What observations can be explained relatively simply by the geocentric model?
8. Using the geocentric model, what happens when you try to predict planetary positions accurately?
9. What terrestrial motions cannot be explained by the geocentric model?
10. Describe the heliocentric model of the universe.
11. Which apparent motions of celestial objects can be explained by the heliocentric model?
12. Why is the heliocentric model preferable to the geocentric?
13. In what way did Kepler modify the heliocentric model?
14. Where is the sun in Kepler's modified heliocentric model?
15. When is the orbital speed of a planet greatest? When is it least?
16. State Kepler's law of planetary periods both in words and mathematically.
17. What is the relationship between a planet's distance from the sun, its average speed, and its period of revolution?
18. What causes the difference between the time that it takes the moon to complete a circuit of the stars and the time it takes to complete a cycle of phases?
19. Why does the length of the apparent solar day vary?
20. What causes the changes in the sun's daily path across the sky, its noon altitude, and the duration of daylight throughout the year?
21. What unit is used to describe distances to stars?
22. What force of attraction exists between any two objects?
23. Express Newton's universal law of gravitation both in words and as a mathematical formula.
24. Describe the cyclic energy transformations that take place as an object moves along an elliptical orbit.

Group B   1. What simple observations can you make of a planet such as Mars to show its apparent motions? Explain whether these observations could be done in one evening or would require a longer time.
2. Describe the behavior of a Foucault pendulum at a mid-latitude location such as 42°. How would the pendulum's motion change if the pendulum were carried to a position closer to the poles? Closer to the equator?
3. a. Where is the earth in the geocentric model of the universe?

     b. Describe one or more observations of the planets' behavior that is (are) successfully explained by the geocentric model.

     c. What feature (or features) of the geocentric model made the model unsatisfactory?

4. a. Where is the earth located in the heliocentric model of celestial motions?

     b. Where is the sun located in the heliocentric model?

     c. How are the moon, planets, and stars located in the heliocentric model?

     d. If a new planet were discovered in the solar system, what prediction, based on the improved heliocentric model, could we make about the motions the new planet would have?

5. What would be the observable effects if the earth's axis were inclined at a greater angle than 23½°? At a smaller angle? (See Table 6-1 and Figure 6-19.)

6. a. What factors affect the force of gravity between two objects?

     b. As the earth orbits the sun, the gravitational force is constantly changing. Describe the pattern of change, relating your description to Figure 7-17, page 114.

REVIEW EXERCISES

1. For an observer at 42°N there are certain stars that never set. Toward which horizon would you look to see these stars? What is the maximum angle above the horizon at which these stars are found? Using Figure 6-3 and the star maps on pages 71 and 72 (Figures 6-4 and 6-5), name some of the stars and constellations that do not set.

2. a. Figure 6-6 on page 73 shows a star trail pattern obtained when a camera was pointed at Polaris. How long was the shutter left open when this photograph was taken? Hint: remember that the earth rotates 360°/24 hours, or 15°/hour.

     b. Does the answer to the previous question depend on which star trail you chose to measure? Explain your answer.

3. a. One of the columns in Table 7-1 shows the distance of the planets from the sun. Explain why these data cannot be used to calculate the distance of the planets from the earth.

     b. Under what conditions is Neptune farthest from the earth? What is this distance in A.U. and in kilometers?

     c. Under what conditions is Neptune closest to the earth? What is this distance in A.U. and in kilometers?

       d. The planet that approaches nearest to Earth would show the greatest change in its position relative to the stars (see page 95). From Table 7-1, which planet would this be?

4. a. One column in Table 7-1 lists the periods of rotation for the planets. Illustrate how these data vary from Mercury to Pluto, either with a generalized graph or by a description. Where are the high points? Where are the low points?

       b. How do the data for the mass, volume, and diameter of the planets compare to their periods of rotation?

       c. Make an overall generalization based on your answers to questions 4a and 4b.

5. Refer to Table 7-1 to answer the following questions.

       a. The primary cause of our seasons is the tilt, or inclination, of the earth's axis. Which planet(s) would have seasons *most like* Earth?

       b. Which planet(s) would have the *least* seasonal change?

       c. Which planet is less dense than water?

6. Make a diagram showing the phases of the earth as seen from the moon for each phase position of the moon shown in Figure 3-4 (page 34).

7. What is the maximum change in altitude of the noon sun at any given location during the course of a year?

8. Describe the sun's daily path at the North Pole on June 21.

9. If you wanted to construct a sundial that could show time in minutes as well as in hours, how much space (in degrees) would there have to be between the minute markings? (Hint: Remember that the sun moves at the rate of 15°/hr.)

10. Suppose we put a satellite in orbit around the sun at a distance of 4 AU from the sun. How many earth years will it take for the satellite to complete one orbit?

11. Four satellites, *A, B, C,* and *D,* are placed in orbit around the earth. Satellites *A* and *B* are orbiting the earth at exactly the same altitude, but *A* has twice the mass of *B.*

       a. How does the gravitational force of attraction between *A* and the earth compare with the force between *B* and the earth?

       b. How do the periods of revolution of *A* and *B* around the earth compare?

       c. Satellites *C* and *D* have the same mass, but *D* is twice as far from the earth as *C.* How does the force of attraction between *C* and the earth compare with the force between *D* and the earth?

       d. How do the periods of *C* and *D* compare?

TOPIC V
ENERGY IN EARTH PROCESSES

The steam and boiling water that erupt from the Old Faithful geyser in Yellowstone National Park are heated by geothermal energy.

CHAPTER 8

You will know something about energy in earth processes if you can:

1. Describe the properties of electromagnetic energy.
2. Explain how energy is transferred.
3. Explain the difference between heat and temperature.
4. Explain how energy is conserved.
5. Describe the various ways in which energy can be transformed from one kind to another.

As we have already noted, little, if anything, happens in this world without energy. We are going to run into energy every time we start to examine an earth process. So it will help to get a clearer idea of what we mean by energy, what its properties are, its different forms, where it comes from and where it goes, and so on. This chapter is about energy and its relation to the earth.

ENERGY

Energy is defined as the capacity to do work. This statement basically means that energy is needed to make something move against a resisting force. Energy cannot be observed or measured unless a change is occurring. Even then, only a *change* in energy is observed. During these changes, one body or system usually loses energy while another gains energy.

Kinds of Energy. Energy appears in many different forms during processes of change, but it always represents a capacity for doing work. *Electrical energy,* for example, is the energy in an electric current; this energy can be used to run a motor.

An important form of energy is the energy of a moving body. This is called *kinetic energy*. The kinetic energy of a hammer, for example, can drive a nail into wood. The kinetic energy of the random motion of molecules of matter is often called *heat energy,* or *thermal energy*.

Another important concept is that of *potential energy*. This is the energy that a body has because of its position or state. As objects are lifted against gravity, they acquire more potential energy. This energy can be released when the objects fall (see Figure 8-1). Water at the top of a dam has more potential energy than the same amount of water at the base of the dam. If water flows down over a water wheel or through a turbine, the change in its potential energy can be used to do work. When a body falls freely, some of its potential energy changes to kinetic energy.

Electromagnetic Energy. *Electromagnetic energy* is a form of energy that can travel through empty space. It can then interact with matter, be changed to other forms, and do work. Visible light is one kind of electromagnetic energy. X rays, ultraviolet rays, infrared rays, and radio waves are other examples.

Everything in the world—even you—gives off electromagnetic energy. The amount of energy given off by an object varies with its temperature. The hotter the object, the more electromagnetic energy it gives off. The colder the object, the less energy it gives off.

Figure 8-1. Potential and kinetic energy. When the ball is lifted against gravity, its potential energy is increased. When the ball drops, some of this potential energy is transformed to kinetic energy.

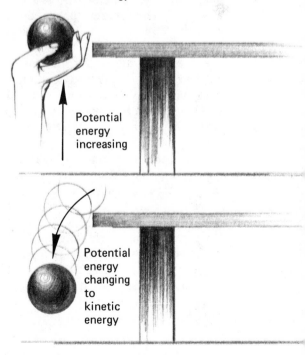

Potential energy increasing

Potential energy changing to kinetic energy

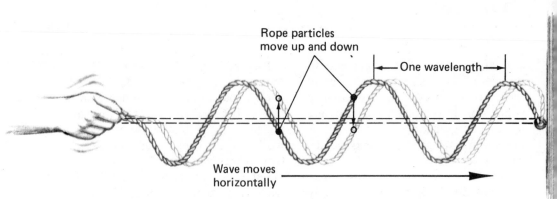

Rope particles
move up and down

One wavelength

Wave moves
horizontally

Figure 8-2. A transverse wave in a rope at two moments a short time apart. As the particles of the rope move up and down, the form of the wave moves to the right. In an electromagnetic wave, there are no moving particles. Instead, there are varying electric and magnetic forces at right angles to the direction of propagation of the waves.

The source of electromagnetic energy is the kinetic energy of moving atoms, molecules, and other particles of matter. As the temperature decreases, the movements of these particles, and hence their kinetic energy, become less. The less the kinetic energy of the particles, the less the electromagnetic energy that is given off. At *absolute zero,* which is theoretically the lowest temperature possible, the particles of matter would have no kinetic energy, and no electromagnetic energy would be given off.

All forms of electromagnetic energy travel in *transverse waves.* This means that the waves vibrate at right angles to the direction in which they are moving (see Figure 8-2). You can see what we mean by a transverse wave if you tie one end of a rope to a solid object and shake the loose end of the rope up and down. The particles of the rope move up and down while the wave passes along the length of the rope. The direction of travel of an electromagnetic wave is often shown by a straight-line arrow called a *ray.*

Since electromagnetic waves travel through empty space, there is nothing actually vibrating in such a wave. Instead, there are electric and magnetic forces that vary in a regular manner as the wave passes. These electric and magnetic forces are directed at right angles to the direction of the wave. Electromagnetic waves are often called *electromagnetic radiation,* or simply *radiation.*

Speed of Electromagnetic Waves. All electromagnetic waves travel through space at a constant speed of approximately 3×10^8 m/sec. This is often called the "speed of light."

The Electromagnetic Spectrum. As we have mentioned, there are many different types of electromagnetic energy, or radiation. The various forms of electromagnetic energy are distinguished from one another by differences in their *wavelengths.* The wavelength is the distance between the *crest,* or peak, of one wave, and the crest of the next wave (see Figure 8-2). The shorter this distance, the shorter the wavelength.

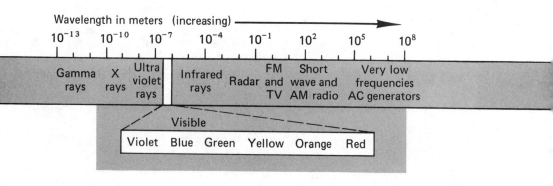

Figure 8-3. The electromagnetic spectrum. Wavelengths are indicated on a logarithmic scale, in which each mark indicates a wavelength 10 times as great as the preceding one. There is no zero point on such a scale.

Figure 8-3 shows the different forms of electromagnetic energy arranged in order of increasing wavelength. The entire range of electromagnetic radiations is called the *electromagnetic spectrum.* You may be familiar with the word "spectrum" as it applies to the colors of the rainbow, from red at one end to violet at the other. This is the spectrum of visible light. You can see from Figure 8-3 that visible light accounts for only a small portion of the much wider spectrum that includes all electromagnetic radiation.

We have already noted that the total amount of electromagnetic energy given off by a body depends on its temperature. The distribution of this energy among the various wavelengths also varies with the temperature of the radiating body. Cool objects give off relatively little electromagnetic energy, and their radiation is mostly of longer wavelengths. As the temperature of an object increases, the amount of electromagnetic energy given off increases, and more and more of the radiation is of shorter wavelengths, and less and less of longer wavelengths.

Interaction of Electromagnetic Radiation with the Environment. When electromagnetic waves come into contact with matter, the waves interact with the particles of the material. There are four possible results of this interaction: (1) The waves can be *refracted,* which means that their direction is changed as they pass through the material. (We say that the waves have been "bent.") (2) The waves can be *reflected,* which means that they are bounced back. Reflected waves do not pass through the material. (3) The waves can be *scattered,* which means that they are reflected and/or refracted in various directions. (4) The waves can be *absorbed,* which means that their energy is taken into the material.

What happens to electromagnetic waves when they interact with matter depends both on the types of radiation (wavelengths) involved and the nature of the material. In most cases, all four of the possible interactions occur in varying degrees.

Electromagnetic energy may also pass through matter without interacting with it. In this case we say that the energy has been *transmitted.*

SUMMARY

1. Kinetic energy is the energy of a moving body. Potential energy is the energy of the position or state of the body.
2. All objects at temperatures above absolute zero give off electromagnetic energy.
3. Electromagnetic energy travels in transverse waves of electric and magnetic forces.
4. The speed of electromagnetic waves through empty space (also called the speed of light) has a constant value of approximately 3×10^8 m/sec.
5. The various forms of electromagnetic energy are distinguished from one another by differences in their wavelengths.
6. All the various forms of electromagnetic energy make up the electromagnetic spectrum.
7. When electromagnetic radiation interacts with matter it may be refracted, reflected, scattered, or absorbed.

ENERGY TRANSFER

We have previously stated that all earth processes involve a transfer of energy. Let's examine some of the ways in which energy is transferred from one place to another or from one body to another.

Radiation. As you have just learned from the preceding section, energy can be transferred across empty space in the form of electromagnetic waves. This method of energy transfer is called *radiation*. (The term "radiation" is used rather loosely. Sometimes it means the energy itself; sometimes it means the process of *giving off* electromagnetic energy; and sometimes—as we are using it now—it means the transfer of energy by electromagnetic waves.)

Atomic reactions inside the sun are continuously releasing enormous amounts of energy. This energy *radiates* from the sun in all directions, traveling in the form of electromagnetic waves at the speed of light, 3×10^8 m/sec. Only a small fraction of the sun's total radiation is intercepted by the earth. However, this energy that reaches us by radiation from the sun is the earth's major source of energy.

Electromagnetic energy can be transferred by radiation here on earth, as well as in space. When you turn on an electric light, the light reaches your eyes by radiation. Heat from a campfire is energy reaching you primarily by radiation (see Figure 8-4).

Conduction. Did you ever wonder why the metal handle of a frying pan gets so hot even though it's not in the flame? How did the heat get from the fire out to the end of the handle? You'd probably say that it traveled through the metal. And you would be right! This form of energy transfer is called *conduction*. Conduction is a method of energy transfer in which heat energy is passed from atom to atom or from molecule to molecule through collisions.

Let's see what actually happens to our frying pan when the stove is turned on. One point you should remember is that when matter is heated,

Figure 8-4. Transfer of heat. Heat from the fire is being transferred in several different ways in this picture. Can you identify them?

its molecules and atoms move faster and faster, because they are gaining energy. So when a burner is turned on, the areas of the pan directly over the flames or in contact with the electric coils immediately begin to heat up. The molecules in these areas move faster and faster. These fast-moving molecules collide with neighboring molecules and transmit some of their energy to them. The neighboring molecules then collide with still other molecules, and so on. In this way heat is transmitted throughout the pan.

Heat energy can be transferrred by conduction through solids, liquids, or gases. However, the solid form of any material usually conducts heat more effectively than the liquid or gaseous forms. The main reason for this is that the atoms or molecules of a solid are held together by strong forces of attraction. In a liquid or gas, the particles move more freely. Therefore, the motion of each particle in a solid has a greater effect on its neighbors than the motion of particles in liquids and gases.

Convection. Did you ever stand on a stool in the kitchen while the oven was on? Did you notice that the air felt much warmer near the ceiling than it did near the floor? You'd probably find the same thing if you measured the air temperature near the floor and near the ceiling of your classroom. Why does this happen? It happens because of the process called *convection*. Of the methods of energy transfer, convection is probably the least direct, and therefore may seem to be most complex. Let's analyze it in some detail.

The air around a stove or radiator is warmed by conduction. The warm air expands, and in expanding, becomes less dense. This less dense, warm air is forced upward by the surrounding cooler, denser air, which moves in underneath it.

When the warm air reaches the ceiling, it spreads out horizontally and begins to give up its heat to the cooler

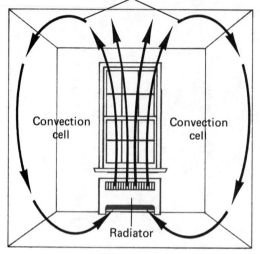

Convection current

Figure 8-5. Heating a room by convection.
The air around the radiator is heated by conduction. The heat is then carried around the room by circulatory movements of the air—convection currents.

ceiling and the surrounding air. As the air loses heat, its temperature drops. Its density increases. After a time, the cooled-off, and now more dense air sinks once more toward the floor. The rising of the heated air and sinking of the cooler air results in a circulatory motion of the air as a whole (see Figure 8-5).

If you think a moment about what is happening, you will see that the circulatory movement of the air is transferring heat energy from one place to another. The heat is entering the air near the source and is being carried upward by the moving air. This kind of circulatory movement can occur in any fluid—either a gas or a liquid. Convection can be defined as the transfer of heat by circulatory movements of a fluid, caused by differences in temperature and density in different regions of the fluid. The moving masses of fluid are called *convection cells,* or *convection currents.* It is the convection currents that actually do the job of transferring heat.

Rooms heated by "radiators" are actually heated by convection. The air around the radiator is warmed, and the heat is distributed around the room by convection currents in the air.

Heat is transferred through the atmosphere and the hydrosphere of the earth by convection currents. It is believed that convection may also occur in the earth's *mantle,* which is the rock layer beneath the lithosphere, or outer crust.

SUMMARY

1. Radiation is a method of energy transfer in which electromagnetic energy travels across empty space in the form of transverse waves.
2. Conduction is the transfer of heat energy from atom to atom or molecule to molecule through contact when the atoms or molecules collide.
3. Convection is the transfer of heat by movements in gases and liquids. These movements are caused by differences in density within the gas or liquid.
4. In convection, heat is transferred from one place to another by a circulatory motion called a convection cell, or convection current.

HEAT AND TEMPERATURE

We have been using the terms "heat" and "heat energy" without being very careful to explain just what they mean. Because heat is such an important concept in earth science, it will help to state more clearly just what we mean by it. At the same time we will find out what we mean by temperature, how it differs from heat, and how the two terms are related.

Temperature. All matter is made up of particles that are in a state of continuous, random motion. Because the particles are in motion, they have kinetic energy. At any moment, the kinetic energies of the individual particles vary widely. *Temperature* is a measure of the *average* kinetic energy of the particles of a substance. The higher the average kinetic energy, the higher the temperature. The lower the average kinetic energy, the lower the temperature. The particles of all objects at the same temperature have the same average kinetic energy.

Heat. What happens when you put a hot object into a container of cold water? The hot object cools off, and the water warms up. Why? Some of the kinetic energy from the particles of the hot object is transferred to the particles of the cold water. As a result, the average kinetic energy of the particles of the hot object decreases. In other words, its temperature drops.

At the same time, the average kinetic energy of the particles of water increases. In other words, the temperature of the water rises. This transfer of energy continues until the particles of the object and the water have the same average kinetic energy, that is, until the object and the water have the same temperature.

Whenever two bodies of matter have different temperatures, energy will flow from the hotter one to the colder one. This energy that flows from one body to another because they have different temperatures is called *heat*. A gas flame is hotter than a pot of water; heat flows from the flame to the pot. The sun is hotter than the earth; heat flows from the sun to the earth.

We have already seen that there are three basic processes by which heat energy can be transferred—radiation, conduction, and convection. But whatever the transfer process is, the energy flow is always from hot to cold—from higher temperature to lower temperature.

Sources and Sinks. A body or region from which heat energy is flowing is sometimes called a heat *source*. A body or region into which heat is flowing is sometimes called a heat *sink*. The concept of sources and sinks is a useful one.

SUMMARY

1. Temperature is a measurement of the average kinetic energy of the particles of a substance.
2. Heat is energy that is transferred from a hotter object to a cooler object because of a difference in temperature.
3. Heat energy flows from a region called a source to a region called a sink.

CONSERVING QUANTITIES OF HEAT

Heat, Mass, and Temperature Change. As we have just seen, an increase in temperature of a body requires an increase in the average kinetic energy of its particles. This means that energy must be added to a body to raise its temperature. In fact, to raise its temperature 2°C will require twice as much total energy as to raise it only 1°C. It is also fairly easy to see that to raise the temperature of 2 grams of a substance by 1°C will require twice as much energy as to raise only 1 gram by 1°C. The reason for this is that 2 grams have twice as many particles as 1 gram. Thus the total amount of heat energy needed to raise the temperature of an object is proportional to both the mass of the object and the desired temperature change.

Measuring Amounts of Heat. Amounts of heat can be measured by making use of the ideas of the preceding paragraph. The unit of heat energy is the *calorie*. You're probably familiar with the term already because it is commonly used to express the energy content of foods. One calorie is the amount of heat needed to raise the temperature of one gram of liquid water by one degree Celsius.

It takes 1 calorie to raise the temperature of 1 g of liquid water by 1°C. How many calories does it take to raise the temperature of 2 g of water by 1°C? If you said 2 calories, you were correct. It takes twice as much heat to raise the temperature of 2 g of a substance by 1°C as it does for 1 g of the same substance.

How many calories would it take to raise the temperature of 1 g of water by 2°C? If you said 2 calories, you were correct again. It takes twice as much heat to raise the temperature of 1 g of a substance by 2°C as it does to raise it by 1°C.

For a given substance, the amount of heat involved in a temperature change is directly proportional to the amount of the temperature change and to the mass of the substance.

Specific Heat. You know that 1 calorie of heat will raise the temperature of 1 g of liquid water by 1°C. But how does the same amount of heat affect 1 gram of other substances? Will their temperatures also be raised 1°C by 1 calorie?

Suppose we take a piece of lead, a piece of iron, and a piece of rock, all with the same mass and all at the same starting temperature. We put them in separate containers, and we heat the three different materials from the same source and for the same period of time. At the end of the heating time you would probably find that the lead was much warmer than either the rock or the iron. In fact, all three substances would probably be at different temperatures.

Different substances heat up at different rates. The amount of heat needed to raise the temperature of a substance by a given number of degrees is a characteristic of the substance.

The amount of heat needed to raise the temperature of one gram of a substance one degree Celsius is called the *specific heat* of that substance. The specific heat of water is 1 cal/g/°C. It takes 1 calorie to raise the temperature of 1 g of water 1°C. If you have a

Substance	Specific heat in cal./g./°C.
Water	1.0
Ice	.5
Water vapor	.5
Dry air	.24
Basalt	.20
Granite	.19
Iron	.11
Copper	.09
Lead	.03

Table 8-1. Specific heats of some common substances.

substance that has a specific heat of 0.3 cal/g/°C, you would have to add 0.3 calorie to raise the temperature of 1 g of that substance 1°C.

Liquid water has the highest specific heat of all naturally occurring substances. This means that all other natural substances heat up (and cool off) more rapidly than water. Table 8-1 gives the specific heats of some common substances.

Heat Calculations. If you want to calculate the amount of heat gained or lost by a substance during a tempera-

ture change, you must know the specific heat of the substance. You must also know the mass of the substance, and the number of degrees the temperature changed. The heat lost or gained (in calories) can be calculated using the formula given in the example below.

Conservation of Energy. Many observations and experiments have led scientists to an important law concerning energy. This law states that in any transfer of energy, the total amount of energy remains the same. That is, the energy lost by a source equals the energy gained by a sink. This is called the *law of conservation of energy.*

Let's conduct an experiment in which we will transfer heat from a heat source to a heat sink. We will then calculate how much heat left the source and how much entered the sink, and see if our results agree with the law of conservati n of energy.

The experiment involves two containers connected by an aluminum

---

EXAMPLE OF HEAT CALCULATION

The temperature of a piece of metal is raised from 20°C to 100°C. Its mass is 30 g and its specific heat is 0.1 calorie/g/°C. How much heat in calories was added to the metal?

Number of calories = temperature change x mass x specific heat

The temperature changed from 20°C to 100°C.

The temperature change was: 100°C − 20°C = 80°C

The mass of the object: 30 grams

Specific heat of the material: 0.1 calorie/gram/°C

The number of calories transferred =

temperature change x mass x specific heat:

↓   ↓   ↓

80°C x 30g x 0.1 calorie/gram/°C = 240 calories

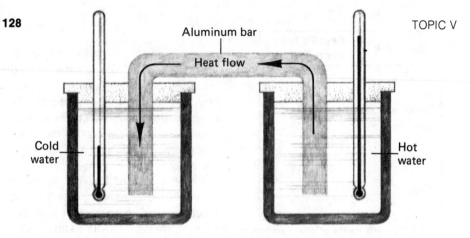

Figure 8-6. Conservation of energy. In this experiment we can observe the flow of heat from a source—the warmer water—to a sink—the cooler water.

bar, as shown in Figure 8-6. The containers are made of Styrofoam or some other material that is a poor conductor of heat (a good insulator). One container is filled with hot water; the other, with cold water. Each container has a thermometer fitted through an insulating cover. To simplify matters, we will make the mass of water the same in each container.

Since the water in one container is at a higher temperature than the water in the other, and since there is a way for heat to flow from one container to the other (by conduction through the aluminum bar), we know that heat will do so. (The rule of nature says that if a way exists, heat will always flow from a hotter body to a colder one.)

We record the masses of water and the two temperatures at the start of the experiment. We then read the temperatures every minute. Knowing the mass of water in each container and the observed temperature changes, we can then calculate the heat loss and heat gain at every stage of the experiment. When we do this in a practical case, we find that the amount of heat gained by the cool water is almost—but not quite—as

much as the amount of heat lost by the hot water. Theoretically, the two quantities of heat should be equal. The heat lost by a source should equal the heat gained by a sink. What has happened to the "missing" energy?

You probably know the answer. Some heat did leave the hot water through the walls of the container and was lost to the surroundings. Some heat also left the aluminum bar by conduction and convection of the air. The law of conservation of energy applies only to what is called a *closed system*. A closed system is one in which energy can neither enter nor leave. The two containers and their metal connector did not form a closed system.

If we cover the metal bar with Styrofoam or some other heat-insulating material and repeat the experiment, we will get a better agreement with the theoretical result. We have brought the system closer to being a closed one, and so less energy is "lost." In our earth science investigations, we will never be dealing with a completely closed system, but we will try to approach that ideal situation as nearly as we can.

SUMMARY

1. The amount of heat involved in a temperature change is directly proportional to the amount of the temperature change and to the mass of the substance.
2. A calorie is the amount of heat needed to raise the temperature of one gram of liquid water by one degree Celsius.
3. The specific heat of a substance is the amount of heat needed to raise the temperature of one gram of that substance by one degree Celsius.
4. Water has the highest specific heat of all naturally occurring materials.
5. Heat lost or gained (in calories) is equal to the mass (in grams) times the amount of temperature change (in degrees Celsius) times the specific heat (in calories per gram per degree).
6. When heat is transferred in a closed system, the heat energy lost by the source (or sources) equals the heat energy gained by the sink (or sinks).

LATENT HEAT

Latent Heat of Fusion. Suppose we take some ice that is below its melting point (0°C). If the ice has been crushed or broken into small pieces, we can stick a thermometer into it and read its temperature. Let's now begin to add heat to the ice, and observe the changes in its temperature. As you would expect, the temperature of the ice begins to increase. This means that the heat energy being transferred to the ice is causing the average kinetic energy of its molecules to increase. The rate of increase of temperature depends on the usual three factors: the rate at which energy is being transferred; the mass of the ice; and its specific heat (about 0.5 cal/g/°C—lower than that of liquid water).

When the temperature of the ice reaches exactly 0°C, it begins to melt. This is no surprise. What *is* surprising is that while the ice is melting, the temperature does not change! Even though we are continuing to add heat at the same rate as before, the temperature of the melting ice remains at 0°C. In other words, the added energy is no longer being transformed into additional kinetic energy of the ice molecules. What is happening to the energy going into the melting ice?

To answer this question, you must know something about the structure of ice. Ice is a *crystalline* solid. That is, its molecules are arranged in a regular, repeating fashion. As the temperature of the ice increases up to 0°C, the added heat energy is transformed into kinetic energy. The molecules in the ice crystal vibrate more and more rapidly, but they do not break out of the crystal pattern.

When the temperature of the ice reaches 0°C, some of the molecules acquire enough kinetic energy to break free of the rigid ice structure. The ice then begins to melt and enter the liquid state. However, it takes energy to break up the crystal structure. While the ice is melting, all the heat energy that enters the ice is used to break up the crystal structure.

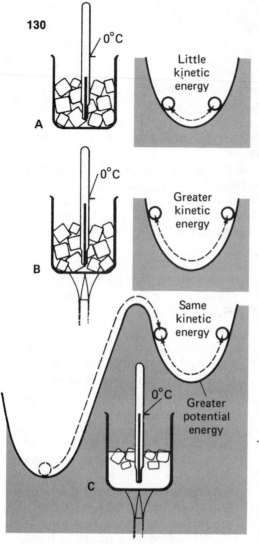

Figure 8-7. Latent heat of fusion. (A) In ice below 0°C, the molecules vibrate back and forth around fixed positions in the crystal. This is like a ball rolling from side to side at the bottom of a trough.

(B) As ice is heated toward 0°C, its molecules vibrate with greater average kinetic energy. This is like giving the ball more kinetic energy. It rides up higher on the sides of the trough, but stays in the trough.

(C) When ice reaches 0°C, it begins to melt. While the ice is melting, the molecules of water are not gaining kinetic energy. They are moving to positions of greater potential energy. This is like giving the ball enough energy to ride up to a trough at a higher level.

None of it goes into increased kinetic energy until the melting process is completed (see Figure 8-7). If heat is added slowly enough, and if there is constant mixing to distribute the heat uniformly, the temperature of the ice-water mixture remains constant at 0°C while the melting is going on. (In an actual experiment, these ideal conditions are usually not maintained, and the temperature does rise slightly before the ice is completely melted.)

The energy transferred during the melting process is transformed into a kind of potential energy called *latent heat*. This is energy that the ice molecules have as a result of changes in their relative positions. The fact that the energy is still there can be shown by letting the water freeze again. The same amount of energy that was stored as latent heat during melting, is released during freezing. This energy is called the *latent heat of fusion*.

Latent Heat of Vaporization. If we continue to add heat after the ice has melted, the thermometer again shows a steady rise in temperature. The added heat is again being transformed into increased kinetic energy of the water molecules.

When the water temperature reaches 100°C (under normal atmospheric pressure), the water begins to boil. It is entering the gaseous state. Once again the temperature stops increasing. And again the transformation of heat to kinetic energy stops, and transformation of heat to potential energy (latent heat) starts.

As in the case of melting, the energy transferred during boiling is being used to change the structure of the substance, that is, to change the relative positions of its molecules. Molecules of water are breaking free of their neighbors in the liquid. These molecules escape into the air and form a gas called water vapor. This process of changing from the liquid state to the gaseous state is called *vaporization*. It requires an input of energy called the *latent heat of vaporization*. The latent heat stored as potential energy during vaporization is returned to the environment when the water vapor condenses to a liquid.

Vaporization of a liquid can occur below the boiling point. It occurs continuously from the surface of any liquid, at any temperature, and is called *evaporation*. Evaporation also involves a transformation of energy to potential energy or latent heat. The chief difference between boiling and evaporation is that in boiling, the vaporization occurs in the interior of the liquid, forming bubbles of vapor. Ordinary evaporation occurs only at the interface between the liquid and its environment.

Although water can evaporate at temperatures below the boiling point, it can't boil unless the water vapor has enough pressure to form bubbles inside the liquid. At normal atmospheric pressure, this happens at 100°C. At lower pressures (for example, on mountaintops), water boils at lower temperatures. In a pressure cooker, water boils at a higher temperature.

Heating Curves. While a substance remains in a single state, either solid, liquid, or gas, added heat energy is transformed into kinetic energy, which raises the temperature of the substance. However, while a substance is changing state from a solid to a liquid or from a liquid to a gas, added heat energy is transformed into potential energy (latent heat), and there is no increase in temperature. While a substance is changing state from a gas to a liquid or from a liquid to a solid, latent heat is released.

These observations are illustrated by the *heating curve* for water, Figure 8-8. This is a graph of the temperature of water (in its three states) as heat is added or removed at a fixed rate. The flat portions are periods of constant

Figure 8-8. Heating curve for water. The graph shows the temperature change of 1 gram of water as heat is added at a constant rate (50 calories per minute). If read from right to left, the graph is the corresponding cooling curve.

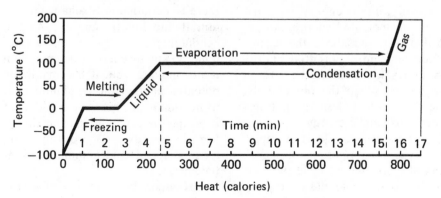

temperature during change of state.

You can see from Figure 8-8 that it takes a great deal more heat to change liquid water to water vapor than it does to change ice to liquid water. In fact, it takes nearly seven times the amount of heat. The latent heat for the change from ice to liquid water is 80 calories/gram, while the latent heat for the change from liquid water to water vapor is 540 calories/gram.

Heat Lost or Gained in Change of State. When a substance is changing state from a solid to a liquid or from a liquid to a gas, it must gain latent heat. When a substance is changing state from a gas to a liquid or from a liquid to a solid, it must lose latent heat. The amount of heat gained or lost during a change of state is equal to the product of the mass times the latent heat per unit mass.

SUMMARY

1. For a change in state to occur, there must be a loss or gain of energy.
2. While a substance remains in a single state, added heat energy is transformed into kinetic energy, which raises the temperature of the substance.
3. While a substance is changing state, heat energy that is added is transformed into a kind of potential energy called latent heat. There is no change in temperature during the change in state.
4. Latent heat is a form of potential energy that is gained or lost during a change in state.
5. A much greater amount of energy is needed to change liquid water to water vapor than is needed to change ice to liquid water.

OTHER ENERGY TRANSFORMATIONS

Gravitational Potential Energy. The movement of matter either away from or toward the earth's center of gravity results in a transformation of energy. In the movement of matter away from the earth, kinetic energy is transformed into potential energy. An object that is raised above the earth's surface has more potential energy than it does at the surface because of its position. When the object falls, some of its potential energy is transformed into kinetic energy.

Let's look at a couple of examples of this type of energy transformation. Think of a boulder sitting at the edge of a cliff. It has potential energy because of its elevation. If the boulder rolls off the cliff, it falls with increas-

ing speed downward, toward the center of the earth. Some of its potential energy is transformed into kinetic energy.

In the swinging of a clock pendulum there is a continuous exchange of potential and kinetic energy. As the pendulum reaches the top of its swing, it has no kinetic energy (the pendulum is not moving), but it has maximum potential energy (the pendulum is at its maximum height). At the middle of its swing the pendulum has maximum kinetic energy (it's moving at its greatest speed) and minimum potential energy.

Absorption. Another type of energy transformation occurs when electromagnetic radiation is absorbed by a material. The quantity and wavelengths of electromagnetic energy absorbed depend on the color and texture of the material. Dark, rough surfaces absorb more visible light than smooth, shiny surfaces. Materials that are good absorbers of electromagnetic energy are also good radiators of electromagnetic energy.

In many processes at the earth's surface, electromagnetic energy of short wavelengths is absorbed by a material, which then reradiates energy of a longer wavelength. For example, in many cases ultraviolet and visible light from the sun are absorbed by a material. This energy is then transformed and reradiated as infrared radiation. This type of energy transformation is important for understanding certain earth changes that will be discussed in Chapter 9.

Friction. Another type of energy transformation occurs at interfaces, where friction develops because of movement along the interface. For example, there is friction between the moving water of a stream and the stream bed. The friction causes the transformation of some of the kinetic energy of the moving water to heat.

Another example of energy transformation at an interface can be found when a boulder rolls down a hill. Friction between the boulder and the ground causes the transformation of some of the kinetic energy of the boulder to heat and sound.

SUMMARY

1. The movement of matter either way from or toward the earth's center of mass results in an energy transformation from kinetic to potential or from potential to kinetic.
2. The characteristics of a surface determine the amount and type of electromagnetic energy that will be absorbed.
3. When electromagnetic energy of short wavelength is absorbed, it can be subsequently reradiated at longer wavelengths.
4. A material that is a good absorber of electromagnetic energy is a good radiator of electromagnetic energy.
5. There is a transformation of energy at interfaces where friction occurs.

REVIEW QUESTIONS

Group A
1. Under what conditions do objects give off electromagnetic energy?
2. In what form does electromagnetic energy travel through space?
3. At what speed do electromagnetic waves travel through space?
4. What is the chief difference between the various forms of electromagnetic energy?
5. What is the *electromagnetic spectrum?*
6. What can happen to electromagnetic radiation when it comes in contact with a material?
7. What happens during the process of radiation?
8. What is *conduction?*
9. Describe the transfer of heat by *convection.*
10. What is *temperature* a measurement of?

11. What is *heat?*
12. What is meant by the terms *source* and *sink?*
13. How is the amount of heat involved in a temperature change of a substance related to the mass and the amount of temperature change of the substance?
14. Give the definition of a *calorie.*
15. What is the *specific heat* of a substance?
16. Of naturally occurring materials, which substance has the highest specific heat?
17. How can you calculate the amount of heat gained or lost by a substance during a temperature change?
18. In a closed system, how does the amount of energy lost by the source compare with the amount gained by the sink?
19. Is energy flow involved in a change in state?
20. While a substance remains in a single state, what happens to any heat energy that is added?
21. While a substance is changing state, what happens to any heat energy that is added? What happens to the temperature of the substance during the change in state?
22. What is meant by the term *latent heat?*
23. How does the amount of energy needed to change ice to liquid water compare with the amount needed to change liquid water to water vapor?
24. What energy transformation occurs when an object is moved away from the earth's center of mass? Toward the center of mass?
25. Which surface characteristics determine the amount and type of electromagnetic energy that will be absorbed?
26. How does the wavelength of electromagnetic energy absorbed by a surface compare with the wavelength of electromagnetic energy reradiated by that surface?
27. If a material is a good absorber of electromagnetic energy, what can be said of its capacity to radiate electromagnetic energy?
28. Give an example of an energy transformation that takes place at an interface where friction occurs.

Group B   1. a. Define the term electromagnetic energy.
　　　　　　　　 b. Define the term wavelength as it applies to electromagnetic energy.
　　　　　　　　 c. List at least 5 different forms of electromagnetic radiation (energy) in order of increasing wavelengths.
　　　　　　　　 d. Describe the relationship between the wavelength of electromagnetic energy emitted by a radiating body and the temperature of that body.
　　　　　　 2. a. Describe the general effect that temperature change has on the density of fluids.
　　　　　　　　 b. Based on the relationship described in 2-a, explain why fluids move as they do within a convection cell. Include in your answer an explanation of the role that the force of gravity plays in this type of heat transfer.
　　　　　　 3. When two objects of unequal temperature are near each other, heat flows from the hotter object to the cooler. The size of the

temperature difference between the two objects will have what effect upon the rate of flow?

4. a. How do the specific heats of most earth materials generally compare to the specific heat of water?

   b. Use Table 8-1, page 127, to answer this question. If equal masses of basalt and water received the same amounts of heat energy, how would their changes in temperature compare?

   c. Based on your answer to 4-a, which would heat up faster in the day during the summer, sand on the beach near a lake, or the water in the lake? Explain your answer. (Note: Both sand and basalt are rock materials whose specific heats are about the same.)

5. Explain what effect (a) the evaporation of ocean water, and (b) the melting of an iceberg would have on the temperature of the environment. Include in your answer references to the terms latent heat of fusion and latent heat of vaporization.

REVIEW EXERCISES

1. The graph below illustrates the theoretical energy transformations that occur as a playground swing moves back and forth. The graph shows the energy transformations of the swing beginning at its backmost point (time = 0) and ending at its frontmost point (time = 100).

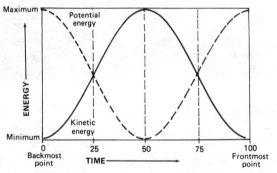

   a. During which time interval, or at which specific time, did the following conditions exist?

   Potential energy increasing, kinetic energy decreasing _____
   Potential energy increasing, kinetic energy increasing _____
   Potential energy decreasing, kinetic energy decreasing _____
   Potential energy decreasing, kinetic energy increasing _____
   Kinetic energy maximum, potential energy minimum _____
   Potential energy maximum, kinetic energy minimum _____

   b. Are the events illustrated by the graph examples of cyclic or noncyclic change?

2. Trace the heat energy given off by your body back to its source—the sun.

3. Convection involves the transfer of energy by a moving fluid. Is the flow of gasoline from the gas tank of a car to the engine an example of convection?

4. Under what conditions could a glacier be a source of heat energy?

TOPIC VI
INSOLATION AND THE EARTH'S SURFACE

The more we learn about solar energy, the better we become at harnessing it for our everyday needs.

CHAPTER 9

You will know something about insolation and the earth if you can:

1. Describe the factors that affect the amount of solar energy reaching the earth.
2. Explain what happens to the solar energy that reaches the earth's surface.
3. Describe the effects of the atmosphere on radiant energy given off by the earth's surface.

In Chapter 8 you learned something about the ways in which energy can be transferred from one place to another, and transformed from one kind to another. In this chapter we are going to study the factors that affect the amount of the sun's energy that is transferred to the earth's surface at any particular time and place. We are also going to learn about the transformations of the energy that reaches the earth from the sun.

INSOLATION

The term *insolation* (from INcoming SOLar radiATION) refers to the portion of the sun's radiation that is received by the earth. It is our share of the sun's total energy output. However, we must remember that when radiation strikes matter, some of it may be reflected, some may be scattered, some may be absorbed, and some may be transmitted. All four of these things happen to the insolation that enters the atmosphere. So the amount and kind of insolation that gets through to the earth's surface is likely to be quite different from the insolation at the top of the atmosphere. We will be mainly interested in the insolation that actually reaches us down here on the ground.

Radiation and Temperature. You will recall from the last chapter that all bodies of matter radiate electromagnetic energy if their temperature is above absolute zero. As a body becomes hotter, it radiates a greater total amount of energy. A hotter body also radiates more of its energy at short wavelengths than a cooler body does.

We can see this happen if we heat an object, such as an iron bar, in a furnace or in a very hot flame. Remember that the longest wavelengths of visible light are at the red end of the spectrum. The shortest wavelengths are at the blue end. As the iron bar heats up, it begins to glow a dull red. This means that it has begun to radiate enough energy at red (long) wavelengths for the eye to detect it.

As the temperature of the bar rises further, its apparent color changes to orange, then to yellow. It is radiating more energy at these shorter wavelengths of visible light. It also appears brighter, because it is radiating more energy altogether.

If the bar becomes hot enough, it turns white hot. White light is a mixture of all the wavelengths of visible light. The iron bar is now radiating strongly enough throughout the visible spectrum to shine with a white light. If the temperature rises even further, the bar begins to radiate less strongly at the longer (red) wavelengths and more strongly at the short (blue) wavelengths. Its light now acquires a distinctly bluish color.

What we have just said about the wavelengths of radiation from a body applies only to radiation given off by the body because of its temperature. This has nothing to do with the color of objects that we see by the light they reflect, or the color of glowing gases in neon tubes and similar devices.

Intensity of Radiation. When we refer to "amount" of energy being radiated, we really mean the *rate* at which energy is given off—the amount given off in a certain time. *Intensity* is the term used to describe the rate at which energy is being transferred. It can be expressed in such units as calories per second. We can say, therefore, that the intensity of radiation from the iron bar increases as its temperature rises. We can also say that the intensity of its radiation at short wavelengths increases as its temperature rises.

Figure 9-1 shows the intensity of radiation at various wavelengths from the earth and from the sun. We see that the wavelengths of maximum in-

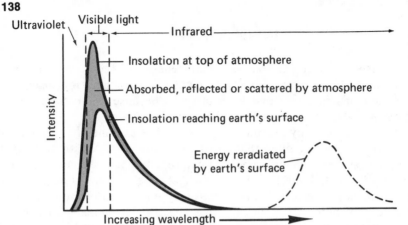

Figure 9-1. Intensity of insolation received and reradiated by the earth's surface.
Total amount of energy is proportional to the area under the curves. About 50% of
the insolation received at the surface is in the infrared range of wavelengths, but
nearly 100% of the reradiated energy is in this range. (The reradiation curve is not
drawn to the same scale as the insolation curves. If drawn to the same scale, it
would be much flatter and would extend much farther to the right.)

tensity from the earth (a fairly cool body) are in the infrared (long) wavelength region of the electromagnetic spectrum. Maximum intensity of radiation from the sun (a quite hot body) occurs in the yellow region of the visible (short) wavelengths.

This does not mean that most of the sun's total energy is in the form of visible light. It still radiates much energy at other wavelengths, both longer and shorter than visible radiation. In fact, about half the energy of insolation that reaches the earth's surface is in the form of infrared radiation.

Intensity of Insolation. Just as we describe the intensity of radiation as the rate at which energy is radiated, we can apply the term "intensity" to the rate at which energy is *received*. The *intensity of insolation* is the rate at which energy of insolation reaches a given area.

Intensity of *radiation* can be expressed in calories per second. Intensity of *insolation* has to have an area factor in it—for example, calories per second *per square meter*. You can see why this is so. There is quite a difference between a rate of 1,000 calories per second per *square meter* and a rate of 1,000 calories per second per *square centimeter!* (Which do you think is more intense? Yes, the second rate is, by a factor of 10,000. If 1,000 calories reach a square centimeter of area in one second, 10,000,000 calories are falling on an area of one square meter. There are 100 × 100, or 10,000, square centimeters in a square meter, each receiving its own 1,000 calories.)

Once you have determined the intensity of insolation for a given area, you can also find the total insolation received by that area over a given period of time. You would find total insolation by multiplying the intensity of insolation by the time.

There are a number of different factors that affect the amount and type of energy received at the earth's surface. In the following section we're going to discuss each of them.

SUMMARY

1. Insolation is that portion of the sun's radiation that is received by the earth.
2. Intensity of radiation is the rate at which radiant energy is being transferred.
3. Intensity of radiation depends on the temperature of the radiating body. As the temperature increases, the total intensity increases, and the wavelengths of maximum intensity decrease.
4. Intensity of insolation is the rate at which insolation is received per unit area.

FACTORS AFFECTING INSOLATION

Figure 9-2 illustrates at least one factor that determines how insolation reaching the earth's surface is related to the seasons. Scene A appears to be summer-like, while scene B seems quite wintery. If you studied these pictures carefully, you probably noticed that the altitude of the sun, or its angle with horizon, is different in the two cases.

In scene A the sun is at a high altitude at noon, while in scene B, at the same hour, the sun is at a low altitude. Does the altitude of the sun affect the temperature? Are there other factors that influence seasonal changes? Let's find out.

Angle of Insolation. Intensity of insolation is determined by the angle at which the sun's rays strike the earth's

Figure 9-2. Season and the angle of insolation. These two scenes show the same view at the same time of day but at different seasons of the year. In scene A, which appears to be summer, the sun is almost directly overhead. In scene B, which appears to be winter, the sun is low in the sky.

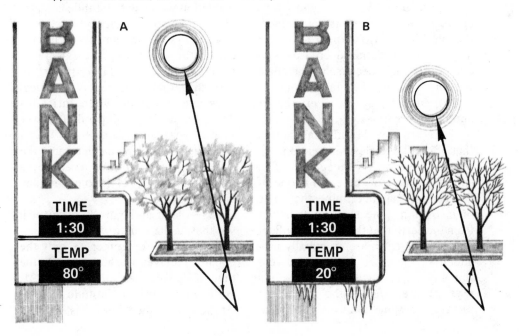

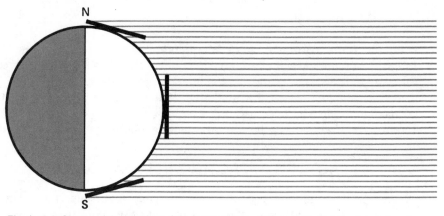

Figure 9-3. Shape of the earth and the angle of insolation. Note that the intensity of insolation is greatest where the rays are perpendicular to the surface.

surface. (This angle is called the *angle of insolation*.) The intensity of insolation is greatest when the angle of insolation is 90°. This is so because when the rays are perpendicular (make an angle of 90°), they are concentrated into the smallest possible area (see Figure 9-3).

As the angle of insolation decreases from 90° to 0°, the intensity also decreases to zero. When the sun's rays arrive parallel to the earth's surface, the intensity of insolation is zero. The intensity of insolation decreases with decreasing angle because as the angle becomes smaller, the same amount of radiant energy is spread over a larger and larger area.

There are several different factors that affect the angle of insolation.

1. *The shape of the earth.* The spherical shape of the earth is one of the factors that determine the angle of insolation. The sun is so distant from the earth that the rays of sunlight reaching the earth are practically parallel to one another. If the earth were flat and perpendicular to the sun's rays, all areas facing the sun would receive the same intensity of insola-

tion. But since the earth is spherical, its surface is curved, and therefore there is only one place on the earth where the rays of the sun can be perpendicular at any given time (see Figure 9-3). At all other locations the angle of insolation will be less than 90°.

2. *Latitude.* From the previous section you can see that intensity of insolation varies with latitude because of the shape of the earth.

The rays of the sun that strike the earth at an angle of 90° are called *vertical*, or *direct*, rays. The only parts of the earth that ever receive vertical rays are those between latitudes 23½°N and 23½°S, depending on the time of year (see Figure 9-4). Therefore, the parts of the earth around the equator have, on the average, a greater intensity of insolation than any other latitudes.

If you look at Figure 9-4, you will see that at the time of the equinoxes, March 21 and September 23, only the equator receives vertical rays. At the time of the summer solstice, June 21, vertical rays strike at latitude 23½°N. At the time of the winter solstice, De-

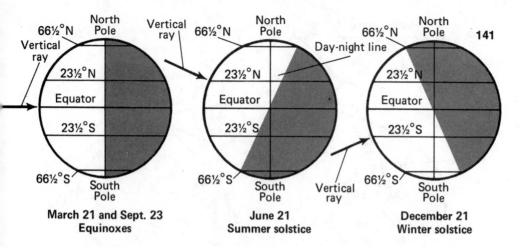

Figure 9-4. Intensity of insolation and latitude. At any given time, intensity of insolation is maximum at the latitude of the vertical rays, and is less at other latitudes.

cember 21, vertical rays strike at a latitude of 23½°S.

3. *Season of the year.* From our discussion of insolation and latitude it should be clear that the season of the year affects the intensity of insolation at any given location.

At the summer solstice, June 21, the vertical rays of the sun strike at their northernmost point, 23½°N, and the noon sun reaches its highest angle everywhere north of 23½°N latitude. On this date the intensity of insolation is greatest in the Northern Hemisphere. This marks the beginning of summer in the Northern Hemisphere and the beginning of winter in the

Southern Hemisphere. During the northern summer, locations at latitudes above 66½°N have 24 hours of daylight, while locations below 66½°S latitude have 24 hours of darkness. At the winter solstice, December 21, the conditions of the two hemispheres are reversed.

So, as the earth travels around the sun in the course of a year, the angle (and intensity) of insolation at a given location varies with the season. Figure 9-5 shows the maximum angle of insolation at noon at four different seasons for a location at 42°N latitude.

Figure 9-5. Maximum angle of insolation (at noon) at 42° north latitude at different seasons.

Sun's rays at noon

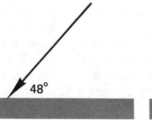

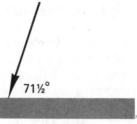

December 21	March 21 and Sept. 23	June 21
Winter solstice	Equinoxes	Summer solstice
Low angle and intensity	Average angle and intensity	Highest angle and intensity

24.5° 48° 71½°

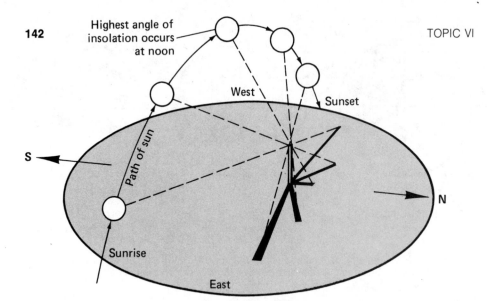

Figure 9-6. Changes in the angle of insolation in the course of one day. The shadow of a vertical post indicates how the angle of insolation varies during the day. The higher the angle of insolation, the shorter the shadow and the greater the intensity. Maximum angle and intensity occur at noon.

4. *Time of day.* Both the angle and the intensity of insolation change constantly during the course of a day. In the morning, when the sun is low in the sky, the insolation arrives at a very low angle, nearly parallel to the horizon (see Figure 9-6). As the day progresses, the sun rises higher and higher in the sky—its angle with the horizon increases—and insolation becomes more and more intense.

At noon the sun is at its highest point in the sky, and the intensity of the insolation is greatest. During the afternoon, the angle of insolation becomes smaller and smaller, and the intensity of insolation decreases accordingly.

Duration of Insolation. The duration of insolation is the number of hours of sunlight received by an area each day. You may remember from Chapter 6 (page 85) that the number of hours of daylight at a location is related to length of the arc, or path, that the sun makes across the sky. Since there is 1

hour of insolation for every 15° of arc, the longer the path, the more hours of daylight.

The duration of insolation depends on a combination of season of the year and latitude. This is illustrated by Table 9-1. In general, the duration of insolation in the Northern Hemisphere is greatest around the time of the summer solstice and least around the time of the winter solstice. However, the *difference* in duration between summer and winter is greatest at high latitudes and least at low latitudes. As we have already noted, the duration of daylight in the polar regions (above 66½° latitude) is 24 hours per day in summer and zero hours per day in winter. At a latitude of 42°N (average for the United States), the duration of insolation is about 15 hours in June and about 9 hours in December. At latitudes near the equator, however, the duration of insolation varies very little throughout the year.

Table 9-1. Angle and duration of insolation.

Latitude	SUMMER SOLSTICE June 21		EQUINOXES March 21 September 23		WINTER SOLSTICE December 21	
	Angle of insolation at 12 noon	Duration of insolation	Angle of insolation at 12 noon	Duration of insolation	Angle of insolation at 12 noon	Duration of insolation
90° N	23½°	24 Hours	0°	12 Hours	— —	0 Hours
80° N	33½°	24	10°	12	— —	0
70° N	43½°	24	20°	12	— —	0
60° N	53½°	18½	30°	12	6½°	5½
50° N	63½°	16¼	40°	12	16½°	7¾
40° N	73½°	15	50°	12	26½°	9
30° N	83½°	14	60°	12	36½°	10
20° N	86½°	13¼	70°	12	46½°	10¾
10° N	76½°	12½	80°	12	56½°	11½
0°	66½°	12	90°	12	66½°	12
10° S	56½°	11½	80°	12	76½°	12½
20° S	46½°	10¾	70°	12	86½°	13¼
30° S	36½°	10	60°	12	83½°	14
40° S	26½°	9	50°	12	73½°	15
50° S	16½°	7¾	40°	12	63½°	16¼
60° S	6½°	5½	30°	12	53½°	18½
70° S	— —	0	20°	12	43½°	24
80° S	— —	0	10°	12	33½°	24
90° S	— —	0	0°	12	23½°	24

SUMMARY

1. Intensity of insolation is determined by the angle at which the sun's rays strike the earth's surface.
2. Maximum intensity of insolation occurs when the sun's rays strike the earth at an angle of 90°. Intensity of insolation decreases as the angle of insolation decreases.
3. The angle of insolation depends upon latitude, time of day, and season.
4. Duration of insolation is the number of hours of insolation received by a given area each day.
5. Duration of insolation depends upon a combination of latitude and season.

TEMPERATURE AND INSOLATION

Why is it hotter in the summer than it is in the winter? The reasons for this difference are connected with two factors that you've probably observed for yourself—the days are longer during the summer and the sun feels stronger. In other words, the two fac-

tors that affect the temperature of a given area are duration and intensity of insolation.

You know that the intensity of insolation is the rate at which energy is received by a given area per unit time. The higher the rate (the greater the intensity), the more energy is received by an area in a given time. The more energy a surface receives, the more it absorbs. And as energy is absorbed, the temperature of the surface increases.

The change in air and ground temperature during the course of a day is a good example of this effect. In the morning, when the intensity of insolation is low, the sunlight is not very effective in heating either the ground or the air. As the sun rises higher in the sky and the angle of insolation increases, the temperature goes up. In the afternoon, as the sun sets, the intensity of insolation decreases, and the temperature drops. So there is a direct relationship between intensity of insolation and temperature at a given location. The greater the intensity, the higher the temperature.

There is also a direct relationship between duration of insolation and temperature. The longer the duration, the higher the temperature. This is true because the total amount of insolation reaching the area increases with increased duration. Figure 9-7

Figure 9-7. Duration of insolation and temperature.

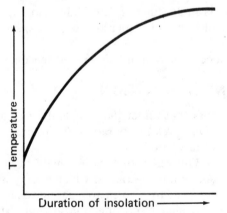

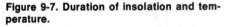

is a graphic model of the relationship between duration of insolation and temperature at a given location.

Seasonal Temperature Changes. In the Northern Hemisphere, both the duration and intensity of insolation are greatest at about June 21, the summer solstice. On that day there are more hours of sunlight than on any other day of the year, and the noon sun is higher in the sky than on any other day of the year.

While duration and intensity of insolation are greatest around June 21, this is not usually the hottest period of the summer. In fact, the average temperature is often considerably higher in July and even August than it is in June (see Figure 9-8). Why does this happen?

To understand this "time lag," you must first remember that every object above absolute zero, such as the earth, continuously gives off electromagnetic radiation. The rate of this radiation depends only on the object's temperature. It is not affected by the rate at which it is *receiving* radiation from other bodies, such as the sun. When the earth's surface is cool, it radiates at a lower rate than when it is warm.

As the earth radiates energy, its temperature tends to drop. But this tendency is offset by whatever radiation it is receiving and absorbing. Therefore, what happens to the earth's temperature depends upon the balance between the rate at which energy is being absorbed and the rate at which it is being lost by radiation. At the winter solstice, the rate of incoming radiation is least. That is, the warming effect of insolation is at its lowest point. At this time the earth's

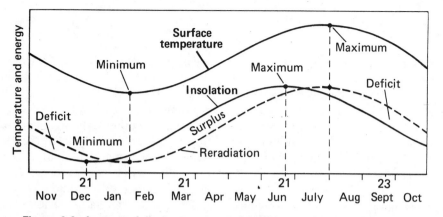

Figure 9-8. Average daily temperatures, insolation, and reradiation for mid-latitudes of the Northern Hemisphere during a year.

surface is losing heat faster than it is coming in. So the temperature of the surface is dropping steadily, day by day, at around this time (December in the Northern Hemisphere).

As soon as the winter solstice is passed, both the intensity and duration of insolation begin to increase. The rate of incoming energy begins to rise. At the same time, the rate of energy loss by radiation is actually dropping, because the earth's temperature is still dropping. At some time toward the end of January or beginning of February, the earth's temperature in northern latitudes has dropped low enough and the rate of insolation has risen high enough so that the two

rates become equal. At this time, equilibrium is reached, and the earth's temperature stops falling. Then, as the rate of insolation continues to increase, there is an overall warming effect. The temperature begins to rise.

The same thing happens in reverse during the summer. The earth continues to warm up even after the point of maximum insolation on June 21. But once again a balance point is reached about 6 weeks later, at the time of peak summer temperatures. Thereafter the warm earth radiates energy more rapidly than it is receiving it, and temperatures begin to fall.

Daily Temperature Changes. There is a daily cycle of temperature change,

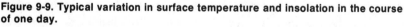

Figure 9-9. Typical variation in surface temperature and insolation in the course of one day.

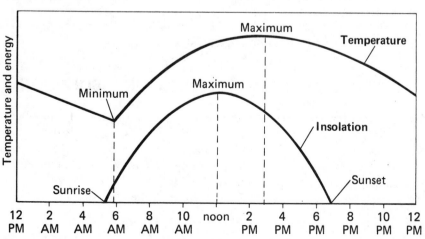

just as there is a seasonal cycle. The earth gives off energy both day and night. But the temperature rises during the day because the earth is receiving more energy than it is giving off. The temperature falls at night because the earth is giving off energy, but is receiving almost none.

The coolest part of the day is usually just around sunrise (see Figure 9-9). This is so because the earth has been losing energy all night. Once the sun comes up, the earth begins to gain energy, and the temperature begins to rise.

The hottest part of the day is not generally at noon, when the intensity of insolation is greatest. Instead, it is in the midafternoon. The reason for this seeming delay in daily temperature change is the same as for the delay in seasonal temperature change. Although the intensity of insolation is greatest at noon, the earth is still receiving more energy than it is losing until some time in midafternoon. The point at which equilibrium is reached between incoming and outgoing radiation marks the hottest part of the day. After that brief and temporary balance, the earth begins to lose energy, and the temperature drops.

This discussion has described only a general tendency or average pattern of temperature changes over a period of time. It does not take into account the effects of weather—winds, clouds, movement of air masses, and precipitation. Because of changes in these conditions, the temperature changes during any particular day can be quite different from the pattern we have just outlined. The effects and causes of weather will be taken up in Chapters 10 and 11.

SUMMARY

1. The temperature at a given location varies directly with the intensity and duration of insolation.
2. Maximum insolation in the Northern Hemisphere occurs about June 21, the summer solstice. Maximum insolation in the Southern Hemisphere occurs about December 21, the winter solstice.
3. Maximum surface temperatures in the Northern Hemisphere occur some time after the summer solstice. Minimum temperatures occur some time after the winter solstice.
4. The highest temperature of the day occurs some time after noon, even though intensity of insolation is greatest at noon.

EFFECTS OF THE ATMOSPHERE ON INSOLATION

Before radiation from the sun can strike the surface of the earth, it must pass through the blanket of gases that surrounds the earth—the atmosphere. What happens as this energy begins to pass through the various layers of air above the surface? Remember that solar radiation is made up of radiant energy of many different wavelengths. The various wavelengths are affected differently as they pass through the atmosphere.

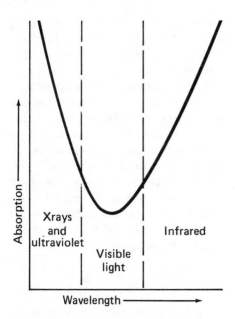

Figure 9-10. Absorption of radiation by the atmosphere.

Absorption. Almost all the X rays and much of the ultraviolet rays are absorbed in the upper part of the atmosphere in a layer called the *ionosphere*. Very little of the energy at these short wavelengths reaches the earth's surface. A large part of the infrared radiation (long wavelength) is also absorbed by the atmosphere, mainly by carbon dioxide and water vapor at lower altitudes. Visible light is affected least by absorption as it passes through the atmosphere.

Figure 9-10 is a graphic model of the absorption of different wavelengths of insolation by the atmosphere. As a result of this absorption pattern, most of the radiation that reaches the surface consists of wavelengths within, or just outside, the visible range.

Reflection. More than 30% of the sun's energy that reaches the vicinity of the earth is reflected back into space without being involved in the

earth's warming process. Most of this reflected energy (25% of the total insolation) is reflected by clouds. One of the most impressive sights from space is the bright light reflected off the clouds covering the earth.

Just as the angle of insolation is important in determining the intensity of insolation, it is also a basic factor in determining how much energy is reflected by a surface. The lower the angle of insolation, the more energy reflected. This is another reason why temperatures are generally lower in the higher latitudes—the angle of insolation is low, and more sunlight is

Figure 9-11. Effects of the atmosphere on insolation.

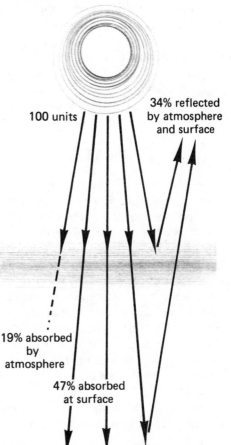

reflected than at lower latitudes. Since less energy reaches the earth's surface, it is not heated as much.

Scattering. In addition to the light reflected off clouds, some light is reflected by gas molecules and by *aerosols*—tiny particles of solid or liquid material in the atmosphere. When insolation strikes these molecules and aerosol particles, some of it is *scattered*—that is, reflected in all directions at random. Some of the scattered rays are turned back toward space, and some are reflected toward the surface of the earth. Figure 9-11 shows what happens to incoming solar radiation as it passes through the atmosphere and strikes the earth's surface.

As the concentration of aerosols in the atmosphere increases, the amount of insolation reaching the earth's surface decreases, and the average temperature in a given location drops. In areas where there is extensive volcanic activity and tons of material are spewed into the air, the amount of insolation reaching the surface is often greatly reduced, resulting in noticeably cooler weather.

SUMMARY

1. Most visible light passes through the atmosphere unchanged, but ultraviolet and infrared radiation are mostly absorbed by the atmosphere.
2. About 25% of insolation is reflected back into space by clouds.
3. The amount of insolation reflected depends on the angle of insolation.
4. Gas molecules and aerosols in the atmosphere cause scattering, or random reflection, of some insolation.
5. The amount of insolation reaching the earth's surface decreases as the amount of random reflection or scattering increases.

INSOLATION AND THE EARTH'S SURFACE

About 50% of the insolation that enters the top of the atmosphere actually reaches the surface of the earth. The rest has been either absorbed, reflected, or scattered by the atmosphere. Of the insolation striking the earth's surface, about 6% is reflected back into space. (Ice and snow reflect almost all the radiation that strikes them.) The rest is absorbed by the earth's surface. (These figures for absorption and reflection are for the earth as a whole, not for any one location.)

Because land surfaces are rougher, darker, and of lower specific heat than water, the surface temperature of land areas tends to rise more rapidly than the surface temperature of water. Also, water is nearly transparent, so insolation tends to pass through it to a greater depth. This, along with convection processes, tends to distribute the heat energy through a much larger volume of water than through land. The overall result is that land surfaces heat up more rapidly than water, even though the same amount of insolation strikes them both.

Reradiation of Insolation. The insolation that passes unchanged through the atmosphere is mostly in

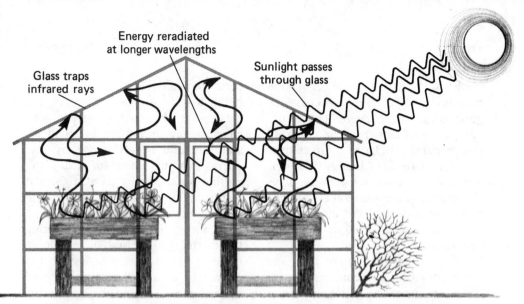

Figure 9-12. The greenhouse effect. Visible light, which is of short wavelengths, passes through the glass of the greenhouse and is absorbed by inner surfaces. This energy is reradiated as infrared radiation, which cannot pass through the glass walls. The energy remains inside the greenhouse and so raises its temperature.

the visible wavelengths. Most of this insolation is absorbed by the earth's surface and thus tends to raise the surface temperature. The earth is constantly radiating electromagnetic energy. The temperature of the earth's surface is such that most of this energy is in the infrared range. This infrared radiation is absorbed by carbon dioxide and water vapor in the atmosphere, and tends to raise the temperature of the atmosphere. Thus, while the atmosphere is not warmed directly by the visible light passing through it, it is warmed indirectly by the reradiation from the earth's surface of energy at infrared wavelengths.

The Greenhouse Effect. Have you ever been in a greenhouse in the winter? If you have, you probably found that it was comfortably warm even though it wasn't heated. Do you know why? The answer is the *greenhouse effect,* which we discussed in the section above, although we didn't give it a name.

Visible light can pass through glass, just as it passes through the atmosphere. Inside the greenhouse, the energy of the light is absorbed by the surfaces of the plants, soil, and other objects, and raises their temperature. This energy is then reradiated at infrared wavelengths. Very little of this infrared radiation passes outward through the glass. Most of its energy is transferred to the air inside the greenhouse by conduction, convection, and absorption. The glass effectively prevents the loss of heat, and the interior of the greenhouse becomes quite warm (see Figure 9-12).

You have probably observed the same effect when entering a car that was closed up and sitting in the sun. The interior of the car is much warmer than the outside air, because radiant energy that passes through the glass windows is trapped inside as heat that cannot escape.

In the section above we described the warming of the atmosphere by infrared radiation given off by the earth's surface. This is also called the greenhouse effect. But in this case, no glass walls are needed. The atmosphere itself absorbs the infrared energy being reradiated by the earth.

Other Methods of Energy Transfer. We have discussed some of the ways that energy is transferred between the earth's surface and the atmosphere, but there are two that we have not discussed.

The first involves latent heat and the evaporation and condensation of water. As water evaporates to form water vapor, it absorbs heat, which is stored as latent heat. So the evaporation of water from the surface of the earth removes heat energy from the earth, thus cooling it. When the water vapor in the atmosphere condenses, forming rain or snow, the latent heat is released, and this heat warms the atmosphere. Thus the evaporation of water removes heat from the surface of the earth, and the condensation of water vapor releases heat to the atmosphere. The net effect is a transfer of heat from the earth to the atmosphere.

The second method involves the direct transfer of heat by conduction between the earth's surface and the atmosphere. Where the land or water is warmer than the air, there is a transfer of heat from the surface to the air that is in contact with it. Circulatory motions of the atmosphere mix this heated air with the cooler air in upper layers. When the air is warmer than the surface of the earth, the flow of heat is in the opposite direction—from the air to the surface.

Radiative Balance. We have mentioned several times that the earth constantly gives off radiation. How does this loss of energy affect the

earth? It is a cooling process—heat is being lost from the surface of the earth. But the earth's surface also gains energy during the hours of insolation, and it is warmed by this energy. In the course of a day the earth's surface cools off at night and warms up during daylight. During the cooling-off period the surface is losing more energy than it is gaining. During the warming-up period, it is gaining more energy than it is losing. In the course of a year the same type of cycle occurs. During the winter the earth is losing heat faster than it is gaining heat. During the summer, it is the other way around.

There may be periods during the daily cycle and during the seasonal cycle when the earth's temperature remains constant for a time. This means that the amount of heat being lost by radiation is equal to the amount being gained from insolation. This is called a condition of *radiative balance*.

As we have seen, any particular part of the earth's surface is usually not in radiative balance. Its temperature is usually rising or falling from hour to hour, from day to day, or from season to season. But can we say anything about the radiative balance of the earth as a whole? Does its overall average temperature change from one year to the next? Over periods of decades or centuries? Over longer periods of thousands or hundreds of thousands of years?

Worldwide temperature data seem to indicate that the earth's average temperature does change from year to year. In other words, the earth as a whole is not in radiative balance on a yearly basis. However, the year-to-

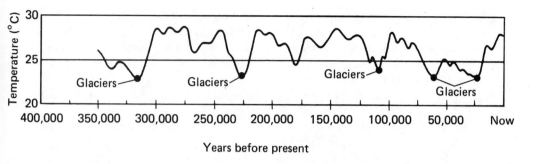

Figure 9-13. Estimated average temperatures of the earth for the past few hundred thousand years.

year fluctuations seem to even out over periods of about a decade (10 years), so we can say the earth is in radiative balance over periods of that length.

Geological records indicate that there have been many periods during the earth's history when the average temperature has dropped, resulting in "ice ages." During such intervals, glaciers spread down from the polar regions and covered large areas of land. The ice ages alternated with warmer periods, during which the glaciers retreated and the earth became warmer than average (see Figure 9-13).

These glacial and interglacial periods lasted for tens of thousands of years. So we can say that the earth is not in radiative balance over periods of that length. At the present time there is much debate among earth scientists as to whether we are in a long-term warming period or a cooling one. There is also disagreement over whether human activities are affecting the radiative balance of the earth, and if so, in which direction.

SUMMARY

1. Land surfaces heat up and cool off more quickly than water.
2. The greatest intensity of outgoing radiation from the surface of the earth is in the infrared range.
3. Visible light passes through the atmosphere unchanged. It is absorbed by the earth's surface and transformed into heat.
4. Infrared radiation from the earth's surface is absorbed by carbon dioxide and water vapor in the atmosphere and converted to heat, which warms the atmosphere. This is called the greenhouse effect.
5. The earth is not in radiative balance on a yearly basis.
6. Over the course of decades the earth does appear to be in radiative balance.
7. Over very long periods of time the earth is not in radiative balance.

RADIOACTIVITY

When an oven is turned on, the interior of the oven becomes quite hot, and its outer surfaces become warm. Heat is radiated from the oven, but it remains hot inside as long as energy is being supplied by burning fuel or an electric current. If the source of energy is turned off, the oven remains hot for a while, but gradually it cools down to room temperature.

Volcanic eruptions show that the interior of the earth is very hot. Even though the earth was probably very hot when it formed about 5 billion years ago, by now it should have cooled off. There must be an internal source of energy that is keeping the interior much hotter than most ovens. We believe that radioactivity is the source of this energy.

Radioactive Decay. In 1896 the French physicist Antoine Henri Becquerel made a discovery of great importance. He had placed a piece of the mineral pitchblende in a desk drawer on top of some unexposed photographic plates. When the plates were developed, Becquerel discovered that they had been partly exposed. He concluded that some form of energy had been emitted by the mineral and had affected the chemicals on the photographic plate. Becquerel found that the mineral constantly emitted radiation that was much like X rays, which had been discovered the previous year by Wilhelm Roentgen. This phenomenon was later named *radioactivity* by Marie Curie.

Pitchblende contains the element uranium. The radiation detected by Becquerel was caused by the uranium atoms, which emit energy as they break down, or decay, to form the more stable element lead. Radioactivity, or radioactive decay, is the natural and spontaneous breakdown of certain unstable elements to form more stable atoms of other elements. Energy is released by radioactive decay. This energy is given off at a rate that is constant for each particular radioactive element. The rate of energy release is not affected by temperature, pressure, or other environmental conditions.

We know that radioactive decay is going on in some of the rocks near the earth's surface. We therefore assume that it is also occurring deep within the crust and providing some of the energy for earth processes, such as mountain building and crustal movements.

SUMMARY

1. Radioactive decay is a process by which the breakdown of atoms releases energy.
2. The decay of radioactive matter is a source of energy for processes within the earth's crust.

REVIEW QUESTIONS

Group A
1. What is *insolation?*
2. What is meant by the *intensity of radiation?*
3. What factor does intensity of radiation depend on? Describe the relationship between temperature, intensity of radiation, and wavelength?
4. What is meant by *intensity of insolation?*
5. How is the intensity of insolation affected by the angle at which the sun's rays strike the earth's surface?
6. At what angle is intensity of insolation greatest?
7. What three factors affect the angle of insolation?
8. What is meant by *duration of insolation?*
9. What factors determine the duration of insolation?
10. What two factors affect temperature at a given location?
11. On what date does maximum insolation occur in the Northern Hemisphere? In the Southern Hemisphere?
12. At what time of year does maximum surface temperature occur in the Northern Hemisphere? Is this before, during, or after the period of maximum insolation?
13. At what time of day is the intensity of insolation greatest? When is the hottest part of the day?
14. Which type of radiation passes through the atmosphere for the most part unchanged?
15. What types of radiation are almost completely absorbed by the atmosphere?
16. What percentage of insolation is reflected back into space by clouds?
17. What determines the amount of insolation reflected?
18. How do gas molecules and aerosols in the atmosphere affect insolation?
19. How does random reflection affect the amount of insolation reaching the earth's surface?
20. Which heats up and cools off more quickly—water or land surfaces?
21. In what part of the electromagnetic spectrum is most of the outgoing radiation from the earth's surface?
22. What happens to visible light that strikes the earth's surface?
23. Explain the *greenhouse effect.*
24. Is the earth in radiative balance? Explain your answer.
25. What is *radioactive decay?*
26. Of what importance is radioactive decay in processes in the earth's crust?

Group B
1. a. What factors affect the amount of solar energy falling each second on a one-square-meter area in the middle of your football field?
   b. Describe the effect that changes in season have upon the duration of insolation.
   c. Describe the effect that changes in latitude have upon the duration of insolation.

2. a. Explain why the highest temperature usually occurs later in the day than the time of maximum intensity of insolation.
   b. List and describe at least 3 effects that the atmosphere may have upon incoming solar radiation.
   c. Define the term radiative balance.
   d. Explain how it is possible for the earth to be in radiative balance over the course of decades, but not be in radiative balance on a yearly basis.
3. Name and describe the type of energy that earth scientists believe is responsible for heating the earth's interior.

REVIEW EXERCISES

1. The graph below shows how the duration of insolation varies with latitude at the time of the summer solstice (dashed line) and at the time of the winter solstice (solid line).

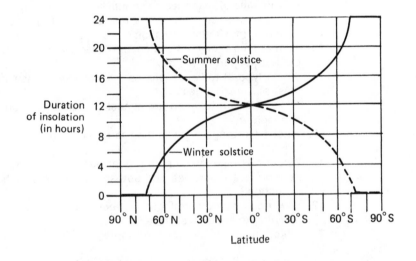

a. Describe the change in duration of insolation as one travels from the equator to each of the poles at the winter solstice.
b. From the graph, determine as accurately as possible the range in duration of insolation for 40° north latitude. Do the same for the latitude of your school.
c. What changes would there be in the graph if the inclination of the earth's axis were less than 23½° or more than 23½°?

2. The table below shows the average number of hours of daylight for the 15th of each month at a location in central New York State. This location is more than 100 km from the ocean. The table also shows the average monthly temperature for this location. Using this data, construct a graph plotting both hours of insolation and average monthly temperature on the vertical axis, using separate lines for each variable. The months of the year are shown on the horizontal axis. Base your answers to the following questions on the graph that you draw and on your knowledge of earth science.

	Hours of insolation	Temp. (°C)		Hours of insolation	Temp. (°C)
Jan.	9.5	−4.0	July	14.8	21.4
Feb.	10.7	−4.4	Aug.	13.8	20.2
Mar.	11.9	.8	Sept.	12.5	16.6
Apr.	13.2	7.4	Oct.	11.1	10.2
May	14.3	14.0	Nov.	10.0	3.6
June	15.0	18.9	Dec.	9.3	−2.0

a. Which of the following graphs represents the relationship between duration of insolation and surface temperature?

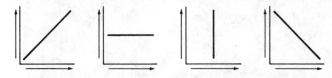

b. Explain why, although the duration of insolation was greatest in June, the average monthly temperature was greatest in July.

c. The location from which the insolation and temperature data was collected is inland. In what ways would the appearance of your graph be different if the data had been gathered from a location at the same latitude, but on an island in the middle of the Atlantic Ocean?

3. The following experiment was set up to show how the angle of inclination affects surface temperature. Three thermometers were placed at equal distances from a light source (see below). Light from the source fell on the thermometers at angles of 30°, 60°, and 90°. Temperature readings from each thermometer were taken at 1-minute intervals for a period of 10 minutes. The results are shown in the table below. Graph the data temperature for all three thermometers on the same set of axes. Base your answers to the following questions on the graph you draw and on your knowledge of earth science.

a. As the angle at which the light strikes the thermometer increases, the temperature _____ (increases, remains the same, decreases). Make a simple graph showing the relationship between temperature and angle of insolation.

b. As latitude increases, the angle of insolation _____ (increases, remains the same, decreases). Make a simple graph showing the relationship between angle of insolation and latitude.

c. The angle of isolation is 0° at sunrise. From sunrise on, it increases until noon, when it reaches its highest point; it then decreases to 0° at sunset. Draw a simple graph showing the relationship between angle of isolation and time of day (sunrise to sunset).

Angle of inclination		Time (in minutes)										
		0	1	2	3	4	5	6	7	8	9	10
	30°	20.0	20.0	20.5	21.0	21.0	21.5	22.0	22.0	23.0	23.5	23.5
	60°	20.0	20.0	21.0	22.0	22.5	23.0	24.0	24.5	25.0	25.0	25.5
	90°	20.0	21.0	21.5	22.5	23.0	23.5	24.5	25.0	26.0	27.0	27.5

TOPIC VII
ENERGY EXCHANGES IN THE ATMOSPHERE

Our local weather is determined by atmospheric patterns that are part of a global system.

CHAPTER 10
Weather

You will know something about weather and its causes if you can:
1. Identify the relationships among the atmospheric variables.
2. Explain how these relationships are used to predict changes in weather.
3. Explain how major weather systems develop and transfer energy in the atmosphere.

In this chapter and in Chapter 11 we will be concerned with that old reliable topic of conversation–weather. What makes weather interesting is that, in our part of the world, it is always changing. We would like to know what the weather is going to be this afternoon, tomorrow, and next weekend. If we're going to have any hope of doing that, we have to study the atmosphere and the kinds of changes that occur there.

ATMOSPHERIC VARIABLES

We know from our own experience that conditions in the atmosphere change frequently. The temperature and the pressure of the air can change. Winds may blow at various speeds and from various directions. There may be different kinds and amounts of clouds and of precipitation. The air may feel dry or damp. These properties of the air that change from time to time are called *atmospheric variables*. We can define *weather* as a description of the atmospheric variables at a particular place during a certain short period of time.

Relationships Among the Atmospheric Variables. In the section of Chapter 2 called "A Weather Watch" (beginning on page 22) there is a brief description of some of the atmospheric variables that you can observe with simple instruments. Weather scientists, or *meteorologists*, have been observing and recording these and many other variables at hundreds of places on the earth and for long periods of time. The National Weather Service makes such records today in a form called a station model. Figure 10-1 shows a typical station

Figure 10-1. A sample station model.

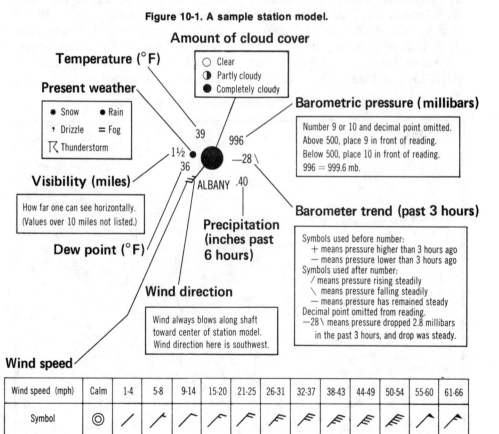

Wind speed (mph)	Calm	1-4	5-8	9-14	15-20	21-25	26-31	32-37	38-43	44-49	50-54	55-60	61-66
Symbol	◎	/	/	/	/	/	/	/	/	/	/	/	/

model, along with an explanation of the symbols used.

We need to mention that at the time this is being written (1976), the National Weather Service is still reporting weather measurements in English units, such as wind speeds in miles per hour, temperatures in °F, and air pressures in inches of mercury. These are the units used at this time in weather reports on radio and television and in newspapers. However, since conversion to the use of metric (SI) units is gradually taking place in the United States, we will use SI units, for the most part, in this chapter. The basic principles of weather observations and predictions will, of course, remain the same, whatever the system of units may be.

Weather Maps. To get back to our story, look at Figure 10-2. This is a simplified weather map for the United States, showing a few of the observations for some of the weather stations around the country. In addition to the station model symbols, the map has a pattern of numbered lines running across it. You will recognize this pattern as a field map, which we discussed in Chapter 5.

This map illustrates the fact that one field map looks pretty much like another. Just by looking at it you can't tell what field quantity is being shown. It could be an elevation field, as in a topographic map; it could be the odor field of a giant national hamburger festival, similar to the much smaller field map on page 59. In this case it is an air pressure field map. Each isoline on this map passes through points that have the same air pressure, as indicated by the number

Figure 10-2. Typical weather map of the United States.

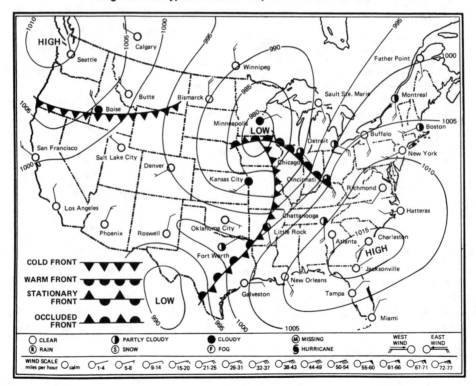

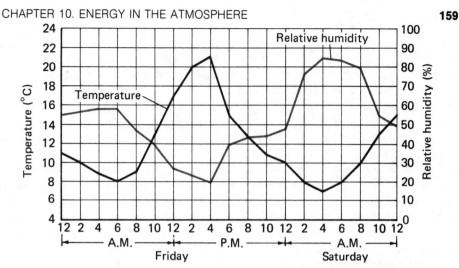

Figure 10-3. Variations in relative humidity and temperature over a period of two days.

on the isoline. Isolines that show points of equal air pressure are called *isobars*. The isobars on the map in Figure 10-2 are labeled in millibars (mb), a metric unit of pressure that has been used in recent years*.

You will notice areas on the map labeled HIGH and LOW. Just as contour lines of increasing elevation "close in" around a mountain peak, so isobars of increasing air pressure close in around regions of maximum pressure, called *highs*. Similarly, isobars of decreasing pressure close in around *lows,* or regions of minimum pressure.

On this weather map you can also see heavy lines with triangular or semicircular bumps along one side or the other. These lines are symbols for *fronts* between air masses. We will have more to say about fronts, air

*The official unit of pressure in the SI (metric) system is the *pascal*. The pascal is a very small unit (1/100 millibar), so the recommended unit for air pressure measurements is the kilopascal (1000 pascals). One kilopascal (kPa) equals 10 millibars. A pressure of 1000 mb equals 100 kPa.

masses, highs and lows, and other details of weather maps as we go along.

Relationships Among Weather Variables. Weather records may be interesting in themselves. But they do not have much practical or scientific value unless they can be used to draw inferences about the causes of weather and to predict future changes in the weather. Meteorologists have studied their records for many years in order to find relationships among the atmospheric variables. Today, computers are used to analyze vast quantities of data for this purpose. From such studies it is possible to state that certain combinations of conditions usually lead to certain other conditions at a later time. Unfortunately, we still cannot predict the weather with absolute certainty. But we can state the *probability of occurrence* of certain changes in the weather.

One way of looking for relationships is to plot two or more variables on the same graph. Figure 10-3, for example, is a graph of observations of relative humidity and temperature for a period of 36 hours. It can be seen that there appears to be an inverse relationship between these two variables. If such a pattern is frequently observed, we can say there is a high probability of its occurrence.

Another method is to keep a record of observations in the form of a table that shows how often one variable occurs along with another. For example, the two variables might be cloudiness and wind direction. Figure 10-4 shows the results an observer obtained over a period of 30 days. Each day he recorded the combination of wind direction and cloudiness as a "hatch mark" in the corresponding box of the table. For example, he noted clear skies combined with westerly winds on 10 days.

A table like this is called a *contingency table.* From the contingency table, you can calculate the probability that westerly winds will be accompanied by clear skies. The table shows that there were 23 days with westerly winds, and the skies were clear on 10 of those days. Therefore, when the winds were westerly, it was clear 10/23 or 43% of the time. This could be taken as the probability of these two conditions occurring together. In

Figure 10-4. A contingency table. This table is a record of daily observations of two weather variables—wind direction and cloud cover—over a period of 30 days. Each day the observed combination of the two variables was marked off in the corresponding box of the table. Wind direction was considered to be either generally easterly or generally westerly. This table could have been expanded to record wind direction more precisely—for example, northeasterly, southeasterly, southwesterly, northwesterly. In that case it would probably be necessary to make observations over a longer period in order to get meaningful probabilities.

WIND DIRECTION	DEGREE OF CLOUDINESS			TOTALS
	Clear	Partly cloudy	Cloudy	
Easterly	1	2	4	7
Westerly	10	8	5	23
COLUMN TOTALS	11	10	9	30

CONDITION	PROBABILITY
Clear with easterly winds	1/7 = 0.14 or 14%
Partly cloudy with easterly winds	2/7 = 0.29 or 29%
Cloudy with easterly winds	4/7 = 0.57 or 57%
Clear with westerly winds	10/23 = 0.43 or 43%
Partly cloudy with westerly winds	8/23 = 0.35 or 35%
Cloudy with westerly winds	5/23 = 0.22 or 22%

similar fashion, many other probabilities of occurrence of weather conditions could be inferred.

What are some of the relationships among weather variables that have been discovered? If you have been conducting a Weather Watch, you can probably find several in your own data. In the following pages we will discuss the most common of these relationships.

SUMMARY

1. Weather is the condition of the atmospheric variables at a given location for a certain short period of time.
2. Weather conditions for a given time and place can be described by the symbols of a station model on a weather map.
3. Weather predictions are based on a probability that the atmospheric variables will change in a certain way.

SOME COMMON WEATHER RELATIONSHIPS

Temperature Variations. In Chapter 9 (page 144) we learned that the average temperature at a given location depends, basically, on the total amount of the sun's radiation received by an area. This, in turn, is determined by the intensity and duration of insolation. The greater the intensity and the more hours of insolation there are, the higher the average temperature of the location.

Intensity and duration of insolation are directly related to daily and seasonal cycles. But they are also modified by various atmospheric factors. For example, if an area is covered by a heavy blanket of clouds, incoming sunlight is reflected by the clouds back into space. Therefore, the amount of insolation received at ground level is decreased, and the temperature at ground level is lower than it would have been without the clouds. Heavy air pollution also cuts down the amount of insolation received at ground level. Cloudiness and even the amount of pollutants that remain in the air are affected by other atmospheric variables.

Pressure Variations. If you watch weather reports on television, you know that they include a lot of talk about highs and lows, sometimes called high-pressure and low-pressure *systems.* They usually tell you what is likely to happen as one of these systems reaches your area. If you have been making the observations and measurements that we discussed in the Weather Watch section of Chapter 2, you have probably had a chance to see what happens for yourself.

A weather report predicting what will happen when a high-pressure system moves into an area might go something like this:

... So, as this high-pressure system moves down from Canada, the rain will end and temperatures will drop. Clear but cold nights can be expected, with daytime high temperatures never getting much above....

This is an example of a relationship that is often observed between atmospheric pressure and temperature—as pressure increases, temperature decreases. A high-pressure system, then, usually contains cooler air than the surrounding regions. In the same way, a low-pressure system usually contains warmer air than the surrounding regions. So, high pressure is usually associated with cooler air, and low pressure with warmer air. The relationship between temperature and pressure is an inverse one. As temperature increases, pressure decreases, and vice versa.

Atmospheric pressure is also affected by the moisture content of the air, and this is also an inverse relationship. The more moisture there is in the air, the lower the atmospheric pressure. The less water vapor present, the greater the atmospheric pressure.

So, high-pressure systems are associated with cooler, drier air, while low-pressure systems are associated with warmer, moister air. Again, these are occurrences of high probability, not guaranteed to occur at all times.

Humidity. We know that the air can feel crisp and dry on a cold winter day, or it can feel damp and "humid." A hot summer day can also feel either dry or humid. We also know from experience that precipitation is more likely to occur when the air feels damp than when it feels dry. Just what is it that we are "feeling" at these times?

We might think that what we are feeling is the *amount* of moisture (water vapor) in the air. This, however, would not be the whole story. The amount of moisture in the air is certainly an important factor. But the degree of dampness or "humidity" that we feel actually depends on how close the air is to being *saturated* with moisture. Warm air can hold more moisture than cold air. Therefore, warm air will feel much drier than cold air with the same amount of moisture content. What counts is not just the amount of moisture in the air, but how close this amount is to causing the air to be saturated.

As stated on page 26, the "closeness to saturation" is described by the *relative humidity* of the air. The relative humidity is the ratio between the amount of moisture in the air and the amount that could be present at the existing temperature. It is usually stated as a percent.

Dew-point Temperature. The dew-point temperature is one of the simplest ways of describing the moisture content of the air. Recall from page 26 that the dew point is the temperature to which we would have to cool the air to make it saturated. It is at this temperature that water would begin to condense out of the air. Therefore, the probability of precipitation will depend on how close the actual air temperature is to the dew-point temperature. If the difference is small, it won't take much change in conditions to reach saturation and start condensation. If the difference is large, the probability of precipitation in the immediate future is small.

It is also important to observe whether the difference between the two temperatures is getting larger or smaller. Only if the difference is getting smaller can we say that the probability of precipitation is increasing. This difference can become smaller in either of two ways. The moisture content of the air can be increasing, thus raising the dew point closer to the air temperature. Or the air temperature can be dropping, thus bringing it down closer to the dew point. (Of course,

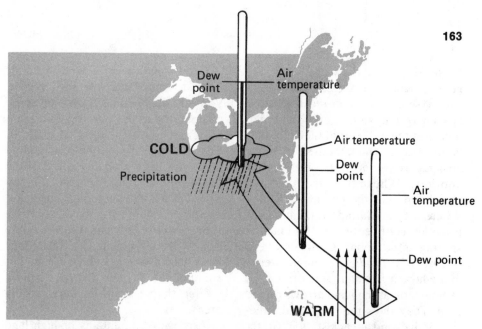

Figure 10-5. Changes in temperature and dew point in a moving mass of warm air.
As warm air passes over the ocean, evaporation increases its water vapor content and raises its dew point. When the air passes over cooler land to the north, its temperature drops. If the air temperature drops to the dew point, precipitation is likely.

both of these effects could be occurring at the same time.)

An example of this relationship is common along the eastern coast of the United States (see Figure 10-5). Warm air moving up from the southeast over the Atlantic Ocean absorbs moisture by evaporation from the ocean, thus raising its dew point. Then the air temperature begins to drop as the air passes over the land farther north. Rain is often the result of such a sequence of events. Later in this chapter we will see that this is an example of the passage of a warm front.

Air Movement. *Wind* is a horizontal movement of air over the surface of the earth. Do you know what makes winds blow and why some winds are light breezes, while others can blow the roof off your school?

A portion of the weather map on page 158 is repeated here in Figure 10-6. Look at the isobars on this map.

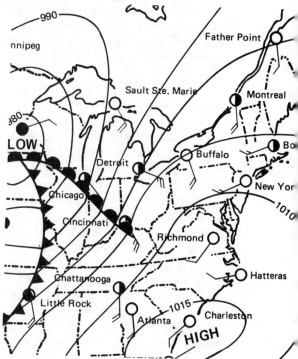

Figure 10-6. Pressure gradients and wind speeds.

In some places they are close together. At other places they are more widely separated. You recall that the spacing of the isolines on a field map indicates the *gradient* of the field, that is, the rate at which the field quantity changes as you go from one point to another. Where the isolines are closely spaced, the gradient is steep. Where they are far apart, the gradient is moderate or gentle. On this map the spacing of the isobars shows us where the *pressure gradient* is large (steep) and where it is small (gentle).

Now look at the wind arrows on the map. They show the speed and direction of the wind at each station. (Refer to the station model on page 157 to recall how to read the wind speed from these symbols.) Notice first of all that the winds seem to be blowing generally away from the high and toward the low. Secondly, the wind speed is generally greater where the pressure gradient is greater. You will see similar relationships on any weather map you examine.

We can infer, then, that it is differences in air pressure that cause winds to blow, and the greater the difference over a given distance, the faster the winds will blow.

Very strong winds often occur around major storm centers, such as hurricanes. In the center of a hurricane the atmospheric pressure is extremely low. So the difference in pressure between the storm center and the air around it is unusually great, and the pressure gradient is very steep. It is this great difference in pressure within a relatively small area that accounts for the winds of very high speed that accompany these storms.

Local Conditions. As you watch or listen to your local weather forecast, you should become aware of some characteristics of your area that seem to affect the local weather pattern. For example, if you live near a large lake, you have probably heard of the *lake effect*. Because a mass of air may pick up water vapor over the lake, your particular area may be hit by more severe storms than nearby areas. But living near a lake does have its advantages, because in hot weather the air near the lake will be cooler than the air in surrounding areas.

A range of mountains or high land may also have a strong influence on the weather. Any change in landscape is going to affect the steady flow of air and the moisture patterns.

If you live in a fair-sized city, you've probably heard many weather reports that go something like this:

. . . High today in the city will be about 90°. Temperatures in the outlying areas in the low 80's.

A forecast like this bears out what every city-dweller has always known —that it's hotter in the city than it is in nearby suburbs or rural areas. Meteorologists refer to this phenomenon as an *urban heat island*. Figure 10-7 shows how this might look on a map of the temperature field around a large city.

There are three basic reasons for this effect: (1) Heat produced by the burning of fuel (to heat homes and offices, run factories, operate cars and trucks, etc.) warms the atmosphere. (2) Man-made materials, such as brick, concrete, and asphalt, heat up more rapidly than open fields or forests, and therefore reradiate

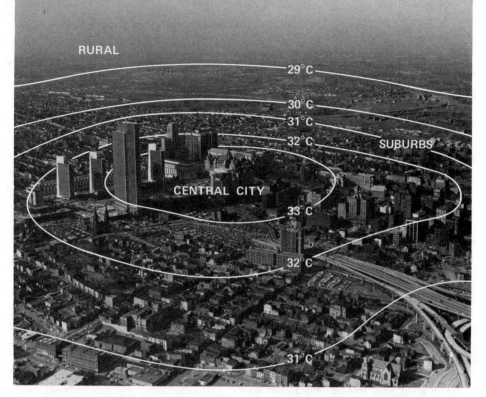

RURAL

29°C

30°C

31°C

32°C

SUBURBS

CENTRAL CITY

33°C

32°C

31°C

Figure 10-7. Urban heat island. The heat given off by large cities changes the temperature pattern of an area.

energy into the atmosphere at a greater rate. (3) Heat that should have been reradiated back into space is trapped by layers of atmospheric pollution. As a result of these processes, the presence of large cities changes the temperature pattern of an area.

Large cities not only heat the atmosphere, but they produce great quantities of carbon dioxide. You should recall from page 149 that carbon dioxide is a good absorber of the energy reradiated at infrared wavelengths by warm surfaces. So an increase in the carbon dioxide content of the atmosphere also contributes to the heating of the atmosphere.

Atmospheric Transparency. Have you ever been fascinated by the dancing specks that can be seen in a shaft of sunlight coming through a window? These are dust particles—tiny bits of material that are always present in the

air. We are conscious these days of the large amounts of smoke particles and other pollutants that our factories, power plants, and even our homes are pouring into the air. But even without these sources, the air would always contain dust from natural sources—bits of decayed leaves, microscopic hairs from the wing of a butterfly, wind-blown soil, and countless others. The air may also contain very small droplets of water, which are almost invisible to the eye.

All of these components of the air affect its *transparency,* and the transparency of the air varies greatly from day to day and from place to place. But the atmosphere tends to clear itself periodically. As we will see in the next chapter, dust particles act as centers around which water vapor can condense to form raindrops and snowflakes. Thus a rainstorm literally washes the air and leaves it cleaner than before.

But how much man-made pollution can the atmosphere handle? Will we come to a point at which it can no longer clean itself by processes like precipitation? This is a serious problem for the future—and the future may not be so far away!

Other Variables. We have seen that some of the atmospheric variables show a simple relationship that is either direct or inverse. For example, the average air temperature shows a direct relationship to intensity of insolation—as the intensity increases, so does the average temperature. Air pressure and moisture content show an inverse relationship—generally, the more humid the air, the lower its pressure. Some of the simple relationships we have observed are illustrated graphically in Figure 10-8.

Other variables, on the other hand, are not related in either a simple direct or a simple inverse manner. Their interrelationships are much more complex. Also, the effects of geographical characteristics, such as lakes and mountains, of cities, and of other local conditions on local weather patterns are complex.

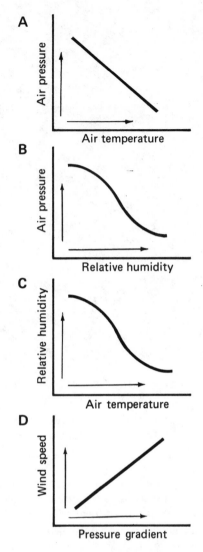

Figure 10-8. Some simple relationships between weather variables. Inverse relationships are illustrated in *A, B,* and *C.* A direct relationship is illustrated in *D.*

SUMMARY

1. Temperature at a given location basically depends on the intensity and duration of insolation. However, it can also be affected by various atmospheric factors.
2. Changes in atmospheric pressure are closely associated with changes in air temperature and water-vapor content.
3. Changes in the dew-point temperature indicate changes in atmospheric moisture.
4. As the difference between air temperature and dew-point temperature decreases, the probability of precipitation increases.

5. Wind is a horizontal movement of air over the surface of the earth.
6. Winds are caused by differences in atmospheric pressure.
7. Wind speed is directly related to the pressure field gradient.
8. In many places, local conditions, including geographical features, have a variety of complex effects on the local weather pattern.
9. Some atmospheric variables are related in a simple direct or inverse manner.

AIR MASSES

If you watch weather reports on television, you're probably familiar with the term *air mass*. An air mass is a large body of air that shows the same temperature and humidity characteristics throughout at a given altitude. That is, within the air mass, all points at the same altitude show pretty much the same temperature and humidity. As you will see, air masses are of basic importance in modern weather forecasting.

The size of an air mass can be equal to that of a fair portion of an entire continent or ocean. An air mass can extend upward to an altitude of 3 to 6 km. An air mass has definite boundaries, and it differs in temperature and humidity from adjacent air masses.

Source Regions. The characteristics of air masses are determined by the region over which they form. Such regions are called *source regions*. An air mass forms when a large body of air remains over an area long enough to pick up the temperature and humidity characteristics of that area. This body of air can be *stagnant* (unmoving), or it can be moving very slowly.

An air mass formed over land will usually be dry. An air mass formed over water will usually be moist. An air mass formed at high latitudes will have a relatively low temperature. An air mass formed at low latitudes will have a relatively high temperature.

Since air-mass characteristics are determined by the source region, air masses are classified and labeled according to their source area. The first factor considered in classifying an air mass is whether it is formed over land or water. The second factor is the latitude at which it forms (see Figure 10-9).

Air masses formed over land are called *continental* (*c*), while those formed over water are called *maritime* (*m*). Air masses formed at high latitudes are called *polar (P)*, while those formed at low latitudes are called *tropical (T)*. As you can see in Figure 10-9, the abbreviations referring to latitude are capital letters, while those for land and water are lower case. For example, an air mass formed over the North Atlantic Ocean would be designated as an *mP* air mass.

Sometimes an air mass can be modified by the area over which it travels. Suppose an air mass forms over central Canada. This would be a *cP* air mass because it formed at high latitudes over land. If this relatively dry air mass travels in a southeasterly direction, it will pass over the Great Lakes. It may then pick up moisture evaporating from the lakes and become a relatively moist air mass.

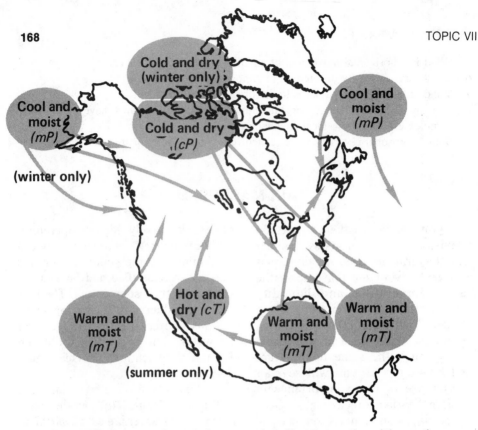

Figure 10-9. Source regions of air masses that affect the weather of the continental United States.

Highs and Lows. Air masses can be of two basic types, depending on their pressure and the direction of circulation of their winds. Low-pressure air masses are called *lows,* or *cyclones.* To most people, the term *cyclone* means a severe tropical storm. To a meteorologist, the term refers to a low-pressure system.

In a low, or cyclone, the pressure is lowest in the center of the system. You might expect the winds to blow in toward the center, directly at right angles to the isobars. However, as explained on page 96, winds in the Northern Hemisphere are deflected to the right by the Coriolis effect. As a result, the winds around a low blow nearly parallel to the isobars, in a *counterclockwise* direction in the Northern Hemisphere. If you examine a weather map, you will see the wind arrows following this pattern around the lows. The result is a counterclockwise rotation of the entire air mass.

High-pressure systems are called *highs*, or *anticyclones.* In a high, the pressure is greatest in the center of the system. You would expect winds to blow outward across the isobars. However, the Coriolis effect again deflects the winds to the right and the result is a *clockwise* circulation or rotation of the air mass.

In the Southern Hemisphere the Coriolis effect deflects winds to the left. Thus the general circulation around highs and lows is the opposite of that in the Northern Hemisphere—that is, highs have a counterclockwise circulation and lows have a clockwise circulation.

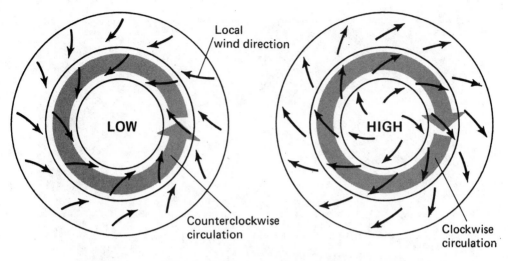

Figure 10-10. Circulation of winds in high- and low-pressure air masses.

SUMMARY

1. Air masses are identified on the basis of their pressure, moisture, and temperature.
2. At any given altitude within an air mass, the temperature field and the humidity field are nearly uniform.
3. The characteristics of an air mass are determined by the region over which it forms.
4. In a low-pressure air mass (a cyclone) the circulation is counterclockwise and in toward the center in the Northern Hemisphere.
5. In a high-pressure air mass (an anticyclone) the circulation is clockwise and outward from the center in the Northern Hemisphere.

FRONTS

The interface where two air masses with different characteristics meet is called a *front*. The interface between the two air masses is fairly distinct, and the two masses of air do not mix together to any great extent. Generally, a front forms when one air mass moves into an area occupied by another air mass of differing characteristics. Weather conditions at fronts are generally unstable, and precipitation is often associated with the passing of a front

Cold Fronts. A cold front forms when a cold air mass moves into an area occupied by a warmer air mass. Cold air masses generally move more rapidly than warm ones. As the cold air mass moves forward, it remains close to the ground because it is more dense than the warm air mass ahead of it. The warm air is therefore forced to rise, as shown in Figure 10-11.

The first sign of an approaching cold front may be the appearance of towering dark clouds in the distance

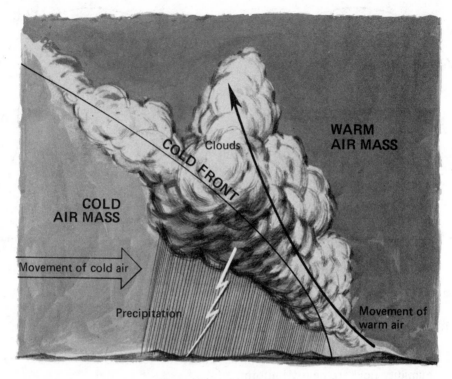

COLD FRONT

Clouds

WARM
AIR MASS

COLD
AIR MASS

Movement of cold air

Precipitation

Movement of
warm air

Figure 10-11. A cold front.

followed by an increase in wind speed (due to an increased pressure gradient). The warm air in the area is forced upward by the advancing cold front. This air cools as it rises until it reaches the dew point. Clouds form, and if condensation is great enough, precipitation will occur. The precipitation that does occur is generally brief, but it can be quite heavy. Thunderstorms are common.

When the front passes, the winds change direction sharply, the pressure rises, and the temperature drops. Small puffy clouds may be left in an otherwise clear sky.

Weather Variables During the Passage of a Cold Front. How would the passing of a cold front look to a meteorologist as he examines the data from his recording instruments? Figure 10-12 shows the variations in air pressure, air temperature, dew point, and relative humidity that were observed in a typical case. To interpret these records, remember that the dew point is the temperature at which the air becomes saturated and the relative humidity becomes 100%. The dew point measures the amount of water vapor in the air, and the relative humidity indicates how close the air is to being saturated.

Looking at the start of the record early Monday morning, we see that the air was moderately warm and humid. The dew point was close to the air temperature and consequently the relative humidity was high. We see, also, that the temperature dropped somewhat during the hours before sunrise, and rose after sunrise—the

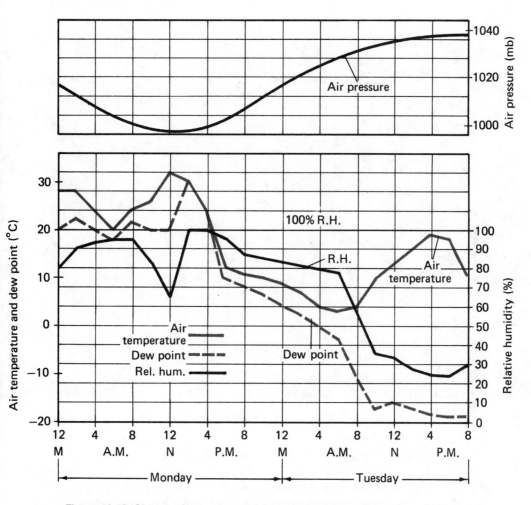

Figure 10-12. Changes in weather variables during the passage of a cold front.

usual pattern described in Chapter 9 (page 145). We also see the inverse relationship between relative humidity and air temperature that we noted in Figure 10-3 on page 157. Air pressure was decreasing during this period.

This pattern continued until noon on Monday. Then something apparently happened to upset it. The temperature began to drop, and it dropped sharply throughout the afternoon. Also, between noon and 2 P.M.

the dew point rose. By 2 P.M., air temperature and dew point were equal, the air was saturated, and the relative humidity was 100%. We can infer that it started raining around noon, and that evaporation of the falling raindrops added water vapor to the air until it became saturated. The air pressure was increasing during this period.

Air temperatures continued to fall through the night, but the dew point decreased even more rapidly. By late

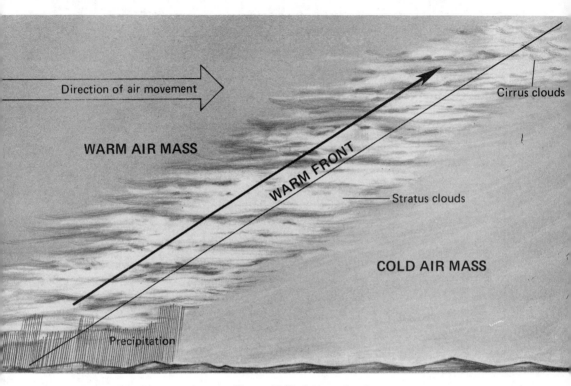

Direction of air movement

WARM AIR MASS

WARM FRONT

Cirrus clouds

Stratus clouds

COLD AIR MASS

Precipitation

Figure 10-13. A warm front.

afternoon on Tuesday, the dew point and the relative humidity had both dropped to low levels. The mid-afternoon high temperature was lower than the lowest temperature of early Monday morning. The air pressure had increased considerably. From all this data it can be quite safely inferred that a cold front went by at about noon on Monday and a cool, dry, high-pressure air mass had moved in. Time elapsed: Less than 24 hours.

Warm Fronts. A warm front forms when a warm air mass moves into an area occupied by a cooler air mass. The cool air remains close to the ground, and the warmer air is forced to rise over it as it moves into the area (see Figure 10-13).

As the warm air rises, it cools. When it cools to the dew point, condensation begins. The arrival of a warm front is marked by the appearance of high, thin, wispy clouds and a gradual decrease in air pressure. As the warm air mass moves into the area, the cloud mass thickens and becomes lower. A light rain or snow begins and continues to fall for a considerable time, sometimes more than 24 hours. Gradually, the precipitation slows, then stops. As the front passes, the wind direction changes, the pressure stops dropping, and the temperature rises.

Figure 10-14 is a graph showing the passage of a warm front as recorded on meteorological instruments. About

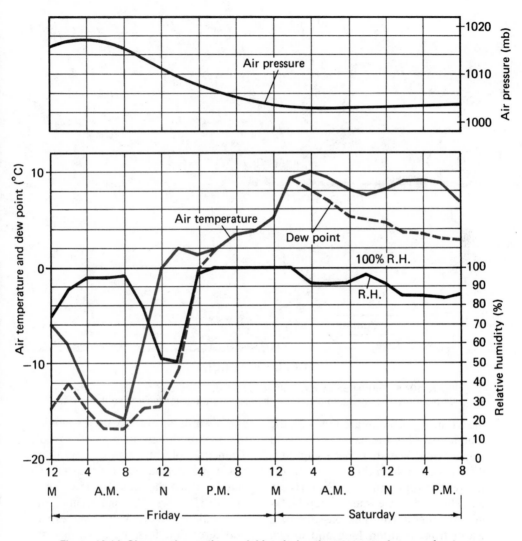

8 A.M. on Friday, the temperature began to rise abruptly, and at first the relative humidity decreased. But within a few hours the dew point also rose sharply. By about 6 P.M. dew point and air temperature became equal, and relative humidity was 100%. Although the air temperature continued to rise through the night, the air remained saturated. It can be inferred that precipitation occurred

from late afternoon to 2 A.M. that night. Air temperatures on Saturday were much higher than on Friday, and relative humidity remained quite high. A warm front had passed through between 2 P.M. and 4 P.M. on Friday, and a warm, moist air mass had arrived.

Notice that the effects of the warm front are still occurring more than 24 hours after the start of the passage of

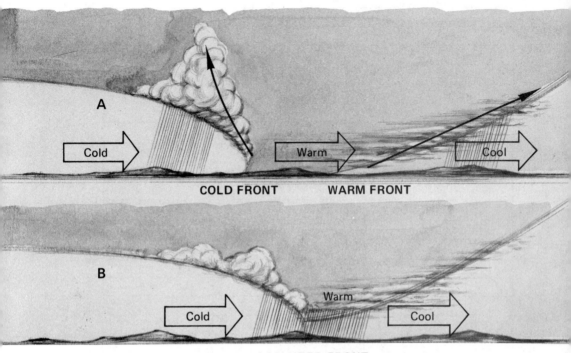

Figure 10-15. Formation of an occluded front. An occluded front forms when a warm air mass is lifted completely off the ground by a faster-moving cold air mass.

the front. If you compare this with the time involved in the passage of a cold front, you'll see that there's quite a difference between them. Cold fronts move through an area relatively quickly, and sometimes violently, as in a thunderstorm. The passage of a warm front is often long and drawn out, taking days before the change is completed.

Stationary Fronts. A stationary front is formed when two adjacent air masses with different characteristics remain in the same positions for a considerable length of time. The weather along a stationary front is similar to that along a warm front.

Occluded Fronts. An occluded front forms in a series of stages. It begins with a stationary front between a cold and a warm air mass, with air moving in opposite directions along the front. Then the cold air begins to turn and move in under the warm air, forming a cold front, as shown at the left of Figure 10-15 A. At the same time, the warm air advances in the same general direction, forming a warm front (see right side of Figure 10-15 A). At the warm front the warm air rides up over the cold air ahead of it. However, the cold front advances faster than the warm front and finally overtakes it. The result is that the warm air mass is lifted entirely off the ground (Figure 10-15 B). This situation is called an occluded front.

Figure 10-16 shows how an occluded front might look on a weather map. Occluded fronts are as-

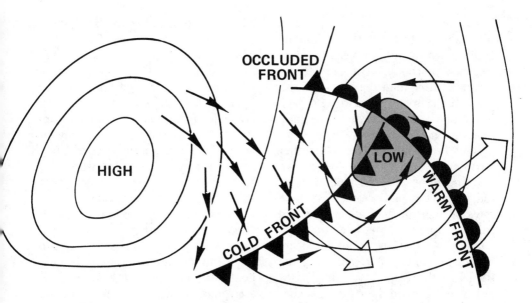

Figure 10-16. Relationships of air masses and pressure systems during formation of an occluded front.

sociated with the formation of low-pressure air masses, or lows, in the mid-latitude. They usually result in heavy precipitation.

Mapping Fronts. Since fronts, or the interfaces between air masses of different characteristics, generally bring changes in the weather, they are of great importance on weather maps. Figure 10-17 illustrates how fronts are shown on weather maps. You can see that a line is drawn along the front, and that the type of front involved is indicated by symbols on the front line.

Tracks of Fronts and Air Masses. In the late 1700's Benjamin Franklin began to keep records of major storms affecting the east coast of the United States. He found that there was a pattern to the movement of these storms.

Figure 10-17. Fronts on a weather map. The positions of fronts are shown by lines on the map, while the type of front is shown by symbols on the front line.

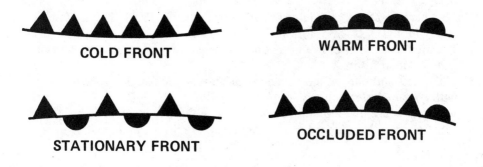

They seemed to move in a northeast direction much of the time. Franklin could not do much with his records, because in those days the storms traveled faster than the news. It was not until the invention of the telegraph in the mid-1800's that weather conditions in one place could be used to predict future conditions in another location.

Using information collected over the years, the paths, or *tracks,* and rates of movement of air masses and fronts can now be predicted quite accurately. Some of the major tracks are shown in Figure 10-9. Knowing the tracks of the fronts and air masses helps meteorologists to forecast weather.

Jet Streams. During World War II, American bomber pilots flying westward in missions over Japan sometimes found strong headwinds at altitudes above 6 km. Some of these winds were strong enough to cancel out completely their plane's forward speed, so that the plane was actually standing still relative to the ground! Flying eastward over the Pacific, the winds were such that planes sometimes doubled their actual flying speed relative to the ground.

These fast-moving streams of air are called *jet streams*. Jet streams appear to be streams of fast-moving air very high in the atmosphere. They occur in many parts of the world and seem to be associated with great waves in the upper atmosphere.

The speeds and positions of the jet stream change with the seasons, and there is even some change from day to day. But certain characteristics do hold fairly constant. The jet streams are found at altitudes of from 6 to 12 km. They are about 500 km wide, and wind speeds near the center range up to 500 km/hr. Jet streams are only several kilometers in thickness.

Meteorologists now think that the day-to-day changes in our weather are strongly influenced by the movements of the jet streams.

SUMMARY

1. The interface where two air masses of different characteristics meet is a front.
2. Weather conditions at fronts are generally unstable. Precipitation often occurs with the passage of a front.
3. The four basic types of fronts are cold fronts, warm fronts, stationary fronts, and occluded fronts.
4. The tracks and rates of movement of air masses and fronts can be predicted with considerable accuracy.
5. Jet streams are fast-moving streams of air in the upper atmosphere.
6. Jet streams may influence day-to-day changes in the weather.

STORMS

Storms are the most spectacular and violent forms of weather. Because storms can be so destructive, they are of great interest to meteorologists. However, until the development of satellites, storms for the most part had to be studied from the ground, and this greatly limited the amount of information that could be obtained about them. Now, with weather satellites, scientists can follow a storm from its initial stages of development until it dies out. Perhaps they will eventually learn to control storms in some way, and to prevent some of the damage done by storms each year.

Let's take a look at three common types of storms: thunderstorms, tornadoes, and hurricanes.

Thunderstorms. The photograph in Figure 10-18, taken from a satellite, shows the Florida peninsula on a typical day in late August. There are thunderstorms in all stages of development in this local region. Over the earth as a whole, it is estimated that more than 2,000 thunderstorms occur *every hour.*

Thunderstorms are generally associated with high temperatures. They occur most frequently in the afternoon over land areas. Thunderstorms are made up of units called *cells.* A cell has a definite life cycle that generally lasts only about an hour. But because a storm may be made up of several cells in various stages of development, it may last much longer than an hour.

Figure 10-18. Thunderstorms forming over the Florida Peninsula, as photographed from a satellite.

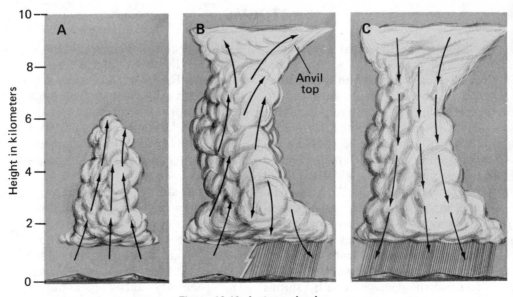

Figure 10-19. A storm cloud.

In the first stages of cell development, parcels of warm, moist air near the ground rise rapidly upward, like air bubbles in a liquid. As the air rises, it cools until the dew-point temperature is reached, and a dark, cumulus storm cloud begins to form. Even though the rising air cools off, it remains warmer than the still air around it, and so it continues to rise. When condensation occurs, large amounts of heat are released; this further warms the rising air, and the upward currents become much stronger. There is heavy precipitation from the condensation, which produces a strong downdraft of air. So within the storm there are areas of strong upward and downward movements of air.

The parcels of warm air continue to rise until they reach heights of 6 to 12 km. At these altitudes condensation decreases, and the temperature of the rising air drops until it is the same as the surrounding air. At this point the mass of air spreads out sideways, forming a flat top on the storm cloud (see Figure 10-19). This is often called an *anvil top* because it resembles the shape of a blacksmith's anvil.

Lightning and thunder occur when the storm clouds become electrically charged. Generally, the top part of the cloud becomes positively charged, while the bottom parts develop both positively and negatively charged areas. The charge builds up until a great spark, or arc, of electricity is discharged between the cloud and an oppositely charged object. This can be another part of the same cloud, another cloud, or the ground. Lightning strokes between a cloud and the ground can be 10 km or more in length.

The tremendous electrical current in the lightning stroke heats the air along its path. The great heat causes the air along the path to expand, and produces a shock wave of sound much like the sonic boom of a jet plane breaking the sound barrier. This sound wave is thunder.

The thunder from a single lightning stroke is usually drawn out in a series of rolls and rumbles, sometimes beginning with a loud crack when the lightning has struck nearby. The reason for the prolonged sound of thunder is that the sound from different parts of the stroke have different travel times, depending on their distance from the observer. Echoes from surrounding hills also add to the combined sound effects.

Tornadoes. Thunderstorms are frightening enough in themselves, but in certain parts of the United States there is always the danger that a squall line of thunderstorms may become the birthplace of a *tornado,* or *twister,* the most violent of all storms. Thunderstorms occur along both warm and cold fronts, but those along cold fronts are generally more violent and more likely to produce tornadoes. Tornadoes have occurred all over the United States, but they are most frequent in Iowa, Kansas, Oklahoma, and Arkansas.

A tornado appears as a funnel-shaped cloud that hangs down out of the towering clouds of a thunderstorm (see Figure 10-20). At the center of the tornado is the *vortex,* an area in which the atmospheric pressure is extremely low. Outside the vortex are winds that swirl in a counterclockwise direction (in the Northern Hemisphere) at speeds that may reach 800 km per hour. Tornadoes are small, some not more than 100 meters in diameter, but the enormous strength of their winds and the sudden and drastic drop in pressure within the vortex leave total destruction in their paths. The sudden drop in pressure may cause buildings

Figure 10-20. A tornado.

to explode or roofs to blow off when the air inside expands suddenly.

Tornadoes generally move in a northeasterly direction at speeds of 40 to 65 km per hour. Most tornadoes last for less than 1 hour. The path of a tornado along the ground is usually from 25 to 65 km long, although some are longer. Very peculiar things have happened to people, animals, and objects caught in the middle of a tornado. Cars, trucks, roofs, and other very large objects are often carried a considerable distance by the winds of a tornado.

Tornadoes leave a path of destruction several hundred meters wide. But the path may be twisted so that one house on a street is completely demolished, while the house next door is untouched. In areas where tornadoes are common, people have underground storm cellars, which provide the best protection against injury.

Hurricanes. The location: 15° north latitude, 65° west longitude, in the eastern Caribbean. The time: late August. A hurricane is born.

A hurricane, which is also called a *tropical cyclone* or *typhoon,* begins as a tightly formed low-pressure system over an ocean. The hurricane characteristics may begin to develop when a high-pressure system forms high in the atmosphere above the low.

The build-up of a hurricane involves the transfer of enormous quantities of energy. Around the center of the low-pressure system, masses of warm air, full of moisture from the warm ocean surface, begin to rise rapidly. Air flows in toward the center of the low-pressure system, causing winds of increasing speed. Until the winds reach a speed of more than 120 km per hour, the system is called a *tropical storm.* But when they exceed this speed, the storm becomes a full-fledged hurricane.

As the air rises, it cools. Towering thunderstorm clouds form. When the rising air cools to the dew point, condensation begins, and with the condensation come torrential rains. Condensation releases tremendous quantities of heat, which further warms the rising air. This creates a warm core in the hurricane. The pressure difference between the storm center and the surrounding air is intensified, wind speeds increase, more moisture is pulled into the system, more condensation occurs, and more heat is released—the entire process gains energy.

The whole hurricane system usually moves in a northwesterly direction at speeds of 15 to 18 km per hour. Figure 10-21 shows how a hurricane might look on a weather map several days after it first formed. Figure 10-22 is a photograph of a hurricane taken from a satellite. Such photographs are used to keep track of hurricanes.

A fully developed hurricane is over 650 km in diameter with winds well in excess of 120 km per hour. Around the center of the hurricane there are rising columns of warm air. But in the center itself the air is descending. This center is the *eye* of the hurricane. In the eye there is almost no wind. The clouds are broken and patchy, and the sky may even be blue. The eye may be as much as 30 to 50 km in diameter. When you are in the eye of a hurricane, you might think the storm is over. But within a short time the "other side" of the hurricane hits, and you're back in the storm again.

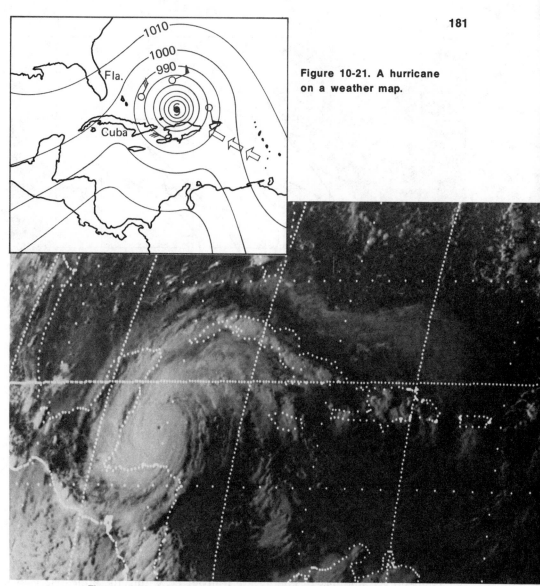

**Figure 10-21. A hurricane
on a weather map.**

Figure 10-22. A hurricane as photographed from a satellite.

But now the winds are blowing from the opposite direction.

The decrease in air pressure as a hurricane moves through an area is about the same as that in a tornado. The low pressure of the tornado causes tremendous damage, but that of a hurricane does not. The difference lies in the length of time during which the pressure drop occurs. In a tornado, the time is measured in minutes, or even seconds. In a hurricane, it is more on the order of hours.

After a number of days, a hurricane dies out. It may smash its way inland, causing great damage as it goes, or it may swing out to sea. In both cases it dies out because it loses its main need—moisture. It requires the constant upwelling of warm, moist air.

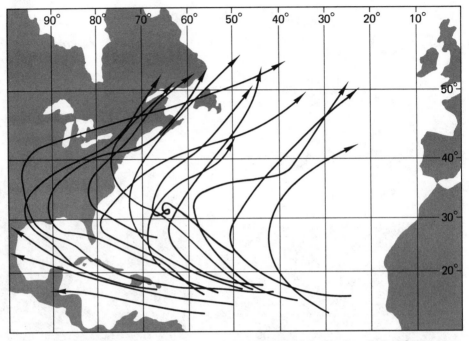

Figure 10-23. General pathways of hurricanes around the eastern United States.

Traveling over land or over the colder northern water cuts off the supply. Figure 10-23 shows typical pathways for hurricanes around the eastern United States.

In this chapter we have moved from the small day-to-day changes in the atmosphere to the most violent and complex of storms. It is this constant changing of atmospheric conditions that makes the science of meteorology such a challenging field. Meteorology is a study of change—and an attempt to understand and predict the course of change in the tremendous energy systems at work in the atmosphere.

SUMMARY

1. Tremendous amounts of energy are transferred within the atmosphere by storms.
2. Thunderstorms are generally associated with high temperatures. They occur most frequently in the afternoon over land areas.
3. Lightning occurs when storm clouds become electrically charged.
4. Thunder is a shock wave of sound. It is caused by the heating and expansion of air in the path of a lightning stroke.
5. Tornadoes are small, short-lived, very violent storms associated with thunderstorms.
6. Hurricanes form over warm oceans.
7. Hurricanes die out as they travel over land or the colder northern oceans, because their supply of moisture is cut off.

REVIEW QUESTIONS

Group A

1. Define the term *weather*.
2. What is a *station model*?
3. What are weather predictions based on?
4. What factors affect temperature at a given location?
5. What factors affect atmospheric pressure?
6. What does a change in dew-point temperature indicate?
7. What happens to the probability of precipitation as the difference between air temperature and dew-point temperature increases? Decreases?
8. What is *wind*?
9. What causes winds?
10. To what factor is wind speed related?
11. Name some of the local conditions, including geographic features, that can affect the local weather pattern.
12. Which atmospheric variables are related in a simple manner? Specify whether these relationships are direct or inverse.
13. What three characteristics are used in identifying air masses?
14. What determines the characteristics of an air mass?
15. What is the direction of circulation in a low-pressure air mass in the Northern Hemisphere?
16. What is the direction of circulation in a high-pressure air mass in the Northern Hemisphere?
17. What is a *front*?
18. How does the passage of a front generally affect weather conditions?
19. What are the four basic types of fronts?
20. What are jet streams and why are they important?
21. What is the importance of storms in terms of energy in the atmosphere?

Group B

1. A. pressure   B. temperature   C. cloud cover
   D. dew point   E. visibility   F. precipitation
   G. wind speed   H. wind direction
   The variables listed above are those shown on the station model on page 157. Choose:
   a. One pair that you would expect to show a *direct* relationship on a contingency table or a graph.
   b. One pair that would show an *inverse* relationship on a contingency table or a graph.
2. Explain how some or all of the variables in Question 1 would change under the following conditions:
   a. The weather changes from warm and humid to cool and dry.
   b. The weather changes from cool and dry to warm and humid.
   (If you would like, organize your answer into a table, using one column for the change listed in 2-a and another column for the change listed in 2-b.)
3. Describe the probable origin, path, and effect on your area of an air mass as it moves from its source region to your location, bringing: (a) warm, moist air, (b) cool, dry air.

Lightning indicates the presence of electrostatic energy in the atmosphere.

CHAPTER 11
Energy in the Atmosphere

You will know something about changes in the atmosphere if you can:

1. Explain how energy and moisture are added to the atmosphere.
2. Describe the factors that affect the density of the air.
3. Describe the circulation of the atmosphere.
4. Explain how moisture leaves the atmosphere.

In Chapter 10 we considered some of the kinds of weather, or conditions of the atmosphere, that we can observe and measure. Among these were air temperature and pressure, relative humidity or dew point, wind direction and speed, and the presence of clouds or precipitation. We saw, too, that we could observe the movement and interaction of large air masses, each with its own distinct characteristics. Even without knowing any of the "whys" or "wherefores" of weather, we could make weather predictions on the basis of the probability of changes in the weather when we observed certain conditions in the atmosphere. But if we can understand the processes of change in the atmosphere, we will have a better chance to make more accurate predictions. This chapter deals with some of the processes that cause changes in the atmosphere.

Figure 11-1. Hang gliders use warm updrafts of the air to stay in flight.

HEATING THE ATMOSPHERE

Solar Radiation. Radiation from the sun is the chief source of energy for the atmosphere. But recall from Chapter 9 (page 147) that *most* of the radiant energy from the sun that enters the atmosphere is either reflected back out to space or passes through to the earth's surface. It has very little *direct* warming effect on the atmosphere.

When radiant energy from the sun reaches the earth's surface, then a large part of the energy *is* absorbed. This absorbed energy heats the earth's surface. The earth's surface then reradiates the energy into the atmosphere. The temperature of the earth's surface is much lower than that of the sun. Therefore, much of the earth's radiation is at long wavelengths in the infrared range. These are the wavelengths that the carbon dioxide and water vapor in the atmosphere can absorb. It is energy *reradiated* by the earth's surface that does most of the warming of the atmosphere.

As you study the picture, you see land and water, and on the land you see darker and lighter areas. From Chapter 9 (page 148) you will remember that these different surfaces heat up at different rates by day and cool off at different rates by night. During the day, the land becomes warmer than the water, and the dark areas of the land become warmer than the light areas. Over the warmer areas, more energy is radiated to the atmosphere than over the cooler ones. Some energy is also transferred from the surface to the atmosphere by conduction at the interface between the surface and the air.

Combustion. Radiation and conduction from the earth's surface are the *main* sources of energy for the atmosphere, together with some direct absorption of insolation. But there are a number of minor sources, and you can see some examples of these in the picture. The charcoal fire in the grill is transferring heat to the atmosphere by radiation and conduction. So is the combustion of fuel in the factory and in the engine of the motorcycle. Each of these is a rather intense source of heat in its immediate neighborhood. But for the atmosphere as a whole, all the combustion around the world pro-

vides only a tiny fraction of the total energy supply. The oxidation of food by living things also adds a bit of heat to the atmosphere. You can think of yourself as one of the sources of atmospheric energy.

Other Sources. Winds are another small source of energy for the atmosphere. Although you cannot see a wind in the picture, you can see evidence of its action. A wind is air in motion. Where winds blow along the earth's surface, the kinetic energy of the moving air is changed to heat by friction at the interface between the air and the surface. This heat raises the temperature of both the surface and the atmosphere to a very slight extent. There are no volcanoes in the picture, but volcanic eruptions are another very small source of energy for the atmosphere.

The various sources of energy in the picture have different amounts of heating effect at different times of the day or year. There are similar variations in heating of the atmosphere on a global scale. At latitudes around the equator, where intensity of insolation is greatest, surface temperatures are highest and the atmosphere receives the most energy. At the poles, heating of the atmosphere is least. These variations from place to place on the earth, and from time to time during the year, are the chief cause of changes in the weather.

SUMMARY

1. The atmosphere is heated mainly by absorption of infrared radiation from the earth's surface.
2. Other sources of heat for the atmosphere include direct absorption of solar radiation, conduction from the earth's surface, combustion, wind friction, and volcanic eruptions.

Figure 11-2. How water enters the atmosphere. The lake, the trees, the freshly plowed soil, and the people all give off moisture to the atmosphere.

ATMOSPHERIC MOISTURE

In Figure 11-1 we saw examples of various ways in which heat energy is transferred to the atmosphere. Figure 11-2 is a drawing in which some of the ways that *water* enters the atmosphere are pictured. How many can you spot? What processes are involved in each case?

Evaporation. You know that if you leave a pan of water out in the air, the water eventually disappears. You can keep watch over the pan to make sure that your pets or other animals don't drink it, or that the water is not carried off in some other obvious way. If you wash your hands, but don't dry them on a towel, they dry anyway in a few minutes. If you rub your hands together or blow on them, the water disappears more quickly. What happens to the water? We say that it dries up. In more elegant scientific language, we say that it *evaporates*. By

this we mean that the liquid water changes to water vapor—a gas. The water has "disappeared" only in the sense that it is no longer visible. But it still exists as a gas mixed with other gases in the air. There are various factors that affect the rate at which this process of evaporation occurs, and we will discuss them later in this chapter.

Where is evaporation likely to be taking place in the scenes in Figure 11-2? Obviously, the lake is a good choice. Evaporation is continuously occurring from large bodies of water, such as lakes and oceans, all over the world. Very likely, the farmer and the camper are perspiring. This water, too, is being evaporated. The freshly plowed soil is probably giving up moisture by evaporation, also. After several minutes, the dark, moist, freshly turned soil may change to a

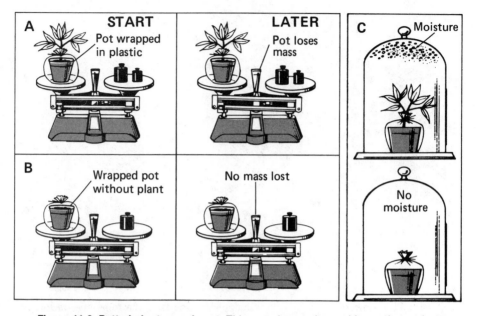

Figure 11-3. Potted-plant experiment. This experiment gives evidence that a plant can remove moisture from the soil and give it off to the atmosphere.

lighter color as it dries out. However, evaporation is not the complete story of how water vapor gets into the atmosphere. There is another important process, not quite as obvious as evaporation, that adds large amounts of water vapor to the air.

Transpiration. Figure 11-3, part A, shows a simple experiment that can be carried out with a potted plant. The soil in the pot was watered. Then the pot and the soil were wrapped in a plastic sheet. The plastic was sealed to the plant stem so that no water could be lost to the air by evaporation. The pot and its plant have been placed on a laboratory balance. After a short time, the balance will indicate that the pot and plant are losing mass.

In part B of the illustration, a pot of watered soil *without* a plant was wrapped in plastic and placed on a balance. In this case, no change in mass is observed as time passes. In part C, a pot-and-plant setup like that in part A has been placed under a large glass jar. After a time, a mist of water droplets will appear on the inside surface of the jar, indicating that the air inside the jar has become saturated with water vapor. This does not happen when a wrapped pot *without* a plant (as in part B) is placed under the jar. If the soil in the pots is examined after a few days, it will be found to have dried out in the setups A and C, but not in B.

These observations indicate that there is a process by which water can leave the soil and enter the atmosphere by passing through a plant. The process by which living plants transfer moisture to the atmosphere is called *transpiration*. In this process, liquid water enters the plant through its roots and is carried upward through its stems to its leaves. The water then passes through the walls of the plant cells into spaces within the leaves, where it becomes water vapor and escapes into the air through openings in the leaf surfaces (see Figure 11-4).

Transpiration is a much more rapid process than simple evaporation would be. It is an essential life process of plants. Many substances that plants need are dissolved in soil water in only very small amounts. Transpiration enables a plant to absorb large quantities of water from the soil, take the minerals they need from the water, and then dispose of the surplus water. Large plants, such as trees, give off great quantities of water by transpiration. It is the process that explains the high humidity that is always present in "steaming" tropical jungles.

In some of the scenes in Figure 11-2, the surface is covered with plants. We can assume that large amounts of water vapor are entering the air by transpiration from these plants, as well as by evaporation from the bodies of water. The two processes of evaporation and transpiration are often referred to, in combination, as *evapotranspiration*.

Energy and Evaporation. After taking a swim on a hot summer day, you feel cool for quite a while, even if you're lying in the sun. This happens because the evaporation of water from your skin is a cooling process. In evaporation, the water molecules that break free of the liquid water to form water vapor are those with the greatest kinetic energy. So the average kinetic energy of the molecules left behind in the liquid water is lowered, which means that the temperature of the water is lowered.

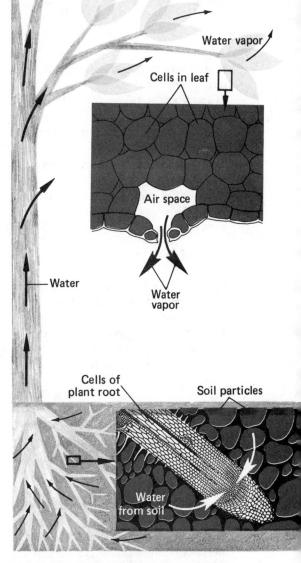

Figure 11-4. Transpiration. In transpiration water enters the plant through the roots and passes upward through the stem into the leaves. The water evaporates into spaces inside the leaves, and then eventually passes out into the air through special openings in the surface of the leaf.

Recall from Chapter 8 (page 132) that the change from liquid water to water vapor requires large amounts of energy. At the boiling point, it takes 540 calories to convert one gram of liquid water to water vapor (steam). In evaporation at temperatures below the boiling point, the heat of vaporization is somewhat less, but still quite large. The heat energy required for evaporation is taken from the water, so the water does drop in temperature. However, the water vapor and the surrounding air are *not* warmed by evaporation. The heat energy is stored in the water vapor as the form of potential energy called latent heat. When the water vapor later condenses back to liquid water, the latent heat then appears as heat energy, and it is at that time that the atmosphere is warmed by it.

Transpiration is basically a process of converting liquid water to water vapor, and the amount of energy used is the same. So transpiration is also an energy-absorbing process. The atmosphere gains energy in the form of latent heat through transpiration as well as through evaporation.

SUMMARY

1. Moisture enters the atmosphere by means of evaporation and transpiration.
2. The oceans and other large bodies of water are the primary sources of moisture for the atmosphere.
3. Energy is required to cause evaporation and transpiration.
4. The atmosphere gains energy through evaporation and transpiration. This energy is in the form of latent heat.

VAPOR PRESSURE

Figure 11-5 shows two mercury barometers. At normal atmospheric pressure, the air pressure can support a column of mercury that is 760 mm in height. This is equivalent to a pressure of 1013 millibars (mb). This is illustrated by the drawing labeled *A*. Remember that the space above the mercury column is empty. We call it a *vacuum*. Therefore, the pressure at the base of the mercury column is due entirely to the weight of the mercury.

In drawing B, a few drops of water have been added to the column. (This can be done by forcing water out of a medicine dropper held under the base of the tube.) When this is done, the mercury column is observed to drop. At 25°C, the height of the column drops about 24 mm, equivalent to about 31 mb.

You might expect the extra weight of the water to cause the mercury level to drop slightly. But the weight of the water alone cannot explain why the whole column drops 24 mm. In fact, since water is much less dense than mercury, the top of the column ought to be slightly *higher* in order to produce the same pressure at the bottom. There must be something in the space above the column that is exerting pressure and adding its effect to the weight of the liquid.

We know that water evaporates, forming water vapor. What has happened in the column is that water vapor has entered the space above the mercury and water. This vapor exerts pressure in the closed space. Look again at the diagram of the normal barometer. We said that the space above the mercury is a vacuum. Actually, it contains some mercury vapor. However, the amount of mercury that evaporates into this space is

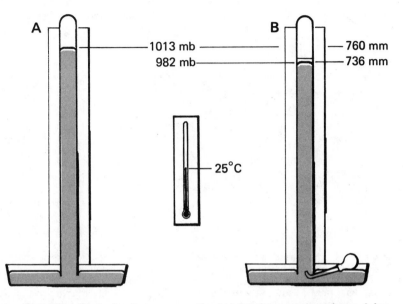

Figure 11-5. The effect of water vapor on the height of a mercury column. A few drops of water inside a mercury barometer causes the column to drop. At 25°C, the drop is about 24 mm.

so small that its pressure can ordinarily be ignored. (In high-precision experiments with mercury columns, the pressure of the mercury vapor does have to be considered.) When water vapor is allowed to form in the space above the column of liquid, the situation is quite different. The pressure of the water vapor is much greater than that of the mercury vapor, and it cannot be ignored.

The pressure of water vapor is called *vapor pressure*. In normal atmospheric pressure, part of the total pressure is due to vapor pressure, part is due to pressure exerted by oxygen, part by nitrogen and so on for all the gases that make up air. The atmospheric pressure is the total of the separate pressures exerted by each of these gases. These separate pressures are called *partial pressures*.

Saturation Vapor Pressure. You will notice that some water in barometer *B*

remains on top of the mercury column. It does not completely evaporate into the space above. Why is this so? As the water evaporates at first, the space at the top of the column begins to be filled with water vapor. But this is not a one-way process. Besides the water molecules leaving the liquid, there are also water molecules entering the liquid from the air. In other words, there is condensation as well as evaporation.

Figure 11-6 illustrates this process. At first, there are more molecules leaving the liquid than are returning to it. The rate of evaporation is greater than the rate of condensation, and the vapor pressure keeps increasing. Eventually, the two rates become equal. The number of molecules leaving the liquid equals the number returning to the liquid. A *dynamic equilibrium* has then been reached. This doesn't mean that evaporation

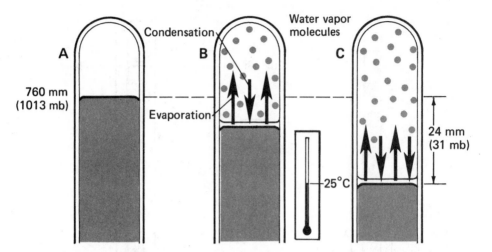

Figure 11-6. The meaning of saturation vapor pressure. In *A*, the normal height of the mercury column in the barometer is shown. In *B*, a small amount of water has been added, and evaporation has just begun. Water molecules are leaving the liquid (evaporation) at a faster rate than vapor molecules are returning (condensation), and vapor pressure is building up above the column. At *C*, equilibrium has been reached. Evaporation and condensation are occurring at the same rate, and the amount of water vapor remains constant. The depression of the mercury column equals the pressure exerted by the water vapor. This is the saturation vapor pressure for the existing temperature. At 25°C, for example, the vapor pressure is 31.4 mb.

and condensation stop occurring. Both processes continue, but at equal rates, so there is no *net* change in either direction. The vapor pressure at this point is called the *saturation vapor pressure*.

The saturation vapor pressure of water is the same in air as it is in the space at the top of a barometer. The presence of the other gases in the air does not affect the equilibrium between water and its vapor. When air is saturated with water vapor, the partial pressure due to the water vapor is the same as the saturation vapor pressure.

Saturation Vapor Pressure and Temperature. From what we have just said you can see that the amount the column drops in barometer *B* is equal to the saturation vapor pressure. The saturation vapor pressure varies with temperature. Barometer *B* in Figure 11-5 shows what happens at 25°C. The saturation vapor pressure at this temperature is 24 mm of mercury, or 31 mb. If we cool the upper portion of the barometer by holding ice cubes against it, the column of mercury will rise. This shows that the vapor pressure has decreased. If we warm the barometer, the column drops, showing that the vapor pressure has increased.

Barometer *B* is thus an instrument that can be used to measure the saturation vapor pressure of water at any temperature between the freezing point and the boiling point. Figure 11-7 is a graph that shows the relationship between saturation vapor pressure and temperature. Note that at 100°C the vapor pressure becomes equal to normal atmospheric pressure

(760 mm or 1013 mb). At this temperature, water will boil if the air pressure is normal. This means that the vapor pressure is great enough to form bubbles of vapor inside the liquid (which is what we mean by "boiling").

Water boils whenever the water temperature is raised to the point where saturation vapor pressure is equal to atmospheric pressure. Therefore, where the atmospheric pressure is lower than normal, water will boil below 100°C. Where the atmospheric pressure is higher than normal, the boiling point of water is raised.

Rate of Evaporation. There are three basic factors that affect the rate of evaporation of a liquid. The first is the amount of energy available. The more energy there is available (the higher the temperature), the greater the rate of evaporation. The second is the surface area of the water. The greater the surface area (the greater the interface between water and air), the greater the rate of evaporation. The third is the moisture content, or vapor pressure, of the air over the water. The lower the vapor pressure, the faster the rate of evaporation. The closer the air is to being saturated, the slower the evaporation rate. This is true because as the air nears saturation, the rate of condensation in the air approaches the rate of evaporation from the surface of the liquid.

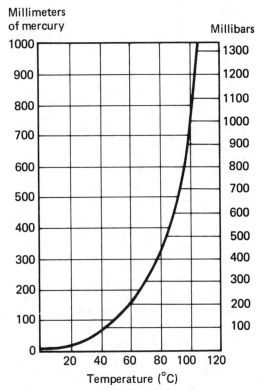

Figure 11-7. **Relationship of temperature and saturation vapor pressure.**

The air closest to the air-water interface will have a higher water vapor content than air at greater heights, and it will also become saturated sooner. If the air above the liquid is not in motion, it will become saturated. If something then moves the air (a fan or wind), then unsaturated air will be circulated over the liquid, and further evaporation will occur.

SUMMARY

1. The pressure exerted by water vapor is called vapor pressure.
2. The vapor pressure of saturated air is called the saturation vapor pressure.
3. Saturation vapor pressure varies directly with temperature.
4. The rate of evaporation depends on the energy available, the surface area, and moisture content of the air.

THE DENSITY OF THE AIR

Up to this point in the chapter we have been examining the ways in which heat and moisture enters the atmosphere. It is time to consider some of the *effects* of these transfers to the atmosphere. One of the most important effects is a change in the density of the air. Changes in density are important because they are the direct cause of movement of masses of air, both locally on a small scale and worldwide on a large scale. How do changes in temperature and moisture content affect air density?

Temperature and Volume Changes in Air. In this chapter, and in other sections of this book, we will frequently refer to the effects of heating or cooling a portion of the atmosphere. It is often stated that "warm air expands" and "cool air contracts." This idea was discussed

briefly in Chapter 2 (page 18). It will be helpful to examine the situation a little more carefully.

Figure 11-8 shows a flask sealed by a stopper. The flask contains air. If the air in the flask is heated by lighting the burner under the flask, will the air in the flask expand? No. Since the flask is airtight, the air inside has no place to go. It can't expand. What does happen is that the *pressure* of the air inside the flask increases as its temperature rises. The pressure increases because the heat being added is causing the kinetic energy of the gas molecules to increase. As a result, the impacts of the molecules on the sides of the flask occur with greater force and with greater frequency, thus creating a greater pressure. If the pressure of the confined gas becomes great enough, it will blow the stopper

Figure 11-8. Increasing pressure of a confined gas that is being heated. As the temperature of the gas increases, the average kinetic energy of its molecules increases, resulting in an increase in the pressure of the gas.

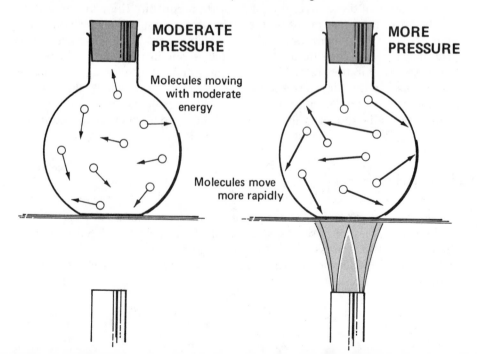

MODERATE
PRESSURE

Molecules moving
with moderate
energy

Molecules move
more rapidly

MORE
PRESSURE

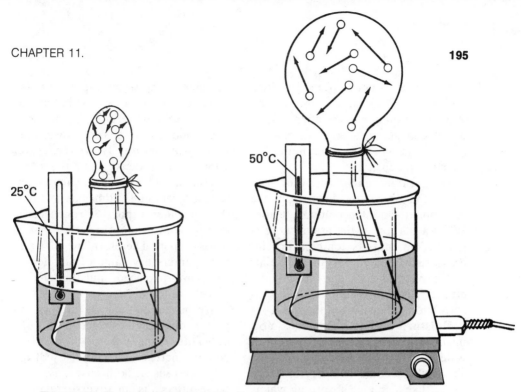

Figure 11-9. Expansion of heated air. If you warm a balloon over a radiator or hotplate, the air molecules inside the balloon acquire more kinetic energy. They are therefore able to expand the balloon to a larger volume. If the balloon is cooled, the air molecules lose kinetic energy and the balloon contracts.

out of the flask or break the glass, whichever gives way first.

But what happens if the flask is open, and we heat it as before? The first effect of the added heat is to increase the air pressure slightly inside the flask. But this immediately drives some of the gas out through the neck of the flask. Thus the pressure inside the flask doesn't rise, but the number of molecules inside decreases. That is, the mass of the gas in the fixed volume of the flask decreases, resulting in decreased density. This effect was discussed in Chapter 2, page 18.

To help visualize the effect of heating a portion of the atmosphere, let us replace the sealed flask by a tied rubber balloon filled with air (see Figure 11-9). What happens when we heat the balloon? Again, the air inside cannot escape. But this time it stretches

the rubber balloon to a larger volume. Again, the density of the air inside the balloon becomes less. But now the density decreases because we have the *same mass* of gas occupying a *larger volume*. The case of the balloon is close to what happens when a region of the atmosphere is heated. The heated "bubble" of the air expands and becomes less dense.

The opposite effects are produced when an air mass loses heat and becomes cooler. Its molecules lose kinetic energy, and the pressure of the surrounding air squeezes the cooler air into a smaller volume, thereby increasing its density. This effect can be demonstrated by cooling a balloon of air. The volume of the balloon will decrease.

You can now see that when we say "warm air expands," we are talking about air that is not confined in a rigid container. That is, we are talking about the situation in the atmosphere, where changes in energy can lead to changes in volume, and hence to changes in density.

Temperature and Density of Air. From the preceding discussion, we can come to an important conclusion. When a portion of the atmosphere is heated, so that its temperature increases, the heated portion of the air will expand and its density will decrease. When air is cooled, it will contract and its density will increase.

Moisture and Air Density. You might expect that when the amount of water vapor in the air increases, the air would become heavier, or more dense, like a sponge absorbing water. Not so! When a sponge absorbs water, there is just as much sponge as before, so the weight of the water is added to the weight of the sponge. But when water vapor enters the air, some of the oxygen, nitrogen, and other gases are "pushed out of the way," or

displaced. The water vapor *takes the place* of these gases, so that in the same volume there is more water vapor and less of the other gases than there was before. However, water vapor is less dense than the other gases in air. Oxygen, for example, has a density about 1¾ times as much as that of water vapor. Nitrogen has a density more than 1½ times that of water vapor. Therefore, when water vapor enters a volume of air, denser gases are displaced, and the average density of the air decreases.

We have just seen that a very important change takes place in air when either its temperature or its moisture content increases. The density of the air decreases in both cases. Each of these effects is an inverse relationship—when one quantity goes up, the other goes down. It will be helpful to keep these inverse relationships clearly in mind as we study their effects on the behavior of the atmosphere.

SUMMARY

1. As the temperature of the air increases, its density decreases.
2. As the moisture content of the air increases, its density decreases.

CIRCULATION OF THE ATMOSPHERE

Convection Cells. We have just seen that wherever the air is being warmed, the air is becoming less dense. Wherever moisture is being added to the air, it is also becoming less dense. We also know that different portions of the atmosphere are receiving heat and moisture at different rates. So it is very common to find a region—which may be quite small or very large—in

which a mass of air of one density is surrounded by air of a different density.

In Chapter 8 (page 124) we considered what happens in a fluid (liquid or gas) when one portion has a different density from another. The more dense portions tend to sink, while the less dense portions rise. This is the process called *convection*. In Chapter 8

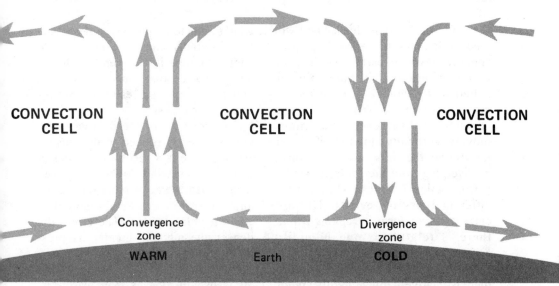

CONVECTION CELL

CONVECTION CELL

CONVECTION CELL

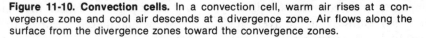

Convergence zone

Divergence zone

WARM   Earth   COLD

Figure 11-10. Convection cells. In a convection cell, warm air rises at a convergence zone and cool air descends at a divergence zone. Air flows along the surface from the divergence zones toward the convergence zones.

we considered convection as a way in which heat energy is transferred in a fluid. In this chapter we will be more concerned with convection as a cause for movement of air and circulation of the atmosphere.

Think of a mass of air over the warm ocean near the equator. This air gains moisture (by evaporation from the ocean surface), and it is warmed by radiation and conduction from the ocean surface. Because the air is both warm and moist, its density is low. It tends to rise. As the warm, moist air rises, its place is taken by cooler, drier air, which moves in underneath it. As this cool, dry air gains moisture and is warmed, it too is forced upward. So, in areas where the air tends to gain moisture and/or heat, there is a steady upward movement of air, with cooler air flowing in from surrounding areas (see Figure 11-10).

We have just described what happens over an area of the earth's surface where the air gains moisture and/or heat. At other locations, conditions are such that the air becomes cooler and drier, and therefore more dense, than the surrounding air. At such locations there is a downward movement of air. This air sinks under the influence of gravity and spreads out horizontally at the surface, forcing less dense air upward. In both situations, we have a circulating system of air currents, which we call a *convection cell.* A region where air is rising in a convection cell is called a *convergence zone (converge* means "to come together"). Air from surrounding areas flows in toward the center of the convergence zone. In the center of the convergence zone the air moves vertically upward.

On the other hand, there are situations in which air loses heat and becomes cooler. This happens to air over cold land masses, such as the northern regions of Canada or Russia.

Such air will become denser and will tend to sink and then spread out horizontally near the earth's surface. A region where this is happening is called a *divergence zone (diverge* means "to move apart"). In the center of a divergence zone, air is moving vertically downward. Near the ground, the air is moving outward, or diverging from the center.

Convection cells can start in two different types of regions. Upward currents of air form in regions where there is relatively high humidity and/or temperature. Downward currents of air form in regions where there is relatively low humidity and/or temperature. So convection cells may form in regions with relatively high humidity and temperature or relatively low humidity and temperature.

Wind. We have defined wind as a horizontal movement of air over the surface of the earth. We experience wind as a local event—as a breeze rustling the leaves of a tree, or as strong gusts causing the entire tree to sway. A wind may, in fact, be the result of local weather factors, such as thunderstorms. But we will see that local winds are also affected by large wind systems that sweep across the earth on a global scale.

When we talk about wind, we must remember that it is a vector quantity—that is, wind must be described in terms of both velocity and direction. As already stated on page 27, winds are named according to the direction they come from. A southeast wind is a wind blowing *from* the southeast toward the northwest.

Air moving in toward a convergence zone or out from a divergence zone is a wind. Here, the wind seems to be the result of convection. Actually, air never moves horizontally unless it is driven by a force, and the force that causes a wind to blow is always the result of a difference in air pressure.

The pressure of the air over a region is directly related to its density. Air pressure is a result of the weight of the air pressing down on a given area. When the air is more dense, the air over a given area weighs more than when it is less dense. Therefore, the denser the air, the greater its pressure.

We have seen (page 196) that cold air is usually denser than warm air. Dry air is usually denser than moist air. We would therefore expect to find that cold, dry air masses are generally centers of high pressure, while warm, moist air masses are centers of low pressure. Observations of air masses show that this is generally the case. Cold, dry air masses are usually present in divergence zones; warm, moist air masses are present in convergence zones. The difference in pressure between the base of a cold, dry air mass and a warm, moist air mass will cause winds to blow outward from the former and in toward the latter.

Although the direction of a wind is basically determined by the location of the centers of high and low pressure, the actual direction of a wind is always affected by the Coriolis force. As explained in Chapter 7 (page 103), this is a force on anything moving along the earth's surface, caused by the earth's rotation. In the Northern Hemisphere, the Coriolis force deflects winds to the right. In the Southern Hemisphere, winds are deflected to the left.

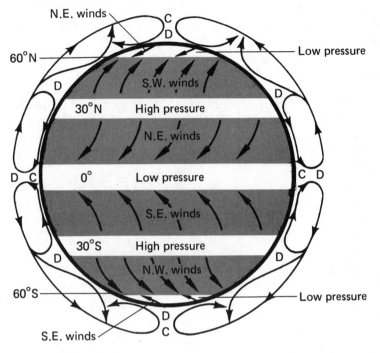

Figure 11-11. Planetary wind and pressure belts in the troposphere. The drawing shows the locations of the belts near the time of an equinox. The locations shift somewhat with the changing latitude of the sun's vertical ray. In the Northern Hemisphere the belts shift northward in summer and southward in winter.

Planetary Winds. We know that the earth's surface is heated unevenly— that the total annual insolation received by areas around the equator is much greater than that received by areas around the poles. Winds transfer heat from regions of high temperature to regions of low temperature and in this way make it possible for life to exist on much of the land areas of the earth.

At the earth's surface, winds blow horizontally from regions of divergence toward regions of convergence. Because of the Coriolis effect, the winds curve to the right in the Northern Hemisphere and to the left in the Southern Hemisphere. Figure 11-11 shows the pattern of winds that flow over the surface of the earth.

It also shows regions of high pressure and regions of low pressure. The positions of the zones of convergence and divergence and of high pressure and low pressure depend on several factors.

You might expect to find a zone of convergence around the equator, the warmest part of the earth. If you look at Figure 11-11, this is exactly what you find. Here the air is warmed by the strong insolation and it also gains moisture because of the high rate of evaporation from the warm oceans. So there are winds blowing in toward the equator from both sides.

At latitudes of 30°N and 30°S there are divergence zones where cool air from the upper atmosphere sinks to the earth's surface. At latitudes of

60°N and 60°S there are zones of convergence, while at both the North and South poles there are divergence zones. During the course of a year, as the sun's direct rays shift northward and southward, the pattern of planetary winds and pressure also shifts.

As you can see from Figure 11-11, the earth's surface is divided into a series of *planetary wind belts,* and within each belt the winds generally blow in a specific direction. Most of the continental United States is within a region in which the wind direction is generally southwesterly.

SUMMARY

1. Wind direction is modified by the earth's rotation—the Coriolis effect.
2. Convection cells in the atmosphere are caused by differences in density of the air and the effect of gravity.
3. Atmospheric convection is affected by variations in insolation.
4. Air moves from regions of divergence to regions of convergence.
5. There is a series of planetary wind belts within which the winds generally blow in a specific direction.

VERTICAL MOVEMENTS IN THE ATMOSPHERE

Atmospheric Pressure and Altitude. The pressure of the atmosphere at any particular place depends on the weight of the air pressing down at that place. When the air above an area is denser, it exerts greater pressure. Our discussion of air density and pressure has been concerned with these conditions at the earth's surface. What happens to air density and pressure as you climb to higher elevations? The pressure of the air at any particular height depends on the weight of the air in a vertical column *above* that height. At the very top of the atmosphere, the pressure is near zero. As you descend toward the ground, the pressure gradually increases, since there are increasing amounts of air above you. Thus we see that the air

pressure depends on altitude, it being less at higher altitudes than at lower. The variation in pressure with altitude is illustrated in Figure 11-12.

Remember, too, that air pressure and density are related. Where the pressure is low, the density will be low. Where the pressure is high, there will be more air compressed into the same volume and the density will be high. Thus, as you rise higher into the atmosphere, not only does the pressure go down, but the density does, also. As a result, most of the mass of the atmosphere is concentrated in its lowest regions. Although traces of air can still be found 1,000 km above the earth's surface, more than half the mass of the atmosphere lies within 6 km of the surface.

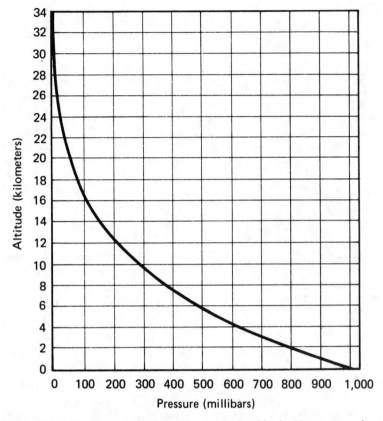

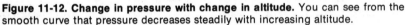

Figure 11-12. Change in pressure with change in altitude. You can see from the smooth curve that pressure decreases steadily with increasing altitude.

Adiabatic Temperature Changes. We know that when heat is added to the air, its temperature rises. This usually results in expansion of the mass of air. When heat is removed from a mass of air, its temperature drops, and the air contracts to a smaller volume. These changes in volume are the results of changes in temperature brought about by adding or removing heat.

What do you think would happen to the volume of a mass of air if the pressure around it was reduced? You are right if you say that the air would expand to a larger volume. Likewise, if the pressure around a mass of air in-creases, the air will be compressed into a smaller volume. In other words, the volume of air will change when its pressure changes, even though no heat has been added or removed. Any change that occurs without the addition or removal of heat energy is called an *adiabatic* change. The changes in volume that we have been talking about in this paragraph are examples of adiabatic changes.

Now here is a big question that is worth some careful thought. Will the *temperature* of the air change when it expands or contracts during an adiabatic change? Logic seems to say that the answer should be no. Since

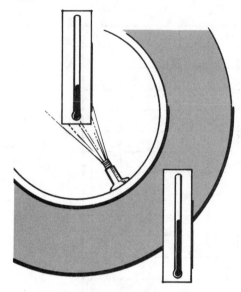

Figure 11-13. Adiabatic cooling. The air leaving the tire is cold because it has gone through an adiabatic expansion.

no heat is added or removed, the temperature should not change. But this is one case where logic lets us down! Experiments show that when a gas expands by an adiabatic process, its temperature drops. Likewise, when a gas is compressed, its temperature rises.

An example of a gas undergoing an adiabatic change is air escaping through the valve of an inflated tire (Figure 11-13). Such a stream of escaping air feels distinctly cold. This is not just the cooling sensation that a breeze may produce. A thermometer will show that the temperature of the escaping air is definitely lower than that of the surrounding air. The escaping air is cold because it expands as it leaves the tire, and the expansion is an adiabatic change.

Changes in the temperature of a gas that occur simply as a result of expansion or compression are called *adiabatic temperature changes*. In an

adiabatic expansion, the temperature of the expanding gas decreases. The reason for this is that an expanding gas is doing work, that is, energy is coming out of it. Since no energy goes into the gas during the adiabatic expansion, the energy coming out must come from energy the gas already contained. In the case of simple expansion, the source of this energy is the kinetic energy of the gas molecules. As the expansion proceeds, the kinetic energy of the gas molecules decreases.

In Chapter 8 we saw that a decrease in the kinetic energy of the molecules of a substance means that the temperature of the substance has decreased. So, as the molecules of an expanding gas lose kinetic energy, the temperature of the gas drops.

All of this is reversed when a gas undergoes an adiabatic compression. Work has to be done on a gas to compress it. That is, energy has to be put into the gas. The energy going in becomes increased kinetic energy of the gas molecules, and the temperature of the gas rises.

Adiabatic Temperature Changes in the Atmosphere. Whenever a mass of air either rises or falls, it undergoes an adiabatic temperature change. For example, consider a mass of air that is rising (Figure 11-14). This upward movement may be caused in various ways. It may be the result of convection. It may be caused by a cold air mass moving in under a warm air mass. Or it may be the result of a wind striking the side of a mountain and being deflected upward. Recall that the atmospheric pressure decreases with increasing altitude. Therefore, as a parcel of air rises, the surrounding

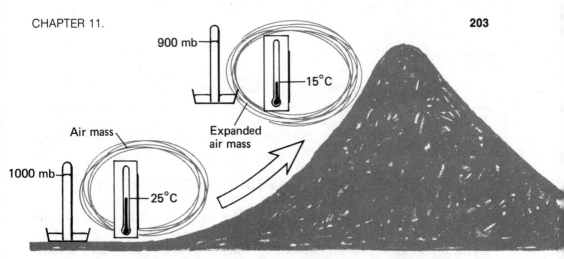

Figure 11-14. Adiabatic expansion in rising air. Whenever a mass of air rises, it undergoes expansion because the pressure is dropping. This expansion is adiabatic, resulting in a drop in temperature.

pressure on it decreases. As a result, the air expands. This expansion is adiabatic, and the temperature of the rising, expanding air decreases. Air rising in the atmosphere is always cooled by the process of adiabatic expansion.

The opposite occurs in descending air. In this case, the descending air meets increasing pressure, and is compressed into a smaller volume. This compression is adiabatic, and the air temperature increases. Air descending in the atmosphere is always warmed by the process of adiabatic compression.

We can see a dramatic example of adiabatic warming in the *chinook*—a wind that blows down from the Rocky Mountains across the Great Plains. Figure 11-15 shows the conditions that can lead to a wind of this type. Cold air moving over the tops of the mountains moves down the slope on the other side. As it descends, it undergoes adiabatic warming, so by the time it reaches the valley, it is a warm, dry wind.

Figure 11-15. Chinooks. Chinooks, which are warm, dry winds, occur when air rising over a mountain sinks to the valley on the other side.

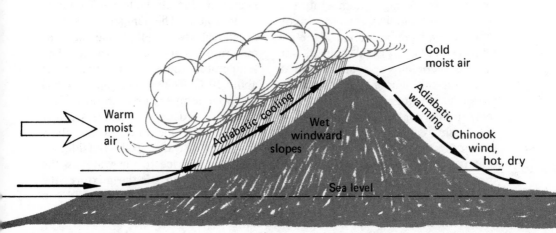

SUMMARY

1. As altitude increases, the atmospheric pressure decreases.
2. As a mass of air rises, its temperature decreases as a result of adiabatic expansion.
3. As a mass of air descends, its temperature increases as a result of adiabatic compression.

HOW MOISTURE LEAVES THE ATMOSPHERE

Earlier in this chapter we considered some of the sources of moisture for the water vapor in the atmosphere. We also looked at the process of evaporation by which liquid water enters the atmosphere as water vapor. There are also ways for water to come out of the air and return to the ground. *Condensation* and *sublimation* are the two processes by which this happens. Condensation refers to the change of state from gas to liquid. Sublimation is the direct change of state from gas to solid, without passing through a liquid state. Let us see the conditions under which each of these processes is likely to occur.

Condensation. At any given time and place, the air contains a certain amount of water vapor. We know that there is a limit to the amount the air can hold, and this limit depends on the temperature. At higher temperatures, the air can hold more water vapor than at lower temperatures. If the air temperature begins to fall, the amount of water it contains does not change at first. But this amount begins to get closer to the maximum. As the air temperature continues to go down, it eventually reaches a point at which the air is saturated. The water vapor that is present is now equal to the maximum that can be present at that temperature. If the air temperature

were to drop any further, the air would be more than saturated. There would be more water vapor present than the air could hold, and some of the vapor would have to come out, either as liquid water or as the solid, ice.

The temperature at which cooling air becomes saturated is called the dew point. If this temperature is above the freezing point of water (0°C), condensation will begin when the dew point is reached. Droplets of water (dew) will appear on the surfaces of objects in contact with the air.

Figure 11-16 shows a simple experiment that you could do to find the dew-point temperature of the air. Your results won't be precise, but they will give you a rough idea of the dew point. The clear plastic cups shown in Figure 11-16 each contain some water. The temperatures vary as shown. Notice that one cup has moisture on its outer surface. The temperature of the water in that cup is about 10°C. The second cup, which is at room temperature (about 20°C), and the third cup, which is warmer than room temperature, do not show any signs of water on the outside.

If you add ice to the water in the second cup and stir the mixture, the temperature gradually drops. If you

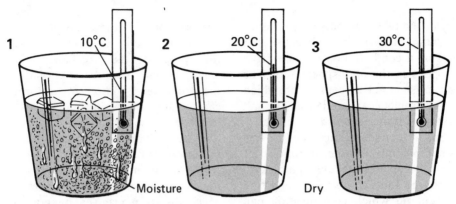

Figure 11-16. Finding the dew-point temperature. You can get a rough idea of the dew-point temperature by adding ice to a cup of water at room temperature and observing the temperature at which condensation begins to form on the outside of the cup.

watch closely, you may be able to find the temperature at which moisture begins to appear on the outside of the cup. The temperature at which it appears is the dew-point temperature.

Condensation Surfaces. There is one important factor in condensation that we have not mentioned up to now. That is, for condensation to occur, there must be a surface for it to occur on. Look at Figure 11-17. On the left is a container filled with moist air. This air has not been filtered—it contains dust, pollen, and many other types of tiny particles called *aerosols*. On the right is a container filled with moist air, but the air has been filtered to remove all dirt, dust, pollen, and other aerosols. Both containers have been cooled to the same temperature. In the container of unfiltered air, we see that a cloud has formed. The air temperature must be at the dew-point temperature or even below it. But the container of filtered air is still clear. No condensation has occurred.

The explanation for this difference between the two containers is that in the unfiltered air the particles act as

surfaces on which condensation can occur. In the pure air there are no such surfaces, and condensation cannot begin without them.

When strong winds blow over the ocean, fine sprays of salt water are blown into the air. The water evaporates, leaving tiny crystals of salt, which are carried throughout the atmosphere. Did you ever notice how

Figure 11-17. Condensation nuclei. Condensation will not occur at the dew point in air that has been filtered to remove all aerosols.

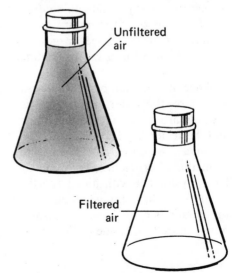

sticky the table salt gets when the air is damp? This happens because salt acts as a condensation surface. This happens in the atmosphere too. The salt crystals act as centers on which water droplets can condense. The salt crystals act as *condensation nuclei*.

So, for condensation to occur, two conditions must be met: (1) moist air must be cooled to the dew-point temperature, and (2) a surface must be present on which condensation can form.

Sublimation. The examples of condensation that we have looked at occurred at temperature above 0°C. What happens when the dew-point temperature is 0°C or below? Does water vapor still condense to liquid water? No. At temperatures below 0°C, water vapor condenses directly into the solid state. Instead of water droplets, it forms ice crystals. This process is called *sublimation*. The frost you find on the inside of your window when it is extremely cold outside is the result of sublimation. Air in the room comes in contact with the window, which is below 0°C because of the cold air outside. The water vapor in the inside air *sublimes* on the window, forming frost. The frost you sometimes see on grass or on cars is also the result of sublimation.

When sublimation occurs in the atmosphere, the water vapor forms ice crystals around condensation nuclei, and the result is a snowflake.

Clouds. We have talked about the formation of droplets of water on surfaces in contact with air at the dew point. What happens when air above the ground is cooled to the dew-point temperature? If condensation nuclei are present (and they almost always are), condensation or sublimation will take place on their surfaces. Very small droplets of water or crystals of ice will appear, and these will form a *cloud*. A cloud is a collection of water droplets or ice crystals so small that they can be kept suspended in the air by upward air currents.

Clouds often form in air that is rising. As we have seen, the temperature of rising air decreases because of adiabatic expansion. As the air cools, its temperature approaches the dew point. When the rising air reaches an altitude at which its temperature has dropped to the dew point, clouds will form. For this reason, the bases of a group of clouds are often at about the same altitude. If the rising air started our fairly dry, it has to rise higher before clouds will form. If the air was nearly saturated to begin with, clouds will form at low altitudes. Clouds can even form at ground level. They are then called *fog*.

Condensation Level. What determines the altitude at which condensation occurs and clouds form? Is there any way of predicting the exact altitude at which the temperature of rising air will reach the dew point?

As a parcel of air rises, it undergoes adiabatic expansion and cooling. It has been found that this cooling occurs at a definite rate, called the *adiabatic lapse rate*. Suppose we start out with unsaturated air at ground level. For each 100 meters of altitude it gains, the temperature of this air will drop 1°C until it reaches the dew-point temperature. This lapse rate is called the *dry* adiabatic lapse rate, and it applies to rising unsaturated air.

When the air cools to the dew-point temperature, condensation begins. We know from Chapter 8 (page 132) that condensation releases latent heat. Therefore, once condensation begins, the temperature of rising air drops at a lesser rate because heat is being added to the air by condensation. For saturated air the adiabatic lapse rate is called the *wet* adiabatic lapse rate, and it is 0.6°C per 100 meters of altitude.

So, unsaturated rising air cools at the dry adiabatic lapse rate of 1°C/100 m, while saturated rising air cools at the wet adiabatic lapse rate of 0.6°C/ 100 m. You might think that if you know the air temperature and dew-point temperature at the surface, you can now figure out the altitude at which condensation occurs. But there is another factor that must be consid-

ered. This is that the dew-point temperature of rising air also drops with increasing altitude. The dew-point temperature decreases because as the rising air expands, the amount of water vapor per cubic meter decreases, and so its vapor pressure is lowered. A lower vapor pressure means a lower dew point. As the air rises, its dew-point temperature decreases at a rate of 0.2°C/100 m.

Putting these two factors together, we find that the temperature of rising unsaturated air approaches the dew-point temperature at a rate of 0.8°C/ 100 m. So, if you know the air temperature at the surface and the dew-point temperature of the air at the surface, you can calculate the altitude at which condensation occurs. An example of this can be seen in Figure 11-18.

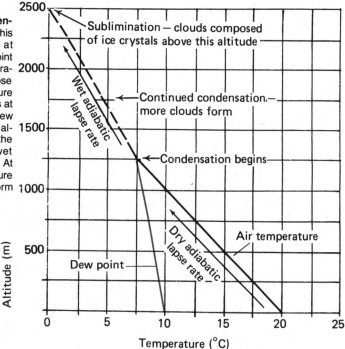

Figure 11-18. Finding the condensation altitude of rising air. In this example, the air temperature at ground level is 20°C and the dew point is 10°C. As the air rises, its temperature drops at the dry adiabatic lapse rate (1°C/100 m) until its temperature drops to the dew point. This occurs at an altitude of 1250 m (where the dew point is only 7.5°C). Above this altitude, condensation occurs and the air temperature drops at the wet adiabatic lapse rate (0.6°C/100 m). At an altitude of 2500 m, the temperature has dropped to 0°C. Ice crystals form by sublimation above this level.

Precipitation. Droplets of water or crystals of ice, no matter how small they are, are still much denser than air and will fall in air. However, because of air friction, small particles fall more slowly than large ones. If the drops or crystals in a cloud are falling through *rising* air, they tend to be kept at the same altitude. That is what keeps a cloud up.

In a dense cloud, tiny droplets of water are constantly colliding. They are therefore constantly joining to form larger and larger drops. As these larger drops form, they begin to fall faster. If the drops become large enough, they fall too fast to be kept up by the rising air currents, and they fall as rain. Any form of water that falls from the atmosphere and reaches the ground is called *precipitation*. Rain is one form of precipitation.

Precipitation and Atmospheric Transparency. Earlier in this chapter we explained how tiny particles—aerosols—in the air act as surfaces on which condensation occurs. These aerosols, including dust, soot, and many other substances, are added to the air both by natural processes, such as volcanic eruptions, and by human activities. The more aerosols there are in the air, the less transparent the air is to insolation. When condensation occurs, some of the aerosols are incorporated into the precipitation, and others are washed down by the falling rain or ice. So precipitation and cloud formation remove some of the aerosols and thus clean the air.

Air-Surface Interaction. As winds blow, there is a direct release of energy by the atmosphere. The moving air sets materials into motion. Dust and small pieces of rock are moved about, resulting in erosion by wind. (This will be considered in Chapters 15 and 16.) Wind also moves water. Waves on lakes and oceans are the result of wind. Wind is one of the factors affecting surface currents in large bodies of water. The Gulf Stream in the Atlantic Ocean is affected by the prevailing wind direction. The wind thus acts as an agent in the transfer of energy from the atmosphere to the surface of the earth.

SUMMARY

1. Condensation can occur when the air is saturated and when a condensation surface is available.
2. Sublimation is the process by which water vapor changes directly to ice at temperatures below 0°C.
3. During condensation and sublimation a significant amount of heat energy is released.
4. Clouds consist of liquid water droplets and/or ice crystals.
5. Precipitation is any form of water that falls from the atmosphere and reaches the ground.
6. Precipitation results when the condensation droplets or ice crystals in a cloud grow large enough to fall.
7. The transfer of energy from the atmosphere can be seen in wind-blown particles of matter and surface ocean currents.

FINDING RELATIVE HUMIDITY

Air at a rather moderate 25°C (77°F) can feel uncomfortably hot and "muggy" if it is humid. On the other hand, the temperature can be well up in the 30's (Celsius)—over 90°F—and still feel fairly comfortable if the air is dry. It's the relative humidity that makes the difference. Physical comfort depends on both the temperature and the relative humidity. That is one reason we would like to be able to measure relative humidity. A comparison of the dew-point temperature and the actual air temperature gives us a general idea of the relative humidity. The greater the difference between them, the lower the relative humidity. But can this information be used to calculate the actual relative humidity in percent? The answer is that it can, but not directly. To see how dew point is related to relative humidity, we need to say something more about vapor pressure.

Relative Humidity and Vapor Pressure. In Figure 11-6 on page 192 you saw how a barometer with a little water in it could be used to find the saturation vapor pressure for any particular air temperature. In the example of Figure 11-6, the air temperature is 25°C and the saturation vapor pressure is 31 mb. The space above the column of liquid inside the barometer is saturated with water vapor. Its relative humidity is 100%.

Suppose that the air had only 25% as much water vapor in it as it has when saturated. The relative humidity would then be 25%. But since there would be only 25% as many molecules of water vapor in the air, the vapor pressure would also be 25% of the saturation pressure. Let us suppose now that more water evaporated into the air, and its vapor content doubled to 50% of saturation. The vapor pressure would also rise to 50% of the saturation pressure. If the air became 75% saturated, the vapor pressure would be 75% of the saturation pressure.

What this tells us is that if we know the actual vapor pressure of the air, and if we know the saturation vapor pressure for the existing air temperature, we can easily calculate the relative humidity. All we have to do is find the ratio of the actual vapor pressure to the saturation vapor pressure and convert it to a percent.

How can we find these two pressures? We have already seen how the saturation vapor pressure can be determined (Figure 11-6). From a series of experiments like this, we can make a table showing saturation vapor pressure for any temperature value. If we measure the temperature of the air, we can then look up its saturation vapor pressure in the table.

Is there any way we can find the actual vapor pressure of the air? We can do this by finding the dew point, as we will see in the next section.

Finding the Dew Point. In Figure 11-16 you saw a method for finding the dew point of the air. This is a difficult and time-consuming process. The dew point can be found in a much simpler way by means of a sling psychrometer (see page 26) and a chart like the one on page 538 in the Appendix. A portion of this chart is shown here (Figure 11-19) in order to explain the method.

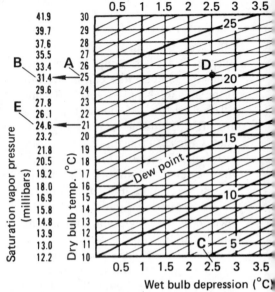

Figure 11-19. Using the Dew Point Chart.
Assume the dry-bulb reading is 25°C and
the wet-bulb is 22.5°C. Then the wet-bulb depression is 2.5°C. Find the dry-bulb temperature along the left edge of the chart (A). The
saturation vapor pressure for this temperature is 31.4 mb (B). Find the wet-bulb depression (2.5°) along the bottom (C). Read across
from (A) and up from (C) to find the dew point
(D). It is 21°. The saturation vapor pressure
for 21° is 24.6 mb (E). This must be the actual
vapor pressure of the air at its present temperature. Relative humidity is the ratio between actual vapor pressure and saturation
vapor pressure, expressed as a percent:

Rel. hum. $= \dfrac{24.6}{31.4} \times 100 = 78\%$

Using the sling psychrometer, we
find the air temperature by reading the
dry-bulb thermometer. We find the
wet-bulb depression by reading the
wet-bulb thermometer and subtract-
ing its reading from the dry-bulb temperature.

Along the lefthand edge of the chart
we find the saturation vapor pressure
for the existing air temperature. The
curved lines running across the chart
are dew-point temperature lines. By
reading across from the dry-bulb reading and up from the wet-bulb depression, we find the dew point. Following
the dew-point line down to the left-

hand edge of the chart, we find the
saturation vapor pressure corresponding to the dew-point temperature.
This is the actual vapor pressure of
the air. Since we now know the actual
pressure and the saturation vapor
pressure, we can calculate the relative
humidity by dividing actual vapor
pressure by saturation vapor pressure
and converting to a percent.

Notice all the information we get
from a single observation with the
psychrometer: air temperature, dew
point, actual vapor pressure, saturation vapor pressure, and relative
humidity.

SUMMARY

1. The vapor pressure of a sample of air is directly proportional to its water
   vapor content.
2. The relative humidity of the air is equal to the ratio of its actual vapor
   pressure to its saturation vapor pressure, expressed as a percent.
3. The vapor pressure of the air can be determined if its dew point is known.

REVIEW QUESTIONS

Group A   1. What is the main source of heat for the atmosphere?
2. Name some of the minor sources of heat for the atmosphere.
3. How does moisture enter the atmosphere?
4. What are the primary sources of moisture for the atmosphere?
5. Do evaporation and transpiration require energy?
6. Does the atmosphere gain energy through evaporation and transpiration? If so, in what form is this energy?
7. What is *vapor pressure*?
8. What is *saturation vapor pressure*?
9. Is the relationship between saturation vapor pressure and temperature direct or inverse?
10. Name three factors that affect the rate of evaporation.
11. Describe the relationship between the temperature of the air and its density.
12. Describe the relationship between the moisture content of the air and its density.
13. What factor modifies wind direction?
14. What causes convection cells in the atmosphere?
15. In which direction does air move between regions of convergence and regions of divergence?
16. What are the regions called where the winds generally blow in a specific direction?
17. Describe the relationship between altitude and atmospheric pressure.
18. What happens to the temperature of a mass of rising air? What causes this change?
19. What happens to the temperature of a mass of descending air? What causes this change?
20. Under what conditions can condensation occur?
21. What is *sublimation*?
22. What energy change occurs during condensation and sublimation?
23. What are *clouds*?
24. What is *precipitation*?
25. Under what conditions does precipitation occur?
26. How can the transfer of energy from the atmosphere to the earth's surface be observed?
27. How is the vapor pressure of a sample of air related to its water vapor content?
28. How is relative humidity related to the vapor pressure of air?
29. What measurement can be used to find the vapor pressure of the air?

Group B   1. a.   Refer to Fig. 11-1 and name several sources of energy that heat the atmosphere.
b.   Describe how the atmosphere is heated through the process of radiation. (Review Chapter 9.)
c.   Describe how the atmosphere is heated through conduction. (Review Chapter 9.)
2. a.   What is the process of evaporation?
b.   What is the process of transpiration?
c.   Describe how energy is involved in each process.
3. a.   How is vapor pressure related to the amount of moisture in the air?

b. What is meant by the statement: "At saturation vapor pressure a condition of dynamic equilibrium exists"?

c. What can be done to increase the saturation vapor pressure of air?

4. Describe two changes in the atmosphere which may cause its density to increase.

5. a. What will happen to a mass of air that is located over the warm ocean near the equator?

b. What do the terms divergence and convergence mean with respect to the circulation of air?

c. What is an adiabatic temperature change?

6. a. What is the dew point?

b. Why are the bases of clouds often flat and at about the same altitude?

7. a. What does relative humidity mean? How is it expressed?

b. Describe two different ways relative humidity can be measured.

REVIEW EXERCISES

1. Assume that at noon on a particular day, the following conditions exist:

The air temperature is 83°F.

The relative humidity is 48%.

The wind speed is 7 miles per hour and its direction is from the north.

The barometric pressure is 1026.6.

Draw a station model showing these weather conditions. See the example of a station model in Figure 10-1, page 157. To find the dew point from the given data, reverse the procedure in Figure 11-19, page 210, using the complete chart on page 538. First find the saturation vapor pressure corresponding to the given air temperature (in °C). Use the given relative humidity percentage to find the actual vapor pressure. Then find the air temperature for which this is the saturation pressure. That temperature is the dew point.

2. Set up a table that will allow you to record the daily weather data for your area for a period of one week. The data should include temperature, barometric pressure, wind speed and direction, relative humidity, precipitation, and cloud cover. This information can be obtained from newspapers, radio, television, or recorded announcements by the National Weather Service. The shorter the intervals between readings, the more meaningful the data will be.

When you have finished collecting the data, analyze it and try to determine (a) whether there are any patterns in the readings (direct or inverse relationships), and (b) how your readings compare with the average readings for your area for the same time of year.

3. Describe the current weather in your area. What type of air mass is present and what is the probable source region for that air mass? Are your current weather conditions caused by the passage of a front? If so, what type of front is involved? Is your weather modified by any local conditions, such as lakes, hills, etc.?

4. From maps in newspapers or from television reports, follow the path of a severe low-pressure system across the country. Plot the path of the system over the course of a few days on a map of North America. Does this storm track follow the normal pathway?

5. Observe and describe the weather conditions during the passage of a front through your area.
   a. What type of front was it? What type of air mass followed the front?
   b. Did precipitation occur? If so, how long did it last? Was it rain, snow, hail, sleet? Was it gentle or violent?

6. Many old weather sayings have some basis in fact, while others do not. Collect some of these sayings and check their accuracy.

7. Figure 11-16 (page 205) shows a simple way to find the dew-point temperature. Suppose that by using that method, we found that the dew-point temperature was 12°C. Also suppose that the air temperature was 23°C at the time of the experiment. What was the relative humidity? What would happen to the relative humidity if the air temperature increased? Decreased?

8. Assume that the same conditions described in the last problem exist outdoors—air temperature 23°C, dew-point temperature 12°C.
   a. Using the information in Figure 11-18 (page 207), find the altitude at which clouds would begin to form.
   b. Suppose the air temperature at the surface is 25°C and the dew-point temperature remains at 12°C. At what altitude will condensation begin? What will the cloud that forms be composed of?

9. To answer the following questions, construct a graph like the one in Figure 11-18, page 207.
   a. If the surface air temperature is 30°C and the altitude of the cloud base is known to be 4.0 km, what is the composition of the cloud likely to be?
   b. What is the dew-point temperature at the surface?
   c. What is the relative humidity at the surface?

TOPIC VIII
MOISTURE AND ENERGY BUDGETS

Scientists are studying the damaging effects of acid rain on this Adirondack lake.

CHAPTER 12
Water in the Earth

You will know something about the water in the earth if you can:

1. Describe the water cycle.
2. Identify the factors affecting water once it reaches the earth's surface as precipitation.
3. Describe the zones of subsurface water.
4. Discuss the problems of the earth's water supply, including pollution.

The part of the earth that is water is called the hydrosphere. When you think of the hydrosphere, you probably imagine the vast oceans first. Then you may recall the lakes, rivers, and streams of the land and the frozen water in glaciers and in the polar ice masses. Perhaps you may even include a rainstorm. Is anything missing from this picture? Yes. A very important part of the hydrosphere is a part we almost never see—the part that is in the rocks and soil of the lithosphere. How does water get into the ground? How does it move underground? How does it leave? This chapter deals with these questions.

FROM HYDROSPHERE TO LITHOSPHERE

The Water Cycle. In Chapter 11 we examined the processes of evaporation and transpiration, which tend to "fill" the atmosphere with water. We also studied the processes of condensation and precipitation, which tend to "empty" the water out of the atmosphere. Since the oceans and other major bodies of water do not seem to be drying up, or steadily rising and flooding the land, there must be a balance between these processes. Water lost from the hydrosphere by evapotranspiration must be returning by condensation and precipitation. This constant circulation of water from hydrosphere to atmosphere and back again is called the *water cycle,* or the *hydrologic cycle.* Its main features are illustrated in Figure 12-1.

The ride that a molecule of water takes around the water cycle may be short and simple. It may leave the ocean by evaporation, become part of a cloud by condensation, and fall right back into the ocean as part of a raindrop. On a water-covered earth, that's about all that would happen. There would be nothing much to say about it, and in fact, there wouldn't be much "earth science." But the earth has a lithosphere, part of which sticks up above the oceans as land. And some precipitation falls on the land.

Figures 12-1. The water cycle. Water lost from the atmosphere by precipitation is returned to it by evapotranspiration, thus maintaining a dynamic equilibrium.

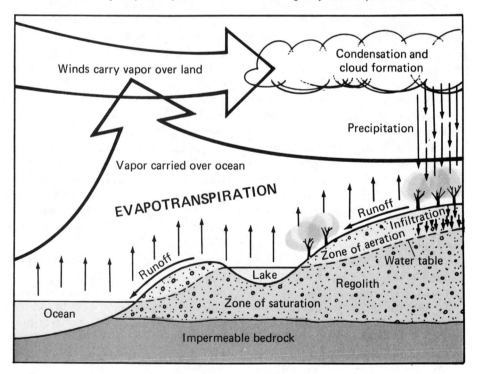

Now the story becomes quite complicated—and also quite interesting. For the next few chapters of this book, we will be talking mostly about how the land is affected by the water that falls upon it.

Where Rain Goes. Picture in your mind a long, steady drizzle such as might occur with the passage of a typical warm front. Where does all that water go? In a town or city, rain that falls on the paved roads runs down the gutters and into sewer drains. But most of the countryside consists of open fields or wooded areas. What happens to rain that falls on ground like that? Think about what you have observed and you will realize that water usually sinks into the ground. This process is called *infiltration.*

Sometimes when it rains very hard, or rains for several days on end, the ground gets soggy and muddy. It seems to have soaked up as much water as it can. Puddles of water collect in the low spots. On slopes, little streams run downhill over the surface. Water flowing over the surface is called *runoff,* and some rain always becomes runoff, at least for a while.

Finally the rain stops. Usually within a few hours the puddles have disappeared and the ground is dry again. Some of the water has evaporated into the air. However, the evaporation rate is too slow to account for the rapid disappearance of so much water. We have to conclude that most of the water has soaked into, or *infiltrated,* the ground.

To sum up, water that falls on the ground as precipitation may *run off* the surface, or it may *evaporate* into the atmosphere. Most of it, however, *infiltrates* the surface. To find out what happens to it after that, we have to dig down and look below the surface.

Infiltration. The infiltration of water into the lithosphere can occur wherever the surface is *permeable,* that is, wherever there are spaces, or *pores,* which the water can enter. If the pores of the surface layers of soil or rock become filled with water, no more water can infiltrate, and the excess water becomes runoff.

Another factor that affects infiltration is the slope of the land. Infiltration takes time to occur. If the slope is gentle, the water has time to infiltrate the ground. But when the slope of the land is very steep, the water tends to run off before much infiltration can occur.

As you know, surface water always runs downhill because of the force of gravity. Gravity continues to act on water as it infiltrates the surface. Water below the surface (which is called *subsurface water)* therefore tends to run "downhill" also. However, the flow of subsurface water is greatly slowed by the resistance of the material through which it flows.

The amount of water that can infiltrate the ground, as well as the rate at which this can occur, depend on two properties of the surface material: *porosity* and *permeability.* These two properties are related, but they are different. Porosity refers to the amount of space into which water could go. Permeability refers to the ease with which water can enter and flow through these spaces. In the following sections we will discover how the characteristics of rocks and soil affect their porosity and their permeability.

SUMMARY

1. The water cycle is the circulation of water from the surface of the earth into the atmosphere and back again.
2. Precipitation may infiltrate the earth's surface, run off, or evaporate.
3. Infiltration can occur if the surface is permeable and unsaturated, and if the slope of the land is gentle enough.
4. The rate of infiltration is determined by the porosity and permeability of the soil.

POROSITY

What happens when you pour water on sand? It sinks right in. But why? The water infiltrates quickly because there are so many spaces between the sand grains. To a varying degree, all soils, and even rocks, have pores. It is the total amount of empty space that determines how much water a soil or rock sample can hold. This gives us the definition of porosity: *porosity* is the percentage of open space in a sample compared with its total volume.

There will be a more complete examination of different kinds of soils in Chapter 14, but for now let's consider the porosity of two very different types—sandy soil and clayey soil. You can see from Figure 12-2 that the particles in the sandy soil are many times larger than those in the clayey soil. You may also notice the difference in shape of the particles and the way they are packed together. What effects do these differences have on the porosity of a sample of soil? Let's examine these facts separately.

Particle Shape. The *shape* of the particles in a soil sample is an important factor in determining porosity. You can see from Figure 12-3 that a sample made up of rounded particles is going to have a greater porosity than one consisting of particles with

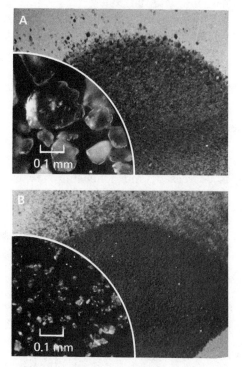

Figure 12-2. Two types of soil. Samples of soil vary with regard to the size, shape, and variety of the particles they contain.

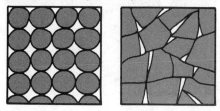

Figure 12-3. Effect of shape on porosity. Rounded particles have more porosity than particles with angular shapes.

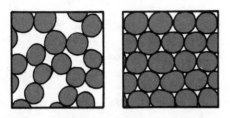

Figure 12-4. Effect of packing on porosity. Loosely packed particles have more porosity than closely packed particles.

angular shapes. The rounded particles just cannot fit together as closely as particles with flat edges.

Packing. Even if the particles in two samples have the same shape, their porosity may differ if one is more tightly *packed* than the other. In Figure 12-4 you can see that the porosity in a loosely packed sample is going to be greater than that in a tightly packed sample. Where the particles are packed closely together, the relative amount of empty space in the sample is decreased, and hence porosity is decreased.

Rounded particles, such as those of sand, usually have only one way of settling together. But what about the

Figure 12-5. Packing of flat particles. Cards thrown into a container at random are likely to be loosely packed with large amounts of empty space between them. If the container is shaken, the cards will settle into a more tightly packed arrangement.

flat particles, such as those of clay? What would happen if cards of irregular shapes were thrown into a container? If the cards were thrown in randomly, the porosity could be quite high (see Figure 12-5). But if the cards are then shaken or pushed down, their porosity drops sharply. *Freshly* deposited clays, in which the particles are mostly flat like cards, may have a porosity of over 90%. But as more material is deposited on top of them, the clay particles become pressed down and tightly packed, and the porosity drops.

Particle Size. What about two soil samples that have particles of the same shape and degree of packing, but of different size? In this case, the two samples can hold about the same

Figure 12-6. Effect of particle size on porosity. Rounded particles of different sizes have about the same porosity, if the particles in each sample are well sorted by size.

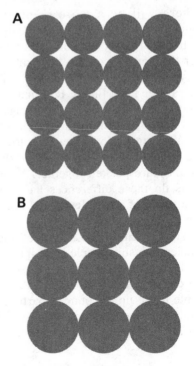

amount of water in their pores. Figure 12-6 shows two samples—one packed with *large* rounded particles, the other with *small* rounded particles. It is true that the individual spaces between the large particles are bigger than those between the small particles. But the *ratio* between the size of the spaces and the size of the particles is about the same. Therefore the *percentage* of empty space is the same in both cases. The porosity of tightly packed round particles is about 35%.

On the other hand, Figure 12-7 shows what would happen if we made up a sample with rounded particles of *two* sizes. The small particles would fill some of the spaces between the large particles. The total volume of

Figure 12-7. Effect of sorting on porosity. If particles of different sizes are mixed together *(B)*, the mixture will have less porosity than well-sorted particles *(A)*.

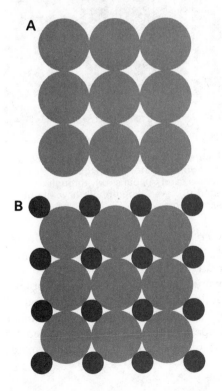

the sample is the same, but the amount of space is less. Therefore, the porosity of this sample would be less than that of the two samples shown in Figure 12-6.

In each sample of Figure 12-6, the particles are said to be *sorted*— they are all approximately the same size. In soils where the particles are sorted, the porosity is greater than in those that are *unsorted*. In unsorted samples, the smaller particles tend to fill in some of the spaces between the larger particles, thus reducing the porosity. Most soils are poorly sorted, or even completely unsorted—that is, they consist of particles of many different sizes, and so they generally have a relatively low porosity— somewhere between 10% and 25%.

Porosity of Rocks. Porosity in rocks is measured in the same way as porosity in soils. However, in soil the particles are loose and separate. They can shift around, and the porosity can change. In rocks, the particles are stuck together in various ways. In some rocks the particles have been locked together by tremendous pressures. In others, the particles are held together by a natural cement. Still other rocks are formed by crystallization of molten material. But in each type of rock there can be some pores left.

Some rocks, such as sandstone, have a porosity of 20 to 25%. In this case the pores are spaces between the grains of what was sand when the material was first deposited. Some rocks consist of crystals that have intergrown, filling most of the spaces between them. The pores in such rocks quite often amount to less than 1% of the total volume.

SUMMARY

1. Porosity is the percentage of open space in a sample compared with its total volume.
2. Porosity is determined by the shape of the particles, how they are packed, and whether or not they are sorted by size.

PERMEABILITY

A material through which water can pass is said to be *permeable*. When considering the permeability of a material, we are mainly concerned with how *rapidly* water can pass through it. Obviously, a rock or soil must have pores if water is to pass through it at all. But the degree of permeability—that is, the rate at which water can pass through—depends not so much on the amount of pore space as on the size of the pores and their interconnections.

Relationship between Porosity and Permeability. Sand has a high porosity. It also has a high permeability. However, the permeability of sand is due not only to its high porosity, but to the fact that the pores are large and interconnected. There is little resistance to the flow of water into and through the pores. On the other hand, a soil made of very small but well-sorted particles may have a high porosity, but low permeability. Water in very small pores is in contact with a large amount of particle surface. Friction and attraction between the water molecules and the particle surfaces prevent rapid flow of water through such a material. (See Figure 12-8.)

A rock may have low porosity, but still be highly permeable. For example, it may have many cracks running through it. Geologists refer to this as

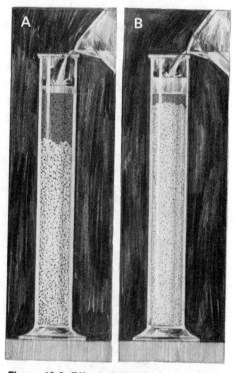

Figure 12-8. Effect of particle size on permeability. Water flows quickly through coarse sand *(A)*, but slowly through very fine sand *(B)*, even though both have about the same porosity.

secondary porosity. The total volume, of the cracks may be only a small percent of the volume of the rock, but water can flow through the cracks quite rapidly. On the other hand, a rock with high porosity may be almost impermeable if its pores are sealed off from one another by cementing material. And in some rocks, such as limestone, water may have increased both the porosity and the permeability by dissolving away some of the rock material.

Infiltration and Permeability. Downward infiltration of water must stop when an impermeable layer is reached. This may happen quite close to the surface, or it may occur at a considerable depth. Is there a limit to the depth of the permeable layer? Evidently, there is. Almost no water can be obtained from wells that are more than 3 km deep, no matter what type of rock is present. Geologists reason that the increasing pressure as depth increases gradually closes all the pores and cracks in the rock structure.

Runoff and Permeability. When rainfall cannot infiltrate the soil, the result is runoff—the water literally runs off over the surface of the land. Runoff will occur when the soil is saturated and can hold no more water. But it can also occur when the ground is not saturated; for example, in a very heavy downpour the rate of infiltration cannot keep up with the rainfall, so the water runs over the surface of the land. Runoff is also common on steep slopes, where the water runs downhill faster than it can sink into the ground. Plantings on hillsides sometimes hold the rainwater long enough for it to infiltrate more or less completely. But of course, in a very heavy storm, there is always the chance that the plantings themselves will be washed away by heavy runoff!

Runoff may gradually infiltrate unsaturated areas of the surface, or it may continue to flow over the surface in streams and rivers. Most runoff eventually reaches the oceans.

SUMMARY

1. The permeability of a material is a measure of the rate at which water can pass through it.
2. Permeability depends on pore size and on whether or not the pores are interconnected.
3. The permeability of loose material increases with increased pore size.
4. Surface runoff can occur when rainfall exceeds the permeability rate, when the soil is saturated, or when the slope of the surface is too great to allow time for infiltration.

ZONES OF SUBSURFACE WATER

We have said that water moves downward in response to gravity until it reaches an impermeable layer. From this statement you might incorrectly conclude that the upper portions of permeable ground are dry except when a recent rainfall is draining through. If this were the case, no plants could grow where the permeable layer extended down very far. Most grasses, for example, have root systems that never go more than about 50 cm into the soil. They would have a hard time between rains where the permeable layer was 3 km deep! Let us take a closer look at what happens to water that infiltrates the surface.

Wetting Action of Water. Dip a finger into water and take it out, and you find that your finger is wet. A thin film of water clings to the surface of your skin. Even violent shaking will not throw it off, although it will gradually evaporate. Water clings to most solid surfaces in this way. It is held on the surface by a force of attraction between the water molecules and the molecules of the other material. This attraction between a liquid and a solid is called *adhesion*.

As water infiltrates the ground, a thin film of water is left behind on all the particles of the soil and on the walls of all the pore spaces through which the water passes. Thus, the upper portions of soil retain moisture that plants can use.

Capillary Action. Dip the corner of a paper towel into water and watch the water wet the towel as it is drawn up into it. Have you ever wondered how water could defy the law of gravity in this way? This behavior of a liquid is called *capillary action*. It is observed whenever the liquid is in contact with very narrow spaces. It can be seen very easily in glass tubes dipping into water, as illustrated in Figure 12-9. Water is drawn up into the tubes by capillary action. The narrower the tube, the higher the water rises in it.

Capillary action is the result of two different forces acting on the molecules of the liquid. One force is the force of adhesion between the liquid and the walls of the tube. The other is the force of attraction between the liquid molecules themselves, called *cohesion*. When a glass

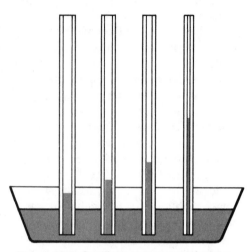

Figure 12-9. Capillary movement of water. Water is drawn up into the glass tubes by capillary action. The water is pulled higher in tubes of smaller diameter.

tube is placed in water, adhesion causes water molecules to climb up the inner walls of the tube. As these molecules move upward, they pull a column of water up behind them by the force of cohesion. The column stops rising when the weight of the water exactly balances the upward force of adhesion. Since a narrow column of water weighs less than a thicker one of the same height, the water can be pulled higher in the narrow column before an equilibrium of forces is reached.

The spaces between the fibers of a piece of paper act like fine tubes. Water rises into these spaces by capillary action. Water will also be drawn upward into the pore spaces of rocks and soil by capillary action from water that has accumulated at lower depths. Depending on the diameter of the pore spaces, water will rise in them to heights of from a few centimeters to a meter or so.

Water clinging to the surfaces of particles in the upper portions of the soil is called *capillary water,* because it is held there by the same forces that cause capillary action. If there is enough capillary water, it will form a continuous film that coats the walls of the pore spaces. If some of the capillary water is drawn off by plant roots, the water may be replaced by a spread of the capillary film from nearby regions. This mainly horizontal movement of water within the soil is called *capillary migration.* It is a very slow process.

There is an inverse relationship between the permeability of a soil and the amount of capillary water it can retain. In a soil with large pores and high permeability, such as a sandy soil, the amount of surface to which water can adhere is relatively small. In soils with small pores and low permeability, such as clayey soils, there is a relatively large amount of surface for holding capillary water.

Zones of Subsurface Water. Infiltration, retention of capillary water, and capillary action combine to produce several distinct regions, or zones, within a permeable surface layer. Compare Figure 12-10 with Figure 12-9 as we discuss these zones of subsurface water.

The Zone of Saturation. Water infiltrates the ground until it reaches an impermeable layer of rock. The water then fills up the pore spaces above this layer under the action of gravity, forming the *zone of saturation.* This corresponds to the water in the container in Figure 12-9. The water in the zone of saturation has settled to its lowest possible level. This water is called *ground water.* The top of the zone of saturation is called the *water table.* If you dig a hole down into the zone of saturation, the hole will fill with water up to the level of the water table.

The surface of the water in the container in Figure 12-9 is horizontal. The

Figure 12-10. Zones of subsurface water.

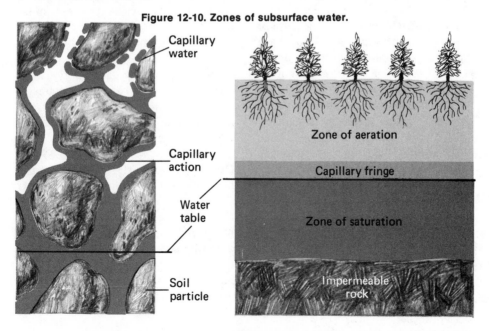

Capillary water

Capillary action

Water table

Soil particle

Zone of aeration

Capillary fringe

Zone of saturation

Impermeable rock

water table is usually not horizontal, because water infiltrating the ground also flows slowly "downhill" below the surface. The water table usually shows a pattern that is similar to the "ups" and "downs," or changing elevation, of the surface above.

The Capillary Fringe. Above the water table there is a zone in which the pores are filled by water drawn up by capillary action. This zone is called the *capillary fringe*. The smaller the pores, the higher the water will rise in the capillary fringe. However, as already noted, this is seldom more than 1 meter and is often only a few centimeters.

Although the pores are filled with water in the capillary zone, a hole dug into this zone will not fill with water. The small pore spaces are needed to hold water at this level.

The Zone of Aeration. Above the capillary fringe the pore spaces are not filled with water, but they are not completely dry, either. As we have seen, water is clinging to the surface of the soil particles here in the form of a thin film. The walls of the pores are wet, but their interior contains air. It is in this *zone of aeration* that most plant roots are found. You might not think there would be enough water there for a plant's needs. But this is not the case. There is plenty of water in the zone of aeration. True enough, it is spread out in the form of a thin film coating the soil particles, but the total surface area of these particles is enormous. Tiny root hairs by the millions, along the tips of growing roots, penetrate the pores and absorb the moisture clinging to the soil particles.

Changes in the Subsurface Zones. Let us review what happens to rainfall that infiltrates the ground. A large part of it clings to soil particles in the zone of aeration as it sinks in. Some of it, however, ends up in the ground water and the capillary fringe. What happens between periods of precipitation? In the zone of aeration, water gradually evaporates from the pore surfaces into the twisting air passages upward to the atmosphere. Water is also removed from this zone by absorption into plant roots and transpiration in the plants. The zone of aeration therefore slowly dries out between periods of rain.

In the capillary fringe, water also evaporates into the pore spaces above. However, this water is replaced by capillary action from below as fast as it is lost by evaporation. Thus, the level of the capillary fringe remains at a constant height above the water table.

The water table itself, however, gradually drops during dry periods, as the ground water slowly flows downward into streams and lakes, or directly into the oceans near seacoasts. As the water table drops, the capillary fringe drops with it.

During and after rainy periods, all these effects are reversed. Water is returned to the surface film of the zone of aeration, to the ground water, and to the capillary fringe.

Subsurface Water and the Water Cycle. From this description of what happens to water beneath the earth's surface, we can see how this water returns to the atmosphere to keep the water cycle going. Water in the zone of aeration returns to the atmosphere mainly by evapotranspiration. On the other hand, very little of the ground water returns naturally to the atmosphere until it has made its way through permeable layers to bodies of water exposed to the air.

We purposely put the word "naturally" into the last sentence in the paragraph above. Much ground water is removed today by human activity. Wells are dug down to the water table, and water is pumped out for our numerous industrial, agricultural, and human needs. Human activities have begun to have serious effects on the water table in many parts of the world. This will be one of the topics we will think about in later sections of this chapter.

SUMMARY

1. Soil particles and pore spaces near the surface are coated by a film of water that clings by the force of adhesion.
2. Water moves upward into pore spaces by capillary action.
3. The extent of capillary action increases with a decrease in the size of soil particles and pore spaces.
4. The lowest portion of a permeable surface layer is saturated with water. Water in this zone of saturation is called ground water, and the top of this zone is called the water table.
5. Above the water table is the capillary fringe in which the pores are kept filled with water by capillary action.
6. The upper portion of the surface layer is the zone of aeration, where the pores are coated with water, but also contain air.

THE WATER SUPPLY

What would you consider to be the most precious substance on earth? Gold? Diamonds? Well, even if you had all the money in the world, it would be of no use to you if you lacked one thing—water. Without water there could be no life as we know it on earth.

Our earliest records show that the quest for water has always been important. Great civilizations rose where fresh water was plentiful, as along the Nile River in Egypt. Today we continue to search for unlimited water supplies, but we are not likely to find them. If you look at Figure 12-11 on the next page, you will see that 97% of the earth's water is salt water, which we cannot use unless the salt is first removed. Only 3% of the earth's water is fresh water, and three-fourths of this exists as ice in glaciers and ice sheets. So, less than 1% of the earth's water is found as fresh surface water or ground water. From these figures you can see that although much of the surface of the earth is covered with water, only a small percentage of this is readily available to us.

In ancient times, large populations could exist only where there were large supplies of fresh water in lakes or rivers. Even today, most centers of population are found where there is enough surface water within a reasonable distance to meet a modern society's needs. Still, many people have

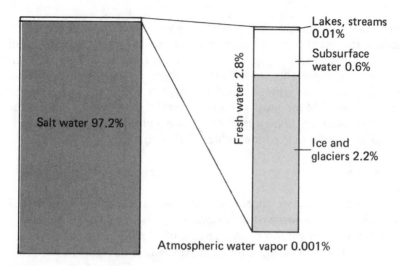

Figure 12-11. Distribution of the hydrosphere. Less than 1% of the hydrosphere is available as fresh water for plants and animals.

always managed to live where there is practically no fresh surface water. Somehow they have made use of the subsurface water stored in the ground. This is usually done by digging wells.

Gravity Wells. If you have ever dug a hole in sand on the shore of a lake or ocean, you may have seen that you don't have to go very far before the hole begins to collect water. You have dug a gravity well.

Most wells are gravity wells, which are holes that are dug or drilled into the ground until they reach the water table (see Figure 12-12). The shaft of a dug well may be lined with brick or a similar material, while in a drilled well, the shaft is a steel pipe. In both types of wells there must be holes around the bottom to allow water to seep in. The water must then be pumped up to the surface. As long as usage does not exceed the rate of infiltration of water into the well, the well will provide water. However, gravity wells depend on precipitation

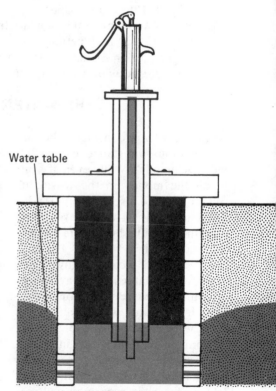

Figure 12-12. A gravity well. In a gravity well, water must be pumped or lifted to the surface.

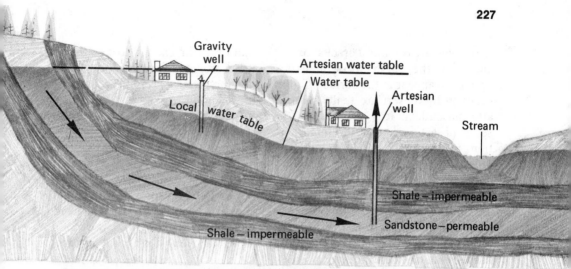

Figure 12-13. Source of water for an artesian well. An artesian well is a well that is dug through an impermeable rock layer to a permeable layer saturated with water. If the water table in the permeable layer is higher than the ground level at the well, water will flow from the well under its own pressure.

in their immediate area. So during prolonged dry periods, the level of the water table may drop, leaving the well dry.

Artesian Wells. A second type of well is the artesian well, which may or may not depend on local rainfall for its water supply. Wherever you can dig down deep enough to reach the water table, you can have a gravity well. But artesian wells can be dug only where there is a layer of permeable material sandwiched between two layers of impermeable material. Figure 12-13 shows the conditions necessary for an artesian well. The precipitation that supplies this type of well may be falling only a short distance away on the top of a nearby hill, or it may be hundreds of kilometers away in a distant mountain range.

As you can see from Figure 12-13, a typical artesian formation might consist of a layer of sandstone, which is highly permeable, sandwiched between layers of shale, which is impermeable to water. The sandstone

layer, which can hold great quantities of water, is exposed on a hilltop. It then runs underground in between the layers of shale. Precipitation on the hilltop infiltrates the sandstone layer. The water is under pressure from the weight of the water above it, just like water in a sloping pipe. When a well is dug into the sandstone layer, the water, since it is under pressure, will rise into the well, often all the way to the surface.

In many parts of the world, artesian wells are a major source of water. In some cases the artesian wells are at a great distance from the source of precipitation. This is true in the Great Plains region of the United States. Here the water comes from precipitation high in the Rocky Mountains. It fills the sandstone bed of a tremendous artesian formation that extends for hundreds of kilometers through Kansas, Nebraska, and North and South Dakota. Similar artesian formations are found in dry plains next to mountains in other parts of the world.

In some areas natural cracks, or fissures, in the earth allow artesian springs to appear at the surface. Some oases in the desert are really natural artesian outlets. It is possible that in some desert regions artesian formations far below the surface could provide life-sustaining water if only they could be tapped.

Glaciers. As we saw in Figure 12-11, three-fourths of the earth's fresh-water supply is in the form of ice, which for the most part is not used by man. There are a few cities that are near enough to use the melt water from glaciers and snow fields in the mountains. Boulder, Colorado, for example, owns a glacier in the Rocky Mountains, which supplies part of the city's water. But this is very unusual. There have been numerous schemes devised for using some of the fresh water stored as ice. It has been proposed that icebergs could be towed to locations in need of water and then melted, but so far there has been no practical test of this idea.

SUMMARY

1. Gravity wells are holes in the ground that extend down to the water table. The water must be pumped to the surface.
2. Artesian wells are found only where a layer of permeable material is sandwiched between two layers of impermeable material. Water in such artesian formations is under pressure, and will often rise to the surface without pumping.

WATER POLLUTION

Since only 3% of the earth's water is fresh water, it seems logical that we should do everything possible to preserve this most vital of all earth resources. The chemical and physical properties of water, however, present a problem that is unique to this substance. Water comes very close to being the "universal solvent". This means that most substances, natural or manufactured, will dissolve in water. When they do, they change or *pollute* the water. Even though the study of water pollution is really just beginning, we already cannot cover the information known about this rapidly-expanding subject. A few examples of water pollution problems should highlight its critical nature.

Sources of Pollution. Some water pollution may occur naturally. For example, a stream may cut its way through a deposit of sulfur compounds in the earth. The sulfur contaminates the water, and may kill fish and other forms of aquatic life. Most pollution, however, is the result of human activities.

There is a direct relationship between pollution and population. As the population has increased, pollution of the environment has increased, sometimes to the point of threatening human life.

A student of history would point out that most cities were established where they are because of the availability of water, often a river or lake. It seemed logical to dump unwanted waste into the water and let the water dissolve the sewage or simply carry it away. As the rate of dumping increased, the natural cleansing process of the water became overburdened. In an attempt to help nature, cities have built expensive sewage treatment plants and industries have spent large sums of money to treat their waste products before they enter the environment.

A special type of pollution problem, called *eutrophication*, occurs in many lakes. As the population around lakes has increased, chemicals present in fertilizers and detergents have seeped into the lakes, where they provide nourishment for certain simple green plants called *algae*. At first, the algae grow in enormous numbers, and form a thick layer on the top of the lake. Algae at the bottom of the layer cannot receive needed sunlight, and die. The process of decay of the dead plants uses up the available oxygen in the water, and all fish and other oxygen-using organisms quickly die off. With eutrophication, the whole process for keeping the lake clean breaks down.

Even groundwater can become polluted. Areas that depend on well water for their water supply must constantly test for harmful bacteria brought in by sewage. Wells near the ocean can become contaminated with salt water. If water is drawn from the well at too high a rate, the level of ground water can drop below sea level. When this happens, salty ocean water enters the water supply. This is an especially serious problem in heavily populated coastal areas, such as Long Island, New York, southern Florida, and parts of California.

Remember that we said that water is almost the "universal solvent"? This chemical property of water becomes a serious problem when we try to dispose of some of the wastes of our industrial society. The Environmental Protection Agency (EPA) estimates that 71 billion gallons (270 billion liters) of hazardous wastes are produced each year in the United States. The EPA has also listed hundreds of old chemical dumps that must be cleaned up before more damage is done to the water supply. This is not really a new problem. Recently, Parisians discovered that part of their water supply is threatened by contamination from a dump used by Napoleon's army to dispose of horse carcasses!

Radioactive wastes cause a special problem since their decay rate into harmless material may be in hundreds of thousands of years. Power plants, whether using traditional fuel or nuclear, present a problem known as *thermal pollution*. These utilities take cold water from rivers and other waterways and use it to remove waste heat. The large quantities of warmed water from the cooling towers are then returned to the waterway. The warmer water can hold less oxygen than the cooler water, and these changes in oxygen concentration and temperature can kill off fish and other organisms.

The high temperature may also stimulate the activity of *aerobic* (oxygen-using) bacteria in the water, which further depletes the oxygen supply. This may eventually lead to an increase in the number of *anaerobic* bacteria (bacteria that do not need free oxygen), and these bacteria and their waste products are themselves pollutants.

One of the most publicized environmental issues of recent years has been that of acid rain. This form of industrial pollution has evidently caused widespread damage to the northeastern United States and Canada. Similar situations have heavily damaged forests in Scandinavia and Germany.

Acid rain forms when sulfur dioxide and nitrogen oxides combine with water in the atmosphere to form sulfuric and nitric acids. The actual chemical pathways traveled by the pollutants is a subject of intense study. Clouds are now considered to be complex "chemical factories" in which the acids are produced in a series of reactions. Small variations such as in the temperature or the pressure of the cloud will greatly change the amount of acid rain and snow delivered to the land below. Other researchers are now finding that the type of soil the acid precipitation flows through must also be considered. An acidic soil will intensify the effect, while a basic soil will minimize it.

Before 1900, lakes in the northeastern United States teemed with fish, and the wildlife in the wilderness was abundant. By the 1920s, trout began to vanish from many of the lakes. Soon, many species of fish and wildlife became scarce. There were many suspected causes such as overlumbering of the forests. It wasn't until the early 1970s that scientists began to identify the cause. Airborne pollution from sulfides produced by industries in the midwest and Canada dissolved in the water vapor in the air to produce acid rain and snow. By the mid-1980s, almost 200 lakes in the Adirondacks of New York had been declared critically acidic. This means that these lakes will not sustain life because of their acid content. Almost 300 other lakes are considered endangered: on their way to becoming critically acidic.

Many agencies, governmental and private, are trying to solve the problem. One method involves 'liming' the lakes. Lime (calcium carbonate) is a *basic* substance. Bases neutralize acids. Adding lime to the lakes reduces their acidity. This is a temporary solution, however, since the lime must be added each year.

One of the major sources of the pollutants causing acid rain is the coal used by midwestern industries. Changing to another fuel would be tremendously expensive, and would have many economic side effects. However, scientists who have studied this problem feel that waiting will only make the solution more expensive. Some worry that we may already be too late.

SUMMARY

1. Pollutants are added to the hydrosphere through the activities of individuals, communities, and industrial processes.
2. Hydrospheric pollutants include dissolved and suspended materials, including organic and inorganic wastes; heat, or thermal energy, from industrial processes; radioactive substances; and abnormal concentrations of various organisms.
3. An increase in temperature or an increase in the activity of aerobic bacteria lowers the concentration of oxygen dissolved in water.

4. Acid rain is a form of industrial pollution that results when oxides of sulfur and nitrogen combine with water vapor in the atmosphere to form weak acids.

REVIEW QUESTIONS

Group A
1. What is the *water cycle?*
2. What three things can happen to precipitation?
3. Under what conditions will infiltration occur?
4. What factors determine the rate of infiltration?
5. Define *porosity.*
6. What determines the porosity of a sample?
7. Define *permeability.*
8. What factors determine the permeability of a sample?
9. How is the permeability of loose material related to pore size?
10. Under what conditions can runoff occur?
11. In what form is water present in soil near the surface?
12. How does water move upward in the soil?
13. What is the relationship between the *extent* of capillary action and the size of soil particles and pore spaces?
14. What is the *water table?*
15. What are the characteristics of the zone of aeration?
16. What is a *gravity well?*
17. What conditions are necessary for an artesian well?
18. What factors are contributing to the pollution of the hydrosphere?
19. Name the various types of pollutants found in the hydrosphere.
20. What types of industry are thought to produce the pollutants that cause acid rain?
21. Where does acid rain occur?
22. Why is acid rain an expensive problem to fix?

Group B
1. Trace the route of a water drop as it travels the complete water cycle. Show some of the "choices" that have to be made as to which part of the cycle the drop follows at various places. You may want to use a diagram to make your explanation easier.
2. a. Describe the characteristics of a soil in which there would be a high infiltration rate.
   b. Describe the characteristics of a soil in which there would be a low infiltration rate.
3. Describe the difference in the characteristics of the zone of aeration and the zone of saturation in the soil. Locate the water table and the capillary fringe in relation to the two zones. A diagram may be used to help you answer this question.
4. What are some of the problems people have in trying to provide themselves with enough water? If you know of any special problems your community is having, describe what these problems are.

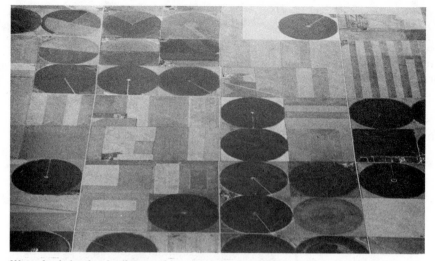

Water for irrigation is dispersed by a variety of means, including huge rotating sprinklers that create patterns when viewed from above.

CHAPTER 13
The Local Water Budget

You will know something about local water budgets and about climate if you can:

1. Analyze the various parts of the water budget.
2. Relate the water budget to patterns of change in the local environment.
3. Describe the factors that affect climate and use them to determine the climate patterns for a continental land mass.

Governments, businesses, and individuals must all keep track of the money they have available for present and future expenses. To do this, they make up a budget of expected income and outgo. They hope that they can at least make income balance outgo, or even have a surplus that can be saved for an emergency or a large purchase in the future. If funds drop too low to cover expenses, they may have to do without something, or else borrow from an outside source.

The water supply of a community or region is at least as important as its money supply. Therefore, many communities work out a local water budget that shows expected income (precipitation), outgo (evapotranspiration), and savings (soil storage of water). With such a budget, a community can plan its use of water. As we will see in this chapter, the water budget of a region is also useful in describing or classifying its climate.

THE LOCAL WATER BUDGET

In Chapter 12 you learned that when it rains, the soil retains some of the water that infiltrates the ground. Between rains, some of this stored water is used by plants and some is lost by evaporation. Thus every region has a local water cycle of income from *precipitation*, outgo through *evapotranspiration*, and variations in soil water *storage*.

A *local water budget* is a mathematical model of the water cycle for a region. It shows how the income, outgo, and storage of water vary over the course of an average year. The local water budget may show periods of water *deficit*, when the total supply is less than the total demand, and it may show periods of *surplus*, when there is more water available than can be used or stored.

During the following discussion of the factors in a water budget, keep in mind that we are talking about the natural water cycle of a region. We are not considering what people may do to alter the supply and demand picture. For example, they can dig wells and draw water from the ground water. They can pump water from a lake or a river. They can bring water in from a distant source through pipes or canals. Nature can do none of these things.

Precipitation (Income). From what has just been said, you can see that the only natural source of water for a region is the precipitation that falls on that region. Precipitation is the source of water income, much like the salary a person receives from an employer. Money income is measured in dollars. How shall we measure precipitation?

You might expect it to be measured by volume, in such units as cubic meters. But a cubic meter of water falling on 1 square meter of land is quite different from a cubic meter of water spread out over 1,000 square meters. What really counts is how much water falls on each unit of area.

The simplest way to describe precipitation per unit of area is in terms of a depth of water. If we say that the precipitation in a given region is 10 mm, we mean that the water that falls on that region could cover it everywhere to a depth of 10 mm. It makes no difference, then, whether we are thinking about a backyard garden of 100 square meters or a farm of 100,000 square meters. As far as the plants and soil are concerned, precipitation of 10 mm is the same amount of income in both cases. For the same reasons we will measure outgo and storage of water in millimeters. In the following discussion we will use P as the symbol for precipitation.

Precipitation may, of course, take several forms, such as snow, hail, or mist. In a water budget, we assume that forms other than rain are changed to their equivalent of liquid water.

Figure 13-1 on the next page shows the pattern of average annual precipitation for the continental United States. You can see that there are regions in the Northwest where precipitation during the year totals more than 1,500 mm, and other regions in the Southwest where annual precipitation is less than 250 mm. You can also see that precipitation can vary a great deal within a relatively short distance. Therefore, water budgets are gener-

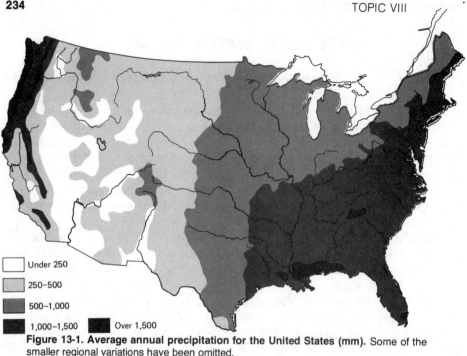

Under 250

250–500

500–1,000

1,000–1,500   **Over 1,500**

Figure 13-1. Average annual precipitation for the United States (mm). Some of the smaller regional variations have been omitted.

ally calculated for small areas, rather than for whole countries or states.

Precipitation also varies seasonally in most regions, being higher in some months than in others. Figure 13-2, for example, shows the average precipitation in Los Angeles by months. We would want a water budget for Los Angeles to tell us what happens during that dry period from May to September. A water budget is therefore usually constructed on a month-by-month basis.

Evapotranspiration (Outgo). As you already know, evaporation and transpiration (evapotranspiration) are the only means by which water passes from the surface of the earth into the atmosphere. Evapotranspiration can be compared to the amount of money an individual spends. There are two kinds of situations, both in personal money budgeting and in water budgeting. In one case, you have all the

money you need to buy whatever you want. What you spend then is the maximum amount you *want* to spend. This is your *potential* maximum. In terms of a water budget, there is also a certain maximum amount of evapo-

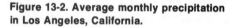

Figure 13-2. Average monthly precipitation in Los Angeles, California.

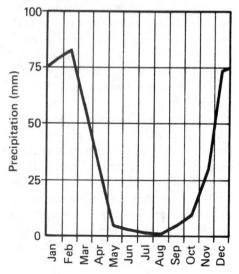

transpiration that could occur in a region. This is the amount of water that will be given up to the atmosphere by evapotranspiration if there is enough water available. We call this the *potential evapotranspiration,* and we use the symbol E_p to represent it.

Factors That Affect E_p. Like precipitation, potential evapotranspiration also varies during the year. The maximum evapotranspiration that *could* occur, assuming plenty of water on hand, is not the same in every month. Evaporation of water and transpiration from plants will vary with the amount of energy available for these processes. In the winter months, when intensity and duration of insolation are both low, there is less energy available than in the summer months. Temperatures are low, so evaporation is reduced. Plants receive less energy from sunlight, so their activities, including transpiration, are also reduced. In regions that have severe winters, surface water may be frozen and plants may be practically dormant. Under such conditions, E_p is very nearly zero.

In the summer, on the other hand, high temperatures tend to produce rapid evaporation. High energy income enables plants to grow actively and therefore transpire more rapidly. We can infer, then, that potential evapotranspiration (E_p) will vary directly with the average temperatures during the year. This relationship is shown graphically in Figure 13-3.

Actual Evapotranspiration (E_a). Most of us do not have all the money we would like to spend. We have to limit our purchases to the amount of money our budget tells us we have available. This may, of course, in-

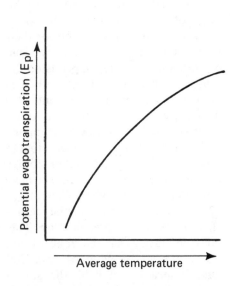

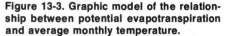

Average temperature

Figure 13-3. Graphic model of the relationship between potential evapotranspiration and average monthly temperature.

clude drawing on our savings. In any case, there is a certain amount of money we do spend. This is our *actual* outgo. Likewise, in a water budget, there is *actual* evapotranspiration (symbol, E_a). This is the amount of water actually given off to the atmosphere in a particular time interval.

There are a few important points to remember about actual evapotranspiration (E_a). In the first place, it is never greater than potential evapotranspiration at any particular time. The actual outgo (E_a) cannot be greater than the maximum that is possible (E_p). Secondly, E_a will be equal to E_p whenever that is possible, that is, whenever there is enough water available to provide that much evapotranspiration. And finally, E_a will be less than E_p whenever there isn't enough water available to meet the potential demand.

Storage (Savings). Water in the pores of the upper layer of the soil is the water that plants rely on for their needs. The amount of water that can be stored in the pores depends on the type and thickness of the soil. The amount that is available to plants also depends on the depth to which their roots go. These factors vary from one region to another, but it is possible to arrive at an average amount of storage that is fairly typical. Scientists have estimated that this average amount of *maximum* soil storage is the equivalent of 100 mm of precipitation. This does not mean that the zone of soil water extends downward only 100 mm. It means that if all the stored water in the plant root zone were collected, it would be equal to 100 mm of precipitation. The relationship of the soil storage zone to the other zones of subsurface water is shown in Figure 13-4.

Storage (symbol, St) is similar to the money that you may have in a savings account. When current income is not enough to cover current expenses, you can draw on your savings to make up the difference. When income is greater than expenses, the excess can go back into savings. Soil storage is the savings account of the water budget. When precipitation is less than potential evapotranspiration during a certain month, water in the soil can be used to make up the difference. When precipitation exceeds potential evapotranspiration, the excess can go into storage.

Surplus (Unusable Funds). There is an important difference between soil storage and a savings account. For all practical purposes, there is no limit to the amount of money that can be added to a savings account. But there *is* a limit to soil storage—the figure of 100 mm that we have already men-

Figure 13-4. The soil storage zone. Only the soil water in the zone of root growth is counted as storage. Maximum storage in this zone is estimated to be equivalent to 100 mm of water.

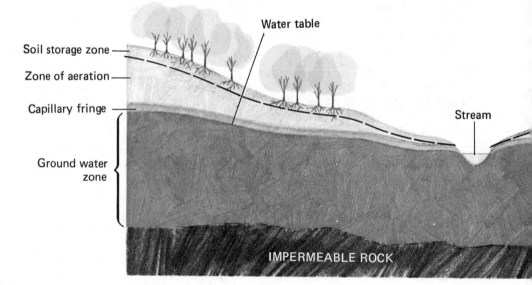

Soil storage zone

Zone of aeration

Capillary fringe

Ground water zone

Water table

Stream

IMPERMEABLE ROCK

tioned. This means that once the soil storage "account" is filled to its maximum of 100 mm, any excess must be wasted. This condition is called a *surplus*. Some of the surplus infiltrates down to the ground water zone, and drains through the ground into streams and lakes. Excess water may also run off the surface. In both cases, the surplus eventually becomes runoff.

Usage (Drawing from Savings). When precipitation (P) during a particular month is less than E_p for that month, evapotranspiration will continue at its normal rate as long as there is water in storage. This means, however, that storage is decreasing. Plants are drawing on the reserves of water in the soil just as you may draw from your savings account during a month when your income is less than your expenses. This reduction of soil storage is called *usage*.

Deficit (Shortage of Funds). Usage can continue as long as there is some storage left, but, of course, it has to stop when St becomes zero. E_a in any month cannot be greater than P + St. Therefore, if P + St is less than E_p, E_a will also be less than E_p that month. This condition is called a *deficit*. The amount of the deficit is equal to E_p − E_a. During the first month of a deficit, St drops to zero. The only source for evapotranspiration after that is the precipitation that falls. The deficit continues until P becomes greater than E_p once again.

This situation is like that of an individual whose savings are used up and whose current income is not enough to cover all the purchases he would like to make. He may borrow money to tide him over his deficit period. But if he can't or doesn't want to go into debt, he would use his income for necessities such as food, and postpone other expenses.

Nature has no way to borrow water. So in periods of water deficit, nature makes do with less. Plants are able to reduce their activities during times of deficit. In desert regions, where conditions are almost a continuous deficit, plants have developed many special traits that enable them to survive long periods without precipitation. The giant saguaro cactus, for example, can absorb enough soil water after a single brief shower, and store it in its stem, to last it for two years. Most cactus plants have no leaves, so transpiration is greatly reduced. Photosynthesis (food-making) occurs in the green stems of cactus, which have a waxy surface to limit loss of water. Sharp spines in many species discourage animals from eating the plants for their stored water.

What we have just said applies only to plants that are native to a region. They don't need man's help to survive in their natural environment. But your prize lawn will have to be watered during dry intervals, and a farmer will probably have to irrigate his crops to keep them growing. These are plants that man has brought into the region or developed for his own purposes, and they do need his help to adjust to conditions that are unnatural for them.

Recharge (Building Up Your Savings Account). Whenever P becomes greater than E_p after a period of usage or deficit, the excess goes back into storage. A period during which storage is increasing is called *recharge*. Recharge continues as long as P is

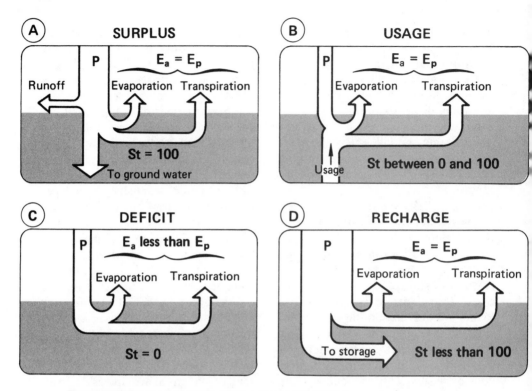

Figure 13-5. The four possible stages of a water budget.
   A. Surplus: Storage (St) is at maximum (100 mm). Precipitation (P) is greater than potential evapotranspiration (E_p). Actual evapotranspiration (E_a) equals potential evapotranspiration. Excess water runs off the surface and infiltrates to the ground water.
   B. Usage: P is less than E_p. Water is drawn from storage. E_a equals E_p, and St decreases.
   C. Deficit: P is less than E_p, and storage is zero. E_a equals P and is less than E_p.
   D. Recharge: P is greater than E_p. E_a equals E_p. Water is added to storage. St increases. There is no loss by runoff.

greater than E_p and St is less than 100 mm. Recharge is similar to building up your savings when your income exceeds your expenses.

   Summary of Water Budget Factors. Figure 13-5 illustrates the four possible conditions of a local water budget—surplus, usage, deficit, and recharge. Note particularly that only during one of the four possible conditions—that of deficit—is E_a less than E_p. The caption will help you review the ideas that have been presented in this discussion.

SUMMARY

1. Precipitation (P) is the only source of water for a local water budget.
2. Potential evapotranspiration (E_p) is the amount of water that a region is capable of giving up to the atmosphere when precipitation plus soil water is sufficient. It varies directly with insolation of the region.

3. Actual evapotranspiration (E_a) is the amount of water that is actually given up to the atmosphere during a stated period. It is never greater than E_p, but may be less than E_p.
4. The soil can store water up to a specific amount equivalent to about 100 mm of precipitation on the average.
5. Usage occurs when P is less than E_p and plants are drawing water out of storage.
6. A deficit occurs when soil storage is zero and P is less than E_p. Under these conditions, E_a is less than E_p.
7. Recharge occurs when P is greater than E_p and soil storage is less than 100 mm.
8. A surplus occurs when P is greater than E_p and soil storage is full at 100 mm. Surplus water is lost either through surface runoff or infiltration to the ground water.

SAMPLE WATER BUDGETS

Let us see how the factors we have been considering apply to an actual case. Table 13-1 is the basic data for the water budget for the region around Buffalo, New York. P is the average precipitation by months, which has been obtained from weather records collected over many years. E_p is the estimated potential evapotranspiration for the region, based on a study of average temperatures, amounts of insolation, types of plants that grow naturally in the region, and other factors. In the third row of the table, labeled P − E_p, the difference between P and E_p for each month has been obtained by simple subtraction. When P is greater than E_p, the difference is positive. When P is less than E_p, the difference is entered as a negative (minus) number. All figures are in millimeters of water.

Figure 13-6 on the next page is the complete water budget for the Buffalo region. It has been constructed from the information in Table 13-1. Let's approach it step by step.

P and E_p. As you can see, precipitation in the Buffalo area is fairly even throughout the year. This is shown on the graph in Figure 13-6 by a solid line. On the other hand, E_p varies greatly

Table 13-1. Buffalo, New York.

	J	F	M	A	M	J	J	A	S	O	N	D	Totals
P	81	72	71	68	73	69	73	74	75	78	80	81	895
E_p	0	0	0	30	72	111	135	122	84	40	15	0	609
P-E_p	81	72	71	38	1	−42	−62	−48	−9	38	65	81	

Buffalo, New York

	J	F	M	A	M	J	J	A	S	O	N	D	Totals
P	81	72	71	68	73	69	73	74	75	78	80	81	895
E_p	0	0	0	30	72	111	135	122	84	40	15	0	609
$P-E_p$	81	72	71	38	1	−42	−62	−48	−9	38	65	81	
ΔSt	0	0	0	0	0	−42	−58	0	0	38	62	0	
St	100	100	100	100	100	58	0	0	0	38	100	100	
E_a	0	0	0	30	72	111	131	74	75	40	15	0	548
D	0	0	0	0	0	0	4	48	9	0	0	0	61
S	81	72	71	38	1	0	0	0	0	0	3	81	347

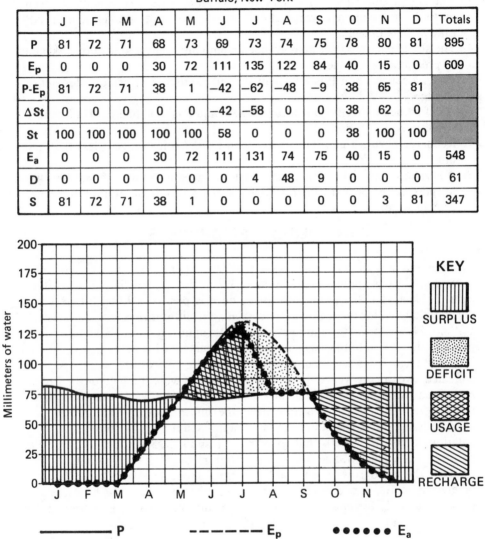

Figure 13-6. The complete water budget for Buffalo, New York.

through the year. During the winter months, it is practically zero. All plant life is dormant, and temperatures are generally so low that almost no evaporation occurs. During the summer months, E_p rises to a peak as temperatures rise and plants become most active. E_p is shown on the graph by a broken line.

The Winter Surplus Months. Look now at $P - E_p$ for October and November. It is 38 mm in October and 65 mm in November. Remember that this is excess moisture that could go into storage. But $38 + 65$ is more than 100. This tells us that certainly by

November soil storage is filled. And it remains filled for many months thereafter. So we see in Figure 13-6 that St (the fifth row down) is 100 at the start of the calendar year in January. The row headed Δ St tells us the change in storage that month. Since St cannot increase beyond 100, Δ St is zero in January.

All the positive amounts of P − E$_p$ that we see in the table while St is 100 are surplus. In Buffalo this surplus in the winter months stays mainly on the surface as snow and ice. It doesn't run off or infiltrate as it might in a warmer region. However, it does eventually do this in the spring, when the snow and ice melt. As far as the water budget is concerned, it makes no difference whether the surplus runs off as it occurs, or whether it accumulates as snow and ice and runs off later. It is surplus in any case. The amounts of surplus are entered in the bottom row of the table in Figure 13-6.

E$_p$ is zero in January, February, and March, so E$_a$ is also zero. This is entered in the row labeled E$_a$. There is, of course, no deficit, so we see zeros in the row labeled D (for deficit).

The Spring Months of Continued Surplus. With the coming of spring, plants become active. Surface ice and snow melt to water. Both evaporation and transpiration begin to occur in increasing amounts. E$_p$ is 30 in April and 72 in May. But there is plenty of water to meet this demand, and E$_a$ keeps up with E$_p$. In fact, there is still a surplus. We see these figures for April and May in the table.

The Summer Months of Usage and Deficit. In June the demand for moisture (E$_p$) exceeds the income (P) for the first time. However, there is enough water in storage to make up the difference. So we see a usage amount (−42) in the Δ St row, and we see the storage drop by that amount to 58. E$_a$ can still equal E$_p$, but there is no surplus. In July E$_p$ is again greater than P, this time by 62 mm. But there was only 58 mm in storage at the start of this month. Adding P of 73 and St of 58 gives us only 131. This, then, is the figure for E$_a$. There is a deficit of 4 mm. The deficits continue through August and September. In these months storage is zero and E$_a$ simply equals P.

The Fall Months of Recharge. By October evaporation is decreasing because of lower temperatures, and transpiration is decreasing because the growing season is ending. Once again, P becomes greater than E$_p$, and there is excess water that can go into storage. In October 38 mm is available for storage. There is still no surplus, however. But in November the storage maximum of 100 mm is reached, and the period of winter surplus begins, completing the yearly cycle.

Annual Summary. Note the totals in the last column of the table in Figure 13-6. Even though there is a short deficit period in this water budget, the annual income of precipitation (895 mm) is well above the total demand of 609 mm. The year as a whole has a surplus of 347 mm of water. In short, the Buffalo region has more than enough precipitation for the natural needs of its vegetation. We will see later what this means in terms of describing the climate of this region.

The Water Budget Graph. To show this cycle on the graph in Figure 13-6, we add the curve for E$_a$, using a series

	J	F	M	A	M	J	J	A	S	O	N	D	Totals
P	10	11	8	7	8	18	40	41	33	17	13	12	218
E_p	11	18	37	75	117	163	171	152	111	62	24	10	951
$P-E_p$	−1	−7	−29	−68	−109	−145	−131	−111	−78	−45	−11	2	
Δ St	−1	−1	0	0	0	0	0	0	0	0	0	2	
St	1	0	0	0	0	0	0	0	0	0	0	2	
E_a	11	12	8	7	8	18	40	41	33	17	13	10	218
D	−	6	29	68	109	145	131	111	78	45	11	−	733
S	−	−	−	−	−	−	−	−	−	−	−	−	−

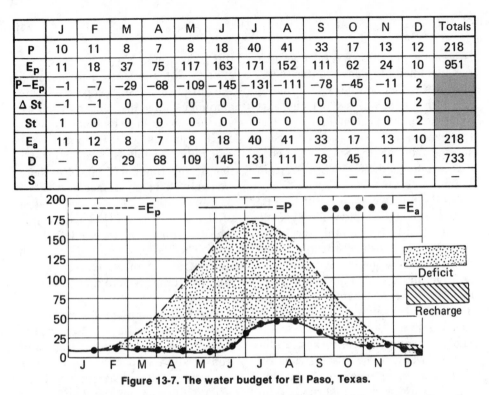

Figure 13-7. The water budget for El Paso, Texas.

of dots. The E_a curve matches the E_p curve except during the deficit period. In this period, the E_a curve drops down and follows the P curve. By using different types of shading, we can show the periods of surplus, usage, deficit, and recharge.

Water Budget for a Dry Region. As an interesting contrast, look at the water budget for the El Paso region in Figure 13-7. Here is a situation in which an almost continuous deficit exists through the year. Only in the single month of December does P exceed E_p, and then only by 2 mm. Most of the time E_p is far greater than the water available. What this means is that there is enough energy (insolation) to support much more abundant plant growth than occurs naturally. This is borne out by the fact that when water is brought in by irrigation, the land will produce a fine growth of crops. The "potential" is there, but the actual moisture supply cannot meet that potential demand.

This is clearly a climate quite different from that of Buffalo. We will have more to say about this later on.

SUMMARY

1. A local water budget can be constructed from monthly data for precipitation and potential evapotranspiration.
2. Monthly changes in soil storage and values of actual evapotranspiration can be calculated from the basic data.
3. Periods of surplus, usage, deficit, and recharge can be determined from the calculations and shown graphically.

STREAMS AND THE WATER BUDGET

In discussing periods of surplus in the water budget we mentioned that some of the surplus water may run off over the surface, while the rest of it infiltrates down to the ground water. Recall that ordinarily the pores in the storage zone near the surface of the soil are not filled with water, even at maximum storage capacity. Stored soil water is only a film on the walls of the pore spaces. During a heavy rain, these pores may be temporarily filled. Surplus will then largely run off the surface. But after the rain, surplus water in the pores will also drain away and join the ground water.

Streams. What happens to surface runoff during heavy rains? Some may gradually infiltrate the soil in less saturated areas. The rest runs downhill into the lowest channels in the local contours, forming little streams. Small streams join to form larger streams, which join other streams, eventually forming the largest streams, usually called rivers, which empty into the oceans.

There is no generally accepted rule for deciding when a stream is big enough to be called a river. The solution to this problem is to avoid the word "river." We will use the word "stream" to mean any natural channel on the earth's surface that carries water downhill.

If the bed of a stream is not below the water table, water will steadily infiltrate the stream bed and drain away. A stream of this kind will be only temporary. Between periods of rain, it will tend to become a trickle and then dry up. However, most streams flow over a saturated bed.

That is, the bed is actually below the water table of the surrounding land, as shown in Figure 13-4 on page 236. Such a stream will flow continuously, even during periods of little rainfall. The stream will be fed not only by surface runoff, but also by flow from the ground water through the pores of the stream bed. This flow from the ground water is very slow, but it occurs continuously all along the stream bed. So it is enough to keep the stream well supplied with water. Water that enters a stream from the ground water is called the *base flow* of the stream.

Stream Discharge. The discharge of a stream is the volume of water that passes a point in the stream during a given amount of time. It is the rate of flow of the stream, not in terms of velocity, but in terms of amount of water. A broad river, slowly and majestically making its way to the sea, may have an enormous discharge. A racing mountain stream is likely to have a relatively small discharge.

The U.S. Geological Survey measures, or *gauges,* the discharge of many streams. Automatic instruments make a continuous record of the discharge, which may then be studied for information that is related to the local water budget.

The discharge of a stream will usually vary from day to day, depending on recent precipitation. Figure 13-8 on the next page shows the record of stream discharge for a stream during a period of about 36 hours, and a record of local rainfall during the same period. As the graph shows, the base flow of this stream is normally around 0.5 cubic meters per second (m³/sec).

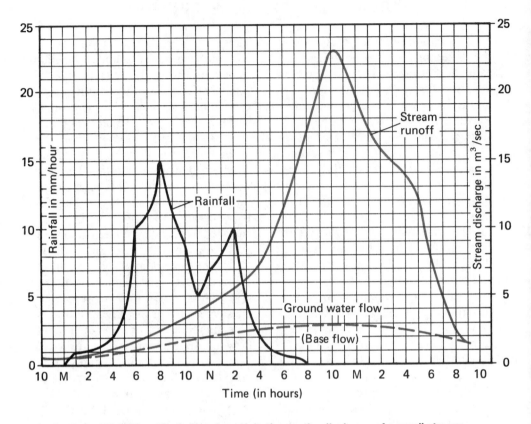

Figure 13-8. The effect of local precipitation on the discharge of a small stream.

This is the discharge during dry intervals. Note what happened to the discharge after the rain started. It reached a peak of about 23 m³/sec. Some of this increase came from an increase in the base flow. This was water that infiltrated to the water table and entered the stream from the ground. Most of the increase, though, was apparently due to runoff from the surface. As you can see, it took about 15 hours for these two factors to have their maximum effect on the discharge.

The discharge of a stream may also vary seasonally through the year. Figure 13-9 shows the discharge record for a stream for a typical year. The water budget for the region is also shown for comparison. As you might expect, the stream discharge is least during periods of usage and deficit, and greatest during periods of surplus. Note, however, that the stream does not stop flowing even at the height of the deficit. It continues to be supplied from the ground water.

The Water Table and the Water Budget. The water table is the level of the ground water, or the level to which the permeable surface layer of rock and soil is saturated. A lake or a stream is in most cases simply a place where the water table comes up above

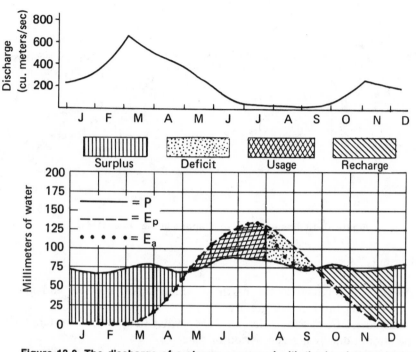

Figure 13-9. The discharge of a stream compared with the local water budget.
Note that although the precipitation is fairly constant through the year, the stream discharge is large during periods of surplus, when there is much runoff, and small during periods of usage and deficit. The peak in March is due to the melting of accumulated snow and ice.

the surface of the land. As explained in Chapter 12, the water table generally follows the ups and downs of the surface, but at some depth below it. Under the action of gravity, the ground water slowly flows through underground pores and enters streams, lakes, and oceans. This steady downhill flow of ground water tends to lower the water table. But infiltration of water from precipitation tends to raise it.

During periods of little precipitation, the water table tends to drop. During periods of heavy precipitation, it tends to rise. The change in the level of the water table over the course of a year is usually not very great. However, the effect may be quite noticeable where the water table is normally above the land surface (See Figure 13-10 on the next page). A stream during the deficit months may be, say, 50 cm deep. With the heavy runoff of surplus during a spring thaw, the stream may rise to a height of 300 cm (3 m). Its depth has increased six times! But the actual change is only 2.5 m. In other words, the water table at the stream has risen 2.5 m.

A change of 2.5 m may make a big difference in the shoreline of a pond. A drop of this amount may cause a marshy area to become quite dry. But except along the margins of streams and lakes, the ordinary changes in the water table in the course of a year have only minor effects.

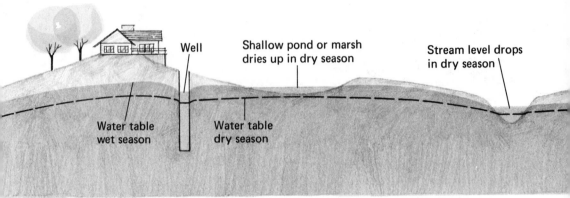

Figure 13-10. Some effects of changes in the water table.

SUMMARY

1. A stream is a channel in the earth in which runoff collects and moves downhill under the force of gravity.
2. The discharge of a stream is the volume of water that passes a certain point in the stream during a given period of time.
3. The discharge of a local stream varies with the amount of runoff from the surrounding area.
4. Streams are fed by ground water and by surface runoff.
5. Stream discharge during dry periods is maintained by the use of ground water.

CLIMATE

When we talk about climate, we are referring to the average weather conditions in a region over a period of many years. Which conditions would you consider the most important in describing climate? Think about the various types of climates that you have heard about or experienced—hot, dry deserts; hot and steaming rain forests; cold, snowy polar climates. In each, the two conditions used to describe climate are temperature and moisture.

Since temperature and moisture are the two most important factors in de-scribing climate, most systems of climate classification begin by breaking down the earth's surface into zones according to temperature patterns and moisture patterns.

Temperature Patterns and Climate. To describe the temperature characteristics of a region, you must know the *average* monthly and yearly temperatures. Another useful temperature characteristic is the yearly temperature *range*. This is the difference between the warmest average monthly temperature and the coldest average monthly temperature.

We know that average temperatures are highest near the equator and become lower as latitudes increase. We can therefore begin to classify climates by dividing the earth into temperature zones by latitude. One common system of doing this is shown in Figure 13-11.

In Figure 13-11, the boundary of the cold zones around the poles has been set by places where the average temperature of the warmest month is 10°C. The line through these places is the 10°C *isotherm* for the warmest month (usually July in the Northern Hemisphere and January in the Southern Hemisphere). Average monthly temperatures along this isotherm are never higher than 10°C. At higher latitudes, average temperatures are even colder. These regions have *polar climates,* in which there is essentially no summer.

The boundary of the *tropical climate zone* around the equator has been set by temperatures of the coldest month. The 18°C isotherm for the coldest month (January north of the equator, July south of the equator) has been selected. Average monthly temperatures inside this zone are never lower than 18°C. Places with a tropical climate have no winter.

The zones between the polar zones and the tropical zone have *mid-latitude climates,* in which there is generally a definite winter and summer.

In drawing the isotherms that are the boundaries of the climate zones in Figure 13-11, the effects of elevation have not been included. The map shows the temperature pattern we would find if all the land areas had elevations near sea level. Actually, there are places within the tropical

Figure 13-11. Latitudinal climate belts of the world. In the tropical climate zone, the average monthly temperatures at sea level never drop below 18°C. In the polar climate zones, the average monthly temperatures never rise above 10°C. Effects of altitude have been omitted.

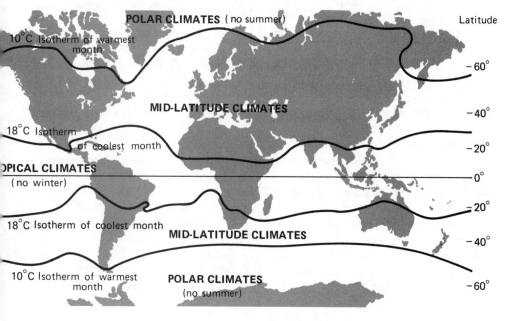

zone that have mid-latitude temperatures, or even polar temperatures, because of their high elevations.

Moisture Patterns and Climate. A classification of climate based on temperature alone gives only half the picture. It may be helpful to know that a certain area has a tropical climate—warm all year long. But it would be just as important to know that it is a desert or that it is a rain forest. To get a truly useful description of any climate, we must include information about moisture.

When we try to classify climates according to moisture conditions, we need to consider the water budget of the region. The water budget tells us not only how much precipitation the region receives, but also how this compares with the natural demand for water—the potential evapotranspiration. Two regions may have the same amount of annual precipitation, say, 500 mm. But one may have tropical temperatures, with a potential evapotranspiration of 1,000 mm. This area would be considered to have a dry climate—less rainfall than it could use. The other area may have cold climate, with a potential evapotranspiration of only 250 mm. This area, with the same precipitation as the other, would have a wet climate—more water than it can use.

To describe the moisture side of climate, then, we should compare P with E_p for the region. One way to do this is to express the comparison as a ratio (P/E_p). When potential evapotranspiration is greater than yearly precipitation, this ratio is less than 1. When precipitation is greater than evapotranspiration, the ratio is greater than 1. Regions in which P/E_p ratio is much less than 1 are said to have an *arid* climate. Where the P/E_p ratio is more than 1, the climate is called *humid*. Intermediate climates are described as *semiarid* or *subhumid*. Table 13-2 shows one system for classifying climates according to P/E_p ratios.

Table 13-2. Classifying climate types.

P/E_p	Climate type
Less than 0.4	Arid
0.4 − 0.8	Semiarid
0.8 − 1.2	Subhumid
Greater than 1.2	Humid

Let's consider two examples using this system.

Example 1: Reno, Nevada

P = 193 E_p = 628

P/E_p = 193/628 = 0.3

Climate type: Arid

Example 2: New Brunswick, N.J.

P = 1183 E_p = 693

P/E_p = 1183/693 = 1.7

Climate type: Humid

As we have already noted, a region need not have a great deal of precipitation to be classified as humid. The yearly precipitation rate could be low, but if E_p is even lower, the climate would still be humid. These points are illustrated by the simplified water budget graphs in Figure 13-12.

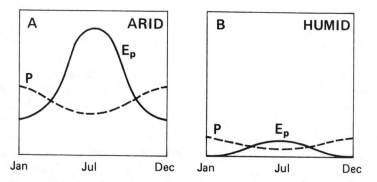

Figure 13-12. Example of the relationship between precipitation and potential evapotranspiration in an arid and a humid climate. Graph *A* shows the relationship between P and E_p for a region in which there is moderate rainfall but high values of E_p. Since there is a net moisture deficit for the year, the region has an arid climate. Some regions around 30° latitudes have climates of this type. Graph *B* represents a climate in which there is little precipitation, but even smaller values of E_p. Since there is a moisture surplus for the year, the climate is humid. Polar regions have climates of this type.

SUMMARY

1. Climatic regions can be described in terms of average monthly temperatures.
2. Climatic regions can be described in terms of the relationship between precipitation and potential evapotranspiration—for example, as the ratio P/E_p.

FACTORS AFFECTING CLIMATE PATTERNS

The climate of a region is determined by a number of different factors, the most important of which is latitude.

Latitude. In Chapter 9 we learned that the intensity and duration of insolation received at the earth's surface varies with latitude. We also learned that temperature depends on duration and intensity of insolation. Latitude, the distance north or south of the equator, is the most important factor in determining the average monthly and yearly temperatures, as well as the yearly temperature range of a location.

At low latitudes, the angle of insolation is high throughout the year. Duration of insolation is about 12 hours a day all year long. Because the inten-

sity of insolation is high all year, and the duration of insolation is about the same throughout the year, the average yearly temperature is high and there is very little variation in temperature. So, at low latitudes, there is relatively constant high temperature all year long, and the annual temperature range is very narrow.

In mid-latitudes, the angle of insolation is quite high during the summer, so the intensity of insolation is high. The duration of insolation during the summer is 15 to 16 hours a day. So, at these latitudes the summer is generally quite warm. During the winter, the angle of insolation is low, so intensity of insolation is low. Duration of insolation is only 8 to 9 hours a day. Thus winter temperatures are low. At mid-latitudes, the average yearly temperature is much lower than around the equator, and the annual temperature range is fairly large.

At high latitudes, average temperatures are very low, because even in summer the angle of insolation is never large, and during the winter insolation may be zero for months at a time. The temperature range is also very great. During the long winter period with little or no insolation, temperatures drop steadily to extremely low readings. During the summer, when the sun shines continuously, temperatures rise steadily and become rather moderate.

If you look back at Figure 13-11 (page 247), you can see that the isotherms that determine the climate zones are roughly related to latitude. But you can see that temperature must be affected by other factors. Otherwise, the isotherms would be straight lines.

Elevation. We know from Chapter 11 (page 202) that as air rises, it expands and cools. So, as altitude increases, temperature decreases. The higher you go, the cooler it gets. Air temperature changes with altitude at a rate of 10°C/km. So increasing altitude, or elevation, modifies the climate pattern in the same way as increasing latitude. There are mountains located on or near the equator that have snow-covered tops all year long.

Altitude also affects precipitation patterns. Air temperature and saturation vapor pressure decrease with increasing altitude. Therefore, as air rises, it approaches the dew-point temperature (see Figure 11-18, page 207). So, areas at higher elevations generally receive more precipitation than nearby areas at lower elevations.

Large Bodies of Water. Figure 13-13 shows average monthly temperatures for the West Coast city of Eureka,

Figure 13-13. Average monthly temperatures for a coastal city (Eureka) and a mid-continent city (Omaha), both at 41° north latitude.

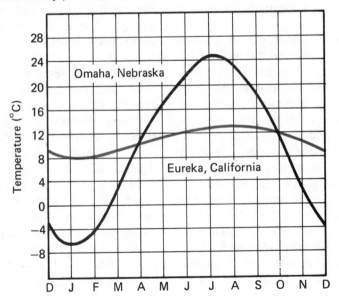

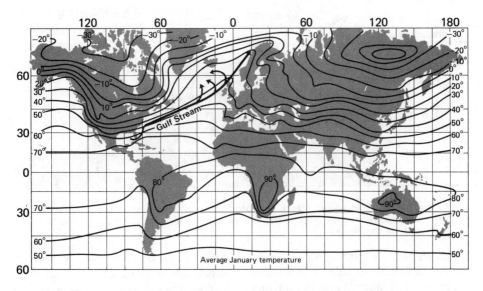

Figure 13-14. Average temperatures for January.

California, and the mid-continent city of Omaha, Nebraska, both of which are at about 41° north latitude. One reason for the difference between these graphs is that climate patterns are modified by the presence of large bodies of water, such as oceans or large lakes. We know from Chapter 9 (page 148) that bodies of water heat up and cool off more slowly than land areas. This modifies the climate pattern of shore areas so that they have warmer winters and cooler summers than inland areas at the same latitude. Such climates are called *marine climates*. Inland areas, which have cooler winters and warmer summers than shore areas, are said to have *continental climates*. Because of the moderating effects of large bodies of water, marine climates show a narrower annual temperature range than continental climates.

Ocean Currents. Study the pattern of the isotherms on the map in Figure 13-14. Notice how much warmer it is in Great Britain and Scandinavia than in other regions at the same latitude. Compare the pattern of the isotherms with the flow of the Gulf Stream as shown on the map. The Gulf Stream is a current of water that is several degrees warmer than the surrounding waters of the Atlantic Ocean. The climates of many coastal areas are modified by ocean currents. Some of these currents, like the Gulf Stream, flow away from the equator to higher latitudes; they raise the average temperatures of coasts and islands they pass near. Others are cold currents flowing from higher to lower latitudes; they have the opposite effect on latitudinal climate patterns.

Mountains. Climate patterns are affected by mountains, which act as barriers to prevailing winds. Figure 13-15 on the next page shows the *orographic effect*—the effect of mountains on climate. The side of the

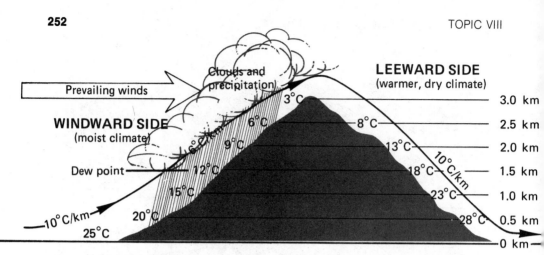

Figure 13-15. Orographic effect. The orographic effect occurs where mountains intersect moist winds. Compare the temperatures at the same altitude on the two sides of the mountain.

mountain hit by prevailing winds is called the *windward side* — in the diagram, the left side. When the air hits the windward side of the mountain, it is forced to rise. As it rises, it undergoes adiabatic cooling (see Figures 11-14 and 11-18, pages 203 and 207). If the air cools to the dew-point temperature, condensation occurs. Clouds form, and precipitation may occur. So the windward side of the mountain will be cool and humid.

The opposite side of the mountain is called the *leeward* side. On this side the air is descending, and as it descends, it undergoes adiabatic warming. So, the leeward side of the mountain will be warmer than the windward side. Also, most of the moisture will have been lost from the air on the windward side, so the leeward side will tend to be arid.

Planetary Wind Belts and Climate Patterns. In Chapter 11 (page 199) we saw the general pattern of circulation of the atmosphere. This pattern produces a belt of low pressure around the equator and belts of high pressure at latitudes around 30°N and 30°S,

with zones of prevailing winds on either side of these pressure belts.

The planentary circulation of the atmosphere affects the general climate pattern at various latitudes, as shown in Figure 13-16. The rising, low-pressure currents near the equator result in much precipitation, so that the climate near the equator tends to be not only hot, but also very humid. In the high-pressure zone of descending air around 30° latitudes, the air is quite dry. This results in a belt of warm, arid climates at these latitudes. At the higher latitudes the climate is generally humid, with temperatures becoming colder as latitude increases. On a continent these basic climates would be modified by distance from the coast, with temperature ranges greater in the interior than along the ocean margins.

This basic latitudinal climate pattern is further modified by continental land masses because of the tendency of land to heat up and cool off to a greater extent than water. As a result, large-scale convection currents between the land and the water disturb

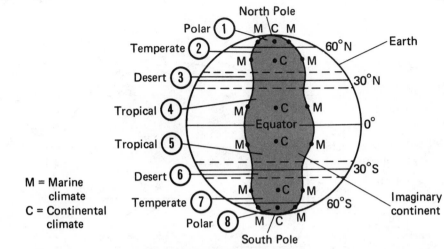

CLIMATE TYPE			
Polar	Temperate	Desert	Tropical
Cold, humid, with large temperature variation	Moderate temperatures, humid, with moderate temperature variation	Hot, arid, with moderate temp. variation	Hot, humid, with little temperature variation
1,8	2,7	3,6	4,5
Zones			

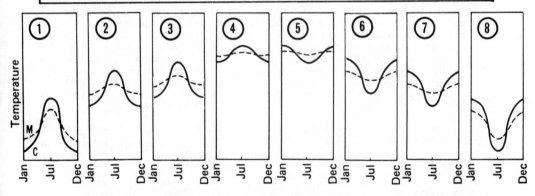

Figure 13-16. Basic latitudinal climate pattern on an imaginary continent. The arid belts around 30° latitudes are the result of descending air in the atmospheric circulation at those latitudes. The modification of this basic pattern by prevailing winds and distance from oceans is illustrated in Figure 13-17.

the normal pattern of the planetary winds. Figure 13-17 on the next page shows how the latitudinal climate pattern is modified by a large land mass. Note that as you move eastward across the continent, the arid belt that is expected around 30° latitudes shifts to higher latitudes and then is cut off, while the humid climate zone is extended to lower latitudes in the eastern portions of the continent. These effects are quite noticeable in the de-

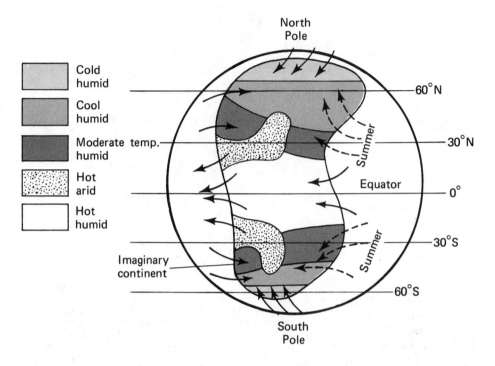

Figure 13-17. Modification of basic climate pattern by prevailing winds. Note that the arid belts around 30° latitudes do not extend across the eastern regions of the continent. One reason for this is that heating of the landmass during the summer produces convection currents that draw moist air over the land from the oceans on the east, thus making the climate more humid. Note also that the central regions of the continent in the mid-latitudes (40° to 50°) are arid. The reason for this is that the westerly winds at those latitudes have lost most of their moisture as precipitation over the western regions of the continent; the high summer temperatures in the central regions also result in lower relative humidity and less chance of precipitation.

sert climate of the southwestern United States and the humid climate of the southeastern states. Re-member, however, that local climate is also affected by other factors, such as mountains.

SUMMARY

1. Latitude affects temperature patterns.
2. Elevation influences both temperature and moisture patterns.
3. Large bodies of water modify the latitudinal climate patterns of their shoreline areas.
4. Ocean currents modify the coastal climate patterns.
5. Mountains act as barriers to atmospheric circulation and so modify the latitudinal climate pattern.
6. Planetary wind and pressure belts affect moisture and temperature patterns.

REVIEW QUESTIONS

Group A   1. What is the only source of water for a local water budget?
2. What is meant by the term *potential evapotranspiration?* How is potential evapotranspiration related to insolation?
3. What is meant by *actual evapotranspiration?*
4. What is the maximum amount of water that can be stored in average soil?
5. Under what conditions does usage occur?
6. Under what conditions does a deficit occur? How does E_a compare with E_p under deficit conditions?
7. Under what conditions does recharge occur?
8. Under what conditions is there a surplus? What happens to the surplus water?
9. What data do you need to construct a local water budget?
10. What is a stream?
11. What is meant by the *discharge* of a stream?
12. What factor affects the discharge of a local stream?
13. From what sources do streams receive water?
14. How is stream discharge maintained during dry periods?
15. In what terms are climatic regions described?
16. What factors affect temperature and/or moisture patterns?
17. What factors modify latitudinal climate patterns?
18. What factor modifies coastal climate patterns?

Group B   1. a. Describe the conditions that exist in a "normal" (humid) climate during the four stages of a water budget. Explain how E_a relates to E_p in each stage.
   b. Describe how the conditions that exist in a dry, desert-like climate affect the water budget in that area.
2. Explain what changes would be observed in (a) a small pond, (b) a small stream, and (c) a very large river, as the water budget went through the four stages of a normal climate.
3. a. The continental United States is regarded as a mid-latitude climate, and yet Reno, Nevada, and New Brunswick, New Jersey, have very different climates. Explain how a difference like this can occur. (See page 248.)
   b. Are there any special local conditions that affect your climate and modify it from that of other locations near you?

REVIEW EXERCISES

1. Determine the source of the water supply for your home. Do you have your own supply, such as a well? Are you supplied by your city or town? If so, what is their source of supply?
2. It is estimated that in the United States, each person uses about 265 l of water per day for personal use. Estimate how much water you use daily. You may have to use a reference source, such as an encyclopedia, to get an idea of how much water is used in certain activities. For example, a bath takes from 115 to 150 l of water.

3. Samples of three different soils were put into glass columns, and the ends of the columns were covered with cloth. The columns were then turned upside down and lowered into a container of water. The height to which the water rose in each column was then measured over a period of time. The results are shown in the graph below. Using the information provided, answer the following questions.
   a. In which soil is the capillary migration the greatest? What soil characteristic affects capillary migration?
   b. Which of the three soils will be the most permeable?
   c. Which of the three soils will have the highest rate of infiltration?
   d. Which of the three soils will have the highest porosity? Which one will have the lowest porosity?
   e. Which of the three soils will be the best for growing crops?

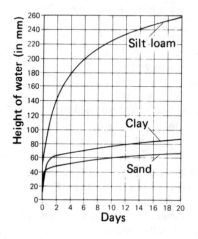
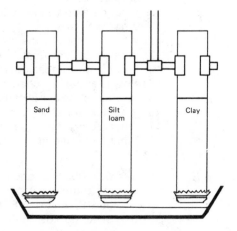

4. To answer the following questions, study the water budget below.
   a. During which months is the available energy for this area the greatest?
   b. During which months did recharge take place?
   c. During which month would the amount of water in the streams of this area be the greatest?
   d. What is the total precipitation for the year?
   e. Why was the potential evapotranspiration of this area approximately 0 mm during January?

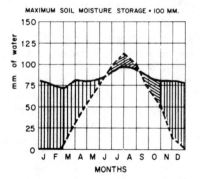

5. The hydrographs below are from two streams in the area of Buffalo, New York, during one year. The Niagara River is a fairly large river, while the Scajaquada Creek is a small stream. Using information from the hydrographs and from the water budget for Buffalo (page 240), answer the following questions.
   a. Which stream has the more irregular flow? What causes this?
   b. Did the Scajaquada Creek run dry during this particular year?
   c. There is an increase in flow in both streams in early December. Is this to be expected from the information given in the water budget, or was it an unusual occurrence during the year the hydrographs were made?

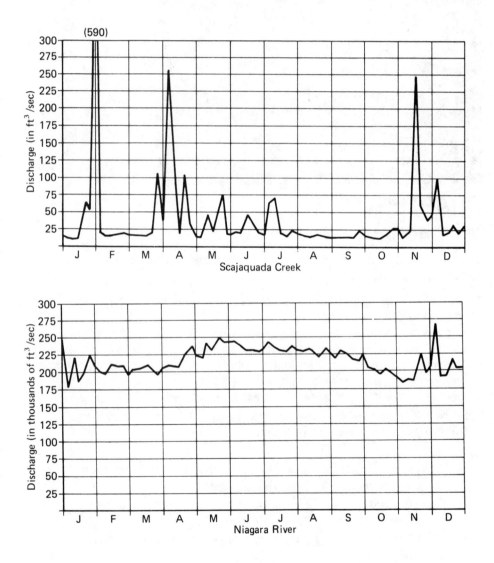

TOPIC IX
THE EROSIONAL PROCESS

These tombstones have been weathered by long exposure to the elements.

CHAPTER 14
Weathering

You will know something about the process of weathering and the factors that affect it if you can:

1. Define weathering in terms of an interaction between the lithosphere, atmosphere, and hydrosphere.
2. Explain the process of physical weathering and give some examples of its effects under different conditions.
3. Explain the process of chemical weathering and give some examples of its effects under different conditions.
4. Identify factors that affect the rate at which weathering occurs.
5. Show the relationship between the weathering process and the soil horizons that develop in a particular area.

Perhaps the most important idea that repeats itself throughout our study of the earth is that we live in an ever-changing world. Even the solid rock of the lithosphere is constantly changing, crumbling, and wearing away. In some ways these tombstones are a model of what is happening wherever the earth's crust is exposed to the air.

WEATHERING

Have you ever wandered through a cemetery, looking at the names and dates on the tombstones? If you have, you probably observed that many of the stones appeared to be "weather-beaten" and worn. Some may have been so badly worn that you could hardly read the lettering on them.

Wherever we observe rocks that have been exposed to the weather for long periods of time, we find evidence that their surface has been changed. The processes that produce changes in the surface of rocks exposed to the atmosphere are called *weathering*.

If weathering were merely the result of exposure to air, we would expect its effects to become more noticeable as time goes by. When we examine many tombstones, we find that this is usually the case. The older ones do seem to be more weathered than the younger ones. However, look at the picture on the opposite page. The stone on the left is cracked and chipped. The one on the right is in very good condition; even the delicate carving at the top of the stone is well preserved. The date on the badly weathered stone is 1844. But the date on the other is even earlier—1835. Thus we see evidence that time is not the only factor that affects the amount of weathering. In this case we can see that the two stones appear to be made of different materials. Apparently, the material a stone is made of may affect the rate at which it weathers.

A Weathering "Laboratory." What are some other factors that may affect weathering? Like most earth processes, weathering occurs very slowly. It is almost impossible to set up an experiment to observe and measure its effects. It might take more than a lifetime to obtain any useful results. A large, old cemetery, however, can be thought of as a "laboratory" in which a weathering experiment has been going on for a long time—in some cases for hundreds of years. By making observations in this laboratory today, we may be able to make inferences about changes that occurred in the past.

One of the authors of this book did conduct such an investigation in cemeteries in Connecticut. His method was to measure the present depth of the figure "1" in many of the tombstones, and compare it with the estimated average depth of the original carvings. He could thus use the "loss of depth" as a measure of the amount of weathering that had occurred since the stones had been put in place.

The investigator measured only tombstones made of a particular type of sandstone. By eliminating the effects of differing materials, he was able to focus his attention on the effects of other factors. One of the factors he considered was the direction in which the stones faced. Data was recorded for stones facing north, east, south, and west. To determine rates of weathering, measurements were made on stones that had been put in place during three different periods: 1810-1820; 1860-1870; and 1895-1905.

The graph in Figure 14-1 shows the results of this investigation. Two inferences may be drawn from the data: (1) the direction in which the stone faces is a significant factor in the rate

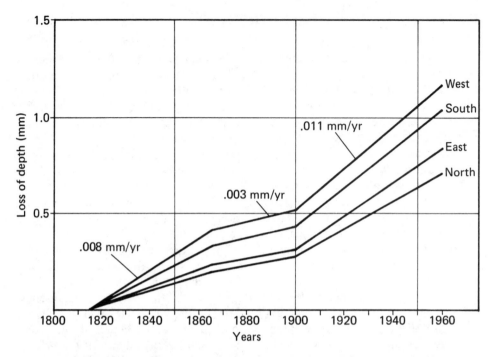

Figure 14-1. **Weathering of tombstones in Connecticut.** This investigation showed that the tombstones facing west underwent the most weathering, while those facing north underwent the least weathering.

of weathering, with the west-facing stones showing the most weathering and the north-facing stones the least; (2) the rate of weathering was not constant over the 150-year period investigated; the rate appears to have decreased in the last half of the nineteenth century, and then increased again in the twentieth century.

This was a single investigation made in a single location. Similar investigations made elsewhere might very well produce different results. Our purpose in reporting this study is only to show how an earth scientist is able to draw inferences about processes that cannot be studied directly. Most of the modern theories of earth changes have been arrived at by similar methods.

The Weathering Process. The process we have been talking about is called "weathering" for good reasons. Weathering is basically the effects of the *weather* on the earth's crust. What is weather? As we saw in Chapter 10, weather is the condition of the atmosphere at a particular time and place. One of the important factors in weather is the presence of water in the air, either in the form of water vapor or in the form of precipitation. In other words, weather involves both the atmosphere and the hydrosphere. Weathering can thus be described as the combined effect of the atmosphere and the hydrosphere on the lithosphere.

The changes that occur in rock during weathering result in a breakdown of the material of the rock. This breakdown may be *physical;* in this case, the rock is simply cracked or broken into smaller pieces. Or the breakdown may be *chemical;* in this case, the substances in the rock are changed to different ones, usually with a simpler chemical composition. Chemical changes, however, usually produce physical changes as well. So weathering is very often a combination of both physical and chemical breakdown. In the following sections we will discuss the various kinds of weathering and the factors involved in each.

SUMMARY

1. Weathering occurs when rocks are exposed to the atmosphere.
2. Weathering is an interaction between the lithosphere and the atmosphere and hydrosphere.
3. The weathering process results in physical and/or chemical breakdown of the rock material.

PHYSICAL WEATHERING

Any process that causes a rock to crack or break into pieces is called *physical weathering.* In this section we will consider three types of physical weathering: the effects of freezing and thawing of water, called *frost action;* the effects of the growth of plants on rocks; and the cracking that may result when pressure on a large mass of rock is reduced.

Frost Action. As you may recall from Chapter 2, when a material is heated, it usually expands, and when cooled, it usually contracts. Furthermore, the extent to which different materials expand and contract under the same temperature change varies a great deal. You might expect, then, that rocks (and tombstones) at or near the earth's surface would break up from the effects of expansion and contraction caused by temperature change alone. This does not seem to be the case. Laboratory experiments have been conducted in which rocks have been exposed to the equivalent of hundreds of years of heating and cooling cycles. Surprisingly, the temperature changes did not cause the rocks to break apart.

What part *does* temperature change play as an agent of physical weathering? Let's look at another factor of weather—precipitation.

Rain or snow wets the surface of rocks. This moisture does not always completely evaporate. It can be found in cracks and pores in the rocks. During temperature changes the water is heated and cooled along with the rock. As discussed in Chapter 2, water has an unusual property—it *expands* upon freezing and *contracts* upon melting. This behavior is contrary to that of most materials.

How does this special property of water affect the solid rock in which it is contained? As the water freezes and expands, the increase in its volume is nearly 10%. The effect of this expansion is similar to driving a tiny wedge into the crack in the rock that holds the water. The crack is made a little wider and longer. When the ice melts, the crack again fills with water. At the next freeze, the process is repeated. Alternate freezing and thawing of the water is like hammering a wedge into the rock. Over a period of time it will cause the rock to split along the crack. (See Figure 14-2.) Rock is weathered by this alternate freezing and melting of water, or *frost action*.

The results of frost action are most noticeable in places where the temperature of the rocks frequently passes through the freezing point of water. Remember that it is the temperature of the rocks and the water in them that matters, and not the air temperature. So, even in a very cold climate, ice and snow may melt during the day where they are exposed to the sun, and then freeze again at night. For this reason, mountaintops are often littered with broken rock frag-

ments produced by frost action. These collections of fragments are called *boulder fields*.

Frost action has other effects besides the physical breakdown of rocks. At one time it was commonly believed that rocks "grew" in fields. When farmers in the colder climates went out into their fields in the early spring, they would discover a new "crop" of rocks and small boulders that had not been there the previous fall. Of course, these rocks had not actually "grown"; they had been pushed up to the surface by frost action in the soil. Another common example of the effect of frost action is the heaving, or warping, of road surfaces in northern sections of the country.

Plant Action. Have you ever seen a small seedling or a clump of grass growing in a crack in the pavement or in a rock? As these plants grow, their roots become longer and thicker. The expanding roots exert pressure, just

Figure 14-2. The effects of frost action on rocks. Where water enters a crack in a rock, its alternate expansion and contraction as it freezes and thaws eventually splits the rock along the crack.

Figure 14-3. Rock being weathered by lichens and other plants.

as freezing water does. This pressure, too, is great enough to widen the crack, and eventually it may split the rock apart.

Small green plants called *mosses* are often found growing on rocks. Mosses are simpler plants than grasses and are able to grow in smaller cracks and pores in rocks. Still simpler and smaller plants called *lichens* also grow on rocks. Lichens vary in color from white to gray to black and often resemble peeling paint. They have very small rootlike parts that can get a "toehold" in the smallest cracks and pore spaces. These small plants often start the physical breakdown of rock surfaces and prepare the way for water and larger plants to do their part later (see Figure 14-3).

Pressure Unloading. Rocks that have formed deep inside the crust often have lines or planes of weakness along which cracks might be expected to occur. However, while these rocks are buried the enormous pressure caused by the weight of overlying rock keeps these cracks from developing. If the overlying material is removed, these buried rocks are brought nearer the surface, and the pressure on them is greatly reduced. This reduction of pressure due to the removal of overlying material is called *pressure unloading*. Pressure unloading allows the rock to split along its planes of weakness. For example, masses of solid granite or basalt, which formed deep in the crust, are often found at the surface with regularly spaced cracks called *joints*. Joints are usually the result of pressure unloading.

The removal of overlying material in most cases occurs by natural processes such as landslides, earthquakes, and erosion (to be discussed in the next chapter). However, human actions, such as mining and rock quarrying, may also relieve pressure on rocks and lead to cracking and jointing.

If physical changes were all that ever happened in weathering, we would expect to find nothing but smaller pieces of the original rock in an area where weathering had occurred. However, in most cases it is usually difficult, if not impossible, to match the smaller pieces of weathered rock with the original rock in the area, especially in terms of chemical makeup. Obviously, then, changes other than simple physical ones must also take place.

SUMMARY

1. Any process that causes a rock to crack or break into pieces is called physical weathering.
2. Physical weathering of rock may occur as the result of alternate freezing and melting of water, a process called frost action.
3. Physical weathering may occur when cracks in rocks are widened by the forces exerted by growing plants.
4. Physical weathering may occur when rocks split along planes of weakness when the pressure of overlying material is removed.

CHEMICAL WEATHERING

How rocks are formed and what materials make up the different rocks of the crust will be discussed in some detail in a later chapter. For now, all we need to say is that rocks are made up of many different substances called *minerals*. A particular type of rock is identified by the minerals it contains. Some rocks contain only one or two minerals; others contain several.

As the term suggests, chemical weathering involves a change in the chemical makeup of a rock. Such a change occurs when one of the minerals in the rock combines, or reacts, with a substance from the environment to form a new substance. This new substance, formed as a result of a *chemical reaction,* has chemical and physical properties different from those of the substances from which it forms. Thus, the rock is changed.

The changes brought about by chemical weathering almost always weaken the rock. Unweathered rock may last for hundreds of millions of years. But once chemical weathering starts, the rock soon goes to pieces. Water, wind, and gravity can then carry the pieces away, exposing fresh surfaces to the forces of weathering. Let us see how chemical weathering works.

There are many substances present in the atmosphere and hydrosphere that play a role in the process of chemical weathering. However, three particular substances are of major importance—oxygen, water, and carbon dioxide. As we consider the action of each of these, we will see how it applies to the weathering of the tombstones in the study we mentioned earlier.

You will recall that the tombstones were all made of a particular kind of sandstone. This sandstone is composed chiefly of two minerals, called quartz and feldspar. If you looked closely at one of the stones, you would see sand-sized grains of these two minerals cemented together, much as in a piece of manmade concrete. The cementing material in this sandstone consists of two other minerals—calcite and hematite. We will refer to this information as we go along.

Oxygen. Oxygen, which makes up almost 21% of the atmosphere, is a chemically active element. That is, it can combine or react with many other substances. The chemical reaction of oxygen with another substance is known as *oxidation*. Oxidation reactions are very important factors in chemical weathering. For example, iron is an element that is present in many rock-forming minerals. Oxygen will combine with iron to form iron oxide, commonly called *rust* (see Figure 14-4).

How does the formation of iron oxide "weather" the rock? In the original rock, the iron is chemically combined with other substances in a definite structural pattern. When the iron reacts chemically with the oxygen, its chemical ties with the other substances in the rock are broken, and the overall structure of the rock is weakened. There are other materials besides iron that can be weathered by oxidation, and the process is basically the same.

None of the minerals we have named in the tombstone rock structure go through any noticeable oxidation. Therefore, oxidation is not a major weathering process in the case of the tombstones.

Water. We have already seen that water is a major agent of *physical* weathering through the frost action it produces in cold regions. It is also an important agent of chemical weathering.

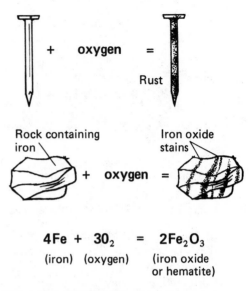

$$4Fe + 3O_2 = 2Fe_2O_3$$
(iron) (oxygen) (iron oxide or hematite)

Figure 14-4. Rusting. When iron is exposed to air, it combines with the oxygen in the air to form iron oxide, or rust.

Have you ever left some garden tools out overnight and in the morning found the grass covered with dew and the tools covered with rust? The same tools could lie in the dry grass all day and show no signs of rusting. (If you don't want to risk your tools, you can try doing this with a few iron nails.) This is an example of the fact that most chemical reactions, including rusting and other kinds of oxidation, are speeded up when water is present.

In the case of rusting, the water simply *assists* the chemical change by speeding up the combination of iron and oxygen. Water itself can also produce chemical weathering by reacting with the minerals in a rock. Some of the new substances formed by the reaction may then dissolve in the water or be washed away, leaving a weakened rock behind.

The chemical action of water is important in the weathering of the sandstone tombstones. It affects two

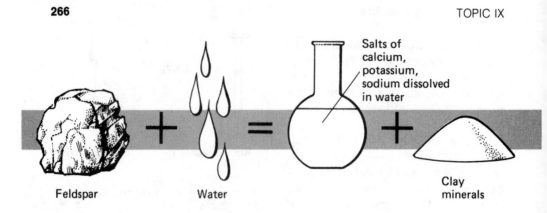

Feldspar   Water   Clay minerals

Salts of calcium, potassium, sodium dissolved in water

Figure 14-5. Chemical weathering of feldspar by water.

of the minerals we named. One of these is hematite, a cementing material in the rock. Chemically, hematite is iron oxide, or rust, and as you might expect, it is a rusty red color. Since the iron in hematite is already oxidized, we can understand why oxygen has no further effect upon it. But water does react with hematite. When it does, it forms *limonite,* an iron mineral that is yellow-red in color. You may have seen these yellow "limonite stains" on rocks or on objects containing iron. If you had left those garden tools out for a week or two while you went on vacation, you would probably have noticed limonite staining on them when you returned. The tombstones in the research study show these stains, especially after a rain. This is an indication that some of the hematite cement is being altered and loosened, thus weakening the remaining stone.

The other mineral in the tombstones that is chemically weathered by water is feldspar. When feldspar reacts with water, some of the elements in the feldspar form substances that dissolve in the water. Among these are potassium, sodium, and calcium. The remainder of the feldspar

forms a fine powder of insoluble substances called *clay minerals.* We will have more to say about clay minerals as we go along. The chemical weathering of feldspar by water is summarized in Figure 14-5. Chemically, the reaction of feldspar and water is very different from that of hematite and water. However, the effect on the tombstone is the same, and that is our purpose in examining each of these processes. The original sandstone materials are weathered to other substances, weakening and eventually crumbling the sandstone.

Carbon Dioxide. Although carbon dioxide gas makes up less than 1% of the earth's atmosphere, it is an extremely important substance. Green plants use carbon dioxide in the process of photosynthesis. This is the process by which food for almost all living things is produced. Carbon dioxide is added to the atmosphere in a number of ways. It is given off by most living things as a waste product of respiration. It is also released by the burning of fuels and the decay of organic (once-living) matter.

By itself, the carbon dioxide in the air has little or no effect on rock minerals. However, carbon dioxide gas

$$CO_2 + H_2O = H_2CO_3$$

Carbon dioxide + water = Carbonic acid

Figure 14-6. Carbonic acid formation. Carbonic acid, which is a weak acid, is formed when carbon dioxide dissolves in water.

easily dissolves in water to form a substance called carbonic acid, as shown in the chemical equation in Figure 14-6. Carbon dioxide in the air combines with water vapor or rain to form carbonic acid. When you hear the term "acid" you usually think of a substance that should be handled with great care. Carbonic acid, however, is a very weak acid—so weak, in fact, that it is safely used in soft drinks ("carbonated" beverages) to produce the "sparkling" or bubbly effect. The bubbles are formed as the carbonic acid breaks down again into water and carbon dioxide.

Carbonic acid may not have the powerful effect of strong acids, but it is still an important agent of chemical weathering. The reaction of carbonic acid with other substances is known as *carbonation.*

The feldspar found in the tombstones of the research study reacts with carbonic acid. As in the reaction with water alone, soluble substances are formed. In this case they are substances called carbonates. Clay minerals are also produced.

The most important example of carbonation, though, is the weathering of the mineral calcite. Along with hematite, calcite is the cementing mineral holding the feldspar and quartz grains together in the tombstones. Calcite is the chemical compound called calcium carbonate. This is an insoluble substance, but when it reacts with carbonic acid, it forms calcium bicarbonate, which dissolves very easily. Just as in the loss of the hematite cement, this loss of calcite cement weakens and crumbles the tombstones.

Limestone, a very common rock, is made up almost entirely of the mineral calcite. Underground caves and slumping land surfaces are quite common in limestone areas. Carbonation dissolves the limestone, usually along the surfaces of joints or cracks. The importance of water in this process should be pointed out. In a dry climate, carbonation would not be as important a process in chemical weathering as it is in a more humid climate.

Other Agents of Chemical Weathering. Although of less importance than carbonic acid, there are other naturally occurring acids that contribute to chemical weathering. Weak acids are produced in the atmosphere by lightning and on the surface by the decay of organic wastes. When these acids are dissolved in rain water or ground water, they will react with and dissolve certain rock minerals.

Figure 14-7 shows a source of some acids that are *not* quite so naturally occurring. This photo is evidence that man is adding weathering agents to his environment at an alarming rate. Many of the gases that we release into the atmosphere combine with water vapor to form very reactive acids.

Figure 14-7. Pollutants act as weathering agents. Substances in the gases being released into the atmosphere combine with water vapor to form acids. For example, oxides of sulfur are found in many waste gases. In the air these combine with water vapor to form sulfuric acid.

The chemical reaction of water with earth minerals has already been described. Water can also *dissolve* many substances. In fact, it is often referred to as the "universal solvent." Some minerals readily dissolve when ground water or rain water comes into contact with them. A good example of this is halite, commonly known as rock salt. If you pour water over a piece of rock salt, it gradually dissolves, leaving you with salty water. The same thing happens in the earth's crust wherever there are salt deposits or other soluble minerals. The salt dissolves, leaving spaces in the rock where more weathering can occur.

SUMMARY

1. Chemical weathering changes the chemical composition of the minerals in rocks and usually weakens the rock as a result of those changes.
2. The agents of chemical weathering include oxygen, water, carbon dioxide, and acids.
3. Water is a major factor in chemical weathering because it speeds up chemical reactions, dissolves many materials, and reacts directly with many mineral substances.

RATES OF WEATHERING

Now that you have learned something about the weathering process, a natural question might be, How long does it take for a rock to be broken down by weathering? To answer that, we will have to examine some of the factors that can affect the rate of weathering.

The type of weathering that occurs in a region is greatly affected by the

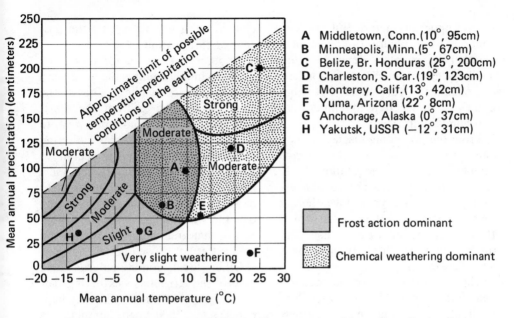

A   Middletown, Conn.(10°, 95cm)
B   Minneapolis, Minn.(5°, 67cm)
C   Belize, Br. Honduras (25°, 200cm)
D   Charleston, S. Car.(19°, 123cm)
E   Monterey, Calif.(13°, 42cm)
F   Yuma, Arizona (22°, 8cm)
G   Anchorage, Alaska (0°, 37cm)
H   Yakutsk, USSR (−12°, 31cm)

Frost action dominant

Chemical weathering dominant

Figure 14-8. Weathering and climate. The amount and type of weathering that occurs in a particular area depends on climate—the temperature and moisture patterns of that area.

kind of weather that region has. However, as indicated by the tombstone study, the weathering of rock materials is a very slow process that extends over long periods of time. So what we are really talking about is the *average* weather conditions of a region, which is more accurately called its *climate*. Climate strongly influences the rate at which weathering occurs and the type of weathering that is most important in a particular region.

Effects of Climate. As you may recall from Chapter 13, the climate of a region can be described in terms of its temperature and humidity. It is easy to see that frost action—the main type of physical weathering—is not going to occur unless the temperature goes below freezing fairly often. So we can expect to find frost action as an important type of weathering at the

higher latitudes. The same conditions can be found on mountaintops, even at the equator.

However, frost action is not going to be very effective without water. So, in cold climates we find that the rate of physical weathering by frost action generally increases with humidity. You can see this pattern in Figure 14-8. You will notice that the diagram shows an interesting exception to the expected pattern. In a climate that is both very cold and very humid, the frost action decreases somewhat. The reason for this is that the rocks are continually buried under deep masses of ice, which get very little chance to melt. Without melting and freezing cycles within the rocks, not much frost action can occur.

As average annual temperatures rise above the freezing point of water, chemical weathering becomes the more important factor. But, as you can see from Figure 14-8, chemical weathering is also dependent on available moisture. Weathering in hot, dry climates is very slight, but it becomes strong where both temperature and humidity are high.

From the preceding discussion you can see that if you know the average temperature and precipitation for a region, you can make a reasonable estimate of the main types of weathering that will occur and the rates at which they will occur. Let's use the tombstone research study again as a specific example.

The tombstones are located in cemeteries near Middletown, Connecticut. The average annual temperature for the area is about 10°C; the average annual precipitation is about 900 mm per year. If you look at Figure 14-8 again, you will see that these data indicate that Middletown should have "moderate chemical weathering with frost action." How does this description apply to the weathering of the tombstones? The information in the preceding sections of this chapter can help to answer that.

1. The climate of the Middletown region is similar to that of other areas in the northeastern United States—cold winters and warm summers. Freezing and thawing cycles do occur, and there is certainly enough precipitation for frost action to occur.

2. One of the cementing materials in the sandstone, the mineral hematite, weathers to limonite by the chemical action of water.

3. Water also reacts chemically with the feldspar grains to form clay and soluble materials.

4. The calcite cementing material is changed to a soluble salt by the process of carbonation.

Another climatic factor that must be taken into account is the local wind pattern. The prevailing wind in the Middletown area is from the west, varying at times from northwest to southwest. The greatest weathering effects would then be expected to show on the west-facing tombstones. Figure 14-1 (page 260) shows this to be so. It would seem logical to expect that the west-facing slope of a mountain in that area would also show the greatest effect of weathering.

Other local conditions can also modify the expected weathering pattern. Figure 14-9 shows what has happened since 1800 to the temperature and carbon dioxide content of the air in the Middletown area.

A partial reason for the increase in temperature shown would be an increase in the size and number of cities, resulting in more extensive "urban heat islands" (see page 164). Another factor that could increase the temperature would be an increase in the carbon dioxide content of the atmosphere (see the discussion of the "greenhouse effect" on page 149). That increase is also shown in Figure 14-9. You will notice that the increase is especially dramatic after 1900. This is usually used as evidence that the increase in carbon dioxide in the air is a result of the development of the internal combustion engine and its use in industry and transportation.

This increase in the amount of carbon dioxide in the atmosphere would also increase the possibility of weathering by the process of carbonation. As you have already seen, one of the cementing materials in the tomb-

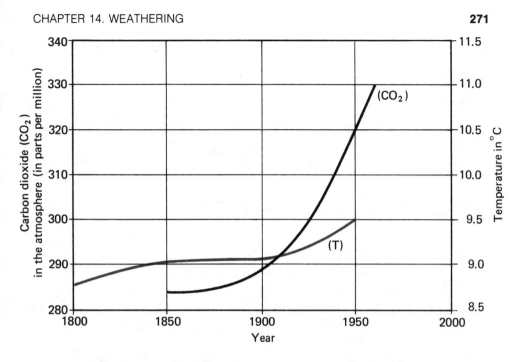

Figure 14-9. Variation in average air temperature and carbon dioxide content in Middletown, Connecticut, since 1800.

stones, the calcite, is especially affected by this type of chemical weathering. The calcite weathers away, allowing the grains of quartz and feldspar to loosen from each other.

Effect of Particle Size. The size of rock pieces being weathered is especially important when considering the rate of chemical weathering. To illustrate this fact, try dissolving a lump of sugar in one cup of coffee and an equal amount of granulated sugar in a second cup at the same temperature. Which sample of sugar will dissolve more quickly? The answer, of course, is the granulated sugar. Similarly, small rock particles will weather faster than larger particles of the same rock under the same conditions. The reason for this difference in rates is that the smaller particles have more surface area exposed to the agents of weathering (see Figure 14-10).

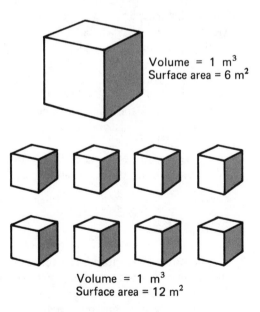

Volume = 1 m³
Surface area = 6 m²

Volume = 1 m³
Surface area = 12 m²

Figure 14-10. Effect of particle size on surface area. As particle size decreases, surface area increases.

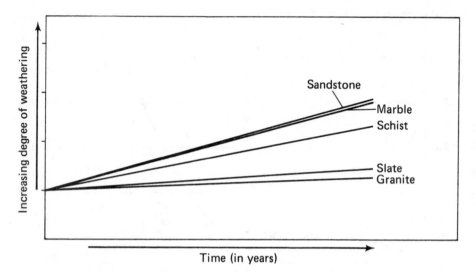

Figure 14-11. Mineral composition and rate of weathering. Rocks of different composition weather at different rates. Of the five rocks in this investigation, granite weathered most slowly and sandstone most rapidly.

Effect of Mineral Composition. We have seen that the rate at which rocks weather varies according to climatic conditions and particle size. Does this mean that any two rocks of approximately the same size and shape that are exposed to the same climatic conditions will weather at the same rate? Would tombstones of different rock materials show the same weathering effects as the sandstone if they were in the same location?

We saw some evidence relating to this question in the photograph on page 258. Another researcher, working in the same region of the northeastern United States, examined this question more thoroughly. His results are shown in Figure 14-11. They indicate that the mineral composition of rock is an important consideration in the rate of weathering.

Thus, it would seem that whenever the *rate* of weathering is being considered, there are three factors that must be taken into account—climate, particle size, and the mineral composition of the rocks.

SUMMARY

1. The rate of weathering is affected by climate, the size of the particles being weathered, and the type of material being weathered.
2. At high latitudes (and high altitudes) frost action is the major form of weathering. In warm climates, chemical weathering is most important. However, low humidity will slow the rate of weathering in both cases.
3. Local climatic conditions—winds, nearness to cities, etc.—can affect the expected weathering rate for a region.

4. A sample consisting of small rock particles will weather faster than a single large sample of the same mass because more surface area is exposed by the small particles.
5. Rocks and minerals weather at different rates because of their different physical and chemical properties.

THE PRODUCTS OF WEATHERING

Weathering, as we have described it up to this point, is essentially a matter of breaking down rocks into smaller and smaller pieces and changing them chemically along the way. How far can this process go? That is, how small can the pieces get? The answer is, quite small. To understand how small that is, we need to know a little elementary chemistry.

Atoms. All substances in the world are made up of combinations of certain simple substances called *elements,* and all elements are made up of *atoms.* Bear in mind that we are talking about mental models, not actual "things" that have been observed. However, our model of the atom works so well in explaining chemical changes that we are fairly sure that something very much like the model actually exists. In this model, an atom has a central part called a *nucleus* in which there are one or more particles called *protons.* Each proton has a single positive charge of electricity (+). In the space around the nucleus, there are particles called *electrons,* each with a single negative charge (−). There are other particles in the nucleus, and these are called *neutrons.* These are neutral in charge. Neutrons are important in the process of radioactivity, but for our purposes in explaining weathering, we can ignore them. Ordinarily, the number of electrons in an atom equals

the number of protons, and the atom as a whole is electrically neutral (shows no sign of an electric charge).

The difference between one element and another is simply the number of protons and electrons in their atoms. Every atom of hydrogen, for example, has one proton and one electron. Every atom of sodium has eleven of each, and every atom of chlorine has seventeen of each. Figure 14-12 shows a model of each of these atoms.

Figure 14-12. Atomic structures of hydrogen, sodium, and chlorine.

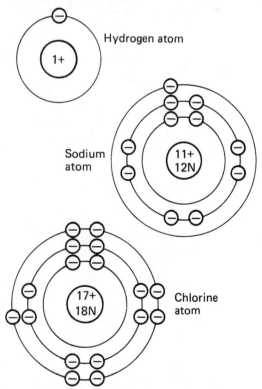

There is a different element for each number of protons and electrons from 1 on up to 106 (at the latest report). The elements that concern us in earth science are those that are fairly common in the earth's rocks. What these elements are and how they form the minerals and rocks of the earth will be more fully explained in Chapter 17.

Chemical Compounds. Chemical *compounds* are substances that are formed when atoms of different elements become joined together in definite ratios. This joining (or *chemical bonding,* as it is called) occurs as a result of a shifting around of electrons when atoms of different elements are close to one another. This shift causes the originally neutral atoms to take on positive or negative charges. The attraction between oppositely charged atoms is the force that holds the atoms together in a compound.

In some cases of chemical combination, the electrons shift so much that some atoms lose one or more electrons altogether, while other atoms pick them up. An atom that has lost or gained electrons is called an *ion.* If an atom has lost electrons (which are themselves negative), it is left with a positive charge, and is therefore a positive ion. If an atom has gained electrons, it is a negative ion. Figure 14-13 shows this diagrammatically.

A simple example of a compound formed from positive and negative ions is rock salt, or sodium chloride. A crystal of sodium chloride is made up of positive sodium ions and negative chloride ions arranged in a definite order in a structure called a *crys-*

Figure 14-13. Ionic bonding. When sodium and chlorine react to from rock salt, the sodium atom loses an electron, which is gained by the chlorine atom. The sodium ion now has one more proton than electrons, so it has a net charge of +1, while the chlorine ion has an extra electron, so it has a net charge of −1.

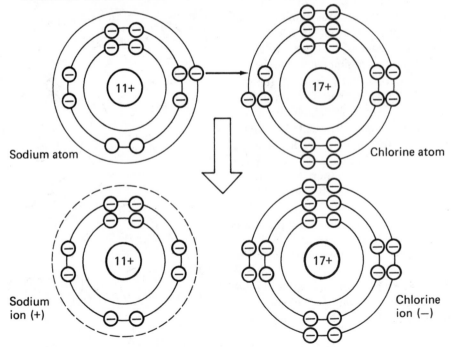

Sodium atom

Chlorine atom

Sodium ion (+)

Chlorine ion (−)

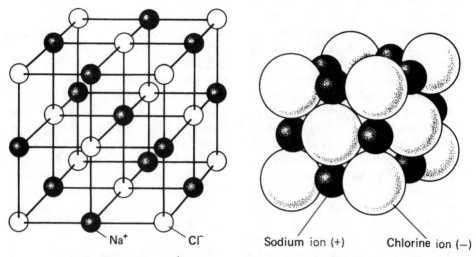

Figure 14-14. Crystalline structure of sodium chloride.

tal lattice. In a crystal lattice, each ion is strongly attracted to ions of opposite charge on all sides of it. It is these forces that give each crystal its characteristic shape and its resistance to breaking. Figure 14-14 illustrates a crystal of sodium chloride.

Most minerals consist of positive and negative ions arranged in a crystal lattice of a definite shape. The positive ions are usually ions of a metal, such as iron, calcium, magnesium, or potassium. The negative ions are usually nonmetals, such as chlorine, oxygen, or sulfur. Some negative ions consist of atoms bonded together and having excess electrons as a group. The carbonate ion, for example, is made up of one carbon atom, three oxygen atoms, and two extra electrons.

Let's go back to the question we raised about how far the weathering process can go. The answer is that it can go all the way to the actual separation of a mineral crystal into its ions. However, this final step can occur only when the compound dissolves in a solvent, such as water.

A Case Study of Weathering. As a specific example of the weathering process and how far it can go, let us follow the weathering of granite, one of the most common rocks in the crust of the earth. For this purpose we will use Stone Mountain, which we mentioned earlier, on page 49.

Stone Mountain is over 3 km long, 1.5 km wide, and more than 200 m high. How could this huge mass of granite ever weather away? Let's look at the specific weathering processes that could affect this mountain. In doing so, we will concentrate on three minerals that make up most of this rock—quartz and feldspar, the two minerals that are always present in granite, and mica, which is almost always present also.

1. *Physical weathering*. The climatic conditions affecting Stone Mountain, Georgia, are similar to those of the nearby region of Charleston, South Carolina (see Figure 14-8).

Unlike Connecticut, where the tombstone study was made, the temperature in the region of Stone Mountain rarely passes through the freezing point. Even if it did, Stone Mountain is relatively joint-free, so any effect of frost action would be primarily on the surface of the rock. Another difference between Stone Mountain and the Connecticut tombstones lies in how the minerals in the two kinds of rocks are joined. The sandstone grains in the tombstones are cemented together by other minerals, and there is a fair amount of pore space into which water can enter. The minerals in the granite of Stone Mountain tend to be intergrown crystals. So, there are few, if any, open pores for water to enter.

Physical weathering, then, is not a major factor in the weathering of Stone Mountain, but it does occur to some extent.

2. *Chemical weathering.* As we mentioned, the region of Stone Mountain is similar in climate to that of Charleston, South Carolina. Therefore, as shown in Figure 14-8, "moderate chemical weathering" is to be expected. Let's look first at the possibility of the chemical weathering of the quartz in the granite rock. Quartz is one of the most common minerals in the crust of the earth, making up more than one-fourth of the crust. Many people are able to recognize it on sight because it is so common. It does not react chemically with oxygen, water, or carbon dioxide. It is therefore affected very little by chemical weathering. If you were able to examine Stone Mountain (or any other granite rock) very closely, you would see quartz crystals remaining in the surface

where other materials have weathered away. If this granite mountain is being weathered chemically, it is not because of its quartz content.

Let's consider the effect of chemical weathering on the other minerals in the granite. As we stated in the discussion of the weathering of the sandstone tombstone, feldspar is weathered chemically by both water and carbonation. The products are clay minerals and soluble salts of certain metals, such as calcium, potassium, and sodium. The chemical weathering of mica has essentially the same results.

Although chemical weathering of the granite does not affect the quartz in it, it does free the quartz particles as the other minerals are weathered away. So we can say that quartz particles are a product of the chemical weathering of granite. Other "hard" minerals in the rock that resist chemical weathering are released in the same way.

3. *Final products.* Now let's summarize what we have discovered about the weathering of a granite mountain. As you read this section, refer to Table 14-1 and Figure 14-15. We mentioned that some physical weathering of Stone Mountain occurs. A greater amount will occur in masses of granite that have cracks or joints, or that are in colder climates. In any case, the effects of physical weathering are mainly to break the rock into smaller pieces of granite. Most of these pieces will be rather large.

Chemical weathering, meanwhile, is affecting the mineral grains at the surface of the rock, both on the original mass and on any pieces that have been broken off by physical weather-

NAME	DIAMETER (mm)	APPROX. NO. OF PARTICLES/GRAM	APPROX. SURFACE AREA (cm^2/GRAM)
Pebbles	60 – 2	2 – 3	2 – 3
Sand	2 – .05	150,000	80
Silt	.05 – .005	6,000,000	500
Clay	Below .005	90,000,000,000	8,000,000
Colloids	Below .0001	Very large	Very large

Table 14-1. Particle size and surface area.

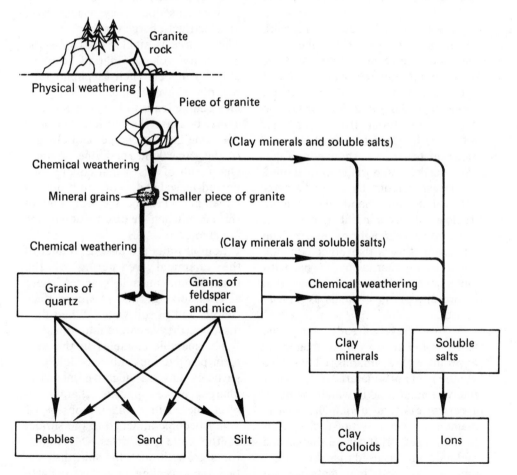

Figure 14-15. Weathering of granite.

ing. As we have seen, the quartz in granite is hardly affected at all by chemical weathering. However, the feldspar and mica are gradually broken down to clay minerals and soluble salts. As this happens, the structure of the rock is weakened. Individual grains of quartz will come free. Small pieces of the granite containing several different mineral crystals may also break off. Chemical weathering will continue to act on the feldspar and mica in these small pieces, so that eventually more crystals of quartz will be freed.

Since the grains of quartz in granite are of many different sizes, the particles of quartz released by weathering of the other minerals will also be of many different sizes. Most of them, however, will be *sand*. Sand is not the name of a material. It is a word that refers to the size of the particles in a loose material. As shown in Table 14-1, particles that range from about 2 mm down to about .05 mm in diameter are called sand. Sand may contain particles of any mineral. However, it often consists mostly of quartz. The reason for this is that other common minerals weather away to particles much smaller than sand, so that what is present in most sands is mainly quartz.

As we have already said, the feldspar and mica weather chemically to produce clay minerals. Clay is also not the name of a material. Clay is any finely divided solid in which the particles are less than about .005 mm in diameter. When it is moist, clay tends to stick together. It can be shaped and molded, and it is used to make pottery and as a modeling material for sculpture.

The particles in clay can range downward in size almost to the size of single molecules. In the magnified view of clayey soil in Figure 12-2 on page 217, you can see particles that are just visible as specks. These are the true clay particles in this photo. There were many particles present that could not be seen at the magnification used.

Clay particles smaller than about .0001 mm in diameter are called *colloids*. Colloid particles are too small to be examined directly with an ordinary microscope. They usually have an electrical charge on their surface. This charge is similar to the "static electricity" charge that makes dust cling to objects such as phonograph records. However, in colloids the surface charge tends to keep the particles apart, because the particles all have the same kind of charge, and charges of the same kind repel one another. One result of this is that colloids dispersed in water do not settle out, as larger particles do. We will refer to this again when we discuss deposition in Chapter 16.

Soluble salts are also a product of the chemical weathering of the feldspar and mica in granite. These salts dissolve in rainwater, in surface runoff, and in soil water. When they dissolve, they separate into ions.

The metallic elements in the salts form positive ions. Most colloid clay particles have a negative electrical charge. Since opposite charges attract, the positive mineral ions in soil water become attached to the surface of the colloid particles. As plant roots grow through the soil, they detach the ions clinging to the soil particles and absorb them into the plant. In this way, plants obtain many elements that they need for growth and other life activities.

In this example, we have followed the weathering of one kind of rock—granite—in one specific location, to its ultimate conclusion. Other rocks, under different conditions, weather differently. Whatever the nature of the original rock may be, and whatever the type and extent of weathering that occurs, the products are particles that may range in size from ions on up to boulders. All particles of weathered rock, regardless of their size, are called *sediments*. From now on it will be convenient to use this term when referring to rock particles.

SUMMARY

1. Atoms are the basic unit of all elements. An atom has a nucleus containing one or more protons (+). The nuclei of most atoms also contain neutrons, which have no charge. Surrounding the nucleus are the electrons, which are equal in number to the protons. The atom as a whole is neutral in charge.
2. An electrically charged atom is an ion. It is positively charged if it is lacking electrons; it is negatively charged if it has extra electrons.
3. Physical and chemical weathering combine to break rocks down into particles of many sizes. The order of particle size (from larger to smaller) is sand to silts to clays to colloids.
4. Some of the substances produced by chemical weathering are soluble in water and break down into ions when they dissolve. All surface and ground water contains the ions of dissolved minerals.

THE END RESULT OF WEATHERING—SOILS

Pick up a handful of dirt. You may very well be looking at the remains of a mountain! When the weathering processes that we have examined act on the solid crust, one of the usual end results is dirt—or what is more correctly called *soil*. The tiny bits of rock and particles ranging in size from sand to colloids and ions make up most of the mass and volume of soil. However, soil is far more than weathered rock, which is merely lifeless mineral particles. Without living things, there would be no true soil. And without soil, there would be no life on land as we see it today.

Perhaps you have looked at some soil under a microscope. Anyone who has knows that ordinary dull "dirt" is crowded with all sorts of things. Bits of twigs appear like logs. Pieces of leaves and bark are difficult to recognize because they are so huge. A tiny bug looks like something from a science fiction movie. Particles of weathered rock like boulders.

Although, as we have mentioned, soil is made up mostly of inorganic material (particles of weathered rock) the most important part of the soil in terms of plant growth is organic matter (the decayed remains of plants and animals). This organic matter is called *humus*. Humus gives soil its dark brown or black color. The decay of organic matter is accomplished by bacteria and fungi, which are found in the soil in tremendous numbers. Through decay, the substances in the

Figure 14-16. Soil profile showing A, B, and C horizons. The A-horizon is the topsoil; the B-horizon is the subsoil; the C-horizon is partially weathered bedrock.

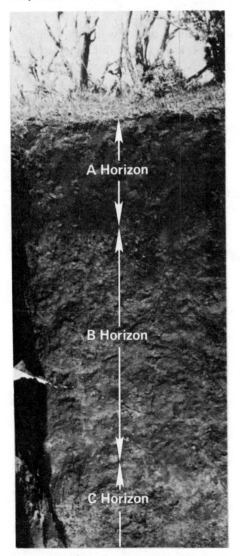

remains of plants and animals are returned to the soil in a form that living plants can use again.

Soil Horizons. You can't learn much about the soil in any given area by looking at it from the top, which is your usual view. Looking down at the soil beneath your feet can be compared to looking down at a three-decker sandwich from the top. With the sandwich, all you see is the top slice of bread. To find out what is *in* the sandwich, you have to view it from the side. The same is true with soil. To see what is *in* the soil, you have to view it from the side. Such a view, as shown in Figure 14-16, is called a *soil profile*. The different layers in the profile are called *soil horizons*.

By examining a soil profile, you can draw inferences about the history of the area, especially about the weathering that has taken place. Soil development, like weathering, is a slow process. Figure 14-17 illustrates the "stages" in the development of a soil from an *immature* soil to a *mature* soil. Immature soils have no topsoil, or at best, only a very thin layer.

A mature soil consists of several identifiable layers, or horizons. For convenience, these layers are usually identified by letters, starting at the top: A-horizon (topsoil), B-horizon (subsoil), and C-horizon (partially weathered bedrock). The unweathered rock, or bedrock, is usually not identified by letter, although it may be labeled as the D or R horizon.

The A-horizon, or topsoil, contains humus formed by the decay of plant and animal matter. The humus furnishes important nutrients to the upper layer of soil. These nutrients make it possible for the soil to support

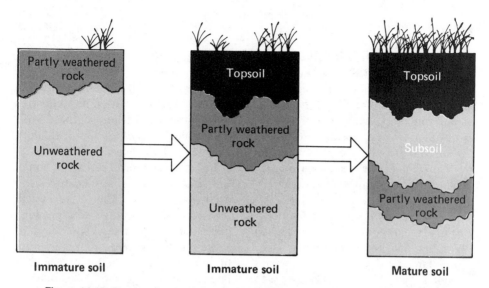

Figure 14-17. Stages of soil development from immature to mature. In the original state there is unweathered bedrock at the surface. Gradually, weathering proceeds downward to deeper levels. Infiltration, capillary migration, plant action, and the movement of sediments by organisms in the developing soil produce horizons with characteristic features.

more and larger plants. As these plants die and decay, still more organic matter is added to the soil, and the layer of topsoil becomes deeper and more fertile.

During the formation of humus, acids are formed. These acids contribute to the breakdown of mineral material in the soil. In addition, there is air and water present in the pores of the soil (see Chapter 12, page 216), which means that chemical and physical weathering can affect the soil and the solid rock under the surface. Besides moving through the pores, the water and air can follow the pathways opened by worms, insects, and larger burrowing animals. In this way, animals help to speed up the weathering process and thus aid in soil formation.

Soil Classification. Earth scientists have attempted to classify the various types of soil found around the world. Such classifications are important aids in soil conservation and in making the most efficient use of each type of soil. In classifying soils, the most

important consideration is the amount and type of minerals present in the upper horizons, since these layers provide most of the nutrients for plant growth. The mineral composition in these upper horizons is closely related to rainfall amounts. The greater the rainfall, the greater the amount of soluble minerals in the soil that will be dissolved and carried away as ions. This removing, or "washing away," of soluble minerals from the soil is known as *leaching*.

Several major kinds of soil can be identified on the basis of the minerals present in the A- and B-horizons. This, in turn, is related to the climate (rainfall and temperature) of the region.

One type of soil, called a *forest soil,* is found in the eastern third of the United States, where precipitation is generally greater than 60 cm/year and average temperatures are moderate. Under these conditions, almost all the soluble minerals (calcium and magnesium compounds) are leached out of the soil and carried into the ground water. Many of the less-soluble minerals, such as aluminum and iron oxides, are also removed from the A-horizon and accumulate in the B-horizon. The minerals left in the A-horizon are therefore mostly the very insoluble ones, such as quartz. Soils of this type are called *pedalfers* (from *ped* = soil, *al* = aluminum, and *fe* = *ferrum*, the Latin name for iron), because the upper horizons are rich in aluminum and iron compounds.

The large supply of water in the soil makes it possible for large trees to grow and for forests to develop. However, the trees block most of the sunlight from reaching ground level, so that very little vegetation can survive on the forest floor. The main source of humus for a forest soil is the decay of leaves and evergreen needles. As a result, only a thin layer of humus develops.

The A-horizon of a forest soil usually has two regions—a dark upper layer called the A_1-horizon, which contains humus, and a grayish layer below it called the A_2-horizon. Both of these layers are poor in the minerals required by most plants. They are also highly acid, partly because acids are a product of decay of organic materials, and partly because leaching removes calcium carbonate and other base-forming compounds. (Bases are the opposite of acids in their chemical effects.) Many trees can live in acid soils, and their deep roots can obtain the nutrients they need from the lower horizons. However, these soils are not very productive for farming or gardening unless the acids are neutralized by adding limestone, and the missing mineral nutrients are added as fertilizer.

In the western United States there is a large region of arid climate. Here, soluble minerals remain in the soil because the small amounts of rainfall produce little leaching. The soil is rich in calcium carbonate, so these soils are called *pedocals* (*cal* = calcium). They are also called *desert soils*.

In the great central plains section of the United States, the climate is generally subhumid. There is enough moisture to support low-growing plants such as grasses. The decay of these plants produces a large amount of humus, which gradually accumulates to fairly large depths (as much as 50 cm). Leaching, however, is not as great as in the forest soils of humid regions. Soluble minerals, including calcium carbonate, are carried down to the lower portions of the B-horizon, but they are not washed away completely. The roots of grasses grow deep enough to reach the mineral nutrients in this horizon. Soils of this type are called *grassland soils*. Because grassland regions have deep topsoil rich in humus and adequate rainfall, they have become the major agricultural centers of the world, supplying large quantities of wheat and corn.

Another major soil type is found in very warm, humid climates. The high temperatures and abundant moisture result in much weathering of the soil material to soluble compounds that are then leached away. The great activity of soil bacteria at these high temperatures also destroys humus as fast as it forms. These *tropical soils* have very little soluble mineral content and very little humus. Soils of this type do not occur in the United States.

More often than not, close examination of a soil profile will turn up rock particles that obviously did not

come from the weathering of the bedrock. In other words, the particles
must have moved from their source

regions. The transportation of weathered materials will be treated in the
next chapter.

SUMMARY

1. A soil profile shows the distinct layers in the soil, which differ in color, texture, mineral composition, etc.
2. Soil profiles develop as a result of weathering processes and biological activity.
3. Soil characteristics are often consistent over large areas. This has allowed the development of soil classification maps.

REVIEW QUESTIONS

Group A
1. What is *weathering?*
2. Under what conditions does weathering occur?
3. What are the effects of weathering?
4. What is *physical weathering?*
5. What factors cause physical weathering?
6. What is *pressure unloading?*
7. What is *chemical weathering?*
8. Name some of the agents of chemical weathering.
9. Why is water a major factor in chemical weathering?
10. What factors affect the rate of weathering?
11. What is the major form of weathering at high latitudes and high altitudes? At low latitudes?
12. Describe the basic structure of an atom.
13. What is an *ion?*
14. Give the names of the different-sized particles produced by physical and chemical weathering.
15. What is shown in a soil profile?
16. How do soil profiles develop?

Group B
1. Describe how the atmosphere and the hydrosphere interact with the lithosphere to cause weathering.
2. a. In what way can mosses and lichens contribute to the physical weathering of rock?
   b. The alternate heating and cooling of a rock will not of itself cause physical weathering. What else is necessary in order for temperature changes to contribute to weathering?
3. a. What kinds of chemical weathering could you expect if you did an experiment like that described in Figure 14-1?
   b. How does chemical weathering differ from physical weathering?
4. Two towns are located at the same latitude, yet the physical and chemical weathering of the rocks in one town is occurring much more rapidly than in the other town. How is this possible?
5. Why might the soil profile in one place be quite different from that in another place only a kilometer away?

This natural bridge in California was carved from the rock by the action of ocean waves.

CHAPTER 15 Erosion

You will know something about the process of erosion if you can:

1. Distinguish between a transported soil and a residual soil and relate the formation of both types of soil to weathering and erosion.
2. Explain the role of gravity in the erosional process.
3. Develop a generalized model of the erosional process, with particular emphasis on the role of running water as an agent of erosion.
4. Name some other agents of erosion and describe their effects on the earth's surface.

The weathering of solid rock is often the first in a series of related changes that alter the face of the earth. What happens to the smaller rock particles that are produced as a result of weathering? Many, perhaps most, of these smaller particles are transported—often great distances—from their point of origin. Thus, the final change in this series may occur hundreds of kilometers from the place where it all started.

EROSION

It is a common occurrence for a homeowner to order a load of topsoil. The soil is delivered by a truck, and if a large area is involved, it may be spread by a bulldozer. Suppose you dug down into such a spot at a later time and examined the soil profile. You would be able to see that the characteristics of the top layer were quite different from those of the layers underneath, for example, in color, mineral composition, and organic content. The differences would be more than could be explained by weathering alone. You could therefore infer that the top layer had been brought in from someplace else.

Natural soil profiles often show this same condition. They differ so much from the bedrock underneath them that it is not likely that they formed from that bedrock and must have been carried in from someplace else. The rock particles in this type of soil are called *transported sediments*. If, on the other hand, it can be shown that the soil particles have been weathered from the original bedrock, they are called *residual sediments* (meaning that they have always "resided" there).

Earth scientists have found that transported sediments are far more common on the earth than residual sediments. This indicates that there are forces on the earth that can move rock particles from one place to another. Any natural process that removes sediments from one place and carries them away to another is called *erosion*. In this chapter we will examine various ways in which erosion is brought about.

As in so much of earth science, we will have to be detectives in many cases of erosion. Just as a bulldozer may leave tread marks as evidence that it has been in an area, so the natural agents of erosion also leave telltale signs. However, there are also many situations in which we can actually observe erosion occurring. So we do not have to rely entirely on inference. Let us then see what we can discover about the forces and agents of erosion.

Gravity—The Driving Force of Erosion. Everything on the earth is continuously being pulled toward the earth's center by the force of gravity. Any particle of matter that is free to move is going to move downward unless some other force interferes. The atoms, molecules, and mineral crystals in a solid rock are, of course, not free to move in response to gravity. So mountains stand tall, resisting the force of gravity.

However, the forces of weathering are constantly attacking the surfaces of the mountains, weakening and loosening bits and pieces of all sizes. These pieces of rock *are* free to move, and when they do move, they move downward in response to gravity. In almost all cases, they also move horizontally away from their original location. Gravity is the driving force of this movement. And as rock particles move down and away from where they were, there is a loss of potential energy. As we will see, all erosion is powered by a conversion of the potential energy of gravitation to other forms, particularly kinetic energy.

Gravity can thus work alone as an

Figure 15-1. Rocks on a slope. Pieces of bedrock, which have broken off as a result of weathering, are found on most slopes.

agent of erosion, tending to pull all loose particles down along every slope. Figure 15-1 shows a common sight wherever the land has rocky slopes. We see sediments that have accumulated near the bottom of a hillside. A study of these rock pieces would show that they are very similar in composition to the solid bedrock of the hillside. They have apparently been weathered from the bedrock and have rolled down the slope. However, most of them have not fallen all the way down. They are resting on the slope, even where the slope is rather steep. This observation agrees with common daily experience. Objects on a slope do not necessarily roll or slide down it.

Angle of Repose. If you put a marble on a glass plate, and lift one end of the glass the slightest amount, the marble will roll downward. But if you put a block of wood on a board, you can lift one end of the board to a considerable angle before the block begins to slide. If you cover the board and the block with sandpaper, you have to tilt the board even higher before the block will move. The force of friction accounts for these observations. This force can resist the effect of gravity—up to a point. What is that point?

The full force of gravity is directed straight downward. If an object is resting on a horizontal surface, 100% of its weight is directed at right angles to the surface (that is, straight down) and none of it is directed along the surface. If, however, the surface is tilted, only a fraction of the force of gravity acts at right angles to the surface. This part of the force presses the object against the surface and produces the frictional force that tends to keep the object from sliding down. Another fraction of the gravity acts downward along the slope. This is the force that tends to make the object slide or roll down the slope. These two parts of the force of gravity on a slope can be shown by diagrams like those in Figure 15-2.

Notice that as the angle increases, the fraction of gravity that causes friction becomes less and the fraction that is pulling the object down the slope becomes greater. At some angle, then, the force down the incline will become greater than the resisting force of friction, and the object will slide or roll down. For a given kind of loose material resting on a given kind of surface, there is some angle at which the effective force of gravity down the slope becomes greater than the resisting force of friction. The material will then move down the slope.

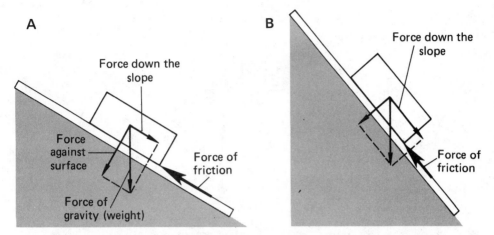

Figure 15-2. Force of gravity on a tilted surface. On a tilted surface the force of gravity is divided into two components. One component acts at right angles to the surface. The second acts downward along the slope.

The greatest angle at which loose material will rest on a surface is called the *angle of repose* (or rest).

You can find the angle of repose for earth materials quite easily. Just make a pile of the material on the ground and measure the angle of the cone that is formed (see Figure 15-3). For most earth materials you will find that this angle is about 35°. This is the angle you are likely to see in piles of sand and gravel at construction sites or in gravel supply yards. On slopes any greater than this, you are not likely to see much loose material, unless it is resting on other sediments below it.

Some Effects of Gravity. On slopes that are close to the angle of repose, the shock of a slight earthquake may send a sudden rush of rocks and soil down the slope in a *landslide*. The reason for this is that the force of friction is greater when an object is at rest on a surface than after it starts mov-

Figure 15-3. Angle of repose. The angle of repose is the greatest angle at which loose material will rest on a surface.

Figure 15-4. Landslide in Madison Canyon, Montana.

ing. Therefore, once a mass of sediments begins to slide down a slope, it tends to keep going and even to build up speed. The effects of one famous landslide are shown in Figure 15-4. In other cases, a heavy downpour may soak the ground and reduce the friction between the soil particles. Again, there may be a landslide, or a kind of slipping of material called *slumping.*

Landslides are not a very common occurrence. They can occur only where the land is steep enough. And even when it *is* steep enough for a landslide to occur, there may not be enough loose material to form one. Sediments may have moved down the slope one piece at a time as they formed.

Near the beginning of this section we said that solid mountains can resist the force of gravity. There is evidence, however, that whole hillsides *can* be affected by gravity over a period of time. On many hillsides you can see fence posts, telephone poles, tombstones, and other objects that were once set vertically, but are now tilted. Sometimes, layers in the bedrock are also seen to be curved downslope. What these observations indicate is that the whole hillside is slowly slipping downward. This is a process called *hillside creep.* It is believed to be caused in many cases by alternate swelling and contracting of the surface during wet and dry seasons. The swelling loosens and separates the soil particles slightly. When they settle back, they also settle down a little lower. Over the course of the years, the upper layers of the soil and rock slowly move downhill.

Agents of Erosion. Landslides, falling rock, slumping, and hillside creep need a fairly steep slope to occur. Where slopes are not very steep, the downslope effect of gravity is just not great enough to move the sediments. Most of the earth's land surfaces have slopes of less than 5°! So, if gravity were the only agent of erosion, most sediments would remain where they formed. But we began this chapter by observing that most sediments appear to have been transported. What, then, are the agents of erosion that transport sediments down these very gradual slopes?

Running water is a rather obvious agent of erosion. In any muddy river you can see the sediments being carried along. In rushing mountain streams, you can see and hear the sand and pebbles being rolled and bounced along the bottom. On a world-wide basis, running water moves far more material than any other agent of erosion. We will therefore concentrate our attention on erosion by running water in the rest of this chapter. But we will consider some other agents, also.

SUMMARY

1. Sediments that have been moved into a region from another place by natural processes are called transported sediments.
2. Sediments that formed in their present location are called residual sediments.
3. The removal and transport of sediments is called erosion.
4. Transported sediments are much more common than residual sediments and are evidence of erosion over large portions of the earth's surface.
5. Gravity is the main driving force of all erosional processes.
6. Gravity may act alone as an erosional agent, producing such effects as landslides, slumping, and hillside creep.
7. Running water is the predominant agent of erosion on the earth.

STREAMS

Imagine yourself on a slope near the top of a mountain range. There is the splash of a raindrop at your feet. Then another. Soon the rain is pelting down. The dry dirt softens as the pore spaces fill with water. Mud forms. The water that was rain begins to trickle downhill across the earth. Tiny dirt particles are carried along. As the dirt moves away, spaces are left in the soil. More and more dirt particles move downhill with the water, following the most direct route downward. Gradually a pathway develops. Particles are picked up from the bottom of this pathway and carried downhill with the water. Other dirt particles slip from the top of the pathway when the support is removed from below. They tumble into the water and are washed along downhill.

The rain stops. The trickles of runoff dry up or infiltrate the soil. But permanent streams continue to flow downward. They are supplied by ground water seeping into the stream bed from the surrounding layers of saturated soil. Where two streams meet at a common low point, they join to form a single larger stream. More

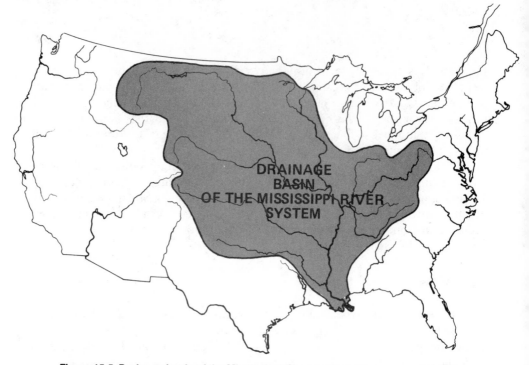

Figure 15-5. Drainage basin of the Mississippi River system. All streams within this drainage system empty into the Mississippi River.

and more small streams join the main stream as the running water descends to lower levels.

Drainage Basins. Follow this growing stream downward. The volume of water it is carrying—its discharge—keeps getting larger. The stream becomes deeper and wider in order to move this growing volume of water. Finally, the stream may become a broad, majestic river like the Mississippi. Near its mouth at New Orleans, the Mississippi River may carry as much as 50,000 cubic meters of water per second down to the Gulf of Mexico.

Now let us retrace our steps. Follow a river like the Mississippi upstream along each of its branches. As you do this, you climb to higher and higher ground. Eventually you reach the source of any branch you are tracing—a point where its flow begins. This may be a pond or lake fed

by ground water, or it may be a spring in the ground where the water table reaches the surface. Beyond the source, the ground continues to rise for a while. Then it reaches a peak or ridge and starts to drop again. Soon you reach the sources of other streams that are flowing down on the other side of the ridge into another river system.

Look at the map in Figure 15-5. A continuous line has been drawn along the high ground above the source of each stream that flows into the Mississippi River. This line is called a *divide*, because it divides the Mississippi River system from all neighboring systems. It completely encloses the Mississippi River and all its branches. There is no stream inside this region that does not flow into the Mississippi or one of its tributaries.

This enclosed area is called the *drainage basin* of the Mississippi

River system. Every drop of the water that flows down the river originally fell as precipitation within that drainage basin. A similar basin can be traced for every river in the world.

Stream Systems. Some drainage basins are very large, like that of the Mississippi system (see Figure 15-5). Others are short and narrow, like those of the rivers flowing down the eastern slopes of the Appalachian Mountains. Whatever its size or shape, each drainage basin contains a single stream system that branches like a tree. All the running water within the basin ends up in the same stream that empties into a large body of water, such as a sea or ocean.

A stream system consists of more than running water. It includes all the land surface drained by the system and all the sediment being transported by the system. The potential energy of gravity that drives the system should also be considered a part of it. We have used the word "system" several times in this section, and we have used it many times before in referring to such things as the solar system, high and low pressure systems, etc. In each case the word means something made of many interrelated parts that work together as a unit. You may recall that we also mentioned "closed" systems (see page 128). In a closed system, nothing enters or leaves the system. A stream system is clearly not this kind. It is an open one. The precipitation that provides the water enters from the atmosphere. The water eventually leaves the system through the mouth of the stream or by evaporation. Some of the sediments also leave through the mouth of the stream. And finally, the potential energy used by the system is lost to the environment as heat. (We will consider energy relationships in a stream system in greater detail in the next chapter.)

SUMMARY

1. Every stream and its branches make up a single system that collects all the runoff within a definite area called the drainage basin of the system.
2. A stream system consists of running water, the land surface it drains, the sediment it transports, and the potential energy used to drive it.

CHARACTERISTICS OF STREAMS

While it is true that no two streams are ever exactly alike, there are certain characteristics that are common to all streams. These characteristics, in turn, affect the "life history" of the stream and the valleys that are carved out by it. Although every stream has branches, we can begin by examining a theoretical stream that does not have any. What we discover about such a simple stream can then be applied to each branch. Then by combining the effects of all the branches, we can put together a picture of the action of the system as a whole.

Velocity. Like the rocks and sediments on a hillside, water on a hillside is pulled downward by the force of

TOP VIEW

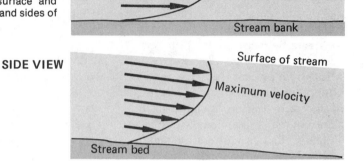

Figure 15-6. Water velocity in a stream. The velocity of the water varies with location in the stream. It is greatest near the surface and least along the bottom and sides of the stream.

gravity. Sediments may be held on a slope by friction, but no force of friction acts on water unless the water is moving. Therefore, water always flows downhill on even the slightest of slopes. However, the speed of its flow does depend on the slope. As the slope increases, the effective force of gravity down the slope also increases. So the velocity of the flowing water increases, too.

As soon as the water starts to flow, forces of friction develop. There is friction between the moving water in a stream and the bed of the stream. There is also friction between the layers of water in the stream as they slide over one another, and between the surface layer and the air. As the velocity of the stream increases, all these forces of friction also increase. There is, then, some velocity at which the force of gravity driving the water down the slope is just balanced by the resisting force of friction. This is the average velocity at which the stream will be moving.

The velocity will not be the same everywhere in the stream. Near the bottom and sides of the bed, it will be least, because that is where the friction is greatest. The velocity will in-

crease as the distance of the water from the bed increases, except near the surface, where friction with the air will slow the water again. Figure 15-6 is a model of the velocity patterns that would be found in the cross section of a typical stream.

Effect of Discharge. As the discharge of a stream increases, the stream becomes deeper and wider in order to move the greater quantity of water being supplied to it. As a result, relatively less of the water is in contact with the bed, and the frictional resistance to the flow has less of an effect on the stream as a whole. The average velocity of the stream therefore increases when its discharge increases. A deep river flowing over a gentle gradient may, then, have a greater average velocity than the same stream near its source, where the gradient is much steeper. However, the velocity of flow *along the bed* will be greater where the gradient is steeper. This is an important factor in the ability of a stream to produce erosion, as we will see later.

Ability to Transport Sediments. In the discussion of gravity as a force of erosion, we pointed out that gravity by itself cannot move sediments very

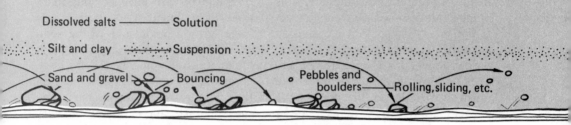

Figure 15-7. Movement of sediments in a stream.

far because most land slopes are not steep enough. The force of gravity acting down a gentle slope is not great enough to overcome the friction between the sediments and the ground. Moving water, however, can provide the additional force needed to move sediments down gradual slopes. Moving water does this in various ways, depending on the size of the sediments (see Figure 15-7).

The smallest sediments—ions—are carried in solution. Colloids, other clays, and silt are kept suspended in the water by its turbulent motion. Sand and small pebbles in a fast-moving stream will be moved by bouncing along the bottom. Larger sediments may be too heavy to be

lifted off the bottom by the moving water, but they may be moved by sliding and rolling. Remember that gravity is always pulling these sediments downward. What the water is really doing is making it easier for the particles to respond to gravity by helping to overcome the resistance of friction.

A large pebble will need more force to start it moving than a particle of sand or silt. If you have ever waded across a stream, you know how much harder it is to keep your footing in a swift part of the current than where the water is moving slowly. The faster a stream is moving, the greater the force it exerts, and the larger the sediments it can move. Figure 15-8 is a graph that shows the average velocity

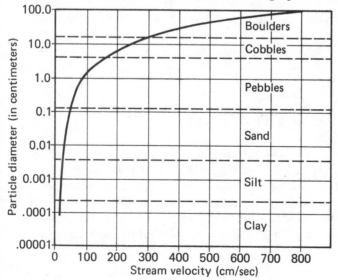

Figure 15-8. Relationship of water velocity to size of sediments transported.

of water that is needed to keep sediments of different sizes moving. This graph confirms what we would expect to find in any stream that is transporting sediment. Where the flow is rapid, we can expect to see sand, gravel, and even rather large stones being moved downward to lower elevations. We expect the water to be quite cloudy or muddy with suspended sediments. Where the stream is moving slowly, we expect to see sand and gravel resting on the bottom, while the finer sediments go drifting by above them.

Quantity of Sediment Transported. The velocity of the water determines the maximum size of the sediments that the stream can move. But that doesn't tell us anything about how *much* sediment the stream will transport. This depends mainly on the discharge of the stream—the amount of water passing a point each second. A river may be carrying enormous quantities of sediment if its discharge is large, even though none of the sediment is coarser than clay or silt. A mountain stream may be moving large boulders, but only a few at a time. So the total mass of sediments moved by the small stream may not be very great.

We may think of erosion as the work that a stream does. In terms of measurable earth changes, it is not just the size of the sediments moved that counts, or the amount of sediments passing a particular point. What is important is the total work of erosion that an entire stream does. In the next section of this chapter we will consider a stream as a total erosional system and see what its effects on its environment may be.

SUMMARY

1. As the slope of a stream bed increases, the average velocity of the stream increases,
2. An increase in the discharge of a stream increases its average velocity.
3. Streams transport sediments as ions in solution, as suspended matter, and by the bouncing and rolling of particles along the stream bed.
4. The size of the sediments that a stream can transport increases as the stream velocity increases.
5. The total amount of sediment that a stream can transport increases as its discharge increases.

EROSION BY STREAMS

Picture in your mind a well-established stream high on a mountainside. Slopes, or gradients, of the surface are steep up here. Imagine, too, that it is spring, and melting snows have saturated the ground. Runoff into the stream is at a seasonal peak, and so is the discharge of the stream. Steep slopes combine with heavy discharge to give the stream a high velocity. It is therefore capable of moving most of the sediments that

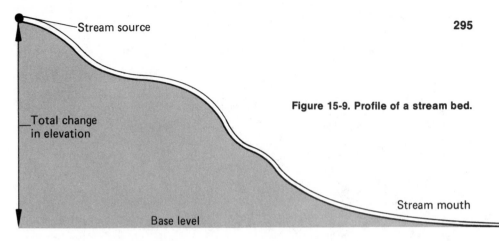

Figure 15-9. Profile of a stream bed.

Stream source

Total change
in elevation

Stream mouth

Base level

may be in it—certainly all the sand and gravel, probably all the larger stones, and perhaps even some boulders.

Where will these sediments come from? Some will be broken loose from the stream bed, but most will come from the bedrock of the surrounding slopes. As weathering breaks the rock into pieces of various sizes, they slide and roll down the steep slopes into the stream. As the stream flows along, it gradually accumulates a greater and greater load of sediments. Irresistibly the stream drags, rolls, bounces, or carries these sediments to ever lower levels.

Is this the only effect of the stream—to transport sediments of weathered rock? Let us see what else the stream may be doing.

The Work of a Stream. Figure 15-9 is a profile of the bed of a stream like the one we have been talking about. The water anywhere along the stream has potential energy due to its elevated position in the earth's gravitational field. When it reaches the lowest point of the profile, it will have lost that potential energy. The amount of potential energy it loses depends only on the difference in height. Whether the water falls straight down over the

edge of a cliff, or runs down a sloping stream bed, the total potential energy lost is the same.

The lowest level to which a stream can flow is called its *base level*. In most cases, this is sea level, although a large lake may act as the base level for a portion of a stream above the lake. The total potential energy of a stream varies with its height above its base level.

Energy, you will recall (page 119), is the capacity to do work. Some of a stream's potential energy may be used to do work. What work may a stream do? Look at Figure 15-10. This is a cross section of the Grand Canyon of the Colorado River in Arizona. Note the V-shape of the canyon with the river at the bottom of the V. Could the stream have cut through the solid rock to carve this canyon? If so, that would certainly be an impressive piece of work. By what process could water cut rock?

First of all, the rushing water can pry loose any grains of material that are projecting into its path. It can also lift flakes of rock that have been weakened by chemical weathering. Most important, however, is the load of sediments being dragged and bounced along the bed. Just as you

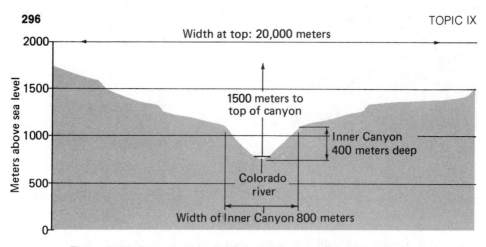

Width at top: 20,000 meters

1500 meters to
top of canyon

Inner Canyon
400 meters deep

Colorado
river

Width of Inner Canyon 800 meters

Meters above sea level

Figure 15-10. Cross section of the Grand Canyon of the Colorado River.

can scrape a hollow into a board with a piece of sandpaper, so a stream can use its sediments to scrape the bottom and sides of its bed. It may take thousands of years for these processes to cut down through a meter of rock. But in the history of the earth, there is time enough for Grand Canyons to be cut many times over.

Youthful Streams. The streams we have been examining are streams with steep gradients, and they have rough sediments flowing rapidly down from high elevations. Such streams usually have V-shaped cross sections. The sharpness of the V will vary, depending on the resistance of the walls to weathering. In some cases, the walls of the canyon are nearly vertical, as in Ausable Chasm along the Ausable River in the Adirondack Mountains of New York (see Figure 15-11). Because of the high velocity of these streams, especially at flood periods, all loose material on their beds is constantly being moved along. Their beds are therefore continuously exposed to erosion and downcutting by the streams. A stream at this stage in its life is called *youthful*. Its actual age in years is not important. One "youth-

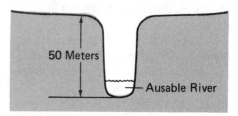

50 Meters

Ausable River

Figure 15-11. Ausable Chasm along the Ausable River in New York State. The Ausable River is an example of a youthful stream.

ful'' stream may be millions of years older than another. It is still youthful if it is still cutting through bedrock.

In this early stage of development, it is quite common to find rapids, where sharp increases in the gradient result in high velocity. Waterfalls are also likely to occur, with the stream dropping almost vertically to a lower elevation. These irregularities in the profile of the stream bed occur because of variations in resistance of the bedrock to erosion. Where the stream runs over a less resistant rock, it will downcut more rapidly, producing the sharp changes in slope that we have mentioned.

These features last only a relatively short time. The very increase in velocity that these features produce gives the stream more cutting power. It therefore tends to remove these steep sections by eroding them away (see Figure 15-12).

Mature Streams. As a youthful stream continues to cut its bed downward, it approaches closer to its base level. Its potential energy for the work of cutting and removing rock becomes less. As a result, its average gradient also decreases. So its velocity near its bed becomes less. It loses the ability to move the larger sediments it has been transporting. The stream bed now becomes covered with this loose material, thus protecting it from further erosion. Only at times of peak flow can the stream move these sediments. Cutting action of the stream becomes very slow, or stops altogether. Meanwhile, weathering and the action of tributary streams have widened the base of the V and formed a valley with gentle slopes, as shown in Figure 15-13.

In its youthful stage, the stream had enough energy to move obstacles or destroy irregularities in its bed. Now

Figure 15-12. Niagara Falls. The stream is eroding the shale more rapidly than the more resistant limestone. Because of undercutting of the falls, they are being moved upstream at a rate of about 1 meter per year.

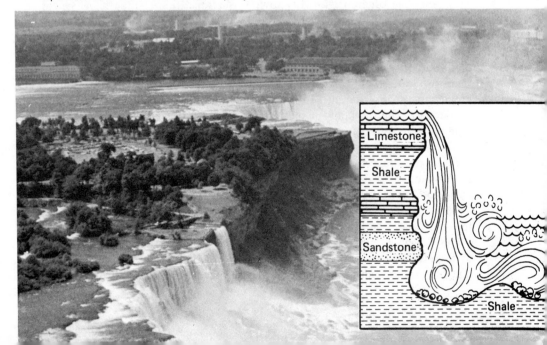

Figure 15-13. Meanders. A stream in the stage of maturity may form loops, or meanders, that swing back and forth across the valley.

the stream is affected more by the obstructions it meets. It goes around them and begins to swing to one side or the other, forming loops called *meanders* and traveling back and forth across its widening valley (see Figure 15-13).

Although the stream is traveling more slowly along its bed than when it was youthful, and therefore cannot transport the larger sediments, this does not mean that its ability to carry sediment has decreased. By now, tributary streams are feeding large volumes of water and sediment into the main stream. Because of the increase in the volume of water, and therefore in its total kinetic energy, a greater mass of sediment can now be carried. But the transported sediment is mostly silt and clay.

The stream is now said to have reached the stage of *maturity*. As in the case of a youthful stream, maturity is not a matter of age in years, but depends only on the characteristics of the stream and its valley.

Old Streams. Finally, the gradient of the stream bed becomes so small that the stream cannot move any but the finest of its sediments. During periods of peak flow, such a stream will usually overflow its banks and flood the nearby portions of its valley. When the flow subsides, a layer of silt and clay is left on the valley surface. This area is called a *flood plain*. The well-sorted sediments of flood plains soon become rich soils.

A stream or river at this stage is considered *old*. One of the features of a river in old age is the shape and behavior of its meanders. A typical pattern for a stream in old age is seen in Figure 15-14. The meanders are strongly looped. From time to time they become cut off from the stream and are left behind as water-filled depressions called *oxbow lakes*. The reason for this is that the water on the outside of a curve has to move faster than that on the inside in order to make the turn. The faster-moving water on the outside of the curve erodes the bank and extends the curve further in the same direction. On the inside of each curve, where the water slows down, sediment tends to be deposited. Figure 15-15 shows how this process leads to the cutting off a loop

Figure 15-14. Stream in old age.

Figure 15-15. Formation of oxbow lakes.

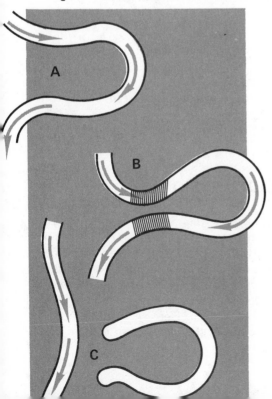

and the forming of an oxbow lake.

The process also causes a stream in old age to weave back and forth across its flood plain, from the base of the hills on one side to the hills on the other. In the course of time (which may be thousands of years), the stream crosses every part of its plain. Wherever it happens to be, it leaves its deposits of silt and clay after every flood. Thus the entire plain acquires a deep cover of soil.

The Life History of a Stream. In this explanation of the life cycle of a stream, we have focused on each stage separately, as if the entire stream changed from one phase to the next as a unit. It is very unlikely that any stream is at the same stage of development throughout its entire length. In fact, most streams tend to have the characteristics of youth near their source and of old age near their mouths, and to be in the mature stage somewhere in between.

The pattern, however, is not often that simple. Look at Figure 15-16, the profile of the Colorado River. Judging by its gradient, the river is almost surely in the youthful stage near its source high in the Rocky Mountains. Near its mouth at the Gulf of California, it is approaching the stage of old age. But the river is certainly in the youthful stage where it is cutting the Grand Canyon, and this is about two-thirds of the way to the river's mouth. The noticeable increase in gradient where the river enters the Grand Canyon explains its "youthfulness" here. We can infer that local conditions can greatly affect the development of a stream all along its course. We will return to this subject in the final chapters of this book.

Figure 15-16. Profile of the Colorado River.

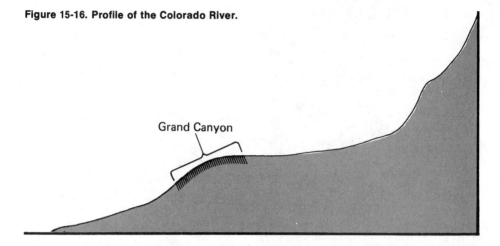

Grand Canyon

Story Without End. How does the life of a stream end? Theoretically, the stream and its branches should eventually reduce its entire drainage basin to a flat plain nearly at sea level. We don't know what such a land would look like because there are no such places on earth. Although weathering and erosion are constantly acting to level the land, other forces seem to be constantly pushing it up again. So a stream in very old age may find itself youthful again as its valley rises. With a fresh supply of potential energy, it begins to repeat its life story.

SUMMARY

1. Youthful streams carrying sediments down steep gradients can cut through solid bedrock.
2. When youthful, streams have V-shaped valleys.
3. In the stage of maturity the valley of a stream widens. The stream ceases to cut through the bedrock.
4. In old age, the stream develops a wide flood plain, across which it wanders in a series of curves, or meanders.

OTHER AGENTS OF EROSION

As we stated earlier in this chapter, running water is by far the leading agent of erosion on a worldwide scale. For those of us who have lived our lives in the humid sections of the United States, running water is the eroding agent that we are most aware of. But there are places in the world, such as the Sahara Desert, where streams almost don't exist. If you lived in such a region, you would be most conscious of the power of the wind to transport sediment. In very cold climates, running water is also seldom seen. Here we would be conscious of the presence of ice and the erosional effects it can produce. You don't have to leave the United States to find places where wind and ice are important agents of erosion. So it will be useful to compare the action of these agents with that of water and to consider briefly the similarities and differences in their effects.

Erosion by Ice. Masses of frozen water on land are called *glaciers.* They are most likely to form in the cold temperatures at high elevations, and fill up the valleys and depressions on mountainsides, somewhat the way water would. Glaciers of this kind are sometimes called "rivers of ice" or "frozen rivers" because they look like rivers that have frozen in place (see Figure 15-17). In some ways they act like very slowly moving water. However, there are some important differences in the way these *valley glaciers* interact with the surface of the land.

Glaciers may also cover vast areas of the earth's surface in the form of sheets of ice, called *continental glaciers.* Long-term changes in the earth's average temperature may cause such ice sheets to extend themselves toward lower latitudes during cooling periods and then to retreat during warmer periods. There is evidence nearly everywhere in the Northern Hemisphere that such an advance and retreat occurred rather recently (in geological terms), ending only about 10,000 years ago.

For our purposes we need not be concerned with the differences between the valley glaciers that resemble rivers and the continental ice sheets that are more like vast seas. Both types have similar transporting properties and both types produce and leave similar results.

Glaciers form by the steady accumulation of snow that falls on their

Figure 15-17. A valley glacier.

Figure 15-18. U-shaped valley formed by glacial erosion.

surfaces. As the snow piles up, its weight compresses the lower portions and turns them to solid ice. If you have ever made a snowball, you may have personally experienced this "icing" effect. The enormous weight of a glacier causes it to move slowly down its valley. The movement of a glacier is like that of a river in very slow motion. The velocity is least at the bottom and sides where the ice is in contact with the valley floor. It is greatest near the center of the top surface of the mass of ice.

When the lower edge of a glacier reaches elevations where the air temperature is above the freezing point, the advance of the ice stops. Streams of water then flow continuously from the melting ice front. The erosional action of these streams will be basically the same as that of any stream.

Where a valley contains a glacier, weathered rock particles continually slide and roll down the slopes, just as they do where the valleys have running streams. However, the sedi-

ments that fall onto a glacier remain on the surface of the ice for a time. Gradually they are covered by fresh snow, and gradually they sink through the ice to the bottom of the mass. Thus the bottom and sides of a glacier become studded with sediments. Unlike the sediments in fast streams, which become rounded and smooth by constant friction among themselves, sediments in a glacier are often sharp and irregular. This is a result of their being ground against the bedrock as the glacier moves. As the glacier moves steadily downslope, it drags these sharp sediments along the surface of the bedrock. The bedrock is thus scratched, torn, and broken, and the surface is eroded wherever the ice is in contact with it—on the sides of the valley, as well as on the bottom. One result of glacial erosion, then, is the carving out of U-shaped valleys, rather than the V's cut by narrow streams (see Figure 15-18).

When, because of climate changes, a glacier is advancing, it pushes a

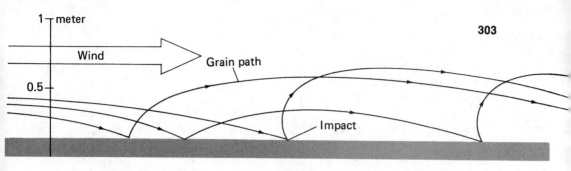

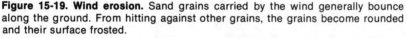

Figure 15-19. Wind erosion. Sand grains carried by the wind generally bounce along the ground. From hitting against other grains, the grains become rounded and their surface frosted.

large load of unsorted sediments ahead of it like a bulldozer. When a warming interval causes the glacier to retreat, it leaves these piles of sediments behind. Thus the remains of glacial erosion are much different from those of stream erosion. These effects will be considered in more detail in later chapters.

Erosion by Wind. If you have ever had a particle of dirt blown into your eye, you know that moving air can transport sediments. For wind erosion to occur, however, there must first of all be a wind, and second, there must be loose, dry particles available for the wind to move. You wouldn't expect a dust storm in a forest, even with winds of 100 km/hr.

Wind erosion is most noticeable in desert regions. Here, weathering has reduced the bedrock to fine particles, mostly of sand size. When a wind blows, the sand grains move in a series of bounces, similar to the movement of sand along a stream bed (see Figure 15-19). Note that the sand grains seldom rise as much as a meter off the ground. However, small piles of windblown sand tend to build up into forms called *dunes*. Sand dunes, which may be 50 meters or more in height, are a common feature of desert regions. They also occur along sandy beaches.

Particles that have been moved by wind erosion have certain noticeable characteristics. They are well rounded by the repeated impact of grain against grain. When examined with a magnifier, their surfaces are seen to have a frosted appearance.

Wind can also erode solid rock, somewhat the way water does, by the grinding action of windblown sand. Such effects of wind erosion are seen in many arid regions that have outcrops of bedrock. Since sand particles blown by wind remain near the ground, their erosional effects are observed only near the base of rocks. An undercutting of a rocky cliff in a des-

Figure 15-20. Erosion of a rock by wind. Because the particles transported by the wind remain close to the ground, the base of the rock undergoes the greatest amount of erosion.

ert region is usually evidence of wind erosion. A striking example of what wind erosion can do is seen in Figure 15-20.

Erosion by Waves. Anyone who has stood on an ocean beach when large waves are rolling in must be aware that enormous forces are at work. There is a constant churning of the sand as the waves break, crash down, ride up the slope, and then fall back. But is erosion going on? There seems to be a constant back-and-forth movement, but is anything being carried *away?* A study of beaches over a period of time shows that transport of the sand does occur. Most of the time there are currents of water flowing parallel to the beach. Although these cannot be seen, their effects are often noticed by swimmers who find themselves being carried down the beach in one direction or the other. Often there are currents flowing in toward the shore at one place and away from the shore at others. These currents have erosional effects that change the shape of the beach and the kinds of sediments on it.

Waves also erode bedrock that is exposed to their action. Weathering produces sediments that are then washed and scraped away by the impact of the waves. So wherever there are rocky slopes along an ocean shore, they are being worn away by the waves. Wave action is another instance of erosion by water—moving water, if not actually "running" water.

Density Currents. The erosional activity of water and wind—and even ice—may be familiar to you. You may have seen their effects in your environment, even if you were not conscious of the process at work before

you started this course. There is another erosional agent that is seldom observed and whose existence has only recently been discovered. Much is still to be learned about it. This agent is called a *density current*. It can form and operate wherever two materials of different densities are in contact and one material is able to flow over or under the other. One detailed example will serve to illustrate some of the properties and effects this erosional agent may have.

In 1935 Hoover Dam was completed, creating a lake (called Lake Mead) almost 130 km long in the original channel of the Colorado River. It was well known before that time that the Colorado carries over a hundred billion kilograms of sediment each year. It was expected that this sediment would gradually accumulate and spread out over the floor of the lake.

Soon after the completion of the dam, scientists began to record a sediment flow along the floor of the lake of an unexpected kind. Once or twice a year, a thick flow of clay and water moved down the lake. This flow might take a week or more to travel the entire 130 km. When the flow reached the dam, the rise in lake floor level was sometimes as much as 10 m, settling out over a period of time to less than 6 m.

These flows were examined in detail in this natural laboratory. Figure 15-21 shows the results of this study. The mechanism of this flow is now understood to be associated with a density difference. The clay-laden water that arrives at the new mouth of the Colorado as it enters Lake Mead settles at first. Soon, however, the balance is upset, usually by a heavy flow of new sediment-laden water.

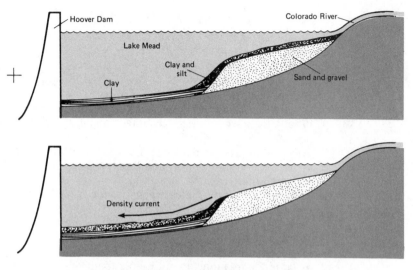

Figure 15-21. Density currents in Lake Mead.

This triggers the flow of a density current—the flow of the denser mixture of water and sediment down under the less dense, clearer water above.

Recent research indicates that this specialized type of transport may be of even greater importance than was first realized. Density flows have been observed along the margins of the continental shelf in the ocean. This may be an important mechanism for moving sediment to the deep ocean floor.

Effects on Sediments. If we review the processes of erosion that have been described in this chapter, we can see that each agent of erosion produces different effects on the sediments it transports. Erosion by running water rounds and smooths the particles it moves. Sediments moved by glaciers tend to retain their original irregular and sharp outlines. Wind-driven particles are well-rounded, but tend to have a frosted or finely pitted surface. These different effects are of importance to the earth scientist because they help him infer the process that brought sediments to where they are found. This, in turn, helps him infer the conditions that existed in the environment at the time the transport occurred. Very often, these conditions are quite different from those of the present environment. In later chapters we will see how some of these inferences can be applied.

SUMMARY

1. Moving ice, called glaciers, can erode rock and transport sediments.
2. Wind can transport sediment of sand size or smaller and can produce distinctive erosional effects, such as sand dunes.
3. Wave action has erosional effects on shoreline rocks and on beaches.
4. Density currents can transport sediments along underwater slopes.
5. Each agent of erosion produces distinctive changes in the material it transports.

REVIEW QUESTIONS

Group A

1. What are *transported sediments*?
2. What are *residual sediments*?
3. What is *erosion*?
4. Are transported sediments or residual sediments most common? Which type provides evidence of erosion?
5. What is the main driving force of all erosional processes?
6. What effects are produced by gravity acting alone as an erosional agent?
7. What is the predominant agent of erosion on the earth?
8. What is meant by the *drainage basin* of a stream system?
9. Name all the parts of a stream system.
10. What is the relationship between the slope of a stream bed and the average velocity of the stream?
11. How does an increase in the discharge of a stream affect its average velocity?
12. Describe the ways in which streams transport sediments.
13. What is the relationship between stream velocity and the size of the sediments that the stream can transport?
14. What is the relationship between the discharge of a stream and the amount of sediment that the stream can transport?
15. What type of stream is most effective in cutting through bedrock?
16. What is the shape of the valley of a young stream?
17. Describe the valley of a stream in the mature stage.
18. Describe a stream in old age.
19. What is a *glacier*?
20. What is the role of wind in erosion?
21. What causes erosion on shoreline rocks and on beaches?
22. How are sediments transported along underwater slopes?

Group B

1. a. Explain what observations would be needed to decide if a soil is residual or transported.
   b. Which is more important, weathering or erosion, in the formation of a residual soil? Explain.
   c. Which is more important, weathering or erosion, in the formation of a transported soil? Explain.
2. Why do earth scientists usually consider gravity to be necessary for erosion to occur?
3. a. The velocity of the water in a stream varies at different points across the stream's width and at different depths. Describe these differences and explain what causes them.
   b. Describe the various types of particles that may be eroded by running water.
   c. Explain what causes a stream to pass from youth to maturity and from maturity to old age.
4. List the observations that would lead you to believe that the following agents of erosion had been active in a particular area: (a) ice, (b) wind, (c) waves, (d) density currents.

REVIEW EXERCISES

1. In the study of weathering of tombstones in Connecticut (page 259), the investigator found that the surface facing west was most weathered and the surface facing north was least weathered. Present an hypothesis that explains this pattern of weathering.

2. Examine the outside walls of several old stone or brick buildings in your area. Determine which wall of each building shows the most weathering.

   a. Is the direction in which the most weathered wall faces the same for every building studied?

   b. In which direction do the walls showing the least weathering face?

   c. Are the results of your investigation the same as the results of the study of Connecticut tombstones? If so, do you think that the causes of the weathering pattern are the same in your area as in Connecticut?

   d. Examine several buildings that are either made of wood or have wooden parts. Can you observe the same kinds of weathering effects in the wood as you saw in the brick or stone? Is the order of weathering (by direction) the same for wood as for the stone or brick?

   e. Are the weathering effects that you have observed caused by physical or chemical weathering?

3. Figure 14-8 (page 269) shows the relationship between climate and weathering (Point *A* in that illustration is Middletown, Connecticut).

   a. What climatic changes would have to occur in the Middletown area for the type of weathering to change?

   b. Referring to Figure 14-8, find which type of weathering occurs in your local area. (To do this, you will have to have some idea of the average annual precipitation and average annual temperature of your area.)

   c. What would happen to the weathering pattern in your area if the average annual temperature increased over long periods of time by 5°C? What would happen if the average annual temperature decreased by 5°C?

4. Below are graphs showing average monthly temperatures and rainfall for locations in five different types of climates. Using information from the graphs and from Figure 14-8 (page 269), describe the type of weathering that would occur at each location.

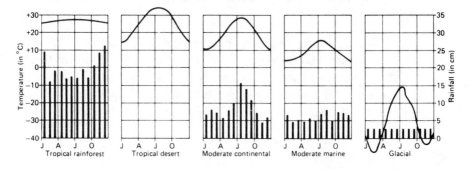

TOPIC X
THE DEPOSITIONAL PROCESS

A page from Leonardo da Vinci's *Notebooks* describing the actions of rivers. Some of the notes are in "mirror writing", that is, written backwards.

CHAPTER 16

You will know something about the depositional process if you can:
1. Describe some of the factors that affect the deposition of particles.
2. Describe some of the characteristics of an erosional-depositional system.

> *The streams of rivers move different kinds of matter which are of varying degrees of gravity, and they are moved farther from their position in proportion as they are lighter, and will remain nearer to the bottom in proportion as they are heavier, and will be carried a greater distance when driven by water of greater power.*
>
> *Leonardo da Vinci*
> *1452–1519*

DEPOSITION

If we wanted to put the important ideas of the last chapter and of this one into a single sentence, we couldn't do much better than the quotation on the preceding page from Leonardo da Vinci's notebooks.

Leonardo da Vinci lived more than 500 years ago. He is best known as a great painter, sculptor, and architect of the period of history called the Renaissance. You may recognize him as the artist who painted the *Mona Lisa* and *The Last Supper*. But Leonardo was also a keen observer of his environment. He left a vast collection of notebooks in which he recorded the inferences he made from his observations. Some of his ideas and conclusions are now known to be incorrect. But most of them show that he was a man of amazing insight. It is remarkable that long before the scientific world had even thought about such things as erosional-depositional systems, Leonardo could describe, in so few words, how a stream transports and deposits earth materials.

Chapter 15 was concerned with the erosional process, that is, the ways in which earth materials are removed from one location and transported to another. We also considered the changes in the environment that are caused by erosion. This chapter will focus on the processes that cause materials to be left or dropped in their new locations. These processes are called *deposition*.

Sediments. The earth materials that are transported during erosion and dropped during deposition are bits and pieces of weathered rock. As you learned in Chapter 14, these pieces of rock may be of almost any size, from ions on up to boulders. Whatever their size, they are called *sediments*. The process of deposition is therefore also called *sedimentation*.

Sedimentation usually occurs in the medium that has transported the sediments. In most cases this is water, and we will focus most of our attention on sedimentation that occurs in water. We will also consider sedimentation that occurs in air and in ice.

Erosional-Depositional Systems. From what we have said thus far, it should be clear that there is no deposition without erosion. The materials have to be removed from one location (erosion) before they can be left at another (deposition). We can also say that there is no erosion without deposition. There is a limit to how far an erosional process can move materials before they have to be dropped. We will shortly be looking at the factors that cause deposition to occur. The continuous removal, transport, and deposition of sediments within a given region make up an *erosional-depositional system*.

One of the discoveries of earth science is that new rocks are continuously being manufactured from old ones. This natural recycling of rock materials is called the rock cycle, and it will be examined in Chapter 18. You will find that the operation of erosional-depositional systems is a key idea in understanding the rock cycle. This is just one more example of how all the processes of earth change interlock with one another.

SUMMARY

1. The processes by which transported materials are left in new locations are called deposition.
2. Rock particles that are transported by erosional processes are called sediments. *Sedimentation* is another term for *deposition*.

FACTORS AFFECTING DEPOSITION

We saw in Chapter 15 how moving water is able to transport sediments. What happens when water carrying sediments slows down, or stops altogether, as when a river enters a lake or ocean? We find that some of the particles settle out. This is to be expected. After all, rock particles are denser than water and should be expected to sink in water. But what we also observe is that some particles settle quickly, others take much longer, and some seem to take forever—that is, they never do get to the bottom. What accounts for these differences in settling rates? Let's try some experiments to find out.

Particle Size. Figure 16-1 shows a plastic cylinder, about one meter tall, nearly filled with water, and a beaker containing particles of matter. These particles are of mixed sizes, but are all of the same shape and density.

When the particles are poured into the column of water, an interesting thing happens. The particles do not all settle to the bottom at the same rate. For the most part, the largest particles settle to the bottom most quickly. The smaller, lighter particles take longer to settle. Figure 16-2 illustrates what the general arrangement of the particles would be after settling to the bottom of the cylinder.

If you were to examine the water in the column closely several minutes

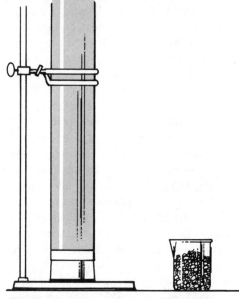

Figure 16-1. Set-up for observing settling patterns of particles of varying densities, shapes, and sizes.

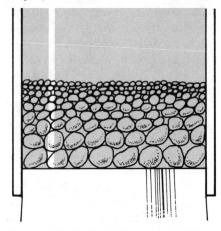

Figure 16-2. Settling pattern of particles of the same density but of different sizes.

after adding the particles, you might notice that some of the tiniest particles had still not settled out. In fact, you might have to wait several days for some of the particles to settle. Particles of colloidal size may remain suspended for an indefinite period.

Colloids are largely responsible for the muddy appearance of many lakes and rivers. Because of their very tiny size, colloids remain suspended for very long periods as they are moved about by the natural motions of the water in which they are present.

Size, then, is one important factor in determining the rate at which particles settle out of water. Notice in Figure 16-2 that, as a result of the sorting of particles according to size, distinct regions or zones within the layer of sediment can be identified. We will return to this observation later in the chapter.

If we measure the time it takes for particles of the same material but of various sizes to settle through the same depth of water, our data will show a definite relationship between particle size and settling time. Figure 16-3 is a graphic model, or graph, of that relationship. You can see that the

graph agrees with the results of the experiment using a mixture of particle sizes. Larger particles take less time to settle out than smaller particles. This is an inverse relationship: as particle size increases, settling time decreases. Or we can turn it around and say that as particle size decreases, settling time increases.

Reasons for this Observed Relationship. Why should smaller particles sink more slowly than larger particles of the same density? Think about the forces that are acting on the particle. The force of gravity is pulling the particle downward. You will recall that this force is called the weight of the particle. It depends only on the mass of the particle. The other force acting on the particle is friction with the water. As the particle sinks through the water, this force resists the motion. That is, the force of friction acts upward on the particle.

The force of friction depends on the speed of the particle. As the speed increases, the resisting force of friction also increases. As long as the downward force of the particle's weight is greater than the upward force of friction, the particle will gain speed as it sinks. But at some speed the two forces will become equal, and the particle will sink from then on at a constant speed. This is the maximum rate at which the particle can sink in still water. (The same thing happens to an object falling in air.)

Now, we have already seen (page 271) that as any material is cut into smaller and smaller pieces, the total surface area of the pieces gets larger and larger. That is, the amount of surface *relative to the weight* of a particle becomes larger as its size

Figure 16-3. Relationship between particle size and settling time.

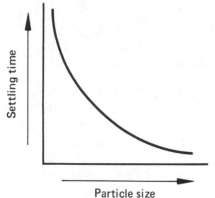

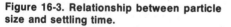
Particle size

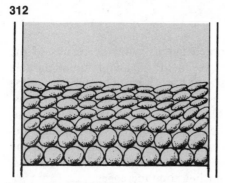

Figure 16-4. Settling pattern of particles of same density and maximum diameter, but different shapes.

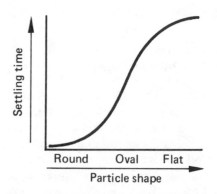

Figure 16-5. Relationship between particle shape and settling time.

gets smaller. Therefore, the frictional resistance is relatively greater for smaller particles, and a balance between the upward and downward forces is reached at a slower rate of descent.

For very small particles, this balance occurs at very slow sinking speeds. If there is the slightest amount of turbulence (random motion) in the water, it will completely offset the slow downward drift of the particles. Since every body of water has some movement in it due to convection, winds, or other disturbances, very small particles are often kept suspended indefinitely by these natural movements of the water.

Particle Shape. Let's consider a second experiment. We will use the same column of water as in the experiment on particle size. We will also use particles of the same density, as we did in that case. This time, however, the particles will all have about the same size, that is, the same maximum diameter, but they will have different *shapes*. Some will be spherical, some will be oval, and some will be flat.

Figure 16-4 shows the probable results of pouring the different-shaped particles into the column of water.

The spherical particles are on the bottom, the oval shapes in the middle, and the flat particles on top. These results indicate that shape is also a factor affecting the rate of deposition. A graph of the relationship between particle shape and settling time is shown in Figure 16-5. This graph indicates that the more spherical the particle, the faster the settling rate. There is a direct relationship between the degree of flatness and the time required to settle to the bottom. As flatness increases, settling time increases.

You should be able to see the reason for this relationship. A flat particle has much less weight than a round one of the same size. It may weigh only a tenth or a twentieth as much, if it is really thin. But its surface area and therefore its friction with the water will be only a little less. So the balance between upward and downward forces will be reached much sooner with the light, flat particle than with the heavy, round one.

A similar effect of shape on the speed of objects falling in air can be easily observed. Take two identical sheets of paper. Crumple one into a ball, and drop both at the same time. The ball of paper reaches the floor much sooner than the flat sheet.

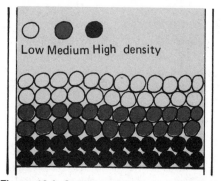

Figure 16-6. Settling pattern of particles of the same size and shape but of different densities.

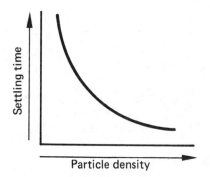

Figure 16-7. Relationship between particle density and settling time.

Particle Density. You may have noticed that in the description of each of the experiments, three characteristics of the particles were mentioned. In addition to size and shape, the density of the particles was included. You have probably guessed that density is also a factor in determining the rate of settling. Once again, we can use the same setup to study the effect of density. This time the particles will be of the same size and shape, but will have different densities. The particles will be spherical in shape, identical in size, but range in density from low to medium to high.

If we pour the particles of mixed densities into the water, the result will be similar to that shown in Figure 16-6. Note the key that identifies particle density. The result of this experiment indicates that there is a direct relationship between particle density and settling rate; that is, the denser the particle, the faster it will settle. Figure 16-7 shows this relationship graphically.

This result is also easy to explain. Since the particles have the same size and shape, the frictional forces on them will be the same as they sink through the water. But the denser particles will be heavier. So they will sink faster.

Deposition of Mixed Sediments. In the three experiments just described, we were careful to have only one factor vary at a time. Thus we were able to observe the effect of that factor—size, shape, or density—by itself. Nature, of course, is not so scientific. In a natural depositional system, particles of many sizes, shapes, and densities are likely to be present. Furthermore, many different depositional events may occur, over a period of time, in a given system.

We can perform an experiment to see what may happen in such a real-world situation. Once again, the cylinder and column of water will be used. This time, however, earth materials consisting of particles of mixed sizes, shapes, and densities will be poured into the water. In addition, we will produce several separate "events" of deposition by adding equal amounts of mixed sediment to the column of water four separate times. After each beakerful of sediment is added to the water, sufficient time will be allowed for most of the particles to settle out before the next beakerful of sediment is added.

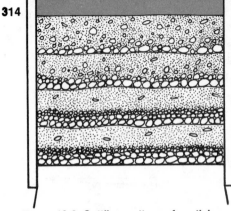

Figure 16-8. Settling pattern of particles of mixed sizes, shapes, and densities.

Figure 16-8 shows the general arrangement of the sediments after the last beakerful has been allowed to settle. If you examine the column of sediments carefully, you will notice that there are four distinct layers and that each layer has similar properties..The roundest, largest, and densest particles are at the bottom of each layer, while the smallest, flattest, and least dense particles are at the top of each layer. This separation of particles during deposition is known as *sorting*. When the sorting occurs from bottom to top throughout a layer, it is called *vertical sorting*.

Graded Bedding. Closer examination of each layer in Figure 16-8 will provide still more information. You will probably notice that the degree of sorting, or separation of particles of different sizes and shapes, is greater in the bottom layer than in the top layer. The reason for this is that the particles in the bottom layer sank through a greater depth of water and therefore had more time to become separated. Remember that the separation occurs because some particles are sinking faster than others. If the particles sink only a short distance before coming to rest, they will not have

a chance to become as well separated, or sorted, as they would in deeper water. So, within each layer the particles are sorted according to size, shape, and density, but the degree of sorting is directly related to the depth of water through which the particles have settled. Layers of sediment that are each sorted, as in this experiment, are said to be *graded*. The layers themselves are referred to as *graded beds* of sediment. (See Figure 16-9.)

Vertical sorting or grading usually occurs in shallow, quiet bodies of water. If the streams entering such bodies of water have seasonal variations in discharge, and therefore in the amount and size of sediments they carry, deposition will occur in the form of graded beds. Each graded bed will be the accumulation from one seasonal flow.

Graded bedding also occurs on the sea floor. As shown in Figure 16-10, the edge of a continent extends underwater as a relatively shallow shelf, called the *continental shelf*. At some distance from the shore, the continental surface descends sharply in a region called the *continental slope*. Along the continental slope there are

Figure 16-9. Graded beds of sediment.

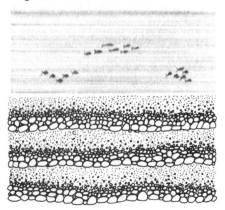

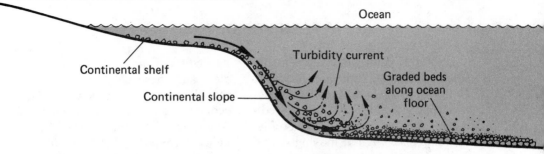

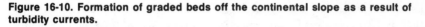

Figure 16-10. Formation of graded beds off the continental slope as a result of turbidity currents.

accumulations of sediments in an unstable condition. Just as landslides of loose rocks, gravel, and sand can suddenly occur on hillsides, it is believed that similar sudden movements of sediment can occur on these underwater slopes. When this happens, the movement results in a flow of water and sediment called a *turbidity current*. The sediments are swirled around by the current and then settle to the flat sea floor beyond the slope. In this settling process, the sediments become well sorted. Each such event of deposition is like the dumping of each beakerful of mixed sediments in the experiment shown in Figure 16-8.

Earth scientists use observations of graded bedding to help them infer the conditions that existed at the time the deposition took place. Where highly graded beds of sediment are found today, it can often be inferred that a lake or some quiet body of water once existed. Sedimentary deposits in which the layers are not well sorted, but instead are a mixture of particles of various sizes, shapes, and densities, usually indicate that deposition took place in water that was either not very quiet or not very deep. Thus, the type of sediments and the degree of sorting help earth scientists determine the location, depth, and extent of bodies of water that once covered the land, but no longer exist. The study of sediments is one of the methods that earth scientists use to trace the history of changes of the earth's surface. We will examine this method and others in more detail in Chapter 18.

SUMMARY

1. If all factors other than size are equal, smaller particles settle more slowly in fluids than do larger particles.
2. Very small particles, such as clay and colloids, may remain suspended in water indefinitely.
3. If all factors other than shape are equal, flatter particles settle more slowly in fluids than do rounded particles.
4. If all factors other than density are equal, particles of higher density settle in fluids faster than do particles of lower density.
5. When several events of deposition in quiet water occur, each involving a mixture of sediments, vertical sorting will take place and graded beds of sediment will be formed.

PATTERNS OF DEPOSITION

Up to this point we have been considering sedimentation in still water. Our objective was to discover the factors that affect the settling of sediments, and this was easiest to do first in water that was not moving. However, a great deal of sedimentation takes place in water that *is* moving, either in streams, or in currents in lakes and oceans. Let us see what some of the characteristics of such sedimentation are.

Effect of Stream Velocity. Every stream is part of an erosional-depositional system. In the preceding chapter we learned how the transport of sediments depends on the stream velocity. As the velocity increases, the stream is able to transport particles of increasing size. It follows that whenever the velocity of the stream *decreases,* it loses some of its ability to move sediments. The largest of the particles being moved will be left behind first. The slower the stream velocity becomes, the smaller the sediments that will be deposited.

Erosion occurs when particles of earth materials are moved from one place to another. Deposition occurs when the particles stop moving and either settle down or get left behind. Thus in every erosional-depositional system, erosion occurs whenever the medium is gaining speed, and deposition occurs whenever it is losing speed.

It is helpful to remember that larger sediments, such as sand and gravel, are moved by water mainly by being rolled, dragged, or bounced along the bottom. When water that is moving sand and gravel slows down, it loses its ability to move the largest particles, and these get left behind. Although it is correct to say that these sediments have been deposited by the water, you should not think of them as being "dropped" like the particles in our experiments with the column of water. The particles of sand and gravel were never very far above the bottom, if at all, even while they were moving.

Silt and clay are light enough to be actually suspended in the moving water. But gravity acts on them all the same, and they are constantly drifting downward through the water even as the water moves along. However, eddies and swirls and other currents in moving streams constantly stir up these fine particles. Even when some of them do touch bottom, they are soon swept up into suspension again. In this way, the particles are steadily carried along. But even these fine sediments will settle out if the stream velocity becomes too low.

Horizontal Sorting. We can now begin to form a picture of what would happen in a stream that is gradually slowing down. At first it will deposit the larger, rounder, denser particles, such as pebbles. If the slowing is gradual, most of these will be left behind before particles of sand begin to be deposited. Further along in the stream's course, after the sand has been deposited, some silt and clay will settle out. The smallest particles of clay and colloids will be carried the farthest and are likely to reach the mouth of the stream before being deposited.

If we look at the bed of a stream that is gradually slowing down over a

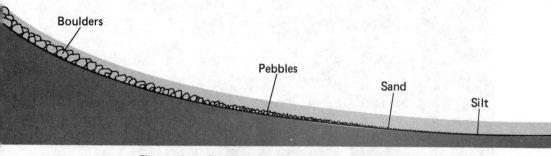

Figure 16-11. Horizontal sorting along a stream bed.

horizontal distance, we see something like Figure 16-11. As we look along the stream bed from the region of highest velocity to the region of lowest velocity, we see a gradual reduction in the size of the sediments. Thus, instead of being graded vertically, the sediments are graded *horizontally*. This is called *horizontal sorting*. It is exactly what Leonardo da Vinci had in mind.

Sedimentation at the Mouth of a River. The model that we used in the last section was a stream that gradually slowed down as it passed along its course. Real streams do not behave this way. The velocity may change in a very irregular pattern, sometimes increasing, sometimes decreasing, as the gradient and width of the stream bed change. But whatever happens along the way, every stream has some velocity as it approaches its outlet. Then, when it enters the sea or other large body of water, the velocity suddenly drops.

The situation is now much closer to that of sedimentation in quiet water. The forces that may have kept sediments suspended and moving are no longer acting, and the sediments therefore settle out. Sediments that may have traveled thousands of kilometers, taking many years to make the journey, have finally come

to rest in a new environment. In later chapters we will see the importance of this event.

Sediments at the mouth of a stream often form a deposit called a *delta*. The term "delta" is derived from the Greek letter Δ. This type of land form was given this name because some of the first ones recognized, such as that at the mouth of the Nile River (Figure 16-12), were roughly triangular in

Figure 16-12. Nile delta.

Figure 16-13. Mississippi delta.

shape. However, not all river deltas are triangular in shape. For example, the Mississippi delta (Figure 16-13) is a branching, or "bird-foot" type, and its outline is much more complex than that of the Nile delta.

As we have just seen, when a stream enters the quieter waters of a lake or bay, its velocity is suddenly slowed. However, the horizontal motion, or current, of the stream does not *stop* completely at the stream's mouth. The current decreases more or less gradually, depending on the discharge at the mouth. The effect of the current can be felt some distance from shore. For example, the flow from the Amazon River in South America, which has the world's largest discharge, is so powerful that its effect

can be felt several kilometers out at sea.

As a result of the gradual slowing of the current at a stream's mouth, some horizontal sorting of sediments occurs. The largest, densest particles are deposited closest to the shoreline, where the decrease in stream velocity is most pronounced. As you move out from the shoreline, the general pattern shows a gradual change from coarse to fine, from roundest to flattest, and from most dense to least dense. The diagram in Figure 16-14 illustrates what this type of sorting might look like. You should be aware of the fact that the process of sorting usually does not produce perfect separation. For example, sand may be found mixed with coarser particles near the

Figure 16-14. Horizontal sorting where a stream enters the ocean.

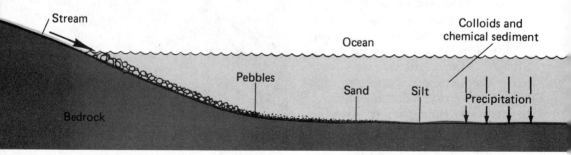

shore and also with silt and clay farther out in deeper water. However, the general pattern is fairly definite.

Particles of colloidal size are usually prevented from settling by the electrical charge they have. This charge is similar to the charge of static electricity that some materials acquire when they are rubbed. The colloidal particles usually have the same kind of charge (either positive or negative). Since like charges repel each other, the colloidal particles repel each other. Any tendency to settle and come closer together is resisted by this force of repulsion.

However, when colloids enter sea water, they meet an environment that contains ions of both kinds of charge. These ions can interact with the colloids and neutralize their charge, and even cause the particles to clump together by electrical attraction. In this way particles large enough to settle out are formed. This clumping process is called *flocculation*.

Sediments that are dissolved in the water and present as ions may also be deposited under certain conditions. In this type of deposition, the water becomes *saturated* with the particular substance. It can no longer hold all the ions that are present, and the ions join together to form solid crystals, which then settle out of the water. Crystals that form in and settle out of a solution are called *precipitates*. The process itself is called *precipitation*. Large beds of the mineral gypsum (calcium sulfate) and the mineral halite (sodium chloride, or common salt) are believed to have been deposited by precipitation from saturated sea water, or from inland seas that have dried up by evaporation.

Deposition in Other Media. We have been concentrating on deposition of sediments in water, since this is the medium in which most erosion and deposition occurs. But there are two other media of erosion—ice and air—and deposition occurs in these media, too. Just as there are depositional patterns that are characteristic of sediments deposited in water, these other agents of erosion also produce characteristic depositional patterns.

Ice. Glaciers, or moving ice, are erosional agents. Sediments deposited by glaciers are divided into two kinds, *direct* and *indirect*. Direct glacial deposits are sediments that are left by the ice itself when it melts. Little liquid water is involved in the process of direct glacial deposition. One characteristic of such deposits is that the sediment is generally unsorted. Particles of all sizes, shapes, and densities are deposited together. A typical direct glacial deposit is simply a pile of unsorted rock material, looking much as if it had just been dumped from a dumptruck (see Figure 16-15).

Figure 16-15. Direct glacial deposit. The rock material in direct glacial deposits is unsorted.

Indirect glacial deposits are also called *fluvio-glacial* deposits. Fluvio-glacial sediments consist of particles that have been carried by the glacial ice to a certain point, and have been carried further by the water produced from the melting ice of the glacier. Because these sediments have been carried at least some distance by water, there is some sorting of sediment particles. Even where there may have been some sorting of particles, other clues help to identify these deposits as being glacial. Examination of individual particles will show that they are partially rounded and are usually grooved and scratched as a result of being dragged by the ice.

Wind. In some parts of the world, wind is responsible for the deposition of large amounts of sediment. Air, like water, is a fluid. Thus, in wind-deposited sediments, there tends to be a pattern of sorting similar to that in water-deposited sediments. However, particles deposited by wind are generally finer or smaller than those deposited by water. When examined under a magnifying glass, individual grains of wind-deposited sediment often appear quite rounded, some nearly spherical. The surface of the particles often appears frosted.

A side view of wind-deposited sediment shows fine layers of well-sorted particles. Individual layers often appear to rest upon one another at varying angles, as seen in Figure 16-16. For example, a series of nearly horizontal layers may be covered by a set of layers tilting down to the right. Other layers, still higher up, may tilt down to the left. Tilted layers such as these are said to be *cross-bedded*. The changes in the directions of the various layers is believed to be caused by changes in wind direction.

Gravity As An Erosional-Depositional Agent. As we already pointed out in Chapter 15, gravity is the force that drives all erosional-depositional systems. Gravity causes streams to flow and glaciers to move. Even winds are caused by gravity acting on masses of air with different densities. Gravity can also act alone as an agent of erosion and deposition, without involving any medium.

Wherever the surface slopes, earth materials may move downslope under the influence of gravity, without the help of water, ice, or wind. These materials will accumulate, or be deposited, at the base of the slope, but will show no evidence of sorting at all (see Figure 16-17). The rock fragments are

Figure 16-16. Wind-deposited sediment.

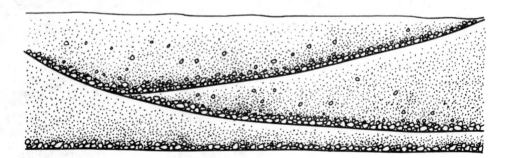

generally sharply angular and blocky in appearance. They will not show any of the characteristics of particles moved by wind, ice, or water, such as pitting, scratching, or polishing.

Earth changes that are brought about by erosion and deposition are predictable and possess identifying characteristics. In later chapters of this book you will discover how earth scientists use their understanding of these processes to help them unravel the mysteries of past earth changes and predict earth changes that are yet to come.

Figure 16-17. Gravity is an erosional-depositional agent.

SUMMARY

1. A decrease in the velocity of an erosional agent, such as moving water or wind, will produce a pattern of horizontal sorting of sediments.
2. Patterns of deposition and the characteristics of the sediments often indicate the medium in which the deposition occurred.
3. Glacial deposits are either completely unsorted, or partially sorted if running water from the melting ice was involved in the deposition.
4. Wind-deposited sediments usually consist of well-sorted, small particles in layers that may be tilted with respect to one another.
5. Gravity acting alone may produce deposits of unsorted rock particles of all sizes at the bases of hills, cliffs, and mountainsides.

CHARACTERISTICS OF EROSIONAL-DEPOSITIONAL SYSTEMS

We now know enough about the factors that affect erosion and deposition to sum up some of the characteristics of erosional-depositional systems as a whole. A good way to do this is by means of a model. But first let us say exactly what we mean by an erosional-depositional system.

An erosional-depositional system has two main parts. One part of the system is a continuous medium of erosion, such as a stream with all its tributaries, extending from its source to its mouth. The other part of the sys-

tem is all the land surface that can be eroded by the medium. In the case of a stream system, this includes all the surface from which runoff can enter the stream. It is the *drainage area* of the stream system. The area of an erosional-depositional system thus has definite boundaries. All deposition that occurs inside those boundaries is the result of erosion that has also occurred inside those boundaries.

To keep our model of an erosional-depositional system simple, we will

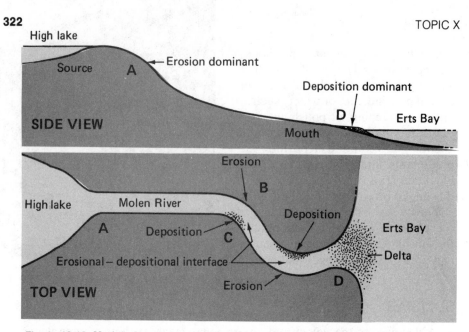

Figure 16-18. Model of a stream representing an erosional-depositional system.

have only a single stream in it, without tributaries. This will allow us to make general statements that apply to all parts of erosional-depositional systems, without being concerned about details that may vary from one system to another.

Figure 16-18 represents a typical model for our purposes. High Lake is the source for the Molen River, and Erts Bay is its outlet. Looking down on the system, we see that the river has curves along its course. Looking at the system in profile, we see that the gradient varies along the river's course.

Erosion and Deposition in the Model System. You have learned that when the velocity of a stream increases, its ability to transport sediment also increases. Erosion therefore becomes dominant at such places. Where the velocity decreases, the stream loses some of its transporting ability, and deposition becomes dominant. Where in our model system is the velocity of

the stream probably increasing? One such place is the region marked A in Figure 16-18, where the gradient is increasing along the stream's course. From your experience with gradients in real life, you expect the stream to pick up speed as it enters the steeper gradient at A, and it does. Region A is therefore a region where erosion is dominant.

Down near Erts Bay, in the region marked D, the bed of the stream flattens out; the gradient is decreasing. Therefore, in region D, deposition is dominant over erosion. At the bay itself, where a delta has been formed, the stream velocity decreases almost to zero, there is practically no erosion, and only deposition is occurring to any noticeable extent.

Where else in the stream is either erosion or deposition likely to be dominant over the other? As you saw in Chapter 15, stream velocity always increases on the outside of curves and decreases on the inside, relative to the average velocity of the stream at that point in its course. Therefore, erosion is dominant at the point labeled *B*, and deposition is dominant at point *C*.

Erosional-Depositional Interfaces. What do we mean when we say that erosion or deposition is "dominant"? To understand this term, remember that the movement of sediments by running water is a very erratic affair. As a stream transports sediments, millions of individual events of erosion and deposition are continuously occurring. Some particles are stopping for a time, others that had been at rest are being moved again. If more particles are being picked up and moved along than are settling down and coming to rest at any given place, then erosion is dominant at that place. But where more particles are being deposited than are being picked up and moved away, deposition is dominant.

Every erosional-depositional system has places in it where erosion is dominant (as on the outside of curves and along steep gradients), and other places where deposition is dominant (on the inside of curves and in regions of small gradient). You can see that there must be regions in between where neither process is dominant. In other words, there are interfaces between erosion and deposition. In our model, such an interface would be found about midway between points *B* and *C* in Figure 16-18 as well as at other places between *A* and *D*. At these interfaces we find a condition we have met many times already—a state of dynamic equilibrium, in which two opposing processes, erosion and deposition, are exactly balanced.

Energy in Erosional-Depositional Systems. It is interesting to examine erosional-depositional systems in terms of energy changes. When we do this, we get a new view of what is actually going on during erosion and deposition. When a rock falls from a cliff, the rock loses potential energy and gains kinetic energy. In an erosional system, the medium and sediments also acquire kinetic energy by losing potential energy. Refer again to our model in Figure 16-18. At the source of the stream (region *A*), the water and the sediments have a certain amount of potential energy. As they begin to move down to lower levels, they gain kinetic energy as their potential energy decreases.

However, the stream and its sediments soon reach a maximum velocity because of the retarding effects of friction. As the water and the sediments rub against the stream bed and against each other, friction transforms their kinetic energy into sound and heat.

Where the stream gradient and bed characteristics are fairly uniform, the velocity will be constant. The decreasing potential energy will be just enough to make up the energy being lost through friction. Where the gradient increases, the stream velocity will increase, and erosion will be dominant. Here, some potential energy is being converted to additional kinetic energy. But as the stream approaches its mouth, its velocity decreases and deposition becomes dominant. Here, the stream and the sediments are losing kinetic energy. Finally, the water and sediments come completely to rest. They have lost some of the potential energy they once had, and they have no kinetic energy to show for it. In short, the erosional-depositional system has lost energy.

In terms of energy then, every erosional-depositional system is a losing proposition. All it accomplishes is to take particles of matter that were at rest at a higher elevation and bring them to rest at a lower elevation. Kinetic energy goes from zero to zero. Potential energy goes from something to something less. Remember, however, that "loss" of energy does not mean the destruction or disappearance of energy. It merely means that energy once possessed by the system has been transferred to the environment, chiefly in the form of heat. The system no longer has this energy available to it.

How did the materials at the source of the stream acquire their potential energy—their energy of position—in the first place? Will they ever regain that energy, to repeat the erosional-depositional cycle once more? That is what most of the remaining chapters of this book will be about.

SUMMARY

1. An erosional-depositional system is a region with definite boundaries, within which all the events of erosion and deposition occur within a single continuous medium.
2. Erosion is dominant over deposition where velocity and kinetic energy of the medium are increasing. Deposition is dominant where velocity and kinetic energy are decreasing.
3. An interface between erosion and deposition can usually be found in an erosional-depositional system. At such an interface, a state of dynamic equilibrium exists.
4. In the erosional phase of an erosional-depositional system, there is a transformation of potential energy to kinetic energy.
5. In the depositional phase, there is a loss of kinetic energy.
6. In an erosional-depositional system, the total energy within the system is always decreasing.

REVIEW QUESTIONS

Group A
1. What is meant by the term *deposition?*
2. What are *sediments?*
3. If all other factors are equal, what effect does particle size have on the rate of settling.
4. What kinds of particles may remain suspended in water indefinitely?
5. If all other factors are equal, what effect does particle shape have on the rate of settling?
6. If all other factors are equal, what effect does particle density have on the rate of settling?
7. Under what conditions will vertical sorting and horizontal layering take place?

8. What effect will a decrease in the velocity of an erosional agent have on the pattern of sorting of sediments?
9. What may be indicated by deposition patterns and sediment characteristics?
10. Describe particle-sorting in materials deposited by glaciers, wind, and gravity.
11. What is an *erosional-depositional system?*
12. Under what conditions is erosion dominant over deposition? Deposition dominant over erosion?
13. In what phase of an erosional-depositional system does a transformation of energy occur?
14. In what phase of an erosional-depositional system does a loss of kinetic energy occur?
15. What is happening to the total energy in an erosional-depositional system?

Group B
1. a. Describe the relationship between the size, shape, and density of sediment particles, and the rate at which they settle in quiet water.
   b. Define the term graded bedding and describe the conditions that must exist in order for graded bedding to occur. Include in your description a reference to the term vertical sorting.
   c. Describe the pattern of sediment deposition that occurs along a stream course at locations where stream velocity is reduced.
   d. Describe the depositional patern that occurs at the point where a stream flows into a lake or pond.
2. Describe the properties of an erosional-depositional system. Include in your answer: A — a definition of the term erosional-depositional system; B — a reference to the relationship between kinetic energy of a stream and deposition or erosion; C — a general statement that describes the overall energy relationships within the system.

REVIEW EXERCISES

1. On a separate piece of paper make a sketch of a delta-type formation. Present both a side view and a top view, and show the size distribution of particles within the deposit.
2. On a separate piece of paper make up a chart describing the characteristics of sediments deposited by the various agents of erosion.
3. To answer the following questions, see Figure 16-18 (page 322), which is a model of an erosional-depositional system. Describe the effects that the following changes might have on that system.
   a. Straightening the meander between point *C* and the delta.
   b. Lowering the level of the bay.
   c. Raising the level of the bay to point *C*.
   d. Increasing the slope of the entire system.
   e. Decreasing the slope of the entire system.

TOPIC XI
FORMATION OF ROCKS

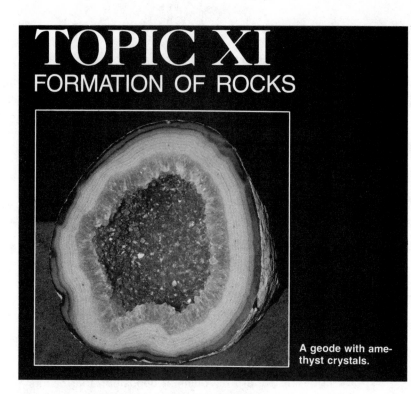

A geode with amethyst crystals.

CHAPTER 17 Minerals

You will know something about the nature of rocks and minerals if you can:

1. Describe some of the differences between a rock and a mineral.
2. List the physical properties of minerals that are used in mineral identification.
3. Explain the importance of silicate minerals.

In Chapters 14 through 16 we found that exposed rocks were continuously weathered, eroded, and deposited as sediment. We examined the processes of erosion and deposition and investigated some of the relationships that exist in erosional-depositional systems. One of the questions that often arises from such a study is, why is it that the earth's surface has not been leveled and covered with a uniformly thick layer of sediment? Part of the answer is that new rock material is continuously being formed, much of it from these sediments. In this chapter we will study the nature and composition of rocks, both old and new, as well as the nature of the minerals of which rocks are made. In the next chapter we will consider the processes by which pieces of old rocks become parts of new ones.

ROCKS

The photograph at the top of page 326 shows a *geode*. A geode is a rocky sphere containing mineral crystals. If you study the photograph you will note the differing properties of the inner and outer portions of the geode. The outer shell looks dull and smooth, while the inner structures appear glassy and jagged. Closer examination would reveal these inner structures to be mineral crystals. They are colored differently than the rocky outer shell. Considering these characteristics, how should we classify the geode? Is it a rock or a mineral? How can we tell the difference?

To begin with, let us try to say what we mean by the term *rock*. In Chapter 4 (page 49) we defined the lithosphere as the shell of solid material around the earth. Any portion of this solid shell is called rock. However, the loose rock material, including soil, that covers much of the earth's land surface is also considered to be part of the lithosphere. This loose material, which can be easily moved, is sometimes referred to as *regolith*. The solid material beneath the regolith is then called *bedrock*. Most of the material that makes up the regolith was produced as a result of the weathering of bedrock.

Rocks and Minerals. If you pick up a handful of soil or other earth material, the chances are pretty good that you will pick up some rock material, either a single piece of rock, or several smaller pieces. If you examine a piece of this rock material carefully, you may find that it is made up of many smaller parts, or *grains*, in a wide variety of colors, shapes, etc. (see Figure 17-1). From this evidence you would be correct to conclude that the rock is made up of several different substances. The different substances that make up rocks are called *minerals*. (We will see later in this chapter that some rocks are exceptions to this "rule." They are *not* made of minerals.)

Most rocks are *mixtures* of minerals. It is important to understand the differences between a mixture and a compound. In Chapter 14 (page 274) we saw that a compound is a chemical combination of two or more elements combined in definite proportions. In a mixture, there are two or more different substances present, but they are not chemically combined. They are only physically mixed and perhaps

Figure 17-1. Piece of rock. Rocks are made up of grains, which vary in size, color, and shape.

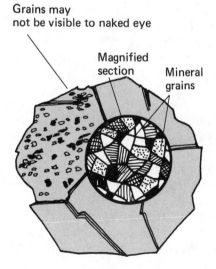

Grains may not be visible to naked eye

Magnified section

Mineral grains

cemented together. The different substances in a mixture may be compounds as well as elements, and they may be present in *any* proportions.

For example, suppose you added 1 g each of sand (quartz crystals), iron filings, and salt to a beaker and then stirred the contents thoroughly. You would have a sand-iron-salt mixture. In this particular mixture, the three substances would be present in a proportion of 1:1:1 by mass. If you added 2 g more of sand and 3 g more of iron, you would *still* have a sand-iron-salt mixture. The only difference would be the proportions of the ingredients, which would now be 3:4:1.

Because the ingredients of a mixture are not chemically combined, their chemical composition and their properties have not been altered by being mixed together. Very often you can see the individual particles of the different substances in the mixture, and they can be separated out of the mixture without changing them.

The substances making up a solid rock are often held together, or cemented, by some other substance, which is also part of the mixture. You could make your own model of a rock by adding the sand-iron-salt mixture just described to a moist paste of plaster of paris. After stirring the entire mixture thoroughly, you would allow it to stand until the plaster of paris hardened. Your "rock" would be a solid mixture composed of sand, iron, salt, and plaster of paris (which is calcium sulfate, a mineral). However, being manmade, it would not be true rock.

If you are familiar with any of the rocks in your area, you may also be familiar with some of the minerals that

FELDSPAR	**AUGITE**
QUARTZ	**GARNET**
MICA	**MAGNETITE**
CALCITE	**OLIVINE**
HORNBLENDE	**PYRITE**
KAOLIN	**TALC**

Table 17-1. Rock-forming minerals.

those rocks are composed of. There are more than 2,000 minerals known, but most of them are very rare. Just a few minerals make up more than 90% of the mass of the lithosphere. These are called the *rock-forming* minerals. The main rock-forming minerals are listed in Table 17-1.

Monomineralic and Polymineralic Rocks. Some rocks are made up of only one mineral, rather than a mixture of minerals. These rocks are called *monomineralic* rocks, "mono-" meaning one. Some examples of monomineralic rocks are rock salt, which is composed of the mineral halite, and limestone, which is composed of the mineral calcite.

Most rocks are composed of more than one mineral. Such rocks are called *polymineralic* rocks, "poly-" meaning many. One of the most common polymineralic rocks is granite (see Figure 17-17 on page 341), which is usually composed of three or more minerals. The composition of granite was discussed in Chapter 14 (page 275). You will recall that granite always contains quartz and feldspar. (Actually, two different varieties of feldspar are usually present.) Other minerals commonly present in granite are mica and hornblende. As you might expect, all these minerals are found high in the list of rock-forming minerals in Table 17-1.

Most of the rocks in the lithosphere are composed of one or more of the rock-forming minerals. Therefore, most rocks have a number of minerals in common. Different rock types have different characteristics partly because of the kind and amount of the various minerals they contain and partly because of the manner in which they were formed. In Chapter 18 you will learn how rocks can be classified and described. You will also discover that the characteristics of rocks can be used to learn about the environment in which a particular rock was formed.

SUMMARY

1. The lithosphere consists of bedrock and regolith. Bedrock is the continuous shell of solid material around the earth. Regolith consists of soil and loose rock material that overlies the bedrock in many places.
2. With few exceptions, rocks are composed of minerals. Most rocks are mixtures of minerals, which may be present in any proportion.
3. Monomineralic rocks are composed of one kind of material. Rocks composed of more than one kind of mineral are called polymineralic rocks.
4. A relatively small number of minerals, called the rock-forming minerals, make up most of the rocks of the earth's crust.
5. Most rocks have a number of minerals in common.

MINERALS

The characteristics of a rock depend, to a large part, on the properties of the minerals it contains. However, before discussing these properties, we should determine exactly what is meant by the term *mineral*. Although earth scientists may differ somewhat in their definitions of the term, it is generally agreed that a mineral must be a *naturally occurring* substance and must have *characteristic physical and chemical properties*. Most geologists also agree that a mineral is *crystalline* and *inorganic*. "Crystalline" means that it is a solid with a definite structural pattern. "Inorganic" means that it is not derived from the complex compounds in the remains of living organisms. Thus the substances in coal, which is organic in origin, are not minerals. In fact, coal is one of the "exceptions" mentioned earlier—a rock that is *not* composed of minerals.

For our purpose then, the following is an acceptable definition: A *mineral* is a naturally occurring, crystalline, inorganic substance with characteristic physical and chemical properties. The expression "characteristic physical and chemical properties" means that each mineral has certain properties by which it can be identified. Some of the properties, especially the chemical properties, require special equipment and complicated laboratory procedures in order to test them. However, several important physical properties are easily observed and can be used for mineral identification.

Physical Properties of Minerals. Some of the important physical properties of minerals include color, streak, luster, hardness, specific gravity, cleavage, and crystal form. Some minerals show a particular property that no others have. In such cases the mineral can be identified on the basis of that characteristic property alone. The ability of mica to cleave, or split, into very thin sheets is one example. The magnetic property of the mineral magnetite is another example. In most cases, however, a combination of properties is used to identify a mineral. Let's take a brief look at each of the properties listed.

Color. Certain minerals do have a distinctive color that aids in identification. Unfortunately, many different minerals are the same color, and many are colorless. Also, certain minerals may be found in a variety of colors. Quartz, for example, is a colorless mineral. However, the presence of just a trace of some impurity can make it pink, or green, or violet, or some other color. Thus, color alone is not usually very helpful in mineral identification.

Streak. Streak is the color of a mineral in powdered form. The powder is left when the mineral is rubbed across a rough surface, such as a piece of unglazed porcelain. Although certain minerals have a very distinctive streak, most rock-forming minerals have a white streak. Therefore, like color, streak alone is of limited use in mineral identification.

Luster. Luster is the way in which the surface of a mineral reflects light. There are two kinds of luster—metallic and nonmetallic. Minerals with metallic luster shine like brightly polished metal. There are several categories of nonmetallic luster, such as glassy, pearly, and dull or earthy.

Hardness. The hardness of a mineral is a measure of its resistance to being scratched. This particular property is quite useful in mineral identification. Hardness is also important geologically, because it determines how easily a mineral is worn away by the processes of weathering and erosion.

Specific gravity. Specific gravity, or relative density, is another property that is very useful in mineral identification. The specific gravity of a mineral is simply the ratio of the mineral's density to the density of water. Since the density of water is 1.0 g/cm^3, specific gravity is expressed by the same number as density in grams per cubic centimeter, but it has no units. A mineral with a density of 3.0 g/cm^3 has a specific gravity of 3.0.

Cleavage. Cleavage is the tendency of a mineral to split along surfaces, or planes, of weakness. These surfaces are called *cleavage planes*. A mineral may have only one cleavage plane, or it may have several cleavage planes at definite angles to one another. For example, mica shows cleavage in one direction and can be peeled into very thin sheets. Halite (rock salt) shows cleavage in three directions, all at right angles to one another. Halite therefore cleaves into cubes (see Figure 17-2). Minerals that do not show cleavage are said to *fracture* when they break.

Crystal form. Crystals are solids with regular geometric shapes. Crystals generally have flat, smooth sur-

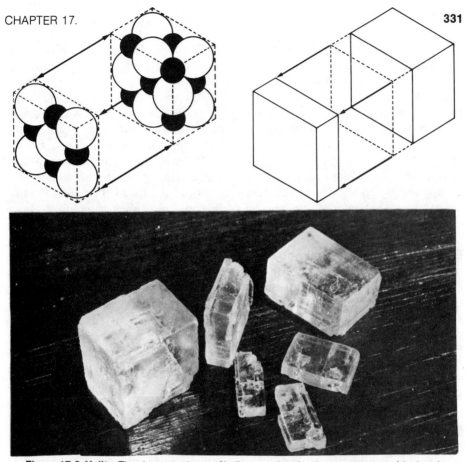

Figure 17-2. Halite. The cleavage planes of halite are related to the arrangement of the ions in halite crystals.

faces called *crystal faces*. Crystal faces are often easy to see in a sample of quartz (Figure 17-3). As discussed in Chapter 14 (page 274), most minerals consist of positive and negative ions arranged in a crystal lattice with a definite pattern. Most minerals form crystals because of the regular and orderly arrangement of the atoms and ions of which they are composed.

The properties discussed here are valuable aids in mineral identification. It is perhaps even more important that many of these physical properties provide evidence about the internal structure of the various minerals—that is, the arrangement of their atoms

Figure 17-3. Quartz crystal.

and ions. Before we look into the structures of minerals in any detail, we should know something about the chemical composition of the minerals. In other words, before we can understand how the "parts" are arranged, we must know what those "parts" are.

Mineral Composition. Minerals are composed of *elements,* which are substances that cannot be broken down into simpler substances by ordinary chemical means. We saw in Chapter 14 (page 274), that 106 elements are known to exist. Eighty-eight elements can be found in the earth's crust, atmosphere, or hydrosphere. The other eighteen are known only from samples produced artificially by man.

Most of the elements are classified as *metals,* or *metallic elements.* Metallic elements have certain physical characteristics in common, such as hardness, shiny luster, and good conductivity of heat and electricity. Another characteristic of metals is that they can be hammered, bent, or pulled into different shapes without breaking. Examples are iron, copper, aluminum, silver, and gold. However, one metallic element, mercury, is a liquid at ordinary temperatures.

The remaining elements are called *nonmetals.* Of these, several are gases at room temperature (for example, hydrogen, oxygen, nitrogen, and chlorine). One (bromine) is a liquid. The others are soft, easily broken solids (for example, sulfur).

Actually, it is chemical properties that make the most important distinctions between metals and nonmetals. In chemical compounds, the metals form positive ions, while the nonmet-als form negative ions (or form compounds that have no ions). A few elements are on the borderline between metals and nonmetals, having some properties of each class. An important example of a borderline element for the earth scientist is silicon.

You probably know that some elements are far more common in the earth's crust than others. That is one reason why iron, for example, is so much less expensive than gold. But perhaps you are not aware that just a few elements account for nearly all the mass of the crust. Figure 17-4 illustrates this fact. Of the elements that occur naturally on the earth, eight make up 98.5% of the mass of the crust, all the others together adding up to only 1.5%. Furthermore, oxygen alone accounts for nearly half the mass of the crust, and silicon more than a quarter. Together, these two elements make up almost 75% of the mass of the crust. The table in Figure 17-4 also shows that in terms of the volume of the crust, almost 94% is taken up by oxygen atoms! So, if you pick up a piece of *any* rock, you can be almost certain that it is mostly oxygen. It would be a fairly safe bet that it contains silicon, too. We'll explore these thoughts later.

When we talk about the percentages of different elements in the crust, we don't mean that the elements are present as separate substances. Elements are not often found alone. They are usually combined with other elements in chemical compounds. The manner in which the atoms of elements join, or bond, together to form compounds was discussed in Chapter 14 (page 274). We learned there that atoms can gain or

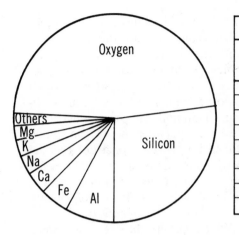

Composition of the Earth's Crust			
Element	Sym-bol	Percent by mass	Percent by volume
Oxygen	O	46.6	93.8
Silicon	Si	27.7	0.9
Aluminum	Al	8.1	0.5
Iron	Fe	5.0	0.4
Calcium	Ca	3.6	1.0
Sodium	Na	2.8	1.3
Potassium	K	2.6	1.8
Magnesium	Mg	2.1	0.3
All others	—	1.5	—

Figure 17-4. Composition of the earth's crust.

lose electrons to form ions, and that crystalline compounds are made up of ions arranged in definite patterns. Some minerals, such as sulfur, copper, and gold, do occur as single elements. Most minerals, however, are crystalline compounds.

Since oxygen and silicon are the two most abundant elements, you might wonder whether they combine to make a mineral. In fact, they do form a fairly common mineral called *quartz,* which is the compound silicon dioxide (SiO_2). Earth scientists refer to silicon and oxygen as the *constituent units* of quartz. The idea of constituent units will be very useful as we examine the *structure* of minerals, that is, the way in which the ions are arranged in their crystal pattern.

SUMMARY

1. A mineral is a naturally occurring, crystalline, inorganic substance with characteristic physical and chemical properties.
2. Several important physical properties of minerals can be used for mineral identification. These properties include color, streak, luster, hardness, specific gravity, cleavage, and crystal form.
3. Minerals are composed of elements. A few minerals, such as copper, are composed of one element. Most minerals are chemical compounds.
4. Of the approximately 88 naturally occurring elements, only a relative few make up most minerals.
5. Of the elements present in the earth's crust, oxygen is the most abundant by mass and volume. Silicon is the second most abundant by mass.

STRUCTURE OF MINERALS

Earlier in this chapter we saw that some of the physical properties of minerals can be used to identify them. Scientists are never content just to describe the properties of something. They wonder why one material has different properties from another. By observation and experiment they try to construct a model of the materials that can explain the observed properties. In the following discussion of mineral structures, we will not go into the methods used to construct the models, since they involve complicated techniques and mathematical calculations. We can say, however, that cleavage and fracture patterns are important clues. Also, much information about the arrangement of atoms and ions inside crystals is obtained by observing what happens to X rays when they pass through the crystal.

Silicate Minerals. We have already mentioned that silicon and oxygen combine to form silicon dioxide, the mineral quartz. Recalling that silicon and oxygen account for almost 75% of the mass of the crust, we should expect to find these two elements in many other minerals, too. We do. Minerals that contain silicon and oxygen in chemical combination with other elements (usually one or more metals) are called *silicates*. About 60% of all minerals are silicates.

Because of their abundance, some knowledge of the nature and structure of silicates is important. Such knowledge will help us understand some of the changes that occur within the lithosphere.

The Silicon-Oxygen Tetrahedron. Since oxygen represents nearly 94%

of the volume of the crust, the lithosphere could be considered to be essentially a framework of oxygen atoms. With most of the space occupied by oxygen atoms (or ions), all the other atoms and ions, such as silicon, aluminum, and iron, must fit in the spaces between the oxygen atoms. Our task now is to construct a model in which atoms of silicon and oxygen can be fitted together to make up the various types, or forms, of silicate materials that are observed.

We begin with the chemist's model of the silicon atom (Figure 17-5). In this model, there are four electrons near the outside of the atom. Each of these electrons can form a chemical bond between the silicon atom and another atom. The silicon atom can therefore be bonded to four oxygen atoms. In this process, each outer electron of the silicon atom enters the outer shell of an oxygen atom. The

Figure 17-5. Model of a silicon atom.

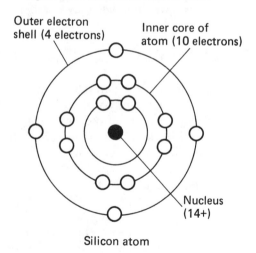

Outer electron shell (4 electrons)

Inner core of atom (10 electrons)

Nucleus (14+)

Silicon atom

result is that the oxygen atom becomes a rather large negative ion. At the same time, the silicon atom becomes a rather small positive ion. Models of oxygen and silicon ions are shown in Figure 17-6.

Remember that the oxygen ions will now be strongly attracted, or "bound," to the silicon ion, since they have opposite electric charges. What is the most compact way that four large spheres can be arranged around one small sphere? A little experimentation shows that the best arrangement looks like Figure 17-7. The large spheres are at the four corners of a structure called a *tetrahedron* (plural, *tetrahedra),* with the small sphere in the center.

Figure 17-6. Models of oxygen and silicon ions.

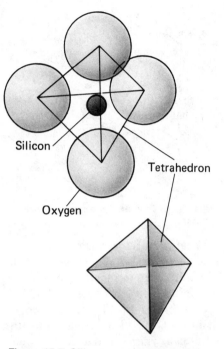

Figure 17-7. Silicon-oxygen tetrahedron.

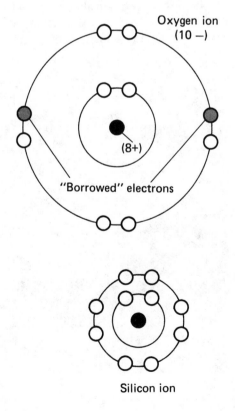

A tetrahedron is difficult to draw on a flat sheet of paper. It is easier to examine a three-dimensional physical model. If you do this, you will see that a tetrahedron has four flat faces, each of which is a triangle with three equal sides. The four triangles fit neatly together to form a regular object with four corners.

Our model of the *structural unit* of silicates, then, is a *silicon-oxygen tetrahedron* (also called a *silica tetrahedron),* in which the four large oxygen ions are at the corners and the small silicon ion is at the center. Notice that almost all the volume of the tetrahedron is occupied by the oxygen ions. Thus we see how the model agrees with our statement that oxygen makes up nearly all the volume of the rocks and minerals of the crust.

Oxygen ion

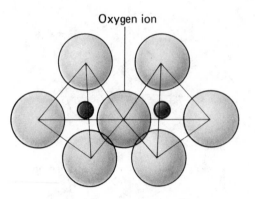

Figure 17-8. Oxygen ion shared by two tetrahedra.

What about the various *forms* of silicate minerals? What role does the silicon-oxygen tetrahedron play in determining their properties? How is it that minerals that are composed mainly of the same basic unit—the silicon-oxygen tetrahedron—can exhibit such a variety of properties and structures? The main reason is that an oxygen ion can act as a corner for two tetrahedra and therefore connect them together as shown in Figure 17-8. In this way, chains, sheets, and networks of tetrahedra can be formed in various patterns. The tetrahedra can also combine with ions of other elements to form a large variety of chemical compounds with many different types of internal structure.

Once again, remember that we are dealing with a model. The larger spheres *represent* oxygen ions and the smaller sphere *represents* a silicon ion. The entire assembly *represents* the arrangement of these ions in the silicon-oxygen tetrahedron. No one has ever seen the real thing. However, indirect evidence suggests that this is the way in which the ions are arranged.

Silicate Families. There are groups, or families, of silicates. These groups look and feel different from one another, but more important, perhaps, is that the minerals in each group *cleave* differently from the minerals in the other groups. You will recall that cleavage is the tendency of a mineral to split along flat, smooth planes. Some minerals cleave readily, while other minerals do not cleave at all. Both extremes are found within the silicates. The type of cleavage (or lack of cleavage) is one kind of physical evidence of the structure of the silicate mineral. Let's look at the silicate families and some examples of minerals in each.

Isolated tetrahedra. Figure 17-9 is a photograph of a sample of olivine, a silicate mineral. Olivine is composed of silicon-oxygen tetrahedrons and ions of either iron or magnesium or both. Notice the rough, sugary ap-

Figure 17-9. Olivine.

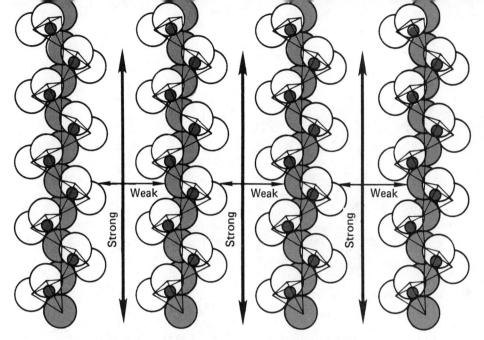

Figure 17-10. Structure of a single-chain silicate.

pearance of the surface of the mineral. Olivine does not cleave along any flat surface. It breaks, or fractures, irregularly. This total lack of cleavage is believed to indicate that the mineral is made up of *isolated tetrahedra,* that is, tetrahedra that are not directly combined with each other.

The tetrahedral structures are present as separate units throughout the mineral. They are held in position by forces of attraction that exist between the tetrahedra and the metallic ions that are present in the mineral. Consequently, when the mineral breaks, there is no "preferred" way of breaking. There are no lines or planes of weakness along which the mineral might split. Hence, there is no cleavage. Silicate minerals composed of isolated tetrahedra usually do not show cleavage.

Chains. Under certain conditions, silicon-oxygen tetrahedra join with one another to form long, chainlike structures. Figure 17-10 is a model of the way scientists think the tetrahedral units combine to form *single-*

chain silicates. Notice that each shaded oxygen ion is a part of two adjacent tetrahedra and thus bonds them together. The bonds continue in a line, forming a chain with great strength along its length. However, the forces of attraction between chains are relatively weak. Thus, a silicate mineral that is constructed of chains of silicon-oxygen tetrahedra holds together pretty well from end to end, but not very well between chains. The chains are held together in the mineral by weak bonds formed with metallic ions. These bonds are similar to those that exist between isolated tetrahedra in olivine.

Minerals in the family of chain silicates tend to break or fracture in splinters or fibers. Figure 17-11 is a photograph of the silicate asbestos, which has a fibrous fracture. Notice the fibrous or threadlike nature of this mineral. Asbestos is an example of a *single-chain* silicate.

Sheets. In the single-chain silicate structure, each silicon ion can be considered to be bonded to the next one

Figure 17-11. Asbestos.

along the chain through the oxygen ion that they share. Two chains could also become bonded side by side as shown in Figure 17-12. In this structure, every second silicon ion along each chain is bonded through an oxy-

gen ion to a silicon ion in the other chain. You can compare this structure to two logs tied together at intervals along their length. This double-chain bonding can be extended sidewise indefinitely, as shown in Figure 17-13. We now have a structure like a series of logs tied together to make a raft. The result is to form a flat layer or sheet made of many silicate chains joined side by side.

Scientists believe that the tetrahedra are combined in this way in the family of silicates known as the *sheet silicates*. Notice that three of the four oxygen ions in each tetrahedron are shared with other tetrahedra, but the fourth is not shared. The result of this bonding is a mineral that holds together very well from end to end and from side to side, but not very well

Figure 17-12. Structure of a double-chain silicates.

Figure 17-13. Structure of sheet silicates.

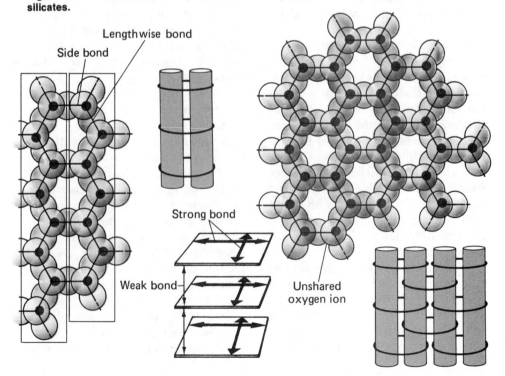

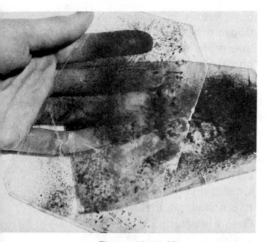

Figure 17-14. Mica.

Figure 17-14 is a photograph of a piece of mica. If you have ever held a sample of this silicate mineral, you know how it cleaves. It peels or separates into thin sheets or layers, often transparent if they are thin enough.

Networks. When a silicon-oxygen tetrahedron shares *all* its oxygen ions with adjoining tetrahedra, the result is a *network* of tetrahedra that are strongly bonded in all three dimensions of space. In these structures, each silicon ion shares four oxygen ions with other silicon ions. Figure 17-15 is a model of such a silicate.

between sheets or layers. The reason for the weakness between sheets is that the forces holding the sheets together (where the oxygen ions are not shared) are not as strong as those holding the tetrahedra together within the sheets. Once again, the result is a mineral that cleaves in a very special way.

How does this three-dimensional bonding affect the way a network silicate will break? Think about it. A chain silicate is weak between chains and splits between them. A sheet silicate is weak between sheets and splits between sheets. Where is the weakness in a silicate mineral that is held together by strong forces in all directions between tetrahedra? The answer, of course, is that there is *no* direction of weakness. Network silicates are very hard, and they are difficult to cleave.

Figure 17-15. Structure of a network silicate.

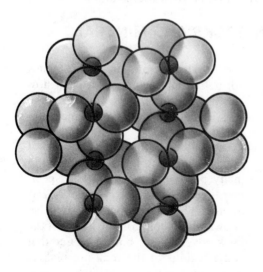

Figure 17-16 shows a photograph of a piece of quartz as it was found in a rock, and after an attempt to cleave it. Quartz is a network silicate and is the hardest of the common rock-forming minerals. The flat surfaces that you see are not cleavage planes; they are crystal faces. Quartz does not cleave. It fractures unevenly, like glass.

At this point we have established what a silicon-oxygen tetrahedron is, how it is put together, and how these units combine to form the different families of silicate minerals, the most abundant minerals in the earth's crust. Some of the silicate minerals

Figure 17-16. Quartz before and after attempted cleavage.

have been used to illustrate the relationship between the inferred structure of the mineral and its observable physical properties. The same *idea* applies to all minerals. However, keep in mind that the relationship between structure and properties is not always as clearly demonstrated as it is in the examples that have been given. You should be aware that the chemical nature of the particular elements in a mineral and the type of bonding between their atoms or ions are major factors in determining the properties of a mineral.

SUMMARY

1. Oxygen and silicon combine with metallic elements to form silicate minerals.
2. The basic structural unit of silicate minerals is the silicon-oxygen tetrahedron.
3. Silicate minerals may consist of separate tetrahedra or of more complex units resulting from the bonding of tetrahedra to form chains, sheets, or three-dimensional networks.
4. The observable physical properties of minerals can be related to the inferred arrangement of their constituent units—that is, their atoms and ions.

DIFFERENCES BETWEEN ROCKS AND MINERALS

At the beginning of this chapter the question was raised as to whether a geode is a rock or a mineral, and how we should be able to distinguish between the two. You have just learned that rocks are mixtures of minerals, but if you were to pick up a piece of earth material, how would you tell whether it was a rock or a mineral?

Sometimes this is an easy task, other times it is quite difficult. Before we examine the different classes of rocks and learn about the environments in which they form, perhaps we should learn how to determine, very roughly, the difference between rocks and minerals.

Let us look carefully at a sample of granite, a very common rock found in many parts of the world. The specimen in the center of Figure 17-17 is granite. (These photographs are also shown in full color on the inside of the back cover of this book.) Notice that some regions of the rock are pinkish and shiny; some are white or gray,

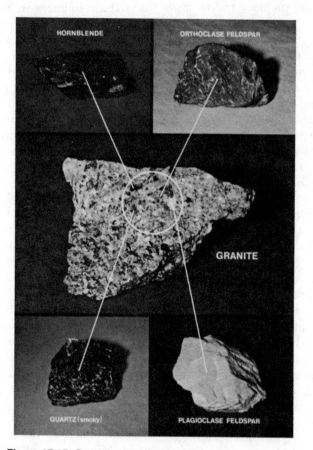

Figure 17-17. Granite and the separate minerals that form it.

with a glassy appearance; others are dark gray or black, some shiny and some dull. These different areas are, in fact, different minerals. They are the mineral *grains* of which this rock is composed.

The photographs around the outside of the illustration show specimens of some of the minerals in this sample of granite. The lines point to regions of the rock where the corresponding mineral grains can be seen. In this granite sample, the grains are not more than a few millimeters across. The mineral samples in the separate photographs are 100 mm or more in size. However, even these large pieces were originally parts of rocks that contained other minerals. On the other hand, mineral grains in a rock may also be very small—so small that a microscope is needed to see them. But whether large or small, each mineral grain is a single material with the same characteristics.

This does not mean that a mineral always has exactly the same appearance. The color of a mineral, for example, may vary greatly from one specimen to another. The color of a mineral depends on how the atoms and ions in the crystal interact with the different wavelengths that are present in the light striking the material. Imperfections in the crystal structure can change this interaction and thus change the color that the observer sees. Some kinds of imperfections are the result of the conditions under which the crystal formed. Other imperfections are caused by the presence of impurities. Impurities are small amounts of elements or compounds that are not really a part of the composition of the mineral.

The quartz in the granite shown in the photo is a variety called smoky, because of its dark color. Another variety of quartz, not found in the sample of granite shown, is rose quartz, which has a rose color. The type of quartz shown in Figure 17-16 on page 340 is clear or colorless. All three are, however, the same substance. Granite always contains one or more varieties of quartz.

Another type of mineral always found in granite is orthoclase, a member of the feldspar group. Note its glassy luster, sharp edges, and uniform color. Orthoclase tends to have two right-angle cleavages that often produce a steplike form.

Plagioclase is another variety of feldspar, and it is almost always present in granite. One of its distinguishing features is a series of fine lines on its cleavage faces. It is otherwise quite similar to orthoclase.

Hornblende is the fourth mineral illustrated in this sample of granite. Most granites contain small amounts of dark minerals, and hornblende is one of the common kinds of these minerals. Hornblende, when examined at close range, appears to be made up of bundles of shiny splin-

ters. These splinters are actually long, narrow crystals.

Mica (which is illustrated on page 339) is another mineral that is very often found in granite. However, it is usually present as tiny, sparkling grains. We have not attempted to show the mica in this specimen.

A number of other minerals may occur in granite, depending on the conditions under which the rock was formed.

If you examine the photograph of granite again and compare it with the photographs of each of its component minerals, you should be able to detect the basic difference between rocks and minerals. A mineral displays similar characteristics throughout; a rock, unless it is monomineralic, will often show different characteristics in different regions of the sample. The characteristics of a given region within the rock will be the characteristics of the mineral in that region.

Just as minerals can be classified and placed in categories, such as the silicates, so, too, rocks can be classified. Minerals are classified according to their chemical composition and the arrangement of their atoms and ions. Rocks, on the other hand, are classified according to their *origin*— that is, *how* they were formed, *what* they were formed from, and the *conditions* under which they were formed. The three basic types, or groups, of rocks are *sedimentary, metamorphic,* and *igneous.* Chapter 18 deals with the formation and characteristics of these rock types in considerable detail. At this point you need only understand that rocks, like minerals, display specific characteristics, and these characteristics are the result of the conditions under which the rocks were formed.

SUMMARY

1. The physical properties of a mineral sample are the same throughout the sample. The physical properties of a rock sample usually vary from one part of the sample to another.
2. Rocks are classified according to origin. The three main classes of rocks are sedimentary, metamorphic, and igneous.
3. All rocks display characteristics that are the result of the conditions under which they were formed.

REVIEW QUESTIONS

Group A

1. Name and describe the two basic parts of the lithosphere.
2. What are most rocks composed of?
3. What is meant by the term *monomineralic* rock? *Polymineralic* rock?
4. What are the *rock-forming minerals?*
5. Define the term *mineral.*
6. Name the physical properties of minerals that are used for mineral identification.
7. Which element is most abundant in the earth's crust both by mass and by volume? Which element, by mass, is the second most abundant?
8. What type of mineral is formed by the combination of oxygen, silicon, and metallic elements?
9. What is the basic structural unit of a silicate mineral?
10. Describe some of the different forms of silicate minerals.
11. To what are the physical properties of a mineral related?
12. On what basis can rocks be distinguished from minerals?
13. How are rocks classified? Name the three main classes of rocks.
14. What determines some of the characteristics of rock?

Group B

1. One student claimed that an object in his hand was a rock. Another student said that it was a mineral. What kinds of observations would be needed to settle the argument?
2. a. List at least two physical properties that are not usually very useful for distinguishing one mineral from another.
   b. List at least three physical properties that are often used for distinguishing one mineral from another. Why are these physical properties useful, while those listed in 2-a are not useful?
3. a. Define the term *silicate,* and explain why silicate minerals are found so abundantly in rock material.
   b. Explain why silicate minerals exhibit such a wide variety of physical characteristics.
   c. List and describe one property of at least three minerals found in granite rock.

The Grand Canyon is made up almost entirely of sedimentary rock.

CHAPTER 18
Rocks

You will know something about rocks and their formation if you can:
1. Name the three basic types of rock and the various materials from which they are formed.
2. Describe how each type of rock is formed.
3. Explain the rock cycle.

Up to this point in the course, we have learned a good deal about rocks. Rocks are the solid, nonliving stuff of the earth. "Big" rocks are changed into "little" rocks by the processes of weathering and erosion. Most rocks are solid mixtures of minerals. The rock-forming minerals combine in many ways and in many different proportions to form a wide variety of rock types. The one area not touched upon seems to be the actual formation of rocks. We say rock-"forming" minerals combine to "form" rocks. The questions, then, are how and under what conditions do rocks form? Where do the "big" rocks come from?

SEDIMENTARY ROCKS

Sedimentary rocks are rocks that are formed from accumulated sediments. Some of the particles of sediment result from the weathering and erosion of preexisting rocks. Others are organic material derived from biologic, or life, processes. Most sedimentary rocks form from materials that have been deposited in water. However, rocks are also formed from wind-deposited and ice-deposited sediments. Sedimentary rocks often retain some of the characteristics of the sediments from which they formed. For example, rocks formed from water-deposited sediments often show the layering or bedding that is characteristic of that medium of deposition.

Sedimentary rocks, then, are formed from accumulated sediments. But there are different kinds of sediments, ranging from the unsorted mass of rock material deposited by a glacier to the ions derived from minerals dissolved in rivers, lakes, and oceans. As you might imagine, the processes involved in forming a rock from the sediments in a glacial deposit will be quite different from those involved in forming a rock from ions in solution. Earth scientists have divided the sedimentary rocks into three groups, based on the way in which the rocks were formed. Let's take a look at these groups.

Clastic Sedimentary Rocks. *Clastic* sedimentary rocks are formed from particles of rock that have been produced by weathering and erosion of previously existing rock. The term "clastic" comes from the Greek word *klastos,* meaning broken. Thus, clas-

tic refers to broken pieces or fragments of rock material. The original particles of sediment can often be recognized in clastic sedimentary rocks. They may be worn and rounded, or sharp and angular, just like the particles in the sediment from which the rock was formed.

When clastic sediments are first deposited, they are easily moved about because the particles are not fastened together. Clastic sediments can be changed into rock, or *lithified,* in two ways. As sediment accumulates, layer upon layer, the added weight of new deposits creates great pressure on the bottom layers. This increasing pressure squeezes the sediment particles closer and closer together, gradually compressing the sediment into a much denser mass (see Figure 18-1). This process, which is called *compaction,* may be sufficient in itself to change very fine sediment, such as silt and clay, directly

Figure 18-1. Compaction of sediments. The weight of the new deposits compresses the underlying sediments into a dense, compact mass.

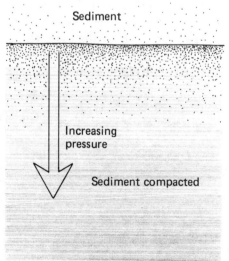
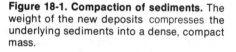

Sediment

Increasing
pressure

Sediment compacted

Figure 18-2. Shale.

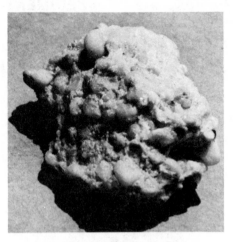

Figure 18-3. Conglomerate.

into rock. The most common sedimentary rock formed by compaction is shale, which is formed from clay particles or a mixture of clay and silt particles. Shales make up the largest proportion (about 70%) of all sedimentary rocks in the earth's crust (see Figure 18-2).

One reason why compaction is sufficient to change clays and silts into rocks is the extremely small size of the particles. When larger-sized clastic particles are involved, such as sand grains or pebbles, compaction alone will not produce sedimentary rocks. These larger-sized particles must be *cemented* together as they are being compressed. Several natural materials are often available for the

process of cementation. Calcium carbonate, iron oxide, and silica (silicon dioxide) all serve as cementing materials in clastic sedimentary rocks. These cementing materials come from minerals that have been dissolved in ground water. As the dissolved mineral matter accumulates in a lake or ocean, it comes out of solution to act as cementing material.

Two common sedimentary rocks whose particles are cemented together are sandstone and conglomerate. As the name suggests, sandstones consist of sand grains cemented together, usually by silica or calcium carbonate. Conglomerate is lithified gravel (see Figure 18-3). This rock consists of fairly large, rounded peb-

Table 18-1. Some common clastic sedimentary rocks.

ROCK NAME	PARENT MATERIAL	GRAIN SIZE
Conglomerate	Pebbles or larger w/cement	Larger than 3 mm
Sandstone	Sand	1/16 to 3 mm
Shale	Mud and clay	Less than 1/16 mm

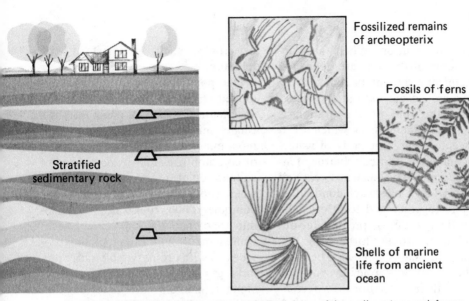

Fossilized remains of archeopterix

Fossils of ferns

Stratified sedimentary rock

Shells of marine life from ancient ocean

Figure 18-4. Stratified sedimentary rock. Each layer of the sedimentary rock formation contains different fossils. These fossils provide clues to the environmental conditions that existed at the time the sediments were deposited.

bles embedded in a mixture of sand and silt. Table 18-1 lists three common types of clastic sedimentary rocks, their particle sizes, and the parent material.

Clastic sedimentary rocks are usually *stratified,* that is, they show the presence of layers. Often the particles are highly sorted, so that the particles within a given layer are all nearly the same size. Stratification is perhaps the most important characteristic of sedimentary rocks. Because it is often the most noticeable feature of a given rock sample, stratification is most helpful in identifying a rock as being sedimentary rather than igneous or metamorphic.

Clastic sedimentary rocks often contain clues that aid in identification and in interpreting the history of the sediments from which the rocks were formed. One important type of clue is *fossils.* Fossils are remains, imprints, or traces of ancient plants or animals. Clastic rocks also tend to resemble quite closely the sediments from which they have formed. They often appear dull and earthy, and are usually found in layers. The presence of fossils and the close resemblance to the parent sediments often represents a record, preserved in rock, of the conditions that existed during sedimentation in the environment in which the rock formed (see Figure 18-4).

Chemical Sedimentary Rocks. Chemical sedimentary rocks are formed from materials that were once dissolved in water. These materials were in the form of mineral ions in solution as a result of chemical weathering of rocks (see Chapter 14). Most of these ions are carried in ground water, and they eventually reach lakes, seas, or oceans, where they accumulate. As described in Chapter 16, page 319, the water in which these materials accumulate eventually becomes saturated with these ions, and can no longer hold all of them in solution. When this happens, some of the ions are deposited as chemical sedimentary rocks.

In some cases, saturation occurs because the rate of evaporation is greater than the rate at which fresh water enters the large body of water. This situation is particularly true of inland seas and lakes, such as Great Salt Lake in Utah. Under such conditions, ions join together and form crystals, which then settle, or precipitate, out of solution. Rocks formed in this manner are called *evaporites,* because of the important role evaporation plays in their formation. Two common evaporite rocks are halite (rock salt) and gypsum.

Chemical sedimentary rocks can also form without evaporation being involved. Under certain conditions, various ions combine chemically to form crystals of insoluble minerals. These minerals precipitate out of solution, accumulate on the sea floor, and form deposits of chemical sedimen-

tary rocks, such as limestone and dolomite.

One point that should not be overlooked here is that all chemical sedimentary rocks are composed of a single mineral. That is, they are monomineralic. For example, halite, or common rock salt, is composed of sodium chloride, a mineral formed when sodium ions and chlorine ions combine. Thus, rock salt is a monomineralic chemical sedimentary rock. Quite a mouthful for the rock that provides us with ordinary table salt! Similarly, gypsum is calcium sulfate, limestone is calcium carbonate (calcite), and dolomite is calcium magnesium carbonate—all monomineralic rocks.

Organic Sedimentary Rocks. The third group of sedimentary rocks are those that form as a result of biologic processes. Some organic sedimentary rocks form directly from the remains of plants and animals. Coal, for example, is a rock formed from leaves, stems, and trunks of trees and

Figure 18-5. Ancient coal-forming swamp forest. This artist's reconstruction is based on fossil evidence discovered in coal deposits.

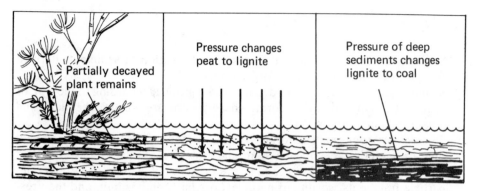

Partially decayed plant remains

Pressure changes peat to lignite

Pressure of deep sediments changes lignite to coal

Figure 18-6. Three stages in the formation of coal.

other plants that lived in swampy areas millions of years ago (Figure 18-5). When these trees and other plants died, their remains were deposited in shallow, stagnant water. This deposition in water prevented the normal processes of decay from taking place. The plant remains were only partially decayed, forming a soft, fibrous material called *peat*. Peat is the first stage in the formation of coal. As more and more sediments accumulated, increased pressure caused peat to be compacted into *lignite*. Also called "brown coal," lignite is the second stage in coal formation. Continued compaction caused lignite to change into the darker, harder, more familiar product known as *bituminous coal*, or "soft coal." (See Figure 18-6.)

Another common organic sedimentary rock is limestone. Many forms of marine life extract calcium carbonate (lime) from sea water and use it in the formation of their shells or skeletons (see Figure 18-7). When these animals die, their soft body parts decay and the hard lime materials are left to accumulate on the sea floor. These lime deposits are eventually cemented or compacted (or both) to form limestone. The lime in these rocks is de-

rived from the mineral calcite, which was weathered from rocks on land, carried to the ocean, and removed from solution by the marine animals. Thus, while organic processes play an important role in their formation, these "organic" limestones are *not* composed of organic matter. Like the chemical limestone described earlier, limestone of organic origin is composed of the mineral calcite.

Figure 18-7. Fossiliferous limestone. This sedimentary rock was formed from the shells of ancient marine animals.

SUMMARY

1. Sedimentary rocks are formed from an accumulation of sediments derived from preexisting rocks and/or organic material.
2. Sedimentary rocks can be divided into three groups, according to the *type* of sediments from which they form. These groups are clastic, chemical, and organic sedimentary rocks.
3. Sedimentary rocks may be formed by one or more of the following: compaction, cementation, chemical action, and biologic processes.
4. Many sedimentary rocks resemble sediments in that they show layering, particle fragments, sorting of particles, organic composition, and the presence of fossils.

NONSEDIMENTARY ROCKS

Nonsedimentary rocks are those rocks that do *not* form from sediments. The nonsedimentary rocks are divided into two groups, according to origin. These two groups are the *igneous* rocks and the *metamorphic* rocks.

Igneous Rocks. Igneous rocks are rocks that form as a result of the cooling and hardening of rock material that was at one time molten or liquid. The hardening of liquid rock is referred to as *solidification* or *crystallization*. There are two classifications of igneous rock. These classifications are based on *where* solidification occurred. Igneous rocks formed at some depth beneath the earth's surface are called *intrusive* or *plutonic*. Igneous rocks formed at the earth's surface are called *extrusive* or *eruptive*.

Melting of Rock. All molten rock originates at considerable depth beneath the earth's surface, some perhaps as deep as the upper mantle. The mechanisms that cause rock to melt at these depths are not clearly understood. However, a combination of high temperature and reduced pressure is believed necessary for melting

to occur. It is believed that the major source of heat energy in the interior of the earth is the radioactive decay of unstable elements in the lithosphere and mantle. Some possible explanations for decreases in pressure on the rock at great depths include faulting and folding within the crust and erosion of overlying rock and soil. These processes will be discussed in more detail in the next topic. For now we will simply assume that conditions are often such that large quantities of rock material can and do melt.

The depth at which molten rock originates may vary from a few kilometers to over forty kilometers beneath the earth's surface. The total volume of a given mass of liquid rock material may be as great as tens or even hundreds of cubic kilometers. This liquid rock beneath the earth's surface is referred to as *magma*. When rock melts, it expands and becomes less dense. The magma is therefore forced upward through cracks and faults in crustal rock, a process known as *intrusion* (see Figure 18-8). Much of this magma does

Figure 18-8. Igneous intrusions. Magma often forces its way (or intrudes) into cracks in surrounding rocks. When the magma cools and solidifies, it forms intrusive igneous rock.

not reach the earth's surface. It slowly cools and solidifies, forming intrusive igneous rock.

Intrusive Igneous Rocks. Intrusive, or plutonic, igneous rocks are usually recognizable because rocks of this group contain fairly large crystals. Magma is a hot solution of silicates from which minerals tend to separate as it cools. The greater the depth at which cooling takes place, the slower will be the rate of cooling. Deep within the crust, magma cools very slowly, perhaps only a few degrees in thousands of years. As cooling progresses, different minerals crystallize and separate out of solution at different temperatures. The minerals with very high melting points crystallize first. These are generally dark-colored, dense minerals. Upon crystallization, these dense minerals tend to sink to the lower regions of the magma, leaving the lighter-colored, less dense minerals to crystallize out later, at cooler temperatures. This results in separation of minerals, a

characteristic often found in intrusive igneous rocks. This separation produces igneous rock of two color types, light and dark. Because the dark-colored minerals are generally denser than the light-colored minerals, darker-colored igneous rock is usually denser than lighter-colored rock.

Another important result of the cooling process is the formation of mineral crystals of different sizes. Crystal size is closely related to the rate of cooling. The more slowly a magma cools, the larger will be the resulting mineral crystals. Thus, rocks formed from magma that cooled deep within the crust tend to have larger crystals than rock formed closer to the earth's surface, where cooling occurs more rapidly. The size of the grains or crystals in a rock determines the *texture* of the rock. Rocks that consist of large crystal grains have a coarse-grained texture. Granite and gabbro are good examples of coarse-grained intrusive igneous rocks. Gabbro is a dark, dense rock. Granite is a light-colored rock of lower density.

Extrusive Igneous Rocks. Fine-textured igneous rock, consisting of small crystals, forms when magma cools quickly. This relatively rapid cooling usually occurs at or near the earth's surface, where surrounding temperatures are much lower and heat can escape more quickly. The most rapid cooling will occur at the surface itself. Magma that reaches the earth's surface is called *lava*. Rocks formed from the solidification of *lava* are called *extrusive* igneous rocks. The terms *eruptive* and *volcanic* are sometimes used to refer to these rocks.

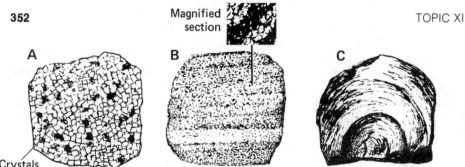

A

Magnified section

B

C

Crystals

Figure 18-9. Texture in igneous rocks. The drawings depict three types of texture found in igneous rocks. *(A)* Slow cooling of the liquid rocks results in the formation of large crystals, which are visible to the unaided eye. *(B)* When cooling is more rapid, the crystals formed are often too small to be seen without magnification. *(C)* If cooling is very rapid, the solid rock has a glassy texture without mineral crystals.

As stated earlier, crystal size is related to the rate at which liquid rock cools. The slower the rate of cooling, the larger will be the crystals that form. Because lava cools quickly, the crystals in extrusive igneous rock are quite small, and the rock has a fine-grained texture (see Figure 18-9). In fact, some lavas cool so quickly that there is no time for crystals to form at all. Rocks formed under these conditions have a glassy texture. Obsidian, sometimes called volcanic glass, is an excellent example of such a rock (see Figure 18-10).

Figure 18-10. Obsidian.

Because they have a fine-grained texture, extrusive igneous rocks are generally more difficult to identify than intrusive igneous rocks. Often, only a general classification, such as whether the rock is light- or dark-colored, can be made in the field. Two examples of fairly common fine-grained igneous rocks are rhyolite, which is light-colored, and basalt, which is dark.

Igneous Rock Identification. As you have seen, several different characteristics are used as aids in classifying igneous rocks in a very general way. These characteristics include grain size (texture), color (light or dark), and density. The chart in Figure 18-11 illustrates the most basic system of igneous rock classification. This chart uses four common igneous rocks as standards against which rock samples can be compared. Notice that the rocks on the left side of the chart, granite and rhyolite, are light-colored rocks of low density. On the right side, gabbro and basalt are dark-colored rocks of high density. The rocks at the top of the chart are coarse-grained in texture, while those at the bottom are fine-grained. Thus, if you were to pick up a dark-colored

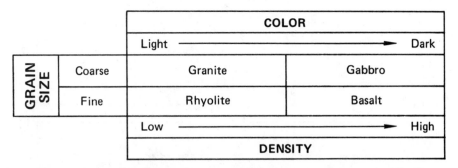

Figure 18-11. Igneous rock classification. This simple chart can be used to classify igneous rocks according to color, texture, and density.

igneous rock with a fine-grained texture, it would "belong" in the lower right-hand box of this chart. It might not be a piece of basalt, but it would be more *like* basalt than it would be like any of the other standard rocks in the chart.

The chart in Figure 18-11 permits only the most basic classification of igneous rocks. The key to actual identification of a rock is, of course, its mineral composition. The color of a rock can serve as a general guide to composition. The term *felsic* is often used to refer to light-colored igneous rocks. Felsic is derived from the word "feldspar." It indicates the presence of light-colored minerals of low density, such as feldspar and quartz. The term *mafic* is used to describe dark-colored igneous rocks. This term comes from the words "magnesium" and "ferrum" (iron), and it indicates the presence of dark-colored minerals of high density, such as olivine and pyroxene.

The diagram in Figure 18-12 is a scheme or chart for use in both classifying and identifying igneous rocks. Notice that it includes all the characteristics contained in the chart in Figure 18-11 *plus* mineral composition. The box at the top of the diagram is

very similar to the chart in Figure 18-11, with light-colored (felsic) rocks of low density to the left and dark-colored (mafic) rocks of high density to the right. Grain size ranges from fine at the bottom of the box to coarse at the top.

The important difference between this chart and the one in Figure 18-11 is in the lower portion of this chart, which shows mineral composition. Notice that each of the different areas inside the box represents a different mineral, and the approximate percentages by volume are shown on scales at the sides of the box. Let's take a brief look at the area between the two dotted lines toward the left side of the chart in order to learn how to use it properly.

Notice that the three most abundant minerals, by volume, enclosed by these dotted lines are orthoclase (a feldspar), quartz, and plagioclase feldspars. From what you have already learned you should recognize that these are the three minerals that are always present in granite. The other minerals between the lines, mica and amphibole (hornblende), are often found in granite, also. The percentages of these minerals present in a granite may vary somewhat. How-

SCHEME FOR IGNEOUS ROCK IDENTIFICATION

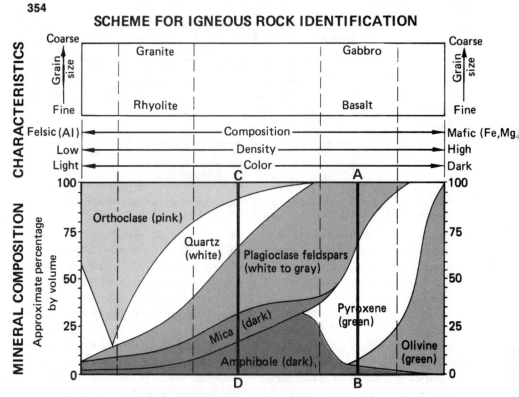

Figure 18-12. Scheme for identifying igneous rocks.

ever, as the diagram indicates, the composition of any rock represented by the region between the two dotted lines will be at least 80% feldspars and quartz by volume.

If mineral composition were the only factor to be considered for identification purposes, any rock represented by this region of the chart would be considered a granite. However, one other important factor must be taken into account—texture, or grain size. Trace the dotted lines up to the box at the top of the diagram. You will find two igneous rocks listed there. If the rock sample being considered had a coarse-grained texture, it would be a granite, an intrusive igneous rock. If it were fine-grained, it would be a rhyolite, an extrusive rock. The mineral compositions of these two rocks are similar. But because they crystallized under different conditions, their textures are different (see Figure 18-13).

Figure 18-13. Rhyolite and granite. These close-up photographs show the fine-grained texture of rhyolite (A) and the coarse-grained texture of granite (B).

Toward the right side of the chart you will find a similar pair of dotted lines. In the box at the top, the two igneous rocks listed between these lines are gabbro and basalt. Consider an igneous rock represented by line AB on the diagram. This rock contains four minerals—plagioclase feldspar, pyroxene, olivine, and amphibole. According to the scale on the right side of the diagram, the approximate percentages of the four minerals in rock AB, by volume, are: plagioclase, 35%; pyroxene, 55%; olivine, 5%; and amphibole, 5%.

What other information about rock AB does the chart provide? Since the rock is dark in color, high in density, and composed of mafic minerals, it is found toward the right side of the diagram. If you were to examine a sample of the rock represented by line AB, you could determine its texture. If it were a coarse-grained texture, the rock would be a gabbro. If it were fine-grained, it would be a basalt.

As a final exercise in using this chart, suppose you are told that line CD represents a sample of a coarse-grained igneous rock. What information about that rock can you get from the chart? First of all, you can determine the composition of the rock and you can find the approximate percentages, by volume, of each mineral present. Next, the position of line CD on the chart (slightly left of center) indicates that the rock is somewhat denser and darker in color than granite. The presence of fairly large amounts of mica and amphibole, both dark minerals, tends to support the idea that the rock is darker than granite. Specifically, rock CD is probably

granodiorite, a relatively unimportant intrusive igneous rock. However, you should be aware that identification of igneous rocks through visual examination alone is a difficult task. Identification of component minerals of a rock sample in the field may, in fact, be impossible. However, the use of a chart such as the one in Figure 18-12 should aid you in understanding the general classification of igneous rocks.

Metamorphic Rocks. Metamorphic rocks are those that have formed from other rocks as a result of the action of heat, pressure, and/or chemical activity. Metamorphic rock may form from sedimentary, igneous, or even other metamorphic rocks. The word "metamorphic" comes from Greek words meaning *to change form (meta = change, morph = form)*. So, metamorphic rocks are rocks that have been changed in form in some fashion. Generally, metamorphic rocks are divided into two groups, *regional* metamorphic rocks and *contact* metamorphic rocks.

Regional metamorphic rock is formed by forces acting over wide areas, perhaps as much as hundreds or even thousands of square kilometers. Essentially, the factors that cause metamorphic rock to form are extreme conditions of temperature and pressure. These factors are often accompanied by increased chemical activity. It should be noted that the formation of sedimentary and igneous rocks also involves temperature and pressure, but the extremes are different. If temperature, pressure, and/or chemical activity are such that existing rock changes, either chemically or

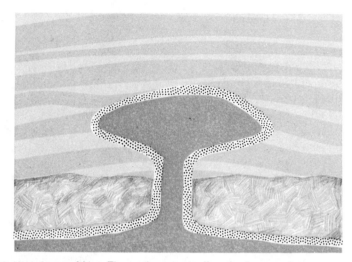

Figure 18-14. Contact metamorphism. The rocks surrounding the igneous intrusions are metamorphosed as a result of their contact with the hot liquid rock.

physically (without melting), the result will be the formation of metamorphic rock.

Metamorphic rock probably forms at great depth (tens of kilometers) within the earth's crust. The extreme conditions of temperature and pressure required for regional metamorphism to take place are not found at the earth's surface. In fact, the conditions required for regional metamorphism to occur are usually associated with mountain-building processes. Therefore, metamorphic rocks are often found in mountainous regions or in regions where mountains once existed, but have long since been eroded away.

Contact metamorphic rocks are formed at the interface of hot magma and existing rocks. As stated earlier, magma is forced into cracks and openings in crustal rocks. The surrounding rock is changed, or metamorphosed, as a result of being in *contact* with the hot magma (see Figure 18-14). The high temperatures alone may be sufficient to cause metamorphism to take place. Often, however, the hot magma

dissolves some minerals from the existing rock. The changes involved are usually chemical in nature, resulting in entirely new minerals being formed.

When existing rocks are changed, or metamorphosed, these changes often produce certain characteristics that may help you to recognize that a rock is metamorphic. A brief description of some of the changes caused by metamorphism follows.

Distortion. During metamorphism, the structure of a rock may be twisted

Figure 18-15. Distorted structure in a metamorphic rock.

and distorted, with no change in chemical composition taking place (see Figure 18-15). This distortion often helps in distinguishing metamorphic rocks from igneous rocks. It is one of the most noticeable characteristics of metamorphic rocks.

Banding or zoning. Banding or zoning of minerals is perhaps the most outstanding characteristic of metamorphic rocks (see Figure 18-16). Casual observation of banding might cause the observer to confuse it with the layering found in some sedimentary rocks. Closer examination will reveal that banding is due to concentrations of various component minerals into zones of different colors. Banding results when conditions of high temperature and pressure cause a rearrangement or recrystallization of the minerals in the rock. Melting does not occur. The bands of minerals form

Figure 18-16. Banding in metamorphic rock.

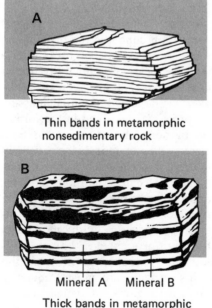

Thin bands in metamorphic nonsedimentary rock

Mineral A   Mineral B

Thick bands in metamorphic nonsedimentary rock

at right angles to the direction in which the pressure was exerted. Usually, the greater the pressure and temperature, the thicker the bands of color will be.

Increased density. Metamorphic rocks are often denser than the rocks from which they are formed. Sedimentary rocks usually contain pore spaces between the grains of sediment. The high pressure involved in metamorphism forces the grains closer together, eliminating the spaces and increasing the density of the rock.

Chemical change. Chemical activity, such as that which often accompanies contact metamorphism, results in the formation of new minerals.

Kinds of Metamorphic Rocks. Although there are many different kinds of metamorphic rocks, only a few are commonly found. Brief descriptions of these common metamorphic rocks follow.

Marble. Marble is metamorphic limestone. It is usually white to light gray in color. If it contains impurities, marble may show a wide variety of colors, such as green, brown, or yellow. Marble is composed of the mineral calcite, and will fizz when dilute hydrochloric acid is dropped on it. Marble is easily cut and polished. For this reason it is often used for tombstones and monuments.

Slate. Slate, which is a very common metamorphic rock, usually forms from shale. Slates range in color from black to green to brown to red.

Quartzite. Quartzite is highly metamorphosed quartz sandstone. It is a tough, hard, dense rock that is difficult to break. It can usually be distinguished from sandstone in that it breaks *through* the quartz grains.

Figure 18-17. Gneiss (top); garnet mica schist (bottom). The large crystals visible in the schist are garnet.

Sandstone fractures *around* the grains.

Gneiss. Gneiss is usually highly distorted and shows banding (see Figure 18-17). This rock is often formed from granite, but it may also form from metamorphism of other rocks or minerals.

Schist. There are many types of schists, but mica schist and garnet schist are quite common. All schists

exhibit a type of layering, known as *schistosity,* which allows them to be easily broken. Schist and gneiss are two of the most commonly found metamorphic rocks.

In summary, then, the key to classifying any rock is to look for characteristic structures or features that give clues to the origin of the rock sample. Once you have decided on the origin, classification becomes easier. For example, if a rock sample appears earthy and you can see bedding or layers, it is probably sedimentary. If the rock is banded and appears to be folded or twisted, it is probably metamorphic. If it is glassy in appearance, or contains crystals, it is most likely an igneous rock. This sort of general observation will often help considerably in classifying rocks. However, there will be exceptions. For these exceptions, or for more specific identification, more sophisticated methods of testing and observing must be employed.

Another helpful but very general observation concerns the distribution of the three classes of rocks. Sedimentary rocks are generally found as a relatively thin layer of rocks covering large continental masses. The processes involved in the formation of nonsedimentary rocks, both igneous and metamorphic, are usually associated with unstable crustal conditions. Extreme conditions of temperature and/or pressure are generally associated with earthquakes and volcanic activity or with mountain-building processes. Thus, nonsedimentary rocks, at or near the earth's surface, are most frequently found in regions of volcanoes or mountains.

SUMMARY

1. Nonsedimentary rocks are classified as either igneous or metamorphic.
2. Igneous rocks are formed from the cooling and solidification of liquid rock.
3. Igneous rocks are divided into two groups. Intrusive igneous rocks form beneath the earth's surface; extrusive igneous rocks form at the earth's surface.
4. Crystal size is directly related to the rate of cooling. The slower liquid rock cools, the larger the crystals that will form.
5. Metamorphic rocks are formed from other rocks in the crust. Metamorphism is caused by extreme conditions of heat and pressure and may be accompanied by chemical changes.
6. Metamorphic rocks are divided into two groups. Regional metamorphic rocks are formed over wide areas of the crust by extreme conditions of heat and pressure. Contact metamorphic rocks are formed at the interface of magma and crustal rock.
7. Some changes caused by metamorphism include: distortion, banding or zoning of minerals, increased density, and chemical changes that result in newly formed minerals.
8. Characteristics exhibited by rocks of the three classes provide information about the environment in which the rocks formed.

THE ROCK CYCLE

From earlier sections of this chapter, you have found that some rocks are related, in some fashion, to other rocks. For example, all metamorphic rocks are formed from preexisting rocks, either sedimentary, igneous, or other metamorphic rocks. In addition, some sedimentary rocks form from sediment composed of weathered fragments of various types of rocks. *Some* rocks, then, are definitely related to, or formed from, other rocks. To carry this idea one step further, *all* rocks are *potentially* related to all other rocks.

To explain this potential relationship among all rocks, we will use a model. You are already familiar with the use of models. We have used them many times in this book. In this instance, our model is called the *rock cycle*. This model is used to show how the three classes of rock are interrelated. It is also used to show the relationships that exist between the processes that produce each of the various classes of rock—sedimentary, igneous, and metamorphic.

As you study the rock cycle model, remember the major ideas upon which the rock cycle is based: *Any rock type can be changed into any other rock type, and most rock material has the potential to move in any direction within the cycle.* This means that any type of rock can contain materials that were once part of another rock type. In addition, any single piece of rock material can remain unchanged for an indefinite period of time, or it can change from type to type an indefinite number of times.

Figure 18-18. The Rock Cycle.

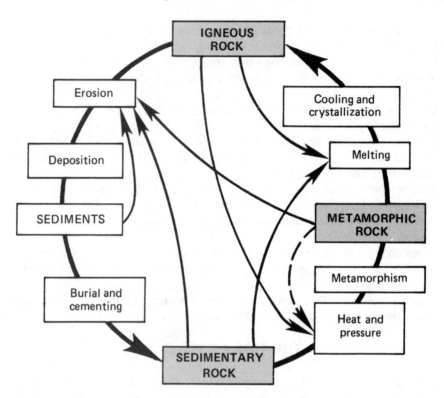

The Rock Cycle Diagram. Figure 18-18 is a diagram of the rock cycle. The diagram is almost self-explanatory, but let's take a look at some of its component parts. Notice that all three classes of rock are represented: igneous at the top, metamorphic at the right, and sedimentary at the bottom. Notice also that sediments are represented in the model, located at the left side of the diagram. You can see that the diagram is basically a closed circle, with interconnecting arrows. The arrows illustrate the pathways that any type of rock might take as it undergoes change to become a different type of rock. Let's examine the model one part at a time, starting with the sediments.

Sediments in the Cycle. Figure 18-19 represents a magnified portion of the rock cycle model. This portion represents the sediment part of the model.

Figure 18-19. Sediments in the rock cycle.

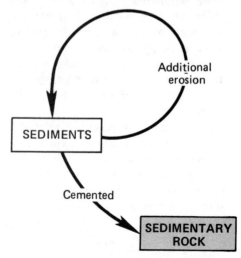

Notice that sediments have two possible routes within the rock cycle. First, they may be further eroded, in which case they remain as sediments. Second, they may be compressed and cemented to become sedimentary rock. It *may* be possible, under certain conditions, for sediments to be changed directly into either igneous or metamorphic rocks; this might happen, for example, by sudden contact with an intrusion of magma. However, such conditions are not likely to occur, and these pathways are not shown on the rock cycle model.

Sedimentary Rocks in the Cycle. The next portion of the rock cycle to be considered is the sedimentary rocks. Figure 18-20 is a magnified version of this portion of the model. This figure shows that sedimentary rock may be changed in any of three ways. It can be weathered and eroded to form sediments again, as often happens. Sedimentary rock might be melted, later to become igneous rock, or it might be changed (without melting) by heat and/or pressure to form metamorphic rock. Remember, these are *potential* pathways of change.

Figure 18-20. Sedimentary rocks in the cycle.

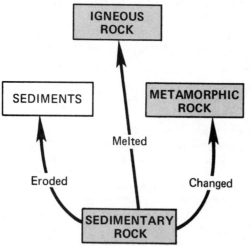

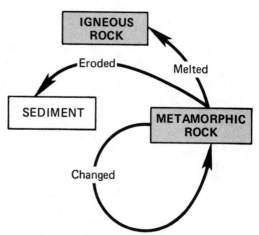

Figure 18-21. Metamorphic rocks in the cycle.

Nothing requires that *any* of these changes take place at any given time. A particular sedimentary rock might remain unchanged for an indefinite period of time.

Metamorphic Rocks in the Cycle. Now examine Figure 18-21, which represents the metamorphic rock portion of the rock cycle. These rocks also have three potential routes of change. A metamorphic rock could be eroded and converted to sediments. Or, it could be melted, later to become an igneous rock. The third possibility, as represented by the dashed line, is that a metamorphic rock could be changed by heat, pressure, and/or chemical action to form a *different* metamorphic rock. This latter change represents a small cycle within the larger cycle. This type of transformation is one reason why metamorphic rocks and the processes involved in their formation are so complex and difficult to interpret.

Igneous Rocks in the Cycle. Figure 18-22 represents the final portion of the rock cycle, the igneous rocks. As you can see, igneous rocks also have

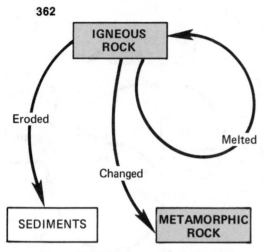

Figure 18-22. Igneous rocks in the cycle.

three potential pathways for becoming other rocks. One pathway, which is available to *all* types, is to be eroded and transformed to sediments. If igneous rocks are exposed to the proper conditions of heat, pressure, and/or chemical action, they can be changed to metamorphic rocks. Finally, igneous rocks may be melted, later to become new igneous rocks. The igneous rocks formed under these conditions will be "new" rocks, because their crystal structure and/or their chemical composition will have been altered.

The rock cycle, then, is a simple means of describing very complex processes of change. Keep in mind that the entire science of "rockology," or, more properly, *petrology,* is very complex. The mechanics of metamorphism, the chemical changes involved, and the energy transformations that occur during the changes from one rock type to another are only partly understood. Keep these thoughts in mind as you examine the rock cycle. Use the model to help yourself to understand the interrelationships that exist between some of the rock samples that you have studied or will study as part of this course.

SUMMARY

1. The rock cycle is a model designed to show how the different rock types are related and the potential pathways rock material may follow in the transformations from one rock type to another.
2. Any one type of rock can be changed into any other rock type.
3. There is no "preferred" direction of rock material within the rock cycle.
4. The composition of some rocks suggests that the materials of which they are composed have undergone several changes within the rock cycle.
5. Changes that rocks undergo within the rock cycle are complex and often not clearly understood.

REVIEW QUESTIONS

Group A
1. From what materials are sedimentary rocks formed?
2. Name three groups or divisions of sedimentary rocks.
3. Describe three processes by which sedimentary rocks may be formed.
4. Describe some of the ways in which sedimentary rocks may resemble the sediments from which they are formed.
5. Name the two groups of nonsedimentary rocks. Describe how rocks of both groups are formed.

6. What are the two divisions of igneous rocks? Describe the factors upon which the system of classification is based.
7. Describe the relationship between the rate at which magma cools and the size of the crystals in the igneous rock formed.
8. From what materials are metamorphic rocks formed? What conditions cause metamorphism?
9. Name the two groups of metamorphic rocks and describe the formation of each.
10. List four important changes that rocks may undergo during the process of metamorphism.
11. For what purpose is the model of the rock cycle designed?
12. According to the rock cycle model, what kinds of transformations can occur among the different types of rocks? Are some transformations more likely to occur than others?

Group B
1. Describe the main characteristics of sedimentary rocks that distinguish them from other types of rock.
2. a.   Describe how igneous rocks are formed.
   b.   Describe how metamorphic rocks are formed.
3. Explain the concept of the rock cycle as it is described in this chapter. Include in your answer a description of the various pathways that a given sample of rock material may take as it is carried through the cycle.

REVIEW EXERCISES

1. Select *six* of the rock-forming minerals listed in the chart below. Use the Mineral Identification Table in the Appendix (page 540) to fill in the properties of each of the minerals you have chosen.

Mineral	Color	Streak	Luster	Hardness	Cleavage
Feldspar					
Quartz					
Mica					
Calcite					
Hornblende					
Kaolin					
Augite					
Garnet					
Magnetite					
Olivine					
Pyrite					
Talc					

Scheme for Igneous Rock Identification

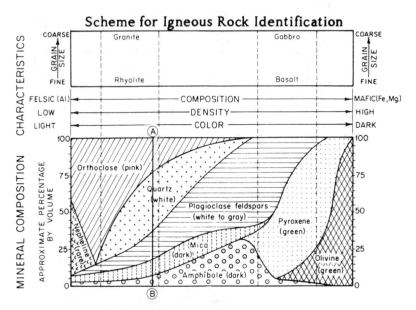

2. Line AB represents an *intrusive* igneous rock. From the diagram, obtain the following information about rock AB: mineral composition, approximate percentage of each mineral present, density, color. From your knowledge of igneous rocks, also determine the grain size and the name of the rock.

3. Identify rock samples A and B, based on the descriptions given below.

	SAMPLE A	**SAMPLE B**
COMPOSITION	Orthoclase 60% Quartz 20% Plagioclase 10% Mica 8% Amphibole 2%	Plagioclase 15% Pyroxene 70% Olivine 14% Amphibole 1%
GRAIN SIZE	Fine	Coarse
COLOR	Light	Dark
DENSITY	Low	High

4. On a separate piece of paper, make a copy of the table below. Use the diagram to determine density, color, grain size, and approximate mineral composition of the igneous rocks listed in the table.

ROCK	MINERALS PRESENT	COLOR	DENSITY	GRAIN SIZE
Basalt				
Gabbro				
Rhyolite				
Granite				

5. Using the rock cycle model (p.360) trace the various pathways that a sample of igneous rock (granite) might take through the rock cycle. List each of the possible changes that the sample could undergo.

6. The table below gives the composition and grain size of five different sedimentary rock samples. Using the Sedimentary Rock Classification Chart found in the Appendix (page 543), identify the five rock samples by name.

	SAMPLE # 1	SAMPLE #2	SAMPLE #3	SAMPLE # 4	SAMPLE # 5
COMPOSITION	Silicate	Carbonate	Carbonate	Silicate	Neither silicate or carbonate
GRAIN SIZE	.5mm to 1.5 mm	Molecular	Pebbles	.001mm to .015mm	Molecular

7. Below are descriptions of characteristics of six different common rocks. From the following list of ten names, select the one that matches the description of each sample: marble, halite (rock salt), bituminous coal, gneiss, conglomerate, rhyolite, limestone, shale, obsidian, granite.

SAMPLE #1

Black, low density, no visible crystals, shows evidence of fossil plants

SAMPLE #2

Light-colored, low density, visible crystals, coarse texture, contains quartz and feldspar

SAMPLE #3

Black, shiny, low density, no visible crystals, glassy texture

SAMPLE #4

Distorted structure, no visible crystals, high density, shows color bands

SAMPLE #5

Mixed colors, low density, pebbles imbedded in a sandy base, cemented

SAMPLE #6

Colorless, no visible crystals, low density, cleaves into tiny cubes

TOPIC XII
THE DYNAMIC CRUST

Mt. St. Helen's spewing hot gases, ash and dust during the 1981 eruption.

CHAPTER 19
Evidence of Crustal Change

You will know something about crustal change if you can:

1. Describe the direct evidence of minor crustal change near the earth's surface.
2. Describe the indirect evidence of major crustal change below the earth's surface.

Until now, we have been concerned with changes in the earth that, for the most part, were either easily measurable or small in scale. But what about large-scale changes in the earth? Changes so enormous that they involve the shifting about of entire continental land masses? Well, this is what the next three chapters are all about—the dynamic, changing earth, with energy transfer and transformation occurring on a planetary, or global, scale.

The authors gratefully acknowledge contributions to Topic XII by Edward Benjamin Snyder, Yorktown High School, Yorktown Heights, N.Y.

EVIDENCE OF CRUSTAL CHANGES NEAR THE SURFACE

When we study the earth's surface, we find many kinds of evidence that the crust has moved and shifted in the past and that such changes are taking place right now. This section of the chapter will consider some of this direct evidence that can be observed at the surface. There are also several types of *indirect* evidence of crustal change, especially change going on deep within the crust or even below it. Although we cannot observe the rocks far below the surface, we can draw inferences about them from certain observations that we can make at the surface. Evidence of deep crustal change will be examined in the next section of the chapter.

Figure 19-1. Sedimentary strata. This sedimentary rock formation near Canyon City, Colorado, consists of alternating layers of sandstone and shale.

Horizontal Rock Strata. When exposed on edge in road cuts, stream banks, and excavations, sedimentary rocks are often found lying in flat layers, or *strata,* that are parallel and horizontal. Figure 19-1 illustrates this arrangement of layers of sedimentary rock. Notice that the flat layers are all parallel to one another and that they lie horizontally.

Isn't this observation what we should expect from what we know about the formation of sedimentary rocks? You should remember from Chapter 18 (page 345) that sedimentary rocks form from the compaction or cementation of sediment. We also know from Chapter 16 that sediment is deposited in quiet water in flat, parallel, horizontal layers. So, if sedimentary rocks are formed from layers of sediment, then we should expect to find those rocks in flat, parallel, horizontal layers, as in Figure 19-1. Earth scientists refer to this characteristic of sedimentary rock layers as *original horizontality.*

Sedimentary Rocks at High Elevations. In the Grand Canyon of the Colorado River in Arizona (Figure 3-1, page 31), sedimentary rocks more than 1,000 m thick are exposed along the canyon walls. The top of these layers of rock is more than 2 km above sea level. Similar sedimentary rocks are found at high elevations over a large area (called the Colorado Plateau) in Colorado, New Mexico, Arizona, and Utah, and in many other high plateau regions of the world.

If the sediments that formed these rocks were deposited in water, how did they get so far above sea level? The most likely explanation is that they

Figure 19-2. Tilted sedimentary rock. The inclination of the once-horizontal layers of these sedimentary rocks is evidence of crustal activity.

were raised to their present elevation by crustal movement.

Fossils. A fossil is the remains or traces of a once-living organism. In Chapter 23 we will discuss the various kinds of fossils, how they were formed, and how their ages can be estimated. For our purposes in this chapter, we will simply note that fossils of marine (sea) animals, such as corals and clams, have been found in sedimentary rock at elevations high above sea level, in some places at elevations of thousands of meters.

Sediments collected from ocean bottoms also contain fossils. Often, fossils of marine animals of types that live only in shallow waters near ocean shorelines are found at great depths and at considerable distance from present shores. In many instances, fossils of animals that are believed to have lived at about the same time are found both at high elevations and in deep ocean sediments.

How can we account for the existence of marine fossils of similar age at such widely different elevations? Again, the most likely inference is that after being deposited in shallow water, some of the rock layers with their fossils were uplifted, while others sank to lower levels.

Tilted Strata. When exposed on edge, some sedimentary rock layers are found to be tilted. Their layers are not horizontal. Figure 19-2 illustrates rock strata that are tilted, or inclined, at an angle away from the horizontal. We know that sediments being deposited today are always found in more-or-less horizontal layers. We infer, therefore, that the strata became tilted by crustal movement after the sediments had hardened into rock.

Folded and Bent Strata. Figure 19-3 is a photograph of sedimentary rock layers that are not only tilted, but also folded almost into the shape of an S. We don't even see *tilted* sedimentary beds today, and we certainly never find them bent and distorted like the layers in Figure 19-3. Sediments are moved too easily for them to remain in such a state, even if they were somehow distorted temporarily.

How did these layers become folded? You may find it difficult to believe that layers of solid rock can be bent and folded like sheets of paper, but that is apparently what happened to the rocks in Figure 19-3. Laboratory experiments have shown that rock *can* slowly change shape if strong forces are applied for long periods of time.

Faults. Observers often find layers of sedimentary rock that appear to have been broken and shifted relative

Figure 19-3. Distorted sedimentary rock.

tion of objects and structures on the earth's surface. Displacements of several meters have been measured in some cases.

Figure 19-4. Faulted sedimentary rock. The rock layers to the left of the diagonal fault line are lower than the matching layers to the right of the fault.

to each other. Examine Figure 19-4 carefully. This photograph illustrates layers of rock that appear to have been broken and moved. Notice the diagonal line cutting across the rock layers. This is the edge of the surface along which movement seems to have occurred. The rock layers on one side of the diagonal line are not continuous with the layers on the other side. But if you compare the layers on both sides, you will find matching *series* of layers. If you shift the layers up or down, they can be made to match exactly.

A break or crack in rock along which motion appears to have occurred is called a *fault*. The process of the displacement of rock along a fault is called *faulting*.

Do masses of solid rock actually break and move against each other along faults? We need not hesitate to answer yes. Observers have seen it happen. After an earthquake, it is often possible to notice a shift in posi-

Volcanic Activity. On February 20, 1943, in the middle of what had been a flat, level corn field, four farmers in Paricutin, Mexico, felt the earth shake and watched in disbelief as "smoke", ash and gasses began to burst forth from a small crack in the ground. These four people, without understanding what was happening, were observing the birth of a new volcano. The surface of their level corn field began to swell causing the surrounding area to be up-lifted by more than two meters in a matter of moments. Within 24 hours, uplifting, accompanied by the accumulation of volcanic ash, dust and cinders, had produced a cone nearly 50 meters high. Within six days, a volcanic mountain more than 160 meters in height had formed where less than a week before there had been nothing but a flat, level corn field! One year later the Paricutin volcano had reached a height of approximately 500 meters.

The type of volcanic cone that was produced by the Paricutin eruption is referred to as a *cinder cone*. Such volcanoes consist mostly of rock particles, ash, cinders and volcanic dust. Different kinds of volcanic eruptions produce different types of cones. Volcanoes which erupt molten rock, or *lava*, create cones which are very broad-based with gently sloping sides. Volcanoes of this type are known as *shield volcanoes*. The volcanoes which produced the Hawaiian Islands are shield-type volcanoes. If a volcanic cone is built up of alternating layers of fluid lava and rock particles or cinders, it is known as a *composite volcano*. Mt. Vesuvius in Italy is an example of a composite volcano.

Figure 19-5. Composite volcano. Volcanoes of this type may erupt only thick lava for a long time and then suddenly spew a mixture of cinders, ash, and rock fragments called *pyroclasts*.

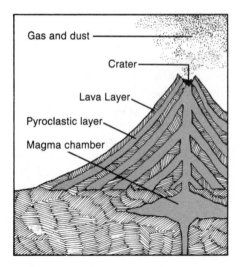

Figure 19-6. Raised beaches. Each of the step-like formations in the background was once at sea level.

Raised Beaches. Along the edges of some of the continents *(continental margins)* there are regions near the shoreline that have a steplike appearance, as in Figure 19-6. That is, as you travel inland from the shore, the elevation of the surface increases in a series of steps. The top surface of each step is usually horizontal, but in many cases the rock layers in the vertical face of the step are tilted.

Earth scientists reason that each flat step was once at sea level, and that the step was a beach cut into the shore by wave action. Then the entire shoreline was raised by an upward movement of the local crust. When the upward movement stopped, the waves cut a new beach. This beach became a second step when another uplift of the crust occurred. The tilting of the strata often observed in the faces of raised beaches may have occurred before the uplift began.

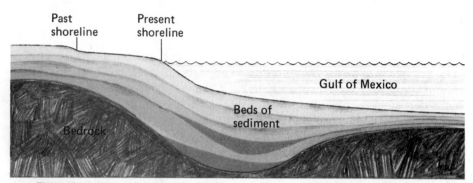

Figure 19-7. Geosyncline on the floor of the Gulf of Mexico. The floor beneath the center of the geosyncline, where sediments are thickest, shows evidence of slow subsidence.

Changes in Bench Mark Elevations. A bench mark is a marker that is set permanently into the ground (usually in solid bedrock) and labeled with its exact elevation above or below sea level. The locations and elevations of bench marks are often shown on topographic maps. When the elevations of bench marks are checked by later measurements, it is often observed that the elevations have changed. These observations are direct evidence of vertical movements of the crust.

Geosynclines. In many parts of the world, great thicknesses of sediments have been found with an unexpected characteristic. The accumulations of sediment are in some cases as much as 15 km thick. But fossils and other types of evidence indicate that all of the sediments were deposited in shallow water. Sedimentary rocks that formed from great thicknesses of shallow-water sediments occur in many places. There are also shallow seas in which such sediments are apparently accumulating today. One of these areas, which earth scientists have studied, is in the Gulf of Mexico. The beds or layers of sediments there are observed to be thicker in the middle than around the edges, as shown in Figure 19-7. They seem to be slowly sinking, or *subsiding,* in the center.

An area of shallow water that appears to be subsiding as sediments collect in it is called a *geosyncline.* Figure 19-8 shows the location of

Figure 19-8. Present-day geosynclines.

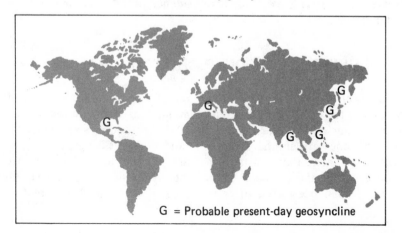

G = Probable present-day geosyncline

present-day regions that are believed to be geosynclines. According to this interpretation of a geosyncline, sediments deposited in shallow water can accumulate to great thicknesses because the underlying crust is subsiding at the same rate that sediments are being added. The beds of sediment are thinner toward the edges because most of the subsidence occurs at the center of the basin.

Minor Crustal Change. Taken all in all, the observations described up to this point are rather convincing evidence that the earth's crust does rise and fall and shift about. We can say that the earth has a dynamic crust, which means that it is constantly active and changing. Would you say that the changes described so far are *major* ones? Let's think about that.

The Colorado Plateau has about 2½ million cubic kilometers of rock that appears to have been lifted 8 to 10 kilometers since the sediments were first laid down. On a human scale, that could be called major! But in relation to the size of the earth, it is not much. On an earth that is 12,000 kilometers in diameter, to shift some rocks by 10 kilometers is really a rather minor change. You would probably think of a scratch in the skin of an apple as a minor change. Yet this would be relatively a much greater change than the crustal changes we have been considering.

Are there more serious events of change going on in the earth's crust —changes that might move whole continents thousands of kilometers across the surface? We will examine evidence of such changes in the next section.

SUMMARY

1. Sedimentary rocks at high elevations suggest past uplift of the crust.
2. Shallow-water marine fossils found today both at high elevations above sea level and at great ocean depths indicate changes in elevation of the crust.
3. Tilted and folded rock strata suggest past crustal movement.
4. Rock faults, volcanoes, displaced strata, raised beaches, and changes in bench mark elevations are all indications of crustal change and movement.
5. Geosynclines provide evidence of subsidence of the crust near some continental margins.

EVIDENCE OF DEEP CRUSTAL CHANGE

We have already mentioned the movements of the crust that are often observed during earthquakes. Eruptions of volcanoes are another example of crustal change that can be directly observed at the surface. Volcanoes have even been seen to rise out of the ground in the space of a few months, as Paricutin did in Mexico in 1943. Earthquakes and volcanic eruptions occur at irregular intervals, and are, as yet, unpredictable. Are they merely random events near the surface of the crust? Or are they evi-

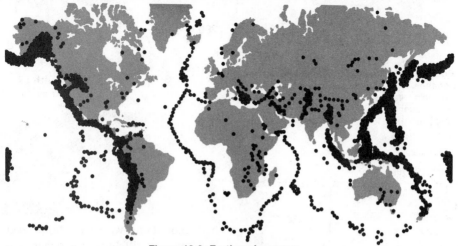

Figure 19-9. Earthquake zones.

dence of major processes going on deep below the surface? Let us look at the evidence for such deep-seated crustal change.

Earthquake Zones. For many years earth scientists have been observing and recording the locations of earthquakes. (Methods of making such observations will be described in the next chapter.) Figure 19-9 is a world map on which each earthquake that occurred during a period of several years was marked by a dot. Where earthquake activity is frequent, the dots have run together to form a thick band. You can see two such heavy zones of earthquake activity—one along the western coasts of North and South America, the other through the chains of islands in the western part of the Pacific Ocean. Other regions of fairly intense earthquake activity can be seen in the eastern Mediterranean, in southwest Asia, and elsewhere. Notice, also, the thin lines of earthquake activity running through the middle of the oceans. Earthquakes may not be as frequent here as along some of the continental margins, but they do show a definite pattern of occurrence.

Zones of Volcanic Activity. Figure 19-10 is a world map showing the locations of volcanoes that are active

Figure 19-10. Zones of volcanic activity.

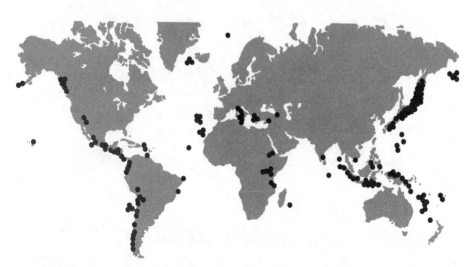

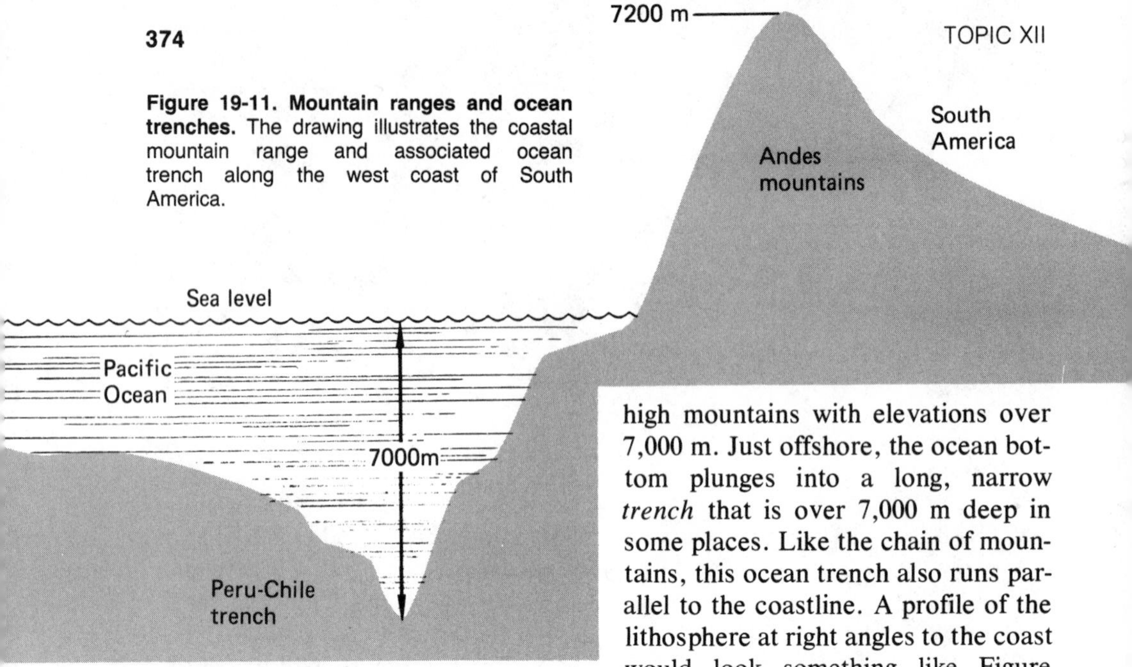

7200 m ——————

South
America

Andes
mountains

Figure 19-11. Mountain ranges and ocean trenches. The drawing illustrates the coastal mountain range and associated ocean trench along the west coast of South America.

Sea level

Pacific
Ocean

7000m

Peru-Chile
trench

high mountains with elevations over 7,000 m. Just offshore, the ocean bottom plunges into a long, narrow *trench* that is over 7,000 m deep in some places. Like the chain of mountains, this ocean trench also runs parallel to the coastline. A profile of the lithosphere at right angles to the coast would look something like Figure 19-11.

today or are known to have erupted in the recent past. Here, again, we see a definite pattern of zones of volcanic activity. We can also see that the earthquake and volcano zones appear to coincide.

Mountain Ranges and Ocean Trenches. All along the Pacific coast of South America there is a chain of

Recall from Figures 19-9 and 19-10 that this coastline of South America is a zone of earthquake and volcanic activity. We have just noted that on the landward side of this zone there is a range of high mountains. On the seaward side there is a deep ocean trench. This association of mountain

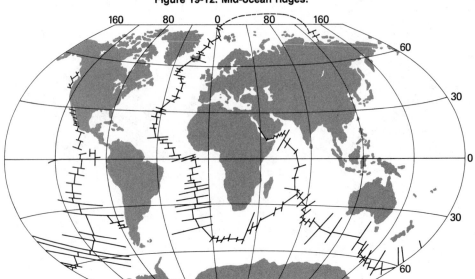

Figure 19-12. Mid-ocean ridges.

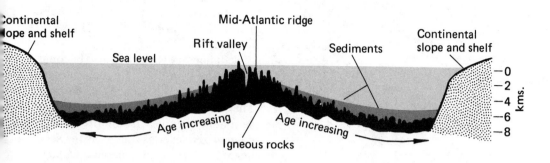

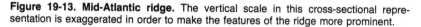

Figure 19-13. Mid-Atlantic ridge. The vertical scale in this cross-sectional representation is exaggerated in order to make the features of the ridge more prominent.

ranges, ocean trenches, and a zone of crustal activity is found at many other places along continental margins. Sometimes, as in the western Pacific, a series of islands, called an *island arc,* is found alongside the ocean trench. In such cases, the islands are actually the peaks of mountains rising from the ocean floor. Is there some large-scale process occurring in the crust to account for this association of features?

Mid-Ocean Ridges. Would you believe that there is a range of mountains on earth that is 80,000 km long and 3 km high, but was unknown until about 35 years ago? This major feature of the lithosphere escaped notice because most of it is under water. Figure 19-12 shows the location of these ridges along the ocean floors. If you compare this map with Figure 19-9 you will discover that these undersea ridges follow exactly along the lines of earthquake activity on the ocean bottoms. In Figure 19-12, notice that the mid-ocean ridges are broken into short lengths, which are displaced from each other by long faults along the ocean floor (represented by the thin lines crossing the ridges). Most earthquakes in the ridge zone occur near these

faults.

Figure 19-13 is a cross section of a typical portion of the mid-Atlantic ridge. Notice the deep rift valley in the center of the ridge. Rift valleys are a characteristic feature of the ocean ridges, although they are not present everywhere along the ridges. Studies of samples of rock from the ridges show that they are igneous. In a later chapter we will study the methods used to determine the age of rocks. Here we will simply state the fact that rocks taken from the center of the oceanic ridges have all been found to be quite young; that is, they were formed relatively recently. Rock material on either side of the ridge appears to be older, the age increasing with distance from the center of the ridge.

Rock Magnetism. As you know, the earth has a magnetic field with one magnetic pole near the North Geographic Pole and the other magnetic pole near the South Geographic Pole. The earth acts as though it has a giant bar magnet along its axis.

If you cover a bar magnet with a sheet of paper and sprinkle iron filings on the paper, the bits of iron will line up in the direction of the magnetic

Figure 19-14. Magnetic field. The pattern of iron filings provides a "picture" of the magnetic field around the bar magnet. The earth is superimposed over the magnet to illustrate similarity to the earth's magnetic field.

field of the magnetized bar, as in Figure 19-14. Many of the rock-forming minerals contain iron. When rock is in a molten state, its atoms and ions are free to move and arrange themselves in any direction. Atoms of iron in liquid magma respond to the earth's magnetic field by aligning themselves in the direction of the field, as the iron filings did in Figure 19-14. When the magma solidifies into rock, its iron atoms become locked into the positions they had just before the rock hardened. The result is that igneous

rocks contain a magnetic record of the direction of the earth's magnetic field at the time and place the rocks were formed.

Sedimentary rocks can also become magnetized in the direction of the earth's field at the time they harden. This happens because many of the sediments come from previously magnetized igneous rocks. As the sediments settle, they become aligned with the earth's field, and come to rest generally lined up with that field. As the sediments harden into rock, the direction of their magnetism is also locked into place.

A study of the magnetism of rocks of many different ages in many parts of the crust has shown that the earth's magnetism has reversed itself many times in the past. Today, one end of a compass needle points toward the earth's magnetic pole near the North Pole. But about 700,000 years ago, that same compass needle would have swung around and pointed the other way. The earth's magnetic poles were reversed at that time from the polarity they have now. Many such reversals have been traced back through millions of years of the earth's history. The record of these reversals for the past 4 million years is shown in Figure 19-15.

Figure 19-15. Reversals in polarity of the earth's magnetic field.

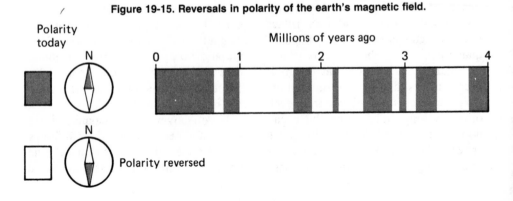

Polarity today

Millions of years ago

N

Polarity reversed

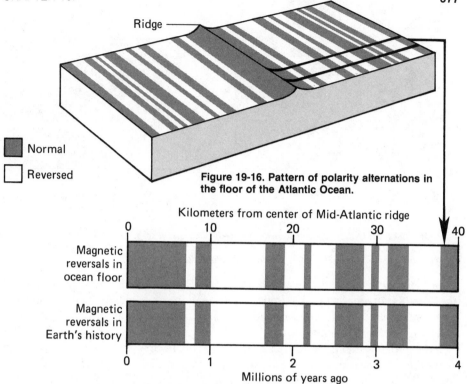

Figure 19-16. Pattern of polarity alternations in the floor of the Atlantic Ocean.

Kilometers from center of Mid-Atlantic ridge

Magnetic reversals in ocean floor

Magnetic reversals in Earth's history

Millions of years ago

Figure 19-17. Pattern of magnetic reversals in ocean floor compared with pattern of reversals of earth's magnetic field.

Magnetism of the Mid-Ocean Ridges. The magnetism of the rocks on the ocean floor can be studied from the ocean surface with a sensitive instrument called a *magnetometer*. An astonishing discovery was made when the magnetism of the crust on either side of the ocean ridges was observed. It was found that there were long strips parallel to the ridge, with alternating magnetic polarity. That is, there may be a strip 10 km wide that is magnetized in the same direction as the earth's magnetic field today. But alongside it is a strip of some other width that is magnetized in the opposite direction. Thus there is a pattern of strips of alternating polarity and of varying width parallel to each mid-ocean ridge. Even more astonishing is the fact that the patterns on opposite sides of the ridge are mirror images of each other. That is, the pattern of magnetic change is exactly the same as you travel away from the ridge in either direction.

Figure 19-16 shows the pattern of magnetic polarity of the rocks on both sides of the ridge in the North Atlantic Ocean. The first reversal is observed about 7 km from the center of the ridge; the next is 1 km further away; the third is 2 km beyond that; and so on.

In Figure 19-17, the pattern of the magnetic strips on one side of the ridge is compared with the time chart of the earth's magnetic reversals in Figure 19-15. We see a practically perfect match of *distance* on the ocean

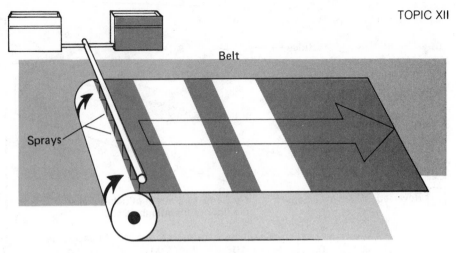

Figure 19-18. Conveyor-belt model of ocean-floor spreading. The moving belt represents the ocean floor. The alternating bands of paint represent the alternating patterns of polarity found in the rocks of the ocean floor.

floor and *time* between reversals of the earth's magnetism. A similarly close match has been found on both sides of every mid-ocean ridge.

What process can explain these remarkable observations? Look at Figure 19-18. This drawing shows a moving belt that is being sprayed with paint. There are two spray tanks, one with black paint and the other with white. When the black spray is on, a black band appears on the belt as it moves along. When the black spray is turned off and the white turned on, a white band begins to appear. If the belt is moving at a fixed speed, the width of each black or white band is directly proportional to the time that the corresponding spray was on. The distance of each band from the spray is also proportional to the time since it passed the spray.

Earth scientists reason that something similar is going on at the mid-ocean ridges. According to the theory of *ocean-floor spreading,* new rock is being formed continuously at the center of the ridge, acquiring the magnetic polarity of the earth at that

time. The rock is then being carried away from the ridge on either side at a constant rate by motion of the oceanic crust. Put in the simplest terms, the ocean floors are moving apart on either side of each oceanic ridge. As the ocean floors spread apart, the opening between them is continuously filled by flows of magma, which cools and hardens into new rock. In our moving-belt model of this process, the belt represents the moving ocean floor. The paint spray represents the magnetism given to the rocks by the earth's magnetic field as the molten rock cools and hardens.

Today scientists agree that this process of ocean-floor spreading is going on and has been going on for millions of years. The big question is, What forces or processes are causing this to occur? We will come back to this question in Chapter 21.

Continental Drift. If you look at maps of South America and Africa, you will see how closely the east coast of South America seems to fit the west coast of Africa, like pieces of a jigsaw puzzle. This similarity was noticed almost as soon as the New World was explored and mapped in the 1500's. The idea that these two continents were once part of a single land mass was proposed many times in the centuries since these early explorations. However, it is only recently that earth scientists have become convinced that this match of coastlines is not just an accident, but that South America and Africa are ac-

tually the separated halves of what was once a single continent. In fact, scientists believe that North America, South America, Europe, and Africa were all once joined as shown in Figure 19-19. There is also evidence that the other continents were once parts of larger land masses.

What kinds of evidence have led to these conclusions? The evidence is very much like the clues you use to

Figure 19-19. Giant jigsaw puzzle. The shapes of the coastlines are only one clue leading to the theory that the continents on either side of the Atlantic Ocean were once joined together in a single landmass.

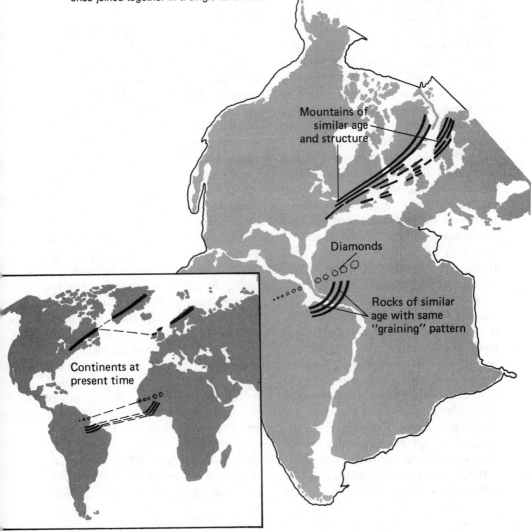

put a jigsaw puzzle together. Before the puzzle was cut into pieces, a picture was printed on it. You match the jigsaw pieces partly by shape, but also by matching parts of the picture. The continents, likewise, carry certain features besides their shape that seem to show that they were originally attached.

Similarity of rocks and minerals. In many cases, the types of rocks and minerals found along one continental margin are very similar to those along the matching edge of another continent. For example, diamonds found in eastern Brazil and in western Africa are similar in composition and show a gradual increase in size from west to east. The size of the diamonds found in eastern Brazil matches the size of the diamonds in western Africa.

Mountain formations. There are many instances of ancient rock formations that seem to match from one continent to another across large stretches of present ocean. For example, parts of the Appalachian Mountains in the northeastern United States seem to be a continuation of a mountain chain that can be traced from Norway and Sweden down through Scotland and Ireland and into Newfoundland in eastern Canada. The western part of these mountains now seems to be in eastern Greenland. These similarities in mountain formations can be explained if we assume that the land masses were grouped as in Figure 19-19 at the time the mountains were being formed. Another example is certain rock formations in the western bulge of Africa, which have a distinct "graining" pattern. An exact continuation of this pattern has been found in similar rocks in Brazil, just where it should be if the two continents were once attached as in Figure 19-19.

The fossil record. A study of fossils on both sides of the Atlantic Ocean shows a remarkable similarity of types of animals. When species develop in widely separated regions, they are usually quite different from one another. The fact that similar species are found far apart today, separated by thousands of kilometers of ocean, suggests that the separation occurred *after* the organisms appeared.

The climate record. Studies of the rocks and fossils in many parts of the world show that the climates of the continents were once much different from what they are today. For example, the evidence indicates that about 300 million years ago there were hot deserts in what is now the north polar region. At the same time there were enormous glaciers covering central Africa, Brazil, and India, where hot climates are found today. The most likely explanation is that the continents have moved over the face of the earth, their climates changing as they moved through different latitudes.

The magnetic record. Perhaps the strongest evidence of continental drift comes from the magnetic record in the rocks. In discussing ocean-floor spreading, we concentrated mainly on the polarity of the magnetism in the rocks. However, we can learn much more than that from a careful study of the direction of the magnetism. Figure 19-20 is a diagram of the lines of magnetic force as they emerge from the earth's surface. When a rock particle becomes magnetized, it becomes lined up along the line of magnetic

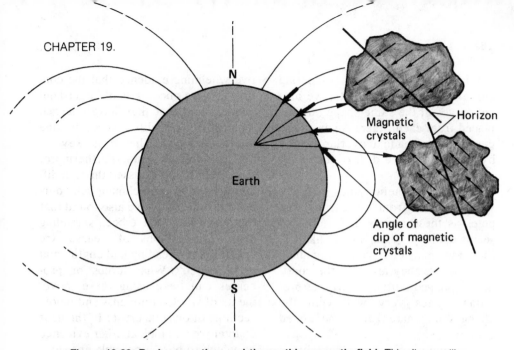

Figure 19-20. Rock magnetism and the earth's magnetic field. This diagram illustrates how the angle of dip of magnetic crystals in rocks will vary with location on the earth's surface.

force passing through its location. This means that it not only lines up in a general north-south direction, but that it also dips away from the horizontal, depending on its latitude. As Figure 19-20 shows, a magnetized rock particle at a high latitude will dip sharply away from the horizontal. A particle near the equator will lie nearly horizontal. Therefore, by studying the dip of the magnetism in a rock, we can calculate not only the direction of the magnetic pole when the rock formed, but also how far away the pole was.

When we do this with rocks of different ages on any continent, we get what is called a "polar-wandering curve." The curve shows where the pole seems to have been at different times in the past. Figure 19-21 shows two polar-wandering curves. One curve shows where the north magnetic pole appears to have been according to studies of North American

rocks. The other curve is based on studies of European rocks. The two curves have the same shape, but they get farther apart as they go back in time.

Figure 19-21. Polar wandering curves for North American and European rocks. Each curve shows where the north magnetic pole seems to have been when rocks of different ages were formed.

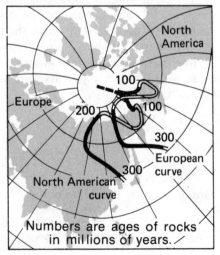

When we plot the polar wandering curves for other continents, we also get curves of the same shape but displaced from each other. Again, these curves can be made to overlap exactly by allowing for the drift of the continents.

Did the magnetic poles actually wander as far from the earth's true poles as these curves indicate? This seems unlikely. What is more likely is that the magnetic poles remained about where they are, and the continents changed latitude. This interpretation agrees very well with the changes in climate that we mentioned earlier.

To sum up, we can say that there is overwhelming evidence that the continents were once parts of larger land masses, and that they have changed their positions with respect to one another during the past several hundred million years. Furthermore, they seem to have passed through different latitudes and climate belts during this time. We have also found that the ocean floors have been spreading apart for millions of years. Are ocean-floor spreading and continental drift related? What forces or processes can be causing these movements of whole continents and whole sections of oceanic crust? In the next chapter we will look at other evidence on which to base a possible answer.

SUMMARY

1. Zones of frequent earthquakes and volcanic activity can be located on the earth's surface.
2. In many places the zones of crustal activity are associated with high mountain ranges and deep ocean trenches.
3. Igneous rock near the center of the ocean ridges is younger than the igneous rock farther from the ridges.
4. The earth's magnetism seems to have reversed itself many times in the past.
5. Strips of rock parallel to the ocean ridges show patterns of reversal of magnetic polarity that match the reversals of the earth's magnetism.
6. The shapes of the continents, combined with comparisons of rocks and minerals, mountain formations, fossils, past climates, and rock magnetism, suggest that the continents were attached at one time and have since drifted apart.

REVIEW QUESTIONS

Group A   1. What type of rocks found at high elevations suggests past uplift of the crust?
          2. In what ways do current positions of marine fossils indicate changes in elevation of the crust?

3. Describe five other types of evidence of crustal movement.
4. List and describe three types of volcanic cones.
5. Name three areas that are zones of earthquake and volcanic activity.
6. What features are associated with zones of crustal activity?
7. What is known about the age of igneous rock in ocean ridges?
8. Describe evidence showing that the earth's magnetic field has reversed itself many times in the past.
9. Describe evidence showing that the continents were attached at one time and have since drifted apart.

Group B

1. a. What is meant by tilted strata, and what might cause strata to become tilted?
   b. What is a marine fossil, and what is unusual about the places where these fossils are sometimes found?
   c. What must happen to a rock in the laboratory to make it bend and change its shape?
   d. What is a raised beach and how are such beaches probably formed?
   e. Define the term geosyncline and explain how geosynclines suggest that there have been changes in the earth's crust near the surface of the earth.
2. a. What is an earthquake zone and how do earth scientists go about determining where they exist?
   b. What relationship is there between earthquake zones and zones of volcanic activity?
   c. What is the mid-Atlantic ridge?
   d. Explain why igeous rocks contain a record of the direction of the earth's magnetic field. Of what significance is this record?
   e. Explain why observations of rocks and minerals, mountain formation, and fossils support the idea that the present-day continents were once attached to each other and have since drifted apart.

A section of the San Andreas fault in California.

CHAPTER 20
The Earth's Crust and Interior

You will know something about the earth's interior if you can:

1. Describe some of the properties of earthquake waves.
2. Explain how the epicenter of an earthquake can be located.
3. Describe models that help to explain the structure and composition of the earth's crust and interior.

Did you ever plan to dig a hole to the center of the earth? Many children start such ambitious projects. Most give up at a meter or so. With modern engineering techniques, we can of course do better. The deepest penetration into the earth's crust by man is a mine about 7.5 km deep. Still this is less than 0.06% of the way to the earth's center. Earth scientists are people who have never lost their curiosity about what they would find at the center of the earth. Since they don't expect to be able to examine the earth's interior at first hand, they have devised ingenious methods of drawing inferences about it. This chapter is concerned with the kinds of observations that enable us to construct a model of the earth's structure without actually cutting it apart.

EARTHQUAKES

In the preceding chapter we mentioned earthquakes as one of the evidences of crustal change. The fact that earthquakes can cause death and destruction on a large scale is reason enough to try to understand their nature and causes. But in the course of studying earthquakes, it has been found that they can be used as a tool to examine the structure of the entire earth. As you will learn, earthquakes produce waves in the earth. By observing these waves we can draw many inferences about the composition and properties of the materials through which the waves have passed. So let us take a closer look at earthquakes and the phenomena related to them.

The Nature of Earthquakes. If you have ever stood near a railroad track as a train went by, or felt the ground vibrate from a passing truck, you have experienced something of what it is like to be an observer during a minor earthquake. Often the experience is more of an "inner" sensation than one of actually feeling the ground move. Well, then, does the ground really move? What *does* happen when an earthquake occurs, and exactly what is an earthquake?

An earthquake is the shaking, vibrating, and sometimes violent movement of the earth's crust. The vibrations and movement are evidence of the release of energy. The sudden release of energy during an earthquake is similar to the transformation of energy that occurs when you break a stick or any other brittle object. At first as you apply force to the object, it bends or twists slightly.

The work you are doing becomes stored in the material as potential energy. At some point the force being applied (called the *stress)* becomes greater than the strength of the material. The bonds between the atoms and molecules break, and the object suddenly separates, usually producing a crack of sound and noticeable vibration of the broken parts.

Earth scientists believe that stress and potential energy accumulate in rocks over a period of time as enormous forces in the crust cause it to bend and twist. Eventually the stress becomes greater than the strength of the rocks at some particular place in the crust. The rocks then suddenly break in that place, and their stored potential energy is converted to kinetic energy, vibration, sound, and heat. Usually, portions of the surrounding rock move relative to each other. An observer would report the occurrence of an earthquake.

Faults and Earthquakes. In Chapter 19 you learned that a break, or fracture, in rock along which motion of the rock has occurred is called a fault. The two portions of the rock on either side of a fault have slipped relative to one another along the fault. This motion may have been mainly up and down, or from side to side, or a combination of these motions, as illustrated in Figure 20-1. Faults can be classified according to the type of movement that has occurred. Different types of faults are identified in Figure 20-1.

Once a fault develops in the crust, it represents a zone of weakness. As stress builds up in the region of the

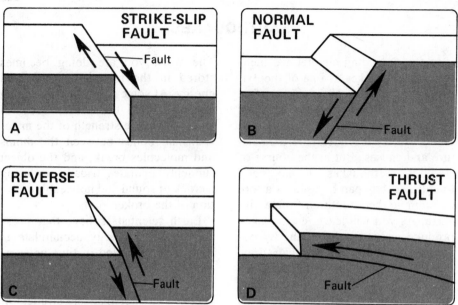

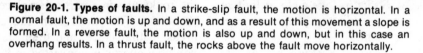

Figure 20-1. Types of faults. In a strike-slip fault, the motion is horizontal. In a normal fault, the motion is up and down, and as a result of this movement a slope is formed. In a reverse fault, the motion is also up and down, but in this case an overhang results. In a thrust fault, the rocks above the fault move horizontally.

fault, the rocks are more likely to give way along existing faults. Therefore, once a movement along a fault has occurred, it is likely to occur again and again in a series of small movements spaced out over long intervals. Each time the rocks move along a fault, an earthquake occurs. Thus earthquakes are most common where active faults are present.

It is believed that most faults in the crust are below the surface, where they cannot be observed directly. But several major faults can be seen at the surface. One of the most famous is the San Andreas Fault, which extends for hundreds of kilometers and runs almost the entire length of California (see Figure 20-2). The cover of this book shows an aerial view of a portion of this fault. The crust on the west side of the fault is moving northward with respect to the east side. How-

Figure 20-2. San Andreas fault. The San Andreas fault, which runs through most of California, is a strike-slip fault.

ever, this movement does not occur uniformly or at the same time along the entire fault. Only a small section of the fault slips at any one time. A major movement along this fault caused an earthquake that destroyed much of San Francisco in 1906.

Earthquake Waves. When masses of rock break or move along a fault, vibrations occur that move outward in all directions from the point of origin, much as ripples on water move outward from the point at which a pebble strikes the surface of a smooth pond. Keep in mind, though, that earthquake vibrations move outward from the point of origin in all three dimensions (see Figure 20-3). Earthquake vibrations produce a wavelike motion in the rock through which they pass. These waves are called *seismic* waves. The point of origin of the waves is called the *focus* of the earthquake. Seismic waves travel away from the focus in all directions through rock within the crust and also along the surface.

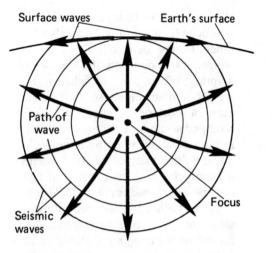

Figure 20-3. Earthquake waves. Earthquake waves move out from the focus in all directions, both through the earth's crust and along the surface.

Seismographs. It is not necessary to be near the focus of an earthquake to detect it. An instrument called a *seismograph* can detect and record seismic waves that may have traveled thousands of kilometers from their source. A seismograph (see Figure 20-4) consists basically of four parts:

Figure 20-4. Seismograph. A seismograph can detect vibrations in the earth's crust.

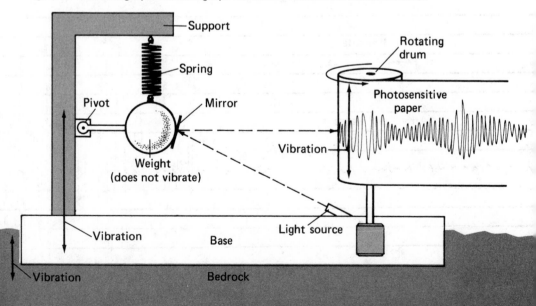

(1) a support, or base, fastened to the bedrock; (2) a rotating drum also fastened to the bedrock; (3) a heavy weight suspended from the support by a spring; (4) a "pen" attached to the weight and arranged so that it can draw a line on a sheet of paper wrapped around the drum. The "pen" in a modern seismograph is not actually a writing instrument. It is usually a mirror that reflects a beam of light onto photographic paper on the drum.

In most other types of recording instruments, the pen that makes the record of a changing variable is attached to an instrument that measures the variable. For example, in a recording barometer the pen could be attached to the diaphragm of an aneroid barometer. As the diaphragm moves, the pen changes position relative to the paper on which it is writing. But a seismograph has to record the *changing position of the bedrock* as an earthquake vibration goes by. How can it do this if the entire instrument is attached to the bedrock? How can the pen be made to move relative to the paper?

The answer to these questions is found in the hanging weight. Because the weight has inertia, and because it is not rigidly attached to the support, it remains fixed in space while the support and the drum move up and down. Since the pen is attached to the weight, relative motion between the drum and the pen occurs. As the drum with its recording paper turns, the pen draws a wavy line on the paper, showing the size, shape, and frequency of the wave to which the seismograph is responding. This record of an earthquake wave is called a *seismogram*. A typical seismogram is shown in Figure 20-5.

Seismographs can be designed to record earth vibrations in either a ver-

Figure 20-5. A seismogram. This is a portion of a seismogram of the Guatemalan earthquake of February 4, 1976, recorded at Albuquerque, New Mexico. This record, which was made on a rotating drum, starts at the upper left and ends at the lower right. It shows the arrival of the P waves, followed by the S waves about 4½ minutes later (see pages 393-397).

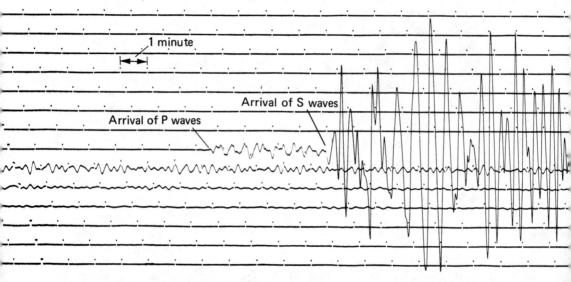

tical or a horizontal direction. They can be adjusted to record very rapid vibrations or very slow ones. Seismograms of the same earthquake recorded in different locations on the earth can be compared to determine travel times and other characteristics of the waves reaching each station.

From studies of thousands of seismograms recorded at many research stations, earth scientists have discovered that there are different types of seismic waves and that they travel at different speeds. Seismic waves may travel completely through the earth and be reflected back from the surface many times. The same wave may sometimes be observed for many days as it passes back and forth inside the earth. Some earthquake waves set the entire earth vibrating like a bell. Later in this chapter we will consider some of these different types of waves in greater detail and see what inferences can be drawn from the information they give us.

Epicenter of an Earthquake. You have learned that the focus of an earthquake is the point of origin of the seismic waves. Very few earthquakes originate at the surface of the crust. The focus is usually at some point below the surface, often tens or hundreds of kilometers deep.

For an observer on the surface, the apparent force of an earthquake is greatest at the point directly above the focus. This point on the surface is called the *epicenter* (see Figure 20-6). The distance from the epicenter down to the focus is called the *focal depth* of the earthquake. The severity of an earthquake at the surface depends partly on the focal depth. For earthquakes of the same energy or inten-

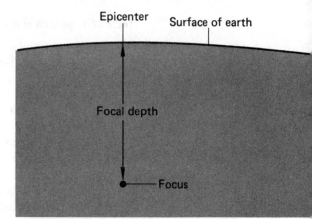

Figure 20-6. Epicenter of an earthquake. The epicenter is the point on the earth's surface that is directly above the focus. The focal depth is the distance from the epicenter to the focus.

sity, the effect at the surface is less as the focal depth becomes greater.

Earthquake focal depths are grouped into three classes. *Shallow-focus* quakes occur from the surface to a depth of about 60 km. Earthquakes that occur at depths between 60 and 450 km are classified as *intermediate*. Earthquakes that occur at depths below 450 km are called *deep-focus* earthquakes. Seismologists have found that earthquake foci are rarely located deeper than 700 km. We will examine the relationship between earthquake focal depth and crustal effects in the next chapter.

Intensity of Earthquakes. As we have said, the severity of earthquakes depends partly on focal depth. Another important factor is, of course, the amount of energy that is released by the earthquake. Seismologists have found that the amount of energy released varies considerably from one earthquake to another. Since the severity of earthquakes at the surface is related both to focal depth and energy released, various

Table 20-1. Mercalli scale of earthquake intensity.

Intensity   Observed Effects (selected)

I   Not felt except by a very few persons in favorable locations.

II   Felt by a few persons at rest, especially on upper floors of build-
             ings.

III   Quite noticeable indoors. Cars at rest may rock slightly. Vibration
             similar to that of passing truck.

IV   Most persons feel it indoors, a few outdoors. Dishes, windows,
             doors rattle.

V   Felt by nearly everyone. Dishes, windows may break. Some ob-
             jects overturned or moved.

VI   Felt by all persons. Many run outdoors. Heavy furniture may
             move.

VII   All persons frightened and run outdoors. Some damage to well-
             built buildings, considerable in poorly built structures. Noticed
             by persons in moving cars.

VIII   Considerable damage, with partial collapse, in even well-built
             structures, great in poorly-designed ones. Chimneys, columns,
             walls fall. Heavy furniture overturned.

IX   Great damage in substantial buildings, Ground cracks. Under-
             ground pipes break.

X   Many masonry and wooden structures destroyed. Ground badly
             cracked. Rails bent. Landslides from river banks.

XI   Most structures collapse. Bridges destroyed. Broad fissures in
             ground.

XII   Total damage to almost all structures. Waves on ground visible.
             Some objects thrown into the air.

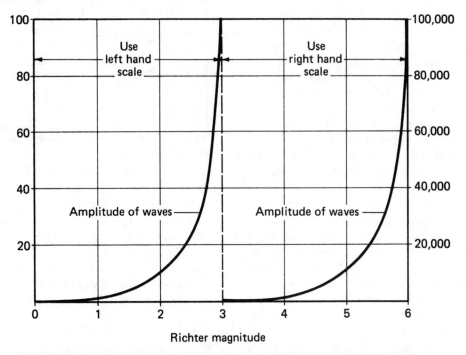

Figure 20-7. Relationship of wave amplitude to magnitude on the Richter scale.

scales of severity have been established.

An *intensity* scale measures the severity of an earthquake in terms of the effects it produces on the local environment. The *Mercalli scale,* summarized in Table 20-1, is such a scale of intensities. As you see, the scale ranges from an intensity of I, which is just barely noticeable, to an intensity of XII, which results in total destruction of all structures and seismic waves that can actually be seen moving across the earth's surface. The Mercalli scale is obviously not a very precise system of measurement and it refers only to the directly observable effects at any particular location. It tells very little of scientific interest or value about the earthquake process.

The Richter Magnitude Scale. A *magnitude* scale is a system of ex-

pressing the severity of an earthquake in terms of the amount of energy released, regardless of the damage or other noticeable effects it may produce. Earth scientists have been able to relate the estimated energy of an earthquake to the *amplitude,* or height, of the waves recorded by a seismograph. Since the amplitude of the waves decreases with distance from the focus of an earthquake, this distance must be taken into account in assigning a magnitude to an earthquake detected at any given station. Methods of determining this distance will be discussed later in this chapter.

The magnitude scale now in general use is the *Richter scale,* named after the scientist who developed it. The scale is based on the amplitude of the waves that would be observed near the epicenter of the earthquake. A magnitude of 0 was assigned to an earthquake that would produce just barely measurable waves. An earthquake of magnitude 1 was then defined as an earthquake that would produce waves ten times as high. Each increase of 1 on the Richter magnitude scale corresponds to a wave amplitude that is ten times as great as the amplitude of the number before it. Thus the wave amplitude of an earthquake of magnitude 2 is one hundred times that of magnitude 0. The same ratios apply everywhere on the Richter scale. For example, the amplitude of a magnitude 6 earthquake is ten times that of magnitude 5, one hundred times that of magnitude 4, and one-tenth that of magnitude 7. These relationships are illustrated by the graph in Figure 20-7.

The amount of energy represented by the Richter scale increases six

	Magnitude
India 1897	8.7 (est.)
San Francisco 1906	8.3 (est.)
Japan 1923	8.3
Chile 1960	8.5
Alaska 1964	8.4
China 1976	8.2

Table 20-2. Richter magnitude for some major earthquakes.

times as rapidly as the amplitude of the waves. Each step on the Richter scale therefore corresponds to a change in energy of sixty times. The wave amplitude of a Richter-6 earthquake, for example, would be one million times as great as that of a Richter-0 earthquake, but the energy would be almost fifty *billion* times as much.

In terms of noticeable effects, an earthquake of magnitude 2 is about the smallest that people at the epi-

Table 20-3. Richter scale of earthquake magnitude.

Magnitude	Equivalent energy by mass of exploding TNT	Remarks
0	600 g	Enough to blast a stump
1	20 kg	Small construction blast
2	600 kg	Average quarry blast
3	20,000 kg	Large quarry blast
4	600,000 kg	Small atom bomb
5	20 million kg	"Standard" atom bomb
6	600 million kg	Small H bomb
7	20 billion kg	Enough energy to heat New York City for one year
8	600 billion kg	Enough energy to heat New York City for 30 years
9	20 trillion kg	The energy in the world's production of coal and oil for five years.

center would feel. An earthquake of magnitude 6 or more would generally be considered a major one. Table 20-2 shows the Richter values for some of the world's major earthquakes in modern times. You can see that a magnitude-9 earthquake has not yet been recorded. Table 20-3 shows the amounts of energy that scientists es-timate are released by earthquakes from Richter 0 to 9.

Magnitude is, for seismologists, a more satisfactory means than intensity for expressing the severity of an earthquake, because it involves fewer variables and it is based on accurately measurable quantities.

SUMMARY

1. An earthquake is the shaking and vibrating of the earth's surface.
2. Earthquakes appear to be associated with sudden displacements of rock along faults in the lithosphere.
3. Energy released during an earthquake travels through the earth in the form of waves of various types, which can be detected and recorded by seismographs.
4. The magnitude of an earthquake is a measure of the total energy released by it.

TYPES OF EARTHQUAKE WAVES

From a study of seismograms, earth scientists have found that there are three main types of earthquake waves that their instruments detect. Two of these wave types travel from the earthquake focus through the interior of the earth to the recording station. The third type travels entirely along the surface. It is the two types that travel through the earth that give us the most useful information about the earth's structure and composition. Since we are interested in building a model of the earth's interior, we will concentrate our attention on these two wave types.

Compressional or Primary Waves (P Waves). What do we mean by the word "wave" as applied to matter? What is the relation between waves and vibrations? A *vibration* is the movement of particles of matter in a cyclic manner back and forth around some average position. A *wave* is a pattern of vibrations throughout a material. As a wave goes through a material, the particles of the material vibrate in place, while the wave pattern moves on. In a *compressional wave* (also called a *longitudinal wave),* the direction of vibration of the particles is parallel to the direction of travel of the wave. For example, if a wave is traveling to the right (or to the left) in a material, the particles of the material will vibrate to the left and right of their normal position (see Figure 20-8).

As the particles move toward one side of their normal positions, they move closer to their neighbors on that side and farther from their neighbors on the other side. This results in a compression or squeezing together of

Direction of wave travel

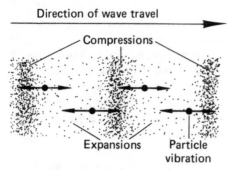

Figure 20-8. Compressional wave. In a compressional wave the vibration of the particles is parallel to the direction of travel of the wave.

the particles on one side and a spreading apart or expansion on the other. The compression causes the particles ahead of it to move in the direction of the wave, thus causing the compressional part of the wave to move on. The particles that started the compression then bounce back, only to meet other particles being pushed along by the next compression. In this way a series of compressions and expansions moves through the material. This wave action can be observed in the coils of a spring, such as a Slinky toy. You can see the compressions and expansions move along the spring, while the individual coils vibrate back and forth.

An important fact about compressional waves is that they can travel through solids, liquids, and gases. Sound waves in air are compressional waves.

Compressional waves are one of the two main types of earthquake waves that travel through the earth. They travel, on the average, faster than other types of seismic waves. As a result, they usually arrive at a given location ahead of the other types of earthquake waves. For this reason, compressional seismic waves are commonly referred to as *primary*, or *P*, waves. P waves travel through earth material at various speeds, but usually greater than 4 to 5 km/sec.

Earth scientists have learned that seismic wave speed also depends, in part, on the density of the material through which the waves pass. As primary seismic waves go deeper into the earth, passing through more and more dense rock, they tend to speed up and move at rates faster than 4 to 5 km/sec.

Let's summarize what we have learned about primary seismic waves, or P waves:

1. They are the fastest-traveling earthquake waves.
2. They cause rock particles to vibrate in the same direction as the wave is traveling.
3. They are capable of traveling through solids, liquids, and gases.
4. They travel faster through denser earth material. It has been observed that P waves generally travel faster as they penetrate more deeply into the earth.

Shear, or Secondary, Waves (S Waves). The second type of seismic wave that travels through the earth is called a *shear wave*. It is the same type of wave as the transverse waves described in Chapter 8 (page 120) and illustrated by a wave in a rope (Figure 8-2, page 120). In a shear, or transverse, wave the particles of the material vibrate at right angles to the direction of travel of the wave.

In a compressional wave, the particles moving into a region of compression give an extra "push" to the particles in front of them. In this way the energy of the wave is passed along through the material. In a shear wave, the energy of the moving particles cannot be passed along the wave by a "pushing" effect. The energy can be transferred from one particle to the next only if the particles are strongly bonded together, so that the motion of one affects the motion of its neighbors. This strong bonding occurs only in solids. Therefore, a shear wave cannot be transmitted through a liquid or a gas. If a shear wave traveling through a solid reaches an interface with a liquid or a gas, the wave cannot continue on. The interface usually acts like a mirror, and the wave is reflected back into the solid, often in a different direction.

Another important fact about shear waves is that they do not travel as fast as compressional waves. Their speeds range from about 1 to 3 km/sec. As a result, shear waves take longer than compressional waves to reach an observer and therefore arrive after the primary waves. For this reason, shear waves are commonly referred to as secondary, or *S*, waves.

Like P waves, the speed of S waves is affected by the density of the material through which they pass. Thus, once the speed of P or S waves is determined, certain inferences can be drawn about the density of earth material that is otherwise not accessible for direct observation.

Let's summarize what we have learned about S waves.

1. They travel more slowly than P waves.
2. They cause rock particles to vibrate at right angles to the direction of travel of the wave.
3. They cannot travel through liquids or gases.
4. Like P waves, S waves travel faster through more dense material.

Travel Times of Seismic Waves. Figure 20-9 shows a typical seismogram that might be recorded at a station a few thousand kilometers from the focus of an earthquake. When the earthquake occurred, seismic waves started through the earth in all directions. These waves followed some

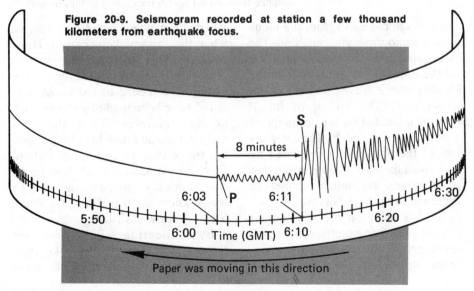

Figure 20-9. Seismogram recorded at station a few thousand kilometers from earthquake focus.

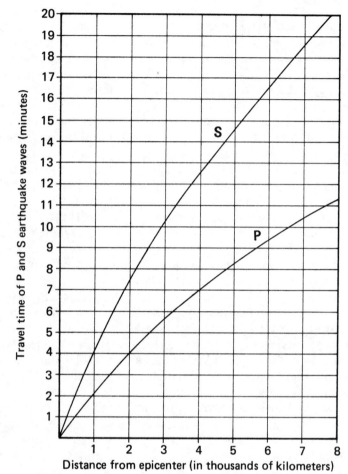

**Figure 20-10.
Travel time vs.
distance, P and
S waves.**

path through the earth from the focus to the seismograph station. Since the P waves and S waves started together, and the P waves travel faster than the S waves, the P waves arrived at the station first. The arrival of the P waves is indicated on the seismogram by the arrow labeled P. The later arrival of the S waves is indicated by the arrow labeled S. You can see that the P waves are much smaller in amplitude than the S waves.

The time scale on the seismogram tells the observer exactly when the P waves *arrived* and exactly when the S waves *arrived*. It does not indicate when the waves started out, that is, when the earthquake occurred. However, suppose that information was obtained in some other way. For example, a record of the exact time could have been made by an observer at the epicenter. Then the seismologist would know how long it took for the waves to reach his station. Since he would also know how far he was from the reported earthquake, he would know the travel time for P and S waves for that distance.

By collecting such data for thousands of known earthquake times and locations, seismologists have been able to construct a graph that relates travel time to epicenter distance for P waves and S waves. This graph is given in Figure 20-10. It shows, for example, that if an observer is 2,000 km from the epicenter of an earthquake, the P waves will arrive 4 minutes after the earthquake occurs, and the S waves will arrive 7 minutes, 30 seconds, after the event. (Readings of the graph are made to the nearest 10 seconds and 100 km.)

Bear in mind that the epicenter distance is measured over the surface of the earth. It is the geographical distance between the observer and the epicenter—the distance that would be measured on a map.

Finding the Epicenter Distance. The travel-time graphs of Figure 20-10 were constructed from data for earthquakes of known time and location. But we can now use them to calculate the distance to the epicenter of *any* earthquake recorded by seismograph. How is this done? Examine the travel-time graphs again. Notice that as the distance from the epicenter increases, the *difference* between the two travel times also increases. It is this difference in travel time that shows up on a seismogram as a difference in arrival time of the two types of waves. For example, if the observer is 1,000 km from the epicenter, the P waves take 2 minutes, 10 seconds, to reach the observer, and the S waves take 4 minutes. The difference in arrival time is 1 minute, 50 seconds. At 4,000 km from the epicenter, it takes 7 minutes for the P waves to arrive and 12 minutes, 40 seconds, for the S waves. The time difference is 5 minutes, 40 seconds.

Consider again the example of an epicenter distance of 2,000 km. The difference in arrival times is 3 minutes, 30 seconds. Could this same difference be observed for any other distance? No. If the distance is less than 2,000 km, the time difference will be less. If the distance is greater than 2,000 km, the time difference will be more. There is only one possible epicenter distance for a difference of 3 minutes, 30 seconds, and that distance is 2,000 km. Likewise, there is a definite distance that corresponds to any given difference in arrival times of P and S waves.

Suppose, then, that we have a seismogram of an earthquake that looks like Figure 20-11. We see that the P waves arrived at 3:21:15 GMT (Greenwich Mean Time in hours, minutes, and seconds), and the S waves arrived at 3:27:15 GMT. The time difference is 6 minutes, 0 seconds. How do we find the epicenter distance that results in a time delay of 6 minutes, 0 seconds? To do this, we have to find the place on the graph of Figure 20-10 where the vertical distance between the two curves is exactly 6 minutes, 0 seconds. One way to do this is to use the lefthand (vertical) scale to mark off this height on the edge of a card, as shown in

Figure 20-11. Seismogram showing difference in arrival times for the P and S waves. This information is used to find the distance of the station from the epicenter.

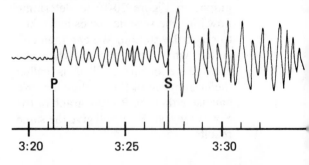

P   S

3:20   3:25   3:30

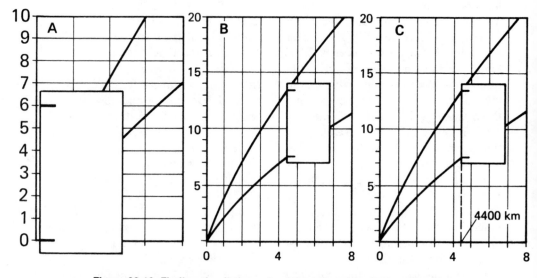

Figure 20-12. Finding the distance from the epicenter of an earthquake.

Step A of Figure 20-12. Then, making sure to keep the edge of the card vertical, we slide it along the curves until we find the place where the curves are the right distance apart (see Step B). Then we can read down to find the distance along the bottom (horizontal) scale. As you see in Step C, the epicenter distance is 4,400 km.

Time of Occurrence of an Earthquake. We mentioned that a seismogram shows the *arrival times* of the P and S waves, but it does not tell us when the earthquake occurred. But once we have found the epicenter distance, we can use the travel time graphs in Figure 20-10 to determine how long the seismic waves had taken to reach the station. We can then calculate what time it was when the earthquake occurred. This is called the *origin time* of the earthquake. We can use either the P-wave graph or the S-wave graph. Both will give the same results.

Try this with the record in Figure 20-11. We have already found that the epicenter distance was 4,400 km. From Figure 20-10 we find that the travel time for P waves for that distance is 7 minutes, 30 seconds. Since the P waves arrived at 3:21:15, and the earthquake must have occurred 7 minutes, 30 seconds, earlier, the origin time was 3:13:45. To test your understanding of the principle, calculate the origin time from the arrival of the S waves in the same way. You should get the same result.

Simplified Travel-Time Graph. You may have realized at this point that the procedure can be made much easier and more accurate if we construct a new graph making use of the information in Figure 20-10. We first find the time delay corresponding to many different distances, for example, for every 500 km. Then we plot time delay as one variable against distance as the other. This gives us a

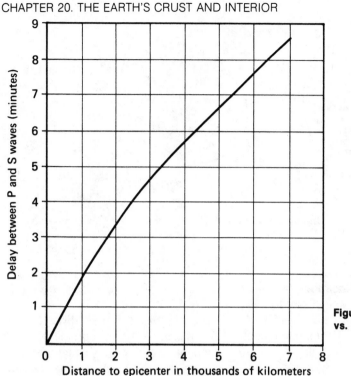

Figure 20-13. P-S interval vs. distance.

single graph that allows us to find the distance directly if we know the time delay. Figure 20-13 is a graph constructed in this manner.

Test this new graph with the data from the seismogram in Figure 20-11. The time delay was 6 minutes, 0 seconds. Read across from 6 minutes, 0 seconds, until you meet the curve. Then read down to find the distance. You obtain the same result, 4,400 km, but much more quickly and easily. Note, however, that this graph does not allow us to determine the origin time.

To be sure you understand the principle of finding epicenter distance, try it by both methods with the seismogram in Figure 20-14. If you get 5,200 km, you are doing it right.

Locating the Epicenter. Suppose now that you are a seismologist at the station where the seismogram in Fig-

ure 20-11 was recorded. As we have seen, you can determine that the epicenter is 4,400 km from your location. Does that tell you where the epicenter is? Obviously not. It could be anywhere on a circle around your station with a radius of 4,400 km, as shown in Figure 20-15A. However, if a record of the same earthquake is obtained at another station, a second circle can be

Figure 20-14. Seismogram.

Seismogram with time delay:
6 min 50 sec

P   S

18:58:40   19:05:30

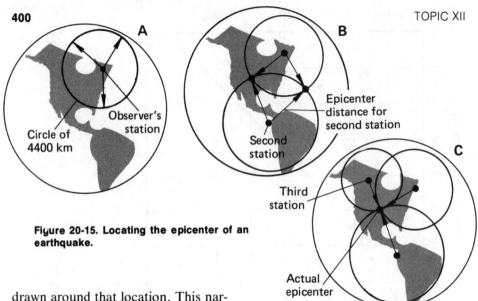

Figure 20-15. Locating the epicenter of an earthquake.

drawn around that location. This narrows the possibilities down to two points, as seen in Figure 20-15B. A third observation will eliminate one of the points and "zero in" on the actual epicenter (Figure 20-15C).

Three observations will usually not be enough in a real case to locate the epicenter exactly. The three circles are more likely to outline a small triangular area within which the epicenter lies. This uncertainty can be narrowed down by adding the data from other stations.

SUMMARY

1. Earthquakes generate two types of seismic waves that travel through the earth's interior: compressional waves and shear waves.
2. In the same material, compressional waves travel faster than shear waves.
3. The speed of a seismic wave varies with the physical properties of the material through which the wave is traveling.
4. Compressional waves can travel through solids, liquids, and gases.
5. Shear waves are not transmitted through fluids (liquids or gases).
6. Differences in travel times of seismic waves can be used to determine the distance between a recording station and the epicenter of an earthquake.

MODEL OF THE EARTH'S CRUST AND INTERIOR

Now that we know a little more of the details of earthquakes, earthquake waves, and the detection of those waves, let's find out how the study of the behavior of seismic waves has led to the development of a model of the earth's crust and interior. We can

then examine that model more carefully.

Boundary of the Crust. In 1909 a Yugoslav seismologist, Andrija Mohorovicic, was studying the records of earthquake waves that had traveled fairly short distances through the upper portions of the lithosphere. He noticed an irregularity in the data that seemed to show that at a certain depth below the surface the waves suddenly increased in speed. The depth at which this happened was different at different places, but it seemed to be about 20 to 30 km below the surface of the continents.

As you may recall, earthquake waves speed up when they enter substances of higher density. Mohorovicic inferred that the waves from the earthquakes were speeding up at these depths because they were entering rock of much higher density. At a certain depth, the lithosphere seemed to change from the kind of rock material found near the surface to material of a much higher average density. It was as if the earth had an outer layer that ended rather sharply, where it met the main body of the interior. This outer layer is what we now call the crust.

Any sudden change in the properties of a material or a system is called a *discontinuity*. On a graph, a discontinuity appears as a break or a sharp change in the direction of the curve. According to the Mohorovicic model, a graph of the density of the lithosphere plotted against depth would look like Figure 20-16. The base of the crust, where the density suddenly changes, is called the *Mohorovicic discontinuity*, or simply, the *Moho*. The region of dense material below the Moho is called the *mantle*. You may recall that a boundary like the Moho, where the properties of materials suddenly change, is also referred to as an interface. Thus, the Moho appears to be the interface between the earth's crust and mantle.

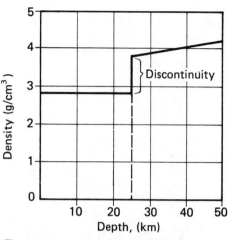

Figure 20-16. Density vs. depth in the lithosphere. The region of rapid increase in density, between 20 and 30 kilometers below the surface, marks the Mohorovicic discontinuity.

The Core of the Earth. We have seen that as the distance from an epicenter to a recording station increases, the travel time of the seismic waves increases. This is to be expected, since the waves have to travel a greater distance through the earth to reach the more distant station. However, an unexpected observation is made when the angle around the earth's circumference from the epicenter to the station is more than 102 ° (see Figure 20-17). This is a distance of about 11,000 km. At this distance, the P and S seismic waves suddenly disappear, although surface waves can be detected. P waves from the earthquake can again be detected if the station is more than 143° away, or about 16,000 km. However, no S waves are observed. Between 102° and 143° from an earthquake epicenter, no P or S waves are observed. The result is a band or belt-like region around the earth, about 41° or 4,500 km wide, in which no waves that have passed through the earth from an earthquake can be observed. Earth scientists refer to this region as the

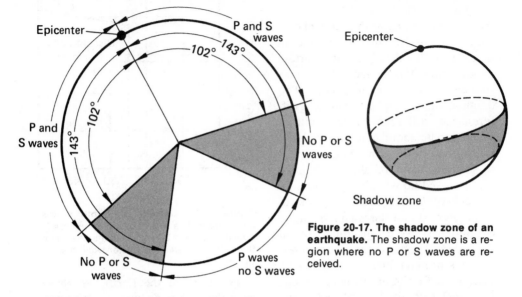

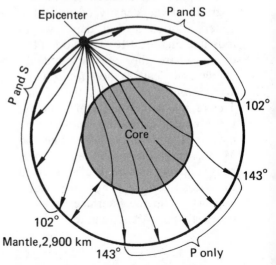

Figure 20-17. **The shadow zone of an earthquake.** The shadow zone is a region where no P or S waves are received.

earthquake's *shadow zone*. The location of the shadow zone will of course depend on the location of the focus of the earthquake. Each earthquake will produce its own shadow zone between 102° and 143° away from it. Beyond the 143° distance, in a circular zone on the side of the earth opposite the earthquake focus, the P waves can be recorded, but no S waves.

These observations lead to the conclusion that deep within the earth there must be a region with properties that have two effects on earthquake waves: (1) P waves must be changed in direction so that they "miss" the shadow zone, and (2) S waves must be stopped altogether. Since this inner region allows P waves to pass through it, but not S waves, we can infer that the region has the properties of a liquid. (Recall that S waves cannot pass through a liquid.) The inner portion of the earth, where the solid mantle ends and a liquid material begins, is called the earth's *core*.

Figure 20-18 shows the paths that

earthquake waves probably follow as they pass through the various regions of the earth's interior. When waves pass through a material in which the density gradually changes, the waves gradually change direction. This accounts for the curved shape of the wave paths through the mantle. When

Figure 20-18. **Paths of earthquake waves through the earth.** Earthquake waves travel a curved path as they pass through the mantle. Notice how the waves are bent as they cross the mantle-core interface.

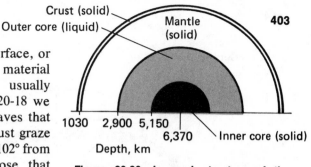
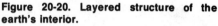

Crust (solid)
Outer core (liquid)
Mantle (solid)

1030 2,900 5,150
6,370 Inner core (solid)
Depth, km

Figure 20-20. Layered structure of the earth's interior.

a wave passes across an interface, or discontinuity, between one material and another, its direction usually changes sharply. In Figure 20-18 we see this happening to the waves that enter the core. Waves that just graze the core reach the surface at 102° from the earthquake center. Those that enter the core are bent sharply inward, and bent again when they leave the core. As a result, there is a zone which cannot be reached by any of the waves. This is the shadow zone we have already observed. Waves either miss the core and come out at 102° or less, or they hit the core and come out at 143° or more. From these observations, earth scientists have calculated that the boundary between the mantle and the core is about 2,900 km below the surface.

Structure of the Core. By studying travel times and other characteristics of the P waves that pass through the core, much additional information about the core has been obtained. First of all, it has been determined that the speed of the P waves drops sharply when they enter the core. Then, at a depth of about 5,150 km, they seem to reach another discon-

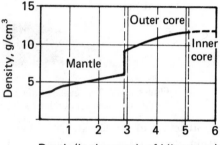

Figure 20-21. Density vs. depth in earth's interior.

tinuity and speed up again (see Figure 20-19). Seismologists believe this means that only the outer 2,250 km of the core is liquid-like, and that the rest of it, all the way to the earth's center, has the properties of a solid. Thus, two regions of the core are believed to exist: the *outer core*, which acts like a liquid, and the *inner core*, which acts like a solid. The model of the structure of the earth as a whole, then, looks like Figure 20-20.

The behavior of earthquake waves passing through the core has also helped scientists estimate the density of the different regions of the earth's interior (see Figure 20-21). It has also been possible to infer the chemical composition of the core. Both the inner and outer cores are believed to be composed almost entirely of iron and nickel.

Figure 20-19. Wave velocity vs. depth. The "disappearance" of S waves at depths of about 3000 meters indicates the presence of a liquid outer core.

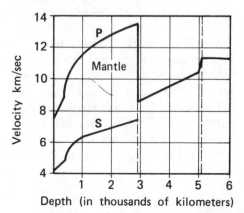

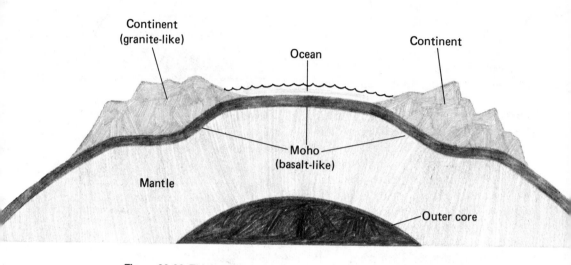

Figure 20-22. Thickness of the crust. The earth's crust is much thicker under the continents than it is under the oceans.

Structure of the Crust. Only waves from earthquakes of large magnitude can pass through thousands of kilometers of the earth's interior and still be strong enough to be detected. Only a few such earthquakes occur each year. It is thus difficult to piece together an accurate picture of the earth's deep interior. On the other hand, about 800,000 shallow earthquakes of small magnitudes (Richter 2.0 to 3.5) occur each year. These can be studied at short range to provide a wealth of information about the crust and the upper mantle. One of the inferences from these studies is that the earth's crust is much thicker under the continents than under the oceans (see Figure 20-22). The Moho (or boundary between the crust and the mantle) is much closer to the surface under the oceans. Notice also in Figure 20-22 that besides a difference in thickness of the continental and oceanic crust, there is also a difference in density. Crustal rock material under the oceans seems to be, on the average, more dense than the rock material that the continents are made of. Samples of crustal material from beneath the ocean usually resembles the igneous rock *basalt,* while most rock material from the continents resembles the igneous rock *granite.* These two kinds of crust are often described as either granite-like (the continents) or basalt-like (the ocean floors).

Look carefully again at Figure 20-22. You will see that the basalt-like layer of the crust is actually continuous, dipping beneath the continental land masses. The Moho is the interface between this lower, basalt-like crustal layer and the mantle beneath it.

Conditions in the Earth's Interior. Earth scientists are very much interested in knowing what the pressures, temperatures, and physical state of the materials are in the interior of the earth. Such information can help them make inferences about the composition of the materials, about the history of the earth's formation, about sources of energy in the earth, and about the causes of crustal change.

Pressure inside the earth can be estimated fairly accurately, because pressure depends only on the weight of the material lying over a given location. The situation is similar to the increasing pressure of the atmosphere as one descends from the upper regions to the ground. However, the magnitudes of the pressures in the earth are millions of times greater than atmospheric pressures, because earth materials are so much denser than air. Scientists have calculated that the pressure inside the earth increases to about 3.5 million atmospheres (1 atmosphere is normal air pressure at sea level). This is equivalent to about 3.5 million kilograms per square centimeter.

Temperatures inside the earth are much more difficult to infer. Measurements made in deep mines and in holes bored into the crust show that

Figure 20-23. Changes in temperature and pressure with increasing depth. The top graph shows the relationship between depth in the earth's interior and pressure. The bottom graph illustrates the depth-temperature relationship.

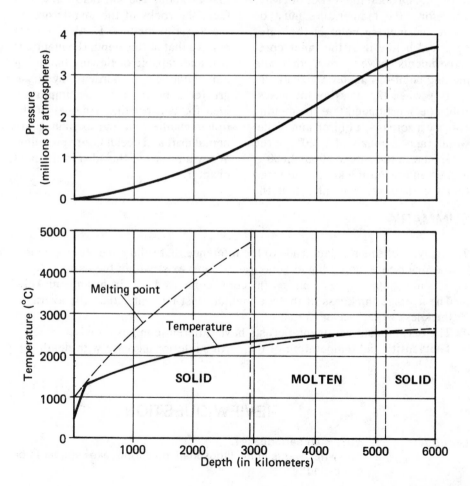

the temperature of the rock increases at a rate of at least 1°C for each 100 meters of depth. If this rate continued through the mantle, the temperature at the bottom of the mantle would be over 30,000°C, far above the melting point of any known material. Almost all the mantle would be liquid. But seismic data indicates that the mantle is solid. Therefore, it is inferred that the rate of increase of temperature observed near the surface does not continue very far into the earth.

We have seen that the core is believed to be liquid part of the way through, and solid the rest of the way. Therefore, the temperature must be above the melting point in the outer core and below it in the inner core. Experiments have shown that the melting point of a material usually increases when the pressure increases. It has been estimated that the melting point of a core made of iron and nickel would range from about 2,200°C at the outer edge of the core to about 2,600°C at the center. Putting all this information together, we can infer that the temperature is above 2,200°C at the boundary of the outer core, but below 2,600°C in the inner core. In other words, the temperature in the deep interior of the earth is around 2,400°C and does not change very much with increasing depth.

It is by reasoning of this kind that the temperature-depth graph of Figure 20-23 has been developed. Notice that the temperature is believed to come close to the melting point of mantle rocks at about 200 km and then to drop below the melting point as depth and pressure increase. This means that at about 200 km below the surface, the rocks of the mantle are on the verge of melting. Earth scientists believe that at this depth the mantle is soft and capable of flowing like a liquid, although it hardens again at greater depths. This is an important idea for constructing a model of the upper mantle that can explain continental drift and ocean floor spreading. We will return to this idea in the next chapter.

SUMMARY

1. Analysis of seismic data leads to the inference that solid zones (crust, mantle, inner core) and a liquid zone (outer core) exist within the earth.
2. Seismic data suggest an earth core composed of iron and nickel.
3. The average thickness of the continental crust is greater than the average thickness of the oceanic crust.
4. The oceanic and continental crusts have different compositions.
5. The density and temperature of the earth's interior increase with depth.

REVIEW QUESTIONS

Group A
1. What is an earthquake?
2. With what events in the lithosphere do earthquakes appear to be associated?

3. What happens to the energy that is released during an earthquake?
4. What does the magnitude of an earthquake measure?
5. Name the two types of seismic waves that travel through the earth's interior.
6. Which of these two waves travels faster?
7. What factor affects the speed at which a seismic wave travels?
8. Which type of seismic wave can travel through solids, liquids, and gases? Which type cannot be transmitted through liquids and gases?
9. How can you determine the distance between a recording station and the epicenter of an earthquake?
10. Name the zones within the earth and state whether they are solid or liquid.
11. What does seismic data suggest that the earth's core is composed of?
12. Explain two of the differences between continental crusts and oceanic crusts.
13. In what way does density and temperature of the earth's interior change with increasing depth?

Group B
1. a. Explain the apparent relationship between earthquakes and faults in the earth's crust.
   b. Define the term seismic wave. Describe the instrument that detects and records seismic waves.
2. Explain how the epicenter of an earthquake can be located. Include in your explanation the following terms: compressional (primary) and shear (secondary) waves, seismogram, seismograph, travel and arrival times, and travel-time graph.
3. a. Describe a model of the earth's interior that is currently being used by scientists to describe the structure of the earth's lower crust and interior.
   b. Describe how the behavior of seismic waves seems to support the model described in 3-a of this question.

This pillow lava in Oman (on the Saudi Peninsula), was uplifted after being extruded underwater from a fissure in the oceanic crust.

CHAPTER 21
Theories of Crustal Change

You will know something about the processes that may cause crustal change if you can:

1. Describe the inferred relationships between continental growth, geosynclines, island arcs, and minor crustal changes.
2. Describe a theoretical mechanism thought to cause major crustal movement, and summarize the inferred relationships between plate tectonics and major crustal change.

In Chapters 19 and 20, we examined a number of observations related to crustal change on the earth. Some of these observations provided evidence of small-scale changes, while others provided evidence of change on a global scale. You have learned about tilted, bent, and broken rock layers, and you have found that large portions of the earth's crust appear to be rising or falling. You have learned about earthquakes and earthquake waves, and how earth scientists use the properties of earthquake waves to create models of the earth's interior. Now it's time to take all the pieces of this gigantic puzzle and to try to put them together in such a way that we can see the "big picture" of the earth's dynamic nature.

CONTINENTAL GROWTH AND GEOSYNCLINES

Before we start putting our puzzle together, let's review briefly some of the evidence of minor crustal change as discussed in Chapter 19.

1. From earlier investigations, we know that most sedimentary rocks are formed from sediments deposited in flat, horizontal, and parallel layers. Yet, sedimentary rock layers are often found that are tilted, folded, and broken.

2. We also know that most sedimentary rocks are formed from sediments deposited in water. Yet, sedimentary rock layers have been found at high elevations, often thousands of meters above sea level.

3. Fossils of ancient plants and animals that once lived in shallow water have been found at the tops of mountains. Other fossils of shallow-water organisms have been found at great depths or at considerable distances from present shores.

4. Many areas of the earth's crust that were thought to be stable have been found to be either rising or sinking.

5. There are places on the earth's surface where sediments are presently being deposited in shallow water. These areas show evidence of subsiding, or sinking, under the weight of the sediments. In many parts of the world, great thicknesses of similar shallow-water sediments have been found. These sedimentary formations are often associated with mountain ranges. As mentioned above, these observations have been used as evidence that the crust has undergone change. This evidence indicates that *vertical* movements of the crust—

uplift or subsidence—have taken place and are presently taking place. The question to be answered now is: What force or forces are responsible for these crustal movements?

There are other pieces to our puzzle, but they will be tied together in the final section of this chapter.

Theory of Continental Growth. If you set out to determine the age of the North American continent, you would discover that it isn't all of one age. Look at Figure 21-1. This map shows how the age of the bedrock varies in North America. If you study the figure carefully, you will see that the continent is oldest at its center and that it gets younger toward the outer edges. It is as though the continent "grew" by

Figure 21-1. Age of bedrock in continental United States. Notice how the age of the bedrock gets younger as you move from the center to the edges of the continent.

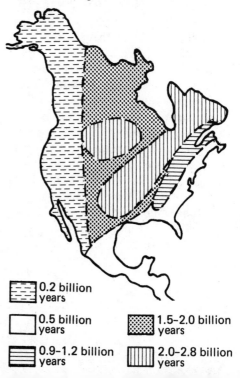

0.2 billion years	
0.5 billion years	1.5–2.0 billion years
0.9–1.2 billion years	2.0–2.8 billion years

adding new material to the edges at different times throughout its history. Many earth scientists believe that this is exactly what happened. In fact, they have a name for this inferred process—*continental accretion*. Continental accretion is the growth of a continent through the addition of material at its edges.

Where does the material come from that is added to the continental edges? Scientists are uncertain because such changes occur so slowly. It is believed however, that the material comes partly from the weathering and erosion of rocks in the older portion of the continent. Earth scientists have observed that every continent has a relatively stable core, or nucleus, consisting of ancient igneous rock. Such a central core is known as a *continental shield.*

According to the theory of continental accretion, the continents we observe today have "grown" through the addition of material along their edges. Some of this material is thought to have been transported from the central portions of the continents to their margins.

It is also believed that continental accretion is associated with the development and eventual erosion of *island arcs*. These narrow chains of volcanic islands are often found adjacent to the margins of continental masses, separated from them by shallow basins or troughs. The troughs collect rock material eroded from both the volcanic island arcs and the continental shields. The weathered and transported sediments deposited in these collection basins, called *geosynclines*, are eventually uplifted to become coastal mountain ranges.

Evidence of ancient volcanic island arcs, now existing as permanent extensions of original continental nuclei, has been observed on several continents. The islands of Japan are considered to be an example of a series of modern island arcs. Many earth scientists consider the Gulf of Mexico and parts of the Sea of Japan to be present day geosynclines. Although geosynclines are shallow, evidence indicates that accumulations of sediments reach thousands of meters in thickness. Why aren't the basins filled in by the addition of sediments? The only explanation for this seeming inconsistency is that, as the sediments pile up, the floor of the geosyncline sinks, or subsides. Further evidence indicates that at some critical point the situation reverses itself. Subsidence stops, sediments are transformed into rock, and the entire mass is uplifted above the water to become part of the continental mass.

From earlier discussions, you should understand how earth material can be weathered from the older sections of the continent, carried by erosional agents to the continental margins, and deposited in the geosynclines. Thus, this theory does answer some questions, such as why the continent gets "younger" as you travel outward from the center. However, the theory raises as many questions as it answers. What causes a geosyncline to subside? How are the

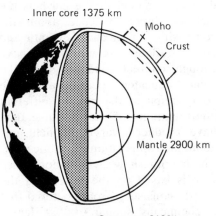

Figure 21-2. The earth in cross section. The crust is shown about ten times its actual thickness if drawn to scale.

sediments transformed into sedimentary, metamorphic, and even igneous rocks? How are these rocks eventually lifted to become mountains?

Isostasy. Figure 21-2 shows a model of the interior of the earth. As discussed in Chapter 20, the development of this model was based on careful analyses of earthquake-wave data. This data revealed that not only are there differences in density between crustal rock and mantle rock, but that there are density differences within the crustal rock itself. Figure 21-3 shows a magnified view of the boxed-in portion of Figure 21-2. The two types of crustal rocks of different densities (granite and basalt), the mantle, and the Moho are labeled. You will recall that the Moho (or Mohorovicic discontinuity) is the interface between the crust and the mantle. Notice that the depth of the Moho seems to be a "mirror image" of the height of the crustal surface. Where the surface rises, the Moho descends.

As this picture of the crust gradually developed, earth scientists attempted to explain the observations by a principle called *isostasy*. ("Isostasy" comes from two Greek words, *isos,* meaning "equal," and *stasis,* meaning "standing.") Basically, the principle of isostasy states that the earth's crust is in a state of equilibrium. Any change in mass of one part of the crust will be offset by a change in another part of the crust to maintain the equilibrium. This "balancing" of masses is called *isostatic compensation*.

The principle of isostasy is based on the idea that the earth's crust is "floating" on the denser rock of the mantle, much as an iceberg floats in water. Thus, if erosion removes rock material from a continent and deposits it as sediment in a geosyncline, the continent will rise a bit and the geosyncline will sink a bit. These changes occur because the continent has *lost* mass, and will therefore float higher in the mantle, while the geosyncline has *gained* mass, and will float lower.

Under the extreme conditions of temperature and pressure present in the mantle, the solid rock loses its rigidity. It becomes plastic and is able to flow very slowly. As sediments

Figure 21-3. Cross section of the earth's crust.

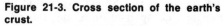

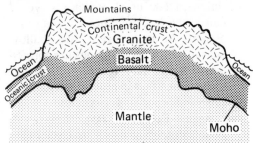

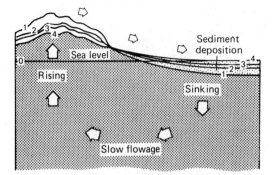

Figure 21-4. Isostasy. This diagram illustrates the isostatic compensation that takes place to adjust for changes in mass due to erosion and deposition.

accumulate in a geosyncline, the geosyncline slowly sinks and some of the mantle rock below the geosyncline is displaced. The displaced mantle rock flows in slowly beneath the continent to occupy the space vacated by the rising continental block. All of these processes are illustrated in the diagram in Figure 21-4.

The principle of isostasy would seem to explain the subsidence of geosynclines. Unfortunately, it provides only a partial answer. Remember the density differences of the materials involved. The material being deposited in the geosyncline is considerably less dense than mantle material. In fact, the compacted sediment in the geosyncline would be only about five-sixths as dense as the rock material it displaces downward. Therefore, if subsidence were due to isostatic compensation alone, the addition of 600 m of sediments would cause the geosyncline to sink only 500 m. At such a rate, the shallow seas in which geosynclines are formed would soon fill up. It seems, then, that some other factor must contribute to the subsidence of geosynclines.

Basalt-Eclogite Hypothesis. A major stumbling block that scientists

have encountered in their attempts to develop a model of the earth is the lack of direct evidence about the composition of the earth's mantle and core. Although scientists do have enough indirect evidence to make some "educated" guesses about the composition of the mantle, different interpretations of the available data have produced varying conclusions about the composition of mantle rock. The hypothesis we will be concerned with is based on the belief that the mantle consists of rock material that is chemically similar to, but denser than, the basaltic rock of the lower crust. One rock that fits this description especially well is *eclogite*.

A series of investigations carried out by a team of earth scientists has provided a plausible explanation for the subsidence and the subsequent uplift that occurs in geosynclines. These scientists were investigating the effects of extreme conditions of temperature and pressure on various earth materials when they discovered the relationship represented in Figures 21-5A, B, and C. As mentioned above, basalt and eclogite are chemically the same, but they differ in density. A difference such as this is known as a *phase difference*. When basalt is subjected to certain temperature and pressure conditions, it can be transformed into the denser eclogite. This transformation occurs when the mineral structure of the basalt changes to a more densely packed arrangement. Such a readjustment is called a *phase transition*.

From data obtained in seismic studies, it has been determined that the Moho is located at depths ranging from about 10 km beneath the oceans

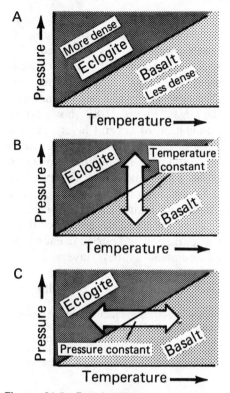

Figure 21-5. Basalt-eclogite relationship.
Basalt and eclogite represent two phases of the same substance. Transitions from one phase to the other are brought about by changes in temperature and/or pressure.

to about 30 km beneath the continents. It has also been determined that the temperature and pressure conditions at a depth of 30 km are about 500°C and 9,000 atmospheres of pressure. The investigations under discussion were designed to simulate the conditions found at depths near the Moho. The investigations revealed the following relationships:

At a constant temperature, an increase in pressure will cause basalt to be transformed to eclogite, while a decrease in pressure will result in eclogite changing to basalt. These relationships are represented in Figure 21-5B.

At a constant pressure, an increase in temperature will cause eclogite to be transformed to basalt, while a decrease in temperature will cause basalt to be transformed to eclogite. These relationships are represented in Figure 21-5C.

Subsidence. If we apply the basalt-eclogite hypothesis to the conditions in a geosyncline, we have a possible mechanism for explaining the subsiding and rising of the geosyncline. Figure 21-6A shows a dashed line drawn across the Gulf of Mexico, which is considered by many to be a present-day geosyncline. Figure 21-6B represents a cross section of the Gulf along the dashed line. This figure shows the Gulf as it probably appeared before any sediments were deposited. Notice the position of the Moho.

Figure 21-6. A present-day geosyncline. Drawing B represents a cross section of the floor of the Gulf of Mexico along the dotted line shown in drawing A.

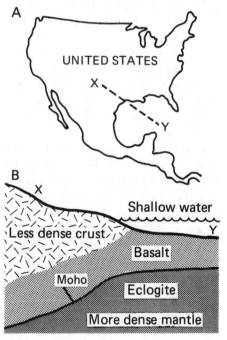

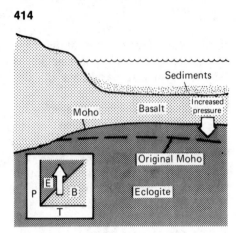

Figure 21-7. Basalt to eclogite transition. The increased pressure due to accumulated sediments causes the basalt at the bottom of the geosyncline to change to eclogite.

The process illustrated in Figure 21-7 is a key to understanding the mystery of the geosyncline. As sediments are deposited on the floor of the geosyncline, the weight of the sediments increases the pressure on the underlying basalt. As shown in Figure 21-5B, such an increase in pressure can cause basalt to be transformed into eclogite. Figure 21-7 shows that some of the basalt above the Moho is changed to eclogite. Because it represents the interface between crustal basalt and eclogite of the mantle, the Moho migrates *upward,* so that it is always positioned above the newly created eclogite.

However, the new position of the Moho is temporary. When the basalt is changed to eclogite, it increases in density. Due to this increase, the newly created eclogite will slowly sink, or subside, into the mantle. When the newly created eclogite sinks, the sediment in the bottom of the geosyncline also sinks, thus making room for more sediments to be deposited.

Figure 21-8A illustrates the situation in the geosyncline *after* the newly created eclogite has subsided. The once flat, horizontal layers of sediment are now bowed. They are thicker in the middle and thinner near the edges. Figure 21-8B shows an accumulation of several layers of sediment in the same geosyncline. Notice that the lower sedimentary layers become more and more deformed as they are forced deeper and deeper. Plants and animals that thrive in the shallow waters of the geosyncline become trapped and buried in each layer of sediment as new layers are deposited one on top of the other. Geologists involved in oil-drilling op-

Figure 21-8. Geosyncline after eclogite subsides. After subsidence, the geosyncline is bow-shaped, as in A. Figure B shows how the geosyncline might look after several layers of sediment have been deposited.

A

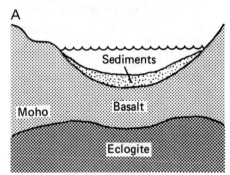

B

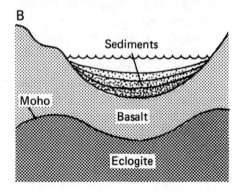

erations in the Gulf of Mexico have discovered fossils of shallow-water organisms in sediments as deep as 10 to 15 km below sea level.

The Gulf of Mexico has been receiving sediments for millions of years. During this time, the amount of sediment deposited would have been more than enough to fill in the Gulf if the floor had remained stationary or if subsidence were due only to isostatic compensation. However, as the sediments accumulate, the increased pressure causes the underlying basalt to be transformed to eclogite. As the dense eclogite subsides to become part of the mantle, the floor of the geosyncline sinks, leaving more room for additional sediments to be deposited.

So, we now have a *possible* explanation of how and why geosynclines sink. But what happens to cause the processes operating in a geosyncline to change? Why does the sinking stop? What causes the materials to be uplifted, eventually producing mountain ranges, such as the Appalachians or the Himalayas? Investigations into the nature of geosynclines indicate that when the sediments have accumulated to a depth of from 15 to 20 km, the conditions seem to favor uplift. Earth scientists are not sure why this is so, but the following represents one *possible* explanation.

Uplift. The accumulated sediments in the geosyncline originate on the continents. Earlier we determined that the rock material of the continents is mainly granitic. Granite is an igneous rock. Scientists have found that many igneous rocks, including granite, contain traces of radioactive elements. As sediments from the continents accumulate in a geosyncline, it is believed that large amounts of heat energy build up. This energy, produced by the decay of the radioactive materials, is transferred to the surrounding sediments, and the temperature at the bottom of the geosyncline is raised considerably. Figures 21-9*A* and 21-9*B* show a possible consequence of this increased temperature.

As the sediments at the bottom of the geosyncline become hotter and hotter, some of this heat is transferred to the eclogite beneath the geosyncline. At constant pressure, an increase in temperature can result in a transformation of eclogite to basalt. Because of its lower density, the newly created basalt will be forced

Figure 21-9. Uplift. Increased temperature at the bottom of the geosyncline causes the eclogite beneath the sediments to change to the less dense basalt.

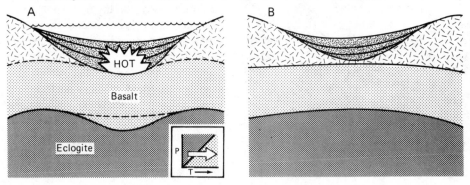

upward by the denser eclogite that surrounds it. As the basalt rises, the entire geosyncline above it is uplifted. In the process, a mountain range is formed.

Figure 21-10 illustrates a hypothetical geosyncline after uplift. The uppermost sediments have been subjected to less extreme conditions of temperature and pressure than the sediments deeper in the geosyncline. These upper layers of sediments have been transformed into sedimentary rock. The sediments exposed to the most extreme temperature and pressure melted to form magma, which later cooled to form igneous rock. Those sediments that were subjected to conditions of very high temperature and pressure but did not melt were changed to metamorphic rock. Thus, as Figure 21-10 shows, igneous rocks form the core of the mountain. Farther from the core, the igneous rock grades into metamorphic rock, which in turn grades into sedimentary rock.

The presence of sedimentary rocks at the surface of mountainous regions accounts for the discovery of fossils of shallow-water plants and animals in

Figure 21-10. Cross section of a geosyncline following uplift.

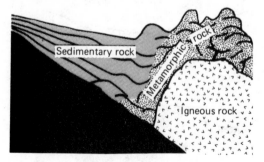

regions well above sea level, sometimes even on mountaintops. Notice that the sedimentary rock units in the mountain region are tilted, folded, and faulted. Eventually, erosion removes the sedimentary rock from the mountain regions, thus exposing the metamorphic and igneous rocks beneath.

Evidence of Past Geosynclines. So much for hypothetical situations. What about factual situations? We have been told that there are several regions of the earth that are considered to be active geosynclines. These regions are shallow-water basins, or troughs, that are receiving sediments from adjacent continents. But what about uplifted geosynclines? Are there any regions that show evidence of once having been sediment-filled troughs?

Figure 21-11A shows a line, labeled XY, drawn across a map of New York State. Figure 21-11B shows a cross section of the rock units along line XY. The cross section was compiled from actual data. Compare Figure 21-11B with the hypothetical uplifted geosyncline shown in Figure 21-10. Do you notice any similarities?

The Appalachian Mountains, which extend from Georgia to New England, have folded, faulted, and tilted sedimentary rock layers. They have an igneous rock core, and they contain a great deal of metamorphic rock. Fossils of shallow-water plants and animals have been discovered on some of the peaks. Many earth scientists believe that these mountains were formed from an old geosyncline. What do you think?

There does seem to be considerable

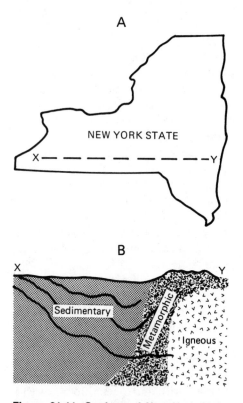

A

NEW YORK STATE

X— — — — — — — — —Y

B

X   Y

Sedimentary

Metamorphic

Igneous

Figure 21-11. Geology of New York State.
Drawing *B* shows a cross section of the bedrock of New York State along the dotted line shown in drawing *A*. Notice the similarity of the bedrock to that of the uplifted geosyncline in Figure 21-10.

evidence in support of the theory of continental growth. This theory, which includes the principles of isostasy and the subsidence and uplift of geosynclines, provides some convincing explanations for the observations listed at the beginning of this section. However, there are some weak points to this theory. The main weakness is that, for the most part, all of the forces involved in crustal movements act *vertically*. Many earth scientists are convinced that these forces alone would not be sufficient to produce the gross distortions that are found in mountains formed from uplifted geosynclines. The rock formations in these mountains have been folded, faulted, twisted, tilted, and, in some cases, overturned. Such distortions are usually associated with strong *horizontal* forces. It is widely believed that such forces were exerted, in combination with the vertical forces already discussed, to produce the complex rock formations found in the Appalachians and in other geosynclinal mountains. The probable source of these horizontal forces will be discussed in the next section of this chapter.

SUMMARY

1. Continental growth and mountain building may be related to the development of island arcs and geosynclinal activity.
2. The principle of isostasy states that the earth's crust is in a state of dynamic equilibrium, which is maintained by vertical adjustments of crustal material due to density differences. These adjustments, called isostatic compensation, may be partly responsible for the uplifting of geosynclinal mountains.
3. The transformation of a material to one of a different density due to conditions of temperature and pressure is called a phase transition. Phase transitions between basalt and eclogite may be the principal factors responsible for subsidence and uplift of geosynclines.

THEORY OF PLATE TECTONICS

As you learned in Chapter 19, the changes associated with geosynclines occur near the earth's surface and are considered to be minor crustal changes. Now let's take a look at a second theory of crustal change, a theory that might explain some of the major crustal changes not touched upon by the geosynclinal theory. To begin, let's quickly examine some of the evidence of these major crustal changes.

1. Earthquakes occur at different depths below the surface. Those occurring near oceanic ridges have, on the average, shallow origins, or foci. Those occurring near mountains and oceanic trenches have deep foci.

2. A series of ridges stretches across all the oceanic floors. It has been found that the rock material nearest the center of the ridges is younger than the rock material at a distance from the center of the ridges. It has also been found that these ridges are regions of high heat flow.

3. Continents often have mountain ranges on their coastal margins. The west coasts of North and South America are examples of this. These mountains are often areas of high earthquake and volcanic activity.

4. Deep oceanic trenches are often associated with coastal mountain ranges. It has been found that these trenches are regions of low heat flow.

5. Earthquakes and volcanoes show a definite pattern of occurrence. Both of these crustal activities seem to occur in certain zones, including the oceanic ridges and trenches and coastal mountain ranges.

6. Although the earth is over 4 billion years old, no sediments older than 200 million years have been found on the ocean floors. There are places on the ocean floors where no sediment has been found at all. These regions are generally associated with oceanic trenches.

7. The continents appear to be moving across the earth's surface. Some are moving apart, others are converging. Rates of movement have been measured, and range from as little as 2 cm per year for some areas to as much as 10-12 cm per year for others.

Are these observations somehow related? Some earth scientists think so. For years, scientists have attempted to formulate a *single* theory of crustal dynamics that would tie all this evidence together. Two of the most promising concepts—continental drift and ocean-floor spreading—were discussed in Chapter 19 (pages 378-382). When considered separately, each of these concepts left many unanswered questions. However, when scientists combined all the evidence into a single theory, they found that they could answer *most* of the questions. Unfortunately, some very fundamental questions remained unanswered: What *forces* cause the continents to move? Where does the new ocean-floor material come from? Where does the old ocean-floor material go?

As the search for answers to these questions continued, one thing seemed clear: great amounts of energy *and* material were involved. This fact led many earth scientists to seek the answers in an obvious place—the earth's interior. Their efforts have not been in vain. In recent years, a single, unified theory has been put forth that many earth scientists feel provides possible answers to most questions about crustal dynamics. It is called the theory of *plate tectonics.* We will examine this theory to see how the questions are answered, but first, let's take a brief look at the new information about the earth's interior that led scientists to the theory.

The Earth's Interior—A Detailed Look. In the last decade or so, earth scientists have conducted an intensive study of the earth's interior. Using sophisticated, precise instruments, these scientists have obtained data from various sources on seismic waves, heat flow, and crustal magnetism. This data has been collected, correlated, and analyzed, and a fairly detailed model of the earth to a depth of about 700 km has been constructed. In Chapter 20 (page 389), we mentioned that no earthquakes deeper than 700 km have yet been recorded. Figure 21-12 shows a cross-sectional view of the earth to that depth. The graph at the right shows a plot of S-wave velocity vs. depth.

The uppermost region of the earth is the lithosphere. This region, which consists of solid rock material, has an average thickness of about 100 km. Earlier in this chapter (page 412), you learned that the crust—the region above the Moho—is relatively thin, ranging in thickness from about 10 to 30 km. Thus, the lithosphere is made up of the crust *and* a region of solid mantle rock.

In the next region of the mantle, from the bottom of the lithosphere to

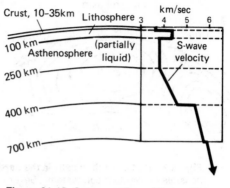

Figure 21-12. Cross section of the earth to a depth of 700 km. The graph shows a plot of S-wave velocities at the various depths within the earth's interior.

a depth of about 250 km, the rock is believed to be partially melted. In Figure 21-12, note the decrease in velocity as S-waves enter this region. This part of the mantle, which is called the *asthenosphere,* is thought to be the source of magma. Evidence indicates that less than 10 percent of the rock material in the asthenosphere is actually molten, but this liquid material is distributed as a thin film between the solid mineral grains. Thus, all of the rock material in the asthenosphere is able to flow very slowly.

Below the asthenosphere, the mantle is solid. Of particular interest to earth scientists are the two regions where phase transitions occur. These regions were identified by marked increases in S-wave velocity (Figure 21-12). The phase transitions, which occur at depths of about 400 km and 700 km, provide evidence of the increase in pressure as you go deeper into the earth's interior.

Now let's see what role this more detailed picture of the earth's interior played in the development of the theory of plate tectonics.

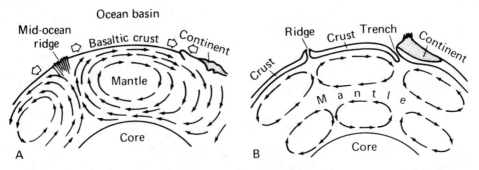

Figure 21-13. Convection cells in the earth's mantle. These drawings represent two *possible* convection cell systems. Several other models have also been suggested.

Convection Cells. According to the two major concepts discussed earlier—continental drift and ocean-floor spreading—the continents and the ocean floor are *moving*. Thus, a fundamental question is: What force is responsible for this motion? The current answer involves the presence of *convection cells* circulating within the mantle (see Figure 21-13).

The convection-cell concept is based on heat-flow data. The information on heat flow was collected using very sensitive instruments that measure the amount of heat energy radiated from the earth's surface. It is believed that this heat is produced by the breakdown, or decay, of radioactive elements within the mantle. It has been determined that, on the average, heat flow is greatest along ocean ridges and least along ocean trenches. The presence of convection cells provides the most logical answer for these differences.

You are already familiar with convection cells. In Chapter 11 (page 196) you learned that there are convection cells in the atmosphere. These cells exist because of differences in density between air masses and the effect of gravity on masses of air of differing densities. You have also learned that

convection cells exist in water for the same reasons. In fact, convection cells will form in *any* fluid if density differences exist and a gravity field is present.

Under certain conditions, rock material seems to behave as a dense, viscous fluid. Thus, it is reasonable to assume that convection cells exist within the earth's interior. We *know* that there are density differences. We *know* that there are differences in heat energy. We *know* that the rock material of the crust is newer and hotter at the ridges and older and cooler at the trenches. Based on this knowledge, scientists have concluded that the ridges and trenches are probably the upwelling and downwelling portions of convection cells.

Figure 21-13 illustrates two possible models of convection cells. Model *A* shows several cells extending from the core to the surface of the mantle. Model *B* shows a second possibility —two (or possibly more) levels of cells circulating within the mantle. There are several other patterns of convection that could exist within the mantle. However, all the models show warmer, less-dense material rising to the surface in one section of the cell and cooler, denser material sink-

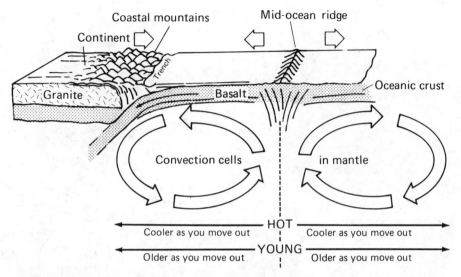

Figure 21-14. Basic mechanism of a convection cell. The rising portion carries warm, less dense material to the surface, while older rock material subsides into the mantle at the downward-moving part of the cell.

ing, or subsiding, into the mantle in another part of the cell (see Figure 21-14). As the new material rises at the mid-ocean ridges, it cools and becomes part of the basaltic crust beneath the ocean. Thus, the material of the crust becomes "older" as you move away from the ridges. As described in Chapter 19 (page 378) the motion of the crust can be compared to that of a moving conveyor belt. Now we will see how the concept of convection cells fits into the larger theory of plate tectonics.

Plate Tectonics. According to the theory of plate tectonics, the earth's crust is divided into a number of separate pieces, or plates. The exact number of plates is uncertain, but it is probably about a dozen. Scientists are still gathering data that will perhaps provide a more exact answer in the near future. In addition to the major plates, there are several smaller plates. As you can see on the map in

Figure 21-15, the larger plates have been named. The map also shows the approximate position of the plate boundaries. Some earth scientists believe that the plate boundaries coincide with regions of either upwelling or downwelling portions of convection cells.

Tectonic plates are often referred to as *lithospheric plates* because each plate is actually an enormous slab of solid lithospheric rock "riding" on the partially molten asthenosphere. The continents, which are roughly lens-shaped in cross section, are "embedded" in the plates, and they move with the plates in response to the ceaseless motion of the convection cells beneath them. Figure 21-16 represents a very simplified model of this system. Notice that not every plate contains a continental mass, and that some plates may carry more than one continent. You can also see this in Figure 21-15.

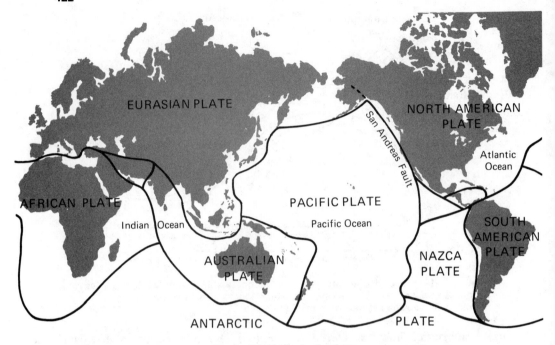

Figure 21-15. Tectonic plates.

Earthquakes—Occurrence and Depth. In Chapter 19 (page 373), it was pointed out that there are *zones* of the earth where earthquake activity and volcanic activity are most frequent. Compare the map in Figure 21-15 with the map of earthquake zones in Figure 19-8 (page 373). This comparison illustrates the fact that earthquake zones coincide closely with the plate boundaries. Thus, the tectonic plate theory helps explain the *pattern* of earthquake occurrence. Most earthquakes occur along the boundaries of the plates.

The depth at which earthquakes occur depends partially on what is happening at the boundary. If the boundary is along an upwelling portion of a convection cell, such as along an oceanic ridge, the plates will be diverging, or moving apart. Earthquakes that occur along such bound-aries tend to be shallow-focus quakes, that is, no deeper than 60 km below the surface. If the boundary is along a downwelling portion of a convection cell, the plates on either side will be converging, or coming together. Such boundaries are known as *subduction zones*. At these boundaries, one plate plunges, or subducts, beneath the other, as shown in Figure 21-17. To a depth of about 60 km, earthquakes in a subduction zone occur along the interface of the two plates. Below this depth, the intermediate-focus and deep-focus quakes occur in the center of the subducting plate. Many of the world's most severe earthquakes, and countless quakes of lesser intensity, have been of the shallow-focus variety that occur along plate interfaces in a subduction zone.

The drawing in Figure 21-17 illustrates what scientists believe occurs in a subduction zone when two plates come together. In most cases, the plunging, or subducting, plate is an oceanic plate. The drawing shows how it is possible for earthquakes of different depths to have roughly the same epicenter. It also illustrates why the focal depths increase as you move inland from the continental margin. The subduction represented in this drawing is similar to that which scientists think is occurring today along the west coast of the South American continent.

Mountain Building. Earlier in this chapter, you learned how some coastal mountains *may* have been created as a result of geosynclinal subsidence and uplift. According to the theory of plate tectonics, coastal mountains are also created as a result of plate collisions. Figure 21-17 illustrates a collision between an oceanic plate and a plate that carries a conti-

nent. In most collisions of this type, the oceanic plate bends and is pushed under the thicker continental plate. The oceanic plate continues downward, and eventually becomes part of the mantle.

Notice the distortion and thickening near the margin of the overriding continental plate. This is a region of faulting, folding, and volcanic activity, which probably account for the presence of mountain ranges at continental margins along subduction zones. It is believed that the Andes Mountains of South America is just such a mountain range. Also notice the trench forming at the surface of the subduction zone.

Ocean-floor Sediments. The theory of plate tectonics also provides logical explanations for the apparent lack of sea-floor sediments older than 200 million years and for the almost total lack of any sediments near ocean

Figure 21-16. A simplified model of the relationship between convection cells in the mantle and the lithospheric plates.

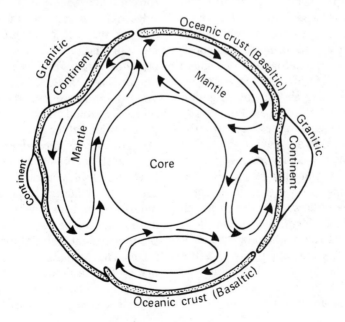

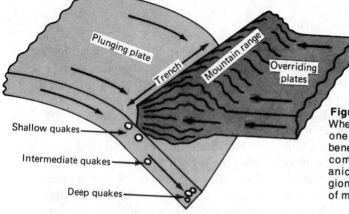

Figure 21-17. Subduction zone. When two tectonic plates collide, one plate plunges, or subducts, beneath the other. Such zones are commonly associated with oceanic trenches, and are often regions of frequent earthquakes and of mountain-building activity.

trenches. Such trenches, as you learned, are located along subduction zones. These are areas where an oceanic plate is plunging beneath a continental plate. Any sediments that are eroded from the continent and deposited in the trench or on the plunging plate will be carried along as if they were on a conveyor belt. These sediments will be pulled into the trench, and eventually they will become part of the mantle below.

Ocean-floor Spreading. Earlier in this section it was stated that the theory of plate tectonics incorporates the concepts of continental drift and ocean-floor spreading. The most popular concept of continental drift holds that at one time all the continents were jointed together in a single landmass. Figure 19-18 (page 379) illustrates how part of this gigantic landmass might have looked before drifting began. You can see how the landmasses that are now separated by the Atlantic Ocean once fitted together like a giant jigsaw puzzle.

According to the theory, as new crustal material was produced at the mid-Atlantic ridge, the ocean floor "grew" and the continents "drifted" apart. If this concept is correct, the rocks of the oceanic crust should be youngest in the region of the ridge, and should grow progressively older

as you move farther from the ridge. This pattern does, indeed, seem to be the case. Much of the evidence in support of this theory comes from studies of the magnetism in the rocks of the mid-ocean ridges and the oceanic crust, as discussed in Chapter 19, pages 377-378). Based on reverses, or anomalies, in the magnetic patterns in the rocks, scientists have been able to construct a map that divides the floor of the North Atlantic Ocean into age zones (Figure 21-18). The figures on the map indicate the time elapsed, in millions of years, since the crustal rock in each zone was formed at the ridge. As you can see, the figures do support the idea of progressive "aging" of the crustal rocks outward from the ridge. Worldwide studies of ocean-floor magnetism have all yielded similar results. The youngest rocks are found near the ridges, and the crust gets older as you move away on both sides of the ridges.

From the figures shown on the map in Figure 21-18, you can determine the age of the Atlantic Ocean basin. The oldest crustal rocks, which are found at the margins of the basin, represent the first crustal material formed at the ridge. The formation of these rocks marks the beginning of ocean-floor spreading and continental drift. It also represents the creation of the floor of

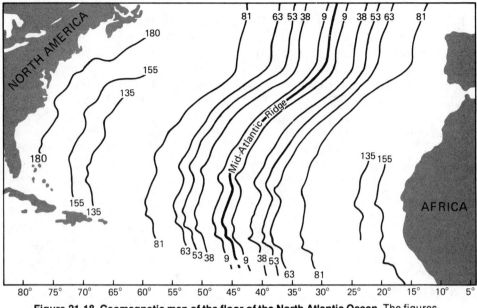

Figure 21-18. Geomagnetic map of the floor of the North Atlantic Ocean. The figures are the ages of the rocks in millions of years.

the Atlantic Ocean. Thus, according to the figures on the map, the Atlantic Ocean is approximately 180 million years old. This age corresponds closely with the ages of the oldest sediments that have been found on the ocean floor. This data also explains the lack of any older sediments. After all, sediments cannot start to accumulate on an ocean floor until *after* the floor has been created.

Rate of Plate Motion. The figures on the map in Figure 21-18 can also be used to determine the *rate* of ocean-floor spreading, and thus, the rate of plate motion. For example, from the center of the ridge to the boundary of the first age zone represents 9 million years of rock-forming activity. The distance from the center of the ridge to the age-zone boundary represents how far the plates have traveled in that time. The *rate* of plate motion can be calculated by dividing the distance traveled by the time required to travel

that distance. Figures for spreading rates at the major ocean ridges are given in Table 21-1. As you can see, the rate of plate motion shows a fairly wide range. The slowest plates are

Table 21-1. Opening rates at the oceanic ridges of the world.

Ridge	Opening rate (cm/yr)
East Pacific rise	10-12
Pacific-Antarctic rise	8
South Indian Ocean North Pacific	6
South Atlantic	3
North Indian Ocean	2-5
North Atlantic	2

found in the North Atlantic, where the spreading rate is 2 cm per year. The fastest rates, 10-12 cm per year, are found along the East Pacific rise.

The discussion of the theory of plate tectonics in this section has barely scratched the surface of the subject. However, in this brief treatment you have seen how this exciting theory does tie together such seemingly diverse activities as continental drift, ocean-floor spreading, earthquakes, volcanic activity, and mountain building. In the few pages of this chapter, you have learned more about the *total picture* of our dynamic earth

than dozens of earth scientists were able to discover over a period of centuries. Keep in mind that there are still some geologic phenomena that are not satisfactorily explained by the theory of plate tectonics. Scientists are only beginning to explore the mechanics of the convection currents in the mantle. However, the theory does provide scientists with a logical framework upon which to hang new theories and ideas. As these new ideas are examined and developed, it is hoped that some of the remaining questions will be answered, and we will better understand our planet.

SUMMARY

1. The occurrence of heat-flow highs in areas of current mountain building and heat-flow lows in areas of subsiding basins suggests the existence of convection cells in the mantle.
2. The close correlation among zones of earthquake activity, volcanic activity, and mountain building suggests that these processes of crustal change are related.
3. The theory of plate tectonics states that the solid lithosphere consists of a series of plates that "float" on the partially molten asthenosphere of the mantle. The convection cells provide the driving force to move these plates, and most of the processes of crustal change occur at the plate boundaries.

REVIEW QUESTIONS

Group A
1. What types of geological events may be related to the process of continental accretion?
2. What is the principle of isostasy?
3. What is meant by the term *phase transition*?
4. How may phase transitions be involved in the uplift and subsidence of geosynclines?
5. What evidence suggests the existence of convection cells in the mantle?
6. What three processes of crustal change are thought to be related to one another? Why do scientists think these processes are related?
7. What is the theory of plate tectonics? Why are convection cells important in this theory? Is there any relationship between areas of crustal change and tectonic-plate activity? Explain.

Group B   1. a.   Describe the process of continental accretion and explain how
                        scientists think this process is related to the development of island
                        arcs and geosynclinal activity.
                    b.   Describe the process of isostatic compensation and explain
                        how scientists think this process is related to geosynclinal
                        activity.
                    c.   Describe the basalt-eclogite hypothesis and explain why this
                        hypothesis is useful to earth scientists. Include in your an-
                        swer reference to subsidence and uplift within geosynclines.
              2. a.   What observations have caused earth scientists to suspect
                        the existence of convection cells within portions of the
                        earth's mantle?
                    b.   Describe the theory of plate tectonics. Include in your an-
                        swer the following terms : earth's mantle, convection cells,
                        subduction zones, granitic and basaltic lithosphere plates,
                        and ocean floor spreading.

REVIEW EXERCISES

1. On a separate sheet of paper, make a diagram illustrating the
   internal structure of the earth as hypothesized by most earth scientists today.
2. The radius of the earth is 6,370 km. The interface between the core
   and the mantle is at a depth of about 3,000 km. What percent of the
   earth's volume is occupied by the mantle? What percent is occupied by the core? (Neglect the volume of the crust.)
3. P waves from earthquakes travel about 1.7 times faster than S
   waves. If both start out from the same source at the same time and
   the P wave travels at a speed of 10 km/sec,
   a. how long will it take the P wave to travel 1,000 km through the
      earth?
   b. how long will it take the S wave to travel 1,000 km through the
      earth?
   c. how far behind will the S wave be after the P wave has traveled
      1,000 km?
4. On a separate sheet of paper, make a diagram showing why there
   is a P-wave shadow zone on the opposite side of the earth from an
   earthquake.
5. Compare the behavior of P waves and S waves in terms of:
   a. the type of vibrational motion they impart to the particles of the
      material through which they travel.
   b. wave velocity through the same medium.
   c. the types of materials through which they can pass.

TOPIC XIII
INTERPRETING GEOLOGIC HISTORY

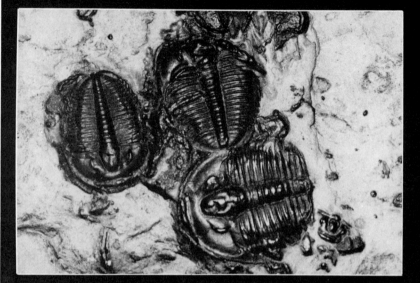

Knowing the time when this species of trilobites lived enables us to date the shale they are embedded in.

CHAPTER 22
Dating Geologic Events

You will know something about determining the relative and/or absolute age of a geological sample or event if you can:

1. Describe the types of evidence to be considered in determining the relative age of a rock or event.
2. Establish a correlation between rocks and/or events at different locations using rock and fossil evidence.
3. Describe how actual geologic ages can be measured using radioactive decay.

Unlocking the mysteries of past geologic events is like putting together a jigsaw puzzle. When you're doing a puzzle, you look for certain clues that can be of help—straight-edged pieces to make up the border, pieces of particular colors, or shapes, etc. Earth scientists also use certain types of "clues," which can help them to reconstruct the history of the earth. In this chapter we are going to see what clues present geologic features offer about past events.

RELATIVE DATING—THE ORDER OF GEOLOGIC EVENTS

As the geologist works to develop a model of the earth's history, he attempts to put events in chronological order—that is, in order of what happened first, what second, and so on. He attempts to find the *relative age* of a rock or event—its age compared with that of other rocks or events. He also attempts to find the *actual,* or *absolute, age,* which is the date that the event occurred or the rock was formed.

Before we get into our discussion of how earth scientists order past geologic events, there is a basic principle of earth science that should be mentioned—the principle of uniformitarianism.

Uniformitarianism. In any discussion of geologic history we describe events that may have occurred in the past in terms of present-day processes. We assume that the forces at work on the earth have not changed with time—that rivers eroded their banks in the past in much the same way they do today, and that rocks weathered in the same way billions of years ago as they do now. This is the principle of *uniformitarianism.*

The principle of uniformitarianism was developed by a Scottish physician and farmer, James Hutton, in the late 1700's. Hutton stated that "the present is the key to the past." That is, by observing the geologic processes now at work on the earth, it is possible to unravel the mysteries of the earth's geologic history. Although Hutton's principle may seem quite obvious today, it represented a major step in geologic thinking at the time. Before Hutton, most 18th-century geologists tried to explain the earth's history in terms of one-of-a-kind, sudden, major changes, or *catastrophes.*

Keeping the principle of uniformitarianism in mind, we can now look at some of the evidence that earth scientists consider in dating events of the past.

Principle of Superposition. Figure 22-1 is an outcrop of rock, that is, ex-

Figure 22-1. An outcrop of rock showing layers.

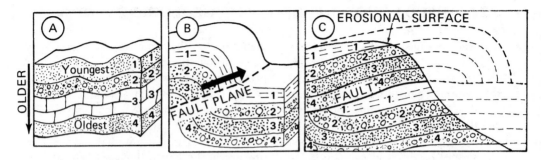

Figure 22-2. The principle of superposition and possible exceptions to it. (*A*) A rock layer is generally older than any layer above it. (*B*) and (*C*) The movement of layers along an overthrust fault can result in an exception to the principle of superposition.

posed bedrock without a covering of regolith. Examine it closely, and you will see that it consists of a number of layers. In Chapter 19 (page 368) we discussed the concept of *original horizontality*—that is, that sedimentary rocks generally form in horizontal layers, with new layers forming on top of existing layers. From this principle it is simple to infer that in sedimentary rock, the bottom layer is the oldest and the top layer the youngest. This idea is the *principle of superposition,* which is a basic concept in relative dating.

Is it always true that the bottom layer of sedimentary rock is the old-

est? No. There can be complications. It is possible that in folded rocks, or where there has been movement along a fault, the layers have been overturned, so that older layers are on top of younger layers. Figure 22-2 shows how exceptions to the principle of superposition can occur.

How can you tell if the rock layers have been overturned? First you might look for general features. Are the rock layers in this outcrop more or less horizontal? Do other outcrops in the area show similar structures? If the answer to both questions is yes, then it is likely that the rock layers have not been overturned.

Figure 22-3. Use of ripple marks and fossils to determine whether rock layers have been overturned. (*A*) Ripple marks in the sand always form with their crests pointing upward. Such ripple marks can be seen in some sedimentary rock. If the crests of the ripple marks point upward, the rocks have probably not been overturned. (*B*) As shells fall to the bottom of the ocean, they usually land with the outside of the shell upward. If most of the fossil shells in a layer are upright, the layer has probably not been overturned.

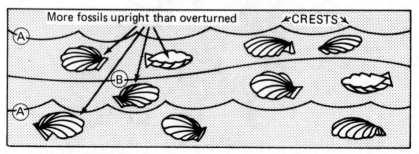

There are also other points that can be checked. You should recall from Chapter 16 (page 314) that sediments deposited in water are generally deposited in a sequence, with coarse ones settling first and finest ones settling last. Thus, within a layer of sedimentary rock you might be able to detect a gradation in the size of particles from top to bottom in a layer. If the finer particles are on top and the coarser ones on the bottom, you can infer that the layer has not been overturned. Ripple marks and fossils may also be useful in answering this question. Figure 22-3 shows how ripple marks in sand and the position of fossils can be used in determining whether or not rock layers have been overturned.

Igneous Intrusions and Extrusions. In Chapter 18 (page 350) we learned that molten rock, or magma, can form intrusions in existing rock (see Figure 22-4). It should be clear that in any formation with an igneous intrusion, the intrusion must be younger than the rock it cuts through.

Figure 22-4 also shows an igneous extrusion—rock formed when magma flowed over the surface and solidified. Again, it should be obvious that the extrusion will be younger than the rock on which it rests. However, the extrusion will be older than any rocks that form on top of it.

Structural Features. Structural features of rocks, such as faults, joints, and folds, are evidence that forces have been acting on the rock and that crustal movement has occurred (see Chapter 19, page 369). (A *joint,* like a fault, is a crack in a rock, but unlike a fault, there has not been movement along the crack.) A rock is older than any fault, joint, or fold it may contain. Such features must have been pro-

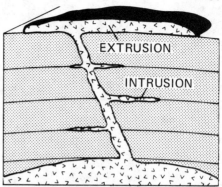

Figure 22-4. Igneous intrusion and extrusion. The intrusion is younger than the rock in which it is found. The extrusion is younger than the rock on which it rests.

duced *after* the rock was formed (see Figure 22-5).

Joints or cracks in rocks may become filled with mineral matter, as shown in Figure 22-5. The mineral deposit is younger than the event that produced the crack, and both the deposit and the crack are younger than the rock in which they occur. A mineral deposit of this type, which is formed from a solution filling a crack in a rock, is called a *vein.*

Internal Characteristics of Rocks. In many igneous intrusions there are fragments of rock, called *xenoliths,* that have not been melted (see Figure

Figure 22-5. Relative ages of structural features of rocks. Folds, faults, joints, and veins are younger than the rocks in which they occur.

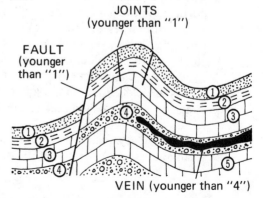

Figure 22-6. Xenolith in an igneous intrusion.

22-6). It appears that the fragments were broken off from surrounding rock and were carried along in the molten igneous material. Such fragments are older than the igneous material in which they are embedded.

In Chapter 18 we discussed the formation of the various types of rocks. From that discussion you should recognize two facts about the relative age of sedimentary rocks. The sediments from which sedimentary rocks are formed are older than the rocks themselves. The sediments must also be older than the mineral cements found in them, because the cement forms after the sediments are deposited.

SUMMARY

1. Relative dating is an attempt to put geologic events or structures into proper chronological order.
2. The principle of uniformitarianism states that the geologic processes that occurred in the past are basically the same as those that are occurring now.
3. The bottom layer of a series of sedimentary layers is the oldest, unless the series has been overturned or has had older rock thrust over it.
4. Rock layers are older than igneous intrusions that cut through them or igneous extrusions that are above them.
5. Rocks are older than faults, joints, folds, or veins that appear in them.
6. Fragments of unmelted material occurring within a rock are older than the rock.
7. In sedimentary rocks, the sediments are older than the cements that bind them and the rock formation itself.

CORRELATION

Using the information given in the last section, geologists can determine the relative ages of the layers in a rock formation. But now another question arises. How can you determine whether the rocks or geologic events occurring at one location are of the same age as those at another location? The process of showing that rocks or geologic events occurring at different locations are of the same age is called *correlation*. Since certain minerals are found in rocks of a particular age, correlation can be an important tool in the search for mineral deposits.

Following are some of the techniques used in correlation.

"Walking the Outcrop." The most direct method for observing a correlation between rocks or events at separate locations is by actually following a particular layer or formation from one location to the other. In this case you actually observe the physical continuity of the structure in question

(see Figure 22-7). As you know, bedrock exposed at the earth's surface is called an outcrop. This method of correlation is called *walking the outcrop,* because you follow the outcrop from one location to another.

Similarity of Rock. Another method of correlation is the direct observation of similarities between layers of rock in different locations. Suppose you are examining an outcrop and notice three layers of rock with particular colors, composition, etc., and in a certain order. In a nearby location you observe three layers of similar color and composition and in the same order. From this evidence you could infer that the rock is the same at both locations. In other words, there is a correlation between the two rocks.

Index Fossils. Fossils are the remains or impressions of ancient plants and animals. They are usually found only in sedimentary rock. Geologists have developed a system for correlat-

Figure 22-7. Correlation by direction observation. A geologist can follow the layers in an exposed hillside by "walking the outcrop," for example, by walking along the road on the left side of this river valley. He may also be able to correlate layers on opposite sides of the valley by observing similarities in color, texture, and sequence of the rock layers.

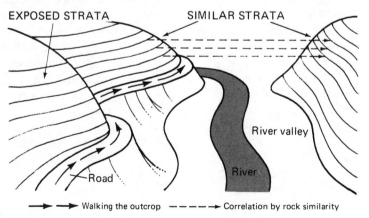

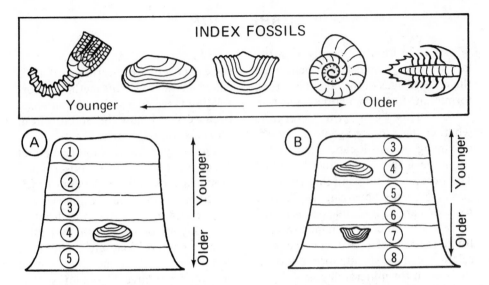

Figure 22-8. Correlation of rocks using index fossils. In (A) a fossil of an organism known to have lived *only* during Period X is found in rock layer 4. This layer was therefore deposited during Period X. The layers above it are younger, and those below it are older. In (B), a similar fossil is found in one of the layers. Therefore, this layer was also formed during Period X. An index fossil of Period Y is found in layer 7. This tells us that layers 5 and 6 are older than Period X, but younger than Period Y. Relative ages of the layers in both formations are indicated by the numbers in order of youngest to oldest.

ing sedimentary rock based on the presence of particular fossils, known as *index fossils*.

An index fossil is the remains or imprint of a particular type of plant or animal that existed for a relatively short period of time but which was found in many different parts of the world. If you think about it, you'll realize why these last two points are important. If the organism existed unchanged for many hundreds of millions of years, its presence would be of no use in dating a rock because it would be found in rock layers of many different ages. If the organism were found only in a few, specific locations, it would be of no use in correlating rock from widely separated regions. Figure 22-8 shows some index fossils and how they are used in relative dating.

Index fossils are one of the best means we have of correlating rocks. The idea of using fossils for such purposes originated about 1800, when William Smith, an English engineer and geologist, made a number of basic observations about fossils and rock formations. He noticed that in a given formation, different layers contained different fossils, but that the fossils in a particular layer of a rock formation were the same throughout the formation. On further investigation, Smith noticed that certain fossils were found in rock layers of the same age, even at widely separated locations. So, the presence of such fossils could be used to correlate the ages of rocks at different locations.

The presence of fossils also reveals something of the past environment. For example, the presence of fossils of marine organisms shows that during a certain period in the past the area was covered by an ocean. If the fossils are index fossils, you can say with some certainty just when, in the past, the ocean covered the area.

Volcanic Ash Deposits. When a volcano erupts, large quantities of volcanic ash are shot into the air. This ash, which consists of small pieces of igneous rock, may be carried for great distances before it falls to earth. So, ash from a single eruption may be deposited over large areas of the earth's surface in a very short period of time. Layers of ash settling in sediments may be incorporated into the rocks formed from the sediments. If these layers of volcanic ash can be identified in rock formations at different locations, they can be used for correlation. Deposits of volcanic ash are good "time markers," because they were deposited over such a short time period. Volcanic ash deposits can be especially useful in correlating rocks that contain no fossils.

Correlation Anomalies. An anomaly is something that does not fit the normal pattern. Anomalies in correlation are conditions or situations in which

the results obtained by common correlation techniques are misleading or incorrect. Figure 22-9 shows one such situation. Here, in a single formation of sedimentary rock, the age of the rock varies by as much as 10 million years. Thus, you can see that even in a single formation, the rock may be much older in one place than in another. In this case the environment of deposition has moved very gradually over millions of years, thereby accounting for the different ages of the rock in the different parts of the formation.

Following is a description of another type of anomaly—one in which there is a clear correlation between certain parts of two separate formations, but apparently unexplainable differences between other parts. As you will see, establishing a correlation between rocks is not always a straightforward process.

A geologist made the following observations at two locations in the Grand Canyon, about 160 km apart. In the first location, ten distinctive rock formations can be identified. These are shown in Figure 22-10. Figure 22-11 shows a section of the

Figure 22-9. Variations in the age of a formation. A sedimentary formation composed of the same type of sediment may be of different ages in different locations because of movement of the environment of deposition. In this diagram, the sandstone at the left is 10 million years older than the sandstone at the right, even though the formation is continuous and similar in composition.

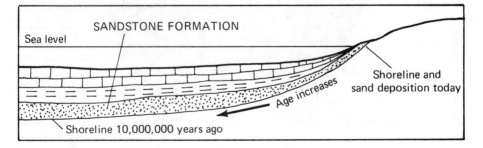

canyon wall along the Bright Angel Trail, about 160 km away, which also contains ten distinctive formations. One easily identified rock formation in the Grand Canyon is the Redwall limestone. It is a tough limestone that is found as bold cliffs wherever it is exposed. The fossils found in the Redwall formation are also distinctive. Furthermore, this formation can be traced along the canyon walls continuously between the two locations. Thus, you can say that the Redwall formation is found at both locations.

Figure 22-10. Section of the wall of the Grand Canyon near the mouth of the Colorado River.

The topmost layer of rock at both locations appears to contain the same fossils, is the same kind of rock (limestone), is about the same thickness, and it, too, can be traced continuously between the two locations. Thus, you can infer that there is a correlation between the topmost layer of limestone as well as between the Redwall formation at the two locations.

At the Bright Angel Trail location, there is a bright red sandstone just above the Redwall formation. This sandstone, called the Supai formation, contains fossil plants and footprints of land animals.

At the second location, the rock lying just above the Redwall formation is a limestone, which is light gray

Figure 22-11. Section of the wall of the Grand Canyon along the Bright Angel Trail.

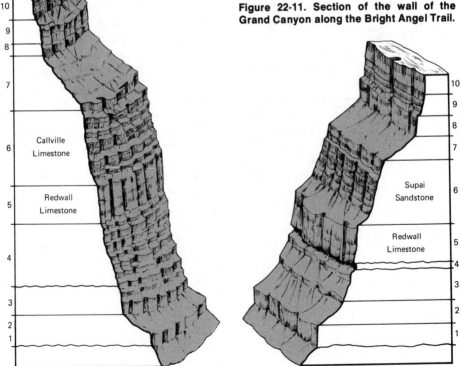

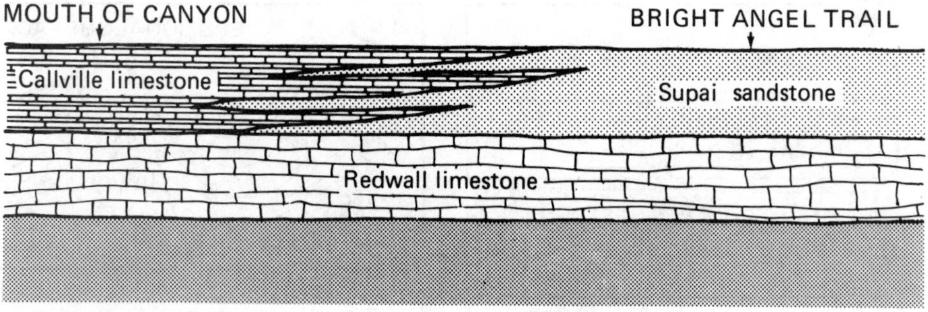

MOUTH OF CANYON   BRIGHT ANGEL TRAIL

Figure 22-12. Alternating layers of sandstone and limestone, indicating a former shoreline.

in color and contains fossils of marine organisms. This limestone is known as the Callville formation.

So, while we have established a correlation between two rock layers at these two locations, we are left with the question of why there is no evidence of the Supai formation at one location and no evidence of the Callville formation at the other location. This is the type of correlation problem that geologists frequently face. Either part of the puzzle is missing, or parts that should fit, don't.

Fortunately, we know the answer to the puzzle in this case. If we follow the Callville limestone toward Bright Angel Trail, we find that the limestone beds become increasingly reddish in color and sandy in texture. Eventually, we reach an area that shows alternating layers of red sandstone and gray limestone, as shown in Figure 22-12. These alternating layers of marine and terrestrial rock indicate the location of a former shoreline. This shoreline moved first one way and then back, as the materials from both environments were deposited. So, we have the answer to our puzzle. The two formations—the Callville

limestone of one location and the Supai sandstone of the other location—were deposited during the same period of time, but in different environments.

Unconformities. In their efforts to work out the geologic history of an area, geologists often find that part of the rock record is missing. Sometimes this is the result of a buried erosional surface, called an *unconformity*. Figures 22-13 and 22-14 show two types of unconformities and how they were formed.

The presence of an unconformity indicates that at some time in the distant past, the area was uplifted by crustal movement. Following uplift, the surface was weathered and eroded away, leaving a gap in the rock record. At a still later period, this area underwent subsidence and was covered by water. New layers of sediment were deposited on the erosional surface, resulting in the unconformity. In most cases, the new layers of sediment and the original rock, which has undergone uplifting, are not parallel to each other. But, as you can see in Figure 12-14, this is not always true.

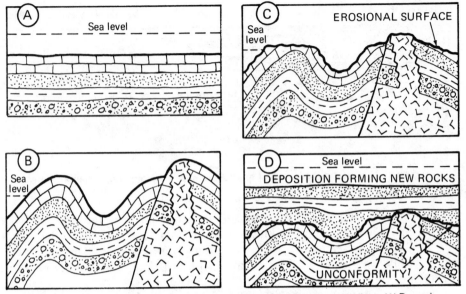

Figure 22-13. Events producing an unconformity with lack of parallelism. (A) Deposition forms sedimentary rock layers. (B) Crustal deformation and uplift occur. (C) Weathering and erosion remove part of the rock record. (D) Submergence and new deposition result in an unconformity along the erosional surface.

Figure 22-14. An unconformity in parallel strata. Uplift, erosion, and submergence have also occurred here, but without deformation. Evidence of a gap in the rock record may be given by widely different ages of the fossils in the layers above and below the unconformity.

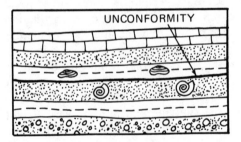

SUMMARY

1. Correlation is the process of showing that rocks or geologic events occurring at different locations are of the same age.
2. In correlation, rock layers may be traced from one location to another directly by "walking the outcrop," thus showing the continuity of layers.
3. Rocks may be correlated on the basis of similarities in appearance, composition, and position in relation to other layers.
4. Fossils are the remains or impressions of ancient plants and animals. They are found almost exclusively in sedimentary rock.
5. Index fossils are the remains or imprints of organisms that existed for a relatively short period of time, but were widely distributed over the earth. The presence of an index fossil in a rock shows that the rock was formed over a definite, relatively short, period of time.

6. Fossils in rocks provide information about the environment in which the rock was formed.
7. Layers of volcanic ash in rock can be useful in correlation because they were deposited over a large area in a very short period of time.
8. Two similar rock formations may be of different ages, or a single formation may be older in some places than in others. These are anomalies to correlation.
9. An unconformity is a buried erosional surface. Where the surface has been eroded away, there is a gap in the rock record.

ABSOLUTE DATING AND RADIOACTIVE DECAY

We have seen some of the ways in which geologists establish the relative age of rocks or the order of events. But how can we find out how many years ago a particular rock was formed or a particular event occurred? Until Henri Becquerel's discovery of radioactivity in 1895, there was no way of finding the actual, or *absolute*, age of a rock or fossil. Only the relative age could be determined. However, within 10 years of the discovery of radioactivity, the English physicist Ernest Rutherford proposed that radioactivity could be used for dating rocks, and within a year he had succeeded in dating a uranium mineral.

Before you can understand what is involved in radioactive dating, you must know something about the structure of an atom and about the phenomenon of radioactivity, or radioactive decay.

Elements and Isotopes. As you know, elements are substances that cannot be broken down into simpler substances by any chemical change. Elements are composed of atoms, which in turn are made up of three different kinds of particles — protons, neutrons, and electrons. Protons and neutrons are found in the dense *nu-*

cleus of the atom, while electrons are found in the space around the nucleus. Protons are positively charged, while electrons are negatively charged, and neutrons show no electrical charge. One element differs from another in the number of protons in its nucleus.

In many cases, there are several different forms of an element, called *isotopes*. All atoms of a given element have the same number of protons in their nuclei. However, the number of neutrons may not be the same. Atoms with the same number of protons but different numbers of neutrons are different isotopes of the same element. For example, ordinary hydrogen has one proton and no neutrons in its nucleus. The two isotopes of hydrogen are deuterium, which has one proton and one neutron, and tritium, which has one proton and two neutrons.

Radioactive Decay. The nuclei of some isotopes are unstable and undergo radioactive decay. These are radioactive isotopes, or radioisotopes. During the decay process, they emit particles and electromagnetic energy, and in this way they are transformed into atoms of other, more stable elements.

In 1905, Pierre and Marie Curie discovered the element radium by painstakingly separating it from pitchblende, a uranium mineral. Radium is even more highly radioactive than uranium, and scientists began to study the radiation given off by this new element. They found that when a beam of radiation was passed through a magnetic field, it separated into three types of rays. One followed a slightly curving path; the second followed a strongly curving path; and the third followed a straight, unchanging path through the magnetic field (see Figure 22-15). The three types of radiation were given the names *alpha, beta,* and *gamma* radiation. (Alpha, beta, and gamma are the first three letters of the Greek alphabet.)

Figure 22-15. Effect of magnetic field on beam of radiation.

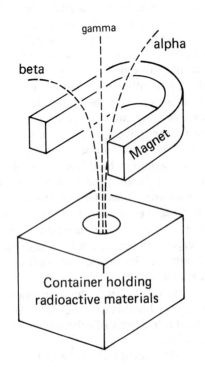

Further investigation showed that alpha radiation, which follows a slightly curving path in a magnetic field, is composed of positively charged particles—alpha particles. Beta radiation, which follows a strongly curving path in a magnetic field, is composed of negatively charged particles—beta particles. Gamma radiation, which is not affected by a magnetic field, does not appear to be composed of particles. Gamma rays are similar to X rays, but they are of shorter wavelengths and are more energetic.

Alpha particles, while positively charged, are heavier than ordinary protons. They have been found to consist of two protons and two neutrons. Thus, when an atom emits alpha particles during radioactive decay, it loses two protons and two neutrons.

Beta particles, which are negatively charged, are electrons. However, they come from within the nucleus. This fact presented a problem to researchers because the nucleus was thought to contain only protons and neutrons. It was eventually found that beta particles—electrons from the nucleus—are produced from the breakdown of neutrons (see Figure 22-16). In radioactive decay, a neutron may split to form a proton and an electron. The proton remains in the nucleus, while the electron is emitted as a beta particle. Thus, when an atom emits beta particles, it loses a neutron and gains a proton.

We know that the identity of an element is determined by the number of protons in the nuclei of its atoms. When alpha or beta particles are emitted from the nucleus of an atom dur-

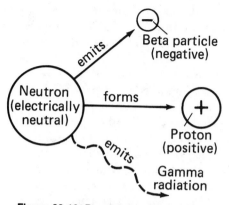

Figure 22-16. Breakdown of a neutron.

ing radioactive decay, the number of protons (and neutrons) in that atom is changed. When an alpha particle is given off, the atom loses two protons and two neutrons. When a beta particle is given off, the atom gains a proton. In this way, the original unstable atom is transformed into a stable isotope of another element.

The transformation of an unstable isotope to a stable isotope of another element by radioactive decay may involve several intermediate stages in which other unstable isotopes are formed. These unstable isotopes also undergo decay, eventually reaching a stable form.

Half-Life of a Radioisotope. The breakdown, or disintegration, of a radioactive element is a random event. Just as you cannot predict which kernel of corn will pop next when you are cooking popcorn, you cannot predict which atom of a radioactive element will disintegrate. However, you can predict that within a given period of time a certain *number* of atoms will decay. How many depends on the particular element involved and the number of atoms present.

The amount of radiation given off by a sample can be measured with an instrument called a *Geiger counter*. With this instrument it is possible to measure the activity of a sample over a period of time. The activity decreases at a steady and predictable rate as the radioactive isotope disintegrates. The rate of radioactive decay is not affected by environmental factors, such as temperature and pressure. Chemical reactions also do not affect the decay rate. Thus, the decay of a radioactive isotope is an "atomic clock," which cannot be affected by external conditions.

Each radioisotope has a definite rate of decay. This means that over a given period of time, a certain characteristic fraction of the atoms in a sample will disintegrate. During the next equal time period, the *same fraction* of the remaining atoms will disintegrate. The length of time necessary for half of a sample of a radioactive element to disintegrate is called the *half-life* of that element.

Suppose, for example, you have a sample of iodine-131, a radioactive isotope of iodine. The half-life of this isotope is about 8 days. This means that after 8 days, half the atoms in your sample will have undergone radioactive decay. After 16 days, half of the remaining iodine-131 atoms will have decayed. Thus, three-fourths of the original sample will have undergone decay. After each 8-day interval, the activity of the original sample will be reduced by half. This is shown in graphic form in Figure 22-17.

The half-lives of radioactive isotopes vary from a fraction of a second to billions of years. To date rocks or fossils, isotopes with long half-lives are needed. Table 22-1 shows the isotopes most commonly used in dating, the stable isotopes produced by their decay, and their half-lives.

Radioactive Dating. When a radioactive isotope decays, an isotope of another element is formed and some form of radiation is given off. Thus, as decay continues, the amount of the original, or parent, isotope decreases, and the amount of the new, or daughter isotope, increases. Figure 22-18 illustrates the changing relationship between the amounts of the radioactive parent isotope and the stable daughter isotope present in a sample.

At the end of one half-life, half of the parent isotope will have decayed to the stable daughter isotope. There should now be equal amounts of the parent and daughter isotopes in the sample. At the end of two half-lives, three-fourths of the parent isotope will have decayed, so the ratio of parent to daughter isotope will be 1:3. The longer the decay process continues, the less parent isotope and the more daughter isotope there is in the sample. As you can see in Figure

22-18, the ratio of the amount of parent isotope to the amount of daughter isotope changes in a predictable manner. Where scientists can accurately measure the amounts of a radioisotope and its stable decay product in a sample, they can, knowing the half-life of the radioisotope, use the relative amounts of the two isotopes to calculate the age of the sample.

As we have mentioned, the radioactive isotopes used to measure the ages of rocks or fossils must have long half-lives. In nature, these isotopes are generally found, in some small proportion, along with the stable isotopes of the same element. For example, potassium is found in many of the rock-forming minerals. Although most of this will be a stable isotope of potassium, some will be the radioactive isotope. As you can see in Table 22-1, the radioisotope potassium-40, with a half-life of 1.3 billion years, decays to the stable isotope argon-40. Scientists are able

Figure 22-18. Curves showing radioactive decay of uranium-238 and formation of the stable decay product lead-206. After one half-life (4.5 billion years), half the original atoms of uranium have become atoms of lead.

Figure 22-17. Decay of I-131.

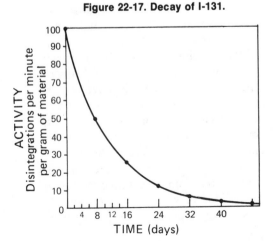

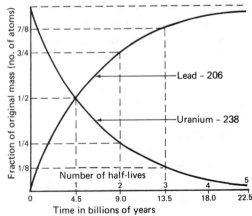

Radioactive Element	Stable Isotope Formed	Radiation Emitted	Half-Life
Uranium—U^{238}	Lead—Pb^{206}	{8 alpha {6 beta	4.51 billion yrs.
Uranium—U^{235}	Lead—Pb^{207}	{7 alpha {4 beta	0.71 billion yrs.
Thorium—Th^{232}	Lead—Pb^{208}	{6 alpha {4 beta	13.9 billion yrs.
Rubidium—Rb^{87}	Strontium Sr^{87}	1 beta	50 billion yrs.
Potassium—K^{40}	Argon—A^{40}	1 electron capture	1.3 billion yrs.
Carbon—C^{14}	Nitrogen^{14}	1 beta	5,770 yrs.

Table 22-1. Radioisotopes used in dating.

to measure even very small amounts of these isotopes in a rock sample. From this information they can calculate the age of the rock. Sometimes more than one radioactive element will be found in a rock sample. In such cases, it may be possible to cross-check results.

For radioactive dating to be done, both the original radioisotope and its decay product must be present in the sample. When rocks undergo melting, both the radioisotope and its decay products are dispersed. For dating purposes, the "atomic clock" is reset at zero. When new rock forms, decay products again accumulate, and dating becomes possible.

Carbon-14 is a radioactive isotope with a half-life of 5,770 years. It is produced in the upper atmosphere by the bombardment of nitrogen-14 by cosmic rays. The carbon-14 produced is incorporated into carbon dioxide, which in turn is taken in by plants. The plants may be eaten by animals, so that their bodies, too, will contain some of this isotope. In living plants and animals the carbon-14 isotope will

be present in approximately the same proportion as it is in the atmosphere. As long as the organism is alive, the proportion of carbon-14 in its tissues remains constant. However, when the plant or animal dies, no more carbon-14 is taken in. The carbon-14 present in the remains, decays, forming nitrogen-14. By measuring the proportion of carbon-14 present in plant and animal remains, scientists can say, with great accuracy, when the plant or animal lived. For example, in a tree that lived about 5,000 years ago the proportion of carbon-14 would be about half that in a tree living now.

Radiocarbon dating, as it is called, is used on the remains of plants and animals up to 50,000 years old. Because of the relatively short half-life of the carbon-14 isotope, it cannot be used to date objects more than 50,000 years old because, for practical purposes, there is no carbon-14 left in the sample after that timespan. It has all decayed. So, for older objects, the potassium-argon isotopes or uranium-lead isotopes are used.

The Age of the Earth. How old is the earth? This question has been asked and the answer sought throughout recorded history. Until recent times, a reliable method for determining the earth's age remained one of the missing pieces to the earth "puzzle." Early efforts by scientists to determine the earth's age included such methods as measuring the salt content of the oceans, the rates of erosion and deposition of sediments, the rate of cooling of the earth, and the luminosity of the sun. As you might expect, the results of such methods were quite inaccurate, and produced a variety of "ages" ranging from 5,000 to 40 million years.

With the discovery of radioactivity and the development of methods of radioactive dating, it has become possible to determine the ages of the rocks of the earth's crust quite accurately. The oldest crustal rocks found to date have been dated at about 4.1 *billion* years. Keep in mind, however, that since the time that the first crustal rocks were exposed to the earth's atmosphere, the processes of weathering and erosion have been at work wearing them down. Most of the rocks that are available for dating purposes— that is, rocks at or near the earth's surface—are *not* part of the original crust. They are considerably younger, and have been formed from the products of weathering and erosion of older rocks. Many of the rocks at the earth's surface have probably passed through the rock cycle more than once.

Fortunately, the earth's crust is not the only source of rock material. Meteorites and rocks from the moon are also available for radioactive dating. Since the moon has no atmosphere, rocks at the moon's surface are virtually unweathered. The oldest moon rocks have been found to be about 4.5 billion years old. Somewhat surprisingly, *all* of the meteorites that have fallen to earth, regardless of their composition, have been found to be of one age—4.5 billion years! Most scientists believe that the meteorites and the moon are parts of the solar system, and thus formed at the same time as the earth. If they are correct, the earth is approximately 4.5 billion years old.

SUMMARY

1. All atoms of a given element have the same number of protons in the nucleus. Different isotopes of a given element have the same number of protons but different numbers of neutrons in the nucleus.
2. The nuclei of some atoms undergo radioactive decay, during which particles and/or electromagnetic energy are given off, and a new element is formed.
3. The disintegration of an individual atom occurs as a random event.
4. The rate at which radioactive decay occurs is predictable, and is characteristic of the element involved.
5. The rate of decay is not affected by external factors, such as temperature, pressure, or chemical reaction.
6. The length of time necessary for half of a sample of a radioactive element to decay is the half-life of that element. Different radioactive isotopes have different half-lives.

7. Radioactive isotopes with relatively short half-lives, such as carbon-14, are used for dating recent organic remains. Isotopes with longer half-lives, such as uranium-238 and potassium-40, are used for dating older remains.
8. As decay continues in a sample, the amount of the original isotope present decreases, and the amount of the stable decay product increases.
9. By finding the relative amounts of the original radioisotope and the decay product in a sample, scientists, knowing the half-life of the isotope, can calculate the age of the sample.

REVIEW QUESTIONS

Group A
1. What is relative dating?
2. What is the principle of uniformitarianism?
3. In a series of sedimentary layers, which is usually the oldest?
4. How does the relative age of an igneous intrusion: (a) compare with that of the rock it cuts through, (b) compare with the age of rocks below and above it?
5. Are faults, joints, folds, and veins younger or older than the rocks in which they are found?
6. Are mineral cements and sediments younger or older than the rocks in which they are found?
7. What is correlation?
8. Describe several ways in which a correlation may be established between rock formations.
9. What are fossils? In what type of rock are they found?
10. What is an index fossil?
11. How can layers of volcanic ash be used in correlation?
12. What is an anomaly of correlation?
13. What is an unconformity?
14. All atoms of a given element have what in common?
15. How do the isotopes of an element differ from one another?
16. What happens to the nucleus of an atom undergoing decay?
17. Can you predict when a particular atom of a radioisotope is going to decay? If not, why not?
18. What can be said about the rate of decay of a given radioisotope?
19. What factors affect the rate of radioactive decay?
20. What is the half-life of an element?
21. Name some radioactive isotopes used in dating. Which are used to date (a) recent organic materials, and (b) older, inorganic materials?
22. In radioactive dating, how is the age of a sample calculated?

Group B
1. Relative dating of geologic events can be done by studying rock phenomena such as superposition, presence of intrusions and extrusions, structural features, and internal characteristics. Which of these phenomena would be most likely to be misinterpreted when used to date events? Explain.
2. List three forms of evidence that you could use to correlate rocks in one place with those in another place.
3. a. The process of radioactive decay is called a random event. What does this mean?
   b. How can the process of radioactive decay provide accurate information about the age of a rock?

These are fossilized dinosaur bones of the Morrison formation, Upper Jurassic period. This assemblage is part of Dinosaur National Monument in Jensen, Utah.

CHAPTER 23
The Record in the Rocks

You will know something about interpreting the record of ancient life and geologic events that is preserved in the rocks if you can:

1. Describe what the geologic column is, how it was compiled, and what it represents.
2. Use the clues and techniques required to infer the geologic history of an area from the rock exposed in the area.
3. Describe how the evolutionary development of life forms can be inferred from the fossil record.

If only rocks could talk, what a story they could tell! Actually, this statement is not as much of an idle wish as it may seem. While rocks cannot talk, they can tell a story. All of the earth's history is recorded in its rocks. The story is there for anyone to read—anyone, that is, who is willing to put in the time and effort to learn to read the "language" of the rock record. Fortunately for us, many earth scientists have believed that the reward of learning and understanding the earth's dynamic history is well worth the effort required.

THE GEOLOGIC COLUMN

What "story" does the rock record tell? Consider the continent of North America. Several times during its history, North America has been invaded by the sea. At times, almost the entire landmass was under water; at other times, water covered only low-lying regions. Mountains were uplifted, eroded away, and uplifted again. Sediments deposited in the shallow inland seas during periods of erosion accumulated to thousands of meters in thickness. Volcanoes were active in various parts of the continent at different times. Great sheets of ice advanced and retreated several times, and the climate changed accordingly. Plants and animals lived and died. Certain species appeared, flourished for a while, and became extinct. Other species appeared to take their places.

This, then, is the story of North America as it has been interpreted from the rock record. The records of the other continents show that all the landmasses of the world experienced similar changes—different changes at different times perhaps, but similar in their total effect.

How did earth scientists tackle the problem of interpreting the record preserved in the rocks? As mentioned in Chapter 22, early geologists were concerned mainly with putting events into chronological order. Thus, they used the "clues" described in Chapter 22 to determine the relative ages of rock formations and the events they represented. These clues included the principles of original horizontality and superposition, igneous intrusions and extrusions, structural features, and internal characteristics of the rocks. However, because these clues are re-lated to physical events only, their usefulness was limited to interpreting the rocks in a local region. Correlation of formations and events at widely separated locations, or even between continents, was difficult, if not impossible.

The big breakthrough came when William Smith recognized that fossils could be used to correlate rock formations. Since the time of William Smith, geologists have learned a great deal about fossils and their importance to the rock record. Geologists now recognize that a definite pattern or sequence exists in the fossil record. In general, the plants and animals found in younger rocks are more complex and more specialized than those found in older rock layers. The evidence of

Figure 23-1. Geologic column. This model of the rock record is a composite made up of rock formations from all over the world.

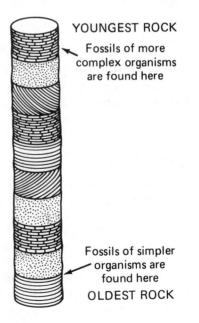

YOUNGEST ROCK

Fossils of more complex organisms are found here

Fossils of simpler organisms are found here

OLDEST ROCK

this evolutionary development will be considered in some detail later in this chapter. Based on this evolutionary trend and the presence of certain index fossils, earth scientists have been able to piece together a chronological record extending from the time of the earliest fossils to the present. The rock record is sometimes referred to as the *geologic column* (see Figure 23-1).

The importance of Smith's contribution to the development of the geologic column cannot be overemphasized. Without using fossils, worldwide correlation of rock formations would not be possible. And without this correlation, scientists could not have pieced together the geologic column, because *no single location on earth contains a complete record of all geologic time*. Not even in the walls of the Grand Canyon, which consist of exposed rock faces over 1,000 m high and 450 km long, is the rock record complete. The geologic column is a *composite* record made up of rock formations (mostly sedimentary) from all over the world. In fact, if all the layered rock formations now recognized were laid one on top of the other, the column of rocks would be more than 150,000 m thick!

SUMMARY

1. Earth scientists are able to trace the geologic history of the earth from the time of the earliest fossils to the present.
2. The geologic column is a composite record put together by earth scientists using rock formations from all over the world.

GEOLOGIC TIME SCALE

Ideally, the geologic column should contain a continuous record of evolutionary progress from the earliest forms of life to the present forms. However, careful study indicates that the story is not quite so simple. Fossils found in one particular formation suddenly disappear as we look higher in the column. Other fossils suddenly appear in the column. Still other fossils are found continuously throughout the column, existing even today as living organisms. Some of these fossil types show little change across geologic time; others show dramatic change.

In the normal course of things, changes through evolution are very gradual and occur over very long periods of time. However, geologists have recognized apparent breaks in the geologic time record. These breaks are usually marked by abrupt changes in the fossil pattern, such as the disappearance of one or more species and/or the appearance of new species. Geologists have also recognized that abrupt changes in the fossil record usually coincide with major physical breaks in the rock record. These physical breaks are often marked by *unconformities* (Chapter 22, page 437). Such breaks are evidence of structural change, such as mountain building or subsidence.

Once all the pieces of the geologic column had been put together and their chronological order determined,

Era			Period (or Epoch)	Millions of Years Ago	Plant Life	Animal Life
CENOZOIC ERA	Age of Man	Quaternary	Recent Epoch	.01	Herbs dominant	Modern man and modern animals
			Pleistocene Epoch	2	Trees decrease; herbs increase	Early man; large mammals become extinct
	Age of Mammals	Tertiary Period	Pliocene Epoch	12	Grasses increase; herbs appear	Mammals abundant; man appears
			Miocene Epoch	26	Forests decrease; grasses develop	Mammals increase; hominids appear
			Oligocene Epoch	37	Worldwide tropical forests	Modern mammals appear
			Eocene Epoch	53	Angiosperms increase	Archaic mammals at peak
			Paleocene Epoch	65	Modern angiosperms appear	Archaic placental mammals appear; modern birds
MESOZOIC ERA	Age of Reptiles		Cretaceous Period	136	Conifers decrease; flowering plants increase	Large reptiles (dinosaurs) at peak, then disappear; small marsupials; toothed birds; modern fishes
			Jurassic Period	190	Conifers, cycads dominant; flowering plants appear	Large reptiles spread; first birds; modern sharks and bony fishes; many bivalves
			Triassic Period	225	Conifers increase; cycads appear	Reptiles increase; first mammals; bony fishes
PALEOZOIC ERA	Age of Amphibians		Permian Period	280	Seed ferns disappear	Amphibians decline; reptiles increase; modern insects
			Carboniferous Period	345	Tropical coal forests; seed ferns, conifers	Amphibians dominant; reptiles appear; rise of insects
	Age of Fishes		Devonian Period	395	First forests; horsetails, ferns	Early fishes spread; amphibians appear; many mollusks, crabs
	Age of Invertebrates		Silurian Period	430	First land plants	Scorpions and spiders (first air-breathers on land)
			Ordovician Period	500	Algae dominant	First vertebrates; worms; some mollusks and echinoderms
			Cambrian Period	570	Algae, fungi; first plant spores	Most invertebrate phyla; trilobites dominant
PRE-CAMBRIAN				?	Probably bacteria, fungi	A few fossils; sponge spicules; soft-bodied invertebrates
				4,500		Life arises; no fossils

Figure 23-2. Geologic time scale.

a geologic scale of relative time was constructed (see Figure 23-2). For most of the more than 4 billion years of the earth's history there is little or no evidence of life. This timespan, which represents the bottom of the geologic column, is known as *Precambrian time,* or, sometimes, as the Precambrian era. Suddenly, about 570 million years ago, a dramatic change took place. There was a "flowering" of living forms. We know this from the abundance of fossils dating from that time. From these earliest known fossils until the present we have a continuous, constantly changing record of life on earth.

As you can see in Figure 23-2, the geologic time scale is divided into three *eras—Paleozoic* (ancient life), *Mesozoic* (middle life), and *Cenozoic* (recent life). The boundaries between these eras are quite clearly marked by major breaks in the rock record. These breaks indicate widespread crustal events, such as mountain building, subsidence, or changes in sea level.

The eras are further subdivided into time units called *periods,* which in turn are broken down into *epochs.* In some cases, periods are named for the geographic area where geologists first identified the rocks of that subdivision. For example, *Devonian* refers to the system of rocks first identified in Devonshire, England. Similarly, *Permian* refers to that part of the record first recognized near Perm, Russia. The names given to some periods refer to certain characteristics of the rocks from that period. Thus, *Carboniferous* indicates the presence of carbon or coal-bearing rocks. The boundaries between geologic periods

are generally considered to be breaks in the rock record. However, the physical and biological events represented by these breaks are less widespread than those that closed out the eras.

Epochs are usually named as simply lower, middle, and upper. Thus, the Cambrian period is divided into three epochs—lower Cambrian, middle Cambrian, and upper Cambrian. For the Cenozoic era, the epochs are assigned names that suggest their chronological order. For example, Paleocene means "ancient recent," while Pleistocene means "most recent." Although geologically very brief, the *Recent* epoch is also generally recognized. This epoch begins at the end of the last ice age, about 10,000 years ago.

As it was originally constructed, the geologic time scale was a scale of relative time. The rocks (and events) were arranged in chronological order. However, once radioactive-dating methods became available, geologists set to work to determine absolute dates and ages for the rocks and events contained in the chart. The results of this effort are also shown in Figure 23-2. The dates on the chart are expressed in millions of years before the present.

Notice that Precambrian time begins with the origin of the earth, about 4.5 billion years ago, and ends about 570 million years ago. So, the earth history record is practically devoid of fossils for about the first 4 billion years. The lack of fossils in Precambrian rocks does *not* mean that there was no life on earth for the first 4 billion years or so. It means, very simply, that the evidence is rather sketchy. The record of life in the Precambrian will be discussed in a later section of this chapter.

The beginning of the Paleozoic era marked a virtual "population explosion" of life forms that has continued to the present. As mentioned earlier, the plants and animals found in younger rocks are generally more complex and more specialized than those found in older rocks. However, this trend of evolutionary development is very slow. The Cambrian period began about 570 million years ago. Yet, the earliest dinosaurs did not appear for almost 350 million years after that.

Evidence of earliest man appears in the rock record about 2 million years ago. Compared to the total span of geologic time, this represents about

$$\frac{2{,}000{,}000 \quad \text{years}}{4{,}500{,}000{,}000 \text{ years}} \text{ or } \frac{1}{2{,}250} \text{ of the en-}$$

tire record! The earliest written record of man dates back to about 4,000 B.C., or about 6,000 years ago. This

event represents only $\dfrac{6{,}000}{4{,}500{,}000{,}000}$

or $\dfrac{1}{750{,}000}$ of the record. As you can

see, modern man's existence can hardly be noticed when compared to the entire span of geologic time!

Interpreting the Geologic History of an Area. We are now familiar with some of the tools and techniques used in reading the rock record. Let's use some of them to try to learn about the earth history of a particular area.

A geologist became interested in the rock structure of the area shown in Figure 23-3. He found exposures, or outcrops, of rock along the river bank, in the road cut and railroad embankment, in the quarries, in a well record, and at occasional outcroppings in the fields. He collected rock and fossil samples at the surface of several locations. Figure 23-4 is a simple map of the locations, showing the type of rock and whether or not fossils were found. Several locations have shale, others have limestone, and still others have sandstone. The map also shows that not all locations contained fossils.

Once the geologist had constructed this map of the surface rocks, he set about to "map" the rocks beneath the surface. He treated each rock type as a field. His next step was to locate the boundaries, or interfaces, between the fields. The interfaces are locations where two different rock types are in contact with each other. Such interfaces are called *contacts*.

Figure 23-3. Area used for geologic field study. The numbers indicate places where outcrops of bedrock are located.

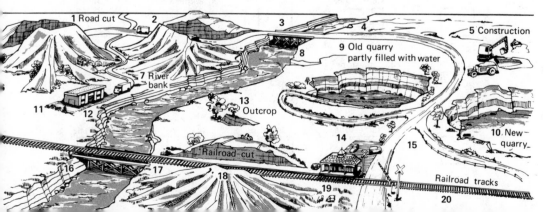

The dotted line in Figure 23-4 shows the probable location of the contact between shale and limestone. Notice that location 19 has no information about the rock-type or fossils. The geologist met a big dog at that location, and he (the geologist) beat a hasty retreat! He believes, however, that there is limestone at that location. Can you see why he would make this assumption? The solid line in Figure 23-4 represents the probable interface between limestone and sandstone.

Thus, based on his surface observations, the geologist has inferred the positions of two contacts—the shale-limestone and the limestone-sandstone. Notice that shale does not appear to contact sandstone anywhere in the area. It seems, then, that a shale-limestone-sandstone sequence may exist in the area. The next problem concerns the relative ages of the rock units. Which unit is oldest and which is youngest?

Notice that the contact lines drawn on the map are not like the isolines drawn to illustrate fields. Isolines connect points of equal value. The lines drawn on this map connect points where change occurs. However, in a sense an equal value does exist along these contact lines. They "connect" the only places where change occurs from one rock type to another. This map, which contains information about rock types and relative positions, is a geologic map. As more information about the area is collected, the geologic map will become more complete.

Let's return to the problem of determining the relative ages of the three rock units. From past experience, we should know that the youngest rock should contain the youngest fossils. In the three-rock sequence, the youngest rock should be on top and the oldest on the bottom. Since the geologist located the contacts by inference, he is not sure of the order of sequence. However, since there is no shale-

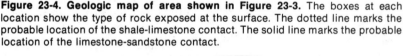

Figure 23-4. Geologic map of area shown in Figure 23-3. The boxes at each location show the type of rock exposed at the surface. The dotted line marks the probable location of the shale-limestone contact. The solid line marks the probable location of the limestone-sandstone contact.

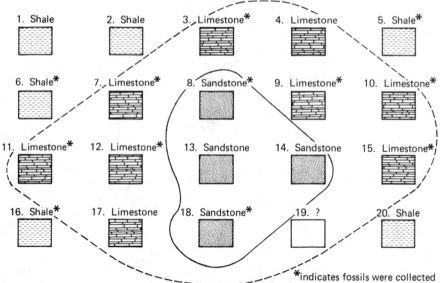

1. Shale   2. Shale   3. Limestone*   4. Limestone   5. Shale*

6. Shale*   7. Limestone*   8. Sandstone*   9. Limestone*   10. Limestone*

11. Limestone*   12. Limestone*   13. Sandstone   14. Sandstone   15. Limestone*

16. Shale*   17. Limestone   18. Sandstone*   19. ?   20. Shale

*indicates fossils were collected

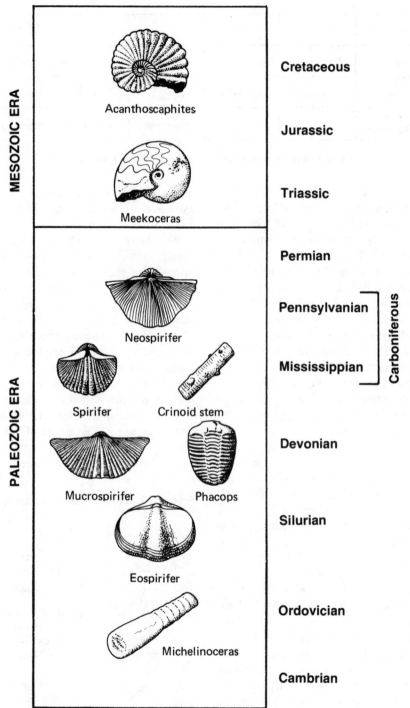

Figure 23-5. Some examples of index fossils from the Mesozoic and Paleozoic Eras.

Location	6	7	8	9	10
Fossil	*Eospirifer*	*Mucrospirifer*	*Neospirifer*	*Mucrospirifer*	*Phacops*
Age	Silurian	Devonian	Pennsyl-vanian	Devonian	Devonian
Age relationship	Oldest	Intermediate	Youngest	Intermediate	Intermediate

Table 23-1. Age relationships of fossils found at locations 6—10.

sandstone contact, he can deduce that the limestone is in the middle of the sequence. However, he is not sure which rock, shale or sandstone, is below the limestone and which is above. Let's see if the fossils he collected can help answer the question.

The only sequence of locations that cuts all of the rock contacts *and* at which fossils were collected is 6, 7, 8, 9, and 10. The following is a list of fossils collected at these locations: location 6—eospirifer; location 7—mucrospirifer; location 8—neospirifer; location 9—mucrospirifer; location 10—phacops.

Figure 23-5 shows some index fossils for the various periods of geologic time. Compare these fossils with the fossils collected at the locations listed above. The information in Table 23-1 shows the fossils, ages, and age relationships of the rocks and fossils at the five locations. The evidence suggests that the rocks at the surface of location 6 are the oldest (Silurian). The rocks at locations 7, 9, and 10 are from the same geologic period (Devonian), but 9 and 10 may be from a different epoch within that period. The rocks at location 8 are the youngest (Pennsylvanian). Although there is probably enough information to suggest an arrangement of the rock

layers, let's see if we can add to the evidence we already have before we make any decision.

We have determined that the youngest rock, sandstone, is at location 8. Are there any other locations we could check out? Referring back to Figure 23-4, we can see that sandstone is at the surface at locations 13, 14, and 18. These rocks should all be of the same age. Since the surface rocks at these locations represent the youngest rock formation in the area, we can predict that limestone of Devonian age should lie immediately below the sandstone. Shale of Silurian age should underlie the limestone. Based on these inferences, the

Figure 23-6. Rock column constructed from fossil evidence.

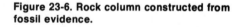
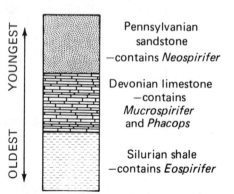

YOUNGEST ← → OLDEST

Pennsylvanian sandstone
—contains *Neospirifer*

Devonian limestone
—contains *Mucrospirifer* and *Phacops*

Silurian shale
—contains *Eospirifer*

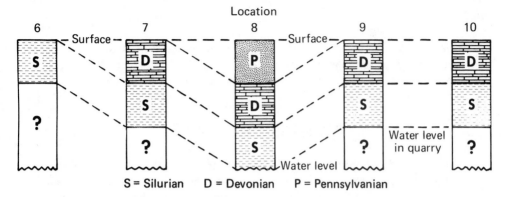

Figure 23-7. Rock columns of various locations in field study. The dotted lines show the probable correlations of the rock units.

geologist constructed the rock column shown in Figure 23-6 for these locations. Working from this model, he constructed columns for locations 6, 7, 8, 9, and 10 as shown in Figure 23-7. The dotted lines show the likely relationships between the columns, that is, the correlations between rock units. Figure 23-8 is a cross section of the area along the five locations described above.

Referring back to Figure 23-4, the geologist noted that the rock contacts form a roughly circular pattern. When this pattern is combined with the cross section of Figure 23-8, the overall picture suggests a depression, or bowl-shaped area. The farther one

travels from location 8, the older the rocks at the surface become. Such a pattern could have been caused by a downwarping of the rock layers, or by an uplifting of the rocks surrounding the area. A pattern of this kind in a layered rock formation is called a *syncline*.

Thus, using rock and fossil samples taken from the surface at a few scattered locations, the geologist has constructed a model of the area. If he wished to verify some of his inferences, he could return to the area and conduct a more detailed study. Undoubtedly, there are some outcroppings where the entire three-rock sequence is complete.

Figure 23-8. Probable bedrock structure across locations 6—10. This cross section was constructed from the rock columns that were inferred for the five locations.

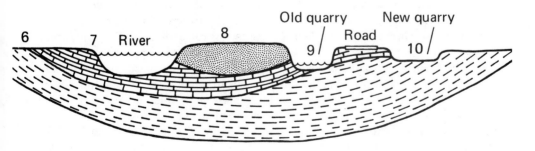

SUMMARY

1. Geologic history can be divided into time units based on fossil evidence.
2. Most of the geologic past is practically devoid of a fossil record.
3. Man's existence is extremely short in comparison with the entire span of geologic time.

THE FOSSIL RECORD

Throughout this chapter, we have been attempting to unravel the puzzle of earth history. Little by little, techniques have been developed that enable the investigator to recognize clues in the rock record. These clues are used to make inferences about the past. As we have seen, the fossil record is one of the most important tools geologists use in their efforts to read the record in the rocks. The fossil record provides evidence about the relative abundance of life in the past, and about the kinds of plants and animals that lived and the changes in life forms that have taken place.

For all practical purposes, the fossil record starts about 570 million years ago, in the rocks of the Cambrian period. However, as stated earlier, the lack of fossils in Precambrian rocks does not mean that there was no life on earth for the first four billion years or so. It means that the evidence is scarce and difficult to read. In fact, the entire Precambrian record is rather sketchy. Let's look at a few of the reasons why this is so.

Most Precambrian rocks are deeply buried beneath layers of younger rock. Therefore, only a small part of the record is available for examination and interpretation.

Most fossils are preserved in sedimentary rock. Precambrian rocks are, for the most part, nonsedimen-

tary—that is, they are igneous or metamorphic. Fossils are never found in igneous rocks. The intense heat of the molten magma destroys any traces of fossils. Likewise, the metamorphism of sedimentary formations would tend to destroy any fossil evidence they might have contained.

Actually, scientists *have* found evidence of life preserved in Precambrian rocks. This evidence consists of microscopic fossils of algae and fungi—plants that existed in a marine environment. The best evidence of animal life are trails and burrows of wormlike creatures preserved in some rocks.

Scientists have also found that many late Precambrian rocks contain large amounts of carbon. Many geologists believe that the carbon is organic in origin, which means that life was probably abundant during the later stages of the Precambrian. Unfortunately for those of us who would like to have a more legible record, most of the life forms were soft-bodied, so there was little chance of preservation as fossils. The Cambrian period marks the appearance of animals possessing hard parts—either shells or some form of skeleton. Such animals had a much greater chance of being preserved as fossils.

Variety of Life. The variety of life forms present and thriving on earth

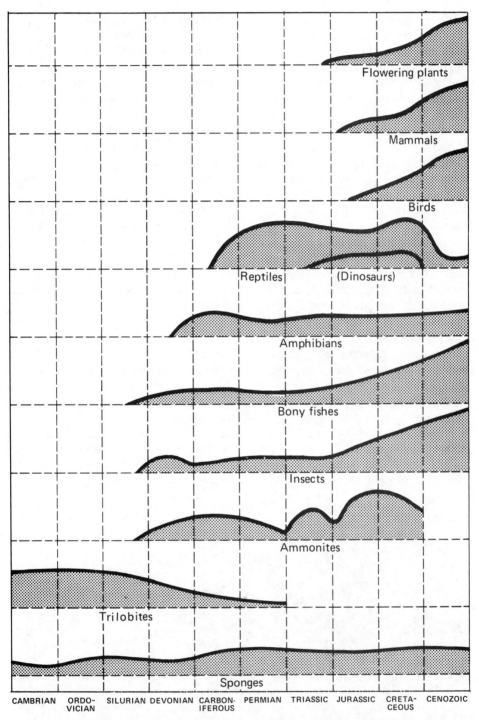

Figure 23-9. Variety of life. This chart shows the geologic time span and the relative abundance and diversity of a few selected types of animals and plants.

today staggers the imagination. And the fossil record indicates that variety has been the order of things since the beginning of the Cambrian, as is illustrated in Figure 23-9. In this diagram geologic time is shown along the horizontal axis, and the number of different kinds of some selected groups of organisms are shown along the vertical axis. These organisms include some invertebrates (animals without backbones), some vertebrates (animals with backbones), and one type of plant.

The horizontal length represents the span of existence of each group of organisms. Trilobites, for example, were present at the beginning of the Cambrian period and became extinct at the end of the Permian, a span of more than 300 million years. The rising and falling of the line representing a group of organisms shows the relative abundance and diversity of that group through time. Diversity refers to the variation in types within the group. More will be said about such variation later in this section.

Even though this diagram includes only a few of the past and present life forms, we can still draw some inferences from it. The record suggests that a wide variety of life forms came into existence, flourished for some period of time, and became extinct. A few organisms, such as the sponges, seem to have been present from the beginning of the Cambrian period and to have survived, relatively unchanged, through the present.

The dinosaurs, a subgroup of reptiles, are an example of a group that appeared, flourished briefly, and died out completely (see Figure 23-10). They existed only during the Triassic, Jurassic, and Cretaceous periods of the Mesozoic era. Man's existence in the Cenozoic era would hardly show in Figure 23-9. Yet how many science fiction movies have you seen that depict man and dinosaurs living at the same time?

Geologists believe that the fossil record contains only a part of the record of past life—probably a very small part. It is quite likely that many different types of organisms left no trace of their existence. Think about it this way — could you become a fossil? What kinds of evidence might be

Figure 23-10. *Tyrannosaurus rex.*

available a million years from now to show that you existed? What are the chances that your footprints left in wet sand might somehow be preserved until the sand was transformed into rock? What are the chances that any part of your body, including your bones, might not become completely decomposed? The chances of preservation are very slim.

In fact, the preservation of fossils is a pretty tricky business at best. If you stop and think about all of the different organisms that have lived and died without leaving a trace, you can begin to see how small the chances are of any particular organism becoming a fossil. Let's take a simplified look at what it takes to become fossilized.

As stated earlier, organisms that possess hard parts, such as shells or skeletons, have the best chance of being preserved. When an organism dies, its remains must be trapped in some medium, such as mud, tar, ice, or volcanic ash. Such burial serves two purposes: it protects the remains from scavengers and it seals them from bacteria, which would act to decompose them. If the organism stays buried long enough, and its remains (or traces of its remains) are *preserved* in some way, it is classified as a fossil. As mentioned above, this is a very simplified description of fossilization. It does not take into account the several means by which the actual preservation may take place. However, it should serve to point out the fact that becoming a fossil is not an "easy" thing to do.

Classification of Living Organisms. All you have to do is look around you to get some idea of the vast number and seemingly endless variety of living organisms. Because of this great

Kingdom	Animal
Phylum	Chordates
Class	Mammals
Order	Carnivores
Family	Felidae
Genus and species	*Felis catus*

Table 23-2. Classification of the house cat.

diversity of living things, and because of man's need to *organize* things into manageable units, scientists have tried for centuries to classify living organisms into groups. The classification of living organisms is called *taxonomy*. In one modern system of classification, living things are divided into three major groups, called *kingdoms*. The three kingdoms are: plant, animal, and protist. (Protists include very simple organisms, mostly single-celled, whose characteristics cannot be classified as either "plant" or "animal.")

Next, consider the organisms in just one of these divisions—the animal kingdom, for instance. Consider the diversity of organisms within this group, from the flea to the elephant, from the minnow to the whale. Obviously, this major division must be subdivided if the classification system is to be of any practical use. Table 23-2 shows the breakdown, or classification, of one type of organism within the animal kingdom—cats.

As you move down the list of subdivision names, each group is smaller and more specialized. For example, a large subdivision, or *phylum,* of the animal kingdom is the chordates. This group includes all animals with backbones (vertebrates) plus two other minor groups that share other characteristics with the vetebrates. By the time you get down to the last two subdivisions—genus and species—the organisms have many characteristics in common. In fact, the "scientific" name of an organism includes both its genus and species. Thus, an ordinary house cat is called *Felis catus.* Similarly, the scientific name for man is *Homo sapiens.*

Variations Within Species. For most purposes, *species* is the smallest subdivision used in the classification of organisms. A species is a group of organisms that live in similar habitats and *interbreed in nature.* However, even within the same species, there is a great deal of variation between individuals. The characteristics used to describe a species will apply to most of its members, but they generally will not apply to all of them.

The differences, or variations, among humans are quite obvious. Some of these differences include height, weight, skin color, hair color, and eye color. There are also less obvious differences, such as blood type. In other species, these differences may be less noticeable, but they do exist. As we will see, this variation among members of a species can be very important for the survival of the species.

Evolutionary Development. Let us consider a species whose members are doing very well in a particular environment. As long as the environment remains unchanged, the species will thrive. However, what happens when the environment very gradually begins to change? Here's where varia-

tion becomes important.

Some members of the species may be better adapted than others to survive under the new environmental conditions. That is, they may possess some seemingly minor, inherited characteristic that gives them a slightly better chance to survive and reproduce than the other members of their species. Under the original, stable environmental conditions this characteristic may have been of no importance whatsoever. But with the change in environment, it becomes important. After long periods of time, most members of the species will probably show this characteristic. Thus the species has undergone a change. Gradual change in a species over long periods of time is known as *evolution.* As the evolutionary process proceeds, the number of changes may be so great that a *new* species comes into existence. In this same way, entirely new groups of organisms evolve. Figure 23-11 illustrates what is thought to happen to species when their environment changes faster than they can adapt.

Extinction. Sometimes the environment undergoes an unusually sudden or drastic change. When this happens, many species become extinct. None (or too few) of their members possesses the characteristics necessary for survival of the species under the new conditions. Since this type of environmental change is not an "overnight" event—it can take many thousands, or even millions, of years—the species does not become extinct immediately after the first sign of environmental change. Extinction follows after relatively long periods of time, during which the population of the species gradually declines.

Figure 23-11. Evidence from the fossil record indicates that mass extinctions have occurred roughly every 26 million years.

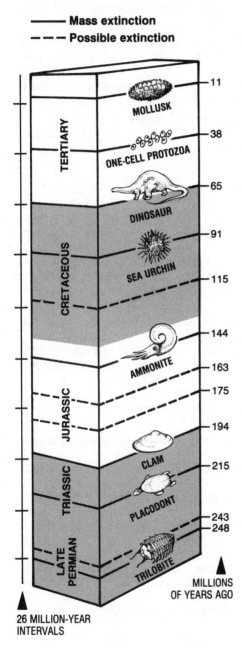

—— **Mass extinction**
‐ ‐ ‐ **Possible extinction**

TERTIARY

MOLLUSK — 11

ONE-CELL PROTOZOA — 38

DINOSAUR — 65

CRETACEOUS

SEA URCHIN — 91

— 115

— 144

AMMONITE — 163

JURASSIC

— 175

— 194

CLAM — 215

TRIASSIC

PLACODONT

— 243
— 248

LATE PERMIAN

TRILOBITE

MILLIONS OF YEARS AGO

26 MILLION-YEAR INTERVALS

Punctuated Equilibria. At the very beginning of this book, in the Prologue, we spoke of *observations* and *inferences* as they related to the development of *theories* about the environment. One theory was discussed that helps to explain why groups of life forms have become extinct in repeating time periods of approximately 26 to 30 million years.

In this section of Chapter 23 you have learned a little about the possible evolutionary development and extinction of life forms as described by the theory of evolution or, more properly, *natural selection.* As explained, most of these changes apparently take place over relatively long periods of geologic time due to environmental changes and variations within a species.

In recent years, however, new fossil evidence has caused some scientists to question the slow and gradual pace of evolution. Some fossil species have shown patterns of change that don't seem to follow the laws of natural selection. One pattern shows that entirely new species sometimes appear abruptly, nearly "overnight" in the fossil record. Accordingly, a new theory has been proposed. The theory of Punctuated Equilibria, in part, states that new species can arise very rapidly when small populations become isolated from large "parent" populations. These new species "punctuate" or interrupt the more gradual evolutionary changes within a large stable population.

One example that illustrates the theory of punctuated equilibria is that of a a new species of snail that appeared in the fossil record within a period of 50 thousand years, a length of time in the geologic record that is a mere "blink of the eye"!

SUMMARY

1. Fossil evidence suggests that a great many kinds of animals and plants have lived on earth in the past under a great variety of environmental conditions, and that most of them have become extinct.
2. Even though a large number of fossil types have been found, it is highly probable that an even greater variety of organisms lived and died, leaving no trace of their existence.
3. Variations within a species can be observed, measured, and described. Such variations may increase the probability of survival of that species.
4. Evolution is the gradual change in a species over long periods of time.
5. New studies of the fossil record have given rise to the theory of Punctuated Equilibria, which helps to explain the appearance of new species in relatively brief periods of geologic time.

REVIEW QUESTIONS

Group A
1. What is the geologic column?
2. On the basis of what evidence can geologic history be divided into time units?
3. At the beginning of what period in the earth's history did there appear to be a dramatic increase in the number and diversity of living forms? What evidence is there of life on earth before the beginning of that period?
4. What does fossil evidence suggest happened to many forms of life that existed on the earth during the past?
5. What can be said about variations within a species? How does variation among members of a species affect the chances for survival of that species?
6. What is meant by the term *evolution*?
7. What is meant by the term Punctuated Equilibria?

Group B
1. a. Why were fossils so important in the construction of the geologic column?
   b. What kinds of information are provided by a completed geologic column?
2. a. What percentage of the earth's total age was the Precambrian era?
   b. What percentage of the earth's total age was the Quaternary period (known as the Age of Man)? Refer to Fig. 23-2, page 449.
3. a. If you wanted to make a map showing the different kinds of rock layers underlying a certain area, what kinds of observations would you try to make?
   b. What is the meaning of the word contact as it is used in the study of rock layers?
4. a. Why have certain species of living things died out?
   b. How are the fossils that are found in recent rock layers different from the fossils found in old rock layers?

REVIEW EXERCISES

1. Analysis of three igneous rocks shows the following ratios of uranium-238 to lead-206.

   rock X — 8 U-238 : 0 Pb-206
   rock Y — 7 U-238 : 1 Pb-206
   rock Z — 3 U-238 : 1 Pb-206

   Refer to Figure 22-18 (page 442) and answer the following questions.
   a. Which sample of rock is the oldest? Which is the youngest?
   b. What is the probable age of each rock sample? (Estimate your answer to the nearest half-billion years.)

2. The five columns shown in the diagram below represent outcrops of rock observed along a highway. Each location is separated from the one next to it by several kilometers. Analyze the rock records carefully and answer the following questions.
   a. Which rock unit is oldest? At which location(s) is it found? Which rock unit is youngest? At which location(s) is it found?
   b. What is the relative order (sequence) of all the rock units?
   c. Describe 3 ways the rocks at the five locations can be correlated.
   d. Describe the probable geologic history of this area. List the sequence of events from oldest to youngest, beginning with the deposition of limestone (seen at location 1).

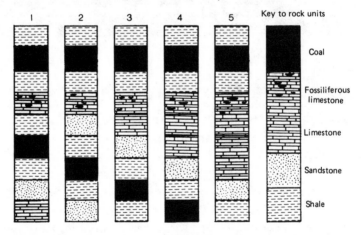

3. Fossils were found at five locations at the surface along a highway, as shown below. Refer to Figure 23-5 (page 453) and answer the following questions.
   a. What sequence of ages can be inferred from locations 1 to 5?
   b. What type of internal rock structure could explain the fossil record as it appears at the surface?

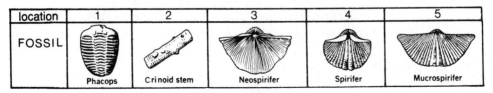

location	1	2	3	4	5
FOSSIL	Phacops	Crinoid stem	Neospirifer	Spirifer	Mucrospirifer

TOPIC XIV
LANDSCAPE DEVELOPMENT

Wind acting on loose sediments can create spectacular forms, like the Dumont Dunes in California.

CHAPTER 24
Landscape Characteristics

You will know something about landscapes if you can:

1. Describe some landscape characteristics that can be observed and measured.
2. Identify and describe landscape regions.

Throughout this course we have been considering changes in the earth. We have studied the processes that act at the interfaces of the atmosphere, hydrosphere, and lithosphere to bring about the changes. We have learned that the forces involved in these processes are constantly at work, ever changing our environment.

These final chapters will include a good deal of summarizing and "bringing together" of information and ideas from topics that were developed earlier in the course, as well as some new ideas about landscape. The study of landscapes is an appropriate one for this summing-up process, because the landscape occupies the unique position of being at the interface of the three "spheres" of the earth.

LANDSCAPE CHARACTERISTICS

Dictionary definitions of the word "landscape" often contain the word "scenery," for example, "a stretch of inland scenery as seen from a single point." Similar definitions could be applied to the words "seascape" and "riverscape." In this chapter, however, the scenic aspects of landscapes will be of secondary importance. We will be interested in the *topography* of the land—that is, the physical features of the earth's surface and their relationships to one another. For our purposes, then, the landscape of a region is the association of the physical features of the earth's surface in that region.

There are many terms that can be used to provide a general description of a landscape. A few such terms are *rugged, rolling, mountainous, flat, high,* and *low-lying.* Such terms are useful for giving a general idea about the *type* of landscape that is being described. However, in order to investigate the processes involved in the development of different landscapes, we must be more specific about the characteristics of a landscape. We will focus on characteristics that are readily observable and can be mea-

sured. Three such characteristics common to all landscapes are hillslopes, stream patterns, and soil associations.

Hillslopes. A *hill* can be defined as a natural elevation of the land surface rising noticeably above the surrounding land. Usually, the term "hill" is applied to features of limited elevation, perhaps 300 m or less from base to summit. A *mountain,* on the other hand, might be described as a very high hill. However, the distinction between "hill" and "mountain" is arbitrary. For example, the highest peaks in the Black *Hills* of South Dakota have higher elevations than do those of the White *Mountains* in New Hampshire.

As far as landscape characteristics are concerned, the *shape* of a hill tells us as much as, if not more than, elevation does about the physical features of a region. The shape of a hill is described in terms of its *hillslopes,* the sloping surfaces that form the sides of a hill.

As the term suggests, the basic characteristic of a hillslope is the slope, or steepness, of its angle from the horizontal. You might not ordinar-

Figure 24-1. Hillslopes. As the landscapes in these two photographs illustrate. hillslopes may range from very steep (left) to almost flat (right).

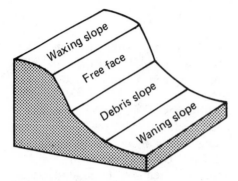

Figure 24-2. Model hillslope. All hillslopes can be described in terms of one or more of the divisions of this model.

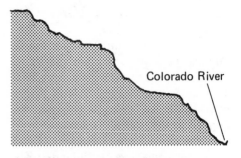

Figure 24-3. Cross section profile of one wall of the Grand Canyon.

ily think that either of the landscapes in Figure 24-1 have hillslopes. They illustrate, however, that hillslopes can range from vertical (90°), as in a sheer cliff, to almost horizontal (0°).

There is no such thing, then, as a "standard" hillslope. The model hillslope shown in Figure 24-2 was developed in order to make it possible to describe a hillslope in terms more specific than "gentle" or "steep." Based on this model, a hillslope can be divided into four regions. The *waxing slope* is the part at or near the crest of the hill. The *free face* consists of bedrock exposed at the surface. The *debris slope* is the part of the slope where fragments that have broken away from the free face accumulate. The *waning slope* is at the base of the hill and has a low angle of slope. The waning slope consists of weathered material transported from the debris slope or the free face. Remember, this is a model hillslope. Not all hillsides are made up of all four divisions. For example, some of the steep-sided hills in Figure 24-1 are almost all free face, with practically no waxing or waning slopes.

The steepness and shape of a hill-slope often varies in an irregular manner. Figure 24-3 is a drawing of the cross section of one wall (or hillslope) of the Grand Canyon at a point along the course of the Colorado River. Notice the varying angles or steepnesses of the slope. Not only can hillslopes vary along their distances, but the general shape or curvature of a hillslope can vary from convex (outwardly curved) to straight to concave (inwardly curved). The drawings in Figure 24-4 represent profiles of several different hillslope shapes.

Thus, hillslopes occur in a variety of shapes and steepnesses. The characteristics of a specific hillslope are a result of the effects of the many factors that shape the landscape. These factors will be investigated in Chapter 25. For now, it is important to realize that hillslopes can be used as *indicators* of the factors that shaped them.

Stream Patterns. Like hills and hillslopes, streams and stream patterns can reveal a great deal about the landscape of a region and the factors that shaped it. As you learned in Chapter 13, streams form when water falls on the earth and, under the influence of gravity, runs off toward areas of lower elevation. When rainfall begins to run

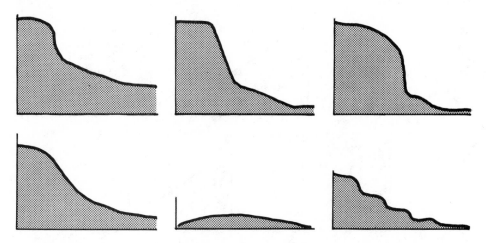

Figure 24-4. Hillslope shapes.

off over the surface, it flows in a layer, or sheet. As it accumulates in the lowest contours along its downhill path, the water forms small rivulets, or rills. These small channels, in turn, combine to form larger channels, which represent the first tributaries of a stream system. Small tributaries combine to form larger tributary streams. This growth of stream size continues until the main stream of the system reaches base level, the lowest elevation possible within the system.

You will also recall that the combination of the main stream and all its tributary streams is a *stream system,* and the region in which these streams flow is called a *drainage basin* (see Figure 15-5 on page 290). The limit, or boundary, of the basin is called the *drainage divide.* All water falling on the earth's surface within this boundary flows away from the divide toward the main stream. The drainage divide is also the line connecting the points of highest elevation surrounding the system.

Streams and stream systems have many characteristics that offer clues about the factors involved in shaping the landscape. The characteristics that we will focus on are stream gradient, drainage pattern, and drainage density.

Stream gradient. As discussed in Chapter 15, the slope of a stream bed, or the stream gradient, is an important factor in determining the velocity of the stream and thus its ability to erode. Erosion, the wearing down and carrying away of rock material, plays a vital role in shaping a landscape. It will be helpful, therefore, to examine stream gradients in profile. We can then measure the gradient and describe its changes for the stream as a whole, or for a particular segment of interest to us. Figure 24-5 shows examples of profiles we may find as we study different streams. Although stream profiles as they exist today may vary greatly, earth scientists have found that streams tend to acquire a certain "average" profile if given enough time to develop. Figure 24-6 shows the shape of this theoretical average stream profile. Note that it is concave all the way, with the

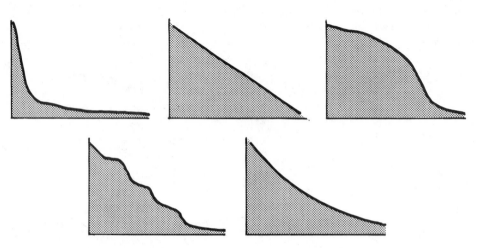

Figure 24-5. Stream profiles. As these drawings indicate, stream profiles vary greatly in shape and gradient.

slope gradually decreasing from source to base level.

The usefulness of the average stream profile is that we can look for variations *away* from the average in an actual stream. Figure 24-7 shows examples of real profiles that vary noticeably from the expected average. By studying the environment of the stream in each case, we may be able to infer the reasons for its particular profile.

Drainage patterns. Within a given region, the streams will form a certain arrangement known as a *drainage pattern.* Figure 24-8 shows several

Figure 24-6. An "average" stream profile.

regions with drainage patterns that differ considerably from one another.

How can we account for these differences? As with hillslopes and stream gradients, we will assume, for now, that the different drainage patterns are produced by the various factors that shape the landscapes. Careful analysis of the landscape characteristics may enable us to infer the reasons for the different patterns.

Drainage density. Another characteristic of stream systems that can be measured is the total length of the

Figure 24-7. Profiles of streams of various sizes. Notice that although the profiles may vary from the expected "average," they all tend to be at least slightly concave.

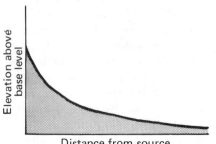

Distance from source

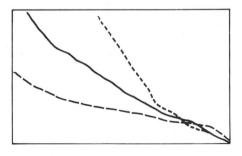

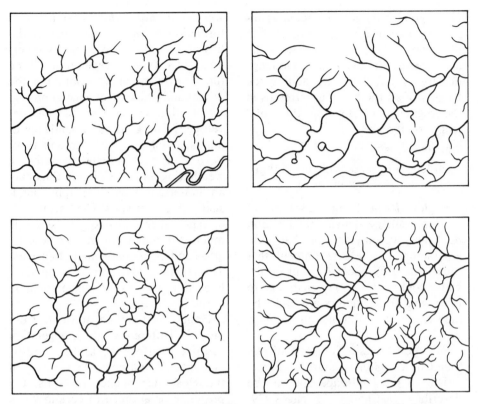

Figure 24-8. Drainage patterns. The different patterns reflect the various landscape characteristics of the regions in which they form.

streams that drain a given area compared with the area drained. Figure 24-9 shows two drainage basins of equal area. It is clear that there is a

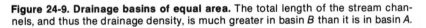

Figure 24-9. Drainage basins of equal area. The total length of the stream channels, and thus the drainage density, is much greater in basin *B* than it is in basin *A*.

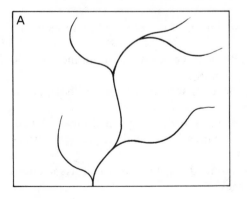
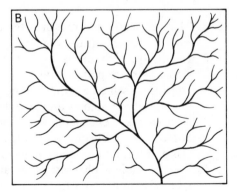

much greater length of stream channels per unit of area in region *B* than in region *A*. This characteristic is the *drainage density* of a region. Drainage density is calculated by adding the lengths of all the tributary streams in the region, and dividing this total length by the area:

drainage density =

$$\frac{\text{total length of stream channels (km)}}{\text{area of region (km}^2)}$$

Region *B* in Figure 24-9 has a greater drainage density than region *A*. Again, we may assume that there are factors in the environment that cause this difference. Careful observation and analysis may enable us to infer what these factors are and why they cause the difference in drainage density.

Soil Associations. The type of soil found in a region is another characteristic of the landscape that can be described. In Chapter 14 (pages 279-282) we considered some of the physical, chemical, and biological processes that produce different soil types. Soils that occur together and have similar characteristics make up a *soil association,* which is similar to a formation in rocks. The characteristics of a soil association partly determine what type of vegetation will be found growing in a region. On the other hand, the type of vegetation also affects the type of soil that has developed. The kind and abundance of plants, combined with the soil type, have important effects on rates of weathering and erosion and thus play an important part in shaping landscape characteristics. The "scenery," or appearance, of wooded hillslopes is much different from that of deserts, grasslands, or bare mountainsides. This surface appearance is also related to processes of change going on in the landscape.

Plants must obtain nutrients from the soil. Different kinds of vegetation require different kinds and/or amounts of nutrients. As a result of the close dependence on soils, the presence or absence of certain kinds of vegetation frequently serves as an indicator of soil type. This aspect of landscape—soil and vegetation—will help us to interpret the factors involved in shaping the landscape.

SUMMARY

1. The landscape of a region is the association of the physical features of the earth's surface in that region.
2. Landscape characteristics that can be observed and measured include hillslopes, stream patterns, and soil associations.
3. Hillslopes, which are the sloping surfaces that form the sides of hills, occur in a variety of shapes and steepnesses.
4. A stream system includes all the streams within a given drainage basin. Some measurable characteristics of stream systems include gradient, drainage pattern, and drainage density.
5. Soils of similar characteristics are grouped together as a soil association, which is similar to a formation in rocks.

Figure 24-10. A mountain landscape.

LANDSCAPE REGIONS

If you have traveled around the country, looked at photographs of different regions, or viewed the scenery in television programs and movies, you are probably aware that the landscape is not the same everywhere. In some parts of the country, a typical view would be similar to that shown in Figure 24-10, a region of jagged peaks, small, rushing streams, and forests. This region is readily identified as a *mountain* landscape.

Figure 24-11. A plains landscape.

Figure 24-12. A plateau landscape.

In other parts of the country, the landscape is like that shown in Figure 24-11, "flat as a pancake." Broad rivers or streams seem to prevail, and the vegetation consists mainly of grasslands. This region has a *plains* landscape.

Still other areas consist of rolling hills, such as those shown in Figure 24-12. There are streams of many different sizes. Forests predominate, and the land is somewhat like a mountain region, but not as rugged. In fact, the tops of all the hills are at about the same elevation. Such a region has a *plateau* landscape.

Essentially, then, we can say that there are three *types* of continental landscape regions—mountains, plains, and plateaus. These three types of landscape are classified on the basis of certain general characteristics. Some of these characteristics are related to elevations. In general, mountains not only have high elevations, but they also have large differences in elevation from point to point, a characteristic called *relief*. Mountains usually have high relief and a great variety of hillslope shapes and gradients. Plains generally have

low elevations (that is, they are near sea level) and very little relief. Plateaus are intermediate between mountains and plains in these respects. They usually have moderate elevations combined with moderate relief.

The characteristics just described are surface features that can be easily observed and measured. These features are related to the structure of the underlying rock formations. Mountains are usually the result of uplift accompanied by distortions of the rock structure, such as faults, folds, and tilted layers. Mountains are usually composed of much nonsedimentary rock. Their internal structure is therefore often complex. Plains are often the result of prolonged periods of sedimentation accompanied by subsidence, or sinking. Their internal structure is horizontal. However, some plains are the remains of old mountains that have been eroded almost to base level. In these cases, the underlying structure may be quite complex. Plateaus are the result of uplift without much distortion. Their structure is, therefore, basically horizontal, with relief resulting from erosion rather than folding or faulting.

Table 24-1 is a summary of the characteristics that are typical of each of the three types of landscape region. Within any continental land mass, we can usually identify examples of all three landscape types. In fact, most large land areas can be divided into landscape regions with distinct boundaries. Figure 24-13 is a photograph of a model relief map of the United States. To make the differences in elevation easier to see, the vertical scale of the map is exaggerated, that is, it is much greater than the scale of horizontal distances. Figure 24-14 shows the boundaries between the main landscape regions of the continental United States. You should be able to match each region in Figure 24-14 with the differences in relief that can be seen in Figure 24-13.

Many of the main landscape regions can be subdivided. For example, the Appalachian Highland region can be subdivided into three specific regions—the Appalachian Plateau, the Appalachian Mountains, and the Piedmont Plateau. These more specific regions are known as *geologic,* or *physiographic, provinces,* which are regions in which *all* parts are similar in structure and climate. For our purposes, it will be sufficient to recognize the landscape regions set off by the boundaries shown in Figure 24-14.

Earlier in this chapter, we mentioned the major soil types found in the continental United States. The map in Figure 24-15 shows the distribution of these soil types. Compare the shapes of the landscape regions shown in Figure 24-14 with the shapes

Table 24-1. Characteristics of the three main types of landscape region.

	Hillslopes	Streams	Soils
Mountains	1. High elevation 2. Steep slopes 3. Small waxing slopes 4. Large free face 5. Variable debris slopes	1. Steep gradients 2. High velocity water 3. Small streams	1. Thin topsoil 2. Very little subsoil 3. Bedrock exposed over large areas
Plains	1. Low elevation 2. Hills very low or nonexistent 3. Mostly waning slopes	1. Low gradients 2. Meandering paths	1. Deep topsoil 2. Subsoil 3. Fertile land for crops
Plateaus	1. Medium to high elevation 2. Steep to gradual hillslopes 3. Shorter free face than mountains 4. Longer waxing slope and waning slope than mountains	1. Steep to gradual gradients 2. Rushing streams to broad, high volume rivers	1. Variable soils thin in uplands, thicker in valleys 2. Valley areas fertile and productive

Figure 24-13. Model relief map of the United States.

©RAND McNALLY & COMPANY, R. L. 76-Y-49

Figure 24-14. The main landscape regions of the United States.

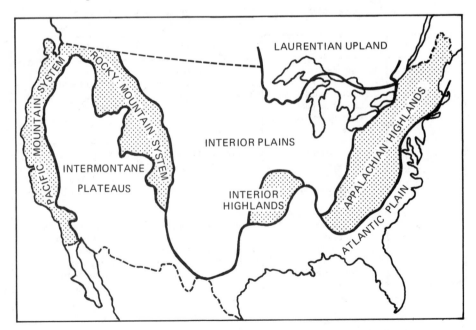

of the various soil locations shown.

In Chapter 15 (page 290) we defined a drainage basin as the area drained by a single stream system. A continental area can also be divided into drainage *regions* in which all streams empty into the *same body of water*. Figure 24-16 shows the map of the continental United States divided in this way. The line running mainly north and south through the western states is called the Continental Divide. It follows the points of maximum elevation through the Rocky Mountain System. All streams to the west of this divide empty into the Pacific Ocean.

A second line separates the streams that flow south into the Gulf of Mexico from those that flow east into the Atlantic Ocean or north into the Great Lakes and the St. Lawrence River (which also empties into the Atlantic). We have already seen (page 290) that the Mississippi River System drains most of the large central region bounded by these two main divides. However, there are many small stream systems that flow directly into the Gulf of Mexico without joining the Mississippi System.

Up to now in this section we have been discussing the general landscape characteristics of a rather large land area—the continental United States. The same methods can be used to study a land area of any size. Of course, the smaller the area studied, the easier it is to be more specific about the landscape characteristics and the factors that influenced the shape of the landscape.

Figure 24-15. Distribution of major soil types in the United States. The soil types represented are (*A*) desert soils, (*B*) grassland soils, and (*C*) forest soils. The unmarked region is generally mountainous. Such regions usually have little, if any, soil development associated with them.

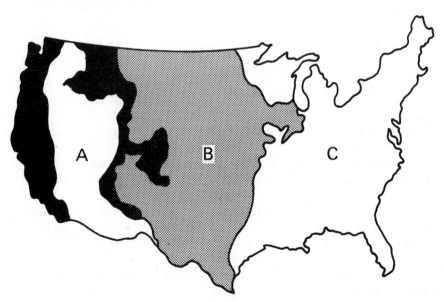

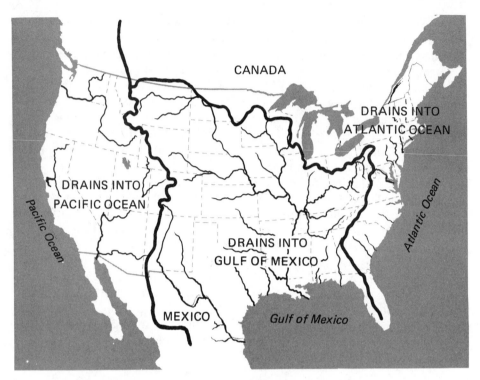

Figure 24-16. Drainage regions of the United States. The heavy lines mark the boundaries, or divides, of the major drainage areas of the country.

SUMMARY

1. Sets of landscape characteristics occur together, forming distinctive landscape regions.
2. There are three types of landscape regions—mountains, plains, and plateaus. These regions are classified according to elevation and internal geologic structure.
3. Mountains are regions of high elevation, great relief, and distorted rock structure; plains are regions of low elevation, little relief, and usually horizontal rock structure; plateaus are regions of medium to high elevation, moderate relief, and horizontal rock structure.
4. Any continental land mass has several distinct landscape regions. The boundaries between landscape regions are usually well defined.

REVIEW QUESTIONS

Group A   1. What are some general characteristics of a landscape that can be observed and measured?
2. What characteristic is used to describe the shape of a hill? Name and briefly describe the four regions of a model hillslope.
3. What are some characteristics of a stream system that can be observed and measured?
4. What is meant by a soil association? What are some characteristics of soils that can be observed and measured?
5. What are the three major types of continental landscape regions? What characteristics are used for classifying these regions?
6. How can you tell when you have traveled from one landscape region to another?

Group B   1. Explain how a hillslope could exist that was missing one of the parts shown in Fig. 24-2.
2. Explain how to find a drainage divide on a road map.
3. Explain why vegetation is a useful indicator of soil types.
4. a.   A term used to describe landscapes is relief. What does it mean?
   b.   Describe the relief of the following : mountainous landscape, plains, plateau.
5. a.   Which type of landscape region shown in Table 24-1, page 473, best describes where you live? Explain.
   b.   Which major drainage region do you live in? See Fig. 24-16.

Glaciers are huge sheets or rivers of ice that can round peaks, carve valleys, and create hills of rock debris.

CHAPTER 25
Environmental Factors in Landscape Development

You will know something about landscape development if you can:
1. Describe the effects of uplifting and leveling forces on the various landscape characteristics.
2. Describe the effects of climate on the various landscape characteristics.
3. Describe the effects of bedrock on the landscape characteristics of an area.

In our investigation of landscape development we have taken the usual first steps in every scientific inquiry – we have looked around us, made observations, and attempted to classify them. We have observed a variety of landscape types and we have devised ways of describing and measuring their characteristics.

We are now ready for the next stage – a search for the "why" and "how" of landscape differences. We are quite sure that we live on a changing planet. We know quite a bit about the changes going on at the surface as well as deep within the earth. Can we use that knowledge to account for the landscapes we see today and perhaps to predict what will happen to them in future ages?

INTRODUCTION

As defined in Chapter 24, the landscape of a region is the association of the physical features of the earth's surface in that region. We also learned that there are certain measurable characteristics that can be used to describe all landscapes. These characteristics are hillslopes, stream patterns, and soil associations. We are now ready to investigate those factors in the environment that act to shape the landscape and to produce the characteristics of the various types of landscapes.

The environmental factors to be considered include uplifting and leveling forces, climate, bedrock, and man's activities. Of these four factors, the first three are all due to natural processes. These three factors will be investigated in this chapter. The fourth factor, human activities, will be considered in Chapter 26.

The overall process of landscape development is very complex. Although there are several factors that can and do influence landscapes, they may not all be operating at a particular time and place. As we investigate the interactions of the environmental factors with landscape characteristics, you may find it helpful to keep a "running account" of the effects of each factor on each characteristic. The table, or grid, shown in Figure 25-1 illustrates one method of organizing the information in a written record. You may want to make a large copy of this table and fill it in as we go along.

There is no practical way to determine the relative importance of the environmental factors, so the order in which they are listed has no particular importance. Likewise, the landscape characteristics are not listed in any particular order. As we investigate each interaction, we can summarize the information gained and place it in the box that represents that interaction. An example of such an interaction would be the effect of climate on stream patterns. This information would be entered in the box in row 2, column 2. After our investigations are completed, we should be able to summarize the effect of any given environmental factor on all of the landscape characteristics. We should also be able to determine how a single characteristic is affected by each of the environmental factors.

Figure 25-1. Relationships between environmental factors and landscape characteristics.

		Hillslopes	Stream patterns	Soils
ENVIRONMENTAL FACTORS	Crustal change— uplift and leveling			
	Climate			
	Bedrock			
	Human Activities			

UPLIFTING AND LEVELING FORCES

Wherever hillslopes exist, the forces of weathering, erosion, and deposition are acting to reduce the slopes and make the surface horizontal. These forces are called *leveling* forces. They are also referred to as *destructional* forces, because they tend to destroy variations in the landscape. The leveling forces act almost entirely at the interfaces between the three "spheres" of the earth.

Although the leveling forces are acting continuously to bring the land down to a uniform, flat surface, they never do accomplish this result. The reason is that there are *uplifting,* or *constructional,* forces that undo the work of the leveling forces. These forces operate beneath or within the crust. They include volcanic activity, isostasy, earthquakes, ocean-floor spreading, and continental drift.

As far as landscapes are concerned, the effects of these two groups of forces are opposite. Uplifting tends to increase elevations and also to roughen, or increase the relief of, the surface. Leveling tends to reduce elevations and smooth the surface. In any particular region at any particular time the rates of uplift and leveling are likely to be different. If the uplifting forces are raising the surface faster than the leveling forces are lowering it, we say that the uplifting forces are *dominant.* In other cases, the leveling forces may be dominant. In some places, the rates of uplift and leveling may be approximately equal, and the landscape will be in a state of dynamic equilibrium.

How can we determine which group of forces is dominant in a region or whether they are in balance? The processes are far too slow for us to observe the changes directly. However, we can observe the present characteristics of the landscape and infer whether uplift, leveling, or neither is dominant at the present time. Let us consider the different effects of uplift and leveling on the various landscape characteristics.

Hillslopes. In regions where uplifting forces are dominant, hillslopes reflect this fact in several ways. Gradients are generally steep, and free face predominates. The other hillslope characteristics—waxing, waning, and debris slopes—are relatively small or even nonexistent. An example of a situation in which uplift is dominant is found where vertical movement along a fault is occurring on a large scale. One result of such crustal movement may be the formation of *fault block mountains,* as illustrated in Figure 25-2. Figure 25-3 is a

Figure 25-2. Formation of a fault-block mountain.

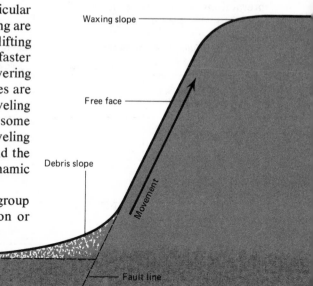

Waxing slope

Free face

Debris slope

Movement

Waning slope

Fault line

Figure 25-3. Region in which uplift has occurred at a faster rate than erosion.

photograph of a typical landscape in which this kind of uplift is apparently occurring. The unbranched, V-shaped gullies in the free face indicate that erosion is just beginning. Sediment carried down the large gulley in the center of the photo has come to rest on the valley floor in a characteristic pattern called an alluvial fan. True debris slopes are absent. Uplift has occurred here at a much faster rate than leveling.

In Figure 25-4 we see a region where leveling has apparently kept in step with uplifting. The many branching gulleys and stream beds indicate that erosion has been going on for a fairly long time. The debris slopes, waning slopes, and valleys between the hillslopes are larger than in the region of Figure 25-3. Much sediment has been transported and deposited in the foreground. Still, the free face of the hillslopes is extensive, and there is little waxing slope. So we can conclude that uplift has been opposing the

effects of leveling and maintaining the features of a recently uplifted landscape.

We have previously seen examples of regions where leveling and deposition are clearly dominant over uplift. Figure 15-13 on page 298 is typical. Erosion by running water is the chief leveling force. Note the gentle gradients, broad waxing slopes, extensive waning slopes, and almost complete absence of free face on the hillslopes still remaining in this landscape. At this time, very little uplift, if any, is occurring here.

Earlier we saw how uplifting forces can change the earth's surface in regions where zones of weakness, or faults, are present. These forces can thrust part of the crust upward along a fault. Uplifting forces can also cause parts of the earth's surface to be elevated without faulting taking place. Internal pressures can cause the crust to *warp* or *fold*. These internal pressures may be exerted vertically, hori-

Figure 25-4. Region in which uplift and erosion have occurred at about the same rate.

zontally, or in both directions at the same time. If these pressures are exerted over a large enough area, extensive regions of the crust may be affected. The result may be a vertical uplifting of a region to form a plateau, or a gentle warping of the crust to form an arch that extends over several hundreds of kilometers. Often, less extensive areas of the earth's crust are deformed by these internal pressures.

If the internal pressure is exerted vertically, the crust may warp upward to form a circular or oval-shaped hill called a *dome* (see Figure 25-5). When internal pressures are exerted horizontally, the result may be a folding of the crust. Such folding can produce a single, elongated hill, or ridge. In other cases, the crust is "wrinkled" into several folds, which results in a series of ridges, as illustrated in Figure 25-6.

The photograph in Figure 25-6 is an aerial view of a series of ridges in the Appalachian Mountains near Harrisburg, Pennsylvania. The streams in this landscape have a surprising characteristic. Instead of following the valleys between the folds, as we might expect them to do, they have

Figure 25-5. A dome.

Figure 25-6. Ridges in the Appalachian Mountains where streams cut across the mountains.

cut into and across the uplifted folds. How could streams have done this?

By studying the exposed rock layers and the fossil record they contain, geologists have reconstructed the history of this region. The methods are similar to those used to unravel the earth history puzzle in Chapter 23 (page 451). The cross-sectional models in Figure 25-7 show the important stages of the landscape development of the region that have been inferred. At one time there were mountains that had been formed by folding of layers of rock. These mountains had been eroded down almost to

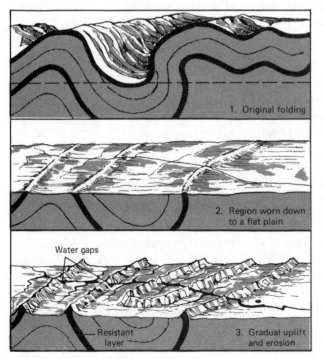

1. Original folding

2. Region worn down to a flat plain

Water gaps

Resistant layer

3. Gradual uplift and erosion

Figure 25-7. Stages of landscape development near Harrisburg, Pennsylvania. The mountains produced by the original folding of the area (1) were worn away by weathering and erosion, producing a flat, plainlike landscape (2). Gradual uplift of the region has resulted in the present landscape (3).

a flat plain, sloping gently to the east. Streams flowed across this plain, following the downward slope. Then the entire region was uplifted again by folding. However, this process was so slow that the streams did not have to leave their channels. They were able to cut down into the folds as fast as they were raised and thus maintain their generally eastward flow. A valley cut across a ridge by a stream is called a *water gap*. Several water gaps in the Appalachian Mountains became important trails and roads across the mountains during the westward expansion of our nation.

Whatever the manner in which uplift occurs, the effect of uplifting forces is to increase the relief of a portion of the earth's surface. This, in turn, changes hillslopes. Their gradients become steeper. As we shall see, these changes have a marked effect on the other environmental factors that influence the shape of the landscape.

Shoreline Landscapes. The shape and characteristics of land adjacent to a large body of water is called a *shoreline landscape*. For our purposes, we will consider a shoreline landscape to be one adjacent to the sea, although lakeshore landscapes are also affected, to a much lesser degree, by many of the same factors that shape a seashore landscape. As you might expect, shoreline landscapes have certain features and characteristics not found in inland landscapes. One reason for this fact is that the leveling activity, or erosion, that occurs along a shoreline is due mainly to wave action, that is, water driven by wind rather than gravity.

Base level in a shoreline region is

sea level, and elevations of the land are expressed relative to sea level. Shorelines are usually classified according to the *change* in elevation of the land surface relative to the surface of the water. Such changes can be due to vertical movements of the land (uplift or subsidence) or changes in sea level. Thus, the three main classes of shorelines are shorelines of emergence, shorelines of submergence, and neutral shorelines.

Shorelines of emergence. As the name suggests, shorelines of emergence are formed when part of the ocean floor near the border of a continent emerges to become part of the landscape. This emergence can be due to crustal uplift, or it can be due to a drop in the level of the ocean. In shorelines of emergence, the water line takes a position against what was once part of the sea floor. Generally speaking, shorelines of emergence are fairly straight or regular.

In some areas, the sea floor adjacent to the continent is part of the continental shelf. The surface of the shelf is relatively smooth and has a gentle slope. Therefore, if part of this shelf emerges, the shoreline landscape produced is a low, smooth, gently sloping coastal plain.

In areas where the sea floor drops sharply, emergence produces a steeply sloping shoreline. In this case, wave action undercuts the hillslope, making it even steeper. Eventually, the oversteepened slope breaks away, forming a *wave-cut cliff*. Wave action and weathering further break down the accumulating debris, reducing it to sand. The sand can be transported by currents and distributed along the shoreline and carried offshore to greater depths in the water. This entire process is summarized in Figure 25-8.

One result of this process is to move the hillslope inland. At the same time a fairly flat beach or *terrace* develops at the base of the hillslope. We have seen an example of this in Figure 19-5, page 370. If emergence occurs at intervals, with periods of stability between them, a series of wave-cut cliffs and terraces at different elevations, looking much like a flight of steps, may develop.

Shorelines of submergence. Whenever the land adjacent to the water subsides, or when sea level rises, a shoreline of submergence is formed. The new water line takes a position along what was a contour of the dry land. Most shorelines of submergence are quite irregular. The outline of the shoreline will depend on what the topography of the land was before submergence.

If the topography consisted of a series of hills, and valleys, submergence produces a very irregular shoreline. Former valleys become deeply indented bays, hilltops become islands, and ridges become promontories or peninsulas. If the topography consisted of a coastal plain of low relief, the new shoreline will be fairly regular, with numerous low-lying offshore islands.

A special type of shoreline of submergence is formed in coastal regions that have been deeply eroded by valley glaciers. When such a coastline submerges, deep, steep-walled, narrow estuaries called *fiords* are formed.

Neutral shorelines. Neutral shorelines develop when there is no relative change in elevation between the land and the water. In such cases, the shorelines tend to become built out further into the water as streams bring sediments down to their mouths. Bays become filled in and deltas or sand bars may form. If there is volcanic activity near the shoreline, the shoreline will be built out by accumulations of debris from the eruptions.

Figure 25-8. Stages in the development of a wave-cut cliff and terrace.

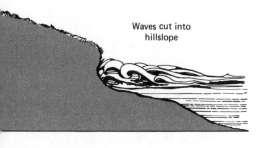

Waves cut into hillslope

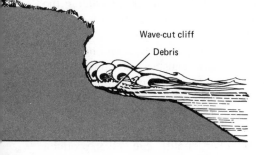

Wave-cut cliff

Debris

Terrace with sandy beach

Figure 25-9. Entrenched meanders in the San Juan River, Utah.

Stream Patterns. As discussed in Chapter 24, stream systems can be described in terms of several characteristics—stream gradient, drainage pattern, and drainage density. Of these three characteristics, the one that is *most* affected by uplifting and leveling forces is gradient.

Whenever uplifting forces produce an increase in hillslope, stream gradients are also increased. Increasing stream gradient increases the velocity, and therefore the eroding power, of a stream, as we learned in Chapter 15. Thus, even as uplifting forces are raising the elevation of the surface, they are also increasing the "leveling" ability of one of the most effective erosional agents—that of running water.

The photograph in Figure 25-9 provides dramatic evidence of the effect that uplift can have on the eroding power of a stream. You can see that the stream in the photograph has a meandering course. As you learned in Chapter 15, a meandering course is usually associated with a river that is

flowing over a relatively flat region that is quite near base level. Such was the case with this river before the region underwent uplift. When the region was uplifted, the stream gradient became steeper and the erosional power of the stream was increased. The "rejuvenated" stream cut vertically into the bedrock, producing the steep-sided *incised,* or *entrenched, meanders* shown here.

We have just seen a second example of uplift causing a stream to erode deeper into its channel, but without changing its course. (The earlier example was the development of water gaps described on page 484.) However, uplift can also produce changes in stream channels and drainage patterns. The patterns that develop are greatly influenced by the characteristics of the bedrock in the region. We will therefore postpone a discussion of drainage patterns until we reach the subject of bedrock composition later in this chapter.

Soil Formation. The formation of soil is influenced mostly by climate and bedrock. The effect of uplifting and leveling forces on soil and its development is confined mainly to determining regions of erosion and deposition. As discussed in Chapters 15 and 16, erosion is generally dominant in regions of high elevation and steep hillslopes and stream gradients. Thus, the earth materials from which soils are formed and developed are being transported from these regions. On the steep hillslopes of mountainous regions, soils are generally thin and poorly developed. On the other hand, deposition is dominant in regions of low elevation and gradual hillslopes and stream gradients. As noted in Chapter 15, this is where deep soils are likely to form.

Crustal change may have a more direct effect on soils when volcanic activity is involved. Volcanic eruptions result in new rock material being deposited on the earth's surface. This new rock material can be weathered to form soil. Volcanic material is often rich in plant nutrients, and as weathering progresses, plants can take root and flourish on the volcanic soil. As more and more plants grow, the soil becomes deeper and more fertile.

In summary, uplifting and leveling forces influence landscape characteristics directly and indirectly. These forces most directly affect surface elevations and hillslopes. In turn, changes in elevation and hillslope gradients influence other factors, such as stream gradients (and, thus, their eroding powers) and soil formation. As you can see, there is a great deal of interaction and interdependence among the processes that act to shape the landscapes.

SUMMARY

1. Landscapes seem to result from the interaction of two groups of opposing forces. These groups are the uplifting, or constructional forces, and the leveling, or destructional, forces.
2. In a particular landscape, one of the groups of forces may be dominant.
3. Shorelines are classified according to the change in elevation of the land surface relative to sea level. The three main classes of shorelines are shorelines of emergence, shorelines of submergence, and neutral shorelines.
4. The rate of crustal change, either uplift or subsidence, may alter, modify, or produce characteristic hillslopes, stream patterns, or soil conditions.

CLIMATE

As you will recall from Chapter 13, climate refers to the average conditions of temperature and moisture in a region over an extended period of time. In this section, we will investigate the influence that climate has on the various landscape characteristics.

Hillslopes. The photographs in Figures 25-10 and 25-11 were taken in two different regions of the United States. The landscape in Figure 25-10 developed in a region where the ratio of precipitation to potential evapotranspiration (P/E_p) is quite high

Figure 25-10. Catskill Mountains of New York State. This region has a humid climate.

(see Chapter 13). This region has a humid climate. On the other hand, the region shown in Figure 25-11 has an arid climate, with a low P/E$_p$ ratio.

One striking difference between the two landscapes is the sharpness of landform features. Arid landscapes have angular or sharp hillslope features, while hillslopes in the humid environment appear more rounded. Free face is much more prominent on arid hillslopes.

As stated earlier, it is just about impossible to pick out one factor as being responsible for producing the particular features of a landscape. Rather, the interaction of all of the environmental factors must be considered. However, the reasons for the differences between the characteristics of the hillslopes shown in the two photographs can be summed up quite accurately in a single word— *moisture*. Moisture is the key to the

Figure 25-11. Death Valley, California. This region has a very arid climate.

processes of weathering, erosion, and soil formation and development. Moisture is also vital to the growth and support of vegetation.

These differences between hillslopes in arid and humid climates are observed all over the world. We may safely infer that the differences are related to the difference in the availability of moisture. How does the amount of moisture influence the landscape development?

Where mountains have formed in an arid region, weathering is most likely to be physical. As explained in Chapter 14, moisture is needed for most processes of chemical weathering. Physical weathering tends to produce large, angular sediments, which roll down the steep free faces. These sediments, transported almost entirely by gravity, form accumulations called *talus* at the base of the hillslopes.

Because rainfall is infrequent, many of the streams in an arid region are *intermittent*. That is, water flows in them only when it rains, or when snow in higher elevations melts. These streams carry sediments to the intermountain areas, the low areas between hillslopes, where the water dries up and the sediments are deposited. These deposits are likely to include evaporites (see page 348). Thus, the hills are worn down, the hillslopes recede, and the intermountain areas become wider and filled with sediments. The overall result is that the relief of the region becomes less rugged.

Another characteristic of arid landscapes is the sparseness of vegetation. Vegetation performs two important functions in landscape development.

The organic matter provided by vegetation is necessary to the development of a mature soil. Of equal importance is the fact that the root systems and surface cover provided by vegetation act to hold the soil in place and thus resist soil erosion by wind and water.

In humid regions, much of the weathering of exposed rock faces is chemical in nature. Chemical weathering tends to produce smoother rock faces than the rough, jagged surfaces characteristic of physical weathering. More important, perhaps, is the fact that most chemical weathering occurs on the rock *surfaces*. As a rock is decomposed by chemical action, its surface often becomes pitted and more easily crumbled. Many of the smaller particles remain in place, forming pockets of thin soil on the hillslope. The adequate moisture makes it possible for grasses and small shrubs to take root and grow in these soil pockets. This vegetation adds to the chemical weathering of the rock beneath. As roots spread, they help hold the soil in place and may also play a role in physical weathering of the rock face.

The abundant rainfall produces permanent stream systems that erode the weathered sediments from the waxing slopes and free faces. These sediments are carried down to lower elevations and deposited, sometimes many kilometers away. The rapid weathering and the erosion by streams combine to reduce elevations and form the rounded hillslopes characteristic of humid regions. In humid regions, the steepness of hillslopes may also be reduced by landslides and slumping, as previously described on page 288. As a result of all these processes, gently rolling landscapes like that in Figure 24-12 on page 472 are produced.

What would happen if the climate in an area changed? It is logical to assume that, if the climate became more humid, landscape features would become more rounded. Similarly, if the climate of a region were to become more arid, and other environmental factors remain unchanged, landscape features would gradually become more angular.

Up to this point, we have been considering the effect of climate on hillslopes. However, hillslopes can also have an effect on climate. In other words, a landscape feature can act as an environmental factor. Suppose, for example, that there is a coastal plain exposed to prevailing winds from the ocean. This region is likely to have a moderately humid climate, as discussed in Chapter 13. Suppose that a crustal disturbance resulted in a chain of mountains being uplifted near the coast. These mountains would present a barrier to the flow of air from the ocean. As explained on page 252, the orographic effect of this mountain barrier would be to force the wind to rise as it moved inland, thus causing the air to cool and to drop more of its moisture on the windward side of the mountains. This loss of moisture, plus the heating of the air by compression as it descends down the leeward side, would produce an arid region on the leeward side of the mountains. Thus, a landscape feature can influence climate.

Stream Patterns. The characteristics of a stream system, as discussed in Chapter 24, are gradient, drainage pattern, and drainage density. As

might be expected, the characteristic most influenced by climate is drainage density. Other environmental factors, such as soil or bedrock conditions, can also affect drainage density. The effect of these factors will be considered later in this chapter.

In considering the effects of climate, it should be remembered that it is not just the *amount* of precipitation that determines the type of climate. It is the *ratio* between precipitation and potential evapotranspiration that is important. Where this ratio is large, the climate is humid. There is much surplus water that can run off over the surface or through the ground. Therefore, in a humid climate the surface and subsurface water can support many streams, and we can expect the drainage density to be high. In the two cases illustrated in Figure 24-9 on page 469, we can infer that the climate of region *B* is much more humid than that of region *A*.

Another difference that we would expect to find between the streams in the two different climate regions would be in stream discharge, the *volume* of water that passes a point in the stream in a given amount of time (see Chapter 13, page 243). The discharge pattern of a stream will reflect, to some degree at least, the environment in which the stream exists.

As mentioned earlier (page 489), in arid regions many streams do not flow all of the time. During periods of little or no precipitation, these intermittent streams dry up. At such times, of course, their discharge is zero. During rainy periods, water will flow and the discharge will go up. Thus, the discharge pattern of streams in arid regions may vary from zero during dry spells to maximum values during and after heavy rains or periods of snow melting. On topographic maps, intermittent streams are shown as broken, rather than solid, blue lines.

The discharge pattern of a stream in a humid region may also show seasonal variation, such as maximum discharge during spring thaw and minimum during a dry autumn. However, discharge rarely, if ever, reaches zero, and the extremes for maximum and minimum values will not be nearly as great as those for intermittent streams of an arid region. Figure 25-14 illustrates the different patterns of stream discharge in arid and humid climates.

Soil Associations. In Chapter 24 (page 470), the importance of soil as-

sociations as a landscape characteristic was explained. From the discussion of soil formation in Chapter 14 (pages 279-282), it is clear that climate is the main factor that determines the type of soil that occurs in a region. However, in that discussion, the emphasis was placed on the rainfall aspect of climate. The temperature factor is also important and should be given some further attention.

One of the most important aspects of temperature, as it relates to soil development, is the effect it has on the rate of decay, or decomposition, of organic matter. When a plant or animal dies, its remains consist of complex organic compounds. In order for these compounds to become a useful

Figure 25-12. Patterns of stream discharge in arid and humid climates. (*A*) Stream in arid region of California. (*B*) Stream in humid region of Florida; fairly uniform monthly P/E$_p$. (*C*) Tributary stream of Missouri River; moderately humid region with seasonal runoff variations.

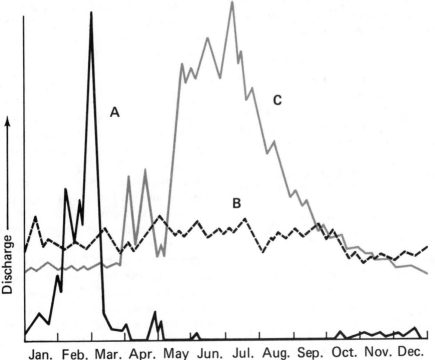

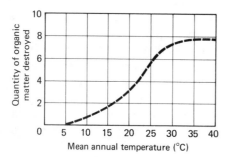

Figure 25-13. Relationship between mean annual temperature and the rate at which organic material is decomposed.

part of the soil for growing plants, they must be partially decomposed. As already mentioned in Chapter 14, partially decomposed organic material in soil is called humus. This decomposition is brought about by the life activities of bacteria. In porous, well-aerated soils, the bacteria are *aerobic,* that is, they use the oxygen in air for their life activities. In poorly drained soils lacking in air spaces, the bacteria present will be *anaerobic,* that is, capable of living without free oxygen.

The rate of bacterial activity is related to temperature. Figure 25-13 is a graph that shows the relationship between the rate at which organic material is completely decomposed by aerobic bacteria and the mean annual

Figure 25-14. Relationship between mean annual temperature and rate of plant growth.

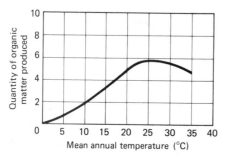

temperature. Plant growth also depends on temperature. As can be seen in Figure 25-14, the rate of plant growth is a maximum when mean annual temperatures are about 25°C. These two graphs are combined in Figure 25-15. We see that below about 25°C, the production of organic material by plants is greater than the rate of complete decomposition by the bacteria. Therefore, in this temperature range, some organic material is only partially decomposed, and humus accumulates in the soil. When average temperatures are greater than 25°C, the bacteria are able to completely decompose organic remains as fast as they are produced. Since completely decomposed material is useless as a soil component, no humus forms under these conditions.

Temperature also plays an important part in soil development on mountains. On high mountains, low temperatures tend to prevent the growth of much plant life, regardless of precipitation. Furthermore, erosion tends to remove weathered rock material as fast as it forms. There is thus little chance for soils of any type to develop. Mountain soils therefore tend to be very thin, with very little development of topsoil and subsoil horizons.

Glacial Action. Another way in which climate affects landscape development is through the action of glaciers. Where climatic conditions are producing glaciers now, or did so in the past, certain definite landscape features appear. In Chapter 15 (pages 301-303), the effects of ice as an erosional agent were discussed. You will recall that one of the chief characteristics of erosion by glaciers is the

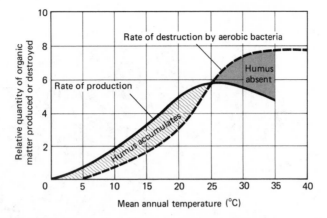

Figure 25-15. Relationship between mean annual temperature and relative rates of production and destruction of organic matter. Where the rate of production is greater than the rate of destruction, humus accumulates. Where the rate of destruction is greater than the rate of production, humus is absent.

formation of U-shaped valleys. In Chapter 16 (page 319), we briefly mentioned the characteristics of deposition by glaciers. In this section, we will examine the effects of glaciers on landscape development in somewhat more detail.

Like shoreline landscapes, landscapes and landscape features produced as a result of glacial activity have special characteristics of their own. As an environmental factor, moving ice would be considered a leveling agent. However, because of the vast amounts of material that can be moved by a glacier, the depositional features of a glaciated landscape are also important. Not only are hillslopes *changed* by glacial action, but some hills are actually *formed* as the result of glacial deposition. Streams are created by glacial melting, and drainage patterns are altered by the erosional and depositional effects of glaciers. Soils are stripped away from some areas and vast amounts of topsoil are deposited in other areas.

There are two classes of glaciers —*alpine* glaciers, which are also called *valley* or *mountain* glaciers, and *continental* glaciers, or *ice sheets.* Alpine glaciers develop wherever mountains are high enough to extend above the snow line. Continental glaciers are huge sheets of ice that cover vast areas of land. Today, thick ice sheets cover most of Greenland and the entire continent of Antarctica. Near the center of the Antarctic ice sheet, ice thicknesses exceed 3000 meters! While the landscapes produced by the moving ice in the two types of glaciers have certain characteristics in common, each has several unique features.

Alpine glaciation. As stated in Chapter 15, alpine glaciers are sometimes called "rivers of ice." The snow and ice collect in basins or depressions high above the snow line. As the snow and ice build up in these basins, the increased pressure causes the ice at the bottom to move, or "flow," as described earlier. Under the influence of gravity, the ice "river" flows

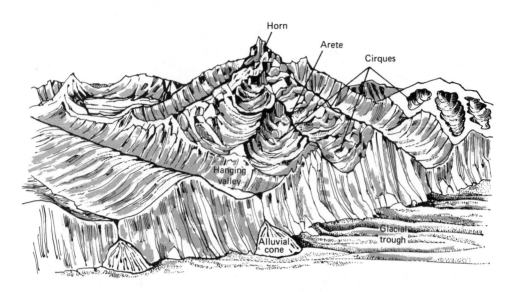

Figure 25-16. Landscape features produced by alpine glaciers.

slowly down the mountainside, gouging and scraping and eroding its valley as it moves. The motion of an alpine glacier is irregular, and the ice at the center moves faster than the ice at the sides. A wide range of speeds have been measured for alpine glaciers, ranging from a few centimeters to a meter or more per day. The leading edge of an alpine glacier reaches its lowest limit at the level where the ice melts as fast as it moves.

Moving ice has the ability to erode all surfaces it touches. As the ice moves, it picks up sediment, much the same as a river does. However, the sediment carried by a glacier includes rocks and boulders in addition to smaller rock and soil particles. As these rocks and rock particles are dragged along by the ice, they scrape and gouge and abrade the bedrock and are an important part of the glacier's erosive power.

In a mountain region where glaciers have not formed, the valleys carved by stream erosion will generally be V-shaped. If the climate then becomes cold enough for glaciers to develop, they may move down these valleys. As a glacier moves through a V-shaped valley, it erodes the valley walls as well as the floor. Most of the waning slopes and debris slopes of the valley walls are removed, leaving only the steep, resistant free face. The result is that the valley cross section is changed to a U shape. (See Figures 25-16 and 25-17.) These U-shaped valleys are called *glacial troughs*.

If the climate later becomes warmer again, the glaciers may melt away, and new streams will flow down the center of the troughs. Where tributary ice streams had been, there may be troughs left high on the valley wall of the main glacier. These are called *hanging valleys*. The presence of glacial troughs and hanging valleys in a landscape today is evidence of past glaciation.

Other landscape features produced by alpine glaciers are found high up on mountain slopes, near the source of the glaciers. The basins or depressions where the snow and ice accumulate become scoured to form amphitheater-like features called *cirques*. When two cirques form in the same region, a sharp, narrow ridge, called an *arete*, is often left standing between them. If glaciation of a mountain is extensive, the peak may be worn away until only a sharp, pyramid-shaped peak called a *horn* remains. All of these features are shown in Figure 25-16.

Thus far, the discussion has focused on erosional features of landscapes influenced by alpine glaciers. Glaciated landscapes also have distinctive depositional features. As glaciers move, they pick up great amounts of rock material, and the particle sizes range from tiny grains to large boulders. All rock material car-ried by glaciers is called *moraine,* and it is all unsorted—that is, all the sizes are mixed together. The material is carried on, in, under, ahead of, and alongside the moving ice. When the ice stops moving, the moraine stops moving also. If the glacier melts, the moraine is left behind. Various moraine deposits are named according to *where* they were located in relation to the ice. The material that was pushed ahead of the ice marks the farthest limit reached by the ice front. This deposit, called a *terminal moraine,* usually consists of a thick ridge of unsorted material. Other deposits include *ground* moraine, which is a thin, fairly even deposit over the floor occupied by the ice, *lateral* moraine, and *medial* moraine (see Figure 25-18).

Continental glaciation. Large areas of the earth that are presently free of glacial ice have landscapes and landscape features that are characteristic of glacial activity. Therefore, it appears that climatic conditions in these areas were once favorable for the de-

Figure 25-17. Formation of a U-shaped valley. (A) V-shaped valley caused by stream erosion. (B) As the glacier moves down the valley, it erodes the walls and floor of the valley, giving it a U shape. (C) If the climate warms and the glacier recedes, new streams will flow down the middle of the glacial trough.

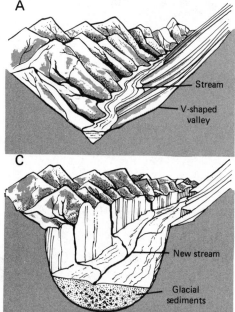

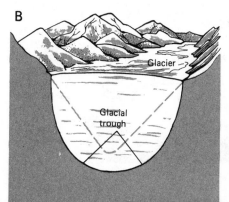

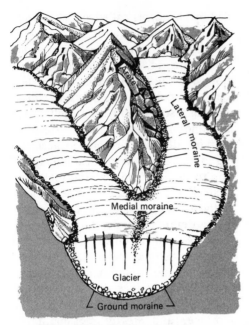

Figure 25-18. Moraine deposits.

velopment of glaciers. In fact, basing their conclusions on evidence from several sources, scientists believe that the climatic conditions in the past were such that the temperate regions of the earth underwent several "ice ages," during which the polar ice advanced and retreated several times. The most recent retreat of ice to its present positions took place sometime between 8000 and 15,000 years ago. Figure 25-19 shows the maximum extent of the glaciation in North America.

Except for the fact that they both consist of moving ice, continental and alpine glaciers have little in common. Alpine glaciers are rather limited in scope, being confined to mountain valleys. The thickness of the ice in these glaciers is measured in tens of meters, and rarely exceeds 100 me-

Figure 25-19. Maximum extent of glaciation in North America. Part of Wisconsin, just south of Lake Superior, was not covered by the ice. This region is called the driftless area.

ters. By contrast, continental glaciers extend over millions of square kilometers of area, and ice thicknesses are measured in thousands of meters.

The movement of ice in a continental glacier is radial. That is, the ice moves outward in all directions from the central part of the glacier, where the ice is thickest. Think about how effective alpine glaciers are in eroding the bedrock over which they move. How much more so the landscape below a great sheet of moving ice must be changed!

In general, the topography of a region eroded by a continental glacier is gentler, or less rugged, than that produced by alpine glaciers. One reason for this fact is that all but the highest of peaks are ground down, abraded, and eroded as the great sheet of ice passes over them. Exposed bedrock in a glaciated landscape has scratches or grooves caused when the rock material carried in the bottom of the ice was dragged over the bedrock.

Many features of a landscape influenced by a continental glacier are depositional. As discussed in Chapter 16, page 319, glacial deposits are of two types, direct and indirect. Direct deposits consist of material left behind when a glacier melts. Indirect, or fluvio-glacial, deposits are carried and deposited by streams of water that flow beneath the glacier or out of the ice front.

Direct deposits consist of unsorted rock material called *till*. Terminal moraines are formed all along the leading edge of the glacier. These moraines may be hundreds of kilometers long, several kilometers wide, and hundreds of kilometers high. The hilly topography of northern Long Is-

land in New York is part of a terminal moraine.

Because indirect deposits are carried by water, they do show some sorting. The largest particles are deposited closest to the ice front and the finer materials are carried farthest from the ice. Broad, fairly flat areas, called *outwash plains,* are often formed ahead of large glaciers.The level, sandy portion of southern Long Island and the prairies of Wisconsin are good examples of outwash plains.

There are several other rather unusual features that are often found associated with glaciated landscapes. *Drumlins* are elongated oval-shaped hills that usually occur in groups or clusters. Drumlins are usually more or less parallel to each other and pointing in the direction of ice movement. Most drumlins consist of unsorted glacial sediments, although some have a solid rock core covered by these sediments. *Eskers* are winding ridges composed of glacial sand and gravel. These ridges form in tunnels beneath the glacial ice, through which streams of water flow. As the ice melts, these tunnels become filled with sediments, which are left behind as eskers. *Kames* are small, cone-shaped hills composed of sand and gravel deposited near the front of a melting glacier. *Kettles* are circular depressions often found on terminal moraines or outwash plains. These depressions form when large blocks of ice break off the glacial front as the glacier is retreating. These large blocks become surrounded by, or covered with, sediments. When the block melts, the kettle is left behind. If the kettle is deep enough to extend below the water table, a kettle lake is formed. Figure 25-20 shows the relationship of the ice and some of the features described above.

Streams and stream patterns are radically affected by continental glaciation. Drainage patterns are altered or interrupted, first by the presence of the ice and later by the deposits left behind. The Finger Lakes of western New York State occupy U-shaped troughs, similar to the troughs formed by alpine glaciers. These troughs were gouged out by the continental glacier in an area previously having a system of stream valleys which ran in a north-south direction.

The actions of glaciers we have described make it very clear that glaciers move enormous amounts of material. Close inspection of soil materials in a glaciated landscape shows that the soils have been transported. They show little resemblance to the parent bedrock of the area.

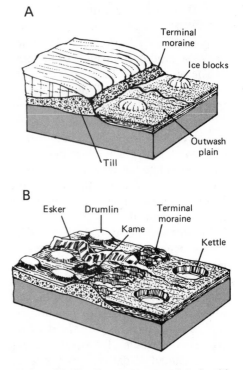

Figure 25-20. Features associated with glaciated landscapes. (A) The features before the glacier melts. (B) The features after the glacier has melted.

SUMMARY

1. A change in climate, such as from a moist to an arid environment, would result in a modification of the landscape.
2. Some landscapes have characteristics that indicate they developed under conditions of climate extremes, such as glaciation.
3. The rate at which landscape development occurs may be influenced by the climate.
4. The steepness of hillslopes in an area is affected by the balance between weathering and erosion.
5. Other factors being equal, hillslopes that evolved in a dry climate have angular features and prominent free face, while hillslopes that evolved in a humid climate have extensive waning slopes and appear more rounded.
6. Stream characteristics, such as discharge and drainage density, are affected by the climate.

7. Soil characteristics, such as soil depth and type of horizons present, are affected by the climate.
8. There are two classes of glaciers—alpine glaciers and continental glaciers. Because glaciers are able to move vast amounts of rock material, glaciated landscapes are characterized by both erosional features and depositional features.

BEDROCK

It has been noted several times throughout this chapter that the bedrock in a particular region must be considered as a factor that influences the development of the landscape. The reason for this fact should be obvious. The landscape—the physical appearance—of any region is the end result of the sculpting of the bedrock by the processes of weathering and erosion.

Essentially, there are two characteristics that help to determine the role that bedrock will play in the development of the landscape in a given region. One characteristic is the class and/or type of rock that makes up the bedrock of a region. Most nonsedimentary rocks are generally tougher—more resistant to weathering and erosion—than are sedimentary rocks. Also, certain types of rocks are tougher than others of the same class. Limestone, a sedimentary rock, is often more resistant to weathering and erosion than other sedimentary rocks, such as sandstone or shale.

The second characteristic of bedrock is its general "condition." What structural features are present? Has it been deformed by internal pressures? If so, how, and how severely? Has it been tilted, folded, faulted, intruded, or perhaps subjected to a combination of some or all of these deformations?

Certain types of rocks are subject to the development of cracks or joints along zones of weakness. All of these characteristics can, and do, have an influence on the landscape that will develop from the weathering and erosion of this bedrock.

As with the other landscape factors, you should keep in mind that bedrock *alone* does not determine landscape. For example, the landscape developed on limestone bedrock in a warm, moist region will probably differ dramatically from the landscape developed on limestone bedrock in a cooler or drier region. It is the interaction of *all* the environmental factors that determines landscape.

In this section, we will take a close look at how bedrock affects the various landscape characteristics.

Hillslopes. The photograph in Figure 25-21 shows a hillslope in Thacher Park, near Albany, New York. This particular hillslope has a prominent feature—a steep-faced bedrock surface, known as a *cliff* or an *escarpment*. The cliff is the free face of this hillslope. Since cliffs are characteristic of many hillslopes, we should know how such features are produced.

On close examination, the cliff face appears to consist of one kind of rock, which seems to be more resistant to weathering and erosion than the rock

Figure 25-21. Limestone cliff. The limestone of this cliff is more resistant to weathering than the rock below it.

below it. Resistance to the processes of weathering and erosion is called *competence*. A rock that resists these processes is said to be a competent rock. The rock in this particular cliff is limestone. The entire free face is one massive layer of competent limestone. Layers below the free face are composed of shale and limestone, and neither is as competent as the limestone in the cliff. Thus, the weaker, less resistant layers or rock wear away faster than the rock of the cliff. Eventually, the erosion of the weaker layers undermines part of the cliff face, and large blocks of limestone fall away from it. The debris slope is made up of rock material from the weaker rock layers and limestone blocks from the free face.

Figure 25-22 is a cross-sectional drawing of one wall (or hillslope) of the Grand Canyon. Notice that this hillslope, which is almost 2,000 meters in length, shows several cliffs, or escarpments, along its length. Beneath each escarpment is a more gradual debris slope. The same erosional pattern exists here as was seen in Figure 25-21.

Assuming that there are no structural features to consider, the general effect of rock competence on hillslope features can be summed up quite briefly. If all of the exposed bedrock has about the same degree of resistance of weathering and erosion, hillslopes will be fairly uniform and will wear down more or less evenly. If, however, the exposed rocks have different degrees of competence, there will be marked differences in slope between the layers of different resistance, with the most competent layers being steepest.

The diagrams in Figure 25-23 represent two regions where the bedrock has not been deformed by crustal disturbances. The bedrock in diagram *A* is nonsedimentary rock of uniform

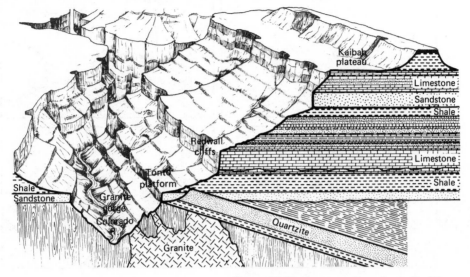

Figure 25-22. Cross section of a wall of the Grand Canyon.

Figure 25-23. Effect of undisturbed bedrock structure on landscape features. (A) This region consists of homogeneous non-sedimentary bedrock. The landscape shows a random distribution of rounded hills. (B) This region consists of horizontal sedimentary bedrock. The landscape shows generally uniform elevation, with steep-sided valleys cut by streams.

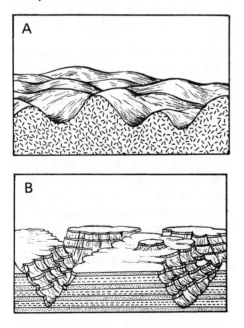

competence. The bedrock of the plateau region in diagram B consists of horizontal layers of sedimentary rock of varying degrees of resistance. The differences in the landscape features of the two regions reflect the differences in their bedrock.

The rate at which hillslope features change is also affected by the type of bedrock present. Generally, hills composed of the least resistant rock will be worn down fastest. Those with more competent bedrock should last longer.

As mentioned earlier, structural features of bedrock, such as faults and folds, will also influence the landscape development. The diagrams in Figure 25-24 depict four different situations of bedrock distortion and the possible landscapes that might develop under the influence of the bedrock features.

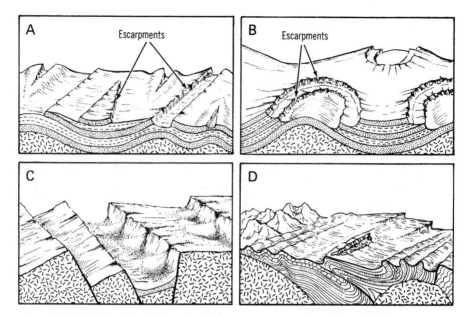

Figure 25-24. Effects of deformed bedrock structure on landscape features. (A) With folded strata of varying resistance the landscape consists of roughly parallel ridges, with steep-sided cliffs of resistant rock. (B) With a domed structure the landscape features resemble those in (A), but ridges and cliffs have a generally circular arrangement. (C) With fault-block mountains the landscape features consist of ridges of varying elevation, with steep slopes along the fault planes. (D) With a complex bedrock structure the landscape varies greatly in elevation and slope.

Another bedrock feature that can affect landscape is the presence of jointing, especially when combined with faults in the bedrock. Any crack in solid bedrock exposes more of the rock to the processes of weathering and erosion. Stream beds will often follow along an area of weakness such as a fault line. A combination of faulting and jointing in a region tends to result in hills or mountains having a definite "squarish" appearance when viewed from above, as on a map. The Adirondack Mountains in New York State show a definite tendency to this squareness.

Stream Patterns. The stream characteristic most affected by bedrock is drainage pattern. If the underlying bedrock of an area is of uniform composition, there will be no specific regions of weakness along which streams will tend to flow. Thus, streams will develop a random pattern, such as the *dendritic* drainage pattern shown in Figure 24-9A on page 469. There will be few, if any, rapid changes in stream gradient in such a region.

When the bedrock in an area consists of rocks with varying degrees of resistance, or when bedrock features such as folding, faulting, and jointing are present, the drainage patterns will be influenced by these features. The drainage pattern shown in Figure 25-25 is known as *trellis* or *block* drainage. Such drainage patterns are found in regions where the bedrock has been extensively folded and consists of rocks with much difference in resistance to erosion. Trellis drainage is also found in regions of faulted and jointed rock.

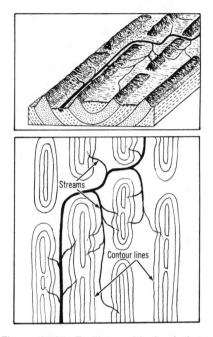

Figure 25-25. Trellis, or block, drainage. This type of drainage is found in folded rocks of differing resistance, and also in faulted or jointed rocks.

The two diagrams in Figure 25-26 illustrate two types of drainage patterns that are found in areas of domed structures. If the bedrock is fairly uniform in resistance, streams will tend to flow in relatively straight courses down the slopes of the dome. The *radial* drainage pattern of these streams is illustrated in diagram *A*. If, however, there are rocks of varying resistance, streams will erode the weaker rocks and tend to follow circular paths around the domes. The annular drainage pattern formed by these streams is shown in diagram *B*.

In regions where there are bedrock features and varying degrees of resistance within the bedrock itself, changes in stream gradient are often present. These changes usually are seen in the form of waterfalls or

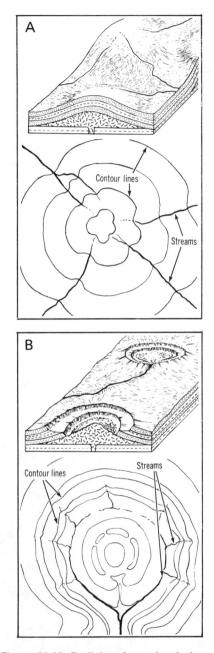

Figure 25-26. Radial and annular drainage patterns. (*A*) Radial drainage patterns occur in areas of domed structure with little difference in rock resistance. (*B*) Annular drainage patterns of concentric circles are found in areas of dome structures with much difference in rock resistance.

rapids. A waterfall is actually a cliff with water flowing over it. Such falls are created where the bedrock beneath a stream changes from erosion-resistant to easily-eroded rock.

Niagara Falls is a typical example of a waterfall formed because of difference in resistance of rocks in the bedrock (see Figure 15-12, page 297). Upstream of the falls, the river flows over a resistant layer of dolomite limestone. Downstream of the falls, the bedrock is much less resistant to erosion. The lip of the falls marks the edge of the limestone layer. As water flows over the falls, the falling water erodes away the rock beneath the lip, thus undercutting the limestone. As the supporting rock is removed, large pieces of the limestone fall into the gorge. Little by little, the edge of the limestone is being worn back.

In regions that have sufficiently humid climatic conditions, there is one type of bedrock that produces an un-usual landscape. The type of rock is limestone. The tendency of limestone to dissolve in groundwater is responsible for producing an *underground* landscape of caverns and streams. The physical appearance of the surface in such a region is known as a *Karst* landscape.

There are few streams on the surface of such a region. Water falling on the surface quickly seeps down through joints and cracks in the bedrock. dissolving more of the rock as it moves downward. Once underground, the groundwater moves through cracks and crevices, dissolving rock material and producing ever larger spaces in the bedrock. Eventually, when the water reaches more resistant rock, it forms underground streams.

The dissolving action of the groundwater forms subterranean caves and caverns, such as the one shown in Figure 25-27. When bedrock

Figure 25-27. Carlsbad Cavern, New Mexico.

Figure 25-28. Sinkhole in limestone.

near the surface is dissolved, the ceiling of the cavern may collapse to form a roughly circular-shaped *sinkhole* (Figure 25-28). Sinkholes are typical surface features of a Karst landscape.

Soil Formation. Of all the factors affecting soil formation and development, climate has the most influence. However, soils do generally form from the bedrock in a region, and thus the bedrock does play a role in the formation and development of soil.

The composition of a residual soil will reflect the composition of the bedrock from which it forms. Soil formed from granite, for example, will consist of partly weathered quartz,

feldspar, and clay (from weathered feldspar), along with bits of mica and hornblende. Another soil, formed from sandstone, will consist mainly of quartz grains, perhaps with some weathered cementing material mixed in.

As a soil develops and becomes older, the material in the upper levels of the soil, farthest from the bedrock. becomes greatly weathered. This weathering, plus the accumulations and decomposition of organic matter, makes it difficult to determine what the parent material might have been. The older the soil, the less it resembles the parent material.

SUMMARY

1. The rate at which landscape development occurs may be affected by the bedrock. The two characteristics of bedrock that most influence landscape development are the type (or class) of rock and the structural features, such as tilting, faulting, and folding.

2. The shape and steepness of hillslopes are affected by the local bedrock composition.
3. Competent, or resistant, rocks are usually found in plateaus, mountains, and escarpments. Weaker, less resistant rocks usually underlie valleys and other low-level areas.
4. Structural features in bedrock, such as faults, folds, and joints, frequently affect the development of hillslopes.
5. Stream characteristics, such as drainage patterns and gradient, are controlled by bedrock characteristics.
6. Soils may differ in composition and are dependent upon the composition of the bedrock. Residual soils resemble the bedrock less as weathering continues. Transported soils may not resemble the bedrock on which they rest.

REVIEW QUESTIONS

Group A

1. What two groups of opposing forces interact to produce landscapes?
2. In any particular interaction, how might the relative influence of the groups of opposing forces be shown?
3. What effect can the rate of crustal uplift or subsidence have on landscapes?
4. On what basis are shorelines classified? What are the three main classes of shorelines?
5. What effect might a change in climate have on the landscape?
6. What inferences can be made from landscape characteristics about the climate conditions under which they formed?
7. What influence might climate exert on landscape development?
8. What characteristic of hillslopes is affected by the balance between weathering and erosion?
9. How do hillslopes which evolved in a dry climate differ in appearance from those which evolved in a humid climate?
10. What two stream characteristics are most affected by climate?
11. What soil characteristics are affected by climate?
12. What are the two classes of glaciers? How is the erosional power of a glacier related to the type of landscape features that are characteristic of most glaciated landscapes?
13. What characteristics of bedrock affect the rate of landscape development?
14. What hillslope characteristics are affected by bedrock composition?
15. What types of landscapes or landscape features are found in regions underlain by competent bedrock?
16. What kinds of structural features in bedrock can influence the development of hillslope?
17. What two factors determine how closely a soil resembles the bedrock on which it rests?

Group B   1. a.   The table in Figure 25-1 lists some environmental factors and some landscape characteristics. Which are the causes and which are the effects?

   b.   In a certain region constructional forces are greater than destructional forces. What hillslope characteristics would you expect to find there? What stream pattern characteristics? What soil characteristics?

2. a.   What hillslope characteristics can be expected in dry climates? In humid climates?

   b.   What effect will a humid climate have on erosion?

   c.   What kind of drainage density is to be expected in a humid climate?

3.   What will be the effect on soils of a high mean annual temperature?

4.   How is an alpine glacier different from a continental glacier? What effects do glaciers have on landscapes?

5. a.   What will be the shape of hillslopes formed in sedimentary rock if the exposed rock layers are of non-uniform competence? If the exposed rock layers are of uniform competence?

   b.   What kind of bedrock conditions will be favorable for the formation of a dendritic drainage pattern? A trellis drainage pattern?

   c.   What kind of bedrock conditions would you expect to find in a radial drainage pattern? In an annular drainage pattern?

People have planted grasses, erected fences, and piled old holiday trees by the shore in an effort to slow erosion.

CHAPTER 26
Human Factors in Landscape Development

You will know something about how landscapes are influenced by man's activities and by the passage of time if you can:

1. Describe some human activities that affect landscape development.
2. Describe some of the long-term effects of environmental pollution and some corrective measures used to combat pollution.
3. Recognize the relative stages of landscape development and describe some of the characteristics of each stage.

In the previous two chapters, we investigated the effects of various environmental factors on landscapes. People may also be classified as an environmental factor. However, unlike other environmental factors, we deliberately exert effects on our surroundings. If a hill stands in the way of "progress," we level it. If the course followed by a river does not meet our requirements, we change it or dam it or build levees along its banks. If a region is arid, we irrigate it. If the soil is nonproductive, we add fertilizer. We remove vast amounts of material from some places and deposit it in other places. Changes that might take thousands, or even millions, of years for nature to bring about, human beings produce in days, weeks, or months.

OUR EFFECT ON THE LANDSCAPE

Human influence on the landscape has been closely related to growth in population and advancements in technology. As the population has grown (world population recently passed the 4 billion mark), people's assault on the landscape has increased. The need for shelter, fuel, and food led to the chopping down of entire forests, plowing of vast areas of land, and the search for and removal of coal, petroleum, and other mineral deposits.

With the onset of the industrial revolution and the advancement of technology in all areas, more changes in the landscape were made. Much of the population moved from farms to cities, more and more land was leveled, paved over, and built upon. In our quest for "progress" and a better standard of living, we have placed a strain on the natural resources of the earth.

Human influence on the landscape is twofold. Many of our activities directly change the landscape, or physical features of the earth's surface. One serious side effect that often accompanies these changes is pollution of the environment. Over a period of time, pollution can and does lead to changes in soils, hydrologic environment, and even local climate conditions. These changes, in turn, can influence the landscape. In recent years, people have come to recognize the

Figure 26-1. Open-pit copper mine.

seriousness of the long-term effects of pollution and depletion of natural resources. This recognition has led to the development of programs designed to conserve our resources, protect the environment, and restore much of the "damaged" environment to a state as close to its original condition as possible.

This section is broken down into three divisions: the direct effects of man's activities on landscape; environmental pollution and the indirect effects on landscape; and conservation, protection, and restoration.

Direct Effects of Human Activities. While not necessarily the most important, the direct effects of human activities on landscape characteristics are certainly the most easily observed.

Hillslopes. The photograph in Figure 26-1 shows a region where open-pit mining for copper is taking place. Where a hill once stood over 450 meters high, there is now a steep-sided pit over 300 meters deep. The slopes are being excavated to remove the rich copper ore. Waste rock is discarded in great piles, forming artificial hills and new hillslopes.

Since the open-pit operation began in 1906, more than 9 million metric tons of copper have been produced at this mine. (A metric ton is equivalent to 1,000 kilograms.) In a single year, about 27,000 metric tons of ore are removed, along with probably an equal amount of waste rock. This quantity of material has a volume of about 125 million cubic meters! In other words, using this material you could form a cube about five football fields long on each side!

Human activities have certainly changed this landscape. The question is, have the changes been beneficial? In terms of the landscape itself, the scenic beauty of the area has been greatly diminished. One hillslope was removed and new slopes around the pit have been created. Artificial ponds have been created for the purpose of leaching out additional metals from the rock. Some of this water may find its way into streams or ground water and possibly cause pollution. The nonrenewable metal resources, which required millions of years to be deposited and concentrated in this rock, are being removed in a hundred years.

On the other hand, the operation of the mine has provided jobs for many people and economic benefits for the company that owns it, its stockholders, and employees. The raw materials that have been removed from the mine have been used to create products that have benefited us all.

Thus, it is impossible to make a blanket statement regarding the "goodness" or "badness" of this activity. Our need for the ore must be weighed against the damage to the environment. In terms of the effect on the landscape, however, it is safe to say that the mining activity has certainly changed the landscape—the physical appearance of the area—for the worse.

Figure 26-2 shows another mining operation. In this case, the material being removed is sand and gravel. In this operation, as in the open pit mine, the process of excavation tends to produce the following changes in a hillslope:

1. Vegetation is stripped off, exposing unweathered soil, rock, or gravel to the elements.

Figure 26-2. Gravel pit.

2. Fertile topsoil is stripped away from the mineable material.

3. A steep, unstable hillslope is produced.

These changes may tend to disrupt a landscape surface that was in a state of equilibrium or balance. Before excavation, erosion may have been controlled by vegetative cover, and the angle of the hillslope may have been gradual enough to make the likelihood of landslides or slippage unlikely. Removal of the cover and steepening of the slope by excavation produces an unstable hillslope. Heavy rain or vibrations could cause a slide.

Geologists have determined that hillslopes consisting of loose materials can be stable up to a gradient of about 37°. The maximum angle at which such a hillslope will be stable depends somewhat on the shape and size of the particles and on the amount of ground water present. Ground water tends to act as a lubricant.

As illustrated in Figure 26-3, highway construction almost always involves some "rearranging" of the landscape in order to have a rea-sonably level road bed. This re-arrangement may involve removal of materials from the uphill side of the roadway and/or the depositing of landfill on the downhill side. Both of these activities may change the gradients of the hillslopes and increase the possibility of landslides. Thus, considerable care should be taken to insure that the "new" hillslopes are stable. Additional conservation practices, such as terracing and planting

Figure 26-3. Highway construction. One effect of this activity is to steepen the hillslopes on both sides of the highway, thus increasing the chance of erosion.

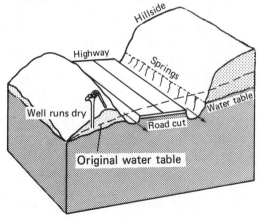

Figure 26-4. Unstable stream bank.

grass and shrubs on the slopes, are usually followed in an effort to minimize soil erosion.

Stream patterns. Rivers and streams have played an important role in the development of the inland regions of this country. Many early settlements were situated near rivers, in order to take advantage of the many benefits, such as transportation, power, and drinking water. However, dependence on rivers involves many problems, not the least of which is flooding. In many areas, seasonal flooding of rivers causes widespread damage to homes, businesses, and crops, as well as loss of life. In attempts to prevent, or at least control, flooding, man has built levees, channelized streams, changed the direction of streams, and erected dams.

In addition to flooding, stream-bank erosion due to undercutting can also be a problem. The bank shown in Figure 26-4 is susceptible to erosion every time flooding or high-water conditions occur. People who live along such streams lose some of their property each time the river bank is carved away. In some areas, a process called channelization is used to eliminate the erosion problem. The stream shown in Figure 26-5 has been channelized. The stream bed has been straightened, obstructions have been removed from the bed, and the bank has been covered with large, flat rocks. This rock material, called riprap, shields the banks from the erosive force of the water. The "new" channel can now act as a sluiceway to speed the runoff of excess rainwater or melted snow.

While channelizing may solve the problems of flooding and bank erosion, certain undesirable side effects may also be produced. By "forcing" a relatively large amount of water to flow along a restricted course, the downward erosion of the stream may be increased, thus increasing the gradient of the stream. The end result may be that the channelized stream entrenches itself, and the armor of rip-rap along the banks may be undercut.

A more serious result of channelizing is often felt downstream. The channelizing results in *more* water being sent downstream, and the flooding and eroding problems are passed along to the downstream areas.

An alternative to channelizing is to hold back excess runoff, help it to infiltrate, and allow it to leave a region in a controlled flow. One method for controlling runoff is to construct recharge basins. These basins serve as collecting areas during periods of runoff. The water is "collected" in temporary ponds, from which it is allowed to infiltrate, thus helping to raise the water table. Eventually, these basins fill up with silt, which is carried to the basin by the running water. A similar silting problem occurs behind river dams. The problem of how to prevent this buildup of silt, or how to get rid of it after it accumu-

lates, is one that has plagued engineers for years. As yet, no satisfactory solution to this problem has been found.

Figure 26-6 shows a number of measures that can be taken to help control runoff and bank erosion in small streams. The combined effect of the devices shown here are to reduce the chance of downstream flooding, control erosion, improve the environment for fish and wildlife, and help retain runoff for infiltration. As far as landscape is concerned, just about all of the characteristics of this stream —drainage pattern, drainage density, and stream gradient—are influenced.

Soils. Perhaps the two most common ways in which man directly alters the soils and soil associations of a region are by removal of vegetation and by excavation. As we learned earlier, the presence of vegetative cover is very important to soils and their development. Plant roots help hold soil

Figure 26-5. Channelized stream. Several measures have been taken to reduce the amount of bank erosion along the course of this stream.

Figure 26-6. Stream improvement structures.

in place, while the organic material derived from the plants aids in the development of a mature soil profile. Whenever the vegetative cover is removed, topsoil is lost—carried away by wind and/or water.

Three industries—farming, logging, and construction—probably account for most of the removal of vegetative cover from the soil. The excavations discussed earlier in this chapter are other examples of ways in which man's activities affect the soil and change the landscape. All of these activities are necessary—in fact, vital—to our existence. We need food, houses, paper, fuel, and the metals and other minerals that are removed from the crust by these activities. However, it has become more and more apparent that improved methods of operation and conservation must be observed.

Pollution and Landscape. As stated earlier, the direct effects of human activities on landscape characteristics are most obvious. However, in the course of our everyday activities, we have been guilty of polluting our environment. While the immediate effects of polluting may not always be obvious or serious, the long-term consequences can prove devastating.

Atmospheric pollution. In recent years, the importance of atmospheric pollution has been recognized. Usually, emphasis is placed on the health hazards presented by unhealthy air. However, there is another very important aspect of atmospheric pollution to be considered. The presence of pollutants in the atmosphere may actually alter the rate at which the sun's energy is absorbed and radiated at the earth's surface. Such changes can modify climate. The importance of climate to many of the factors that affect landscape characteristics has been discussed in earlier chapters.

Water pollution. Some of the causes and effects of water pollution were discussed in Chapter 12. Unfortunately, just as people found rivers and streams to be invaluable sources of transportation and power, we also found them to be convenient for carrying away unwanted wastes. As population increased, the amount of waste dumped into the waterways also increased. The quality of the water gradually decreased until it was unusable, even for transportation. Today, some rivers are so badly polluted they have been declared fire hazards!

The dumping of wastes is not the only way man pollutes water. Figure 26-3 (page 511) shows the long-term effects of improper planning for construction of a highway. As the drawing shows, the highway excavation cut down through the water table on the uphill side of the roadcut. Thus, ground water seeped out of the rock, and it was necessary to install a drainage system along the sides of the road to carry off this seepage.

On the downhill side of the roadcut, the water table level dropped, because the main source of infiltrating water had been cut off. Wells below the roadway dried up. Water flowing in the drainage system beside the highway easily became polluted with dissolved substances from the automobile exhausts and from chemicals spread on the road surface in winter to melt snow and ice. This polluted water then seeped into the ground to become part of the ground water.

Another source of water pollution is pesticides and other chemicals used in farming. Some of these chemicals become dissolved in rainwater, infiltrate, and enter the ground water. The most serious aspect of this type of pollution is that many of these chemicals enter the food chain. The pollutants are absorbed into the roots of plants, which in turn are eaten by animals. The addition of these substances into the food chain represents a definite health hazard to all of the consumers involved.

Prevention, Conservation, and Reclamation. Public awareness of the problems of pollution and depletion of natural resources is greater than ever before. In the past, many inefficient, wasteful, and even dangerous practices were permitted, even encouraged, because they were faster, cheaper, and/or easier. However, the undesirable, long-range results of many of these practices are now being seen and understood. People recognize the fact that their way of life—perhaps their very existence—is threatened by the abuse and misuse of the environment. Programs for conservation and reclamation of the environment and natural resources have been initiated in recent years.

Air pollution. The federal government and many state and local agencies have passed and are enforcing legislation designed to clean up the air and keep it clean. Emissions from automobile exhausts and industrial plants have received special attention. The efforts to cut down on the most harmful pollutants released from these sources have met with some success. While more remains to be done, the outlook for achieving and maintaining a cleaner, healthier atmosphere is encouraging.

Water. The nation's waterways have been used as convenient "dumping grounds" for wastes. The major pollutants are sewage and industrial wastes. The shortage of good drinking water is only one part of the pollution problem. Not only are many of these waters too polluted to drink, they are also too polluted for recreational activities, such as swimming and boating. Some waterways are so polluted that fish and other wildlife can no longer survive in them. Thus, the ecological balance of nature in and around these waterways has been disturbed.

As was the case with air pollution, the recognition of this problem by the general public has led to efforts to stop the pollution and to improve the conditions. There is a new emphasis on the removal of harmful substances from the waste products *before* they are dumped into the lakes and streams. The technology for treating waste products and rendering them harmless is available. However, putting the technology to work is a very costly proposition, and is being opposed at various levels for this reason. In the end, the public will have to decide where the priorities lie.

Soil. Figure 26-7 illustrates a landscape produced by a combination of poor soil-use practices and drought. There is little that man can do to control the latter—weather and climate control are still beyond our capabilities. However, the scene shown in this photograph would not have been so devastating had proper methods of soil use and conservation been followed. The land in this region had been overgrazed and overcultivated

for years prior to the drought. Bare of vegetation, the topsoil was simply blown away. Whenever land is plowed and cultivated, vegetative cover is removed and topsoil is exposed to the processes of wind and water erosion. However, there are methods by which topsoil can be conserved and erosion kept to a minimum.

When left unchecked, wind blowing across unprotected fields can strip away tons of valuable topsoil. Windbreaks, consisting of trees or fences, will serve as barriers to slow down the winds, thus decreasing their erosional power.

Figure 26-8 shows the use of contour plowing as a soil conservation measure. The furrows, plowed to follow the contours of the hilly land, slow down runoff as it moves downhill after a rain storm.

Figure 26-7. Dust Bowl, U.S.A. A combination of poor soil management and drought produced the devastating results shown in this photo.

Figure 26-8. Contour plowing.

Erosion is not the only "enemy" in the battle to conserve the soil and to use it most efficiently. Continuous use of topsoil for the raising of crops will use up, or deplete, certain nutrients in the soil. For the same soil to support crops year after year, these nutrients must be replenished. This can be accomplished by adding fertilizer, rotating crops, or a combination of the two. Different crops remove different nutrients from the soil. Thus by rotating the crops—planting different crops in different fields each year or so—the depletion of certain nutrients can be avoided. By planting certain "alternative" crops, such as alfalfa, nutrients can be replaced.

Farming is not the only activity that affects the soil. Consider the excavations discussed earlier in this chapter. Strip mining is one example of how the landscape can be drastically changed for the worse by human ac-

tivities. The reason for employing this method of mining, especially for coal, is that it is fastest and most economical. Both of these reasons are valid ones, especially during these times when all sources of energy are in great demand. However, rather than leaving the area as a scarred, unattractive mass of excavations and discarded piles of rock and soil, new programs of reclamation are being undertaken as joint efforts of community and industry. After the coal or ore is removed, the area is restored to a condition as close to the original as possible. The "reclaimed" landscape is then available for recreational areas or construction sites, whatever the needs of the community might be. While reclamation is relatively expensive, the long-range benefits derived from such projects can far outweigh the dollar cost.

Other projects directed at reclamation of land and resources are being conducted, and more are starting all the time. The recycling of metals and paper is designed to help conserve ore deposits and forests. Disposal of solid waste on land is being carried out by more orderly and purposeful methods. Much solid waste is being used in landfill operations, whereby unusable land areas are being developed and converted into land for parks, playgrounds, or other recreational uses.

In the last several sections we have been investigating interaction between landscape characteristics and the environmental factors that influ-ence those characteristics. Early in Chapter 25, a grid was provided as a suggested method for organizing the information (Figure 25-1, page 479). Figure 26-9 shows the same grid with the information entered in the appro-priate boxes. The information in each box summarizes the major effects a given factor has on a specific charac-teristic. If you read across the grid, you can summarize the effects of one environmental factor on the three landscape characteristics. If you read down one column of the grid, you can summarize the changes in one charac-teristic that can be caused by the dif-ferent factors.

SUMMARY

1. Human activities frequently affect the landscape. The results of these activities may be beneficial at first, but the long-term effects are often harmful.
2. Such activities as excavation and field cultivation may disrupt a stable land-scape by exposing the surface to agents of erosion. Certain measures, such as contour plowing, help to minimize erosion.
3. Activities such as highway construction can disrupt ground water flow and surface drainage.
4. The uncontrolled addition of soluble and insoluble materials to surface and ground water supplies can lead to harmful levels of pollution. Waste water treatment facilities can help reclaim or protect water quality.
5. Ground water levels can be maintained and surface runoff controlled and conserved through the use of such devices as recharge basins, dams, and stream bank protectors.
6. Uncontrolled use of soils for agricultural purposes can lead to a depletion of soil nutrients and eventual loss of topsoil. Conservation measures, such as fertilization, crop rotation, and pest control, help to maintain or reclaim soil.
7. Uncontrolled disposal of solid waste can lead to landscape pollution. Sani-tary landfill methods can help reduce the negative effects of solid-waste disposal, and can be used to reclaim unusable areas for recreational pur-poses.

	Hillslopes	Streams	Soil
Crustal Change (Uplifting and Leveling)	During uplifting, land elevations increase, mountains form, hillslopes steepen, distinctive hills form due to folding and faulting. Shorelines emerge or submerge.	During uplifting, stream gradients increase.	New soil material may be produced by volcanic activity.
	During leveling, land elevations decrease, mountains are worn down, hillslopes become more gradual, surfaces approach base level.	During leveling, stream gradients decrease. Distinctive stream drainage patterns form.	Erosion removes soil material from steeper slopes and transports material for soil-making processes to lower elevations.
Climate	Arid climates produce sharp, angular hillslopes. Humid climates produce rounded hillslopes. Weathering and erosion generally occur faster in humid regions.	In arid environments streams may flow intermittently. Drainage density is higher in humid regions (other factors being equal).	In arid regions the soils may be shallow or non-existent. Few plants exist, and there is little or no leaching. Development of soil horizons is poor. In humid regions deep soils may form and plants may be abundant. Leaching is extensive. Very humid regions may have no humus because of complete breakdown of organic matter by bacteria.
	Hillslopes can affect wind and precipitation patterns.		
	Glaciation produces unique hillslope shapes in valleys and causes new hills to form.	Glaciation causes distinctive stream characteristics.	Soils may form from material transported and deposited by glaciers.
Bedrock	Bedrock features may affect the shape of hillslope surfaces. Hillslope steepness depends on rock resistance. Resistant rock forms cliffs; less resistant rock wears away rapidly.	Homogeneous bedrock may cause distinctive stream patterns. Complex bedrock may alter stream patterns. Waterfalls form where cliffs occur. Limestone regions may have few surface streams, but numerous sinks or sinkhole lakes.	Bedrock composition directly affects soil composition.
Human Activities	Excavations make hillslopes too steep, and the surface becomes unstable, increasing the chances of landslides. Removal of vegetation and topsoil also leave the surface unstable, and it erodes more easily.	Ground-water drainage may be altered by highway construction. The courses of rivers may be altered for irrigation, to control flooding, and to produce power.	Improper soil usage may deplete topsoil. Clearing land for agriculture may result in erosion and further loss of soil.
			Fertilizers increase soil productivity.
	Relatively small hills can be either created or removed by man.	Use of streams and lakes for sewage disposal results in water pollution.	Addition of pollutants to the soil may make it unusable.

Figure 26-9. Completed grid from Figure 25-1 .

TIME AND LANDSCAPE DEVELOPMENT

One aspect of landscapes that has not yet been considered is the time required for a landscape to develop. In other words, how *long* does it take for the environmental factors to produce landscape characteristics? There are two ways to look at this question. One is to try to determine the *actual* amount of time required. The other is to describe the time in terms of the *relative* stage of development of the characteristics of a landscape. Knowing the actual time is always preferred by scientists. However, it is often necessary to settle for finding the relative ages.

Stages of Landscape Development. One common method used to describe the relative stages of landscape development makes use of the terms youth, maturity, and old age as subdivisions of the development process.

Figure 26-10 shows one interpretation of the erosional development of a fault-block mountain. You can note the changes in the characteristics from the initial, or youthful, stage to the stage of old age. It is difficult to assign a specific amount of time required for any stage to develop, because different changes take place at different rates, and the rates often depend on the conditions under which the changes occur.

Table 26-11 lists some general characteristics that are often used to distinguish the stages of landscape development. Keep in mind that these are general guidelines, not hard and fast rules. The function of such guidelines is to aid in classifying the characteristics of a landscape. The stages are "points" along a continuous path of development. They do not

Figure 26-10. Erosional development of a fault-block mountain. This drawing illustrates the stages of development, from uplift (left) to old age (right).

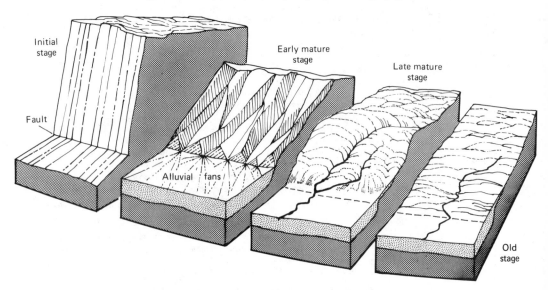

	Hillslopes	**Streams**	**Soils**
Youth	High elevations Rugged surfaces Steep slopes	Steep gradient Small volume Waterfalls and rapids common Relatively straight paths High velocity	Little development of horizons Parent material still easily visible Shallow development
Maturity	Lower elevations Less rugged surfaces May be more rounded, especially in humid environment Less steep slopes	More gradual gradient Broad meanders Flood plains Few or no waterfalls Medium velocity	Horizons developed Parent material less recognizable Thicker development
Old Age	Little or no elevation above surrounding area	Very low gradient Meander cut-offs are common Very broad flood plain Low velocity	Parent material completely gone Materials highly weathered Thick humus present in certain environments Thickest development

Figure 26-11. Characteristics of stages of landscape development.

represent abrupt changes.

Landscape and Dynamic Equilibrium. As stated earlier, a landscape may be in a state of dynamic equilibrium. Opposing forces acting on the landscape may be occurring at equal rates, so that no overall change *seems* to be taking place.

If a landscape is in a state of dynamic equilibrium and one of the forces influencing that landscape should change, the equilibrium could be upset. For example, suppose that the rock material making up a hillslope were to change. Such a change could be caused by a rock face of different composition being exposed by weathering and erosion. If the newly exposed rock were less resistant to weathering and erosion, the hillslope would wear down faster than before.

As the hillslope grew smaller and the gradient less steep, the streams eroding it would slow down and have less erosional power. Gradually, the stream would adjust its rate of erosion until the landscape again was in a state of dynamic equilibrium.

The existence of a state of dynamic equilibrium has the effect of making the process of landscape development seem to stand still. In such a state, a landscape might retain the features of the youthful stage for an undetermined period of time. The process of landscape development involves many variables, or environmental factors, as we have seen. A change in the action of any of these factors could have the tendency to upset an existing state of equilibrium, or to cause such a state to be established.

SUMMARY

1. The amount of time during which environmental factors have been active will determine the stage of development or condition of the landscape.
2. The stages of landscape development are youthful, mature, and old.
3. The interaction of environmental factors with landscape characteristics occurs as a delicately balanced process. The state of balance can be altered by changing any of the factors in the interaction. The system tends to move toward a state of dynamic equilibrium unless one or more of the factors affecting the system changes.

REVIEW QUESTIONS

Group A
1. How might the immediate, or short-term, effects of human activities on the landscape differ from the long-term effects?
2. What effect do activities like excavation and cultivation have on hillslopes?
3. What undesirable effects can highway construction have on the environment?
4. What kinds of activities often lead to harmful levels of water pollution? What actions can be taken to offset these harmful effects?
5. What kinds of devices can be used to control and conserve ground water and surface runoff?
6. What could be the effect of uncontrolled use of soils for agricultural purposes. What conservation measures can help maintain or reclaim soil?
7. What is one major cause of landscape pollution? Describe some methods that can be used to avoid this situation and, at the same time, reclaim useless land areas for recreational purposes.
8. What factor determines the stage of development or condition of the landscape?
9. How can stages of landscape development be classified or described?
10. Describe the state of balance of the factors that interact to cause the landscape. How can this state of balance be changed? What condition does a landscape development system move toward in a natural process?

Group B
1. Human activities may affect the landscape in a beneficial and in a non-beneficial way.
   a. List at least three "benefits" that could be caused by highway construction such as that shown in Fig. 26-3. List at least three "costs" that could be caused by the same construction.
   b. List at least three "benefits" caused by people's attempts to control rivers. List at least three "costs" caused by these same attempts.
   c. List at least three "benefits" caused by people's activities with the soil. List at least three "costs" caused by these activities.
2. a. What are the effects of air, water, and land pollution occurring where you live?

    b. What corrective measures can you see are being taken in your area to overcome environmental pollution?

    c. What additional measures can you identify that need to be taken in your area to further overcome local environmental pollution?

    d. Identify which groups, agencies, or individuals have the responsibility or power to correct the unresolved problems of environmental pollution.

3. Using your descriptions of your local landscape made, earlier, write a summary describing the type of landscape region in which you live, its stage of development, and its condition with regard to environmental pollution. Assume the description is going to be sent to someone who is not familiar with your area. Include ample information so that the person will be aware of your climate and of the landscape characteristics that make your area unique.

REVIEW EXERCISES

1. The profile of an average or ideal stream can be simulated using a model called a random walk. Use the procedure as described by your instructor to produce several random-walk profiles. Compare your profiles with those produced by other students in your class and with the profile shown in Figure 24-6 (page 468).

2. The drainage densities shown in Figure 24-9 (page 469) do not appear to be equal. Measure the stream lengths, calculate the drainage area, and determine the drainage densities. Use a scale of 1 cm = 1 km. List some reasons that could explain why the two areas have such a difference in drainage density.

3. Refer to Figure 25-15 (page 493) to answer the following questions.

    a. Three cities have mean annual temperatures of 20°C, 25°C, and 30°C respectively. How will the humus production and accumulation compare among the cities?

    b. Two cities have the same mean annual temperature. One city is at an elevation of 2 km, the other is at sea level. How does humus production compare at the two locations?

    c. Determine the mean annual temperature for several cities from an atlas. Describe the relative rates of production and destruction of plant matter that you would predict for the areas

4. Concrete for building purposes consists of cement, sand, water, and gravel. The amount of gravel commonly used in concrete is about 50%. How large a gravel pit would have to be excavated to build a highway 500 kilometers long, 1/50 kilometer wide, and 1/5,000 kilometer thick?

    Assume the gravel pit is excavated to an average depth of 20 meters. What area would the pit cover? How does the area compare with the size of your community?

5. Figure 26-6 (page 514) illustrates some structures that man can use to improve stream conditions and control erosion. Select a stream near where you live. Walk the stream and observe its condition. Compile a list of suggestions that could improve its condition. Consider possible negative effects of these suggestions. Present your report to your class.

Epilogue

According to the dictionary, the epilogue of a book is the concluding section. It serves to "round out" or interpret what has gone before.

We began this book focusing on the processes of making observations and drawing inferences from those observations. These two activities are basic to the work of the earth scientist. It is from a base of carefully made observations that the observer is able to find patterns of change in the environment. The information, or data, derived from these observations also helps to explain the patterns.

Isolated or unrelated bits of information are of little use in determining patterns. Thus, we attempt to organize information or classify it so that it is useful. One frequently used method of organizing data is to construct a model. A model is a device designed to use data or evidence in such a way as to show how events occur or processes operate. The model is a *simulation* of an actual object or event being studied.

Throughout this book, we have attempted to focus on the model concept. We have tried to add to the model as we went, hoping to obtain a model complete enough to explain all our observations. Our approach to earth science has been to think of the earth and its processes as resembling a jigsaw puzzle. The more information (data) we gathered, the more of the puzzle we were able to complete. Each little bit of information was like a piece of the jigsaw puzzle, which had to be identified and fitted into place. Sometimes we identified pieces of the puzzle, but we weren't sure where they fit. Finding the solution is part of the fascination of science and the process of inquiry.

The first steps in our model-building process concentrated on physical characteristics—dimensions, shapes, and motions. Very early in the development of our model, we realized that earth changes involved a transfer of energy. Thus, it became apparent that any earth model would be incomplete without relating energy changes to our observations.

The sun was recognized as our most important energy source, and its part in earth processes was added as a piece of the puzzle. Gravity was also recognized as an important energy source, and its role in shaping the earth was incorporated into the model.

As more parts of our model became identified, we found that we could use observations to make certain predictions. For example, by studying the changes that take place in the atmosphere, and the energy relationships involved in those changes, it became possible to recognize certain atmospheric conditions. From this, we gained greater understanding of weather and climate and were able to predict what weather (or climate) changes would be caused by changes in the atmosphere.

Observations of changes occurring in the atmosphere and at the earth's surface led naturally to the concept of interaction, or cause-and-effect relationships. We learned to try to identify effects, in the hope that inferences drawn from these effects would lead us to their cause. Studies were made of the interaction between the atmosphere and the earth's surface. The results were interpreted, and we developed a model of moisture and energy budgets, and, finally, of climates.

Studies of the effect of climate on the lithosphere led to investigations of the erosional process. We became aware of the factors that cause the wearing away of the earth's surface. In our studies of erosional-depositional systems, an understanding of energy changes and equilibrium conditions was necessary in order to fit this piece of the puzzle into the earth model.

Our studies of deposition led naturally to the rock-forming processes. As we investigated how rocks formed, the evidence suggested that the changes were part of a cyclic process in which "all rocks originate from other rocks." The study of the rock cycle brought to light the extreme environmental conditions under which rocks form. Questions about these conditions presented new puzzles to be solved to complete the earth model.

Investigations of the earth's crust and interior provided more evidence about the importance of interactions in earth processes. This part of the model seemed to suggest a restless planet, whose crust undergoes constant change. Some of these changes, such as volcanic eruptions and earthquakes, are abrupt; others, such as mountain building and subsidence, are much more gradual, but not less spectacular. We became aware that these processes of change had been at work for extremely long periods of time and are continuing today. Thus, our attention was shifted to the problem of reconstructing the history of the earth.

We discovered that the rocks of the earth hold a wealth of information about the earth's past. We learned the clues and techniques that are used to interpret the rock record. From the evidence in the record, we drew inferences about the geologic and biologic history of the earth, from its origin to the present.

We investigated changes or interactions that occur at the earth's surface to produce and influence landscapes. Cause-and-effect relationships helped us gain an understanding of the interaction of landscape characteristics and environmental factors.

Human activity as an environmental factor was investigated in some detail, with considerable concern expressed over our influence on and abuse of our natural resources. We considered how our very survival on this planet may depend on our being able to control our effect on the delicate balance that exists among processes of the earth model. Particular stress was placed on ways in which the current trend of pollution and misuse of resources can be halted, or at least brought under control. These methods were summarized under three headings—prevention, conservation, and reclamation.

We have explored together the development of an earth model. The model includes the physical characteristics of the planet and the processes that affect the characteristics. We have added all of the pieces of the puzzle that we have at hand. Many parts are still missing. As more pieces become identified, the model will become more complete. The model may even be changed dramatically, as it was when Copernicus reshaped the earth model by putting the pieces of the puzzle in a new relationship.

How have you changed as you proceeded through this course? You might try to recall what you were like at the beginning of this school year. You were a few months younger, probably a little shorter, maybe a little bit lighter. These are physical differences. How have you changed in terms of your knowledge of the earth and your attitudes toward it? What are you now that you weren't before? What will you be from here on?

Some expressions that occur to us as highly desirable responses to these questions include: aware, concerned, more knowledgeable, somewhat awed by the earth, confident of our ability to gain understanding about the earth. Finally, we would hope that you feel a certain sense of duty to act as a steward, or caretaker, of the environment.

We can hope for these responses, but we can't require them from you. If we have been successful in the interactions we have had with you throughout this book, then the "forces" that we have applied to you may result in an "effect" that will help make the environment a little better for all.

Glossary

absolute zero—the coldest, or lowest, temperature possible at which all heat energy has been removed from an object. 0° Kelvin or -273° Celsius.

acid rain—precipitation with a pH of 5.6 or less.

actual evapotranspiration (E_a)—in a local water budget, the actual outgo of water due to evaporation and transpiration.

adiabatic change—any change that occurs without the addition or removal of heat energy.

aerobic bacteria—bacteria that require oxygen for their life processes.

aerosols—tiny solid particles, such as dust, pollen, and salt, that are found suspended in unfiltered air. Aerosols serve as nuclei on which water droplets can condense.

air mass—a large body of air that shows the same temperature and humidity characteristics throughout at a given altitude.

amplitude—the strength of intensity of a wave.

anaerobic bacteria—bacteria that do not require oxygen for their life processes.

angle of repose—the greatest (steepest) angle at which loose material will rest on a surface.

aphelion—the point in a planet's orbit that is farthest from the sun.

asthenosphere—a region of the upper mantle that is thought to be partially molten; that region of the mantle in which convection cells are believed to be circulating.

atmosphere—the layer of gases surrounding the earth.

base flow—water that enters a stream from ground water.

bedrock—the solid rock beneath the regolith.

capillary action—the upward movement of water through narrow passageways resulting from the forces of adhesion and cohesion.

carbonation—the reaction of carbonic acid with other substances. It is an important reaction in the chemical weathering of rocks.

celestial sphere—a model of the sky, consisting of an imaginary sphere (with the earth at the center) on which the heavenly bodies are projected.

chemical compound—any substance composed of atoms of different elements joined together in a definite ratio.

chemical weathering—the breakdown of rock by chemical action, during which there is a change in chemical composition of the minerals in the rock.

cleavage—the tendency of a mineral to split along surfaces, or planes, of weakness; a physical property used in mineral identification.

climate—the average weather conditions in a region over a period of many years.

cloud—a collection of water droplets or ice crystals so small that they can be kept suspended in the air by upward currents. Clouds at ground level are called *fog*.

colloid—a solid particle that is too small to be seen with an ordinary microscope and too light to settle in water.

compressional (P) waves—seismic waves in which the particles vibrate in a direction parallel to that of the wave path. Also called *primary waves,* their motion is due to alternating compression and expansion of the rock.

condensation—the change of state from gas to liquid.

conduction—the transfer of heat energy from molecule to molecule through direct contact (collision).

conservation of energy—the scientific law that states that in any transfer of energy, the total amount of energy remains the same.

constructional forces—forces operating beneath or within the crust that tend to raise the earth's surface. Also called *uplifting forces*.

continental drift—a theory that states that the earth's continents are continuously moving and changing their relative positions on the earth's surface.

contour map—a map on which surface elevations are shown by means of isolines called contour lines. Also called *topographic map*.

convection—the transfer of heat within a fluid by means of circulatory movements (currents) of the fluid.

convection cell—a circulating system of motion within a fluid in which temperature and density differences exist. In the warmer, less dense portion of the cell, motion is upward; in cooler, more dense portions, motion is downward.

convergence zone—a region in a convection cell where air is coming together (converging) near the earth's surface and then rising.

coordinate system—any system for assigning two numbers to every point on a surface.

core—the innermost zone of the earth's interior. Based on seismic evidence, the core is believed to consist of two regions—the outer core, which behaves like a liquid, and the inner core, believed to be solid.

Coriolis effect—an effect of the earth's rotation that causes the shifting, or deflecting, of the paths of projectiles, ocean currents, and winds.

correlation—the process of showing that rocks or geologic events that occurred in different places are of the same age.

crust—the uppermost portion of the lithosphere, including the soil and loose rock material (regolith).

crystal—a solid with a regular geometric shape. Most crystals have smooth, flat surfaces, or *faces*.

crystal lattice—the arrangement of atoms (or ions) in a definite, repeating pattern that is characteristic of each crystal.

cyclic change—a change that goes through an orderly series of events that repeat at regular intervals.

density—a measure of the concentration of matter (mass) in a given space (volume); mass per unit volume.

density current—any current or flow of material that is set in motion by the contact of two materials of different densities, where one of the materials is capable of flowing over or under the other. Such currents often act as erosional agents.

deposition—the "dropping" of transported materials (sediments), or the processes by which transported materials are left in new locations. Also called *sedimentation.*

destructional forces—forces operating at the earth's surface that tend to destroy variations in elevation of the landscape. Also called *leveling forces.*

dew point—the temperature at which the air would be saturated with water vapor.

discontinuity—any sudden change in the properties of a material or a system.

divergence zone—a region in a convection cell where air is sinking and then spreading out (diverging) near the earth's surface.

drainage basin—the entire area enclosed by a drainage divide and in which all of the water that falls as precipitation eventually drains into the main stream of the basin, e.g., the Mississippi River basin.

drainage density—the ratio of the total length of all stream channels within a drainage basin to the total area of the basin.

drainage divide—the line drawn along the high ground that encloses a drainage basin or marks the boundary between two adjacent drainage basins; a line across which no water flows.

dynamic equilibrium—a situation in which changes are occurring, but a balance among the changes keeps the overall conditions the same.

earthquake—any movement of the earth's crust, usually along a fault or zone of weakness; the shaking, vibrating, and sometimes violent movement of the crust.

ecliptic—the apparent path that the sun follows among the stars.

element—any substance that cannot be broken down into simpler substances by ordinary chemical means.

energy—the capacity to do work. Energy can be transferred from one body to another. The total quantity of energy remains constant during any change.

epicenter—the point on the earth's surface directly above the focus of an earthquake.

epoch—the shortest time unit in the geologic time scale.

equator—a line around the earth connecting all points midway between the North and South Poles; the 0° latitude line.

equinox—time of year when the sun is directly over the equator and day and night are of equal length (12 hours) everywhere on earth. The *vernal* (spring) *equinox* occurs on or about March 21; the *autumnal* (fall) *equinox* occurs on or about September 23.

era—the largest division of the geologic time scale.

erosion—any natural process that removes sediments from one place and transports them to another.

erosional-depositional system—a region with definite boundaries, within which all the events of erosion and deposition occur within a single continuous medium.

evaporation—the change of stage from liquid to gas; the vaporization, or escape of molecules, from the surface of a liquid.

evapotranspiration—the transfer of moisture to the atmosphere by the combined processes of evaporation and transpiration.

evolution—the gradual change in the characteristics of a species over long periods of time, which eventually results in a new species.

fault—a break or crack in the earth's crust along which motion occurs or appears to have occurred.

field—a region of space in which there is a measurable quantity of a given property at every point, e.g., the earth's magnetic field.

focus—the point within the earth at which an earthquake and its associated earthquake (seismic) waves originate.

fossils—remains, imprints, or traces of ancient plants or animals.

Foucault pendulum—a pendulum with a very long radius of swing, used to illustrate the fact of the earth's rotation.

front—the interface where two air masses with different characteristics meet.

frost action—the physical weathering of rock by the alternate freezing and melting of water in the pores or cracks in the rock.

geocentric model—any model of the universe that is designed with the earth at the center.

geologic column—a composite, chronological model of the rock record extending from the time of the earliest fossils to the present.

geologic province—a landscape region in which all parts are similar in structure and climate. Also called *physiographic province*.

geologic time scale—the division of geologic time into units, based on evidence contained in the rock record.

geosyncline—an area of shallow water that appears to be subsiding as sediments accumulate in it.

glacier—any mass of frozen water on land. Glaciers are powerful agents of erosion. *Valley* or *alpine* glaciers form at high altitudes in mountainous regions; *continental* glaciers, or *ice sheets,* form at high latitudes.

gradient—rate of change between two points; quantity of change per unit of distance. Also called *slope*.

greenhouse effect—the heating of the atmosphere by the reradiation of energy from the earth's surface at long wavelengths, which are absorbed by the air.

ground water—the subsurface water in the zone of saturation.

H-R diagram—a chart that classifies stars according to their temperature and brightness.

half-life—the length of time necessary for half of a sample of a radioactive element to disintegrate.

heat—energy of the random motion of molecules in a substance; energy that flows from one body to another because they have different temperatures.

heat sink—a body or region into which heat is flowing.

heat source—a body or region from which heat is flowing.

heliocentric model—any model of the universe that is designed with the sun at the center.

high-pressure system—an air mass in which the pressure is greatest at the center. In such a system, winds blow outward from the center in a clockwise circulation. Also known as a *high,* or *anticyclone.*

horizon—the edge, or rim, of the celestial sphere; any point on the circle 90° from the observer's zenith.

humidity—a measure of the amount of water vapor in the air.

humus—partially decayed organic matter that gives topsoil its dark brown or black color.

hydrosphere—the thin layer of water that rests on or penetrates the lithosphere. The hydrosphere consists of *all* the earth's water, including polar ice and subsurface water.

igneous rocks—rocks formed by the hardening of once-molten or liquid rock.

index fossil—fossils that are typical of a particular geologic period or epoch. Such fossils are very useful in correlating rock formations.

inertia—the property of a mass to resist a change in its motion; the tendency of an object at rest to remain at rest and an object in motion to continue moving in a straight line at constant speed.

infiltration—the sinking, or soaking, of rainwater into the ground.

insolation—from *in*coming *sol*ar radi*ation;* that portion of the sun's radiation that is received by the earth.

interface—a boundary between regions of different properties. Changes and energy flow usually occur across an interface.

ionosphere—a region of the earth's atmosphere that contains a high concentration of electrically charged particles. Most of the harmful rays (X rays and ultraviolet rays) of the sun are absorbed by the ionosphere.

isoline—on a map of a field, a line connecting all points having the same field value.

isostasy—the principle that states that the earth's crust is in a state of equilibrium, and that any change in mass of one part of the crust will be offset by a change in another part. This "balancing" of masses is called *isostatic compensation.*

isosurface—in a three-dimensional field, a surface that passes through all points having the same field value.

isotope—different forms of the same element. Isotopes have the same atomic number but different atomic weights or masses.

kinetic energy—energy a body has because of its motion.

landscape—the association, or relationships, of the physical features of a region of the earth's surface.

latent heat—a form of potential energy that is gained (or lost) by the particles of a substance during a change in state of that substance.

latent heat of fusion—the latent heat involved in a change of state from solid to liquid or from liquid to solid.

latent heat of vaporization—the latent heat involved in a change of state from liquid to gas or from gas to liquid.

latitude—a measurement of angular distance north or south of the equator, which is the 0° latitude line.

lava—liquid rock (magma) that reaches the earth's surface.

leaching—the removing, or "washing away," of soluble minerals from the soil by infiltration of surface water.

light-year — the distance light travels in 1 year; a unit for expressing distances of stars.

lithosphere—continuous shell of solid rock around the earth. The lithosphere includes the crust and part of the mantle.

lithospheric plate—an enormous slab of lithospheric rock. According to the theory of plate tectonics, the earth's lithosphere consists of a number of these individual plates.

local water budget—a mathematical model of the water cycle of a region.

longitude—a measurement of angular distance east or west of the prime meridian.

low-pressure system—an air mass in which the pressure is lowest in the center. In such a system, winds blow in toward the center in a counter-clockwise circulation. Also called a *low,* or *cyclone.*

luster—the way in which the surface of a mineral reflects light; a physical property used in mineral identification.

magma—liquid rock beneath the earth's surface.

mantle—region of dense material in the earth's interior between the crust and the outer core.

mass—the amount, or quantity, of matter in an object.

meander—a winding or looping bend in a stream bed. Meanders are characteristic of a mature stream.

mean solar day—an average solar day (exactly 24 hours).

meridian—a semicircle on the earth's surface connecting the North and South Poles.

metamorphic rock—rock formed from other rocks as a result of the action of heat, pressure, and/or chemical action.

mid-ocean ridge—a mountain chain running along the middle of an ocean basin. All ocean basins have such a feature on their floors.

mineral—a naturally occurring, crystalline, inorganic substance with characteristic physical and chemical properties.

model—anything that represents the properties of an object or a system in such a way as to help describe or predict its behavior.

Mohorovicic discontinuity—the boundary, or interface, between the crust and the mantle. Also called the *Moho*.

monomineralic rock—a rock composed of a single mineral, e.g., halite (rock salt).

nova—a very bright star that is left-over when a Red Giant explodes off its outer layer.

oblate spheroid—a sphere that is flattened along one diameter and bulges around the middle. The earth's shape is that of an oblate spheroid.

ocean-floor spreading—a theory that states that the ocean floors are spreading apart as new rock material is added to the crust in the regions of the mid-ocean ridges.

original horizontality—the principle that sedimentary rocks were formed from layers of sediment that were once in a horizontal position.

orographic effect—the effect of mountains on the climate of a region, particularly an increase in precipitation on the windward side and a decrease on the leeward side.

outcrop—any bedrock formation that is exposed at the earth's surface.

oxidation—the chemical reaction of oxygen with another substance. It is a common and important reaction in chemical weathering of rocks.

parallax—the apparent shift of one object relative to other objects due to the motion of the observer.

parallels of latitude—east-west lines above and below the equator made by passing planes through the earth parallel to the equator.

perihelion—the point in a planet's orbit that is closest to the sun.

period—the second largest time unit in the geologic time scale. Each era is subdivided into periods.

permeability—the ability of a material to allow fluids to pass through it.

phase transition—the transformation of one mineral form into another form under extreme temperature-pressure conditions.

physical weathering—the breakdown of rock into small pieces without chemical change.

physiographic province—see **geologic province.**

plate tectonics—a theory of crustal motion that states that the earth's crust is divided into a number of separate plates that are "floating" on the dense, liquid-like zone of the upper mantle called the *asthenosphere.*

pollutant—anything that, if added to the environment in sufficient concentration, adversely affects (pollutes) the environment for human purposes.

polymineralic rock—a rock composed of two or more minerals. Most rocks are polymineralic.

porosity—the percentage of open space in the volume of a sample of a material.

potential energy—energy a body has because of its position or state; "stored" energy.

potential evapotranspiration (E_p)—in a local water budget, the maximum possible outgo of water due to evaporation and transpiration.

precipitation—(1) weather: any form of water that falls from the atmosphere and reaches the ground. (2) chemical: the formation of a solid (precipitate) in a liquid solution. Such formation may be due to a chemical reaction or to the cooling or evaporation of the solvent.

pressure—the amount of force exerted on a unit of area; force per unit area.

prime meridian—the semicircle connecting the North and South Poles that passes through Greenwich, England; the 0° longitude line.

Punctuated Equilibria—a theory that explains rapid episodes of evolution that appear in the fossil record.

radiation—(1) the transfer of energy by electromagnetic waves; (2) the emission, or giving off, of electromagnetic waves or, in the case of radioactive substances, the emission of high-speed particles.

radiative balance—condition in which the amount of heat lost by radiation is equal to the amount gained from insolation.

radioactive dating—any method of determining the age of a sample that is based on radioactive decay of natural elements.

radioactivity—the natural and spontaneous breakdown of certain unstable elements to form atoms of other elements. Energy in the form of waves or high-speed particles is released during the decay process. Also called *radioactive decay*.

regolith—the loose rock material, including soil, that covers much of the earth's land surface.

relative humidity—the ratio of the amount of water vapor in the air to the maximum amount that could be present at that temperature. Expressed as a percent.

relief—the difference in elevation between the highest and lowest points in a region.

residual sediments—sediments that have been weathered from the bedrock on which they are situated.

rock—any portion of the lithosphere. Most rocks are mixtures of minerals.

rock cycle—a model designed to show how the three classes of rock are interrelated.

rock-forming minerals—those minerals that make up more than 90% of the mass of the lithosphere. These minerals, in various combinations, make up most of the rocks of the earth.

runoff—water flowing over the surface of the ground.

saturation vapor pressure—the pressure exerted by water vapor in a sample of air that is saturated with water vapor. Saturation vapor pressure is directly related to temperature.

sedimentary rocks—any rocks formed from accumulated sediments.

seismic waves—wavelike motions in the earth caused by earthquakes.

seismograph—an instrument designed to detect and record earthquake (seismic) waves.

shear (S) waves—seismic waves in which the particles vibrate at right angles to the direction of travel of the wave. Also called *secondary* waves, shear waves cannot be transmitted through a liquid.

sidereal day—a day whose length is measured by two successive appearances of a star at a given meridian. A sidereal day is about four minutes *shorter* than a solar day.

sidereal year—the time required for the sun to make one complete circuit of the ecliptic. A sidereal year is about 20 minutes longer than a solar year.

silicate mineral—any mineral that contains silicon and oxygen in chemical combination with other elements. About 60% of all minerals are silicates.

silicon-oxygen tetrahedron—the structural unit of silicate minerals, which consists of four oxygen ions bonded to a silicon ion centrally situated among them.

soil association—the grouping together of soils of similar characteristics.

soil horizons—the different layers in a soil profile. Each horizon has its own characteristic properties.

soil profile—a side view of a vertical section of soil showing all horizontal layers.

soil storage (St)—in a local water budget, the amount of water in the soil that is available to plants. Soil storage has a maximum possible value for a given situation.

solar day—a day whose length is measured by two successive appearances of the sun at a given meridian; the period from one noon to the next.

solar year—the time between two successive summer solstices or two successive winter solstices.

solstice—the time of year when the sun's vertical rays reach farthest north or south of the equator. On June 21 (*summer* solstice) the vertical rays strike at 23½°N; on December 21 (*winter* solstice) the vertical rays strike at 23½°S.

source region—the region over which an air mass originates and which determines the properties of the air mass.

species—a distinct type of organism that produces offspring of the same type.

specific gravity—the ratio of a substance's density to the density of water; a physical property used in mineral identification.

streak—the color of a mineral in powdered form; a physical property used in mineral identification.

stream—any natural channel on the earth's surface that carries water downhill.

stream discharge—the volume of water that passes a point in the stream during a given amount of time.

stream system—a combination of the main stream of a region and all of its tributary streams.

subduction zone—the boundary where two converging lithospheric plates come together. At such a boundary, one plate plunges (subducts) beneath the other.

subsidence—any sinking or downward motion of a portion of the earth's crust.

superposition—the principle that states that in a sedimentary rock formation, the bottom layer is the oldest and the top layer is the youngest.

surplus (S)—in a local water budget, any precipitation that is received when soil storage is at its maximum.

temperature—a measure of the *average* kinetic energy possessed by the particles of a substance.

topographic map—see **contour map.**

topography—the physical features of the earth's surface.

transported sediments—sediments that have been carried from some other place. Such sediments usually differ considerably from the bedrock on which they are found.

turbidity current—a swirling current produced by sudden movements of sediments down the continental slope.

unconformity—a buried erosional surface. There is a discontinuity in the ages of the rock layers that are in contact at an unconformity.

uniformitarianism—the principle that states that the forces and processes that affect the earth today are basically the same as those that operated in the past.

vapor pressure—the pressure exerted by the vapor of a solid or a liquid; often used to refer to the pressure of water vapor exclusively.

water cycle—the constant circulation of water from the hydrosphere to the atmosphere (by evapotranspiration) and back again (by condensation and precipitation). Also called the *hydrologic cycle.*

water table—the top of the zone of saturation.

weather—the atmospheric variables that prevail at a particular place during a short period of time.

weathering—the breakdown of rock material as a result of chemical and/or physical action.

weight—a measure of the force of gravity on a body. The weight of an object is proportional to its mass.

wind—a horizontal movement of air over the surface of the earth.

zenith—the highest point on the celestial sphere; the point in the sky directly above the observer.

Appendix

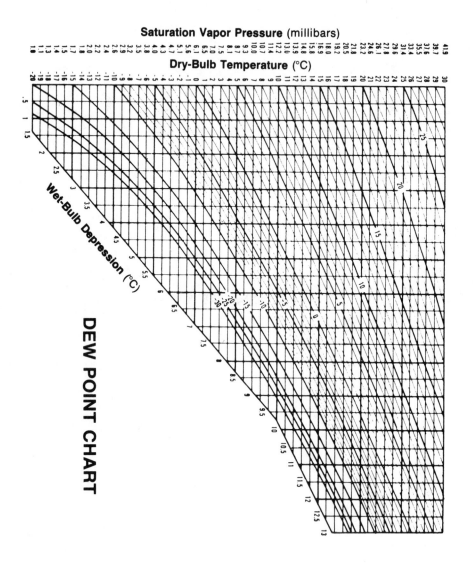

Saturation Vapor Pressure (millibars)

Dry-Bulb Temperature (°C)

Wet-Bulb Depression (°C)

DEW POINT CHART

Using the Dew-Point Chart

Practice using the Dew Point
Chart with the following data:

> Dry bulb temperature = 17°C
> Wet bulb temperature = 13°C

Example 1.
To find the *dew-point temperature*,
a) Find the dry-bulb temperature on
the left side of the chart (17°C).
b) Find the difference between dry-
bulb and wet-bulb temperatures (4°C).
This is the wet-bulb depression.
c) Find the point where the graphs of
the dry-bulb temperature and the wet-
bulb depression meet. Read the dew-
point temperature by following the
sloping line that passes through this
point to the left side of the chart
(10°C).

Example 2.
To find the *relative humidity*,
a) Read the value of the saturation
vapor pressure for the dry-bulb temperature at the left side of the chart
(19.2 mb).
b) Read the value of the saturation
vapor pressure for the dew-point
temperature, also at the left side of the
chart (12.2 mb).
c) Divide the second value by the first,
and multiply the result by 100.

$$\frac{12.2}{19.2} \times 100 = 64\%$$

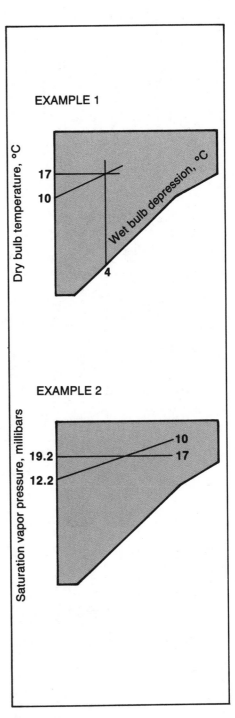

MINERAL IDENTIFICATION CHART

Color: varies considerably

Cleavage: one, two, three, or more direction

Fracture: uneven, shell-like, splintery, or fibrous

Luster: metallic (like polished metal) or nonmetallic (glassy, waxy, silky, dull or earthy, greasy, pearly)

Streak: dark-colored with opaque and metallic minerals; light-colored with translucent and nonmetallic minerals

Specific Gravity: light weight (up to 2.5); medium weight (2.6 to 3.0); heavy weight (over 3.0)

Hardness: one to ten on the standard hardness scale

Other Characteristics: taste, odor, feel, magnetism, crystal form, flexibility, elasticity, brittleness, transparency, translucency, opaqueness, acid reaction

Mineral	Color	Cleavage	Fracture	Luster	Streak	Specific Gravity	Hardness	Other Characteristics
Asbestos	white to light green	none	splintery	silky	white	2.2	2-5	fibrous; greasy feel
Augite	black to green	2	uneven splinters	glassy	grayish green	3.1-3.5	6	short, stubby-sided crystals
Azurite	blue	none	fibrous	glassy	light blue	3.8	3.5	bubbles in HC1
Bauxite	red to brown	none	none	dull	red to brown	2.5	1-3	lumpy appearance; odor of wet clay when wet
Calcite	all colors	3	none	glassy, dull	white	2.7	3	transparent to opaque; bubbles in HC1
Cassiterite	red-brown	none	uneven	dull	white-brown	7	6-7	heavy, rounded masses
Chalcopyrite	brassy yellow	none	uneven	metallic	green-black	4.2	3-4	iridescent
Galena	gray to black	3	none	metallic	gray to black	7.5	2.5	cubic crystals; heavy

Mineral	Color	Cleavage	Fracture	Luster	Streak	Specific Gravity	Hardness	Other
Garnet	red to black	none	uneven	waxy to glassy	white	3.1-4.3	6.5-7.5	brittle; rounded; translucent
Graphite	dark gray to black	none	flaky	metallic	black	2-3	1	greasy feel; soft;
Gypsum	colorless or white to gray	3	uneven	pearly to dull	none or white	2	2	fibrous; flexible
Hematite	red to black	none	uneven	metallic to dull	red-brown	5.1	6	brittle; opaque; never crystalline
Hornblende	black to green	2	uneven splinters	glassy	dark green	2.9-3.5	6	long, 6-sided crystals
Kaolinite	white to gray	none	earthy	dull	white	2.2	1.5-2.5	clay odor; crumbles greasy feel
Limonite	yellow, brown	none	shell-like	dull	yellow-brown	3-4	1-5	earthy; dull; brittle
Magnetite	black	none	uneven	metallic	black	5.2	6	magnetic; brittle; heavy
Malachite	green	none	fibrous	dull	light green	4	3-4	bubbles in HC1
Mica	black to brown, colorless	1	uneven	glassy, pearly	white	2.7-3.1	2-2.5	elastic; transparent thin sheets; flexible

Mineral	Color	Cleavage	Fracture	Luster	Streak	Specific Gravity	Hardness	Other Characteristics
Olivine	yellow-green	none	uneven	glassy	pale green	3.2-3.6	7	granular masses; sugary; glassy grains
Orthoclase feldspar	white, pink	2	uneven	glassy, pearly	white	2.5	6	translucent on thin edges
Pitchblende	grayish to black	none	uneven	dull	black	6-9	5-6	pitchlike appearance
Plagioclase feldspar	white, gray	2	uneven	glassy, pearly	white	2.7	6	striations on one surface; opaque
Pyrite	pale brass	none	uneven	metallic	greenish-black	5	6	striations on crystals; commonly called "fool's gold"
Quartz	white, gray, pink	none	shell-like	glassy	white	2.6	7	translucent
Salt	colorless	3	uneven	glassy	none	2.3	2.5	salty taste; dissolves in water
Sphalerite	brown to black	6	none	waxy	light	4	3-4	brittle
Sulfur	yellow	none	shell-like	greasy	white	2.0	2	crackles in heat of hand; brittle; burns with blue flame
Talc	white, light	1	uneven	glassy, pearly	white to green	2.6	1	greasy feel; foliated

SEDIMENTARY ROCK CLASSIFICATION CHART

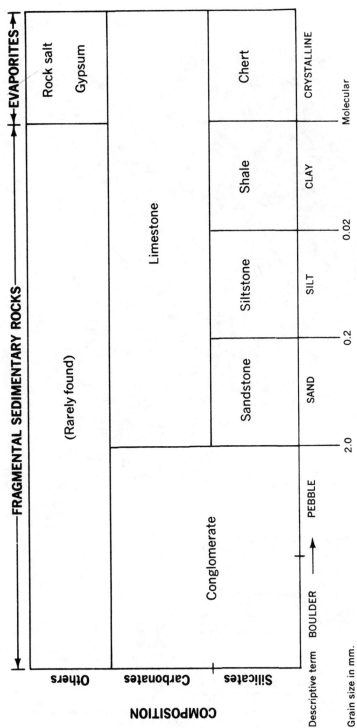

BEDROCK GEOLOGY

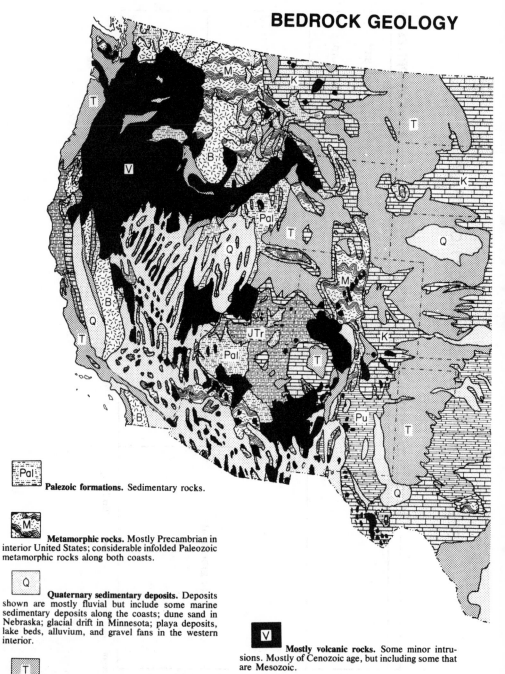

Palezoic formations. Sedimentary rocks.

Metamorphic rocks. Mostly Precambrian in interior United States; considerable infolded Paleozoic metamorphic rocks along both coasts.

Quaternary sedimentary deposits. Deposits shown are mostly fluvial but include some marine sedimentary deposits along the coasts; dune sand in Nebraska; glacial drift in Minnesota; playa deposits, lake beds, alluvium, and gravel fans in the western interior.

Tertiary formations. Sedimentary and mostly of marine origin along the coasts; some volcanic along the Washington-Oregon coast; in western interior mostly lake and stream deposits but includes considerable volcanic material.

Mostly volcanic rocks. Some minor intrusions. Mostly of Cenozoic age, but including some that are Mesozoic.

Granitic batholiths. Late Mesozoic and early Cenozoic.

OF THE UNITED STATES

 Late Mesozoic. Mostly sedimentary cretaceous formations; marine and continental deposits intertongued.

 Early Mesozoic formations (Triassic and Jurassic). Red beds in eastern U.S.; mostly red beds and canyon-forming sandstones in Rocky Mountain region; mostly marine and metamorphic rocks in westernmost U.S.

 Upper Paleozoic formations (Mississippian, Pennsylvanian, and Permian). Marine and continental sedimentary deposits; not metamorphosed except in the Pacific Mountains where formations include volcanics and metamorphics.

Lower Paleozoic formations (Cambrian, Ordovician, Silurian, and Devonian). Sedimentary deposits, mostly of marine origin.

EARTHQUAKE S-WAVE AND P-WAVE TRAVEL TIME GRAPH

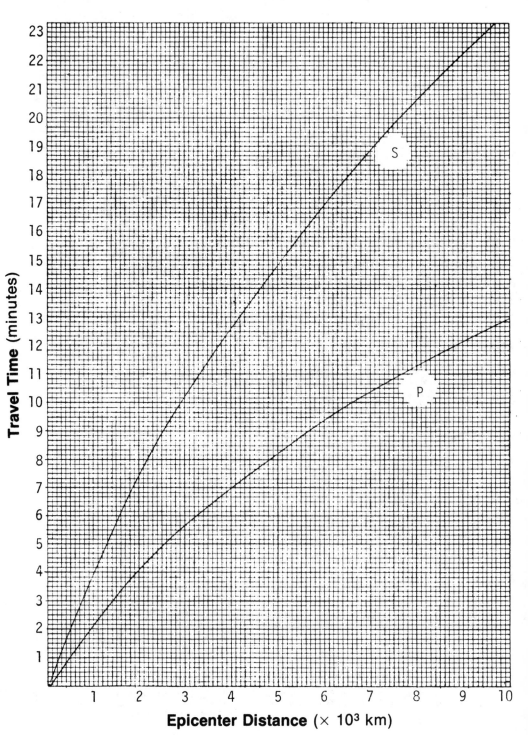

Travel Time (minutes)

Epicenter Distance ($\times$ 10³ km)

Index

ART AND PHOTOGRAPH CREDITS